Taking Sides: Clashing Views
in Media and Society, 15/e

Alison Alexander
Jarice Hanson

http://create.mheducation.com

ISBN-10: 1260180220   ISBN-13: 9781260180220

Contents

Unit 6   283

Detailed Table of Contents

Unit 1: Media and Social Issues

Issue: Do Media Reflect Contemporary Family Relationships?
Yes: Leigh H. Edwards, from "Reality TV and the American Family," University Press of Kentucky (2010)
No: Sarah Boxer, from "Why Are All the Cartoon Mothers Dead?" *The Atlantic* (2014)

Associate Professor Leigh H. Edwards examines how families are portrayed in television and discusses how certain narrative tropes, trends, and genres present us with real family relationships representative of American society and culture. She raises the important point that reality television in particular presents viewers with real conflicts to which many families can relate, because the programs portray real cultural problems that have no easy answers. She concludes her argument with an assessment that public debates about family and marriage often frame the content of the families we see on television. Sarah Boxer examines the content of animated movies and questions why so many mothers in fairy tales and children's films represent the absent mother. Since more American households are headed by married couples or single mothers, she questions the portrayals of mother figures, father figures, and step parents. Without mother figures, she claims, other characters have to step in to teach the lessons mothers often provide for their children, and audiences are left with questionable role models.

Issue: Have Media Representations of Minorities Improved?
Yes: Drew Chappell, from "'Better Multiculturalism' through Technology: *Dora the Explorer* and the Training of the Preschool Viewer(s)," Lexington Books (2013)
No: Elizabeth Monk-Turner, et al., from "The Portrayal of Racial Minorities on Prime Time Television: A Replication of the Mastro and Greenberg Study a Decade Later," *Studies in Popular Culture* (2010)

Professor Drew Chappell-juxtaposes facts about recent actions attempting to ban ethnic studies and restrict immigration in parts of the United States with the television show, *Dora the Explorer's* portrayal of a bilingual (English/Spanish) speaking girl, and discusses how the show introduces children to bilingualism, border identities, and multicultural discourse. Chappell discusses how the performance of identity in Dora's world can teach children about what brings all humans together. Elizabeth Monk-Turner et al. revisit what has become a classic study in the portrayal of minorities in media and finds that even though how minorities are represented have changed within context, no serious changes to stereotypes have really occurred. In this study of prime-time television programming, little has changed within the 10-year time span between the classic Mastro and Greenberg study, and the analysis provided by the authors.

Issue: Have More Women Become Involved as Decision Makers in Media Industries?
Yes: Hannah McIlveen, from "Web Warriors: The Women of Web Series," *Lydia Magazine* (2014)
No: Martha M. Lauzen, from "Boxed In: Portrayals of Female Characters and Employment of Behind-the-Scenes Women in 2014–15 Prime-time Television," Center for the Study of Woman in Television & Film (2015)

Hannah McIlveen challenges the dominant male culture of decision makers in television to discuss how women have been making inroads in nontraditional programming on the Web. Working in low-budget situations does not stop their creativity, and even television network executives are paying attention to new content from women creators on the Web. Every year, Professor Martha M. Lauzen, Ph.D., conducts a survey of the roles of women in prime-time television at the Center for the Study of Women in Television and Film at San Diego State University. In this report, she provides data for the 2014–2015 television season, and women are still underrepresented in prime-time television.

Issue: Do Digital Technologies Influence Our Senses?
Yes: Saga Briggs, from "Six Ways Digital Media Impacts the Brain," informED (2016)
No: Tristan Harris, from "How Technology Hijacks People's Minds—From a Magician and Google's Design Ethicist," tristanharris.com (2016)

Saga Briggs is a writer and the Managing Editor of InformEd, an online resource for educators based in Australia. In this article, she compiles recent data to suggest how our brains adapt to the use of digital technologies over time. Based on the work of neuroscientists, she argues that there are several ways in which technology influences our behavior and "rewires" our brains. She discusses six ways in which we become conditioned by our interaction with technology. Her article particularly focuses on users (like teens) who seem to use digital technology 24 hours a day, 7 days a week. Tristan Harris was the design ethicist for Google for 3 years. Based on his experience and his knowledge of how technology companies operate, he argues that the companies exert much more influence over our behaviors than we do. In other words, he believes that we are being conditioned by the companies to behave in certain ways, rather than our minds or bodies responding to the type of influences caused by technologies themselves. He does however note that technology companies have become experts in structuring information that exploits our human vulnerabilities.

Unit 2: A Question of Content

Issue: Do Media Cause Individuals to Develop Negative Body Images?
Yes: June Deery, from "The Body Shop," Palgrave Macmillan (2012)
No: Michael P. Levine and Sarah K. Murnen, from "'Everybody Knows That Mass Media Are/Are Not [*Pick One*] a Cause of Eating Disorders': A Critical Review of Evidence for a Causal Link between Media, Negative Body Image, and Disordered Eating in Females," *Journal of Social and Clinical Psychology* (2009)

June Deery examines the role of reality television and body makeover programs and concludes that these types of programs normalize the idea that bodies can and should be improved by plastic surgery, weight loss, and control programs, and that women in particular should subject themselves to all measures to find "success" and "happiness." She theorizes that these programs assume that women in particular do have negative body images, and that the real messages of these programs are that surgical steps can and should be taken to improve one's poor body image. Michael P. Levine and Sarah K. Murnen also investigate magazine ads, but find the assumption that media cause eating disorders to be too limited. Instead, they cite a wide range of social, behavioral, and cultural issues over time to understand the complex conditions under which girls begin to adopt negative body issues that result in eating disorders.

Issue: Is Product Placement an Effective Form of Advertising?
Yes: Kaylene Williams, et al., from "Product Placement Effectiveness: Revisited and Renewed," *Journal of Management and Marketing Research* (2011)
No: Ekaterina V. Karniouchina, Can Uslay, and Grigori Erenburg, from "Do Marketing Media Have Life Cycles? The Case of Product Placement in Movies," *Journal of Marketing* (2011)

Professors Kaylene Williams et al. chronicle the evolution of product placement and define the term as incorporating "commercial content into noncommercial settings." They discuss the subtle differences between brand placement and product placement and raise the topic of how product placement is becoming more common in many media forms, including music and games. Professors Karniouchina, Uslay, and Erenburg analyzed 40 years of movies (1968–2007) to uncover the idea that product placement has become a tactic that no longer interests viewers of major motion pictures. As a result, they suggest that marketers should investigate other ways of trying to connect ideas and brand identities.

British journalist Elizabeth Day thinks of selfies as modern-day self-portraits. Despite their popularity, she sides with critics who consider selfies to be narcissistic and expressions of our self-absorbed lifestyles. *The New York Times* reporter Jenna Wortham claims that our predilection for responding to faces is just a part of a more technologized world, and that while we shouldn't discount the selfie phenomenon, we should also keep in mind that selfies are a type of visual diary.

Unit 3: News and Politics

Technology writer Farhad Manjoo has interviewed Mark Zuckerberg, founder of Facebook, on many occasions. In this article, he discusses how Zuckerberg and the Facebook staff reacted to what was being written and said about Facebook's role in disseminating "fake news" prior to, and during the 2016 Presidential election. The article discusses whether Facebook's attempts to create connections among users have actually contributed to the spread of lies, misinformation, and fake news, and whether social media has a responsibility to monitor information that can mislead the public, particularly through its News Feed feature. Providing an overview of news gathering and dissemination processes for the last hundred years, David Uberti highlights some of the historical precedents that stirred up controversy about whether the news media spreads misinformation or not. He shares the perspective that over time, different forms of media have participated in misleading the public. Even though he cites PolitiFact as the source of calling fake news in 2016 the "Lie of the Year," he is critical of how mainstream media have contributed to the public's distrust of all forms of news media.

Journalist and editor Mark Follman reports that mass shooters claim to be inspired by previous massacres. A desire for fame is enhanced by the coverage achieved in previous shootings. Copycats plan their actions to be seen by the media and the public. Changing how media covers these stories may reduce the likelihood of subsequent copycats. Follman urges media organizations to create industry standards for coverage of mass shootings. While Professor Charlie Beckett acknowledges that terrorism relies on publicity to disrupt society, provoke fear, and demonstrate power. Journalism has a responsibility to help society cope with this complicated problem, but faces challenges of verification, dealing with propaganda, and the speed of the news cycle. Better reporting is needed, but journalists cannot shirk the responsibility to be independent, critical, and trustworthy.

Sheldon R. Gawiser and G. Evans Witt have a vast experience in developing polls and analyzing the results of polls. Their belief in the accuracy of polls to reflect public opinion is grounded in decades of experience, and in the scientific accuracy of the poll. They provide advice to journalists on how to measure the worth of a poll in terms of its scientific rigor as opposed to its casual approach toward accuracy. Herbert J. Gans discusses how news media personnel often portray public opinion through polls inaccurately. He makes an important distinction between the way people answer polls and the definition of public opinion.

Issue: Are Twitter and Other Social Media a Good Source of Political Information?
Yes: John H. Parmelee and Shannon L. Bichard, from *Politics and the Twitter Revolution: How Tweets Influence the Relationship between Political Leaders and the Public*, Lexington Books (2012)
No: Clay Shirky, from "The Political Power of Social Media: Technology, the Public Sphere, and Political Change," *Foreign Affairs* (2011)

In these sections of their longer study on the role of Twitter and politics, Professors John H. Parmelee and Shannon L. Bichard examine how political leaders use Twitter to influence the public. While politicians establish personal relationships with followers, some tweets are intended to influence policy. They examine the potential for the one-way form of communication provided by Twitter to engage with the public. Clay Shirky turns this issue around by asking about the use of social media to effect change within authoritarian regimes. He describes situations in which protests have been arranged by text. It is in the use of social media to coordinate actions and develop shared awareness that their power resides. But, he warns that these tools can be ineffective and cause as much harm as good.

Unit 4: Law and Policy

Issue: Does Technology Invade Our Privacy?
Yes: Daniel J. Solove, from "The All-or-Nothing Fallacy," Yale University Press (2011)
No: Stewart Baker, from "The Privacy Problem: What's Wrong with Privacy," *Tech Freedom* (2010)

Daniel J. Solove, professor of law at George Washington University and authority on privacy issues, argues that privacy is too often sacrificed for security concerns. He argues that there are often solutions that do not involve such sacrifices, but that they are dismissed by an all-or-nothing attitude. Stewart Baker, former assistant secretary for Policy at Homeland Security, argues vigorously for better collection and use of technological information. Its importance in preventing acts of terrorism, in tracking potential criminals, and in protecting the interests of the country far outweighs privacy concerns of individuals.

Issue: Should Corporations Be Allowed to Finance Political Campaigns?
Yes: Thomas R. Eddlem, from "Citizens United Is Breaking Up Corporate Dominance of Elections," *The New American* (2012)
No: David Earley and Ian Vandewalker, from "Transparency for Corporate Political Spending: A Federal Solution," Brennan Center for Justice at New York University School of Law (2012)

Conservative author Thomas R. Eddlem makes the case that corporate media institutions influence the messages that the public sees and hears. As a result, the Supreme Court's 2010 *Citizens United* decision, which gives corporations the right to make political contributions and creates the possibility of the establishment of SuperPACs, also results in the exercise of freedom of speech. David Earley and Ian Vandewalker, two counsels at the Brennan Center for Justice at the New York University School of Law, argue that the rise of political spending that resulted from the Supreme Court's *Citizens United* decision has created a situation in which political elections can be "bought" by corporate donors. Because of the new law, they argue that the only way to ensure transparency is to create a situation in which all political donations are disclosed to the public.

Issue: Does Drone Journalism Challenge Journalistic Norms of Privacy?
Yes: Margot E. Kaminski, from "Enough with the 'Sunbathing Teenager' Gambit," *Slate* (2016)
No: United States of America National Transportation Safety Board, from "Brief of Amicus Curiae to Safeguard the Public's First Amendment Interest in the Free Flow of Information," www.hklaw.com (2014)

The access afforded by drones is rewriting privacy laws according to Law Professor Kaminski. She explores the complexity of privacy issues, including the range of national, state and local regulations and practices that often conflict. Drone regulation, she notes, is about much more than sunbathing teenagers. The Amici Curiae brief filed with the Federal Aviation administration represents media industries arguments to protect First Amendment rights of newsgathering organizations in the evolving regulatory environment. They warn against the "chilling effect" on news of several actions including banning the use of drones for newsgathering.

Issue: Can Anything Be Done about Trolls and Online Harassment?
Yes: Andy Greenberg, from "Inside Google's Internet Justice League and Its AI-Powered War on Trolls," *Wired* (2016)
No: Elisabeth Witchel, from "Why a Troll Trolls," The Committee to Protect Journalists (2016)

Technology writer Andy Greenberg discusses the problem of online harassment and argues that many people are being driven off of the Internet because they cannot speak or write what they feel, even in jest, because social media organizations are not set up to police personal expressions. But now, Google has a subsidiary called Jigsaw that can moderate political or personally motivated cyberattacks through artificial intelligence. Drawing heavily on the experiences of a number of women, some of whom were victims of online harassment through Gamergate, Greenberg believes that technological solutions may be found to curb online trolling and personal harassment. Elisabeth Witchel consults with the Committee to Protect Journalists, an independent non-profit dedicated to journalistic integrity and protecting the rights of journalists around the world. In this article she discusses the problem of trolling from some people who have acted as trolls, but also, from people whose lives have been affected by trolls. She addresses the psychology of people who troll, and addresses the question of whether trolling is a manifestation of cultural sickness. She also identifies people who have been the victims of trolls and their responses.

Unit 5: Media Business

Issue: Is Streaming the Future of the Music Industry?
Yes: Joan E. Solsman, from "Attention, Artists: Streaming Music Is the Inescapable Future. Embrace It," CNET News (2014)
No: Charles Arthur, from "Streaming: The Future of the Music Industry, or It's Nightmare?" *The Guardian* (2015)

Journalist Joan E. Solsman discusses the rise of streaming services like Pandora and Spotify, and identifies three business models that are emerging for the number of streaming services. Her article shows how divergent the forms of distribution for music have become, and the impact on artist revenue for some of those new services. Journalist Charles Arthur discusses some of the same streaming services, but identifies how little profit many of them are making because consumer tendency to download free music cuts into the revenue of many of the emerging services.

Issue: Is There a Future for Digital Newspapers?
Yes: Gabriel Snyder, from "Keeping Up with the Times," *Wired* (2017)
No: Michael Rosenwald, from "Print Is Dead. Long Live Print," *Columbia Journalism Review* (2016)

An in-depth analysis of *The New York Times* digital strategies by Gabriel Snyder illustrates how traditional companies can move into the world of digital newspapers. The *Times* strategy is to invest heavily in their core journalism offerings while continually adding new online features. By 2016, the *Times* was making nearly $500 million in digital revenues. They now believe they can make the economics work. Michael Rosenwald quotes early digital journalist, "I have come to realize that replicating print in a digital device is much more difficult than what anybody, including me, imagined." Digital editions have not proved to be the replacement revenue stream that was envisioned and the assumption that readers prefer the immediacy of digital now seems questionable. To this author, the future of print journalism will be the traditional newspaper.

Issue: Are Digital News Services Good for the News Business?
Yes: David Weinberger, from "The Rise, Fall, and Possible Rise of Open News Platforms: The Twisty Path towards a Net Ecosystem That Makes News More Discoverable, Reusable, and Relevant," Shorenstein Center on Media, Politics, and Public Policy (2015)
No: Jonathan Stray, from "The Age of the Cyborg," *Columbia Journalism Review* (2016)

When he was a Shorenstein Fellow at Harvard University, David Weinberger investigated the brief history and impact of open source news gathering and dissemination. His study of how open source architecture influenced the quality of news at National Public Radio, the *New York Times*, and *The Guardian*. Calling the system API (application programming interface), Weinberger examines the impact of sharing information with other media companies and individuals over the Internet. Though the systems started slowly, he is optimistic that in time most news gathering will be conducted with APIs. Jonathan Stray, a technology writer and teacher at Columbia Journalism School addresses the technologies and sharing sites as a more automated method of gathering and disseminating news and information. With artificial intelligence (AI) and algorithms that scour social media (like Twitter and Google), these "cyborg" technologies notice what is trending and what people are sharing. This type of topical news generation can result in stories and videos that are put together more quickly than a person could assemble the pieces for a finished story. However, Stray thinks that it will be a long time before AI can be effectively used to replace human journalists.

Unit 6: Life in the Digital Age

Issue: Can Digital Libraries Replace Traditional Libraries?

Yes: Robert Darnton, from "A World Digital Library Is Coming True!" *The New York Review of Books* (2014)
No: Jill Lepore, from "The Cobweb: Can the Internet Be Archived?" *The New Yorker* (2015)

Harvard University Library Director Robert Darnton suggests that a new model of publishing scholarly work may need to be created to preserve ideas in electronic form. The traditional library, he says, relies on a financial model that is no longer sustainable. The result, he suggests, is to continue to convert scholarly research to digital data and for libraries to specialize, and cooperate in their lending processes. Historian and Harvard University Professor Jill Lepore examines the efforts to collect digital information—particularly Websites—through the Internet Archive, but provides frightening data on how incomplete the archive of digital data is, why that happens, and what consequences occur because of incomplete records of digital data.

Issue: Can Journalism Stand Up To Attacks on Freedom of the Press?

Yes: Marvin Kalb, from "Current Challenges to the Freedom of the Press," *Shorenstein Center on Media, Politics and Public Policy* (2017)
No: Philip Bennett and Moises Naim, from "21st-Century Censorship," *Columbia Journalism Review* (2015)

Marvin Kalb sees Trump's dismissive treatment of news media as a significant attack on freedom of the press. Calling media "enemies of the American people" was reminiscent of the language of Mao Zedong and Stalin. Undercutting the media is a strategy of authoritarianism; preserving democracy requires a free press. Philip Bennett and Moises Naim look at press freedom in a global and digital context and find censorship on the rise. They argue that governments are having success in disrupting and undercutting independent media to determine the information that reaches society.

Preface

Communication is one of the most popular college majors in the country, suggesting that students are interested in the way in which messages are created and exchanged. We are surrounded by media and media technology today that continually mediate our experiences with ourselves, with others, and with the broader group we identify as "society." We've moved from traditional "mass" media that operated with large institutions sending messages to a large, heterogeneous audience to using media forms to interact in real-time with others, or just to amuse, entertain, or inform ourselves. Large-scale media producers have had to change business models to also cater to niche audiences, as well as to maintain their former practices and battle for the attention of audiences.

Today, people have the capacity to become producers of mediated content that can be shared online, through blogs, websites, social networking sites, and podcasts. Never before have we had the capacity to consume mass media, as well as produce our own forms of media and have a platform for low-cost or free distribution over the Internet.

This book addresses a number of controversial issues in media and society. The purpose of these readings and indeed of any course that deals with the social impact of media is to create a literate consumer of media—someone who can walk the fine line between a naive acceptance of all media and a cynical disregard for any positive benefits that media and media technologies may offer.

The study of media and society is very much a part of the way in which we live our lives by blending technologies and services, public and private media uses, and public and private behaviors. In the near future, many of the technologies we use today may be subsumed by yet newer technologies, or greater use of those that we already use. Film, television, music, radio, and print all come to us today over the Internet (through wired or wireless means), and smart phones are well on their way to replacing laptop computers as the "all-in-one" portable technology.

Since many of the topics for these readings are often in the news (or even constitute the news), you may already have opinions about them. We encourage you to read the selections and discuss the issues with an open mind. Even if you do not initially agree with a position or do not even understand how it is possible to make an opposing argument, give it a try. Remember, these problems often are not restricted to only two views; there may be many. We encourage you to discuss these topics as broadly as possible, and we believe that thinking seriously about media is an important goal.

These readings have been chosen to be used for students in introductory courses in media and society. We know that some instructors have found these selections useful for courses in writing about communication topics, ethics, and public speaking. The topics are such that they can be easily incorporated into any media course regardless of how it is organized—thematically, chronologically, or by media form.

Each issue includes an introduction to set the stage for debates argued in the YES and NO selections. We also pose a number of Learning Outcomes to help guide reading. We offer a starting point for discussion in the section titled, "Is There Common Ground?" We also offer suggestions for further reading on the issue and suggested Internet References to expand upon the material in each section. The introductions and the suggestions for additional resources and Internet sites do not preempt the reader's task: to achieve a critical and informed view of the issues at stake.

In reading an issue and forming your own opinion, you should not feel confined to adopt one or the other of the positions presented. Some readers may see important points on both sides of an issue and may construct for themselves a new and creative approach. Such an approach might incorporate the best of both sides, or it might provide an entirely new vantage point for understanding.

Editors of This Volume

ALISON ALEXANDER is a Professor of Telecommunications and Senior Associate Dean at the Grady College of Journalism and Mass Communication at the University of Georgia. She is the past Editor of the *Journal of Broadcasting & Electronic Media*, and past President of the Association for Communication Administration and the Eastern Communication Association. She received her PhD in communication from Ohio State University. She is widely published in the area of media and family, audience research, and media economics.

JARICE HANSON is Professor Emerita in the Department of Communication at the University of Massachusetts at Amherst. Her research focuses on the impact of new technology. She formerly held the Verizon Chair in Telecommunications at Temple University, and was the founding Dean of the School of Communications at Quinnipiac University. She received her MA and PhD at Northwestern University's Department of Radio-TV-Film. She is the author or editor of numerous books and articles, including *The Economic Encyclopedia of Social Media: Friending, Following, Texting, and Connecting* (Greenwood, 2016) and *24/7: How Cell Phones and the Internet Change the Way We Live, Work and Play* (Praeger, 2007), *Constructing America's War Culture: Iraq, Media, and Images at Home* (coedited with Thomas Conroy) (Lexington Books, 2007), and *The Unconnected: Participation, Engagement, and Social Justice in the Information Society* (coedited with Paul M. A. Baker and Jeremy Hunsinger) (Peter Lang, 2013).

Acknowledgments

We wish to acknowledge the encouragement, support, and detail given to this project. We are particularly grateful to Debra Henricks, who has carefully and painstakingly worked with us to produce the best edition possible and who has guided us through many editions and substantial revisions of this book.

We would also like to extend our appreciation to the many professors who reviewed our previous edition, and we are grateful for the advice they have provided in the preparation of this edition.

We would also like to thank our families and friends for their patience and understanding during the period in which we prepared this book.

Academic Advisory Board Members

Members of the Academic Advisory Board are instrumental in the final selection of articles for the Taking Sides series. Their review of the articles for content, level, and appropriateness provides critical direction to the editor(s) and staff. We think that you will find their careful consideration reflected in this book.

Introduction

Ways of Thinking about Media and Society

Media are everywhere in the industrialized world today. It is likely that anyone reading this book has access to more forms of media than their grandparents could ever dream of. Many readers are probably adept at multitasking—a term unheard of when this book series began in 1987. Many readers are probably adept at using so many technologies that deliver content over tablets or smart phones that it almost seems strange to think that broadcast TV, cable TV, film, radio, newspapers, books and magazines, and the recording industry all once were thought of as different forms of media, all delivered in different ways, and all with different economic structures. The digital revolution has a price as many traditional or legacy media face this disruptive technology that has upended traditional business models. The convergence of these media over wired and wireless distribution forms now presents us with words, sounds, and images that often blur former distinctions among media forms and industries.

Media are also often scapegoats for the problems of society. Sometimes the relationship of social issues and media seems too obvious *not* to have some connection. For example, violence in the media may be a reflection of society, or, as some critics claim, violence in the media makes it seem that violence in society is the norm. But in reality, one important reason that the media are so often blamed for social problems is that media are so pervasive. Their very ubiquity gives them the status that makes them seem more influential than they actually are. If one were to look at the statistics on violence in the United States, it would be possible to see that there are fewer violent acts today than in recent history—but the presence of this violence in the media, through reportage or fictional representation, makes it appear more prevalent.

There are many approaches to investigating the relationships that are suggested by media and society. From an organizational perspective, the producers of media must find content and distribution forms that will be profitable, and therefore, they have a unique outlook on the audience as consumers. From the perspective of the creative artist, the profit motive may be important, but the exploration of the unique communicative power of the media may be paramount. The audience, too, has different use patterns and varying desires for information or entertainment, and

demonstrates a variety of choices in content offered to them, as well as what they take from the media. Whether the media reflect society or shape society has a lot to do with the dynamic interaction of many of these different components.

To complicate matters, the "mass" media have changed in recent years. Not long ago, "mass" media referred to messages that were created by large organizations for broad, heterogeneous audiences. This concept no longer suffices for the contemporary media environments. While the "mass" media still exist in the forms of radio, television, film, and general interest newspapers and magazines, many media forms today are hybrids of "mass" and "personal" media technologies that open a new realm of understanding about how audiences process the meaning of the messages. Audiences may be smaller and more diverse, but the phenomenon of using media to form a picture of the world and our place in it is still the fundamental reason for studying the relationship of media and society.

As we look at U.S. history, we can see that almost every form of media was first subject to some type of regulation by the government or by the media industry itself. This has changed over the years so that we now have a media environment in which the responsibility for the content of media no longer rests entirely in the hands of the FCC or the major corporations. We, as consumers, are asked to be critical of the media we consume. This requires that we become educated consumers, rather than relying on standards and practices of industry or government intervention into questionable content. While this may not seem like a big problem for adult consumers, the questions and answers become more difficult when we consider how children use the media to form judgments, form opinions, or seek information.

Our habits are changing as the media landscape grows. The average American still spends over three hours a day viewing television, which is in the average home over seven hours a day, but recent statistics indicate that the "average" American actually spends about 10 hours a day facing a screen of some sort—whether that is a TV screen, computer screen, tablet, or cell phone screen. That interaction with media clearly warrants some understanding of what happens in the process of the person/media interaction and relationship.

Politics and political processes have changed, in part, due to the way politicians use the media to reach voters. A proliferation of television channels has resulted from the popularity of cable, but does cable offer anything different from broadcast television? DVDs, Blu-Ray, and streaming services like Netflix deliver feature-length films to the home, changing the traditional practice of viewing film in a public place, and video distribution via cable or the Internet is now a practical option for anyone with transmission lines large enough and wireless broadband fast enough to download large files. The recording industry has been transformed by technology that allows consumers to sample, buy, or steal music online. The communications industry is a multibillion-dollar industry and the third fastest-growing industry in America. From these and other simple examples, it is clear that the media have changed American society, but our understanding of how and why remains incomplete.

Dynamics of Interaction

In recent years, the proliferation and availability of new media forms have changed on a global scale. In the United States, 98 percent of homes have at least one telephone, but by 2008 the number of cell phones outnumbered land phones. On a global scale, the number of cell phones nearly exceeds the world's population. In the United States, over 98 percent of the population has access to at least one television set, but in some parts of the world, televisions are still viewed communally or viewed only at certain hours of the day. The use of broadband and wireless connections continues to grow in the United States, while some other countries (usually smaller countries, with high GDP) are reaching saturation with broadband technologies, and other countries still have limited dial-up services for the Internet.

But apart from questions of access and available content, many fundamental questions about the power of media in any given society remain the same. How do audiences use the media available to them? How do message senders produce meaning? How much of the meaning of any message is produced by the audience? And increasingly important for discussion is, How do additional uses of media change our interpersonal environments and human interactions?

Progress in Media Research

Much of media research has been in search of theory. Theory is an organized refinement of everyday thinking; it is an attempt to establish a systematic view of a phenomenon in order to better understand that phenomenon. Theory is tested against reality to establish whether or not it is a good explanation; so, for example, a researcher might notice that what is covered by news outlets is very similar to what citizens say are the important issues of the day. From such observations came agenda setting (the notion that the media confer importance on the topics they cover, directing public attention to what is considered important).

Much of the early media research was produced to answer questions of print media because print has long been regarded as a permanent record of history and events. The ability of newspapers and books to shape and influence public opinion was regarded as a necessity to the founding of new forms of governments—including the U.S. government—and a good number of our laws and regulations were originally written to favor print (like copyright and freedom of the press). But the bias of the medium carried certain restrictions. Print media necessarily were limited to those individuals who could read. The principles that emerged from this relationship were addressed in an often-quoted statement attributed to Thomas Jefferson, who wrote, "Were it left to me to decide whether we should have a government without newspapers, or newspapers without a government, I should not hesitate a moment to prefer the latter." But the next sentence in Jefferson's statement is equally important and often omitted from quotations: "But I should mean that every man should receive those papers and be capable of reading them." Today, however, the newspaper is no longer the primary distribution form for information that is critical to living in a democracy.

Today, media research on the relationships among media senders, the channels of communication, and the receivers of messages is not enough. Consumers must realize that "media literacy" and maybe even "technological literacy" are important concepts too. People can no longer take for granted that the media exist primarily to provide news, information, and entertainment. They must be more attuned to what media content says about them as individuals and as members of a society, and they need to be aware of how the ability for almost everyone to create media (like blogging or social networking) challenges traditional ownership and privacy laws and regulations. By integrating these various cultural components, the public can better criticize the regulation or lack of regulation that permits media industries to function the way they do.

The use of social science data to explore the effects of media on audiences strongly emphasized psychological and sociological schools of thought. It did not take long to move from the "magic bullet theory"—which proposed that media had a direct and immediate effect on the receivers of the message, and that the same message intended by the senders was the same when it was "shot" into the receiver—to other ideas of limited, or even indirect, means of influencing the audience.

Media research has shifted from addressing specifically effects-oriented paradigms to exploring the nature of the institutions of media production themselves, as well as examining the unique characteristics of each form of media and the ability of the media user to also produce media products. What most researchers agree upon today is that the best way to understand the power and impact of media is to look at context-specific situations to better understand the dynamics involved in the use of media and the importance of the content. Still, there are many approaches to media research from a variety of interdisciplinary fields: psychology, sociology, linguistics, art, comparative literature, economics, political science, and more. What these avenues of inquiry have in common is that they all tend to focus attention on individuals, families or other social groups, society in general, and culture in the broad sense. All of the interpretations frame meaning and investigate their subjects within institutional frameworks that are specific to any nation and/or culture.

Many of the questions for media researchers in the twenty-first century deal with the continued fragmentation of the audience, caused by greater choice of channels and technologies for traditional and new communication purposes. The power of some of these technologies to reach virtually any place on the globe within fractions of a second will continue to pose questions of access to media and the meaning of the messages transmitted. As individuals become more dependent upon the Internet for communication purposes, the sense of audience will further be changed as individual users choose what they want to receive, pay for, and keep. For all of these reasons, the field of media research is rich, growing, and challenging.

Questions for Consideration

In addressing the issues in this book, it is important to consider some recurring questions:

1. Are the media unifying or fragmenting? Does media content help the socialization process, or does it create anxiety or inaccurate portrayals of the world? Do people understand what they are doing when they post personal information online or open themselves to immediate criticism and feedback?

2. How are our basic institutions changing as we use media in new and different ways? Do media support or undermine our political processes? Do they change what we think of when we claim to live in a "democracy"? Do media operate in the public interest, or do media serve the rich and powerful corporations' quest for profit? Can media find a successful business model in the digital age? Can the media do both simultaneously?

3. Whose interests do the media represent? Do audiences actively work toward integrating media messages with their own experiences? How do new media technologies change our traditional ways of communicating? Are they leading us to a world in which interpersonal communication is radically altered because we rely on information systems to replace many traditional behaviors?

Summary

We live in a media-rich environment where almost everybody has access to some forms of media and some choices in content. As new technologies and services are developed, are they responding to the problems that previous media researchers and the public have detected? Over time, individuals have improved their ability to unravel the complex set of interactions that tie the media and society together, but they need to continue to question past results, new practices and technologies, and their own evaluative measures. When people critically examine the world around them—a world often presented by the media—they can more fully understand and enjoy the way they relate as individuals, as members of groups, and as members of a society.

Alison Alexander
University of Georgia

Jarice Hanson
University of Massachusetts—Amherst

Unit 1

UNIT

Media and Social Issues

Do media reflect the social attitudes and concerns of our times, or are they also able to construct, legitimize, and reinforce the social realities, behaviors, attitudes, and images of others? Do they operate to maintain existing power structures, or are they symbolic communication central to our culture? Do we use stereotypes to form ideas of appropriate ways of behaving, or to give us a sense of what we can do in the world? The ways media help us to shape a sense of reality are complex. How much do media influence us, versus how we use media to fit our already preconceived ideas? Should concern be directed toward vulnerable populations like children? If we truly have a variety of information sources and content to choose from, perhaps we can assume that distorted images are balanced with realistic ones – but is this a likely scenario in our society? Questions about the place of media within society, and within what many people call the "information age," are important for us to understand, whether we use media, or whether media use us.

Selected, Edited, and with Issue Framing Material by:
Alison Alexander, *University of Georgia*
and
Jarice Hanson, *University of Massachusetts—Amherst*

ISSUE

Do Media Reflect Contemporary Family Relationships?

YES: Leigh H. Edwards, from "Reality TV and the American Family," University Press of Kentucky (2010)

NO: Sarah Boxer, from "Why Are All the Cartoon Mothers Dead?" *The Atlantic* (2014)

Learning Outcomes
After reading this issue, you will be able to:
• Consider how children learn from media content.
• Understand the role different genres play in constructing a "mediated" world for audiences.
• Reflect on how often media distort images of real-world relationships.
• Think broadly about whether media reflect or distort sociological facts.
• Think about the images you see when you watch television or film, and consider whether these images have shaped your expectations.

ISSUE SUMMARY

YES: Associate Professor Leigh H. Edwards examines how families are portrayed in television and discusses how certain narrative tropes, trends, and genres present us with real family relationships representative of American society and culture. She raises the important point that reality television in particular presents viewers with real conflicts to which many families can relate, because the programs portray real cultural problems that have no easy answers. She concludes her argument with an assessment that public debates about family and marriage often frame the content of the families we see on television.

NO: Sarah Boxer examines the content of animated movies and questions why so many mothers in fairy tales and children's films represent the absent mother. Since more American households are headed by married couples or single mothers, she questions the portrayals of mother figures, father figures, and step parents. Without mother figures, she claims, other characters have to step in to teach the lessons mothers often provide for their children, and audiences are left with questionable role models.

Do media reflect social reality as though we were looking into a mirror, or do they frame the issues within social life so that we see them in a different way? Do we learn from the images we see in the media? Do we favor certain types of representations because they resonate with our own values? These basic questions support all studies that focus on the relationship of media and society. From early studies that suggested that the values portrayed in media would be immediately seized by the public, to models of limited and indirect effects, scholars, citizens, and students have grappled with the way media and society inform and relate to each other. Today we no longer question whether the media do affect our values—the question is now, *how* media affect our values.

Since television's early days, families have been represented as the focus of many genres and formats. The assumption that "everyone" can relate to domestic conflict and the roles family members play in their social lives seems to be a basic construct for drama as well as for comedy. Some theories support the idea that a "family structure" is such a basic social group with such universal understanding and appeal that every cast member in a show—whether representing members of a family or not—actually reflects an archetype of some member of a family unit. Some theorists even claim that we learn about the different roles each family member plays in a family unit, and we exhibit behaviors to fit those roles.

In these two selections, different genres are examined, but representation of real family members and situations families may encounter are the contexts for the authors' analyses of the impact media content has on the intended audience. The authors of these selections approach the topic of family representations in media with particular viewpoints. Professor Leigh H. Edwards's selection gives some history of the representations of the American family in television over the years, but she examines the genre of reality programming to suggest that four narrative structures have evolved: a nostalgia for the traditional nuclear family; representations of a new, modified nuclear family norm in which the husband and wife both work outside the home; an ideal of family pluralism; and a questioning of norms that give us a different sense of family diversity. She cites many contemporary reality television shows in which some semblance of "family" is represented, but claims that what unites all of these diverse family structures is the sense that people have to deal with cultural conflicts.

Sarah Boxer raises the question of why so many fairy tales and animated children's films seem to situate the mother outside of the picture. In most cases, she claims, the mother is dead, so who helps the children (or innocent characters of any species) learn about motherly love and guidance? When you consider the primary audience for this type of content—children—her observation of the dead mother becomes a more important factor to consider when we focus on how children learn from media, and what they learn from media.

Furthermore, Boxer examines the family relationships in animated films and finds that the father-figures sometimes take on mythic proportions. Is this presentation of gender roles (or lack of them) harmful to the development and socialization of some children? Are fathers in children's media content made to be superheroes? These are only some of the types of questions she raises.

In addition to examining representations of families (and changing families) in America, these selections remind us that media can often be an important form of entertainment that conditions audiences to have certain expectations, or teaches them about gender roles and social responsibilities. We know media are powerful, but their power is not always easy to understand, and we know that some of the early media content children see stays with them throughout their life. From ideas such as the "agenda setting theory" of communication, which posits that media do not tell us what to think, but rather, tell us what to think about, to studies of para-social interactions (the relationship we form with people whom we see in media), and ideas of *resonance*, which describes how we relate to the images we see in media, there are several assumptions and theories to guide an inquiry into the relationship of media content and its presentation of social values.

Some of the earliest television programs in the 1950s featured fathers who played the role of the "all knowing," eternally "understanding" parent. *Father Knows Best* was perhaps the quintessential glorification of fatherhood and the father as the "rock" of the family. Over the years, however, the "hapless" dad became more common in television. Homer Simpson is one such example, but even in the popular comedy *Modern Family*, all of the fathers are loving, and good providers, but occasionally helpless. Television mothers, though, have often played the roles of the "behind-the-scenes" fixer of problems, homemakers, and moral centers of the family.

For this reason, Sarah Boxer's observations of missing mother figures in children's animated features is a particularly interesting shift in media content. The overwhelming number of stories in which the mother is replaced by a strong father figure or even a helpful animal (!) suggests that mothers are expendable in these stories.

In general, however, the many representations of family roles and family relationships as portrayed in media suggest one of the most fundamental themes in all of media studies today. From fictionalized portrayals to shows that emulate "reality," we interpret media content according to our own experiences, beliefs, assumptions, and values. At the same time, we think of media portrayals as either "believable" or "unbelievable." Animation is a special category that presents viewers with a world that might or might not be true. The tension suggested by images that create assumptions about "reality" and representation gives us an "in between" place where we see how our favorite stories or portrayals of families provide a yardstick by which we gauge our own sense of what is "normal" or "abnormal." All in all, these media representations of families and family relationships provide a context by which we measure our own lives and experiences.

YES ↵

Leigh H. Edwards

Reality TV and the American Family

Reality television shows are reframing ideas of the family in U.S. culture. The genre titillates by putting cultural anxieties about the family on display, hawking images of wife swapping, spouse shopping, and date hopping. Its TV landscape is dotted with programs about mating rituals, onscreen weddings, unions arranged by audiences, partners testing their bonds on fantasy dates with others, family switching, home and family improvement, peeks into celebrity households, parents and children marrying each other off on national television, and families pitching their lives as sitcom pilots. Though obviously not the only recurring theme pictured, family is one of the genre's obsessions. Scholars have begun to draw attention to certain questions surrounding family, gender, and sexuality, but we have yet to address fully how the genre debates . . . reshapes the family or to account for the centrality of that theme in reality programming. This discussion of the family is important, since TV has always played such a vital role in both shaping and reflecting fantasies of the American family.

Using historicized textual analysis, this essay demonstrates how the reality TV genre both reflects and helps shape changing "American family" ideals. A significant number of reality shows picture a seemingly newfound family diversity. For every traditional "modern nuclear family," with its wage-earning father, stay-at-home mother, and dependent children, we see a panoply of newer arrangements, such as post-divorce, single-parent, blended, and gay and lesbian families. What is the significance of this family diversity as a recurring theme in factual programming? Concurrent with images of demographic change, we also see a familiar rhetoric of the "family in crisis." Witness the emergency framework of *Nanny 911* (a British nanny must save inept American parents who are at their breaking point) or *Extreme Makeover: Home Edition* (a design team must renovate the home of a family otherwise facing disaster). Their premise is that the American family is in trouble. Many scholars have noted how the family has

constantly been described as being in crisis throughout its historical development—with the calamity of the moment always reflecting contemporaneous sociopolitical tensions. The idea of crisis has been used to justify "family values" debates, which usually involve public policy and political rhetoric that uses moral discourses to define what counts as a healthy family.

I would argue that reality programs focused on the familial settings and themes implicitly make their own arguments about the state of the American family, entering long-running family values debates. In their representation of family diversity (which different series laud or decry) and in their use of family crisis motifs, reality narratives capture a sense of anxiety and ambivalence about evolving family life in the United States. Reality TV market[s] themes about our current period of momentous social change: the shift from what sociologists term the "modern family," the nuclear model that reached its full expression in the context of Victorianera industrialization and peaked in the postwar 1950s, to the "postmodern family," a diversity of forms that have emerged since then. Indeed, a key theme in reality TV depictions is that family is now perpetually in process or in flux, open to debate. Social historians define the modern family as a nuclear unit with a male breadwinner, female homemaker, and dependent children; its gendered division of labor was largely only an option historically for the white middle class whose male heads of household had access to the "family wage." This form was naturalized as universal but was never the reality for a majority of people, even though it was upheld as a dominant cultural ideal. Diverse arrangements have appeared since the 1960s and 1970s, constituting what the historian Edward Shorter termed "the postmodern family." New familial forms have emerged, spurred by increases in divorce rates and single-parent households, women's entrance into the labor force in large numbers after 1960, the decline of the "family wage," and the pressures on labor caused by postindustrialism and by globalization.

Taken as a whole, reality series about the family alter some conventional familial norms while reinforcing others. I would agree with critics such as Tania Modleski and Sherrie A. Inness, who argue that popular culture texts that address issues such as gendered roles and the real contradictions in women's lives often both challenge and reaffirm traditional values. These reality programs picture some updated norms (frequently, the edited narratives validate wider definitions of familial relations or urge men to do more domestic labor). The genre's meditation on the shift in norms is not radical, however, because it occurs within TV's liberal pluralism framework. Various programs construct their own sense of the contradictions of family life, such as tensions involving women juggling work and child care, gender role renegotiations, further blurring of public and the private "separate sphere" ideologies, racialized family ideals, and fights about gay marriage. Such shows celebrate conflict, spectacularizing fraught kinship issues as a family circus in order to draw more viewers and advertising, but they most often resolve the strife into a liberal pluralist message by episode's end (for example, using the liberal discourse of individualism to represent racism as an interpersonal conflict that can be resolved between individuals through commonsense appeals rather than as a structural social issue).

I would contextualize these themes both in terms of television's long history as a domestic medium and in reference to ongoing family values battles. The new household models and demographic changes, such as increased divorce rates, sparked a political backlash beginning in the 1970s: the family values media debates that have intensified since the 1990s. These skirmishes, such as Dan Quayle's attack on the sitcom character Murphy Brown as a symbol of unwed motherhood in the 1992 presidential debates, are an important sociohistorical context for the current reality programming trend. For my purposes here, I date the full advent of the current genre to the premiere of MTV's *The Real World* in 1992, although related forerunners like police and emergency nonfiction series emerged in the late 1980s, and factual programming has, of course, been around since the medium's origins. Though critics debate the looseness of the term *reality TV* as a genre, I use it to refer to factual programming with key recurring generic and marketing characteristics (such as unscripted, low-cost, edited formats featuring a mix of documentary and fiction genres, often to great ratings success).

The links between TV and the family are foundational, as long-running research on television and the family has established. The television historian Lynn Spigel has shown how early TV developed coextensively with the postwar suburban middle-class families that the

medium made into its favored topic and target audience. The historian Stephanie Coontz has noted how current nostalgia for the nuclear family ideal is filtered through 1950s domestic sitcoms like *Leave It to Beaver*. As critics have illustrated, family shows comment not only on society's basic organizing unit but also on demographic transformations by tracing their influence on the family. Ella Taylor traces a family crisis motif in 1970s series such as *All in the Family*, *The Jeffersons*, and *One Day at a Time*, noting network efforts to generate socially "relevant" programming to grab a targeted middle-class demographic as well as to respond to social changes prompted by the women's and civil rights movements. Herman Gray, likewise, in *Watching Race*, has detailed assimilationist messages, reflecting prevailing social discourses, in portraits of black families in the 1980s, like *The Cosby Show*. I demonstrate how reality TV opens a fresh chapter in TV's long-running love affair with the family—the medium has birthed a new genre that grapples with the postmodern family condition.

Reality TV mines quarrels about family life, producing, for example, gay dating shows (such as *Boy Meets Boy*, 2003) at the precise moment of national deliberations over gay marriage. The genre sinks its formidable teeth into these controversies. Much as domestic sitcoms did in the 1950s, it gives us new ways of thinking about familial forms in relationship to identity categories like gender and sexuality or to larger concepts like citizenship and national identity. It does so in part by illuminating the cultural tensions underlying family values debates, such as the family's contested nature as a U.S. institution that legitimates social identities, confers legal and property rights, and models the nation imagined as a family, whether a "house united" or a "house divided."

Tracing recurring tropes in reality programs about the family, I would argue for four key narrative stances toward social change: nostalgia for the traditional modern nuclear family; promotion of a new, modified nuclear family norm in which husband and wife both work outside the home; a tentative, superficial embrace of family pluralism in the context of liberal pluralism; and an open-ended questioning of norms that might include a more extensive sense of family diversity. These narrative trends are particularly evident in some specific reality subgenres: family-switching shows (*Trading Spouses*, *Wife Swap*, *Black. White*, *Meet Mister Mom*); observations of family life (*The Real Housewives of Orange County*; *Little People, Big World*); celebrity family series (*The Osbournes*, *Run's House*, *Meet the Barkers*, *Being Bobby Brown*, *Breaking Bonaduce*, *Hogan Knows Best*); home and family makeover programs (*Extreme Makeover: Home Edition*, *Renovate My Family*); family workplace series (*Dog the Bounty Hunter*, *Family Plots*, *Family*

Business); family gamedocs (*Things I Hate about You, Race to the Altar, Married by America, The Will, The Family*); parenting series (*Nanny 911, Supernanny, Showbiz Moms and Dads*); and historical reenactment programs with family settings (*Colonial House, Frontier House*).

These programs watch middle-class "average joes," perhaps the viewer's friends and neighbors, navigate the shoals of domesticity, grappling with cultural problems such as the tension between kinship and chosen bonds, the effect of the media on the family, and the state's efforts to define "family" as a matter of national concern and to legislate access to marriage rights. Ultimately, these shows convey a kind of emotional engagement, what Ien Ang would term "emotional realism," regarding changes in family structures in the United States, capturing a recent shift in middle-class attitudes toward the American family, a change in what Raymond Williams would call that group's "structure of feeling."

Narrative Tropes

Reality TV spectacularizes such issues as a family circus in order to draw viewers and sell advertising. Part of its vast ratings appeal stems from the fact that it portrays real people struggling with long-running cultural problems that have no easy answers: tensions in the ties that bind, between kinship and chosen bonds, between tradition and change; personal versus social identity; and competing moralities. The genre explores angst about what "the American family" is in the first place. Such widespread worries are not surprising, given that this unit is a social construction that is notoriously difficult to define, particularly since it has historically encoded gendered roles and hierarchies of class, race, and sexuality that define ideas of social acceptance, a crucible for selfhood and nationhood. Critics have noted the regulatory nature of the modern nuclear family model, and official discourse has traditionally framed that unit as a white, middle-class heterosexual norm to which citizens should aspire.

Reality TV does not explicitly solve those family values disputes. Instead, it concentrates on mining the conflict between the two familial forms, one residual and one emergent. Rather than answering questions about what the postmodern family will become, it rehearses sundry arguments about how the familial unit is getting exposed, built up, torn down, and redefined. Some programs offer wish-fulfillment fantasies, smoothing over rancorous public squabbles and social changes but not resolving those tensions.

For example, Bravo's *Things I Hate about You* (2004), reflecting this panoply, turns domesticity into a sport in which snarky judges determine which member of a couple is more annoying to live with and partners happily air their dirty laundry on TV (sometimes literally). One week we see an unmarried heterosexual couple with no children, the next a gay domestic partnership. No one model dominates. The series fits all these groupings into the same narrative framework: a story about family and the daily irritations of domesticity. . . .

Trends in Reality TV's Textual Representations of the Family

Drawing on the sociopolitical and media history of the family values debates, reality TV offers viewers the voyeuristic chance to peer into other people's households to see how all this cultural ruckus is affecting actual families. As the genre takes up the modern and postmodern family in various ways, it often explicitly engages with public policy and media discussions. The way reality serials address familial life illuminates an uneasy shift from modern nuclear family ideals to the postmodern reality of diverse practices.

One main trend in reality programming is for series to look backward with a nostalgia for the modern nuclear family that reveals the instability of that model. Some series revert to older concepts, such as the sociologist Talcott Parsons's mid-twentieth-century theories of functional and dysfunctional family forms. He argued that the modern nuclear family's function under industrialized capitalism was to reproduce and socialize children into dominant moral codes, as well as to define and promote norms of sexual behavior and ideas of affective bonds associated with companionate marriage. Dysfunctional families that deviated from norms were functionalism's defining "Other," and some critics argue that this paradigm still influences sociological research on family life (Stacey, *In the Name of the Family*). Pop psychology concepts of functionalism and dysfunctionalism certainly circulate widely in today's mass media, and we see their influence in reality shows.

A particularly apt example is the spouse-swapping subgenre, which includes shows like ABC's *Wife Swap*. The titillating title implies it will follow the wild exploits of swingers, but the show instead documents strangers who switch households and parenting duties for a short period. Similarly, on Fox's *Trading Spouses: Meet Your New Mommy* (the copycat show that beat ABC's to the air), two parents each occupy the other's home for several days. Both series focus on the conflict between households, revealing a fierce debate among participants as to whose family is healthier, more "normal," or more "functional."

On *Trading Spouses*, one two-part episode swaps mothers from white suburban nuclear families, each comprising a husband, a wife, two kids, and a dog ("Bowers/Pilek"). Both clans want to claim modern nuclear family function-ality for themselves, but economic tensions ensue, even though each woman describes her family as middle class. A California mom with an opulent beach house judges her Massachusetts hosts, with their modest home and verbal fisticuffs, as unkempt, whereas her outspoken counterpart deems the beach household materialistic and emotionally disconnected. Each woman characterizes the other family as dysfunctional. Their conflict reveals not only the degree to which many people still use these older ideals as their own measuring sticks, here staged as issues such as tidiness or appropriate levels of emotional closeness, but also the tenuousness of those ideals, given the intense contradic-tions between two supposedly functional families.

Through the premise of swapping households or roles for several days, these programs explore Otherness by having participants step into someone else's perfor-mance of kinship behaviors. In so doing, they illuminate identity categories that are performed through the family. This dynamic was perhaps most notably executed on the series *Black. White,* which used makeup to switch a white and black family for several weeks and staged racial ten-sions between them. In this subgenre more generally, par-ticipants reproduce a version of their counterparts' social identity. Thus, the switch highlights the arbitrariness of such identity performances. Since the shows allow the participants to judge each other, family appears as a topic of open-ended debate.

These programs depend on conflict generated by social hierarchies of race, class, gender, and sexuality, and they privilege white male heteronormativity. Their narra-tives often focus on gender, encouraging men to take on more child care and domestic chores. Yet they still rely on ideologies of gender difference to explain household units and to reaffirm the mother's role as nurturer-caregiver. By absenting the mother, the wife-swap series imply that hus-bands and kids will learn to appreciate the woman of the house more.

These series encourage a liberal pluralist resolution to conflicts, one that upholds an easy humanist consen-sus, or what critics term "corporate multiculturalism," which markets diversity as another product rather than picturing and validating substantive cultural differences. The framing narratives resolve competing ideas, most often by defining as normal a modified modern nuclear family (two working parents). In shows about alterna-tive households, for example, the narratives sympathize

with the single mom or the lesbian couple but uphold the intact nuclear family as more rational and functional. Yet the narratives also often critique participants' overly intense nostalgia for the bygone modern nuclear ideal, and they sometimes allow for some validation of alter-native models, such as an African American extended family. They depend on sensationalism and conflict over values to spark ratings.

This open warfare over functional and dysfunctional families includes a huge helping of nostalgia, as epitomized by a series like MTV's *The Osbournes*. This hit show sup-ports the sense that if the modern nuclear ideal has been replaced by a diversity of family forms, U.S. culture still has an intense nostalgia for the older norm. Is nostalgia for the fantasy nuclear unit actually a defining characteristic of the postmodern family? It is for *The Osbournes*. Viewers flocked to the show because it juxtaposes a famously hard-living, heavy-metal family with classic sitcom family plotlines, edited to emphasize the irony of seeing the curs-ing, drug-abusing rock star Ozzy and his brood hilariously butchering *Ozzie and Harriet*–style narratives.

The entertainment press dubbed them "America's favorite family," and a series of high-profile magazine cover stories tried to explain the show's wild popular-ity by pointing to how the Osbournes "put the fun in dysfunctional." The show garnered MTV's highest-rated debut at that time and enjoyed some of the strongest rat-ings in the channel's history during its run from 2002 until 2005. Part of the appeal lies in how the Osbournes seem to capture on videotape a more accurate sense of the pressures of family life, ranging from sibling rivalry to teen sex and drug use to a serious illness (such as Sharon's cancer diagnosis and treatment). Even though their fame and fortune make them unlike home view-ers, the family can be related to because of the strug-gles they confront openly. Likewise, they reflect current family diversity because they are a blended family; their brood includes their son and two daughters (one of whom declined to appear on the series), Ozzy's son from his first marriage, and their children's teen friend whom they adopted during the show after his mother died of cancer. Ozzy himself suggested that he did the series in order to expand understandings of the family: "What is a functional family? I know I'm dysfunctional by a long shot, but what guidelines do we all have to go by? *The Waltons*?" Ozzy here is both arbiter and agent; he notes TV's power to define a range of meanings for the family, whether through the Waltons or the Osbournes.

Yet even while the program's narrative meditates on entertaining dysfunctionality and new family realities, it also continuously tries to recuperate the Osbournes as a functional nuclear family. Story arcs are edited to frame them as dysfunctional (cursing parents, wild fights, teen-age drug use), but also to rescue them as functional; there are sentimental shots of the family gathered together in their kitchen or clips of them expressing their love and loyalty despite the titillating fights. Even though Ozzy tells his family they are "all f—ing mad," in the same breath he says he "loves them more than life itself" ("A House Divided"). The edited narrative purposefully emphasizes the bonds of hearth and home, sometimes trying to establish functionality by cutting out serious family events that would have made Parsons blanch: Ozzy's drug relapse, severe mental illness, and nervous breakdown during taping; trips to rehab by Jack and Kelly, the son and daughter; and Sharon's temporary separation from Ozzy over these issues. Press coverage of the show and fan response likewise emphasized a recuperative dynamic, both looking for the loveable, reassuring nuclear family beneath the rough exterior. As an *Entertainment Weekly* cover story noted, Ozzy Osbourne went from being boycotted by parents' groups in the 1980s for bat biting and supposedly Satanic lyrics to being asked for parenting advice from men's magazines. Thus, even while registering the limitations of Parsons's model, the series still tries to rehabilitate this celebrity family as functional. As a result, this program and others like it explore the postmodern family, but at the same time they look back wistfully on the old modern nuclear paradigm.

The Osbournes is also a prime example of a program that explicitly comments on the influence of television on family ideals. Part of the show's insight comes from registering how much the media, whether the popular music industry or television, have shaped this family unit. Brian Graden, then president of MTV Entertainment, described the program's draw as "the juxtaposition of the fantastical rock-star life with the ordinary and the everyday"; summarizing one episode, he laughed, "Am I really seeing Ozzy Osbourne trying to turn on the vacuum cleaner?" Graden noted that after they collected footage on the Osbournes, producers realized that "a lot of these story lines mirrored classic domestic sitcom story lines, yet with a twist of outrageousness that you wouldn't believe." Watching footage of their daily experiences, Graden immediately views them through the lens of earlier TV sitcoms; everywhere he looks, he sees the Cleavers on speed. And the show Graden's company makes of this family's life might one day comprise the plotlines other viewers use to interpret their own experiences in some way. After their smash first season, the Osbournes were feted at the White House Correspondents' dinner and managed to parlay such national attention into more entertainment career opportunities, with a new MTV show, *Battle for Ozzfest* (2004–), hosted by Sharon and Ozzy and featuring bands competing to join their summer tour; Sharon's syndicated talk show that ran for one season (2003–2004); and their children's slew of TV, movie, and music ventures growing out of their exposure from the reality program.

Though most families could not follow the Osbournes into celebrity, what many do share with the rockers is the knowledge that TV significantly shapes familial ideals. This media awareness marks a parenting trend. In their recent audience study of family television-viewing practices, Stewart M. Hoover, Lynn Schofield Clark, and Diane F. Alters found that parents had a highly self-reflexive attitude toward the media. They were well conscious of how the mass media both reflect and shape social beliefs, and they worried about the daily influence of television in their children's lives. Hoover et al. identified this media anxiety as part of what they term "self-reflexive parenting" behaviors stemming from increased concerns about child rearing since the 1960s. They see this model of parenting as part of what Anthony Giddens calls the project of self-reflexivity in modernity, in which people are reflective about their interaction with the social world as they continually incorporate mediated experiences into their sense of self. . . .

Cultural Histories and Family Values Media Debates

I would argue that reality TV is the popular media form with the most to say about the current status of the American family. The television historian Lynn Spigel has shown that early TV developed coextensively with the post–World War II suburban middle-class family—a specific kind of modern nuclear family model the medium made into its favored subject and audience. As Spigel notes, while sociologists like Talcott Parsons were arguing in the 1940s and 1950s that the modern nuclear family is the social form best suited to capitalist progress, the new electronic TV medium targeted the postwar white, middle-class families flocking to the suburbs, encouraging the development of the modern family as a consumer unit.

As a new genre now exploring the self-conscious imbrication of family and the media as one of its main themes, reality TV raises vital issues of marketing and consumerism. If television enters the home to become, as Cecelia Tichi has shown, "the electronic hearth" around which the family gathers, so too does the family envision itself through the tube. TV addresses the family as ideal viewer, imagined community, and the basis for democracy mediated through mass communication; the nation is figured as a collective of families all watching their television sets (a collective that can now exercise its democratic rights by calling in to vote for a favorite singer on *American Idol*). If the domestic sitcom was like an electronic media version of a station wagon trundling the modern family along in the 1950s, reality TV is the hybrid gas-electric car of the postmodern family today. . . .

Not surprisingly, recent public arguments about family and marriage often turn reality TV into prime fodder. Conservative groups frequently protest reality fare. Most spectacularly, complaints made by conservative activists from the Parents Television Council prompted the Federal Communications Commission (FCC) to threaten Fox with a fine of $1.2 million, the largest to date, for *Married by America* when it was on the air. The show had audiences pick mates for couples who could have gotten married on air (though none did and all the arranged couples stopped dating after the show). The protestors found it a vulgar trivialization of the institution of marriage.

On the flip side of the coin, progressive thinkers have used reality TV to make public arguments advocating a greater diversity of marriage and household arrangements. The cultural theorist Lisa Duggan, in a 2004 *Nation* article, explores public policy about state-sanctioned marriage in the context of the debates over gay marriage, critiquing, for example, "marriage promotion" by both the Clinton and the Bush administrations as a way to privatize social welfare. Duggan calls for a diversification of democratically accessible forms of state recognition for households and partnerships, a "flexible menu of choices" that would dethrone the privileged civic status of sanctified marriage and "threaten the normative status of the nuclear family, undermining state endorsement of heterosexual privilege, the male 'headed' household and 'family values' moralism as social welfare policy." She uses reality TV as an example of current dissatisfaction with gendered, "traditional" marriage and a marker of its decline, describing "the competitive gold-digging sucker punch on TV's *Joe Millionaire*" (which tricked eager women into believing they were competing to marry a millionaire) as an entertainment culture indicator of the statistical flux in marriage and kinship arrangements. She argues that the franchise confirms social anxiety that "marriage is less stable and central to the organization of American life than ever." Notably, Duggan pairs her *Joe Millionaire* example with the pop singer Britney Spears's rapidly annulled 2004 Las Vegas wedding (to a high school friend, Jason Alexander) as similar social indexes; the celebrity life and the reality show plot

represent similar kinds of evidence, both equally real (or equally fake) in current entertainment media culture.

Regardless of the different ways the genre enters into existing political discussions, what is striking is that it continually becomes a site for family values debates. A case in point is how a couple competing on the sixth season of CBS's *The Amazing Race* (2005) made headlines because critics accused the husband of exhibiting abusive behavior toward his wife in the series footage. The couple, Jonathan Baker and Victoria Fuller, made the rounds of talk shows to protest that characterization, but the main dynamic of press coverage has been to turn them into a teaching moment. Both went on the entertainment TV newsmagazine *The Insider* and were asked to watch footage of themselves fighting and answer the charge that it looked abusive; Baker responded: "I'm a better person than that. I have to say I had a temper tantrum, you know, I pushed her, I never should have, and you know, I regret every moment of it and you know what, hopefully that experience will make me a better person. That's our story line, you know, that's who we were on television. That's not who we are in real life."

Such a framing of that reality TV footage is emblematic: the show is perceived as somewhat mediated and constructed but still real enough to warrant a press debate. Through a bit of internal network marketing, Dr. Phil actually made them the topic of one of his CBS prime-time specials on relationships. Noting that the show sparked reams of hate mail and even death threats toward the couple, Dr. Phil explicitly argues that America was watching the couple and wants to debate them in TV's public sphere. At the outset of the interview, he invokes and calls into being an imagined national public, saying, "America was outraged and appalled by what they've seen." After he exhorts the husband to correct his behavior, he concludes, "So America doesn't need to worry about you?" (*Dr. Phil Primetime Special*). Dr. Phil does not completely buy Baker's argument that he was only acting aggressively for the camera or that the editing heightened his behavior, and he admonishes the man for exhibiting bad behavior in any context, mediated or not. Dr. Phil is well aware of the construction of images that he himself perpetuates, and he even draws attention to how Baker tries to manipulate this on-camera interview by coaching his wife, yet he insists on a substantial component of actuality in all these depictions. In the press and popular response, the gamedoc show couple becomes a paradigmatic reality TV family example that can be used to analyze the state of the American family more generally.

Ultimately, reality programs add a new wrinkle to television's family ideas. The genre illuminates how the current definition of the family is up for grabs, and reality TV enters the debate arena in force. Instead of having nostalgia for the Cleavers as a model of the modern American family, viewers might one day have nostalgia for the Osbournes as a model of the postmodern American family. The amplified truth claims of reality TV comment on the social role of television itself as an electronic medium offering "public scripts" that, as the medium evolves, viewers increasingly want to interact with on the screen and participate in themselves.

Leigh H. Edwards is an Associate Professor of English at Florida State University, where she specializes in nineteenth- and twentieth-century literature and popular culture.

Sarah Boxer

NO

Why Are All the Cartoon Mothers Dead?

Bambi's mother, shot. Nemo's mother, eaten by a barracuda. Lilo's mother, killed in a car crash. Koda's mother in *Brother Bear*, speared. Po's mother in *Kung Fu Panda 2*, done in by a power-crazed peacock. Ariel's mother in the third *Little Mermaid*, crushed by a pirate ship. Human baby's mother in *Ice Age*, chased by a saber-toothed tiger over a waterfall.

I used to take the Peter Pan bus between Washington, D.C., and New York City. The ride was terrifying but the price was right, and you could count on watching a movie on the screen mounted behind the driver's seat. *Mrs. Doubtfire*, *The Man Without a Face*, that kind of thing. After a few trips, I noticed a curious pattern. All the movies on board seemed somehow to feature children lost or adrift, kids who had metaphorically fallen out of their prams. Gee, I thought, Peter Pan Bus Lines sure is keen to reinforce its brand identity. The mothers in the movies were either gone or useless. And the father figures? To die for!

A decade after my Peter Pan years, I began watching a lot of animated children's movies, both new and old, with my son. The same pattern held, but with a deadly twist. Either the mothers died onscreen, or they were mysteriously disposed of before the movie began: *Chicken Little, Aladdin, The Fox and the Hound, Pocahontas, Beauty and the Beast, The Emperor's New Groove, The Great Mouse Detective, Ratatouille, Barnyard, Despicable Me, Cloudy With a Chance of Meatballs*, and, this year, *Mr. Peabody and Sherman*. So many animated movies. Not a mother in sight.

The cartoonist Alison Bechdel once issued a challenge to the film industry with her now-famous test: show me a movie with at least two women in it who talk to each other about something besides a man. Here's another challenge: show me an animated kids' movie that has a named mother in it who lives until the credits roll. Guess what? Not many pass the test. And when I see a movie that does (*Brave, Coraline, A Bug's Life, Antz, The Incredibles, The Lion King, Fantastic Mr. Fox*), I have to admit that I am shocked . . . and, well, just a tad wary.

But I'm getting ahead of myself. The dead-mother plot has a long and storied history, going back past *Bambi* and *Snow White*, past the mystical motherless world of Luke Skywalker and Princess Leia, past Dickens's orphans, past Hans Christian Andersen's Little Mermaid, past the Brothers Grimm's stepmothers, and past Charles Perrault's Sleeping Beauty and Cinderella. As Marina Warner notes in her book *From the Beast to the Blonde*, one of the first Cinderella stories, that of Yeh-hsien, comes from ninth-century China. The dead-mother plot is a fixture of fiction, so deeply woven into our storytelling fabric that it seems impossible to unravel or explain.

But some have tried. In *Death and the Mother From Dickens to Freud: Victorian Fiction and the Anxiety of Origins* (1998), Carolyn Dever, a professor of English, noted that character development begins "in the space of the missing mother." The unfolding of plot and personality, she suggests, depends on the dead mother. In *The Uses of Enchantment* (1976), Bruno Bettelheim, the child psychologist, saw the dead mother as a psychological boon for kids:

> The typical fairy-tale splitting of the mother into a good (usually dead) mother and an evil stepmother... is not only a means of preserving an internal all-good mother when the real mother is not all-good, but it also permits anger at this bad "step-mother" without endangering the goodwill of the true mother.

You may notice that these thoughts about dead mothers share a notable feature: they don't bother at all with the dead mother herself, only with the person, force, or thing that sweeps in and benefits from her death. Bettelheim focuses on the child's internal sense of himself, Dever on subjectivity itself. Have we missed something here? Indeed. I present door No. 3, the newest beneficiary of the dead mother: the good father.

Take *Finding Nemo* (Disney/Pixar, 2003), the mother of all modern motherless movies. Before the title sequence, Nemo's mother, Coral, is eaten by a barracuda, so Nemo's father, Marlin, has to raise their kid alone. He starts out as an overprotective, humorless wreck, but in the course of the movie he faces down everything—whales, sharks, currents, surfer turtles, an amnesiac lady-fish, hungry seagulls—to save Nemo from the clutches of the evil stepmother-in-waiting Darla, a human monster-girl with hideous braces (vagina dentata, anyone?). Thus Marlin not only replaces the dead mother but becomes the dependable yet adventurous parent Nemo always wanted, one who can both hold him close and let him go. He is protector and playmate, comforter and buddy, mother and father.

In the parlance of Helen Gurley Brown, he has it all! He's not only the perfect parent but a lovely catch, too. (Usually when a widowed father is shown onscreen mooning over his dead wife's portrait or some other relic, it's to establish not how wonderful she was but rather how wonderful he is.) To quote Emily Yoffe in *The New York Times*, writing about the perfection of the widowed father in *Sleepless in Seattle*, "He is charming, wry, sensitive, successful, handsome, a great father, and, most of all, he absolutely adores his wife. Oh, the perfect part? She's dead." Dad's magic depends on Mom's death. Boohoo, and then yay!

In a striking number of animated kids' movies of the past couple of decades (coincidental with the resurgence of Disney and the rise of Pixar and DreamWorks), the dead mother is replaced not by an evil stepmother but by a good father. He may start out hypercritical (*Chicken Little*) or reluctant (*Ice Age*). He may be a tyrant (*The Little Mermaid*) or a ne'er-do-well (*Despicable Me*). He may be of the wrong species (*Kung Fu Panda*). He may even be the killer of the child's mother (*Brother Bear*). No matter how bad he starts out, though, he always ends up good.

He doesn't just do the job, he's fabulous at it. In *Brother Bear* (Disney, 2003) when the orphaned Koda tries to engage the older Kenai as a father figure (not knowing Kenai killed his mom), Kenai (who also doesn't know) refuses: "There is no 'we,' okay? I'm not taking you to any salmon run . . . Keep all that cuddly-bear stuff to a minimum." In the end, though, Kenai turns out to be quite the father figure. And they both live happily ever after in a world without mothers.

So desperate are these kids' movies to get rid of the mother that occasionally they wind up in some pretty weird waters. Near the beginning of *Ice Age*, (Blue Sky/20th Century Fox, 2002), the human mother jumps into a waterfall to save herself and her infant, drags herself to shore, and holds on long enough to hand her child to a woolly mammoth. To quote an online review by C. L. Hanson, "She has the strength to push her baby up onto a rock and look sadly into the eyes of the mammoth, imploring him to steady her baby with his trunk," but—hold on—she doesn't have the strength to save herself? And by the way, if Manny the woolly mammoth is such a stand-up guy, why doesn't he "put his trunk around *both of them* and *save them both*" rather than watching her float downriver with a weary sigh? Because, as the reviewer noted, "the only purpose of her life was to set up their buddy adventure." Her work is done. Time to dispose of the body.

Many movies don't even bother with the mother; her death is simply assumed from the outset. In *Despicable Me* (Universal/Illumination, 2010), three orphaned girls, Margo, Edith, and Agnes, are adopted from an orphanage by Gru, a supervillain. Gru adopts them not because he wants children but because he plans to use them in his evil plot. He wants to shrink the moon and steal it. (Hey, wait, isn't the moon a symbol of female fertility?) But by the end of the movie, Gru discovers that his girls are more dear to him than the moon itself. And, as if this delicious father-cake needed some sticky icing, Gru gets to hear his own hypercritical mother—remember, it was *her* negativity that turned him evil in the first place!—admit that Gru's a better parent than she ever was. The supervillain becomes a superfather, redeemer of all bad mothers.

Quite simply, mothers are killed in today's kids' movies so the fathers can take over. (Of course, there are exceptions; in *Lilo and Stitch*, for instance, both of Lilo's parents die and it's her big sister who becomes the surrogate parent.) The old fairy-tale, family-romance movies that pitted poor motherless children against horrible vengeful stepmothers are a thing of the past. Now plucky children and their plucky fathers join forces to make their way in a motherless world. The orphan plot of yore seems to have morphed, over the past decade, into the buddy plot of today. Roll over, Freud: in a neat reversal of the Oedipus complex, the *mother* is killed so that the children can have the *father* to themselves. Sure, women and girls may come and go, even participate in the adventure, but mothers? Not allowed. And you know what? It looks like fun!

Dear reader, I hear your objection: So what? Hollywood has always been a fantasyland. Or, to quote the cat in *Bolt* (Disney, 2008), a kids' movie about a dog who thinks he's actually a superhero because he plays one on TV: "Look, genius . . . It's entertainment for people. It's fake! Nothing you think is real is real!" Get over it. It's just a movie. Or, to quote the empowerment anthem from *Frozen* (in which both parents die), "Let it go."

Okay, I will. But first, a brief dip into reality. Did you know that 67 percent of U.S. households with kids are headed by married couples, 25 percent by single mothers, and only 8 percent by single fathers (almost half of whom live with their partners)? In other words, the fantasy of the fabulous single father that's being served up in a theater near you isn't just any fantasy; it's close to the opposite of reality. And so I wonder: Why, when so many real families have mothers and no fathers, do so many children's movies present fathers as the only parents?

Is the unconscious goal of these motherless movies to paper over reality? Is it to encourage more men to be maternal? To suggest that fathers would be better than mothers if only they had the chance? To hint that the world would be better without mothers? Or perhaps we're just seeing a bad case of what the psychoanalyst Karen Horney called "womb envy." Or maybe an expression of the primal rage that the psychoanalyst Melanie Klein described as the infant's "uncontrollable greedy and destructive phantasies and impulses against his mother's breasts."

Consider *Barnyard* (Paramount/Nickelodeon, 2006), a deeply lame reworking of the *Lion King* plot, in which the father bull, Ben, teaches his reckless, motherless, goof-off son, Otis, how to be a man. ("A strong man stands up for himself; a stronger man stands up for others.") As pathetic as *Barnyard* is, there's something truly staggering in it. Whenever the bulls stand up on two hooves, they reveal pink udders right where their male equipment should be—rubbery teats that resemble, as Manohla Dargis described them in *The New York Times*, "chubby little fingers waving toodle-oo."

In the whacked-out, reality-denying world of animated movies, these chubby, wiggly four-fingered udders, which appear on both females and males, are my favorite counterfactuals, bar none. I love, love, love them. The first time I laid eyes on those honkers, my jaw dropped. Even Walt Disney himself, who cooked up pink elephants on parade, never tried *this*. It was as if the comical leather phalluses of ancient Greek theater had come back to life. As if the directors' very ids were plastered on the screen. Not only do *Barnyard*'s bulls have bizarre phallic teats, but Otis rudely swings his out the window of a speeding stolen car while drinking a six-pack of milk—yes, *milk*—and, as the police chase him, shouts, "Milk me!" Is he saying what I think he's saying? In a kids' movie? Could udder envy be any more naked?

When I finally shut my jaw, I realized that *Barnyard* isn't the only kids' movie with a case of udder confusion. (In the third *Ice Age*, Sid the Sloth, while trying to feed the three baby dinosaurs he's adopted, starts to milk a musk ox before discovering that it's a guy—ack!) But as far as I know, the *Barnyard* scene is the most violent instance; when the teated bull yells "Milk me!" it's like he's shouting

at women everywhere: "You think you're so hot with your tits and your babies. Well, suck on this! (And then die.)"

That's how I see it, anyway, and I don't think I'm alone.

In *How to Read Donald Duck* (1975), Ariel Dorfman, the Chilean American activist and writer, and Armand Mattelart, a Belgian sociologist, discuss the insidiousness of "the absence of woman as *mother* in Disney." Rather than presenting any really maternal figure, they say, Disney offers up only "the captive and ultimately frivolous woman," who lacks any tie to "the natural cycle of life itself"—Cinderella, Sleeping Beauty, Snow White. And in the natural mother's place, they note, Disney erects a "false mother Mickey," a creature of "chivalrous generosity" and "fair play" whose authority looks benign and cheery. The absence of a real mother thus makes way for a new authority, a new "natural" order. The road to social repression, in other words, is paved with Mickey Mouse.

In today's movie fathers, there's plenty of Mickey Mouse. They're magnanimous, caring, and fun. And I imagine these animated fathers look great to most kids. But let's call a spade a spade. The ineluctable regularity of the dead-mother, fun-father pattern is not just womb envy at work, and not just aggression against the breast; it's Mickey's glove displacing the maternal teat. It's misogyny made cute.

Dear reader, I hear you objecting again. Perhaps you're getting irritated. Perhaps you like Pixar. Perhaps you'd like to remind me of some living mothers in a few animated movies: Isn't that a single mother raising two kids in *Toy Story*? (Yes, she's the one who keeps trying to give away the toys.) And isn't that a mother at the end of *The Lego Movie*? (Yes, she's the one who cuts short the nascent father-son bonding moment in the basement by announcing that supper is ready.)

What about Fiona, the ogre-princess in *Shrek* (DreamWorks, 2001)? She certainly seems to be someone's caricature of a feminist—tough, competent, belching earthily with the boys. By *Shrek the Third* (2007), she's pregnant. At her baby shower, she makes all her beautiful, single friends—Snow White, Sleeping Beauty, Cinderella, and Rapunzel—seem like spoiled, materialistic wimps. But when it comes time for Fiona's own father, a frog king, to pass down the crown, he offers it not to *her* but to her ogre-husband, Shrek—who eventually turns it down because he has "something much more important in mind." (He's going to be a father!) That's right: the male gallantly refuses all that power (sweet old Mickey) while the female, who should have been next in line for the throne, isn't asked, and doesn't complain.

Patriarchy is slyly served. We've been slipped a Mickey!

A similar thing happens in *Ice Age: Dawn of the Dinosaurs* (2009). When Ellie, a sassy woolly mammoth, goes into labor, she's stuck on a cliff and her man, Manny, is off fighting predators. This leaves Diego, the saber-toothed tiger, to play birth coach. At one puzzling point, Ellie, the very picture of strength, yells to Diego, "You can do it! Push, push!" as if he were the one giving birth. He snaps back: "You have no idea what I'm going through!" (He's fending off vicious blue dinosaurs—more work than childbirth, from the looks of it.)

It's funny! The filmmakers, after all, don't *really* think Diego is working harder than Ellie. (Sexism always slides down better with a self-ironizing wink and giggle.) But once the baby pops out, we get patriarchy in earnest: the father, Manny, fresh from his own heroics, reenters the scene. Ellie hands him the baby, which he secures with his trunk and declares "perfect."

This cozy family scene reprises the original *Ice Age*, when Manny the woolly mammoth saved the human baby—and not the mother—with his trunk. This time, though, the mother is allowed to live. Why? Because she never upstaged the buddy plot. Her death would have been, well, overkill.

Have we moved beyond killing mothers, to a place where it no longer matters whether they live or die? From the newest crop of kids' animated movies, which are mostly buddy movies—*Planes, Turbo, Cloudy With a Chance of Meatballs 2, Monsters University, Free Birds, The Lego Movie*—it sure looks that way. It seems as if we have entered, at least in movie theaters, a post-mother world.

In March, when I took my son to see *Mr. Peabody and Sherman* (DreamWorks, 2014), I suspected that we'd be watching a buddy movie, pure and simple, in which the presence or absence of mothers was immaterial. I was wrong.

Apparently, it was finally time to blast mothers out of history. At the start of the movie, Mr. Peabody—a dog, a Harvard graduate, a Nobel laureate, and the inventor of Zumba, the fist bump, and the WABAC (pronounced "wayback") machine—says his dearest dream is to be a father. He adopts a human boy, Sherman; vows "to be the best father"; and is wildly successful at it. (He uses the WABAC to teach his son history by introducing him to figures like Benjamin Franklin, Vincent van Gogh, and William Shakespeare.)

The movie thus begins where other kids' movies end, with the perfect father-son relationship. Nothing can threaten them—except, alas, two gals, Ms. Grunion,

an ugly social worker (the evil-stepmother figure), who wants to tear dog and boy apart, and Penny, a bratty girl who is jealous of Sherman's knowledge and gets him to take her on a trip in the WABAC. And there the adventure begins.

They go to Leonardo's Italy. (Why won't the Mona Lisa smile?) They go to ancient Troy. ("Don't even get me started about Oedipus. Let's just say that you do *not* want to be at his house over the holidays! It's awkward.") And they go to ancient Egypt, where Penny herself is inserted into history. Tellingly, she's not given the obvious, powerful role—Cleopatra—but instead becomes the bride of King Tut, who's destined to die early. (Her reaction to learning this bit of history? Vintage Valley Girl with a hint of gold digger: "Oh, trust me, I've thought it through. I'm getting everything!")

But the key moment comes at the end of the movie, when we get to see George Washington muttering about changing the Declaration of Independence. I held my breath. Would the Founding Father (yes, Father) correct one of the most famous, glaring faults of the document? I listened for the magic words, and this is what I heard: "We hold these truths to be self-evident, that all men—and *some dogs*—are created equal." What?!?! (Insert spit take.) Given the chance to rewrite history, the filmmakers give rights to *some dogs*? But not to the bitches (I mean to the women)? Sure, it's funny. Funny like udders on male cows. Funny sad. Funny infuriating. Funny painful.

The power of the WABAC to rewrite history, if only in fantasy, made me remember why I like animation so much. Just as time travel imagines the way things might have been, so does animation give the creator total omnipotence. With animation you can suspend the laws of physics and the laws of society and the laws of reason and the laws of biology and the laws of family. You can have a dog adopt a boy. You can turn a rat into a French chef. You can make male cows with big pink udders. You can change the Declaration of Independence. You can have a family in which every member is a doggone superhero.

As the Soviet film director and theorist Sergei Eisenstein wrote of Disney's early work, you can have "a family of octopuses on four legs, with a fifth serving as a tail, and a sixth—a trunk." You can do anything. Eisenstein marveled, "How much (imaginary!) divine omnipotence there is in this! What magic of reconstructing the world according to one's fantasy and will!"

And yet, in this medium where the creators have total control, we keep getting the same damned world—a world without mothers. Is this really the dearest wish of animation? Can mothers really be so threatening?

I'd like to end on a hopeful note, with a movie that passes my test with flying colors—*The Incredibles* (Disney/Pixar, 2004), which happens to feature not only three major female characters, including a great mother figure, Elastigirl (a k a Helen Parr), who lives for the whole movie, but also a pretty credible father figure, Mr. Incredible (a k a Bob Parr). Unlike just about every other movie dad, Mr. Incredible is far from perfect. He daydreams during dinner. He is more interested in getting back to hero-work (he has been forcibly retired, along with all the other heroes) than in how his kids are doing at school. He even lies to his wife about where he's going and what he's doing. He is super-angry. When his car door won't shut, he slams it so hard that the window shatters.

The hero of the movie isn't Mr. Incredible, but the mother, who turns back into Elastigirl, a really flexible, sexy, and strong superhero, in order to save her husband. ("Either he's in trouble or he's going to be!") At one point during the rescue mission, the plane that the mother is flying is hit by missiles and she and the kids have to eject. The mother uses her elasticity to reach out and grab her children and parachute them, with herself as the chute, to the ocean below. Then she transforms her body into a speedboat (her son, who has super-speed, is the motor) to reach the shore. It's a view of what animated movies could be—not another desperate attempt to assert the inalienable rights of men, but an incredible world where everyone has rights and powers, even the mothers.

I should point out that Elastigirl's superpower—flexibility, stretchiness, or what Eisenstein, back in the 1940s, termed "plasmaticness"—happens to be the very attribute he singled out as the most attractive imaginable in art, a universal sign of the ability to assume any form. He found this elasticity not only in his beloved Mickey Mouse but also in Lewis Carroll's long-necked Alice, in the 18th-century Japanese etchings of "the many-metred arms of geishas," in the rubber-armed snake dancers of New York's black nightclubs, in Balzac's *La Peau de Chagrin*, in Wilhelm Busch's *Max und Moritz*, and in the stretched noses of the Tengu. Elastigirl, then, is not only a great character and a great mother, but the very picture of protoplasmic freedom.

For some reason, though, what really sticks in my mind is not Elastigirl stretching the limits of plasticity but rather a scene from *Ratatouille* (Disney/Pixar, 2007). Colette, the sole female in the kitchen of Gusteau's restaurant, is trying to teach the basics of cooking to Linguini, the bumbling orphan boy who gets a job in Gusteau's kitchen only because his mother slept with the great chef before she (yes) died.

As Colette chops away frenetically at some celery stalks, she shouts: "You think cooking is a cute job, eh? Like Mommy in the kitchen? Well, Mommy never had to face the dinner rush, when the orders come flooding in . . . Every second counts—and *you cannot be Mommy*!" Who is she shouting at? Linguini the lucky orphan? Herself? Men in general? Men who want to have it all? Women who want to have it all? Animators? Fathers? I really don't know, but it's a fantastic moment of pure rage. And it sure rings true.

SARAH BOXER is a writer and illustrator who has published two graphic novels, *In the Floyd Archives* and its sequel *Mother May I?*. She occasionally writes for *The Atlantic* on a wide range of subjects.

EXPLORING THE ISSUE

Do Media Reflect Contemporary Family Relationships?

Critical Thinking and Reflection

1. In what family portrayals in media do you most experience resonance? By that, we mean, which portrayals seem most similar to your own experience?
2. Do you think that the family relationships you observe in reality television are realistic?
3. Can you think of any fairy tales or children's films that feature a strong maternal birth mother?
4. Do you see family relationships in different media genres that you think "reflect reality" or those that might reflect the perspective of a "window on the world"?

Is There Common Ground?

Both of the authors of these selections ground their approach in a different way of seeing the world. They also primarily write about media content that targets different age groups. Professor Edwards is searching for the themes that media families portray, and Sarah Boxer examines content that is most often targeted toward children, though adults often see this content with children. But there is some common ground in the sense that we learn from the family portrayals we see, and we constantly measure our own experiences against the representations reflected in media content. Gender roles are particularly important issues for children to learn, so do children come away with different expectations when they view content that eliminates mothers, while fathers are portrayed as superheroes? Undoubtedly we reflect (consciously or unconsciously) on our own experiences as we consume media content, but do these extreme situations suggest other dynamics that you should consider?

Over decades, our society changes, but different people within our society judge these changes according to different criteria. There are a wider range of family units today than ever before. Nuclear families may not be the norm everywhere, but don't they still set the standard for the way families are represented in so many forms of media? Only 50 years ago, it might seem odd for a single person to adopt a child, but today families with only one parent, same sex parents, or extended families may live in the same household. By examining these questions and the authors' perspectives, you should gain a better sense of your own ideas about families and the representation of role models and gender relations, and how the two selections provide ideas about how media condition us to think of what is "normal" and what is not.

Additional Resources

Leigh H. Edwards, *The Triumph of Reality TV: The Revolution in American Television* (Praeger, 2013). Edwards examines a number of approaches to gauge the impact of reality television and the way it produces representations of social groups and individuals.

Richard M. Huff, ed., *Reality Television* (Praeger, 2006). This collection of essays includes additional perspectives on family portrayals in the media, reality television, and celebrity culture.

Dafnah Lemish, *Children and Media: A Global Perspective* (Wiley-Blackwell, 2014). By examining a wide range of media forms, the author takes an interdisciplinary approach to explaining how and why children perceive content in special ways.

Leonard Maltin, *The Disney Films,* 4th Edition (Disney Editions 2000). This collection of Disney films references plot, character, action, and impact of most of the cartoons produced by Disney Studios.

Internet References . . .

Animation World Network

www.awn.com

Beyond Remote Controlled Childhood: Teaching Young Children in the Media Age

www.naeyc.org/books/beyond_remote_controlled _childhood

Center for Media Literacy

www.medialit.org/media-values

Common Sense Media

www.commonsensemedia.org/blog/family-media

Henry J. Kaiser Family Foundation

www.kff.org/other/the-media-family-electronic-media -in-the/

Maria Konnikova, "What Grown Ups Can Learn From Kids Books," *The Atlantic*, August 6, 2012.

www.theatlantic.com/entertainment/archive/2012/08 /what-grown-ups-can-learn-from-kids-books/260738/

Selected, Edited, and with Issue Framing Material by:
Alison Alexander, *University of Georgia*
and
Jarice Hanson, *University of Massachusetts—Amherst*

ISSUE

Have Media Representations of Minorities Improved?

YES: Drew Chappell, from "'Better Multiculturalism' through Technology: *Dora the Explorer* and the Training of the Preschool Viewer(s)," Lexington Books (2013)

NO: Elizabeth Monk-Turner et al., from "The Portrayal of Racial Minorities on Prime Time Television: A Replication of the Mastro and Greenberg Study a Decade Later," *Studies in Popular Culture* (2010)

Learning Outcomes

After reading this issue, you will be able to:

- Think about the ways representation of race in the media affects our perceptions of individuals.
- Reflect on how what we see and hear in media influences our concept of self and others.
- Evaluate whether social change occurs through the images presented by media.
- Consider the role media play in the lives of different generations of users.

ISSUE SUMMARY

YES: Professor Drew Chappell juxtaposes facts about recent actions attempting to ban ethnic studies and restrict immigration in parts of the United States with the television show, *Dora the Explorer's* portrayal of a bilingual (English/Spanish) speaking girl, and discusses how the show introduces children to bilingualism, border identities, and multicultural discourse. Chappell discusses how the performance of identity in Dora's world can teach children about what brings all humans together.

NO: Elizabeth Monk-Turner, et al. revisit what has become a classic study in the portrayal of minorities in media and finds that even though how minorities are represented have changed within context, no serious changes to stereotypes have really occurred. In this study of prime-time television programming, little has changed within the 10-year time span between the classic Mastro and Greenberg study, and the analysis provided by the authors.

Intense controversy exists about how racial and ethnic groups are portrayed in the media. Many scholars argue that racial representations in popular culture help mold public opinion and set the agenda for public discourse on race issues in the media and society as a whole. Do members of an audience identify with the characters portrayed? Do expressions of images in the media communicate effectively about specific races, ethnicities, or cultures? How much can we learn about other cultures and personal difference through the portrayals of characters in the media? While there may not be one answer to each of the questions posed, we do know that some people are more highly influenced by images of the "other," and that for many people who live in homogeneous communities, their only exposure to people who are different than themselves come through media. In this way, television (and other media forms) can be considered our "windows to the world" as we store the images from media, and make sense of them as we learn more about society.

Extrapolating the images portrayed in media to real life is a complicated process, but often involves some aspect of stereotyping. Despite such shows as the infamous *Amos'n'Andy,* portrayals of African Americans were for the most part absent from early television programming. In the 1970s, many all African American casts found their way to prime time television. Shows like *Good Times, The Jeffersons*, and in 1984, *The Cosby Show*, were all financially successful and showed that popular television, especially comedy, could portray loving families that had an appeal to a broad, multiracial audience.

While the presence of minorities in television have increased with more shows targeting similar racial and ethnic groups, and many shows including members of minority groups within the cast, how those actors and actresses are portrayed still remain one of the most fundamental questions of examining television content. For example, what role does the character "Winston" plays in the popular prime-time comedy, *New Girl*? Does his race matter to the relationships within the show? Can race be represented without resorting to stereotypes, and if and when minority characters are portrayed in nonstereotypical ways, do viewers experience that character differently? Do the parasocial relationships we have with actors/characters in media influence our expectations of people we meet in real life?

The role of stereotyping in media has been a subject of intense study for scholars in media and society. Stereotypes are often thought about as primarily negative images, and yet, if more minorities were portrayed in positive roles, those stereotypes might actually suggest greater accomplishment and challenge negative stereotypes. At the same time, this question could also be extended to thinking about the stereotypes presented by women in the media, representations of age, body type, disability, and class. So the issue of stereotyping is a broad and important one for us to consider.

Many studies have been conducted to examine how minority ownership of programming outlets (like BET, or Telemundo, for example) influence the type of portrayals in media, and questions of ownership and decision making are central to understanding representation of minorities in general. But some larger questions still remain. How do news outlets portray people in the news? Is there a bias that might creep in and change the nature of the story being reported? Are minorities represented across the board in all media forms? What is the relationship of how any one of us learns about other people and difference, to those forms of media we consume?

Professor Drew Chappell takes an interesting approach from performance studies to examine how the animated character, in *Dora the Explorer,* engages in the performativity of multiculturalism. In so doing, the television show creates opportunities for young viewers to learn language, culture, and social values in a context of creating interactive experiences through the medium of television. Though programs like *Dora the Explorer* may not be the solution to introducing a more multicultural world, Chappell identifies issues that have heretofore been nonexistent in terms of how television can normalize relationships in a multicultural world.

In contrast, Elizabeth Monk-Turner, Mary Heiserman, Crystle Johnson, Vanity Cotton, and Manny Jackson adapt the methodology used in a study from 2000 by Mastro and Greenberg who examined representations of Caucasian, African American/Black, and Latino characters in primetime television to help us understand if, within a 10-year period, any significant difference could be discerned from prime-time representations of these groups. Comparing their data to the realities of the U.S. population by race, the authors demonstrate that minorities are still considerably underrepresented, and portrayed differently, and with different characteristics.

The issues represented by these selections should lead you to think broadly about the roles represented by racial and ethnic groups in media, and hopefully, the complex web of media content, ownership of media outlets, writers, actors, and directors. Furthermore, the number of cable channels and the increasing internationalization of media forms (especially film) should make you think more broadly about the issues of representation that go beyond your own school, community, and social relationships. Do you seek images that conform to your own preconceived notions about what is accepted in society? Can you think of situations or images in which some of your ideas about stereotypes have been challenged? How have you dealt with the deviation of what may, on the surface, seem "normal?"

It is also interesting to think about whether programs targeted to special groups, like children, have the potential to create social change, or whether these programs actually support more mainstream, prime-time media fare. Will *Dora the Explorer,* for example, be one of the television shows that shape a generation's expectations for life in the future when, according to the U.S. Census (2008), Latinos comprise one-fourth of the U.S. population? What shows did you watch when you were a child, and which ones do you remember most fondly? Did they all have representations of characters to whom you could relate? Or, did you learn some of your stereotypical reactions to "others" through those media you consumed?

Perhaps a basic question as you approach these two selections should be: how long does it take to change stereotypes? Intense controversy exists about how racial and ethnic groups are portrayed in the media. Many scholars argue that racial representations in popular culture help mold public opinion and set the agenda for public discourse on race issues in the media and society as a whole. Do members of an audience identity with the characters portrayed? Do expressions of images in the media communicate effectively about specific cultures? How much can we learn about other cultures and personal difference through the portrayals of characters in the media?

YES ⤶

Drew Chappell

"Better Multiculturalism" through Technology: *Dora the Explorer* and the Training of the Preschool Viewer(s)

By the late twentieth century, our time, a mythic time, we are all chimeras, theorized and fabricated hybrids of machine and organism; in short, we are cyborgs. This cyborg is our ontology; it gives us our politics.
—Haraway, 149

Arizona, April 23, 2010. Governor Jan Brewer, promoted from Secretary of State when Governor Janet Napolitano left office to serve as the Secretary of Homeland Security under Barack Obama, signs Senate Bill 1070, giving state police broad power to detain and question those people they suspect of being undocumented immigrants to the United States ("Arizona Enacts Stringent Law on Immigration," "Senate Bill 1070"). This legislation has touched off a firestorm of controversy, inspiring protest on both sides of the immigration issue. Emboldened by perceived support for such draconian policies, conservative lawmakers and education officials in Arizona followed up SB 1070 with a ban on ethnic studies ("Arizona Bill Targeting Ethnic Studies Signed into Law") and a crackdown on teachers who speak English with an accent ("Arizona Grades Teachers on Fluency"). In 2011 a bill denying birth certificates to children born in the United States to undocumented individuals is expected was introduced but defeated in Arizona (Rau 2011).

Four years earlier, in the 2006 midterm election, citizens in Arizona, Colorado, and New Mexico voted on measures aimed at discouraging "illegal immigration" from Mexico and South America. Among these measures were Arizona's Propositions 103, which would establish English as the official language of the state, and 300, which would deny public program eligibility to any person who was not a lawful resident of the United States (Arizona Secretary of

State's Office). Both propositions passed into law. These were not the only attempts to respond to perceived abuses of immigration policy. Bilingual education had previously been targeted; in 2000, Arizona banned bilingual programs in schools and established English as the only instructional language.

In this politically charged climate, the Nickelodeon Jr. show *Dora the Explorer,* featuring a bilingual English/Spanish speaking girl and her friends, remained a television hit, with 21.9 million viewers in November 2005 in the United States (Wingett). Preschool children (who are approximately ages 2.5–5 in the United States) watched on television what they were discouraged from encountering in their daily lives: a Spanish speaking girl who, together with her diverse group of friends, leaves her home and family and crosses multiple borders with impunity in order to pursue various objectives.

Dora the Explorer (Dora) constitutes a cultural phenomenon; the television show's popularity has spawned a host of commercial products including toys, games, clothing, books, music albums, and home furnishings. In fact, in the 2006 holiday season, Dora was the number one toy license (Frenck 2). The show has won numerous awards, including a Peabody (for Broadcast Media) in 2003 and two Imagens (for positive portrayal of Latino characters/culture) in 2003 and 2004 ("Awards for Dora" 1–4). It also spun off a second show featuring Dora's cousin Diego, called *Go, Diego, Go.* The show's reach and its cultural currency led me to choose *Dora* as a research site. Even before I had a preschool-age child, I could not escape the show's marketing and media coverage. I wondered what was behind its popularity. What specific narratives and performances did the show employ, and how did it construct dominant and subaltern identities that contribute to what I have elsewhere called "colonizing the imaginary": "an ideological process in which adults write their own culturally bound values, beliefs, and ideas onto narrative structures and performances intended for children's consumption (Chappell 18)?"

To interrogate this topic, I chose twelve episodes of the show that represented a cross-section of the show's storytelling strategies. I watched special double-length episodes ("Dora's Pirate Adventure," "Dora Saves the Mermaids," "Dora's World Adventure"), and standard episodes that reflected a number of tropes, ideas, and curricular goals. In watching these episodes, I paid close attention to the narratives created and the ways they called for children's embodiment—physically (speaking back to the show, moving with Dora), relationally (identifying with Dora and Boots's problems), and ideologically (grappling with the issues and values presented in the show, such as friendship). As I watched the program, with its deceptively simple formula and insistence on communicating directly to its audience, I became aware of subtle ways that the characters engage in an implicit dialog around multiculturalism (more on this term later). There is certainly more to *Dora* than there appears; the show cleverly uses surface-level representations to engage complex social and political concepts (perhaps without the viewer's awareness). Once I collected data, I used typologies and assertion development to analyze my findings. I created the typologies based on a semiotic reading of the *Dora* episodes in relation to contextual information found in the sites and spaces surrounding the show. This context included intended social use, promotional material, contemporary political discourse, and *Dora* merchandising outside the show itself. The typologies allowed for interpretation and analysis of the data (Bogdan and Biklen, Wolcott), and pointed toward a common theme put forth by the image of Dora as cultural traveler who bears the markings of a number of different subaltern identities, from a white middle-class U.S. perspective (non-white, female, child, Spanish speaker), and uses networks of friends and various technologies to solve each issue she faces. I then used assertion development (Erickson) to construct a theoretical understanding of the nature of embodiment and power in the show, as follows: *Dora the Explorer suggests that technology is the road to a multicultural society, and this society will focus on similarities rather than differences.*

Television as Performance

Children's television enters the child's own space; it "invades" the private sphere of the home via a broadcast signal, cable, or other device. To watch a program, young people must gather around a television screen, often located in a common area where parents can monitor their children's viewing. Watching television is a bit like a small-scale film screening; a screen becomes the center of focus, and images tell the story. Unlike in a movie theater, however, a child can feel free to move around as much as desired, take breaks, or "multitask," playing with toys, books, and so on while watching. Also, the characters on a television screen are (typically) miniaturized, easily controlled by the viewer (wielding a remote). This use of space may lead to a familiarity, an intimacy between viewer and television character(s). There is a sense that the program is "only for me," although I know there are many others watching the same program, not being able to see them "erases" their presence. Television uses time in specific, regimented ways; programs appear according to a schedule, thus allowing the practice of viewing to become routinized. On non public broadcasting channels (such as Nick Jr.—Dora's network) programs are "interrupted" for commercial content—product and service advertising. There is a "rhythm" to watching television shows and waiting out commercials—an embodied sense of when the program will institute a twist or when a commercial is coining up. Like other media, TV trains users (starting in childhood) in its effective use.

Like film, television controls the viewer's gaze through its use of camera shots. These are typically more "claustrophobic" than in film, as many shows are filmed in studios using sets that are reused from week to week. Animated programs like *Dora* add another layer of mediation; they offer two-dimensional representations of people, places, and objects that the audience recognizes from outside experience. These referents, however, are recombined, exaggerated, and otherwise distorted through the animation process until they become more simulacra than simulations (Baudrillard). As in comic books, the tendency is for animated settings and events to transcend reality. In these worlds, extraordinary things may happen quite easily, as the animator's only limitation is what he or she can draw. Animation sets up a fantastic realm in which rules are malleable, conflict is explicitly handled, and objectives are clearly defined. Animated characters, again like their comic book counterparts, tend to be less psychologically complex and more emblematic. They bear only a passing resemblance to actual people, typically having one characteristic that defines and limits them.

As with film, television audiences are expected to sit relatively quietly and pay attention to what is happening on-screen. However, as mentioned above, television offers more opportunity for freedom of movement and "outside" actions. Typically, the viewing experience is framed as "passive," an engagement with the screen images connotes a detachment with the world at large. Much is made in the media of television's detrimental effects on children's health, as television replaces more "active" entertainment (I use quotes with active and passive to suggest that the dichotomous framing of these terms is troubling in light of the [potential] critical and semiotic activity performed while watching television). *Dora's* creators specifically sought to get children's bodies moving when they view the program. They built in multiple opportunities for children to speak back to the characters and engage in other physical activities. The desired outcome of such a strategy is to make the viewer feel even closer to the characters, as if he or she is inhabiting and exploring Dora's world alongside her.

Most television programs have a two-pronged narrative strategy. They try to create stand-alone episode; so that viewers will have a complete experience during the half-hour or hour they spend watching. But producers also want to reward faithful viewing, and so they create larger narratives that build slowly over time. In the case of *Dora*, this larger story is not as explicitly handled; episodes are self-contained and similar, and the "rewards" for repeat viewing are a knowledge of minor characters and following Dora through multiple settings and genres and watching her persona flourish in each. The strategy of giving viewers a little at a time is part of the training process; like giving an animal a treat when it performs a desired action, a show that comes on at a specific time offers an anticipated and constant return. But children's knowledge of this predictable structure within an episode is also a form of power.

Dora, Her World, and Borders

Dora revolves around a young Latina girl and her friends traveling through various landscapes in search of missing articles or characters, or collaborating on a group objective. Each show follows a similar format, based around the narrative style and strategies of a computer game. Dora and Boots, her monkey best friend, introduce themselves, and a complication emerges. To achieve their objective, they call upon Map, a talking, rolled-up map who identifies a series of locations to which they must travel. Often during their journey, they encounter Swiper the Fox, who attempts to steal an item that Dora needs. Sometimes

Swiper succeeds, and sometimes Dora and Boots foil him by chanting "Swiper, no swiping!" three times. Also on the journey, Dora utilizes her backpack (herself a character) to retrieve some necessary item from the myriad of objects she contains. Eventually, Dora and her friends achieve their objective, and sing a victory song: "We Did It." They then ask the viewer to recall his/her "favorite part" of the journey, before sharing their own. Every show follows this formula; elements such as locations, objects needed, and characters encountered may change, but the journey structure never alters.

Dora takes place in a borderland; its main character speaks two languages and Dora seems caught between Mexican and U.S. culture. Author/theorist Gloria Anzaldúa defines borders as more than physical boundaries: "Borders are set up to define the places that are safe and unsafe, to distinguish *us* from *them*. A border is a dividing line, a narrow strip along a steep edge. A borderland is a vague and undetermined space created by the emotional residue of an unnatural boundary" (3). I find this definition a useful space to begin talking about the discourse around Dora's explorations. Although Dora lives in a borderland, the only "borders" she encounters are spaces between locations, which are easily traversed. In her travels, she might be seen as a *border crosser*—someone who belongs to multiple cultures simultaneously and is able to move freely between and among them. Anzaldúa suggests that those who exist in this state are often feared, mocked, or seen as illegitimate, but Dora encounters no such prejudice. Although she holds several real-world markers of the historically subaltern or marginalized—female, nonwhite, child, Spanish speaker—she is centered in her own constructed society, and so represents the dominant identity (yet the audience has intertextual knowledge of her as a marginalized identity—at least in the U.S.).

By dominant identity, I mean that Dora represents a normative middle class U.S. childhood. She lives in a home, attends school, plays safely with her friends, and does not worry about money for meals (in fact, she sometimes gives Boots money when he doesn't have it available, as in "Ice Cream"). Her mother is an archaeologist, as we learn in "Job Day," but her father's employment (if any) is not addressed. He is mostly seen cooking and caring for Dora's younger siblings. As she is represented as a normative U.S. child, Dora also demonstrates the strategy of "selective incorporation of cultural elements from the various cultural worldviews and practices to which [she] has been exposed during . . . her life" (Chen, Benet-Martinez, and Bond 806). This reflects her positioning as bicultural within a globalized/mediatized environment. Could Dora's border identity point to a growing knowledge and expectation of multicultural identity? Educational theorists Cameron McCarthy and Greg Dimitriades describe the current social condition: "Indeed, if this is an era of the 'post,' it is also an era of difference—and the challenge of this era of difference is the challenge of living in a world of incompleteness, discontinuity, and multiplicity" (202). This paradigm organizes Dora's world, with its border-crossing protagonist and easy acceptance of various cultural backgrounds against an external lived backdrop of controversy over immigration policy and border politics. The show may aspire to Homi Bhabha's discursive "Third Space," with narratives and environments focused not around cultural distinction, but hybridity. In *Dora,* speaking more than one language is taken for granted and imparted as useful. In her world, various cultures (and even species) collaborate and celebrate their common goals and values. In fact, the show represents a liberal humanist societal outlook in which differences are minimized and unity centered.

Yet, the ethos of the *Dora* show also reflects some of the troubling discourse around the term "multiculturalism." Rusom Bharucha writes: "There is almost an in-built expectation written into the 'multi' which assumes that 'we *have* to get along and live together.' In short, it would seem to deny the 'right to exit' a particular society or to subvert the premises of 'living together'" (10). When presented to young people, is the ideology associated with use of this term a forward-looking worldview? Or, does it seek to establish a basic and official knowledge to which all cultures should be exposed in order to mold their cultural understandings while keeping their folkloric character (Torres 198)? In other words, is Dora's border crossing transgressive, challenging accepted notions of identity as "this" or "that," or is it monolithic, attempting to homogenize multiple blended identities into a singular "human" experience? Do the characters in *Dora* have the "right to exit" their common journeys and objectives, or to question the ways in which these objectives are pursued?

Bilingualism and Border Identities

At the beginning of most *Dora* episodes, she greets the audience: "Hola! Soy Dora!" Boots joins in: "And I'm Boots." This bilingual greeting sets the tone for the show, which includes dialogue in both Spanish and English. One of the stated goals of *Dora*'s creators was to teach Spanish vocabulary ("More about Dora" 1), and so episodes introduce Spanish words for numbers, greetings, and simple phrases. Some of these are translated into English, and some are not; the viewer must make meaning of the non-translated words through context. Yet, although the program includes bilingual elements, in its U.S. form, the "default language" is English. A child who spoke no Spanish at all would have no trouble following the narrative of Dora's journey.

Media and communications scholar Richard Popp suggests that the bilingual nature of *Dora* distinguishes the show within the field of educational programming. The focus on language learning becomes a motivation for parents to encourage their children to watch the show: "Language becomes a means of advancing into the upper echelons of education, work, and even taste groups. Bilingualism can open doors and act as a symbol of one's tolerance and refinement" (17). He points out, however, that parents of children watching the show must value the cultural capital associated with being bilingual. They must also have the means to "take the next step" and provide assistance to their children in order for them to progress beyond the simple words and phrases the show teaches (12). This attention to the *kind* of bilingualism being taught by *Dora* is important; the show's educative merit is in teaching English speaking children beginning Spanish, not in assisting Spanish speakers to maintain their language. (This is also true of dual-language schools in Arizona, which can only be attended by Englishproficient students—there is no provision for using Spanish to develop English-speaking skills.) Essentially, Dora is a "helpful native," a guide whose purpose is to introduce her own language to outsiders, and to translate for them when they encounter unfamiliar contexts. But where does Dora "live"? What is the terrain the show guides the audience through?

Dora's home is not specifically located in a single country, but more of a borderland, a "no-place/everyplace." This home space is a verdant landscape with tropical trees and green hills. Dora's family's house has a Spanish tile roof, and the walls around its door and windows are painted with turquoise designs. The landscape and animal clues—Dora's friends include an iguana, monkey, and bull—seem to locate the show in Mexico or South America, but even this is a computer game-style simulation, a politically charged sedimentation of U.S. fantasies of travel/ exploration/colonization. Because she lives in this borderland, Dora seems to be a cultural hybrid, a combination of multiple traditions and folkloric elements. She is drawn as a Latina girl, but plays out (for example) European fairy tale and transatlantic pirate narratives. In an interview, one of the show's writers stated: "We often combine a Latino character with a fable character. But really, it's all a legacy of imagery" (Sigler 43). The "legacy of imagery" the writer speaks of suggests a view of Dora as symbolically formed from multiple imaginary strains.

She is a multicultural cipher, a hybrid in the most surface-level sense of Bhabha's meaning. Without a specific racial or ethnic identity, each viewer can "download" his or her own cultural background onto Dora, molding her into whatever that child or adult needs or wants her to be. (Thus adding to her great crosscultural appeal.)

Dora's family celebrates Christmas, with a tree in their living room and luminaria on the path outside ("A Present for Santa"). Yet the focus of the Christmas episode is on presents and their suitability for those who receive them, not on the religious or family-centered aspects of the holiday. When Swiper attempts to make off with their present for Santa, Boots hopes Christmas will bring out the fox's better nature: "Swiper wouldn't swipe on Christmas, would he, Dora?" In fact, Swiper takes the present, but returns it once he realizes it's for Santa. The present is "una guitarra" (a guitar), on which Santa serenades Boots and Dora with "Feliz Navidad." So Santa serves as a kind of universal bringer of good cheer rather than a Christian icon (this draws from his status in the culture at large, in which he has been largely stripped of religious context). Santa hails a liberal humanist/morality tale view of "Christmas" as unifying and peaceful—and yet, despite his secularization, he still represents Christian ideology; fully decontextualizing such a religious figure is not possible. In 2009, Nickelodeon premiered the episode "Dora Saves Three Kings Day,' which presents a surface treatment of Latino celebrations of Epiphany and the arrival of the three kings or magi (Reyes Magos). In the episode, Dora and her friends rescue animals which are to bring them to their village for the Three Kings celebration. . . .

When Dora travels, she does so almost instantaneously by stepping into a method of conveyance (that helpfully appears when she needs it) and then stepping off in a new location, usually after singing a brief song. These vehicles can take her across lakes, around the world, or even to another planet ("Journey to the Purple Planet"). She can also enter fairy tales by climbing into books ("Dora Saves the Prince") and breathe underwater using a magic crown to transform into a mermaid ("Dora Saves the Mermaids"). In her travels, Dora never buys a ticket or rides with other children. She has complete freedom to cross borders without documentation, and she never passes through any kind of immigration post. When she arrives at her destination, the local people and animals happily accept her. (One exception to this is when she enters Swiper's home space in "Berry Hunt" and picks berries—in this episode she is chased by a bear.) All this traveling suggests the space-bending possibilities of the Internet, a technology that allows communication and virtual travel across great distances. Because of its simulated nature, travel via

the Internet does not require documentation or funds. Like Dora's transportation, it occurs instantaneously and whenever needed by the user. But, again like Dora, those who travel in this fashion are limited by the environments, people, and information available through the technology used. And these travelers must always return "home" to their physical bodies. Although Dora may cross geographic borders, she cannot escape those of the television frame; she is at the mercy of her journey narrative and when her show ends, she disappears—or transitions into a Dora controlled by the child fan, assisted by branded dolls, clothing, and so on.

Children and Technology

Dora's narrative takes the form of a computer game, and Dora herself utilizes various technologies during her adventures. Thus, the show engages questions about the relationship of young people to technology such as: How is Dora's life structured as a computerized series of binary decisions? How does Dora's use of technology engage specific forms of embodiment and identities? And how does it reflect children's experience with technology in the "outside world"?

Theorists such as Neil Postman argue that children's use of media decreases their capacity for imaginative play and exposes them to harmful stimuli. On the other side of the continuum, David Buckingham argues that new media, such as computer software, the Internet, and text messaging, provide additional venues for communication and enhance young people's ability to extend their knowledge and influence. This utopic vision positions technology as generating new forms of learning, democratic literacy, liberation from bodily identity, and creative expression (Buckingham 44). Facility with multiple media also produces the ability to adapt to change, experiment creatively with different modalities, and learn to solve problems by "doing"—without rule books or manuals (McDonnell 115–16).

Through watching Dora, children learn the ritualized semiotic and performative aspects of machine use (Oravec 253). As they become accustomed to technology—through representations in entertainment or use of computers at home or school—children prepare to use machines in their daily lives. But cultural theorist Jo Ann Oravec cautions that: "Technology rituals can thus displace efforts to establish or participate in more human-centered rituals, rituals that involve higher levels of human response and permit more spontaneity, playfulness, and even magic" (Oravec 254). Notice the parallel here with Postman's view. As shows like Dora engage the binary structure of computer functions (calling for one right answer), might they curb children's creative use of the technology or ability to imagine alternative solutions and narratives?

When we use technology, we participate in an exercise of control over ourselves as users. We must use the technology in the way it demands; otherwise, it will not fulfill its function. Oravec suggests that adults have explored the "strategic use of technological ritual" to reinforce structure and establish discipline over children (262–263). Teaching such processes as launching a program, starting a file, saving work, researching on the Internet, etc. constitutes an imposition of structure, a discipline of children's minds and bodies focused toward particular uses of machines. This discipline imposes a technological layer on top of other daily structures such as mealtimes, class schedules, and bedtimes. The process assists in socializing children to become technological workers in a modernist paradigm (Callahan). As Donna Haraway suggests in the quote I led with, such a process moves society into an ever closer, cyborglike relationship with its machines.

Another issue raised by Oravec is the purpose of introducing children to technology in a consumerist culture. She states: "Through these consumption rituals, children learn that technology is a consumer item, and that the purpose of human interaction with computers is to collect various devices and then follow the programmed instructions, experimenting within their affordances and constraints" (261). As children add more technological devices and media, they increase their cultural capital. Rather than calling on children to master a single program or tool, as a parent or teacher might, the consumer market suggests that diversifying one's technological portfolio provides a more direct key to success. This is reflected in the *Dora* program; Dora relies on a multitude of mechanical devices (transportation, tools, reference materials) to get where she needs to go and acquire necessary items. But she also consistently utilizes her map to access information and mark her progress. Indeed, having access to technology and exhibiting mastery in its use ensures Dora is able to complete her objectives successfully each episode. (Such consumerism/collection is also promoted through the proliferation of *Dora* merchandise, electronic and non-electronic.)

Technology in/as Dora's World

Dora makes extensive use of technology during her adventures. Some is "low tech" or magic, like the map that shows her the locations she needs to travel through to reach her objectives, or her backpack that magically holds whatever items she might need. And some is quite sophisticated—as

mentioned, she has access to whatever mode of transportation she requires at any given time. In "Dora's World Adventure," she makes use of a collection of video screens that project images of her friends around the world and allow her to speak with them, as if on videophone. These screens, like Dora's instantaneous travel, suggest the possibilities of Internet communication. Dora's cousin Diego has a computerized "field journal" that he uses to collect information on animals ("Meet Diego"). The field journal seems to be linked not only to an information network about zoology, but also to a satellite feed—Diego can use it to locate any animal in seconds. The journal looks something like a Blackberry or GPS device, and its key function in the narrative gives it a "cool" factor that makes such devices attractive to the viewer.

Boots and Dora also like to "catch stars," reaching up and grabbing smiling stars that fly by them on their journey. Dora stores the stars in a special rainbow pocket on the side of her backpack. These "captive" stars, with diverse abilities and properties, prove useful as she applies them to various problems. Rocket Star, for example, can enable her to move more quickly. Glowy can light up dark places. In *Dora the Explorer: The Essential Guide,* a companion book to the television series aimed at emerging readers and their families, the author states that these small pieces of technology are "giggly star friends" (Bromberg 16), yet they seem unwilling to be caught and always fly away after being "helpful." The stars contribute to the framing of Dora's world as a video game, as they fly above the characters' heads and suggest the idea of "bonuses" when they are caught—they are objects, tools without any agency or function other than to aid Dora.

Other elements of the show suggest the mediated nature of Dora's world as well. In the original title sequence for the show, the camera zoomed in from outside a (non-animated) child's room and focused on a desktop computer. Dora and her friends appeared on that computer. In each episode, including those currently running, a mouse pointer clicks on Dora's name to transition from the title sequence to the main part of the program. This pointer then becomes the audience's avatar in Dora's world, allowing the assumed viewer to access ("click on") objects and elements in the landscape, as he or she would if playing a computer game. Once clicked, objects activate—they fly around the screen, or appear on Dora, or perform some other useful action. Of course, this "mouse pointer" access is not personalized to each viewer; there is one master narrative it portrays. This narrative is also centered around the "correct" answer; for example, if Dora asks for a flashlight, the pointer would choose the picture of a flashlight, not (for example) a maraca that, when shaken, could attract fireflies to light her way. In this way, Dora's technology maps onto Oravec's notion of technological rituals as discipline, as it prepares the viewer to interact with machines in a specific, linear, binary fashion. Rather than imagine multiple possibilities, preschoolers are taught to choose the most obvious, straightforward answer.

Behavioral Responses

As mentioned above, another stated objective of Dora's creators was that the show's audience "be active participants— not only by answering questions, but by getting off the couch and moving their bodies" ("More about Dora" 2). Several times each episode, the show calls for audience members to engage in various types of physical embodiment. In order to issue this call, Dora and the other characters speak directly to the audience, breaking the mediated fourth wall. Dora begins each episode by telling the viewers: "I need your help," and then asking if they will help her. Regardless of the children's response, Dora assumes an affirmative, and begins her journey with the viewer compelled alongside. This participation is touted by Nickelodeon executive Brown Johnson as empowering to the preschool viewers: "It makes them feel smart, and it makes them feel strong, and it makes them feel powerful . . . No one had ever asked for that degree of audience participation before" (Ralli C2). Yet, all of the participation is carefully choreographed to overlap with Dora's success along her journey.

After gaining the viewers' support, Dora, Boots, Map, and Backpack implicate them in their activities through various physical performances. Sometimes these are in the form of compelled speech—the characters tell the children watching that they "have to say" a key word, such as "backpack" or "map." Occasionally, Dora and Boots follow this demand with "louder!" Some of these speech acts engage learning through rote: viewers learn Spanish words by repeating them after Dora, for example. Often the characters employ close-ended questioning as a teaching strategy, asking children where a certain shape or animal is that Dora somehow is having trouble seeing. Sometimes the physical performance is focused on larger movements; children are asked to jump, or reach, or point to an object. Sometimes, viewers will "earn" some reward for engaging in these performances—a friendship bracelet, for example, at the end of the World Adventure story. When this happens, the reward is "given" to the viewers by passing it under (or around) the "camera" so that it appears to have been moved out of Dora's space and into the viewer's. The show thus establishes a token economy, based on

following Dora's instructions, but the token is virtual and disappears as soon as the show is over. Yet, with all these compelled actions and rewards, the fourth wall is a blurry boundary—in many ways—in Dora.

In all these performances, as with the computer pointer avatar, there is one "right" answer, gesture, or other response, and it is assumed that the viewer embodies this correct performance. Thus, there is essentially only one way to engage with the program's narrative, except for interpretations of animal movements or other gestures called for in a general way. The major exception occurs at the end of each episode, when viewers are asked to tell Dora and Boots their favorite part of the day's journey. The characters leave a few seconds of time for children's open responses before validating them: "I liked that part, too." After this, Dora and Boots relate their favorite parts, which may be the same as the viewers'. Only here does the viewer get to express creativity, or break out of the binary right/wrong answer structure.

The interactivity in Dora functions as a metanarrative of the series as a whole, since it is structured as an interactive game—perform correct action, receive reward, progress along journey. But, because it is mediated, the interactivity is false, ultimately resulting in the audience's consumption of the "correct" performance. In the "bargain" of sitting down to watch Dora, viewers lose the ability to express themselves creatively, but gain the comfort of knowing they can never give the "wrong" answer. This is similar to technology use; a calculator cannot give a "wrong" answer, as long as the user inputs the question correctly. Is the bargain beneficial to the viewer? What are the right answers being imparted, and what alternate solutions are left out? Ultimately, Dora leaves little room for resistant viewing or "play."

Implications: Completing the Training

As Dora explores, she transmits specific ideologies regarding childhood and society. The viewers' assumed complicity with her actions places them at the center of debates over border identity and multiculturalism, and the place of technology. Dora's journeys are carefully constructed to serve as conduits for certain values, often having to do with being a "good" person—saving a friend, finding some useful or sentimental item, working as a team. As she travels, Dora sees her world not for what it *is,* but rather as a series of locations to be passed through. Locations serve less as significant journey markers than as staging points for challenges—the no places/every places of computer games. The objective matters most—again, a linear and structural standpoint—and the show cannot end until Dora meets that objective.

The way space is used in *Dora* also serves as a marker for how the show treats other concepts. As mentioned earlier, Dora's world is a simulacrum, a decontextualized version of real landscapes, a place that never was. Sociologist Henri Lefebvre suggests that space can be *abstract,* existing in the realm of the conceptual (we will use this kitchen to cook food), or *lived,* suggesting practical, material usage (the kitchen can also be used for playing with toys, or brushing the cat, or bandaging a cut). Literary theorist Nicholas Spencer argues: "Lefebvre describes abstract space as a homogenizing and fragmenting social force that seeks to destroy the potential for oppositional cultural space that lived space represents" (142). The flattening of space creates a unilateral expectation of how it will be used, disregarding possibilities for play. As Dora moves through her own abstract space, her possibilities for use of space are limited; she cannot bring her space to the realm of the material. Like a character in a novel who is similarly confined, "she cannot integrate her various spatial experiences into a social map of her world" (144). Since Dora cannot and does not bring her experience into the material, it is up to the children viewing the show to do it for themselves. They define their own sense of Dora's space, of who she is as a pretend or aspirational peer, and how her world culturally maps onto their own. Through this relational and ideological embodiment, the show imparts its training.

Multiculturalism—that contested term—is presented in *Dora* as a sort of extended series of friendships, a liberal humanist outlook exemplified by her team's cheer: "When we work together as a team, there's nothing we can't do. 'Cause being on a team means you help me and I help you" ("We're a Team"). Dora and her friends never encounter any hardships based on difference; they don't have difficulties understanding languages, traditions, gestures, or geographies. Their challenges are skills based: they search for objects, pass through locations, outwit Swiper the Fox, and cheer up a grumpy troll by making him laugh. The characters' differences easily coalesce into a network of abilities—accentuated by technological or magic objects that conveniently appear when needed, removing any struggle connected with building assemblages—that serve a common good. The *Dora* vision of community might thus be seen as an idealistic "happy multiculturalism." The characters share a common identity, even though they are of multiple species, cultural backgrounds, and genders. (Class is not specifically represented

or addressed.) Dora and her friends are brought together by common, humanistic objectives that are supposed to transcend their perceived differences.

Educational theorist Carlos Alberto Torres proposes that under such a liberal humanist vision: "Unfortunately the tension between and among these differences is rarely interrogated, presuming a 'unity of difference'— that is, that all difference is both analogous and equivalent (201). This treatment of difference tends to reject radical notions and reproduce structure in its attempts to forge a unified "personhood" (Ladson-Billings and Tate 62). In its attempts to build a liberal humanistic third space—a hybridizing, democratic borderland—*Dora* defers conversation around issues of culture and power. Children do not learn about the relationships between injustice and common cause, or misunderstanding and friendship. Both contained and enabled by the technology that frames it, the show's multicultural discourse is ultimately imaginary and temporary. Everything in *Dora* comes too easily; it is decontextualized and abstracted from cultural and linguistic tensions. In the outside world, those who look like Dora may be stopped and detained by the police if they live in Arizona. Spanish speakers contend with a state system that enforces English as a sole mode of literacy, spoken and written. Yet, *Dora's* determination to exist in a highly simulated environment, with a mysterious avatar pointer and instantaneous travel, sets it apart from the outside world and ignores complex questions around the very issues it engages. The show colonizes the imaginary around the avoidance of cultural conflict and a false sense of unity, while outside, restrictive legislation is signed, protestors gather, and children respond in English when their parents speak to them in Spanish.

Works Cited

Anzaldúa, Gloria. *Borderlands: La Frontera.* San Francisco: Aunt Lute Books, 2007.

"Arizona Bill Targeting Ethnic Studies Signed into Law." *Los Angeles Times,* May 12, 2010. articles.latimes.com/2010/may/12/nation/la-na-ethnic-studies-20100512 (accessed April 29, 2012).

"Arizona Enacts Stringent Law on Immigration." *New York Times,* June 11, 2010. (accessed May 12, 2010). www.nytimes.com/2010/04/24/us/politics/24immig.html).

"Arizona Grades Teachers on Fluency." *Wall Street Journal,* June 11, 2010. online.wsj.com/article/

SB10001424052 7487035725045752138832764 27 528.html. (accessed April 29, 2012).

Arizona Secretary of State's Office. *2006 Proposition Guide: Proposition 103.* 16 October 2007. www. azsos.gov/election/2006/Info/PubPamphlet/Sun_ Sounds/english/Prop 103.htm (accessed April 29, 2012).

———. *2006 Proposition Guide: Proposition 300.* 16 October 2007. www.azsos.gov/election/2006/Info/ PubPamphlet/Sun_Sounds/english/Prop300.htm (accessed April 29, 2012).

"Awards for *Dora the Explorer.*" Internet Movie Database. www.imdb.com/title/tt0235917/awards (accessed April 29, 2012).

Baudrillard, Jean. *Simulacra and Simulation.* Ann Arbor: University of Michigan Press, 1994.

"Berry Hunt." *Dora the Explorer.* Nick Jr. 2000.

Bhabha, Homi. *The Location of Culture.* New York: Routledge, 1994.

Bharucha, Rusom. *The Politics of Cultural Practice.* London: Athlone Press, 2000.

Bogdan, Robert, and Sari Knopp Biklen. *Qualitative Research for Education: An Introduction to Theories and Methods,* fourth ed. Boston: Allyn and Bacon, 2003.

Bromberg, Brian. *Dora the Explorer. The Essential Guide.*

London, New York: DK Publishing, Inc., 2006.

Buckingham, David. *After the Death of Childhood: Growing up in the Age of Electronic Media.* Cambridge, UK: Polity Press, 2000.

Callahan, Raymond. *Education and the Cult of Efficiency.*

Chicago: University of Chicago Press, 1962.

Chappell, Andrew. *Colonizing the Imaginary: Children's Embodiment of Cultural Narratives.* Diss Arizona State University, 2008.

Chen, Sylvia Xiaohua, Veronica Benet-Martínez, and Michael Harris Bond. "Bicultural Identity, Bilingualism, and Psychological Adjustment in Multicultural Societies: Immigration-Based and Globalization-Based Acculturation." *Journal of Personality* 76, no. 4, 2008.

"Dora Saves the Mermaids." *Dora the Explorer.* Nick Jr. 2007.

"Dora Saves the Prince." *Dora the Explorer.* Nick Jr. 2002.

"Dora Saves Three Kings Day." *Dora the Explorer.* Nick Jr. 2009.

"Dora's Pirate Adventure." *Dora the Explorer.* Nick Jr.2004.

"Dora's World Adventure." *Dora the Explorer.* Nick Jr.2006.

Erickson, Frederick. "Qualitative Methods in Research on Teaching." In *Handbook of Research on Teaching.* 3rd ed, edited by. M. C. Wittrock, 119-161. Washington, DC: American Educational Research Association, 1986.

Fernández, Idy. "Go, Diego Go." *Hispanic* 18 (2005): 68.

Frenck, Moses. "Toy Treatment." *MediaWeek* 17, no. 8 (October 19, 2007): MyMl-MyM4.

Haraway, Donna. *Simians, Cyborgs and Women: The Reinvention of Nature.* New York: Routledge, 1991.

"Job Day." *Dora the Explorer,* Nick Jr. 2004.

"Journey to the Purple Planet." *Dora the Explorer.* Nick Jr. 2006.

Ladson-Billings, Gloria and William Tate. "Toward a Critical Race Theory of Education." *Teachers College Record* 97 (1995): 47–68.

McCarthy, Cameron and Greg Dimitriades. "Globalizing Pedagogies: Power, Resentment, and the Re-Narration of Difference." In *Globalization and Education: Critical Perspectives* edited by Nicholas C Burbules and Carlos Alberto Torres, 187–204. Lanham, MD: Rowman & Littlefield Publishers, 1998.

McDonnell, Kathleen. *Honey We Lost the Kids: Rethinking Childhood in the Multimedia Age.* Toronto, Canada: Second Story Press, 2001.

"Meet Diego." *Dora the Explorer.* Nick Jr. 2003.

"More about Dora." *Dora the Explorer.* Nick Jr. 2005. October 12, 2007. nickjr.co.uk/shows/dora/more.

aspx#about (accessed April 29, 2012).

Oravec, Jo Ann. "From Gigapets to Internet: Childhood Technology Rituals as Commodities." In *Rituals and Patterns in Children's Lives,* edited by. Kathy Merlock Jackson, 252–268. Madison: University of Wisconsin Press, 2005.

Popp, Richard K. "Mass Media and the Linguistic Marketplace: Media, Language, and Distinction." *Journal of Communication Inquiry* 30 (2006): 5–20.

Postman, Neil. *The Disappearance of Childhood.* New York: Vintage, 1994.

"A Present for Santa." *Dora the Explorer.* Nick Jr. 2002. Ralli, Tania. "The Mother of 'Blue' and 'Dora' Takes a

Step Up at Nickelodeon." *New York Times,* February 28, 2005. www.nytimes.com/2005/02/28/business/media/28kid.html (accessed April 29, 2012).

Rau, Alia Beard. "Arizona State Rejects 5 Major Immigration Bills." *The Arizona Republic.* February 2, 2012. http://www.azcentral.com/news/election/azelections/articles/2011/03/17/20110317arizona-birthright-citizenshipbills-rejected.html?nclick_check=l (accessed October 24, 2012).

Salaňda, Johnny. *Fundamentals of Qualitative Research.*

Oxford; New York: Oxford University Press, 2011. "Senate Bill 1070." *State of Arizona Senate.* June 11, 2010. www.azleg.gov/legtext/491eg/2r/bills/sbl070s.pdf

(accessed April 29, 2012).

Sigler, Eunice. "A Girl Named Dora." *Hispanic* 16 (2003): 42–5.

Spencer, Nicholas. *After Utopia: The Rise of Critical Space in Twentieth-Century American Fiction.* Lincoln: University of Nebraska Press, 2006.

"Sticky Tape." *Dora the Explorer.* Nick jr. 2001.

Torres, Carlos Alberto. *Democracy Education, and Multiculturalism: Dilemmas of Citizenship in a Global World.* Lanham, MD: Roman & Littlefield Publishers, 1998.

"We All Scream for Ice Cream." *Dora the Explorer. Nick Jr.* 2000.

"We're a Team." *Dora the Explorer.* Nick Jr. 2006.

Wingett, Yvonne. "'Dora' Unlocks Bilingual Treasure" *The Arizona Republic.* February 15, 2006. http://www.azcentral.corn/arizonarepublic/news/articles/0215earlyspanish0215.html (accessed April 29, 2012).

Wolcott, Harry F. *Transforming Qualitative Data: Description, Analysis, and Interpretation.* Thousand Oaks, CA: Sage, 1994.

Drew Chappell is a performance studies scholar who teaches at California State University, Fullerton. In addition to his research on play, globalization and visual and narrative research methods, he is also an award-winning playwright.

Elizabeth Monk-Turner et al.    **NO**

The Portrayal of Racial Minorities on Prime Time Television: A Replication of the Mastro and Greenberg Study a Decade Later

Exploring how racial minorities are portrayed on television is valuable for two primary reasons (Mastro & Greenberg 2000). First, it is socially important to document how minorities are depicted on television as well as how such portrayals have changed over time. Second, as a cultural artifact, television reaches a wide audience. Many maintain that the way racial minorities are represented contributes to stereotypical images, whether positive or negative, that viewers develop (Potter, 1994; Potter & Chang, 1990; Bodenhausen et al., 1995; Devine & Baker, 1991; Persson & Musher-Eizenman, 2003; and Ford, 1997). As Signorielli (2001) observed, television has become the "nation's primary story-teller" (36).

This study replicates earlier work by Mastro & Greenberg (2000) who explored the representation and depiction of Caucasian, African American/black and Latino characters on prime time television. Mastro & Greenberg (2000) found that, compared to Caucasians and African Americans, Latinos were under-represented on prime-time television, where they comprised only 3% of television characters. The Mastro & Greenberg (2000) study is important because they reported that Latino television characters were not as negatively stereotyped as African American television characters. While they found more African American representation on television, the roles and behaviors portrayed were negative characterizations (see too Weigel et al., 1995; Greenberg & Brand, 1994; Ford, 1997). Specifically, Latino characters were generally respected and the least lazy of any group, while African Americans were the laziest, least respected, and dressed most provocatively (see too Fyfe, 1999). The conversations of African American characters fared better in that they were most relaxed and most spontaneous, while the conversations of Latinos were least articulate, most accented,

and least spontaneous. The work of this article replicates the earlier study by Mastro & Greenberg (2000) by exploring the representation, appearance, conversational characteristics and personal characteristics among Caucasian, Latino and African American characters on prime time television a decade later.

Mastro & Greenberg's (2000) work is notable because Latino representation was included in better understanding minority portrayal on prime time television. According to the U.S. Census, Latinos are the nation's largest ethnic or race minority as well as the fastest growing minority group (2008). Today, 15% of the U.S. population is Latino and one of every two people added to the population is Latino (U.S. Census, 2008). The U.S. Census estimates that by 2050, a fourth of the population will be Latino. While the size of the Latino population grows, research attention, notably representation and portrayal on television, lags. Therefore, it is important to track media images and how they have changed over time.

According to Nielsen Media, CBS, NBC, Fox, and ABC remained the top viewed networks on prime time television which were broadcast over the air (2009). CBS came in first place with 5.81 million prime time, with ABC trailing at 5.51 million prime time viewers. Over the period of this study, cable and satellite programs, as well as other niche networks, have competed for viewers; however, the major networks remain in the lead for the television viewing audience in general (Nielsen Media, 2009). Still, other outlets, such as the Spanish language network's Univision, which claims 3.21 million viewers, have changed the landscape of the media and television (Nielsen Media, 2009). Nevertheless, we argue that the images viewers see on major over-the-air channels continue to have the potential to impact how minority and majority group members are perceived in the wider society.

Monk-Turner, Elizabeth; Heiserman, Mary; Johnson, Crystle; Cotton, Vanity; Jackson, Manny. From *Studies in Popular Culture*, vol. 32, no. 2, Spring 2010, pp. 101–114. Copyright ©2010 by Popular Culture Association in the South. Used with permission.

Background

Early work by Goffman (1974) posited that media images and messages work as a cognitive filter to help individuals make sense of the world. Others (Tan, Ling & Theng, 2002) have argued that television has the "potential to reach the most private realms of the human psyche" (853). If television images contribute to stereotypes, Graves' (1999) finding that racial minorities were generally negatively stereotyped on television is troublesome (see too Mastro & Robinson, 2000). Such negative stereotypes could shape how viewers think about racial minorities (see Graves, 1999).

Gerbner et al. (2002) argued that television continuously feeds "mainstream" views over a period of time. Proposing a cultivation hypothesis, Gerbner et al. (1994) posited that television images inform public opinions about the social world (see too Gerbner & Gross, 1976). Specifically, cultivation theory proposed that heavy exposure to media, television in particular, shaped how viewers saw the real world. What such viewers deem as appropriate role portrayals, values and ideologies are, over time, increasingly in line with those delivered on screen (Gerbner et al. 2007). Likewise, Robinson et al. (2007) argued that media images, along with lived experience, significantly shaped children's feelings of others.

Content analyzing animated Disney film images, Robinson et al. (2007) maintained that media images can "form, change, and reinforce stereotypes" (203; Editor's note: See Alexander M. Bruce, *Studies in Popular Culture* 30.1). Even if one does not accept the proposition that such images shape mental formations, Berg (1990) found that images seen on television validated existing stereotypes of the viewing audience and gave them additional credibility (see too Potter, 1994). Further, Greenberg (1988) suggested that certain images, particularly those that stand out to the viewing audience, may be more important in shaping racial attitudes than the mere number of minorities characters shown.

Bodenhausen et al. (1995) found that exposure to media images of successful African Americans may have positive effects on the racial attitudes of whites. Specifically, Vrij et al. (1996) argued that television images may change prejudiced racial attitudes. They found three characteristics were critical for such change to occur. First, television images needed to stress similarities between majority and minority group members. Further, these images needed to include multiple minority group members, not merely a token minority group member. Finally, the anti-discrimination message should be clear in the images shown (see Vrij et al., 1996). If minority characters were presented in a positive way, according to the fivepoint Likert scale used in our content analysis, we examined the explicitness of such positive characterizations. Again Vrij et al. (1996) argued that these factors were essential components of media portrayals of minority characters if negative racial stereotyping is to be lessened.

Method

Prime time television shows (8–10 p.m. EST) were content analyzed during a two-week period beginning in early March 2007. During this period, a one-week sample of all shows and characters shown on ABC, NBC, CBS and FOX was recorded and content analyzed (sports and news programs were excluded from the analysis). Thus, one complete prime time week (Monday to Friday) for each of the four networks was content analyzed. Our unit of analysis was the television character that appeared on these prime time shows, and both major and minor characters were included. The use of a one-week sample followed the pattern established by others who have maintained this type of sample provides a reliable portrait of television portrayals (see Gerbner & Gross, 1976; Pfau, Muller & Garrow, 1995).

Coded variables replicated those used by Mastro & Greenberg (2000), who originally selected variables "to reflect the frequency and prominence of minority portrayals" (p. 693). These variables, they argued, were the attributes that past literature found "as primary components of image formation and stereotyping" (Mastro and Greenberg, 2000: p. 693; see also Berg, 1990). Coded variables included: race, age, network, income level, gender, and role prominence. If characters were major or main characters, those essential to the plot or story line, then their *role* prominence is coded as 1. Other characters were considered minor characters (0). Background characters who appeared on screen but were non-essential (people on the street or characters seen in the background in public areas) were excluded. *Race* is operationalized as Caucasian, African American, Latino/Hispanic, Asian American and all others. This categorization is in line with new Census race categories as well. *Age* is coded as less than 10, 10–20, 20s, 30s, and 40+. Perceived *income* level is coded as low (,$20,000 per year), middle ($20,000–$70,000), or high (over $70,000).

Next, we coded four sets of variables, again in line with Mastro and Greenberg (2000), on a five-point scale (bipolar adjective scales) (p. 694). Again, these items were originally selected because they reflected "an attribute or characteristic which has been associated with an ethnic stereotype" (p. 694). Five *physical characteristics* are content analyzed: weight (thin-obese), height (short-tall), hair color (blonde-black), skin color (fair-dark skin), and accent (no accent-heavy accent). A second set of six variables content analyzed *behavioral characteristics*: articulate-inarticulate, quiet-loud, passive-aggressive, lazy-motivated, ridiculedrespected and dumb-smart. Next, we coded a set of six variables to capture *appearance differences*: excessive makeup-no makeup, excessive accessories-no accessories, provocative attire-conservative attire, casual attire-professional attire, disheveled-well-groomed, and dirty-clean.

Finally, we note attributes that pick up *conversational characteristics*, whether the conversation was tense-relaxed and/or premeditatedspontaneous. To ensure reliability in coding, two coders content analyzed each television program. Intercoder reliability was high (89% agreement across all categories). When there was a disagreement with regard to coding, coders came to an agreement as to the best way to categorize the characterization. Clearly, coding television images is subjective as is how viewers see such images on screen.

Results

Most (74%) of our sample was comprised of Caucasian television actors, 16% of prime-time actors were African American, 5% were Latino, ,2% were Asian Americans and ,3% were of another racial category. In their work, Mastro & Greenberg (2000) also found that 16% of primetime television actors were African American; however, in their work only 3% of such actors were Latino. Over a period of ten years, the racial representation of television actors has not changed significantly. White actors continue to be in a distinct majority position, African American representation is in line with their percent of the U.S. population and the representation of Latinos continues to be in a distinct minority.

Like Mastro & Greenberg (2000), we did not find a significant difference by race, gender, or income. Mastro & Greenberg (2000) found that female characters, regardless of race, were in a minority position (around 37%) among prime time television actors. Our results show that female actors were better represented in prime time—especially among African American actors. Three fourths of African American actors on prime time, a decade later, were female, while 64% of Latino characters and 56% of white characters were female. The vast majority (74% and 73% respectively) of white and Latino characters fell in the middle income category; however, only 67% of African American characters were located here.

In their work, Mastro & Greenberg (2000) found Latinos were significantly younger than other characters.

We did not observe significant age differences by race. In our sample, approximately a third of all characters were in their 30s. On the other hand, Mastro & Greenberg (2000) did not observe a significant difference by race and whether the television character was in a major or minor role. Our results show that the vast majority (91%) of Latino characters were portrayed in major television roles, along with 77% of white characters; however, only 61% of African American characters were observed in this role (X2 5 5.43; p 5 .06).

Next, we explored differences in appearance, conversational style and personal attributes among racial groups. Mastro & Greenberg (2000) found significant differences by race in four of their six appearance characteristics. They found that Latinos wore more accessories and jewelry than whites and that they were the best groomed. Alternatively, African Americans were least well groomed and were more provocative in dress than white characters. A decade later, we found no significant differences by race on any of these six measures. Likewise, Mastro & Greenberg (2000) found significant conversational differences by race. They found that Latinos were most tense and least spontaneous especially compared to blacks. As was true for appearance characteristics, a decade later we found no significant differences by race with regard to these two conversational characteristics (tension and premeditation).

Finally, we content analyzed 11 personal characteristics. Mastro & Greenberg (2000) found significant differences by race for eight of these measures while we found significant differences for six personal characteristics. Mastro & Greenberg (2000) found significant race differences for height, hair, skin color, accent, articulation, respect, aggression, and laziness. We found significant differences for all of these variables save height, aggression, and laziness; however, unlike Mastro & Greenberg (2000), we found significant race differences by intelligence. Mastro & Greenberg (2000) argued that significant race differences by these personal characteristics was an indication of straightforward stereotyping.

Our results show that Latinos continued to be portrayed as having a heavier accent than other racial groups. Most (64%) Latino characters have a heavy accent; however, few (,1%) white or black (3%) characters were portrayed in this way (X2 5 139.56; p 5 ,.0001). Likewise, the trend continues that Latino characters were portrayed as the least articulate of all television characters. A fourth of all black characters were depicted as most articulate along with 30% of white characters; however, no Latino characters fell in this category (X2 5 25.68; p 5 .003). Not surprisingly, we noted that Latino and African American characters had the darkest hair (X2 5 79.66; p 5 ,.0001) and African Americans had the darkest skin color with Latinos intermediate and whites the fairest (X2 5 226.99; p 5 ,.0001). Unlike Mastro and Greenberg (2000), we found significant race difference by intelligence. Half (52%) of all African American actors were depicted as the most intelligent compared to 43% of whites and 27% of Latinos. At the same time, more African Americans (15%) and Latinos (18%) were depicted as least intelligent compared to ,4% of whites (X2 5 23.86; p 5 .02). This finding offers limited support for the idea of counterstereotyping; however, the fact that so many more minority characters were deemed least intelligent compared to whites is of concern.

Mastro and Greenberg (2000) found three relationships that ran counter to traditional stereotypes. They found that Latinos were the least ridiculed (or most respected) characters shown on prime-time—a counterstereotypical finding. A decade later; however, we found a reversal of fortune as Latino characters were most likely to be ridiculed and least likely to be respected compared to either white or black characters (X2 5 30.41; p 5 .002). Mastro and Greenberg (2000) also found that Latino characters were least lazy and most motivated and that African American characters were least aggressive especially compared to whites. Our work found no significant differences by laziness or aggression. Thus, our work found no counter-stereotypical findings by race. In fact, with regard to being respected, our work shows that Latinos were negatively portrayed in this respect.

Finally, we content analyzed whether television actors were depicted as moral-immoral and whether or not they were portrayed as more admirable or despicable. Our work shows that significantly more African Americans and Latinos were shown as immoral (9% and 18% respectively) compared to only 2% of white television actors (X2 5 22.12; p 5 .04). Likewise, significantly more African American and Latino characters were portrayed as despicable, rather than admirable, on television (9% and 18% respectively) compared to only 3% of white television actors (X2 5 22.93; p 5 .02). This finding, coupled with the fading of counter-stereotypes observed by Mastro and Greenberg (2000) ten years ago, is troublesome.

Discussion

This work replicated the earlier work of Mastro and Greenberg (2000), who explored the portrayal of racial minorities on prime time television. Significant race differences in appearance and conversational style, observed by Mastro & Greenberg (2000), were not present a decade later. Unlike the earlier work, our results show that the vast majority of Latino (91%) and white (77%) characters were

in main roles, while only 61% of African Americans were depicted in such a television role. Thus, the few Latino actors that appeared in prime time were in main roles. While African American characters were three times more likely than Latinos to appear on television, they were more likely to be depicted in minor roles. Still, the sheer representation of minority characters is lacking—especially Latino and other minority characters. Only 5% of all television actors observed were Latino, up only two percentage points from the prior study a decade earlier. The representation of African Americans remained constant over this time period at 16% of all television prime time actors. Thus, while some similarities appeared between characters, regardless of race, salient differences were present as well.

Mastro & Greenberg (2000) found counter-stereotypical images for three of the 11 personal characteristics they content analyzed. They found that their Latino characters were the least lazy and the least ridiculed (or most respected) among prime time television characters. Further, blacks were least aggressive, especially compared to white characters. Vrij et al. (1996) argued that such positive characteristics of minority characters were essential to diminish negative stereotyping by race. Unfortunately, we did not find such counter-stereotypes in our work. We found no significant differences by race with regard to being lazy or the display of aggression. Notably, we observed that more Latinos were ridiculed than was true for either whites or blacks (18%, ,1%, and 0% respectively). Both African American and white characters were most likely to be respected and least likely to be ridiculed. Thus, if there was a counter-stereotype in our data, it was that black characters were frequently (45%) portrayed with the most respect along with white characters (36%). However, we posit that it is troubling that significantly more Latino (18%) and African American (9%) characters were portrayed as immoral compared to white (2%) characters. This coupled with the fact that significantly more Latino (18%) and black (9%) characters were viewed as despicable television characters, rather than admired ones, compared to white (3%) characters does nothing to counter negative racial stereotypes.

Like Mastro & Greenberg (2000) we found significant differences by race with regard to hair, skin color, accent and articulation. Notably, no Latino characters were portrayed as most articulate; however, approximately a fourth of black characters and 30% of white characters were shown in this way. Unlike Mastro and Greenberg (2000), we found that black and Latino characters were significantly more likely to be shown as being less intelligent compared to whites. Only 3% of all white characters were perceived as least intelligent compared to 15% of blacks and 18% of Latino characters. At the same time, the majority of African American television characters were portrayed as most intelligent (52% of all African American characters) compared to 43% of whites and only 27% of Latinos. One could argue that these images send mixed messages rather than the clear positive stereotype that Vrij et al. (1996) maintain is necessary to dismantle negative racial stereotyping.

The counter-stereotypical racial images Mastro and Greenberg (2000) observed were lacking in our sample. If positive characterizations are essential to lessening negative racial stereotyping, then prime time television is not providing such portrayals of minority characters. Rather, viewers still see Latinos as having heavy accents, with little articulation skills, and as generally not well respected—especially compared to either African Americans or whites. It seems that Latino representations have lost the most ground over this ten-year period. Viewers of prime-time television see few images to dent any negative stereotypes they may harbor about racial minorities; however, positive images of white characters continue. White prime-time television characters are solidly middle income, fair with regard to skin and hair color, devoid of a heavy accent, articulate, respected, viewed as moral and admirable characters.

Media images contribute to both positive and negative social stereotypes. Race differences in appearance and conversational style have significantly diminished over time; however, the representation of minorities on prime time has not changed over time. What message do viewers take away from media exposure when so few characters are Latinos? Do they notice that many of the African American characters on prime time appear in minor roles? Counter stereotypes observed by Mastro & Greenberg (2000) were not as marked ten years later. Now, of the few Latinos one sees on prime time, significantly more are ridiculed compared to other characters. On a positive note, African American characters were depicted, along with whites, as respected and intelligent characters. This is negated, though, by more minority characters, both Latino and African American, being portrayed as more immoral and despicable compared to whites.

Why, academics and viewers alike might ask, do significant differences remain in the depiction of prime time characters by race? Why hasn't the media done more in producing counter stereotypes of racial minorities to help diminish race stereotyping and social prejudices? Even if one does not accept that the media can reduce such social beliefs, why do the negative minority stereotypes continue? If Goffman (1974) correctly posited that such images are cognitive filters and shape popular meaning,

what responsibility must the media accept in the creation and perpetuation of negative racial stereotyping? We argue that the depiction of minority characters on prime time has changed little over recent time. Counter stereotypical images have faded for Latinos and mixed media messages exist for African American characters. Given that media images are viewed not only by a national but by a growing international audience, we argue that the media must wrestle with these constructed images.

References

Allan, K., & Coltrane, S. (1996). Gender Displaying Television Commercials: A Comparative Study of Television Commercials in the 1950s and 1980s. *Sex Roles*, 35, 185–204.

Atkin, D. (1992). An analysis of television series with minority-lead characters. *Critical Studies in Mass Communication*, 9, 337–349.

Bartsch, R., Burnett, R., Diller, T. & Rankin-Williams, E. (2000). Gender representation in television commercials. *Sex Roles*, 43, 735–743.

Bazzini, D., McIntosh, W., Smith, S., Cook, S., & Harris, C. (1997). The aging woman in popular film. *Sex Roles*, 36, 531–543.

Berg, C. (1990). Stereotyping in films in general and of the Hispanic in particular. *The Howard Journal of Communications*, 2, 286–300.

Bodenhausen, G., Schwarz, N., Bless, H., & Wanke, M. (1995). Effects of Atypical Exemplars on Racial Beliefs: Enlightened Racism or Generalized Appraisals? *Journal of Experimental Social Psychology*, 31, 48–63.

Coltrane, S. & Adams, M. (1997). Work-Family Imagery and Gender Stereotypes. *Journal of Vocational Behavior*, 50, 323–347.

Coltane, S. & Messineo, M. (2000). The Perpetuation of Subtle Prejudice. *Sex Roles*, 42, 363–389.

Craig, R. (1992). The Effect of Television Day Part on Gender Portrayals in Television Commercials. *Sex Roles*, 26, 197–211.

Davis, D. (1990). Portrayals of women in prime-time television. *Sex Roles*, 23, 325–332.

Devine, P.G. & Baker, S.M. (1991). Measurement of racial stereotype subtyping. *Personality and Social Psychology Bulletin*, 17, 44–50.

Ford, T. (1997). Effects of stereotypical television portrayals of African-Americans on person perception. *Social Psychological Quarterly*, 60, 266–278.

Fyfe, J.J. (1999). Police use of deadly force: research and reform. In L.K. Gaines and G.W. Cordner (Eds.), *Policing Perspectives: An Anthology*. Los Angeles: Roxbury.

Gerbner, G. & Gross, L. (1976). Living with television: the violence profile. *Journal of Communication*, 26, 173–199.

Gerbner, G., Gross, L., Morgan, M. & Signorielli, N. (2002). Growing up with television: The cultivation perspective. In J. Bryant and D. Zillmann (Eds.), *Media effects:*

Advances in theory and research. Hillsdale, NJ: Lawrence Erlbaum Associates.

Goffman, I. (1974). Frame analysis. Cambridge, MA: Harvard University Press.

Graves, S.B. (1999). Television and prejudice reduction: When does television as a vicarious experience make a difference? *Journal of Social Issues*, 55,707–725.

Greenberg, B. (1988). Some uncommon television images and the drench hypothesis. In S. Oskamp (Ed.), *Applied Social Psychology Annual* (Vol. 8) Television as a social issue. Newbury Park, CA: Sage.

Greenberg, B. & Brand, B. (1994). Minorities in the mass media: 1970s to 1990s. In J. Bryant and D. Zillmann (Eds.), Media Effects: *Advances in Theory and Research*. Hillsdale, NJ: Lawrence Erlbaum.

Greenberg, B. & Collette, I. (1997). The changing faces on TV: A demographic analysis of network television's new seasons. 1966–1999. *Journal of Broadcasting and Electronic Media*, 41, 4–13.

Hurtz, W. & Durkin, K. (1996). Gender role stereotyping in Australian radio commercials. *Sex Roles*, 36, 103–114.

Lauzen, M. & Dozier, D. (2005). Recognition and Respect Revisited. *Mass Communication and Society*, 8, 241–256.

Lee, E. & Li, K. (1997). The myth of the Asian American super-student. *A Magazine*, 1, 44–47.

Leslie, M. (1995). Slow Fade to ?: Advertising in Ebony Magazine, 1957–1989. *Journalism and Mass Communication Quarterly*, 72, 426–435.

Mastro, D. & Greenberg, B. (2000). The Portrayal of Racial Minorities on Prime Time Television. *Journal of Broadcasting and Electronic Media*, Fall, 690–703.

Mastro, D. & Robinson, A. (2000). Cops and crooks: images of minorities on primetime television. *Journal of Criminal Justice*, 28, 385–396.

Mayeda, D. (1999). From model minority to economic threat. *Journal of Sport and Social Issues*, 23, 203–217.

McArthur, L.Z. & Resko, B.G. (1975). The Portrayal of Men and Women in AmericanTelevision Commercials. *Journal of Social Psychology*, 97, 209–220.

Merlo, J. & Smith, K. (1994). The Portrayal of Gender Roles in Television Advertising. Society for the Study of Social Problems Paper.

Millard, J. & Grant, P. (2006). The Stereotypes of Black and White Women in Fashion Magazine Photographs. *Sex Roles*, 54, 659–673.

Nakayama, T.K. (1988). Model minority and the media.

Journal of Communication Inquiry, 12, 65–73.

Nielsen Media. (2009). Nielsen Media Research Data. Most Watched Prime Time Televison.

Paek, H. & Shah, H. (2003). Racial Ideology, Model, Minorities, and the "No-So-Silent Partner." *The Howard Journal of Communications*, 14, 225–243.

Persson, A. & Musher-Eizenman, D. (2003). The impact of a prejudice-prevention television program on young children's ideas about race. *Early ChildhoodResearch Quarterly*, 18, 530–546.

Pfau, M., Mullen, L. & Garrow, K. (1995). The influence of television viewing on public perceptions of physicians. *Journal of Broadcasting and Electronic Media*, 39, 441–458.

Potter, W. (1994). Cultivation theory and research. *Journalism Monographs*, 147, 1–3.

Potter, W. & Chang, I. (1990). Television exposure measures and the cultivation hypothesis. *Journal of Broadcasting and Electronic Media*, 34, 113–333.

Robinson, M., Callister, M., Magoffin, D., & Moore, J. (2007). The portrayal of older characters in Disney animated films. *Journal of Aging Studies*, 3, 203–213.

Shim, D. (1998). From yellow peril through model minority to renewed yellow peril. *Journal of Communication Inquiry*, 22, 385–409.

Signorielli, N. (2001). The picture in the nineties. *Generations*, 25, 34–38.

Signorielli, N. (2004). Aging on television. *Journal of Broadcasting and Electronic Media*, 48, 279–301.

Steenland, S. (1990). *What's wrong with this picture: The status of women on screen and behind the camera in entertainment TV*. Washington, D.C.: National Commission on Working Women of Wider Opportunities for Women.

Stern, S. & Mastro, D. (2004). Gender Portrayals across the Life Span. *MassCommunication and Society*, 7, 215–236.

Tan, T.T., Ling, L.B., & Theng, E. (2002). Gender-role portrayals in Malaysian and Singaporean television commercials: an international advertising perspective. Journal of Business Research, 10, 853–861.

Tang, J. (1997). The model minority thesis revisited. *The Journal of Applied Behavioral Science*, 33, 291–315.

Taylor, C. & Lee, J. (1994). Not in vogue: Portrayals of Asian Americans in magazine advertising. *American Behavioral Scientist*, 38, 608–621.

Taylor, C. & Stern, B. (1997). Asian Americans: Television advertising and the model minority stereotype. *Journal of Advertising*, 26, 47–61.

U.S. Census. (2007, 2008). (Online). http://www.census.gov/population/projections/nation/nsrh/nprh0610.txt.

Vrij, A., van Schie, E. & Cherryman, J. (1996). Reducing ethnic prejudice through public communication programs. *Journal of Psychology*, 4, 413–420.

Weigel, R., Kim, E. & Frost, J. (1995). Race relations of prime time television reconsidered: patterns of continuity and change. *Journal of Applied Social Psychology*, 25, 223–236.

Wilkes, R. & Valencia, H. (1989). Hispanics and Blacks in Television Commercials. *Journal of Advertising*, 18, 19–25.

ELIZABETH MONK-TURNER, Mary Heiserman, Crystle Johnson, Vanity Cotton, and Manny Jackson all teach at Old Dominion University in Virginia.

EXPLORING THE ISSUE

Have Media Representations of Minorities Improved?

Critical Thinking and Reflection

1. Perhaps the best question is the one stated at the conclusion of the introduction; how long does it take to change stereotypes?
2. Do different generations have a different interpretation of what society is like, because of the media they consume?
3. Are representations of minorities in the media true to the minority—or is the minority actor/actress playing a role that could be played by someone of another race—and does it matter?
4. Should content in the media be broad enough to appeal to audiences of a range of backgrounds?
5. Should program providers conscientiously work toward reversing negative stereotypes?

Is There Common Ground?

The authors of both of these selections question the role of stereotypes and their real impact on audiences, but are less certain of what impact the images they discuss can have on actually creating change in society, or a change in the perceptions of minorities. While Monk-Turner, Heiserman, Johnson, Cotton, and Jackson all note that there are no major changes in the representation of minorities within a 10-year period, they do acknowledge some small changes in tone and the way minorities are represented. Chappell cites a great deal of evidence to show that *Dora the Explorer* creates opportunities for children to learn about multiculturalism, but he is still somewhat pessimistic about the long-term prospects for how such a program can normalize a major change in society.

For these authors, the impact of stereotyping and representations of minorities is of utmost importance, but what we still need to grapple with is how and why stereotypes persist, who pays attention to them, and how these images make a difference or confirm previously held beliefs by individuals. Examinations of content through these types of analysis are critical to understanding the realities of media content, but the multi-dimensions of how we make sense of these images are still more complex processes.

Additional Resources

Simon Cottle, ed., *Ethnic Minorities and the Media: Changing Cultural Boundaries* (Open University Press, 2000).

Bradley S. Greenberg, Dana Mastro, and Jeffrey E. Brand, "Minorities and the Mass Media: Television into the 21st Century," in Jennings Bryant and Dolf Zillman, eds., *Media Effects: Advances in Theory and Research* (Taylor and Francis, 2008).

Mark Lloyd, "Remove the Barriers to Minorities in Media," *Center for American Progress* (August 5, 2005).

Internet References . . .

Center for American Progress, "Race and Beyond: The Media's Stereotypical Portrayals of Race"

    www.americanprogress.org/issues/race/news/2013/03/05/55599/the-medias-stereotypicalpor-trayals-of-race/

Center for Media Literacy, "A Long Way to Go: Minorities and the Media"

    www.medialit.org/reading-room/long-way-gominorities-and-media

Moyers and Company, "Why Is Cable News So Obsessed with the Zimmerman Trial?"

    http://billmoyers.com/2013/07/12/why-is-cable-newsso-obsessed-with-the-zimmerman-trial/

ReachingBlackConsumers.com, "Portrayal of Blacks in the Media"

    www.reachingblackconsumers.com/2011/09/portrayal-of-blacks-in-the-media/

Smith, Aaron, "Explaining Racial Differences in Attitudes Toward Government Uses of Social Media," Pew Internet and American Life Project

    www.pewinternet.org/Commentary/2010/May/Explaining-racial-differences-in-attitudes-towardsgovernment-use-of-social-media.aspx

Selected, Edited, and with Issue Framing Material by:
Alison Alexander, *University of Georgia*
and
Jarice Hanson, *University of Massachusetts—Amherst*

ISSUE

Have More Women Become Involved as Decision Makers in Media Industries?

YES: Hannah McIlveen, from "Web Warriors: The Women of Web Series," *Lydia Magazine* (2014)

NO: Martha M. Lauzen, from "Boxed In: Portrayals of Female Characters and Employment of Behind-the-Scenes Women in 2014–15 Prime-time Television," Center for the Study of Women in Television & Film (2015)

Learning Outcomes

After reading this issue, you will be able to:

- Consider how new technologies present opportunities to groups of people who may have previously been marginalized from decision-making opportunities.
- Think about the unique contributions women bring to the workplace.
- Reflect on media content to consider whether the gender of decision makers really makes a difference.
- Assess opportunities in media industries for everyone in a changing media landscape.
- Think about whether different segments of society have equal opportunities in the workplace.

ISSUE SUMMARY

YES: Hannah McIlveen challenges the dominant male culture of decision makers in television to discuss how women have been making inroads in nontraditional programming on the Web. Working in low-budget situations does not stop their creativity, and even television network executives are paying attention to new content from women creators on the Web.

NO: Every year, Professor Martha M. Lauzen conducts a survey of the roles of women in prime-time television at the Center for the Study of Women in Television and Film at San Diego State University. In this report, she provides data for the 2014–2015 television season, and she states that women are still underrepresented in prime-time television.

For many years, the media industries have been referred to as "old boy industries," meaning that women rarely get the opportunity to make it to the executive, or decision-making level. Some claim that in time this will change, but many of the legacy industries have continued to slot women into some of the lower paid work that often features "soft" news, and women often are not given as many opportunities in media as men, though women make up 51 percent of the population in the United States. As Gloria Steinem stated in *The New York Times*, "It's hard to think of anything except air, food and water that is more important than the media. . . . Especially for groups that have been on the periphery for whatever reason: If we can't see it, we can't be it." Studies over many years continue to show that women are often stereotyped in legacy media content, and that opportunities for women in programs as well as behind the scenes are relatively few. In Professor Martha M. Lauzen's annual report, we see that women remain underrepresented in prime-time television content as well as in executive and creative jobs behind the camera.

But Hannah McIlveen, writing in the online magazine *Lydia Magazine*, says that the emerging world of Web television is still open to women, and that many of the most creative series that are emerging are from women who write, produce, direct, and occasionally, star in original Web series. Furthermore, the Web platform allows a wider range of stories to be told, so there are more images of underrepresented groups, like Latino/Latina characters, characters with disabilities, and Lesbian, Gay, Bisexual, Transgender, and Queer (LGBTQ) characters. The creative opportunities for women on the Web then are far more open to women's creativity and choices. These series have been so successful that even the traditional legacy media are sitting up and taking notice. But even though the Web gives women an opportunity to explore their creative voices, the money to be made in Web television is significantly less than in traditional media forms. Still, the Web can provide an excellent training ground for women and all marginalized groups to learn about the craft of media content construction, and possibly benefit from their own creative initiatives.

Gender inequities in the workplace have a long tradition, and media industries are no exception. From representation of women in media content to opportunities for women to get jobs in media industries, the problem has been long acknowledged as contributing to the perpetuation of distorted representations of American society. This topic cuts across topics of social standards of beauty, expectations of womanhood, role models available to young girls, and many more aspects of our social world that consider media as a reflection of reality. At the same time, we should be aware that gender discrepancies are not the only problems in media industries, and some of the other selections in Taking Sides bring to the discussion of equity and balance in media and in the media industries additional issues such as ethnicity, race, and class diversity.

It is always difficult for people who have been marginalized (for whatever reason) to break the barriers of entry to jobs that have long been held by certain gender groups that may also reflect gender and class biases. But one might feel justified in assuming that in the twenty-first century, it's time for a change. Over the years many good intentions have backfired or completely stalled. In 1963 the Equal Pay Act was supposed to level the discrepancies in men's and women's pay when both were doing the same work, but a "gender gap" in pay persists. In most career- or job-related areas, full-time women workers' earnings are only about 78 percent of their male counterparts' earnings. The gender gap for pay gets even worse for African American and Latina women, with African American women earning approximately 64 cents and Latina women earning 56 cents for every dollar earned by a white, non-Hispanic man. These problems are shared by every country in the world, where pay equity for women always falls behind that of their male counterparts.

In media industries, the pay gaps not only often exist, but opportunities for traditionallymale dominated jobs are rare. This raises an important question for anyone who hopes to work in the media industries: will you be compensated fairly? Furthermore, if you are successful in getting a job in the media industries, can you be an agent of change? Will your generation be the one that shifts male domination to equal opportunity for men and women, as well as other marginalized groups, no matter what their gender? Practically, what can anyone do to be an agent of change?

These issues are not confined to media industries. Discrimination can exist in any profession, but it is often a secret that is hidden from prospective employees. Some companies have rules prohibiting employees from discussing their salaries, and others ask potential employees to sign documents that restrict what they can talk about with other employees on a number of issues that might come up in the workplace. These rules and practices, while not illegal, may tip you off to a situation in which the value of one's labor (and opportunities afforded to them) are steeped in corporate culture that might hide internal inequities.

Before embarking on a career, every individual should do as much homework as possible to see whether the salaries in the field are competitive and fair. Women often have to learn how to be better negotiators in early salary talks, because the longer you stay with one company, the more likely you are to make incremental leaps in salary that are still predicated on your initial salary. Perhaps as people become more aware of the inequities that exist in traditional companies, the more they may be willing to take some risks on lesser known opportunities where job satisfaction and creative control are important.

A number of online sources are now available to help potential employees have a better sense of what starting salaries are in different fields, and women in particular may want to explore some books and training courses on negotiating salary and benefits. Unfortunately, many of the opportunities in new media, like Web television production, may not be compensated. If this is the case, maybe it will be necessary to think about how you might raise the money you need to create an online show or series. Crowdfunding through Kickstarter or Indiegogo, or any one of the online fundraising campaigns, may be helpful to get you over a production budget hurdle or pay for living expenses while you create content for an alternative platform. New media distribution platforms may actually be a means of creating an important wedge in traditional business models and practices, but anyone entering this field should be aware of the potential problems for long-term employment from the start.

These selections raise a number of important points for discussion and hopefully will prompt you to examine your own belief system about equity and balance in the workplace. They also ask us to be more critical about looking at bylines in media, thinking about the gatekeepers of traditional and emerging content, and considering whether there are "women's issues" that are actually more attuned to issues that affect everyone. The media landscape is changing quickly. Does this mean that old problems will persist, or might these problems offer some alternatives to the way media has reflected society in the past?

YES ⤶

Hannah McIlveen

Web Warriors: The Women of Web Series

Imagine this: every television network has a team of people dedicated to finding the next Tina Fey (or, at the slightly edgier networks, the next Lena Dunham); the next female powerhouse who has the kind of talent, charisma and chutzpah they can really build a show on.

These imaginary people sit around a table into the wee hours, drinking too much coffee and wracking their brains, the walls behind them lined with white boards, names frantically scribbled and circled and crossed out. They're looking for the next big woman to shake up TV comedy.

As much as we wish this fantasy team dedicated to finding the next "funny femme" actually existed, comedy TV is still mostly a man's game. And for every Tina Fey, Amy Poehler or Mindy Kaling, there are countless other men making it in lieu of women.

But there is hope. Rather than continue to struggle to make it in traditional comedy television, many women are heading online to make their own opportunities in digital TV.

Through online video sharing and streaming sites, female creators, screenwriters, directors, producers and actors are telling exciting stories from viewpoints that Hollywood tends to marginalize—not only sharing their own experiences as women but exploring the viewpoints of racial minorities, people with disabilities and LGBTQ individuals, proving that web is the home of inclusive comedy that television just isn't ready for.

In bypassing Hollywood's structured institution of television production, the women of web series are able to worry less about getting permission, following rules and fighting sexism. Instead, they can put all of their creative energy into telling stories, many of which touch on deeply personal subject matter (embarrassing sex and struggles with prejudice, anyone?) that reach out to a very specific and dedicated audience. Furthermore, these women always retain a commitment to bringing something new—something that matters and that isn't being seen elsewhere—to TV culture.

Take web series *East WillyB*, co-created and executive produced by star Julia Ahumada Grob, which features a cast of Latino characters of all shapes, sizes and ages. Telling the stories of gentrification in Bushwick, Brooklyn (dubbed East Williamsburg in an effort by realtors to sell the neighborhood, traditionally known as crime-heavy, to new, often White, tenants) the show features singing, fighting, loving and everything in between. Not only does *East WillyB* tell a story that a massive portion of the American population can relate to, it does so without the stereotypical portrayal of Latino culture that is often seen on network television.

Then there is Teal Sherer's *My Gimpy Life*. The series explores the prejudices, exploitation and condescension that the disabled face daily.

Sherer asks people to re-examine their assumptions about disabilities, but she does so in such a fun and self-deprecating way that it never sounds like preaching; just like damn good comedy. Sherer's goal with *My Gimpy Life* is to represent people who deserve a voice in television, but who aren't getting one.

"As a disability advocate," says Sherer, "I want to share my perspective and broaden people's minds. Disabled people are out in the real world, but we're underrepresented in films and on TV. I want producers and casting people to consider disabled actors for any role, not just ones that are written as disabled characters. It's so important to have people in the media that you can relate and connect to."

Another marginalized demographic that's flourishing in web series is a group that has been perhaps inelegantly titled "the uncool LGBTQ" set. While lesbian, gay, bisexual, and transgender characters and storylines gain more attention on network shows like

FOX's *Glee* and HBO's *Looking*, the focus still remains squarely on the young, hip and impossibly beautiful. Meanwhile, on the web, women like Ingrid Jungermann and Amy York Rubin are telling the less glamorous (read: more realistic) stories of LGBTQ life. For Rubin, the game is all about celebrating life's wonderfully awkward and painfully relatable moments in a way that feels authentic.

For Jungermann, the act of bringing verisimilitude to lesbian storylines also has everything to do with relatability—most notable in the age of her characters.

She's dubious about traditional television's interest in LGBTQ people past a certain age saying, "I don't know if networks or cable are ready for a lesbian show about a gay lady approaching 40."

But she's used her two web series, *The Slope* and *F to the 7th*, to represent a broader range of gay characters. While networks continue to employ mustachioed hipsters and Naya Rivera-lookalikes in gay and lesbian roles, women like Rubin and Jungermann cast a refreshingly matter-of-fact (and touchingly amusing) light on LGBTQ culture.

On the lighter, though no less meaningful, side of women bringing innovative comedy to digital television are series like *Ghost Ghirls* and *Seeking the Web Series*. The women behind (and starring in) these shows each bring their own exciting additions to TV culture.

When Amanda Lund and Maria Blasucci co-wrote, executive produced and co-starred in *Ghost Ghirls* for Yahoo! Screen, they brought a whole new genre of comedy to the table: the ghost hunter spoof. Their deadpan delivery, sharp dialogue, and seamless rapport with impressive guest stars like Molly Shannon and Bob Odenkirk shot this Jack Black co-production to viral fame and made many wonder how something like it had never been done before.

With her own series, *Seeking*, up-and-comer Ronit Aranoff is also bringing something undeniably refreshing to comedy by updating the stale genre of rom-coms through crowdsourcing.

She wanted to tell what she calls "real life dating stories" by pulling from strangers' lives; to make an engaging comedy by using stories that literally happened to real, live people—and not just the oft-bland fictional people whose stories you're used to hearing.

"I was tired of watching shows that told stories of a very small cross-section of the population," says Aranoff, "So I decided to ask everyone across age, race, ethnicity, socioeconomic background, [and] religion what their dating experiences were. We're so proud that it's a show about everyone's story." Because of this deeply human framework, *Seeking* never feels contrived. Even when the storylines are silly, it somehow manages to make the silliness ring true—freaky Confederate hipsters and all.

The individual reasons women head online to exert their creative energy may vary, but they usually fall into two broad categories: accessibility and creative freedom.

The most obvious benefit of going digital (as every film school student with a sock puppet and a borrowed Handycam knows) is the low barrier for entry. Anyone who can rent a camera and sign up for a YouTube account is free to start a show—though, of course, it helps if you've got something interesting to say. The lower barrier of entry for web series has a lot to do with money, of course, but it also has to do with rules and permission.

Making a network TV show is one giant rule-following, permission-seeking party. The process of how to submit spec scripts and proofs of concept, the political back-and-forth with executives and all the spoken and unspoken rules to follow before you even go so far as to make that first exploratory contact can stop creators before they've even begun. If you hear back at all from a network, what you hear will probably be a "no."

But as Aranoff so blithely puts it, with digital content, "the only person you have to wait for a yes from is yourself."

When it comes down to it, many women creators get into digital content because it feels like the only option, which is hard to believe considering they're bringing us some of the most exciting, hilarious, and emotionally brave content out there. Even Jack Black's main gals, Lund and Blasucci, fell into this camp before they got hooked up with Black's production company.

"We started writing and making web shorts because we couldn't get any auditions," says Lund. "It was kind of a last resort that we also really enjoyed."

With self-directed digital content, the "yes's and no's" and rules of Hollywood are moot, fostering an environment that's a lot more comfortable to many creatives.

Jungermann remarks that "the web series form is perfect for people who are comfortable making their own rules." Many of the women in web series are excited about finally being able to do their own thing, playing by their own rules.

"*Seeking* is on my terms and I'm really proud of that," says Aranoff.

Jungermann's personal tactic for making content (which seems like something that applies to many web series creators) is to "reshape ideas in a way I can understand them, rely on humility and honesty and hope that whatever I put out there will be understood." A decidedly more zen approach to content creation than you would find from any network executive.

The digital realm is not only a creatively fulfilling place for writers and producers, but for whole casts and crews. The deeper sense of ownership and creative control that comes with going independent and digital can also lead to a greater sense of community for everyone on set. According to Grob, the set of *East WillyB* really felt this impact.

"There was a real family, community energy to the series," she says. "Everyone felt like they were contributing to something very special, a series that was unlike anything that ever existed before, so they gave everything to [it]."

Rubin also experienced the innate sense of community that comes with independent productions on the set of *Little Horribles*.

"Anything indie—which is more the defining factor than it being for web or TV—[is] a really collaborative environment," she says. "There's no client, no studio—it's just about making something everyone feels good about." And that's something viewers can in turn feel good about, too.

Of course, for every benefit of going digital, there's a corollary negative aspect; nothing as beautiful as creative control and freedom of expression comes without a cost. While digital content is inclusive, democratic, and exhilarating in its endless possibilities, it's also unstable. Web series are rarely lucrative and the format is still struggling to gain the recognition it deserves from advertisers and TV's power players.

"I think the web is a great place to explore your creative voice, experiment artistically, learn, and show 'proof of concept' of what you are capable of," says Grob. "It's a very hard place to make money, though. That is the largest challenge indie creators face."

Money continues to be a big issue for web series producers, even as the medium gains popularity among viewers and consideration among critics. Sure, web series are easier to make on the cheap than a multi-cam sitcom, but there's still the need for capital to get that Handycam recording. The trouble with digital content and the almighty dollar isn't just a concern for starving artists who need to pay their rent, either; it's also something viewers should be worried about. As Jungermann is quick to caution, "No matter what anyone says, making work without enough money is detrimental to creativity."

But as the struggles increase for these women, so do the rewards, which is what will keep the creative juices flowing through the web series genre for as long into the future as people have stories to tell. Lund puts it most eloquently when she remarks that holding all the creative power on a series is "way more rewarding . . . You just have this adrenaline kick when you're super passionate about a project. Like when a mother lifts a car up because her child is stuck under it. It's *exactly* like that."

In a way, though, all the common limits of web series are also a big part of what make them so special. A tiny budget, low space allotments, and limited mobility of a production can lead to appealingly intimate results. As creators like Jungermann have no choice but to "keep it small and focus on characters and writing," viewers get the benefit of seeing thoughtful, tightly written, and carefully pared down episodes that encompass only what they really need to. Nothing is stretched to fill time or cut down to allow for commercial breaks. Things just are the way they need to be, with a compelling story front and center. It's a refreshing departure from bombastic network shows with their extraneous sets and scene-stealing CGI. In contrast, an episode of a web series that takes place exclusively in someone's living room—but that feels as emotionally grand as any pearl-clutching scene from *Game of Thrones*—feels fresh.

And that freshness is leading to great strides for women in content creation. Issa Rae, unofficial queen of the web series genre, has built a digital content empire for herself, proving that it *is* possible to have a career in web content as a female minority. And though it feels a little bit like saying every computer science major has the ability to be the next Mark Zuckerberg (not quite realistic) the inclusivity of the space will continue to foster creative growth—and the hope is that financial sustainability isn't too far off. Rae, creator and star of *Awkward Black Girl*, believes this is the case.

"The corporate world has started to embrace digital content in a major way," Rae says. "Companies and networks alike are scrambling to try to figure out the digital world and advertisers are putting out *a lot* more money toward digital content than they were before. The first web series I took seriously (*Fly Guys present The 'F' Word*) was back in 2009, and I remember asking a colleague about trying to get sponsorships and hopefully taking the series to television. She told me nobody was checking for the web, and that there was no money there. She said my best bet was to go the traditional route. That was only five years ago and things have done a 180."

Hollywood's gender and diversity gaps, both in front of and behind the camera, narrow year by year. And though the stats have a long way to go before they're anything close to equal, it's not unreasonable to question how much longer network executives can ignore all of the incredibly talented women out there (though Comedy Central's adoption of Abbi Jacobson and Ilana Glazer's web series, *Broad City*, was a step in the right direction.)

As much as this is about feminism and equality and fairly recognizing talent where recognition is due

("It shouldn't be a newsflash in 2014 that we are hilarious!" jokes Aranoff), the truth is that traditional TV production is largely about money—and good talent and good content lead to good money.

Perhaps this will come as digital content continues to gain respect and raise its profile with critics and the general viewing public. Lund agrees, "I think digital content and traditional TV are eventually going to be indistinguishable. Digital content is now equal to, if not far beyond, the quality of TV. Shows that Netflix does like *Orange is the New Black* and *House of Cards* are better than most shows on TV."

Rubin's also optimistic that the distinction between digital and traditional television is on the way out. She says, bluntly, "It's all just content." If the critics are behind it, and the creators, screenwriters, and actors are behind it, then digital content is well on its way.

As frustrating as it can be for creatives trying to make their voices heard online (according to Grob, to sustain a web series financially you need to aim for at least 100,000 views per episode—no small feat), the tides are indeed changing. Maybe the eventual financial success of web series will rely on the continued expansion of streaming services like Netflix, Hulu, Amazon Prime, and *Ghost Ghirls'* home base Yahoo! Screen. The global takeover of these services does seem kind of impending. Netflix's subscribership gains points each year while HBO's and Amazon Prime's original content gets sharper and more critically acclaimed with each new pilot season.

Techno-financial wizards are working on new ways to eek dollars out of online video, and general awareness about the high quality of web content continues to grow. Perhaps in ten years' time, it'll be possible for new digital content creators to skip the aspiration of traditional television altogether and spend their time appealing to the likes of Reed Hastings instead of Richard Plepler.

In the meantime, these women's work is smart, hilarious and often brave, and it's going to shape the TV landscape of the future in big ways. These are the women the networks need to watch.

HANNAH MCILVEEN writes on a wide range of topics for *Lydia Magazine*, an online journal targeted to women in their 20s and early 30s. All articles are by women and about women, and McIlveen's articles span a range of popular culture topics.

Martha M. Lauzen

 **NO**

Boxed In: Portrayals of Female Characters and Employment of Behind-the-Scenes Women in 2014–15 Prime-time Television

In 2014–15, female characters comprised 42% of all speaking characters on broadcast television programs and 40% of all characters on broadcast, cable, and Netflix programs.

Behind the scenes, women accounted for 27% of creators, directors, writers, producers, executive producers, editors, and directors of photography working on broadcast programs and 25% of those working in these key roles on broadcast, cable, and Netflix programs.

Programs with at least one woman executive producer or creator featured a higher percentage of female characters and employed substantially greater percentages of women writers, directors, and editors than programs with exclusively male executive producers or creators. For example, on broadcast programs with no women executive producers, females accounted for 37% of major characters. On programs with at least one woman executive producer, females comprised 43% of major characters.

On broadcast programs with no women executive producers, women accounted for 6% of writers. On programs with at least one woman executive producer, women comprised 32% of writers.

The findings in this year's report are divided into two major sections. The first section provides the on-screen and behind-the-scenes findings for the broadcast networks, offering historical comparisons for 2014–15 with figures dating from 1997–98. This section also includes an overview of important relationships between women in key behind-the-scenes roles such as executive producers and creators, and the representation of female characters and employment of women as writers, directors, and editors.

The second section provides the behind-the-scenes and on-screen findings for the total sample of programs appearing on the broadcast networks, basic and pay cable (A&E, AMC, FX, History, TNT, USA, HBO, Showtime), and Netflix, and includes a summary of important on-screen and behind-the-scenes relationships.

The study examines one randomly selected episode of every series. Random selection is a frequently used and widely accepted method of sampling episodes from the population of episodes in a season.

Findings for Broadcast Networks

Females on Screen

- 42% of all speaking characters and 42% of major characters were female in 2014–15. This represents no change from 2013–14, but an increase of 3 percentage points from 1997–98.
- Programs airing on ABC featured the highest percentage of female characters (45%), followed by CW (43%), NBC and Fox (40%), and CBS (39%).
- Reality programs were more likely to feature female characters than programs in other genres. Females comprised 47% of characters on reality programs, 41% of characters on situation comedies, and 40% of characters on dramas.
- Female characters continue to be portrayed as younger than their male counterparts. The majority of female characters were in their 20s and 30s (60%), whereas the majority of male characters were in their 30s and 40s (55%).
- Female characters experience a precipitous decline in numbers from their 30s to their 40s. 31% of female characters were in their 30s but only 18% were in their 40s. Male characters also experience a decline but it is not as dramatic (from 30% to 25%).
- Few female or male characters age past 60. Only 2% of female and 4% of male characters were in their 60s or above.

- 77% of female characters were white, 15% were African-American, 3% were Latina, 4% were Asian, and 1% were of some other race or ethnicity.
- Viewers were less likely to know the occupational status of female characters than male characters. 35% of female characters but only 24% of male characters had an unknown occupational status.

Women Behind the Scenes

- In 2014–15, women comprised 27% of all individuals working as creators, directors, writers, producers, executive producers, editors, and directors of photography. This represents no change from 2013–14 and an increase of 6 percentage points since 1997–98.
- Overall, women fared best as producers (38%), followed by writers (26%), executive producers (26%), creators (23%), editors (21%), directors (14%), and directors of photography (2%).
- 45% of programs employed 4 or fewer women in the roles considered. Only 4% of programs employed 4 or fewer men.
- Women comprised 23% of creators. This represents an increase of 3 percentage points from 2013–14 and an increase of 5 percentage points from 1997–98.
- Women accounted for 26% of executive producers. This represents an increase of 3 percentage points from 2013–14 and an increase of 7 percentage points since 1997–98.
- Women comprised 38% of producers. This represents a decrease of 5 percentage points from 2013–14, and represents an increase of 9 percentage points since 1997–98.
- Women accounted for 26% of writers. This represents an increase of 1 percentage point from 2013–14 and an increase of 6 percentage points since 1997–98.
- Women comprised 14% of directors. This represents an increase of 1 percentage point from 2013–14, and an increase of 6 percentage points since 1997–98.
- Women accounted for 21% of editors. This represents an increase of 4 percentage points from 2013–14, and an increase of 6 percentage points since 1997–98.
- Women comprised 2% of directors of photography. This represents no change from 2013–14 and an increase of 2 percentage points since 1997–98.
- 70% of the episodes considered had no female creators, 86% had no female directors, 70% had no female writers, 78% had no female editors, and 98% had no female directors of photography.

Important Relationships

- Broadcast programs with at least one woman executive producer featured more female characters and employed more women directors, writers, and editors than programs with no women executive producers.
- On programs with at least one woman executive producer, females comprised 43% of major characters. On programs with no women executive producers, females accounted for 37% of characters.
- On programs with at least one woman executive producer, women accounted for 32% of writers, compared to 6% of writers on programs with no women executive producers.
- On programs with at least one woman executive producer, women accounted for 15% of directors, compared to 9% of directors on programs with no women executive producers.
- On programs with at least one woman executive producer, women accounted for 25% of editors. On programs with no women executive producers, women comprised 13% of editors.
- Programs with at least one woman creator featured more female characters and employed more women directors, writers, and editors than programs with no women creators.
- On programs with at least one woman creator, females accounted for 45% of major characters. On programs with no women creators, females comprised 41% of major characters.
- On programs with at least one woman creator, women accounted for 50% of writers. On programs with no women creators, women comprised 15% of writers.
- On programs with at least one woman creator, women accounted for 23% of directors. On programs with no women creators, women comprised 10% of directors.
- On programs with at least one woman creator, women accounted for 36% of editors. On programs with no women creators, women comprised 14% of editors.

Findings for Broadcast Networks, Cable & Netflix Programs

On Screen Females

- Females accounted for 40% of all speaking characters and 40% of major characters.
- 78% of female characters were white, 13% were African American, 4% were Latina, 4% were Asian, and 1% were of some other race or ethnicity.

- The majority of female characters (60%) were in their 20s and 30s. The majority of male characters (57%) were in their 30s and 40s. The percentage of female characters drops dramatically from their 30s to their 40s. 32% of female characters were in their 30s but only 19% of female characters were in their 40s. Male characters experienced only a slight decline in numbers (from 29% to 28%).
- Male characters were much more likely than female characters to be seen working. 55% of male characters and 43% of female characters were seen at work and working.

Behind-the-Scenes Women

- Women comprised 25% of individuals in key behind-the-scenes roles on programs airing on the broadcast networks and cable channels, and available through Netflix in 2014–2015. This figure represents no change from 2013–14 and a decline of 1 percentage point from 2012–13.
- Women fared best as producers (38%), followed by writers (25%), executive producers (23%), creators (22%), editors (20%), directors (12%), and directors of photography (1%).
- 57% of the programs employed 4 or fewer women. Only 5% of programs employed 4 or fewer men.
- Women comprised 22% of creators. This represents an increase of 3 percentage points from 2013–14.
- Women accounted for 23% of executive producers. This represents an increase of 2 percentage points from 2013–14.
- Women comprised 38% of producers. This represents a decline of 2 percentage points from 2013–14.
- Women accounted for 25% of writers, a decline of ƒ1 percentage point from 2013–14.
- Women comprised 12% of directors. This represents a decrease of 1 percentage point from 2013–14.
- Women accounted for 20% of editors. This represents an increase of 4 percentage points from 2013–14.
- Women comprised 1% of directors of photography. This represents no change from 2013–14.

Important Relationships

- Broadcast and cable programs with at least one woman executive producer featured more female characters and employed more women directors, writers, and editors than programs with no women executive producers.
- On programs with at least one woman executive producer, females comprised 42% of major characters. On programs with no women executive producers, females accounted for 35% of major characters.
- On programs with at least one woman executive producer, women comprised 12% of directors, compared with 11% of directors on programs with no women executive producers.
- On programs with at least one woman executive producer, women accounted for 32% of writers, compared with 8% on programs with no women executive producers.
- On programs with at least one women executive producer, women comprised 24% of editors, compared with 12% on programs with no women executive producers.
- Broadcast and cable programs with at least one woman creator featured more female characters and employed more women directors, writers, and editors than programs with no female creators.
- On programs with at least one woman creator, females accounted for 46% of major characters. On programs with no women creators, females comprised 39% of major characters.
- On programs with at least one woman creator, women comprised 49% of writers, compared with 15% on programs with no women creators.
- On programs with at least one woman creator, women accounted for 18% of directors, compared with 10% on programs with no women creators.
- On programs with at least one woman creator, women accounted for 37% of editors, compared with 13% of editors on programs with no women creators.

MARTHA M. LAUZEN is a professor in the School of Theatre, Television, and Film at San Diego State University. Her annual report, *Boxed In*, has been providing current data on women in prime-time television in front of and behind the camera for over 18 years.

EXPLORING THE ISSUE

Have More Women Become Involved as Decision Makers in Media Industries?

Critical Thinking and Reflection

1. What harm is there, and who is harmed by perpetuating media images of society that focus on men and marginalize women or other groups?
2. Can new distribution forms of technology change the way marginalized groups get access to audiences?
3. Can new business models be created that disrupt traditional career opportunities and result in a greater range or equitable distribution of upper-level decision-making jobs in media?
4. How might issues of the "pay gap" among different groups be addressed more systematically in society?
5. What can women do to become better advocates for themselves, and what can men do to support greater equity for women in the workplace?

Is There Common Ground?

The authors of these two selections agree that the status quo is not acceptable for women in the workplace, but differ on the possibilities for the future. Martha M. Lauzen's *Boxed In* study for 2014–2015 shows that there is still a huge gender gap in the creative jobs in television, and that women still remain underrepresented in prime-time television.

Hannah McIlveen focuses on a specific emerging form of media in terms of Web content, and describes how dynamic women are becoming in this new medium. She also asserts that when women are creative and productive, traditional media executives sit up and take notice, thereby offering some hope that alternative distribution forms for media may be the way change ultimately comes about. It may be too soon to see how Web content disrupts the media industries, but at least she offers some hope for change.

Gender and pay inequity is a problem in all fields, and the media industries are no exception, but the media industries are in a prime position to publicize change in terms of what they produce. Both women and men have to be aware of these problems and make concerted efforts to create opportunities for everyone in a media landscape that is increasingly serving niche audiences. Awareness of the problem is the first hurdle to tackle.

Additional Resources

Linda Babcock and Sara Laschever, *Women Don't Ask: Negotiation and the Gender Divide* (Bantam, 2007). This book provides useful tips to women on negotiating salary and job opportunities.

Andrew Dawson and Sean P. Holmes, *Working in the Global Film and Television Industries: Creativity, Systems, Space, Patronage,* (Bloomsbury Academic, 2012). This survey of labor opportunities in media reflects cultural values that influence how, why, and when women are treated fairly.

Suzanne Franks, *Women and Journalism* (Reuters Institute for the Study of Journalism at Oxford University, 2013). This study examines opportunities for women in the field of journalism, and discusses the gender pay gap.

Lois P. Frankel, *Nice Girls Don't Get the Corner Office: Unconscious Mistakes Women Make That Sabotage Their Careers* (Business Plus, 2014). This is a self-help book that shows behaviors that keep women from being assertive in male-dominated workplaces.

Internet References . . .

Geena Davis Institute on Gender in Media

http://seejane.org/

Half the Sky Movement

www.halftheskymovement.org/

International Women's Media Center

www.iwmf.org/

Journalism and Women Symposium (JAWS)

www.jaws.org/

Nieman Reports, "Where Are the Women?"

http://niemanreports.org/articles/where-are-the-women/

Selected, Edited, and with Issue Framing Material by:
Alison Alexander, *University of Georgia*
and
Jarice Hanson, *University of Massachusetts—Amherst*

ISSUE

Do Digital Technologies Influence Our Senses?

YES: Saga Briggs, from "Six Ways Digital Media Impacts the Brain," *informED* (2016)

NO: Tristan Harris, from "How Technology Hijacks People's Minds—From a Magician and Google's Design Ethicist," *tristanharris.com* (2016)

Learning Outcomes
After reading this issue, you will be able to:
• Understand how different forms of media influence our senses.
• Consider how businesses operate in ways that will increase their number of users.
• Think about how people adapt to changes in their media systems and their environment.
• Reflect on the way the media you use may impact the way you behave.
• Evaluate the ways in which different generations become "conditioned" to think in certain ways.

ISSUE SUMMARY

YES: Saga Briggs is a writer and the Managing Editor of InformEd, an online resource for educators based in Australia. In this article, she compiles recent data to suggest how our brains adapt to the use of digital technologies over time. Based on the work of neuroscientists, she argues that there are several ways in which technology influences our behavior and "rewires" our brains. She discusses six ways in which we become conditioned by our interaction with technology. Her article particularly focuses on users (like teens) who seem to use digital technology 24 hours a day, 7 days a week.

NO: Tristan Harris was the design ethicist for Google for 3 years. Based on his experience and his knowledge of how technology companies operate, he argues that the companies exert much more influence over our behaviors than we do. In other words, he believes that we are being conditioned by the companies to behave in certain ways, rather than our minds or bodies responding to the type of influences caused by technologies themselves. He does however note that technology companies have become experts in structuring information that exploits our human vulnerabilities.

In the 1960s, a Canadian literature professor became a celebrity with his theories concerning how media "mediate" our realities. Marshall McLuhan was one of the first popular academics to take the approach that "the medium is the message." By that, he meant that every form of media has unique characteristics that influence how we use it, and what meaning we take from the way the message is distributed. One of his popular concepts was that every form of media alters our "sense ratios." So, for example, radio enhanced our hearing, print media relied on the ability of our eyes to make sense of the messages, and so on. As part of this theory, he posited that the more a form of media enhances one sense, the less our other senses are aware of what is taking place. When we use multiple forms of media such as eyes and ears when we partake of film or television, we engage more fully with the senses we're using and further repress our other senses.

McLuhan died in 1980, before the Internet and cell phones became the dominant communication technologies, but it is interesting to think of what he might have said about how each of them influence our senses today. Contemporary McLuhan scholars have different opinions of what he might have thought of a computer, for example, but in general, he might have said that the computer extends our brains, allowing us to give the memory functions over to the superior operating system of the computer. It is not insignificant then, that both of the authors for this issue question what becomes of a person's ability to remember details, when using digital technologies that operate faster than we intellectually reason.

McLuhan also stated that the content of any new form of media was that of old media forms, and he would undoubtedly be fascinated by the way people use digital technologies today. Certainly one aspect of contemporary use is that portable, small technologies like cell phones can be used somewhat unobtrusively anywhere, anytime. Even though cell phones were initially offered to allow people to talk to each other, (following the content of "old" technology), newer developments have allowed users to migrate to many of the cell phone's other qualities, like using the texting features, camera, and multiple apps designed for mobile lifestyles. He would probably be amused and somewhat disappointed that cell phones, for example, are actually used less today for people to talk to each other than they are used to send texts and function as handheld computers.

Many scholars agreed with at least some of McLuhan's ideas, and developed those ideas more fully over time. Neil Postman, for example, wrote a number of books based on the idea that the unique characteristics of a form of media influence the way we make sense of messages and the way we adapt the ethos of the technological form and extend it to other situations. One of his most successful books was *Amusing Ourselves To Death: Public Discourse in the Age of Show Business* (2005), which argued that television had become the dominant medium of the day and that everything else was influenced by the way television and television industries presented information. He accurately predicted that the entertainment function of television would begin to affect other aspects of our lives, and he discussed how educational institutions would begin to favor teachers and methods of teaching that amused students, rather than perpetuating pedagogical forms that favored lectures and traditional, rote learning. Both McLuhan and Postman would note that the election of a president who was a former reality TV star was perfectly in line with the way the public thought of celebrities and what they expected of people who became familiar to them through the televisual image.

Over the years, scholars, parents, and social observers have worried about how children, in particular, become "conditioned" to behaving in ways that are stimulated by current technologies. Think if you will, about the way our sense of time is influenced by the speed of the technologies we use. How long are you willing to wait for a response to a message you send someone? How much time are you willing to spend in looking for information online when you're doing a research paper? How do you read? Have the short messages typically used in cell phone texts and skimming the Internet for information influenced how long you are willing to work on a particular idea? Have you lost the ability to read long-form journalism?

The topic of whether our attention spans are becoming shorter and our ability to read in-depth information is of great concern to educators and the idea of multitasking, as identified as a major issue by Briggs, is a factor in how our bodies and minds may or may not adapt to newer digital technologies over time. This has an impact on our memories and on our ability to think and reason thoroughly. As Briggs reminds us, we can experience both information overload (when too much information is coming at us so that we can't possibly think about it) and relying on technology to do the memory work for us.

Both Briggs and Harris address concepts of addiction to digital technologies, but they differ in how those technological forms structure the interplay between people, their brains, and the way they make sense of information distributed over digital media. According to the psychologist Dr. Kimberly Young, an expert in Internet addiction, many young people first become addicted to Internet use when they leave their homes and live on college campuses. Whether the connectivity provided by schools is superior to what they're used to, or whether it becomes easier to use technologies away from the vigilant eyes of parents, first year students tend to suffer most from Internet addiction. But college students are certainly not the only people to become addicted to a certain form of digital technology; we're learning more every day about how "average" users become compulsive or addictive users for any number of reasons. Internet gambling, shopping, Facebook or Instagram use, or even news addiction are common in the United States and elsewhere. In some countries, interventionist programs have been started to help people break the addiction to cell phones or Internet use. And, it should be noted that Internet addiction or compulsive use of any digital form of media is not just the purview of children or teens. Adults of all ages have been diagnosed with various forms of compulsions or addictions when it comes to digital technologies.

But to return to McLuhan's ideas and the concept that digital technologies influence our senses (or sense ratios), we need only to become more vigilant about our own behaviors, and, we can look around to see how often people in restaurants, walking down streets, or even sitting in class, are tied to their digital technologies. For this reason, Briggs, Harris, and the authors of some of our additional resources and Internet references show how many different approaches are taken to trying to understand the role and impact of digital technology, and how technologies influence our behaviors and our lives.

YES ⬅

Saga Briggs

Six Ways Digital Media Impacts the Brain

We are what we spend our time doing. The average adult now spends over 20 hours online each week. Nearly a third of that time is spent on social media platforms, with Facebook taking up 50 minutes of each day. According to the Bureau of Labor Statistics, that's more time than we spend reading, exercising, or socializing most days. It's almost as much time as people spend eating and drinking (1.07 hours).

Teens rack up even more tech time, with some spending 9 hours engaging with digital media each day.

"It just shows you that these kids live in this massive 24/7 digital media technology world, and it's shaping every aspect of their life," says James Steyer, chief executive officer and founder of Common Sense Media. "They spend far more time with media technology than any other thing in their life. This is the dominant intermediary in their life."

So what happens to the brain, over time, when we engage with digital technology at such a high rate? Two specialists, neuroscientist Susan Greenfield and cognitive scientist David Chalmers, offer somewhat opposing views on the matter.

Greenfield suspects that we're generally worse off, with weaker memories, attention spans, and information processing ability.

"As a neuroscientist I am very aware that the brain adapts to its environment," she says. "If you're placed in an environment that encourages, say, a short attention span, which doesn't encourage empathy or interpersonal communication, which is partially addictive or compulsive . . . all these things will inevitably shape who you are. The digital world is an unprecedented one and it could be leaving an unprecedented mark on the brain."

Chalmers has a more optimistic perspective.

"Technology is increasing our capacities and providing us with newly sophisticated ways of thinking," Chalmers says. "In a way, it's automating work we used to have to do for ourselves painstakingly. It's taking stuff we had to do consciously and slowly and making it happen fast and automatically."

Where do these arguments leave us, especially when we have to make daily decisions about the tools and methods we use for learning about and navigating the world?

The bottom line is this: Whether digital media is changing our brains for the better or the worse, it's our choice to allow or deny that change.

"Because of the plasticity of our brains . . . if you change your habits, your brain is happy to go along with whatever you do," says neuropsychologist Joyce Schenkein. "Our brains adapt, but the process of adaptation is value-neutral—we might get smarter or we might get dumber, we're just adapting to the environment."

This means we actually have more control over the impact of digital media than we think. The point is to be mindful of how our brains are being affected so that we can adjust our tech time accordingly. Let's take a closer look at what kinds of changes can occur, and explore a few ways we can respond when they do.

How Digital Media Impacts the Brain

1. Attention

Digital media encourages us to multitask, if only because it's so easy to switch between tasks when you can open multiple windows in your browser or turn on multiple devices. But is this a good thing?

Stanford neuroscientist Russ Poldrack has found that learning new information while multitasking can cause that information to go to the wrong part of the brain. Normally, new information goes into the hippocampus, which is responsible for the long-term storage of knowledge. If a student is studying while watching TV, Poldrack warns, that same information might instead go to the striatum, which is responsible for storing new procedures and skills, not facts and ideas. This means it will be stored in a shallower way, preventing quick retrieval in the future.

"Multi-tasking adversely affects how you learn," Poldrack says. "Even if you learn while multi-tasking, that learning is less flexible and more specialized, so you cannot retrieve the information as easily."

Nicholas Carr, author of *The Shallows: What the Internet Is Doing to Our Brain*, agrees:

"What psychologists and brain scientists tell us about interruptions is that they have a fairly profound effect on the way we think. It becomes much harder to sustain attention, to think about one thing for a long period of time, and to think deeply when new stimuli are pouring at you all day long. I argue that the price we pay for being constantly inundated with information is a loss of our ability to be contemplative and to engage in the kind of deep thinking that requires you to concentrate on one thing."

If you can filter the important from the unimportant, though, shouldn't instant access to loads of data facilitate the opposite—that is, allow you to devote more brain space to thinking deeply about the things that matter most?

2. Memory

Researchers at the University of California, Santa Cruz and University of Illinois, Urbana Champaign have found that "cognitive offloading," or the tendency to rely on the Internet as an aide-mémoire, increases after each use.

Examining how likely people are to reach for a computer or smartphone to answer trivia questions, Storm et al. divided study participants into two groups: those who were allowed to use only their memory to answer questions and those who were allowed to use Google. Participants were then given the option of answering subsequent easier questions by the method of their choice.

Participants who had previously used the Internet to gain information were "significantly more likely to revert to Google for subsequent questions than those who relied on memory." In fact, 30 percent of participants who previously consulted the Internet "failed to even attempt to answer a single simple question from memory." They also reached for the phones more quickly each time.

"Memory is changing," Storm says. "Our research shows that as we use the Internet to support and extend our memory, we become more reliant on it. Whereas before we might have tried to recall something on our own, now we don't bother. As more information becomes available via smartphones and other devices, we become progressively more reliant on it in our daily lives."

Storm acknowledges that more research needs to be conducted to determine whether these findings spell trouble for the brain: "It remains to be seen whether this increased reliance on the Internet is in any way different from the type of increased reliance one might experience on other information sources, such as books or people."

The question is, does it matter if the information fails to stick? One study out of Columbia University showed that when people know that they'll be able to find information online easily, they're less likely to form a memory of it.

While Storm argues that "the need to remember trivial facts, figures, and numbers is inevitably becoming less necessary to function in everyday life," others might point out that conversation becomes far less enjoyable when we can't recall facts or must always pause to look something up.

And what about memory for other types of knowledge, such as social and emotional cues or the kind of scaffolded understanding that defines expertise? Storm concedes that tech is best used as a supplement, not a substitute, for memory in these cases:

"Although the Internet may be effective in helping people access certain types of information, it may be much less effective in helping people access other types of information. In such cases, using the Internet to access information could prove detrimental. Furthermore, there are forms of expertise that require the possession of vast amounts of knowledge and the ability to rapidly and flexibly use that information is unlikely to be attained when it is stored externally."

3. Thought

According to a new study published in the proceedings of the ACM Conference on Human Factors in Computing Systems, reading on digital platforms might make you "more inclined to focus on concrete details rather than interpreting information more abstractly."

The research focused on a person's "construal levels," defined as "the fundamental level of concreteness versus abstractness that people use in perceiving and interpreting behaviors, events, and other informational stimuli." Over 300 participants, aged 20 to 24 years old, took part in the studies. Participants were asked to read a short story by author David Sedaris on either a physical printout (nondigital) or in a PDF on a PC laptop (digital), and were then asked to take a pop-quiz, paper-and-pencil comprehension test.

For the abstract questions, on average, participants using the nondigital platform scored higher on inference questions with 66 percent correct, as compared to those using the digital platform, who had 48 percent correct. On the concrete questions, participants using the digital platform scored better with 73 percent correct, as compared to those using the nondigital platform, who had 58 percent correct.

Participants were also asked to read a pamphlet of information about four, fictitious Japanese car models on either a PC laptop screen or paper printout, and were then asked to select which car model is superior. Sixty-six percent of the participants using the nondigital platform (printed materials) reported the correct answer, as compared to 43 percent of those using the digital platform.

Assistant professor Geoff Kaufman, who led the study, said: "Given that psychologists have shown that construal levels can vastly impact outcomes such as self-esteem and goal pursuit, it's crucial to recognize the role that digitization of information might be having on this important aspect of cognition."

His colleague Mary Flanagan added: "Compared to the widespread acceptance of digital devices, as evidenced by millions of apps, ubiquitous smartphones, and the distribution of iPads in schools, surprisingly few studies exist about how digital tools affect our understanding—our cognition. Sometimes it is beneficial to foster abstract thinking, and as we know more, we can design to overcome the tendencies—or deficits—inherent in digital devices."

The study was inspired by earlier research on the public health strategy game "POX: Save the People®" which found that players of the digital version of the game were more inclined to respond with localized solutions and players of the nondigital version more often looked at the big picture.

Jordan Grafman, chief of cognitive neuroscience at the National Institute of Neurological Disorders and Stroke, explains it this way: "The opportunity for deeper thinking, for deliberation, or for abstract thinking is much more limited. You have to rely more on surface-level information, and that is not a good recipe for creativity or invention."

4. Empathy

In *The Shallows*, Carr includes a study showing that the more distracted you are, the less able you are to experience empathy. "Distractions could make it more difficult for us to experience deep emotions," he explains. "This kind of culture of constant distraction and interruption undermines not only the attentiveness that leads to deep thoughts, but also the attentiveness that leads to deep connections with other people."

One method of connecting that's quickly becoming obsolete is handwriting, especially in the context of written correspondence. Melbourne handwriting analyst Ingrid Seger-Woznicki believes the discipline of writing legibly was once "a mark of respect between author and reader."

"The lack of writing is reflective of our lack of clarity of communication," she says. "We don't see communication as an art as we used to. Writing by hand forces you to stop and think a bit, and it makes you more aware of how you affect others. Poor handwriting used to be seen as a lack of consideration."

"When you write cursive you are wanting to connect with people's minds at a deeper level, and as a society we don't want to do that anymore."

Some researchers even believe there is an "essential link between the movement of the hand and the creation of thoughts and memories that typing simply cannot replicate."

Good penmanship takes deliberation, consideration, and concentration—qualities we're starting to see less and less of as digital media pulls our attention in multiple directions.

5. Meta-awareness

Some studies suggest that heavy digital media use leads to a loss of cognitive control—not just a loss of attention, but a loss of our ability to control our mind and what we think about.

"One researcher from Stanford pointed out that the more you acclimate yourself to the technology and the constant flow of information that comes through it, it seems that you become less able to figure out what's important to focus on," Carr says. Instead, your mind gets attracted just to what's new rather than what's important.

What's new may be completely devoid of meaning, but the part of the brain that responds to it tends to trick us into thinking it's significant.

"Each time we dispatch an email in one way or another, we feel a sense of accomplishment, and our brain gets a dollop of reward hormones telling us we accomplished something," says Daniel J. Levitin, author of *The Organised Mind: Thinking Straight in the Age of Information Overload*. "But remember, it is the dumb, novelty-seeking portion of the brain driving the limbic system that induces this feeling of pleasure, not the planning, scheduling, higher-level thought centers in the prefrontal cortex."

So, in a sense, the more we pursue empty rewards like Facebook "likes" and Twitter "favorites," the dumber we get, and the harder it is to maintain some level of self-awareness over our habits.

"Make no mistake," Levitin warns, "email, Facebook, and Twitter checking constitute a neural addiction."

Dr. Nicholas Kardaras, author of *Glow Kids: How Screen Addiction Is Hijacking Our Kids* and *How to Break the Trance*, agrees there's a very real reason why it's so hard to coax people away from their devices:

"We now know that those iPads, smartphones and Xboxes are a form of digital drug. Recent brain imaging research is showing that they affect the brain's frontal cortex—which controls executive functioning, including impulse control—in exactly the same way that cocaine does. Technology is so hyper-arousing that it raises dopamine levels—the feel-good neurotransmitter most involved in the addiction dynamic—as much as sex."

Grafman says this kind of addiction is especially dangerous for youth.

"The problem is that judicious thinking is among the frontal-lobe skills that are still developing way past the teenage years," he says. "In the meantime, the pull of technology is capturing kids at an ever earlier age, when they are not generally able to step back and decide what's appropriate or necessary, or how much is too much."

The best thing we can do for our brains—and the brains of our students—is to bring the reality of tech addiction to the attention of the people it impacts most.

6. Attitude

"Hundreds of clinical studies show that screens increase depression, anxiety and aggression and can even lead to psychotic-like features where the video gamer loses touch with reality," says Kardaras.

A Finnish study published last May in the *Journal of Youth and Adolescence* linked depression and school burnout to adolescents' excessive Internet use. Interestingly, it works both ways: The researchers also found that digital addiction is more likely to happen if adolescents already lack interest in and feel cynicism toward school.

Some research, though, casts a more positive light on tech-induced attitudes. For instance, the Pew Research Centre found last year that Facebook users have more close friends, more trust in people, feel more supported, and are more politically involved compared to nonsocial media users. A 2013 study found that teenagers often feel that "social media helps them to deepen their relationships with others."

The bottom line is that, despite its undeniable boons, digital media does pose a threat to optimal brain function and healthy relationships with others. Remain as aware as possible of the way it influences your behavior and you'll be able to ride the wave instead of getting lost in the undertow.

SAGA BRIGGS is a writer and the managing editor of InformEd, an educational think tank based in Australia. Her articles pose intriguing questions about behavior and social interaction with technology and the companies that market new uses for technology.

Tristan Harris

NO

How Technology Hijacks People's Minds—From a Magician and Google's Design Ethicist

I'm an expert on how technology hijacks our psychological vulnerabilities. That's why I spent the last three years as Google's Design Ethicist caring about how to design things in a way that defends a billion people's minds from getting hijacked.

When using technology, we often focus optimistically on all the things it does for us. But I want you to show you where it might do the opposite.

Where does technology exploit our minds weaknesses?

I learned to think this way when I was a magician. Magicians start by looking for blind spots, edges, vulnerabilities and limits of people's perception, so they can influence what people do without them even realizing it. Once you know how to push people's buttons, you can play them like a piano.

And this is exactly what product designers do to your mind. They play your psychological vulnerabilities (consciously and unconsciously) against you in the race to grab your attention.

I want to show you how they do it.

Hijack #1: If You Control the Menu, You Control the Choices

Western Culture is built around ideals of individual choice and freedom. Millions of us fiercely defend our right to make "free" choices, while we ignore how we're manipulated upstream by limited menus we didn't choose.

This is exactly what magicians do. They give people the illusion of free choice while architecting the menu so that they win, no matter what you choose. I can't emphasize how deep this insight is.

When people are given a menu of choices, they rarely ask:

- "what's not on the menu?"
- "why am I being given these options and not others?"

- "do I know the menu provider's goals?"
- "is this menu empowering for my original need, or are the choices actually a distraction?" (e.g. an overwhelmingly array of toothpastes)

How empowering is this menu of choices for the need, "I ran out of toothpaste"?

For example, imagine you're out with friends on a Tuesday night and want to keep the conversation going. You open Yelp to find nearby recommendations and see a list of bars. The group turns into a huddle of faces staring down at their phones comparing bars. They scrutinize the photos of each, comparing cocktail drinks. Is this menu still relevant to the original desire of the group?

It's not that bars aren't a good choice, it's that Yelp substituted the group's original question ("where can we go to keep talking?") with a different question ("what's a bar with good photos of cocktails?") all by shaping the menu.

Moreover, the group falls for the illusion that Yelp's menu represents a complete set of choices for where to go. While looking down at their phones, they don't see the park across the street with a band playing live music. They miss the pop-up gallery on the other side of the street serving crepes and coffee. Neither of those show up on Yelp's menu.

Yelp subtly reframes the group's need "where can we go to keep talking?" in terms of photos of cocktails served.

The more choices technology gives us in nearly every domain of our lives (information, events, places to go, friends, dating, jobs)—the more we assume that our phone is always the most empowering and useful menu to pick from. Is it?

The "most empowering" menu is different than the menu that has the most choices. But when we blindly surrender to the menus we're given, it's easy to lose track of the difference:

- "Who's free tonight to hang out?" becomes a menu of most recent people who texted us (who we could ping).
- "What's happening in the world?" becomes a menu of news feed stories.
- "Who's single to go on a date?" becomes a menu of faces to swipe on Tinder (instead of local events with friends, or urban adventures nearby).
- "I have to respond to this email." becomes a menu of keys to type a response (instead of empowering ways to communicate with a person).

All user interfaces are menus. What if your email client gave you empowering choices of ways to respond, instead of "what message do you want to type back?"

When we wake up in the morning and turn our phone over to see a list of notifications—it frames the experience of "waking up in the morning" around a menu of "all the things I've missed since yesterday."

By shaping the menus we pick from, technology hijacks the way we perceive our choices and replaces them new ones. But the closer we pay attention to the options we're given, the more we'll notice when they don't actually align with our true needs.

Hijack #2: Put a Slot Machine In a Billion Pockets

If you're an app, how do you keep people hooked? Turn yourself into a slot machine.

The average person checks their phone 150 times a day. Why do we do this? Are we making 150 *conscious* choices?

If you want to maximize addictiveness, all tech designers need to do is link a user's action (like pulling a lever) with a variable reward. You pull a lever and immediately receive either an enticing reward (a match, a prize!) or nothing. Addictiveness is maximized when the rate of reward is most variable.

Does this effect really work on people? Yes. Slot machines make more money in the United States than baseball, movies, and theme parks combined. Relative to other kinds of gambling, people get 'problematically involved' with slot machines 3–4× faster according to NYU professor Natasha Dow Shull, author of Addiction by Design.

But here's the unfortunate truth—several billion people have a slot machine their pocket:

- When we pull our phone out of our pocket, we're playing a slot machine to see what notifications we got.
- When we pull to refresh our email, we're playing a slot machine to see what new email we got.
- When we swipe down our finger to scroll the Instagram feed, we're playing a slot machine to see what photo comes next.

- When we swipe faces left/right on dating apps like Tinder, we're playing a slot machine to see if we got a match.
- When we tap the # of red notifications, we're playing a slot machine to what's underneath.

But in other cases, slot machines emerge by accident. For example, there is no malicious corporation behind all of email who consciously chose to make it a slot machine. No one profits when millions check their email and nothing's there. Neither did Apple and Google's designers want phones to work like slot machines. It emerged by accident.

But now companies like Apple and Google have a responsibility to reduce these effects by converting intermittent variable rewards into less addictive, more predictable ones with better design. For example, they could empower people to set predictable times during the day or week for when they want to check "slot machine" apps, and correspondingly adjust when new messages are delivered to align with those times.

Hijack #3: Fear of Missing Something Important (FOMSI)

Another way apps and websites hijack people's minds is by inducing a "1 percent chance you could be missing something important."

If I convince you that I'm a channel for important information, messages, friendships, or potential sexual opportunities—it will be hard for you to turn me off, unsubscribe, or remove your account—because (aha, I win) you might miss something important:

- This keeps us subscribed to newsletters even after they haven't delivered recent benefits ("what if I miss a future announcement?")
- This keeps us "friended" to people with whom we haven't spoke in ages ("what if I miss something important from them?")
- This keeps us swiping faces on dating apps, even when we haven't even met up with anyone in a while ("what if I miss that one hot match who likes me?")
- This keeps us using social media ("what if I miss that important news story or fall behind what my friends are talking about?")
- But if we zoom into that fear, we'll discover that it's unbounded: we'll always miss something important at any point when we stop using something.

There are magic moments on Facebook we'll miss by not using it for the 6th hour (e.g. an old friend who's visiting town right now).

There are magic moments we'll miss on Tinder (e.g. our dream romantic partner) by not swiping our 700th match.

There are emergency phone calls we'll miss if we're not connected 24/7.

But living moment to moment with the fear of missing something isn't how we're built to live.

And it's amazing how quickly, once we let go of that fear, we wake up from the illusion. When we unplug for more than a day, unsubscribe from those notifications, or go to Camp Grounded—the concerns we thought we'd have don't actually happen.

We don't miss what we don't see.

The thought, "what if I miss something important?" is generated in advance of unplugging, unsubscribing, or turning off—not after. Imagine if tech companies recognized that, and helped us proactively tune our relationships with friends and businesses in terms of what we define as "time well spent" for our lives, instead of in terms of what we might miss.

Hijack #4: Social Approval

Easily one of the most persuasive things a human being can receive.

We're all vulnerable to social approval. The need to belong, to be approved or appreciated by our peers is among the highest human motivations. But now our social approval is in the hands of tech companies (like when we're tagged in a photo).

When I get tagged by my friend Marc, I imagine him making a *conscious choice* to tag me. But I don't see how a company like Facebook orchestrated him doing that in the first place.

Facebook, Instagram, or SnapChat can manipulate how often people get tagged in photos by automatically suggesting all the faces people should tag (e.g. by showing a box with a 1-click confirmation, "Tag Tristan in this photo?").

So when Marc tags me, *he's actually responding to Facebook's suggestion*, not making an independent choice. But through design choices like this, *Facebook controls the multiplier for how often millions of people experience their social approval on the line.*

Facebook uses automatic suggestions like this to get people to tag more people, creating more social externalities and interruptions.

The same happens when we change our main profile photo—Facebook knows that's a moment when we're vulnerable to social approval: "what do my friends think of my new pic?" Facebook can rank this higher in the news feed, so it sticks around for longer and more friends will like or comment on it. Each time they like or comment on it, I'll get pulled right back.

Everyone innately responds to social approval, but some demographics (teenagers) are more vulnerable to it than others. That's why it's so important to recognize how powerful designers are when they exploit this vulnerability.

Hijack #5: Social Reciprocity (Tit-for-tat)

- You do me a favor, now I owe you one next time.
- You say, "thank you"—I have to say "you're welcome."
- You send me an email—it's rude not to get back to you.
- You follow me—it's rude not to follow you back. (especially for teenagers)
- We are vulnerable to needing to reciprocate others' gestures. But as with Social Approval, tech companies now manipulate how often we experience it.

In some cases, it's by accident. Email, texting and messaging apps are social reciprocity factories. But in other cases, companies exploit this vulnerability on purpose.

LinkedIn is the most obvious offender. LinkedIn wants as many people creating social obligations for each other as possible, because each time they reciprocate (by accepting a connection, responding to a message, or endorsing someone back for a skill) they have to come back through linkedin.com where they can get people to spend more time.

Like Facebook, LinkedIn exploits an asymmetry in perception. When you receive an invitation from someone to connect, you imagine that person making a conscious choice to invite you, when in reality, they likely unconsciously responded to LinkedIn's list of suggested contacts. In other words, LinkedIn turns your unconscious impulses (to "add" a person) into new social obligations that millions of people feel obligated to repay. All while they profit from the time people spend doing it.

Imagine millions of people getting interrupted like this throughout their day, running around like chickens with their heads cut off, reciprocating each other—all designed by companies who profit from it.

Welcome to social media.

After accepting an endorsement, LinkedIn takes advantage of your bias to reciprocate by offering *four* additional people for you to endorse in return.

Imagine if technology companies had a responsibility to minimize social reciprocity. Or if there was an "FDA for Tech" that monitored when technology companies abused these biases?

Hijack #6: Bottomless bowls, Infinite Feeds, and Autoplay

Another way to hijack people is to keep them consuming things, even when they aren't hungry anymore.

How? Easy. *Take an experience that was bounded and finite, and turn it into a bottomless flow that keeps going.*

Cornell professor Brian Wansink demonstrated this in his study showing you can trick people into keep eating soup by giving them a bottomless bowl that automatically refills as they eat. With bottomless bowls, people eat 73 percent more calories than those with normal bowls and underestimate how many calories they ate by 140 calories.

Tech companies exploit the same principle. News feeds are purposely designed to auto-refill with reasons to keep you scrolling, and purposely eliminate any reason for you to pause, reconsider or leave.

It's also why video and social media sites like Netflix, YouTube or Facebook autoplay the next video after a countdown instead of waiting for you to make a conscious choice (in case you won't). A huge portion of traffic on these websites is driven by autoplaying the next thing.

Tech companies often claim that "we're just making it easier for users to see the video they want to watch" when they are actually serving their business interests. And you can't blame them, because increasing "time spent" is the currency they compete for.

Instead, imagine if technology companies empowered you to consciously bound your experience to align with what would be "time well spent" for you. Not just bounding the quantity of time you spend, but the qualities of what would be "time well spent."

Hijack #7: Instant Interruption vs. "Respectful" Delivery

Companies know that messages that interrupt people immediately are more persuasive at getting people to respond than messages delivered asynchronously (like email or any deferred inbox).

Given the choice, Facebook Messenger (or WhatsApp, WeChat, or SnapChat for that matter) would prefer to design their messaging system to interrupt recipients immediately (and show a chat box) instead of helping users respect each other's attention.

In other words, interruption is good for business.

It's also in their interest to heighten the feeling of urgency and social reciprocity. For example, Facebook automatically *tells the sender when you "saw" their message, instead of letting you avoid disclosing whether you read it* ("now that you know I've seen the message, I feel even more obligated to respond.") By contrast, Apple more respectfully lets users toggle "Read Receipts" on or off.

The problem is, while messaging apps maximize interruptions in the name of business, it creates a tragedy of the commons that ruins global attention spans

and causes billions of interruptions every day. This is a huge problem we need to fix with shared design standards (potentially, as part of Time Well Spent).

Hijack #8: Bundling Your Reasons with Their Reasons

Another way apps hijack you is by taking *your reasons* for visiting the app (to perform a task) and *make them inseparable from the app's business reasons* (maximizing how much we consume once we're there).

For example, in the physical world of grocery stories, the #1 and #2 most popular reasons to visit are pharmacy refills and buying milk. But grocery stores want to maximize how much people buy, so they put the pharmacy and the milk at the back of the store.

In other words, they make the thing customers want (milk, pharmacy) inseparable from what the business wants. If stores were truly organized to support people, they would put the most popular items in the front.

Tech companies design their websites the same way. For example, when you want to look up a Facebook event happening tonight (your reason) the Facebook app doesn't allow you to access it without first landing on the news feed (their reasons), and that's on purpose. *Facebook wants to convert every reason you have for using Facebook, into their reason which is to maximize the time you spend consuming things*.

In an ideal world, apps would always give you a direct way to get what you want separately from what they want.

Imagine a digital "bill of rights" outlining design standards that forced the products that billions of people used to support empowering ways to navigate towards their goals.

Hijack #9: Inconvenient Choices

We're told that it's enough for businesses to "make choices available."

- "If you don't like it you can always use a different product."
- "If you don't like it, you can always unsubscribe."
- "If you're addicted to our app, you can always uninstall it from your phone."
- Businesses naturally want to make the choices they want you to make easier, and the choices they don't want you to make harder. Magicians do the same thing. You make it easier for a spectator to pick the thing you want them to pick, and harder to pick the thing you don't.

For example, *NYTimes.com* let's you "make a free choice" to cancel your digital subscription. But instead of just doing it when you hit "Cancel Subscription," they force you to call a phone number that's only open at certain times.

NYTimes claims it's giving a free choice to cancel your account.

Instead of viewing the world in terms of choice availability of choices, we should view the world in terms of friction required to enact choices.

Imagine a world where choices were labeled with how difficult they were to fulfill (like coefficients of friction) and there was an FDA for Tech that labeled these difficulties and set standards for how easy navigation should be.

Hijack #10: Forecasting Errors, "Foot in the Door" strategies

Facebook promises an easy choice to "See Photo." Would we still click if it gave the true price tag?

People don't intuitively forecast *the true cost of a click* when it's presented to them. Sales people use "foot in the door" techniques by asking for a small innocuous request to begin with ("just one click"), and escalating from there ("why don't you stay awhile?"). Virtually all engagement websites use this trick.

Imagine if web browsers and smartphones, the gateways through which people make these choices, were truly watching out for people and helped them forecast the consequences of clicks (based on real data about what it actually costs most people?).

That's why I add "Estimated reading time" to the top of my posts. When you put the "true cost" of a choice in front of people, you're treating your users or audience with dignity and respect.

In a Time Well Spent internet, choices would be framed in terms of projected cost and benefit, so people were empowered to make informed choices.

TripAdvisor uses a "foot in the door" technique by asking for a single click review ("How many stars?") while hiding the three page form behind the click.

Summary and How We Can Fix This

Are you upset that technology is hijacking your agency? I am too. I've listed a few techniques but there are literally thousands. Imagine whole bookshelves, seminars, workshops and trainings that teach aspiring tech entrepreneurs techniques like this. They exist.

The ultimate freedom is a free mind, and we need technology to be on our team to help us live, feel, think, and act freely.

We need our smartphones, notifications screens, and web browsers to be exoskeletons for our minds and interpersonal relationships that put our values, not our impulses, first. People's time is valuable. And we should protect it with the same rigor as privacy and other digital rights.

Tristan Harris is a strong believer in using technology, but also, taking "time out" from technology so that we can better balance complicated lives that are often "controlled" by technology. He left his position as Google's Ethicist and began a nonprofit movement called *Time Well Spent* to better align technology with our human needs.

EXPLORING THE ISSUE

Do Digital Technologies Influence Our Senses?

Critical Thinking and Reflection

1. Are the authors stating their opinions, or do they back up their positions with research? How valid is that research?
2. Have you examined your own behavior? How has your use of digital technologies influenced your expectations and way of thinking?
3. The philosopher Marshall McLuhan called the balance of our senses "sense ratios." When you enhance information that influences some senses, what happens to the other senses?
4. Does everyone perceive of the use and meaning of digital technologies in the same way(s)?
5. What is the difference between using technology and compulsive use of technology?

Is There Common Ground?

Both Briggs and Harris are concerned about the relationship of digital technologies and human behavior, though they may differ on the instigating influences that cause us to think in certain ways. In many ways, their inquiries are part of the oldest questions posed about the relationship of media and human beings. The search for both a cause and effect of how technology influences us, and by logical extension, how technology influences society, is one of the fundamental questions of media, technology, and human interaction.

Another common theme in these two selections is that there are several ways of approaching the problem, and different perspectives on the evolution of using technology. Over time, will our biological organisms adapt to technologies that process information faster and more accurately than our brains? Are our brains becoming "rewired" because of the number of issues that influence social use of digital technologies? Is becoming aware of the problems an adequate solution to understanding the social upheaval caused by widespread use of a form of media or a technology?

Finally, both authors take the position that something very important is happening to us, and to society because we have so many digital technologies from which to draw. Both authors also examine the complex nature of the interplay of human behavior and the development of multiple technologies in our lives. Will we eventually be able to better understand how and why we use digital technologies, or will our daily use make critical inquiry irrelevant, as we attempt to integrate digital tools into our daily lives?

Additional Resources

Nicholas Carr, *The Shallows: What the Internet Is Doing To Our Brain*, (NY: W.W. Norton and Co., 2011). Carr explores the ways we read and remember information, and argues that we are becoming more "shallow" in what we know, and how we know it. His approach is very "McLuhanesque," and while many people have criticized his approach, the book was a finalist for the 2011 Pulitzer Prize in General Nonfiction.

Hilarie Cash, Cosette D. Rae, Ann H. Steel, and Alexander Winkler, "Internet Addiction: A Brief Summary of Research and Practice," *Current Psychiatry Review*, Nov. 2012. The researchers identify a number of approaches toward understanding the issues behind addiction to technologies, with an emphasis on the importance of the Internet. This is an overview of studies related to addiction and compulsive behavior, and current research in dealing with the problem.

Dave Mosher, "High Wired: Does Addictive Internet Use Restructure the Brain?" *Scientific American* June 17, 2011. In this brief article, Mosher examines the problem of addiction, the addictive personality, and the way some people who become addicts justify their use of the Internet.

Nicholas Thompson, "Our Minds Have Been Hijacked By Our Phones. Tristan Harris Wants to Rescue Them," *Wired Magazine*, July 26, 2017. In this in-depth article, Harris discusses the way Silicon Valley has perfected protocols for cell phone use that give users "prompts" to encourage them to stay online longer.

Internet References . . .

Academic Earth, "How the Internet is Changing Your Brain" (video), 2017.

http://academicearth.org/electives/internet-changing-your-brain/

Jared Milfred, "Is Google Ruining Your Memory? The Science of Memory in the Digital Age," Yale Scientific, May 11, 2013.

http://www.yalescientific.org/2013/05/is-google-ruining-your-memory-the-science-of-memory-in-the-digital-age/

Jia-Rui Cook, "Digital technology can be harmful to your health," *UCLA Newsroom*, March 29, 2016.

http://newsroom.ucla.edu/stories/digital-technolgy-can-harm-your-health

Jim Taylor, "How Technology is Changing the Way Children Think and Focus," *Psychology Today*, December 4, 2012.

https://www.psychologytoday.com/blog/the-power-prime/201212/how-technology-is-changing-the-way-children-think-and-focus

Pamela DeLuatch, "The Four Negative Sides of Technology," *Eududemic*, May 2, 2015.

http://www.edudemic.com/the-4-negative-side-effects-of-technology/

Unit 2

UNIT

A Question of Content

*W*e no longer live in a world in which all of our media are directed toward mass audiences. Today we have both mass media and personal media, like video games, iPods, and cell phones. Because people use media content in many different ways, and so much of how we make sense of media depends on our own ages and life experiences, the issue of media content that is appropriate for certain audiences takes on a new importance. In this section, we deal with issues that often influence people from all ages and all walks of life – but the questions for discussion become more pointed when we consider that different audiences may perceive different things in the content of some forms of media. In this section, we consider issues that affect our sense of body, behavior, and expression of self to others.

Selected, Edited, and with Issue Framing Material by:
Alison Alexander, *University of Georgia*
and
Jarice Hanson, *University of Massachusetts—Amherst*

ISSUE

Do Media Cause Individuals to Develop Negative Body Images?

YES: June Deery, from "The Body Shop," Palgrave Macmillan (2012)

NO: Michael P. Levine and Sarah K. Murnen, from "'Everybody Knows That Mass Media Are/Are Not [*Pick One*] a Cause of Eating Disorders': A Critical Review of Evidence for a Causal Link between Media, Negative Body Image, and Disordered Eating in Females," *Journal of Social and Clinical Psychology* (2009)

Learning Outcomes

After reading this issue, you will be able to:

- Evaluate the media messages about body image in a better way.
- Analyze how the images influence children and people who may have a particular viewpoint about standards of beauty and attractiveness.
- Understand the power of advertising and marketing lifestyle to a range of age groups.
- Apply the critical skills to other aspects of your lives.

ISSUE SUMMARY

YES: June Deery examines the role of reality television and body makeover programs and concludes that these types of programs normalize the idea that bodies can and should be improved by plastic surgery, weight loss, and control programs, and that women in particular should subject themselves to all measures to find "success" and "happiness." She theorizes that these programs assume that women in particular do have negative body images, and that the real messages of these programs are that surgical steps can and should be taken to improve one's poor body image.

NO: Michael P. Levine and Sarah K. Murnen also investigate magazine ads, but find the assumption that media cause eating disorders to be too limited. Instead, they cite a wide range of social, behavioral, and cultural issues over time to understand the complex conditions under which girls begin to adopt negative body issues that result in eating disorders.

Often media are accused of representing images that result in people's negative behaviors. Sometimes, media are so present in our lives that it seems apparent that there is, or should be, a direct link between media images and real-life manifestations of those images. We know that media have some influence over the way some people construct their ideas of reality, but the most difficult considerations have to do with who is affected, and under what conditions.

The authors of these two selections look at the impact of reality television and the assumptions so many shows make about the normalization of a negative body image, and how magazines send mixed messages to readers.

The authors of the selections for this issue examine the content of reality television shows and magazines, but start from different perspectives. June Deery focuses on reality shows and basic assumptions about body image, while Michael P. Levine and Sarah K. Murnen start with the question of whether images in magazines foster eating disorders and concepts of body image in general. What both selections have in common though is the idea that mediated images assume that there is an ideal body type, and that we as media consumers, measure our own bodies in comparison to the images we see.

We have evidence that plastic surgery for body sculpting is a growing business for both women and men, so the representations in the makeover and reality shows discussed by Deery suggest that television can play an extraordinary role in fostering one's own body image and sense of control over their body. We also know that in extreme cases, some people develop eating disorders based on the ideal body image as superthin, and that extreme measures can harm health. Professors Levine and Murnen evaluate the literature on what causes girls (in particular) to develop eating disorders, and find out that other cultural, social, and psychological issues play a much larger role in causing girls to actually harm themselves by extreme behaviors. Their perspective examines how behavior and self-image are formed over time, and in a world that has several competing causes for why someone psychologically succumbs to extreme eating behavior. Since the Levine and Murnen articles were written, much more evidence has come to light concerning the growing problem of adolescent boys with eating disorders too.

The complexities between media images and self-image are many indeed, and we know that not everyone is influenced by media in the same way. Socialization, family pressures and expectations, the type of media one consumes, and how peers talk about media images all have the potential to influence us in different ways, and still, probably all of us at some time know that something we saw in media made us feel a certain way, or think about something in a special way. When it comes to internalizing those images, our minds often register reactions in ways which we may not be aware.

Advertisers often seek to understand the underlying motivations that cause us to respond—especially for buying products, but sometimes we look to support from other people to confirm what we want to believe. Celebrities also tend to project body images that are often significantly underweight, thereby providing role models that may influence conscious or unconscious desires to be "like them." American culture is rife with stories about

the perils of obesity and unhealthy lifestyles. As a result, it is difficult to seek one particular cause that could be the definitive answer to why anyone develops the self-image that he or she does. But the process of trying to understand the range of psychological and sociological processes that come along with media images is fascinating, and sometimes, frightening.

There have been occasional stories of how product manufacturers have tried to overcome the typical media image of body type. For example, in 2004 Dove soap's "Campaign for Real Beauty" featured girls and women who did not have the media-ideal body type. The campaign used real people and identified them as beautiful for being who and what they were, but in 2008, Unilever (Dove's parent company) and Ogilvy and Mather, the product's advertising company, came under fire for retouching the pictures of the real people in the ads. In a May 12, 2008 article in *Advertising Age*, it was reported that the alleged retouching had created a "ruckus" that was one of the largest scandals in the history of advertising.

The issues of body image and media image are closely aligned to the question of whether advertising is ethical. The social role of advertising suggests that the consumers are suggestible, and that they are motivated to improve themselves, their lifestyles, and attitudes by consuming the products and images they see in media. Often people make assumptions that ads reflecting body type are primarily a female-only issue, but as these authors allude, there are increasing similarities to female and male advertising, especially when it comes to body image and health.

Today we often hear about the problem of obesity—particularly for children. This is a particularly pointed problem for children in school who may not get the type of physical fitness they need, and who often play videogames rather than cultivating an active lifestyle. If these children are influenced by the images in reality TV and as portrayed in magazines, will they look to surgical solutions, or find answers in creating lifestyles that allow them to be comfortable with their own bodies, and concerned about their health? These cultural realities are difficult to reconcile with the idea that the products we buy actually can help us look or feel a certain way, but advertisers know that by praying on our weaknesses, we are often tempted to buy more. But along with our own consumption habits, body modification can also become a way of buying what we think of as the ideal, despite the physical consequences.

YES ↵

June Deery

The Body Shop

For some time, people have accepted the responsibility of maintaining and making fashionable their living space. Surgical makeovers mainstream the idea that we should do the same for our bodies—not just by arranging hair and clothing but by altering the body's very architecture. While some superficial body modification is as old as human culture (piercings, tattoos), recent technologies render the body more radically malleable than ever before. Thanks to surgical techniques, the body's flaws are fixable: therefore, says a consumerist society, they ought to be fixed. Exactly what motivates any given individual to request a surgical makeover is impossible to fully determine—even for the subject involved—but there is no question that mediaadvertising has already played a significant role before anyone lines up for their makeover audition. My aim in examining on-screen transformations is to follow the logic presented in each series and offer an interpretation of its cultural significance.

Although it has been exported around the world, the surgical makeover is another particularly American form of reality television which appeals to this culture's intense and early interest in physical appearance, in glamour, in self-improvement, and in what amounts to a cult of youth. In other countries cosmetic surgery is less socially acceptable, as in many parts of Europe (Franco 2008), or people are more reserved when it comes to showing the body in general, as in China or other parts of Asia. My account will consider a variety of mostly American formats, including *Extreme Makeover, The Swan, 10 Years Younger, Bridalplasty,* and the docusoap *The Real Housewives.* These programs put into popular view rarefied postmodern discourses about the fluidity of the self, about sex and gender, and about the self as a project; however, they are generally noncommittal about whether this project involves multiple selves or the linear evolution of one core self. . . .

Every culture has taboos and prohibitions about which body parts may be subject to another's view, when, and in what circumstances—taboos that are often understood as a matter of ethics but also signal underlying economic arrangements (e.g., the female body as property in capitalist patriarchy). On surgical makeovers, shots of nipples and genitalia are conventionally blurred but otherwise makeover subjects have to display and discuss with a doctor, while on camera, what they perceive to be their specific physical flaws. Ordinarily, this filming of a patient consultation would of course be judged highly unprofessional. The fact that the critique of the body comes largely from the subject herself, a lifelong witness of media images, rather than from another judge, is at this stage a fairly minor distinction. The scenario is uncomfortable for the patient and this is, of course, the point, for their humiliation is the price they have to pay for securing a media audience/surgery. The patients are exposed according to the producers' stipulations in a process that has no medical use or justification. The inappropriateness of this voyeurism was particularly flagrant on *Bridalplasty* when the surgery candidates had to bare all not only to the surgeon or anonymous others (TV audience) once the episode aired, but also to a small, face-to-face group of rival brides on the show. Having their disgraced body parts displayed as they sit in a known group has a particular note of impropriety and it made one candidate burst out with: "No one should have to do this!" accompanied by an awkward laugh. Sue Tait suggests that such sequences are in part designed to get viewers on board with the surveillance and its normative judgments in order to justify the upcoming surgery. The audience is "to share the candidate's assessing and disciplinary gaze and assent with the identification of the aberrant features of the displayed body. This ostensibly 'proves' that surgical intervention is warranted. . .". That may be the plan anyway.

The Temple

The typical makeover has a female patient seeking help from a male surgeon. His bending over her mute and supine body in the operation room brings to mind the old narrative of the male scientist dissecting Nature depicted as a female body. Or his incisions could be seen in purely sexual terms as a male penetration. A more pecific account which dominated Western thought for centuries is Aristotelian reproduction. Without benefit of empirical research, this most influential natural philosopher forthrightly asserted that during reproduction the male shaped formless matter that lay within the female and so he was likened to, among other things, a carpenter creating objects out of wood. So here we have at least fragments of the tropes of body as house and male as builder embedded in early Western patriarchal thought. In the case of the modern makeover, the surgeon resembles a builder not of another body within a woman's body but of the woman herself. Indeed, one of the most striking and repeated images on televised surgeries is of the male surgeon marking up with ink areas of the patient's body that he will be work upon, like a carpenter marking up a piece of wood before he cuts into it. Aristotle's account reflected the tradition of according superiority to form over matter, to intellect and skill over dull substance. The modern makeover does not deviate significantly from this account. . . .

Yet while it is an intimate space, the body is also potentially a site of separation and alienation. Having a body is why subjects can be taken as objects or as things and one could argue that this is the stance being advocated on TV shows that solve problems by fixing the body's material and surface—a glib conclusion, perhaps, but an understandable one. For example, during their initial consultation both surgeons and patients tend to distance themselves from body identity and personal biography by agreeing on the importance of general principles of design such as proportion and symmetry, as one would when working on an architectural project. We saw in style makeovers a similar invocation of principles in order to impress upon subjects that there can and should be an objective assessment of body topology. This is even more the case in surgical makeovers where redesigning the body is presented as an objective task based on neutral factors such as geometric space and proportion, a sublimation most noticeable on *Extreme Makeover* when a photo of the patient's body is displayed like a blueprint, either static on the UK edition or rotating against a geometric grid in the American. In both instances, graphics label problem areas that need to be fixed, an early mapping which reinforces the idea that the person has become part of the object world. In actual fact, surgery is a violent act involving the breaking, tearing, and sawing of human bone and tissue, but on makeover shows clean spatial graphics largely overshadow blood and gore. Contrast this with procedural crime dramas such as CBS's *CSI* (2000–), another popular strain of television that focuses on the narratives that bodies reveal but that relies on sadistic

violence and trauma. The surgical makeover focuses on more containable abstract images which suggest that its procedures are almost a matter of mathematical measurement and redistribution of mass: for women, the redistribution involves smaller waists, larger breasts, smaller noses, bigger lips, while for men the results are "stronger" chins, wider chests, and straighter noses. In addition, one effect of surgery is to make these bodies more like buildings by being static and taut.

In common parlance, patients employ phrases such as "getting work done" or having "a nose job" to euphemistically attach their cosmetic surgery to the more impersonal notion of commercial construction and there may be a form of relief or even liberation in this transaction as depicted on television makeovers. For seeing their body as an object to be worked upon perhaps removes culpability from these subjects, especially as their assessment of their body's flaws is not challenged by sympathetic doctors who simply ratify that their concerns are justified and deserving of attention. Hosts on house makeovers are often careful to avoid blaming inhabitants for the dilapidated condition of their home, stressing financial and time constraints for lack of upkeep and repair. Similarly, blaming subjects is not part of the discourse of *Extreme Makeover or Bridalplasty*. Patients simply hand over their body as an unsatisfactory project for someone else to fix. Surgeons say little about the reasons for excess flesh: they simply suck the offending matter out (avoiding phrases like "you are fat"). However, culpability does emerge on *10 Years Younger* where being put on public display in a glass box has a whiff of the village stocks. This time subjects are held accountable for their state of disrepair: usually the problem is lack of prevention (sunscreen) or bad habits (diet, smoking). Blame and personal accountability are at the forefront of weight loss programs such as *The Biggest Loser*, programs that do not resort to surgery and instead encourage people to modify their bodies themselves over time. Programs that focus on surgery incorporate diet and exercise guides to some extent, but their emphasis is on promoting the rapid transformation achieved by putting one's body in someone else's hands, and the magic happens when the patient is not even conscious of being worked upon by others (under anesthetics). . . .

No one calculates more closely how to make the most of this synthetic narcissism than the women of *The Real Housewives* franchise, whose extrovert behavior exposes the more muted transactions occurring in a series like *Extreme Makeover* or *The Swan*. On *The Real Housewives*, making the body look good is a serious business and while cosmetic surgery is not a central narrative focus it is a vital element in the lives of those being filmed. It appears that most of the women have had some "work" done and increasingly they acknowledge this on camera. Unlike the modest "ugly ducklings" of charitable makeovers, the housewives rely fairly heavily on cosmetic surgery to advance their ambitions, which for many of these women is circumscribed by the finding and keeping of a wealthy husband. For others, an attractive body is also good for their professional careers (e.g., models, realtors, marketers, designers). In either case, these women recognize that body upgrades are essential for maintaining their market value and so for them cosmetic surgery is calculated and routine. In one scene, a husband rewards his wife for having her breasts augmented by surprising her in the recovery room with a gift of diamond earrings. Drowsy but gratified, she gets the message and says (with a laugh of sorts) that she should have cosmetic surgery more often, presumably because of the immediate financial gain.

So much is surgery normalized that one mother and daughter go in for a cozy surgery together (Lynne and daughter in *The Real Housewives of Orange County*) and another woman has almost a drive-thru experience when she has her fourth breast augmentation at a "Same Day Surgery" clinic in a strip mall (Danielle in *The Real Housewives of New Jersey*). The casual nature of the clinic and its setting is one reason why other medical practitioners look aghast at some cosmetic surgeons because they don't legally have to operate within hospitals and can conduct business anywhere. Several other *Real Housewives* women are filmed having minor cosmetic procedures as a fairly regular part of their lives and sometimes they bring friends along as though on a shopping trip. Botox parties are especially popular, both in home and work settings: for example, Vicki (*The Real Housewives of Orange County*) thinks it a nice reward for her employees to have a surprise office Botox party where she coerces them into getting injected, while also acknowledging that having an attractive appearance is good for (her) business. This brings office management into a new (and possibly illegal) area. But her intentions are pure to the extent that she, like the other women in this series, are convinced that working on physical appearance is a sound investment in one's financial future and so she is mentoring others in how best to succeed. Some of the housewives openly discuss how much they paid for various procedures and whether it was a good deal. Certainly they are not shy about displaying the results.

For many of these glamorous, sexualized, post-feminist women, turning their bodies into objects of desire is their chief career and it is their success at this selfcommodification that allows them to spend most of their lives consuming other goods and services. Those

who secure and rely on a wealthy husband's money are shown working hard to "maintain their body" and keep their side of the bargain. They may not work but they "work out," a distinct form of labor usually undertaken by those who don't otherwise have to exert themselves manually. In societies of abundance, part of being beautiful is being toned and slim. This signals discipline and has become an indication of prestige, of success, even of class. *The Real Housewives* series do not depict charity makeovers but those who are able to afford surgery (mostly thanks to their husbands) and who come across, for the most part, as irredeemably superficial and hollow. Their harping on about how it is their choice to trade physical attraction for money (or, less bluntly, achieve a "successful" marriage) hardly masks their subordinate position or the fragility of that marital arrangement. For all their faith in improvement through consumption, there is still an unease and a defensive attitude about their body's status as a commodity, even if within a marriage contract. The specter of being a "prostitution whore" looms over these well-groomed and surgically enhanced women who are in many ways caricatures, but, as caricatures, effectively illustrate some of the negotiations, ambivalences, and even hypocrisies of many other contemporary women and men who similarly invest in their body's appearance. In one sense it seems these women trade their bodies for real estate and in this way one property is exchanged for another. The wealthy husbands become a means to an end, the end being a luxurious home. At least this is where editors often focus their attention; for example, outside shots of each opulent dwelling is ritualistically used to identify the person who will be featured next. Only to the extent that they are wedded to the house (as a signifier of economic position) are they "house-wives," for certainly there is little evidence of the housewifery that is traditionally associated with this term given that many of these women employ nannies, maids, and personal assistants. However, as the various series have evolved, an unintended consequence of the franchise's success is that several of these women are growing more financially and socially independent (for them it appears the two are connected). . . .

On *The Swan* even the subject was not permitted to see her transformed body until it was simultaneously revealed to viewers. Prior to the reveal ceremony, the show's "mirror police" forbade every candidate from looking in any reflecting surfaces on penalty of being thrown out. When she is first allowed to see herself in a staged ceremony in front of a mirror, each subject's re-imaging of her new body is, in Foucauldian terms, a quite literal internalization of the mechanisms of surveillance and the gaze of the Other. She is now not only an object, but "an object of vision: a sight" a sight that seems to both fascinate and alienate her. The fact that her body is the product of others' work is perhaps why the subject is not usually modest about expressing delight in how it looks: in praising her appearance she is praising those who created it. On the more punitive *10 Years Younger* subjects who request a makeover have to stand in a glass box in the equivalent of the town square while passing strangers (literally the-person-on-the-street) are polled about the subject's age and physical appearance. Their appearance (i.e., market value) is assessed while on display, as though a retail object. To compound their status as a thing, they are deaf and mute while in the box and are unable to hear what these casual others are saying about them.

Here is how the *Queer Eye* website describes their style makeovers:

> With help from family and friends, the Fab Five treat each new guy as a head-to-toe project. Soon, the straight man is educated on everything from hair products to Prada and Feng Shui to foreign films. At the end of every fashion-packed, funfilled lifestyle makeover, a freshly scrubbed, newly enlightened guy emerges—complete with that "new man" smell

Each episode, we are told, boils down to a "onehour guide to building a better man." This description of a person in terms of an industrial product like an automobile is intended to be comic because it is not exactly appropriate. But it is not entirely inapplicable either. The made-over person does resemble a product to the extent that his new identity is produced and produced by others. This is especially the case with surgical makeovers where some surgeons refer to the post-op body as, indeed, "the final product." Moreover, when these made-over bodies conform to a fairly narrow range of looks this homogeneity increases the sense that they have not been born but produced: like any manufacturing process, it is a matter of finding cheap raw material ("ordinary" subjects), processing and designing it in line with market forces, and then packaging the results. . . .

In any society, the treatment of the body indicates some of the ways power circulates. Crucially observed in the modern era a shift away from obviously coercive legal and militaristic control of the body to today's more commonly administrative, medical and psychocultural mechanisms. We witnessed the producers' attempts at coercion on style makeovers but on surgical makeovers their control tends to be more firm. On these shows just about all of the patient's movements are dictated in another example

of private, commercial forces being acceptable where public and government overtures are not. Rather than formal, institutional restrictions, there is a therapeutic imperative distributed through private channels (mediaadvertising) urging the subject to conform. To a deeper extent than with shopping makeovers, this handing over of the body for surgery creates an alienation in the labor of self-reproduction. However, television shows such as *Extreme Makeover* and *The Swan* have also helped create a new relationship between patient and surgeon beyond the TV screen. When these series were being filmed they reflected the still authoritarian relationship between uninformed patient and all-knowing doctor where the patient does not question, negotiate, or critique. But since most of these shows have aired and the Internet has opened up further sources of information, patients are more likely to shop around for a surgeon who will best perform what they already judge needs to be done. Meredith Jones observes that, in part because of information circulating through popular channels like reality television, cosmetic surgery patients are now more inclined to approach their doctors as customers looking for a good service provider. So the commercial basis of the transaction is more marked today despite the public relations exercise of makeover TV that tried to erase these finances. In an era when such surgery has become another thing you buy, surgeons report a loss of status but an increase in business.

Attractive bodies attract and very attractive bodies attract even more, so it is no surprise that media-advertising skews toward representations of ideal beauty. More than this, advertising enjoins us to aspire to achieve the extraordinary appearance it uses to capture our attention. As numerous studies have suggested, one of the strongest effects of the media's daily parade of ideal beauty is that this alters what viewers regard as normal and what they aspire to be. That the logic of television prioritizes the superficial and the visual has had profound and still evolving cultural ramifications. For instance, if our models of ideal beauty were textual only there would be more room for our own standards and input, whereas a visual model fixes and imposes the image in exact detail. This opens up an almost infinite market for selling products to those who will never meet this image. On surgical makeovers we witness a diligent and procrustean chopping of bodies to

meet a beauty ideal, but there is no suggestion that media representations should instead be altered. The previously unmediated become fulfilled not just by being mediated but by being *mediatized*, meaning conforming to media images. Surgical candidates appear to have little interest in media exposure as an end in itself, but this kind of programming teaches them, and by extension us, that being mediated can be very beneficial and life transforming and therefore something to be desired.

What particularly struck Fredric Jameson about Guy Debord's depiction of the "society of the spectacle" was the latter's observation that the ultimate form of commodity reification in contemporary society is the image itself. With surgical makeovers, the media image is reified "in the subject and then resold as a TV image. In other words, if ever discourse impacted the material realm it is at this point, the human body. As Baudrillard observed, today we find not only "the forced extraversion of all interiority"— which almost any reality series pushes to the limit—but also the "forced introjection of all exteriority", meaning the internalizing of media imagery. RTV makeovers don't just display the ideal bodies we see everywhere else in the media, they show people imposing this ideal on real bodies: so that they become a simulation of an ideal. In some instances, as in MTV's / *Want a Famous Face* or TV Guide Channel's (nonsurgical) *Look-a-Like*, participants wish to resemble specific media products such as Brad Pitt or Pamela Anderson. Others wish to emulate an iconic figure who is not human, as in Cindy Jackson's 29 plastic surgeries to make her look like Barbie. (Cindy, incidentally, is the name of a British version of the Barbie doll.) RTV's mainstreaming of surgical procedures that offer to realize a hyperbolic image raises the bar for what people are expected to do and to spend in order to achieve a satisfactory status. Producers are tapping into a media effect (the near obsessive desire for an attractive body) within a media product (the makeover series) in order to create a media product of the body.

But it is not an internal feedback loop entirely. Nor is the significance of physical attractiveness an illusion arbitrarily impressed upon us by a cynical media simply in order to secure its own profits. People pay heed to media images, to what the culture deems attractive, because there are real-world consequences. We observe anecdotally and through more formal study that those who look attractive are admired and rewarded. Some of this response may be due to biological mechanisms and some to more socially constructed and culturally variant preferences, but whatever the origins of our attitudes there is little dispute that in real life being judged attractive has distinct advantages. On the biological front, certain body types may be favored because they signal fertility and virility while, for example, symmetrical features may indicate freedom from harmful genetic mutations, traumas, or residual effects of disease. Sociological studies suggest that the physically attractive are more likely to be promoted and to achieve other forms

of success in all stages of life. In any case, whatever the validity of such results, the perception that appearance matters becomes important and largely self-fulfilling, a logic at least reinforced on makeover TV.

Gender Construction

One of the most compelling roles played by media-advertising is that of defining what is feminine or masculine, and it is striking how often female makeover patients report that they wish to be "more feminine," a concept that is almost always tied to being more "sexy." The men's desire for masculinity is generally more muted and indeed there is a possibility that their seeking surgical enhancement will be coded as feminine. Whatever the case, on-screen doctors treat anyone's desire to accentuate their gender as natural and are happy to support heterosexist and sexist norms. As Brenda Weber notes, they appear to support the idea that "sex or biology is malleable while gender is constant," and so the former is shaped to match the latter. One pragmatic advantage of invoking "feminine" or "masculine" in a surgical context is that if doctors and patients have a similar understanding of what this means then it will provide a commonly agreed upon diagram of what an improved body should look like, and so doctors, patients, and presumably viewers will be similarly impressed by the results. But two things are being communicated here: that being strongly gender-marked is a desirable goal and that this effect can be produced through fairly rapid and superficial changes in bodily appearance. As though upholding, and in fact enacting, Judith Butler's notion that biological matters, too, are culturally determined, surgeons redesign the patient's body in order to better meet their culture's gender template. This is a remarkable process since it is only in recent times that there been such an opportunity for a culture to not only interpret but also to physically carve the body and to do so radically, swiftly, and with reasonable safety. In this manner, discourse physically shapes materiality and, if we maintain a gender/ sex distinction, then cosmetic surgery imposes notions of gender (femininity) on to sex (the female body).

The women on some of these shows emerge not just as feminine but as hyperfeminine, most notably on *The Swan* and *The Real Housewives* where the glamour version of femininity produces women who hark back to more patriarchal times: big hair, high heels, lots of "curves," and so on. These shows appear to offer enclaves of "enlightened sexism" where it is deemed acceptable to resurrect retrograde stereotypes and diffuse offense to more progressive viewers with mockery and ironic amusement. The matter takes an absurd turn when what seems like sexism is extended even to the design of teeth. *Extreme Makeover's* Dr. Bill Dorfman is of the opinion that a woman gets what she wants by "flashing her pearly whites" and that a "feminine smile is bright, soft, and beguiling. . . . Not unlike a feminine-looking body, a feminine-looking smile is all about curves." Masculine teeth, on the other hand, should appear "more angular" with the central incisors "square, strong, and more powerful" than the surrounding teeth. If biology doesn't mark gender in this way, then the surgeon is there to help fix this oversight.

One main reason for the surgical redesign of the body is that it is a place that exists in time, and there are two things that we have always known about aging: that it is inevitable and that it is universal. Both of these facts enhance the profitability of addressing nature's planned obsolescence. Fighting time's effects on the flesh is, indeed, a billion dollar segment of the "fashion-beauty complex" in which scientific-sounding ingredients and techniques (with adjectives like bio and molecular) are marketed as powerful "defense" mechanisms, often incorporating but reengineering natural substances. For example, Garnier offers "Ultra-LiftPro gravity defying cream" (Newton, never mind NASA, would be impressed). But this is the essence of commodification: adding value by offering the techné (craft, technology) that works on and even against nature. In many consumer cultures women of any age, despite other accomplishments, are expected to look as slim and adolescent as when they first started out in the market (or as they never did). The fat deposits and stretch marks that are natural testaments to the nurturance of others are matters for self-loathing, while wrinkles are pathologized as a disease that must be cured. As its title suggests, *10 Years Younger* makes reversing the signs of aging its particular focus. On the British version of this format the host walks the subject through a gallery of blown-up photos each sitting on its own easel and each documenting the subject's gradual physical deterioration over time: as they penetrate this spatialization of time's passing, the sense of failure and public condemnation could not be more bleak. Aging, or rather allowing the signs of aging to go uncorrected, is treated as at least a misdemeanor if not a larger crime. But as Sadie Wearing points out, there is a contradiction about the attitude to aging in this and other makeover programming that reflects an ambivalence in postfeminist thinking. On the one hand, postfeminism suggests that aging need not mean loss of femininity, of fun, of self, and so on. But, on the other hand, it insists that people take on the responsibility of making the body look as young as possible by making the right consumer choices.

We have seen how makeover TV, in conjunction with media-advertising, supports what sociologists have identified as a shift in postindustrial society to where "The body is less and less an extrinsic 'given'. . . but becomes itself reflexively mobilized". The extent to which surgical work on this self is either empowering or a sign of victimhood has for some time been a polarizing topic and has given rise to some debate among feminist scholars. There are those such as Naomi Wolf, Susan Bordo, and Germaine Greer who assert that opting for cosmetic surgery cannot be reconciled with feminism and that the practice is little more than a reprehensible effect of patriarchy.[22] Even when an individual feels they are freeing themselves, "In fact, what is happening is a more intense policing of the body" Then there is Kathy Davis who argues that such scholars need to respect the fact that for any individual the option may be empowering and rational given the sociopolitical conditions under which they act. However, it seems the majority of scholars today have adopted a more mixed or ambivalent approach which recognizes both empowerment and oppression. They are unwilling to dismiss cosmetic surgery patients as deluded or vain or victimized, but they underline that individual choice is constrained by the larger sociopolitical structure within which the decision to have surgery is made. As we have seen, makeover TV presents an upbeat narrative of individual empowerment with no serious acknowledgment of social pressures or constraints. Almost invariably TV subjects maintain that their surgery confers on them more "self-esteem," a term that is today very much in vogue (though, remarkably, only since the late 1990s). This benefit is regarded as deeply and individually empowering, though it could be considered a disingenuous claim since this self-esteem is so clearly yoked to the esteem of others (the reveal) and the frequent assertion that "I am doing it for myself" becomes almost meaningless since they are clearly improving their appearance in such a way as to better impress others. In any case, one of the problems with research in this area is that so much depends on self-reporting from patients and this can only take us so far. Even if this input is genuine and reliable, people tend to repeat the available repertoires (self-esteem, I'm doing it for myself) without necessarily realizing how they are being influenced and it is difficult to see how anyone else could prove influence either. However, this much we can say: that reality shows provide some insight into what people say (publicly) about why they want surgery, that they provide information about what surgeons can accomplish, that there appears to be an interest (on television and in real life) in accentuating sexual differences, and that according to both patients and surgeons these series have contributed to an increase in requests for various procedures. Deeper psychological or collective reasons why people elect for surgery are worth speculating about but are not easily proven.

Seeking surgery could, for example, be another form of compensation symptomatic of large sociopolitical trends. This was the opinion of Christopher Lasch and has been implied by others since. When studying narcissistic behavior in the 1970s, Lasch suggested that the focus on the self and on self-improvement was a reaction to the individual's feeling of helplessness in a wider sphere (in his own period, the failure to effect political change after the 1960s and the ever-present threat of nuclear warfare). Lasch believed that the self-empowerment that comes from working on the self was acting as a palliative for larger forces bearing down on individuals which they could not alter. Noting the recent intense focus on body improvement, Anthony Giddens similarly traces its origins to a deeper unease and further institutional unraveling. "What might appear as a wholesale movement towards the narcissistic cultivation of bodily appearance is," he maintains, "an expression of a concern lying much deeper actively to 'construct' and control the body". It may be that the body is targeted because it is a malleable material whose change is feasible and evident, and whose alteration produces both social and financial benefits. As we have seen, improving one's body can be presented as a pragmatic way to prosper in a climate of instability and job insecurity in which individuals are being urged to make the most of their own public relations. More broadly, it may be a comfort in a society of increasing complexity and risk to focus on something one can control. Sociologist Chris Shilling backs this up when he identifies a contemporary reaction where "if one feels unable to exert influence over an increasingly complex society, at least one can have some effect on the size, shape and appearance of one's body". If we accept this explanation, then the accelerated embrace of cosmetic surgery is a sign of a cultural and political ill health that goes far beyond somatic concerns.

Whatever the reasons—and no doubt they are diverse and complex—what is clear is that record numbers of people in Western nations report dissatisfaction with their body image, even in childhood. In this context, TV's surgical fixes are likely to lead to increased pressure to change, which statistics suggest is already happening. As surgery becomes more widespread, we can speculate that the end result will be a form of commercial eugenics linking beauty, money, and rank even more firmly than in epochs past; for if, as these makeovers insist, we can fix our body image but we don't, then an unimproved body would signal either indolence or lower socioeconomic status. Beyond this, if the focus rests on body as the locus for change this inward turn promises to provide little political counterbalance to the prioritization of public image, whether of the individual or of larger social bodies, thus contributing to a future when both micro and macro politics could implode entirely to media-advertising and PR.

. . . .

June Deery is an Associate Professor at Rensellaer Polytechnic Institute. Her research focuses on television and the Internet, and her primary areas of study are gender, class, commercialization, and politics.

Michael P. Levine and Sarah K. Murnen

"Everybody Knows That Mass Media Are/ Are Not [*Pick One*] a Cause of Eating Disorders": A Critical Review of Evidence for a Causal Link between Media, Negative Body Image, and Disordered Eating in Females

Numerous professionals, parents, and adolescents find the media's status as a cause of body dissatisfaction, drive for thinness, and eating disorders to be self-evident: *"Of course,* mass media contribute to unhealthy beauty ideals, body dissatisfaction, and disordered eating—haven't you seen the magazine covers in the supermarket newsstands lately? No wonder so many girls have body image issues and eating disorders." On the contrary, a growing number of parents, biopsychiatric researchers, clinicians, and cynical adolescents find proclamations about media as a *cause* of any disorder to be an irritating distraction. Their contention is, in effect: *"Of course,* we know now that eating disorders, like mood disorders and schizophrenia, are severe, self-sustaining psychiatric illnesses with a genetic and biochemical basis. So, *of course,* no scientist seriously thinks that mass media and the escapades of actors, models, and celebrities have anything to do with causing them." . . .

The relationships between mass media, negative body image, and unhealthy behaviors (e.g., use and abuse of steroids and food supplements) in males are receiving increasing attention. The gender differences (conservatively, 6 to 8 females for each male) in the prevalence of anorexia nervosa, bulimia nervosa, and eating disorder not otherwise specified (EDNOS) other than Binge Eating Disorder are among the largest reported for mental disorders.

Although the matter of dimensions and/or categories is complex and unresolved, substantial evidence suggests that the serious and frequently chronic conditions recognized as the "Eating Disorders" are composite expressions of a set of dimensions, such as negative emotionality, binge eating, and unhealthy forms of weight and shape management. The latter includes restrictive dieting, self-induced vomiting after eating, and abuse of laxatives, diuretics, diet pills, and exercise.

The adhesive drawing together and framing these intertwined continua is negative body image. In most media effects research the multidimensional construct of body image is represented by various measures of what are essentially perceptual-emotional conclusions (e.g., "I look too fat to myself and others" + "I am disgusted by and ashamed of this" = "I hate how fat I look and feel"). For females "body dissatisfaction" results from—and feeds— a schema that integrates three fundamental components: idealization of slenderness and leanness; an irrational fear of fat; and a conviction that weight and shape are central determinants of one's identity. . . .

Researchers in many fields have stopped thinking about "the" cause of a disorder as "the agent" that directly brings about the undesirable outcome. Instead, there is an emphasis on variables that are reliably and usefully associated with an increase over time in the probability of a subsequent outcome. Such variables are called risk factors.

Thinking in terms of risk factors has two major implications for investigating mass media as a "cause" of eating disorders. The first concerns the oft-heard "relative rarity" argument: How could mass media be a cause when the vast majority of girls and young women are exposed to ostensibly toxic influences, but only a small percentage develop eating disorders? This critique dissolves when one considers multiple risk factors as multiplicative probabilities. Assume, conservatively, that 35% of adolescent girls are engaged with those mass media containing

From *Journal of Social and Clinical Psychology,* vol. 28, no. 1, January 2009, pp. 9–16, 19–26, 30–34 (excerpted, refs. omitted). Copyright ©2009 by Guilford Publications. Reprinted by permission via Copyright Clearance Center.

various unhealthy messages. Assume also that three other risk factors—such as peer preoccupation with weight and shape; family history of overweight/obesity; and being socialized by parents and older siblings to believe firmly that a female's identity and worth are shaped primarily by appearance—each have a probability of .35 of occurring in the population. . . .

Second, if mass media constitute a *causal risk factor* for the spectrum of negative body image and disordere-deating, then the following will be the case. *Cross-sectional studies* will show that the extent of exposure to mass media, or to various specific forms of mass media, is a correlate of that spectrum. *Longitudinal studies* will demonstrate that exposure to mass media precedes and predicts development of negative body image and disordered eating. *Laboratory experiments* should show that well-controlled manipulation of the media risk factor (independent variable) causes the hypothesized changes in "state" body satisfaction and other relevant dependent variables, while *controlled analog (laboratory) or field experiments* should demonstrate that prevention programs designed to combat known risk factors do indeed reduce or delay the onset of disordered eating.

These criteria are demanding in and of themselves. Nevertheless, it is also important to incorporate the contributions to knowledge of two further sources: common sense and people's "lived experience." Specifically, if mass media are a causal risk factor, then *content analyses* should document that media provide the raw material from which children and adolescents could *readily* extract and construct the information, affective valences, and behavioral cues necessary to develop the components of disordered eating. Similarly, *surveys and ecological analyses* will reveal that engagement with mass media is frequent and intensive enough to provide multiple opportunities for this type of social-cognitive learning. Finally, *surveys and qualitative studies* should find that, beginning at the age where they can think critically about themselves in relation to personal and outside influences, children and adolescents will report that mass media are sources of influence, and even pressure, on themselves, their peers, and others. . . .

Appearance, status, sexuality, and buying and consuming are, for many reasons (including the power of mass media), very important aspects of life throughout many countries. Consequently, the content of mass media provides daily, multiple, overlapping, and, all too often, unhealthy messages about gender, attractiveness, ideal body sizes and shapes, self-control, desire, food, and weight *management*. These messages sometimes intentionally, sometimes incidentally indoctrinate developing girls and boys with the following easily extracted themes: (a)

being sexually attractive is of paramount importance; (b) the sources of ideals about attractiveness ("being 'hot'!"), style, and the best, most competitive practices for becoming and staying beautiful are obviously located outside the self; and (c) mass media are the most important and inherently enjoyable "external" source of the information, motivation, and products necessary to be attractive and fashionable.

Mass Media and the Thinness Schema

Thus, with respect to the cultural foundations of negative body image and disordered eating, even girls (and boys) as young as 4 or 5 have no trouble finding in mass media the raw materials for various maladaptive but *entirely normative* media-based *schemata* concerning gender and attractiveness. The *"thinness schema"* for females is a set of assumptions, "facts," and strong feelings that are organized so as to establish a readiness to think and respond in terms of, for example, the following themes: (1) Women are "naturally" invested in their beauty assets and thus beauty is a woman's principal project in life; (2) a slender, youthful attractive "image" is really something substantive, because it is pleasing to males and it demonstrates to females that one is in control of one's life; and (3) learning to perceive, monitor, and indeed experience yourself as the object of an essentially masculine gaze is an important part of being feminine and beautiful.

Transnational Idol: The Exaltation of Thinness and the Vilification of Fat

There is a wealth of evidence from content analyses that the ideal female body showcased on television, in movies, in magazines, and on the internet reflects, indeed embodies, the proposition that "thin is normative and attractive." While (because?) American girls and women are becoming heavier, the current body *ideal* (idol) for women has become and remains unrealistically thin. In fact, mass media are one of many sociocultural sources for the normative prejudice that fat is "horrible and ugly," and that "getting fatter" is a sign of at least 4 of the classic "7 deadly sins"—extravagance, gluttony, greed, sloth, and, maybe, pride. . . .

The presence of a positive correlation between level of exposure to mass media, or to certain types of mass media, and the spectrum of disordered eating is a necessary but not sufficient condition for determination of causal agency. However, absence of a positive correlation negates the argument for causality. . . .

Longitudinal Correlates of Exposure to Mass Media

. . . Compared to cross-sectional studies, longitudinal research linking media exposure with body image is sparse. The few published studies do suggest that early exposure to thin-ideal television predicts a subsequent increase in body-image problems. For a sample of Australian girls aged 5 to 8, viewing of appearance-focused television programs (but not magazines) predicted a decrease in appearance satisfaction 1 year later. For European American and African American girls ages 7 through 12 greater overall television exposure predicted both a thinner ideal *adult* body shape and a higher level of disordered eating 1 year later. The results of both studies were valid regardless of whether the children were heavy, or perceived themselves to be thin or heavy, at the outset of the research. The thrust of these two studies is consistent with Sinton and Birch's finding that, among the 11-year-old American girls they studied, awareness of media messages about thinness was related to the strength of appearance schemas a year later.

The importance of a longitudinal design is revealed in recent studies of older children and young adolescents conducted by Tiggemann and by Field and colleagues. In a sample of 214 Australian high school girls (mean age = 14), Tiggemann found that the only measure of television exposure, including total hours of exposure, to produce meaningful cross-sectional and longitudinal correlations was the self-reported extent of watching soap operas. Crosslagged correlational analyses showed that Time 1 exposure to soap operas predicted, to a small but significant degree, internalization of the slender ideal and level of appearance schema at 1-year follow up (Time 2). Time spent reading appearance-oriented magazines, but not other magazines, at Time 1 predicted, also to a small but significant degree, Time 2 levels of internalization, appearance schema, and drive for thinness. However, none of the media exposure variables was a significant longitudinal predictor of body dissatisfaction. Moreover, hierarchical regressions controlling for Time 1 level of each of the four criterion variables (e.g., internalization) found that none of the media exposure measures added significantly to prediction of the Time 2 criteria.

Although Field and colleagues used only single-variable measures of media exposure, their longitudinal research also casts doubt on exposure as a causal risk factor for older children and younger adolescents. Field et al.

investigated a sample of over 6900 girls who were ages 9 through 15 at the 1996 baseline. Preliminary crosssectional work did produce the expected positive linear association between frequency of reading women's fashion magazines and intensity of weight concerns. However, subsequent longitudinal research revealed that over a 1-year period the key predictor of the *development* of weight concerns and frequent dieting was "making a lot of effort to look like same-sex figures in the media." A 7-year follow-up showed that initiation of binge-eating, but not purging, in (now) adolescent and young adult females was predicted independently by frequent dieting and by Time 2 level of attempting to look like persons in the media.

The only longitudinal investigation of young adult women we could locate was Aubrey's 2-year panel study of college-age women. In support of Criterion 4, the extent of exposure to sexually objectifying media at Time 1 predicted level of self-objectification at Time 2, especially in women with low self-esteem. Measures of the tendency to self-objectify are positively correlated with eating disorder symptoms such as misperceptions of weight and shape, body shame, drive for thinness, and restrictive dieting.

Conclusion

Evidence from a very small number of longitudinal studies indicates that for children and very young adolescents, extent of media exposure does appear to predict increases in negative body image and disordered eating. Tiggemann's suggests that by early adolescence the causal risk factor is not media exposure, or even internalization of the slender beauty ideal, but rather the intensity and extent of "core beliefs and assumptions about the importance, meaning, and effect of appearance in an individual's life." . . .

Multimethod studies by Hargreaves and Tiggemann in Australia produced compelling evidence for the contention that mass media have negative and cumulative effects on body image in girls and young women. The adolescent girls whose body image was most negatively affected by experimental exposure to 20 television commercials featuring the thin ideal tended to have greater levels of body dissatisfaction and drive for thinness 2 years later, even when initial level of body dissatisfaction was controlled statistically.

The most vulnerable girls may well have a self-schema dominated by the core importance of physical appearance. In a study of girls ages 15 through 18 Hargreaves and Tiggemann found that appearance-focused TV commercials did activate an appearance-related self-schema, as reflected in several measures of cognitive set. Moreover, as predicted, appearance-focused commercials generated greater appearance dissatisfaction for those girls who began the study with a more extensive, emotionally charged, self-schema for appearance. Interestingly, the negative impact of the thin-beauty ideal in television commercials was, unlike previous findings with magazine images, unaffected by either the girls' initial level of body dissatisfaction or whether their viewing style was more personal (self-focused) or more detached (imagefocused).

Positive (Assimilation) Effects. Durkin and Paxton found that 32% of the 7th grade girls and 22% of the 10th grade Australian girls who were exposed to images of attractive models from magazines exhibited an *increase* in state body satisfaction. Similarly, two studies of Canadian college students found that restrained eaters showed moderate to large increases in body satisfaction following exposure to similar magazine images, whereas unrestrained eaters had very large decreases in body satisfaction.

Two studies in the United States by Wilcox and Laird suggest that young women who focus on the slender models in magazines while defocusing attention on themselves are more likely to identify with the models and thus to feel better about their own bodies. Conversely, women who self-consciously divide their attention between the models and themselves are more likely to evaluate themselves and reach a conclusion that leaves them feeling inferior and worse. This finding is supported by research showing that self-evaluative processes, as opposed to self-improvement motives, are more likely to reflect and activate "upward" social comparison processes, which themselves tend to generate negative feelings about one's body.

Pro-Ana Web Sites. The internet offers many proanorexia (pro-ana) and pro-bulimia (pro-mia) web sites. Some of the most prominent pro-ana sites defiantly and zealously promote AN as a sacred lifestyle rather than a debilitating psychiatric disorder. Their "thinspirational" images of emaciation and their explicit behavioral instructions for attaining and sustaining the thin ideal are intended to reinforce the identity and practices of those already entrenched in AN or BN.

If concentrated exposure to typical images of slender models have negative experimental effects, then we might well expect the images and messages from pro-anorexia web sites to have even more negative effects. Two recent experiments by Bardone-Cone and Cass examined the effects of a web site that they constructed to feature the prototypical content of pro-ana sites. As predicted, exposure to this site had a large number of negative effects on young women, independent of their dispositional levels of thin ideal internalization and disordered eating. At present, we do not know what effects pro-ana and promia sites have on the adolescent girls and young women who avidly seek them out because they already have a full-blown eating disorder. . . .

Media Literacy: Laboratory Investigations

. . . Media literacy (ML) is a set of knowledge, attitudes, and skills that enable people to work together to understand, appreciate, and critically analyze the nature of mass media and one's relationships with them. Systematic investigations of ML can be categorized into analog laboratory studies, brief interventions, and longer, more intensive programs.

. . . Several controlled experiments show that very brief written or video interventions can inoculate college-age women, including those who already have a negative body image, against the general tendency to feel worse about their bodies and themselves after viewing slides or video containing media-based images of the slender beauty ideal. The most effective ML "inoculation" highlights the clash between the artificial, constructed nature of the slender, flawless, "model look" versus two stark realities: (1) the actual shapes and weights of females (and males) naturally vary a great deal across a population; and

dieting to attain an "ideal" and "glamorous" weight/shape that is unnatural for a given individual has many negative effects, including risk for an eating disorder. . . .

Several programs for high-school and college-age females used slide presentations or Jean Kilbourne's video *Slim Hopes* (www.mediaed.org/videos/Media-AndHealth/SlimHopes) to help participants consider the history of changing, but consistently restrictive, beauty ideals and then to answer some fundamental questions: Do *real* women look like the models in advertising? Will buying the product being advertised make me look like this model? These programs emphasize how fashion models, working with the production staffs of magazines and movies, use "cosmetic" surgery, computer graphics, and other technologies to *construct* idealized *images*. Participants are encouraged to explore how these manipulations are carefully orchestrated to stir up the desire to purchase products, many of which will supposedly reduce the discrepancy between such unreal, "perfect" images versus the body shapes and weights of normal, healthy females.

These ML programs are brief, so positive effects are necessarily limited. Nevertheless, it is noteworthy that they tend to reduce, at least in the short run, one important risk factor for disordered eating: internalization of the slender beauty ideal.

Well-controlled studies of multi-lesson, multifaceted media literacy programs that unfold over 1 to 2 months have shown that media literacy training can help girls *and* boys ages 10 through 14 to reduce risk factors such as internalization of the slender or muscular ideal, while increasing the potentially protective factors of self-acceptance, self-confidence in friendships, and confidence in their ability to be activists and thus affect weight-related social norms. In addition to spending considerable time working on the same components as those in the analog and brief interventions, intensive ML programs address the process and costs of social comparison. They also get participants involved in working within their ML groups, their school, and their larger community to translate their increasing literacy into peer education, consumer activism, and creating and promoting new, healthier media.

Recent investigations with college students also show ML to be a promising form of prevention. For example, Watson and Vaughn developed a 4-week, 6-hour intervention consisting of psychoeducation about the nature and sources of body dissatisfaction; group-based content analysis of beauty ideals in popular women's magazines; discussion of media ideals and beauty enhancement techniques; and a brief cognitive intervention designed to help participants dispute negative beliefs and feelings activated by media images of the thin ideal. Compared to a 1-day, 90-min version of this intervention, a one-time viewing of a 34-min media literacy film, and a no-intervention control, the extended intervention was the most successful in reducing the following risk factors for disordered eating: unhealthy social attitudes, internalization of the slender ideal, and body dissatisfaction. . . .

Presumed Influences on Others

In thinking about the subjective experiences of media pressures and influences, it is worth examining more closely the construct of "awareness" of the thin ideal. The perception that peers and people in general (e.g., employers) are influenced by thin-ideal media can itself be a form of subjective pressure that motivates young people to diet in an attempt to meet that ideal. In fact, it appears that the mere presumption of media effects on others may exert its own effect, at least on older females. Park's analytic study of over 400 undergraduates found that the more issues of beauty and fashion magazines a young woman reads per month, the greater the perceived prevalence of the thin ideal in those magazines. The greater this perceived prevalence, the greater the presumed influence of that ideal on *other women;* and in turn the greater the

perceived influence on *self,* which predicted the desire to be thin. More research of this type with younger samples is needed to test this "cultivation of perceived social norms" hypothesis: Greater consumption of beauty and fashion magazines or of appearance-focused TV and internet content will foster stronger, more influential beliefs that the slender ideal is ubiquitous and normative for peers. This logic will, in turn, be a source of pressure and inspiration for the person's own desire to be thin(ner). . . .

And, yet, in light of the important research by Tiggemann and by Field et al. there remains a need to demonstrate more conclusively that either (1) direct engagement with mass media or (2) media effects that are mediated by parents and/or peers *precede* development of the more proximal risk factors such as negative body image. Similarly, despite the preliminary but encouraging evidence from media literacy interventions of varying intensities, to date no studies have tested the deceptively simple proposition that prevention programs can increase media literacy and thereby reduce or eliminate negative media influences—and in turn reduce or delay development of proximal risk factors (e.g., internalization of the thin ideal, social comparison tendencies) *and* attendant outcomes such as EDNOS.

What We Need to Know but Don't Know Yet

This review suggests five principal gaps in our knowledge about mass media as a potential causal risk factor for the spectrum of disordered eating. The first three are derived from the conclusion immediately above. First, there is a need for longitudinal research that examines the predictive validity of media exposure, motives for media use, and the subjective experience of media influences. Second, as noted by an anonymous reviewer of this manuscript, there remains a dearth of information about whether it is the thinness-depicting aspects of magazine, TV, and other media content that exert negative effects. Thus, survey-based longitudinal investigations of media exposure should strive to determine as precisely as possible not only frequency and intensity of consumption, but also the nature of the images, articles, programs, and such to which participants are exposed. Third, there is a need for prevention research that capitalizes on and extends the promising findings of extended media literacy interventions.

The fourth research direction concerns the relationship, particularly from a developmental perspective, between engagement with mass media and other causal risk factors. We need to learn much more about the ways in which body image disturbance and disordered eating are influenced by perceived social norms, by the confluence of media, family, and peer messages about weight and *shape,* and by *indirect* media exposure, such as acquisition of body ideals and eating behaviors via interactions with family, peers, and significant adults (e.g., coaches) who learned them directly from television and magazines. Direct media effects may be small to modest, but the combination of direct and indirect effects, that is, the cumulative media effect, may be substantial.

Finally, the transactions between the developing child (or adolescent) and media constitute another set of important research questions to address. A cross-sectional study by Gralen, Levine, Smolak, and Murnen (1990) indicated that the correlates of negative body image and disordered eating in young adolescents tended to be more concrete and behavioral (e.g., onset of dating, pubertal development, teasing about weight and shape), whereas the predictors in middle to later adolescence were more psychological, such as the experience of a discrepancy between perception of one's own shape versus an internalized ideal shape. More recently, a longitudinal study by Harrison found that the number of hours that children ages 6 through 8 watched television per week predicted an increase in disordered eating without predicting idealization of a slender body. This raises the interesting and testable proposition that exposure to various salient media messages, including those contained in the onslaught of advertisements for diet-, fitness-, and weight-related products, might have little effect on the "thinness beliefs" of young children, while leading them to vilify fat, glamorize dieting as a grown-up practice, and yet still think of fattening, non-nutritious foods as desirable in general and useful for assuaging negative feelings.

With respect to the transformation of relevant psychological processes over late childhood, early adolescence, and later adolescence, Thompson and colleagues have developed and validated various features of the Tripartite Model in which media, family, and peers influence directly internalization of the slender beauty ideal and social comparison processes. This valuable model reminds us that, after nearly 25 years of research on media and body image, we still know relatively little about the automatic, intentional, and motivational processes involved in the role of *social comparison* in media effects. Basic questions remain: What dispositional and situational factors determine when people will make upward social comparisons with highly dissimilar fashion models whose "image" has been constructed by cosmetic surgeons, photographers, and computer experts? And under what circumstances will such comparisons result in negative effects (contrast) or positive effects (assimilation)?

Multidimensional models such as Thompson's also emphasize the need to determine when and how in the developmental process a number of important mechanisms such as appearance schematicity, thin-ideal internalization, social comparison processes, and self-objectification begin to play key roles. Further experimental and longitudinal studies of these mediators will be a very positive step toward understanding the emergence, particularly around puberty, of attentiveness and vulnerability to thin-ideal media images *and* to the many other potentially negative influences that emanate from family, peers, and influential adults such as coaches.

MICHAEL P. LEVINE is the Samuel B. Cummings Jr. Professor of Psychology at Kenyon College, where he teaches and conducts research on abnormal psychology, eating disorders, body image, and the development of personality.

SARAH K. MURNEN is Professor and Chair of the Department of Psychology at Kenyon College. Her research focuses on gender-related issues from a feminist, sociocultural background.

EXPLORING THE ISSUE

Do Media Cause Individuals to Develop Negative Body Images?

Critical Thinking and Reflection

1. What media celebrities or personalities do you emulate? What type of body image do they portray? Do you see your own sense of self influenced by the standards media people exemplify?
2. How are stories about eating disorders framed in the media? Are we told that eating disorders are a choice or that they are detrimental to our health?
3. How would you identify a healthy lifestyle for children and adults?
4. What evaluative measures do you have to assess beauty, health, or eating disorders? How do you describe each? What does your description say about your own views on each of these topics?
5. How do you form standards of what is "appropriate" and what do you do to measure your own behaviors? For example, do you have a weak self-image because you feel you can't measure up to mediated standards of health or beauty? What types of control do you exercise (if you do exercise control) to make you feel that you have a healthy attitude about body image?

Is There Common Ground?

June Deery's analysis of reality television programs that include extreme measures such as plastic surgery, and Michael P. Levine and Sarah K. Murnen's research that sees "two sides of the coin" in response to magazine advertising and body image each make assumptions about the impact of media in our lives, but the perspectives they offer give us much to think about.

The psychology of how one thinks of their body is an important and worthy subject for contemplation. Many books and articles have been written to untangle the many possible threads that lead to how self-image is constituted and maintained. For many years, self-improvement and self-help books have been among the best sellers in bookstores. Critical self-reflection about how one sees themselves and how one judges others is one of the most complex, but important subjects in examining the relationship of media and society.

Additional Resources

Naomi Wolf, *The Beauty Myth: How Images of Beauty Are Used Against Women* (William Morrow and Company, 1991)

This book crafted a persuasive argument that the concept of beauty was a political issue that kept women stuck in a patriarchal system. By media and social issues preying on women's insecurities about their bodies, women's ability to fully participate in the labor force and in the social world was undermined. In 2002, Wolf published the second edition of the book with a new introduction, and in reviewing the new version, critic Emily Wilson, writing for *The Guardian* in the U.K., noted, "The world has changed—a bit—over the past decade and a half, but not enough."

Vickie Rutledge Shields and Dawn Heinecken, *Measuring Up: How Advertising Affects Self-Image* (University of Pennsylvania Press, 2002), or Ellen Cole and Jessica Henderson Daniel, eds., *Featuring Females: Feminist Analyses of Media* (American Psychological Association, 2005)

For more reading on images of ideal bodies in the media and the impact on consumers who may find their own bodies lacking, check out the above-mentioned books.

Arnold E. Andersen, *Making Weight: Men's Conflicts with Food, Weight, Shape & Appearance* (Gurze Books, 2000)

For a study of body image from the male perspective, the above-mentioned book is a helpful analysis of men's increasing sensitivity to issues of weight and appearance.

The U.S. Department of Health and Human Services has posted a Healthy Weight Chart on the Internet:

www.nhlbisupport.com/bmi

The popular magazine, *Psychology Today* occasionally writes about self-esteem issues. One such article that can be helpful to consult is

www.psychologytoday.com/basics/self-esteem

Internet References . . .

The U.S. Department of Health and Human Services

www.womenshealth.gov/body-image/

Selected, Edited, and with Issue Framing Material by:
Alison Alexander, *University of Georgia*
and
Jarice Hanson, *University of Massachusetts—Amherst*

ISSUE

Is Product Placement an Effective Form of Advertising?

YES: Kaylene Williams et al., from "Product Placement Effectiveness: Revisited and Renewed," *Journal of Management and Marketing Research* (2011)

NO: Ekaterina V. Karniouchina, Can Uslay, and Grigori Erenburg, "Do Marketing Media Have Life Cycles? The Case of Product Placement in Movies," *Journal of Marketing* (2011)

Learning Outcomes

After reading this issue, you will be able to:

- Consider the role of product placement as an advertising tool.
- Critically think about the ethics of product placement.
- Evaluate how advertising techniques influence media content.
- Think more carefully about how persuasive advertising in general can be, and product placement in particular.
- Understand the range of influences that shape media content.

ISSUE SUMMARY

YES: Professors Kaylene Williams et al. chronicle the evolution of product placement and define the term as incorporating "commercial content into noncommercial settings." They discuss the subtle differences between brand placement and product placement and raise the topic of how product placement is becoming more common in many media forms, including music and games.

NO: Professors Karniouchina, Uslay, and Erenburg analyzed 40 years of movies (1968–2007) to uncover the idea that product placement has become a tactic that no longer interests viewers of major motion pictures. As a result, they suggest that marketers should investigate other ways of trying to connect ideas and brand identities.

In May 2007, the United States House of Representatives' Committee on Energy and Commerce held sessions on the "Digital Future of the United States." Among the invited speakers was Philip Rosenthal, an actor/writer who had created and became the executive producer of the popular television series *Everybody Loves Raymond,* which ran on CBS from 1996 to 2005. Rosenthal was speaking on behalf of the Writers Guild of America—West, and the Screen Actors' Guild, so his comments on product placement were particularly relevant to the way product

placement has become a part of the production process of television, in particular. While he acknowledged the subtle ways product placement influences shot composition in media, such as the actor's taking a drink out of a can with the label prominently displayed so that the camera can record the product, he cautioned; "Some of these commercial insertions could be dismissed as trivial . . . . This often subtle but always insidious blurring of the line between content and commerce is an issue not just for the creative community, but for the American viewing public as well."

Rosenthal continued to identify how product placement—a seemingly insignificant feature of underwriting the cost of media production by advertisers who pay for the use of their products in media content—has influenced the way writers write, how children learn to consume, and how the public has been exposed to media messages that exploit their emotional connection to shows and characters for the purpose of selling merchandise. The most egregious forms of product placement, he cautioned, occur when business deals between advertisers and production companies make the product a part of the storyline, which forces characters to talk about the product in what then becomes a long infomercial.

The Representatives in the room were shocked to learn that product placement has become such a component of our media landscape. This leads us to question whether the public too would be shocked to learn about the prevalence of product placement, and the potential of this technique to influence our thoughts and behaviors.

Both selections in this issue start with the perspective that product placement is neutral and natural—a change in the discourse about the prevalence in society, as well as a comment on how the public seemingly accepts the content presented to them by media producers. The authors of the two positions focus on more fundamental questions, concerning the effectiveness of product placement rather than the moral or ethical dimensions of whether product placement may be good, bad, or both.

Professors Williams, Petrosky, Hernandez, and Page approach the issue through the lens of advertisers who are seeking to understand the conditions under which product placement may be most effective. Professor Cowley and marketing executive Barron examine the same approach, but go in-depth to uncover a theoretical perspective that integrates social psychology with the act of product placement to show that some of the same techniques can have negative consequences. These two selections help us understand the power of product placement in terms of its history, practice, and how it influences the various media industries, but we have to inject the moral dimensions of questioning whether product placement contributes to our consumer society in positive or negative ways, and, we can ask the question, "Do we really need product placement?"

Historically, questions concerning advertising and techniques used to persuade or influence the public have made the assumption that misleading or deceiving the public is generally something that should be discouraged.

If product placement is normalized through the "behind the scenes" business of raising money for media production, the possibility of the public being misled is hidden from plain view. If product placement has become so prevalent that it is no longer a part of the discourse of advertising and the way the public is "manipulated" by media, perhaps we're really saying that we've lost the fight to make our media industries more ethical.

Some people might say that they don't mind, or don't consciously notice when the judges of *American Idol* all sip from cans of Coca-Cola, but the fact that the judges do shows that product placement has become big business. Similarly, popular television shows like *Biggest Loser*, make-over shows, and many genres of reality television blatantly call attention to products and product placement. What is really at stake, however, is the recurring question of whether advertising makes us buy things, and whether it matters at all, and that's why the normalization of product placement in media matters to us all.

In the United States our media industries grew as primarily commercial entities, but this is not the case in many other countries. Certainly, an argument could be made that the more "international" media become in their distribution arrangements, the more of a "global" norm develops and influences the type of content that can be created, but isn't this also a justification for multinational firms that seek to expand their product sales to other countries? Can consumer desire for a product develop by seeing the product represented in media, over and over? It's not enough to just say "that's the way it is." The real questions are: (a) how did media business get this way? and (b) are there other options for the way businesses operate that might be in the public's interest?

Our media institutions are changing constantly as producers look for ways to attract viewers, and product placement is just one example of how both advertising and television (or advertising and film, music, or video industries) are blurring the distinctions between industries and commercial activity. The power of the media industries, their practices, and the way in which media and society are connected through dozens, if not hundreds, of threads make us more aware of the power of media to influence the way we think, behave, develop attitudes, and function in society.

While this issue and the two selections pose a specific question for discussion, perhaps the bigger questions are all about what this specific example says about how the media and society have evolved over time.

YES ↵

Kaylene Williams et al.

Product Placement Effectiveness: Revisited and Renewed

Product placement is the purposeful incorporation of commercial content into noncommercial settings, that is, a product plug generated via the fusion of advertising and entertainment. Product placement—also known as product brand placement, in-program sponsoring, branded entertainment, or product integration—is a marketing practice in advertising and promotion wherein a brand name, product, package, signage, or other trademark merchandise is inserted into and used contextually in a motion picture, television, or other media vehicle for commercial purposes. In product placement, the involved audience gets exposed to the brands and products during the natural process of the movie, television program, or content vehicle. That is, product placement in popular mass media provides exposure to potential target consumers and shows brands being used or consumed in their natural settings. Ultimately, the product or brand is seen as a quality of the association with characters using and approving of the product placement, for example, Harold and Kumar on a road trip to find a White Castle, Austin Powers blasting into space in a Big Boy statue rocket, Will Ferrell promoting Checkers and Rally's Hamburgers in the NASCAR comedy *Talladega Nights*, MSN appearing in Bridget Jones' Diary, BMW and its online short films, Amazon.com's Amazon Theatre showcasing stars and featured products, Ford and *Extreme Makeover*, Tom Hanks and FedEx and Wilson, Oprah giving away Buicks, Curious George and Dole, Herbie and VW, Simpsons' and the Quik-E-Mart, *Forrest Gump* and the Bubba Gum Shrimp Co. restaurants, Jack Daniels and *Mad Men*, and LG phones in *The Office*, just to name a few. In addition, Weaver gives numerous examples of product placements related to tourism, for example, the film *Sideways* promoting wine tourism in California's Napa Valley, the Ritz-Carlton hotel chain selling Sealy mattresses on the Internet, Holiday Inn Express selling Kohler's Stay Smart shower head, Showtime and HBO in many hotels and motels, and Southwest Airlines serving Nabisco products.

Even though product placement was named and identified formally only as recently as the 1980s, product placement is not new. Originally, product placement served as a way for movie studios and television networks to reduce the cost of production through borrowed props. Brand/product placement first appeared in Lumiere films in Europe in 1896. In the early years of U.S. product placements, the idea of connecting entertainment with consumption messages showed up in the entertainment films of Thomas Edison featuring shots of products from the Edison factory and Edison's industrial clients. Beginning in the 1930s, Procter & Gamble broadcasted on the radio its "soap operas" featuring its soap powders. Also, television and film were used by the tobacco companies to lend glamour and the "right attitude" to smoking. However, due to poorly organized efforts and negative publicity about the surrender of media content to commercialization, product placements were relatively dormant after the Depression. Product placements were recatalyzed in the 1960–70s with a growth spurt during the 1980s and 1990s.

Movies and programs are watched many times, accordingly, product placements are not limited in time to the original filmed item. In addition, today's technology can insert product placements in places they were not before. This digital product integration is a new frontier for paid product placement. As a result, consumers will see more and more product placements that are strategically placed in the media. Most product placements are for consumer products, yet service placements appear more prominently. Service placements tend to be woven into the script and are probably more effective than product placements that are used simply as background props.

Product placements may be initiated by a company that suggests its products to a studio or TV show, or it might work the other way around. Intermediaries and

Williams, Kaylene; Petrosky, Alfred; Hernandez, Edward; Page Jr, Robert. From *Journal of Management and Marketing Research*, vol. 7, April 2011, pp. 132–155. Copyright ©2011 by Kaylene Williams. Used with permission by the author.

brokers also match up companies with product placement opportunities. Costs for product placements can range from less than $10,000 to several hundred thousand dollars. However, television and movie producers routinely place products in their entertainment vehicles for free or in exchange for promotional tie-ins.

In terms of the Internet, consumers want to communicate with companies and brands so that they can get the information they want or need. So, companies need to listen to online conversations and establish what interests their online community. Then, they can provide that information in an engaging format including storytelling, articles, images, and video. For example, Yahoo! has produced branded video content—5–10 minute "webisodes" that usually feature story lines around a specific product such as a show about someone driving cross country in a Toyota Hybrid, sponsored by Toyota. "Being able to creatively brand interesting and valuable online content that attracts readers and viewers might just turn out to be the shortest way to consumer's hearts and minds."

While product placements have been used prolifically to target ultimate household consumers, they are beginning to expand into the business-to-business domain. In general, buying-center participants find the practice to be acceptable for a wide array of B2B products and services. In particular, when buying-center participants are exposed to experimental B2B influence through placement within major motion picture products, participants demonstrate an impressive level of recall and a modestly favorable attitude and purchase intention.

Use of Product Placement

Even though measures of its effectiveness have been problematic, product placement is a fast growing multi-billion dollar industry. According to the research company PQ Media, global paid product placements were valued at $3.07 Billion in 2006 with global unpaid product placements valued at about $6 Billion in 2005 and $7.45 Billion in 2006. Global paid product placement spending is expected to grow at a compounded annual rate of 27.9% over 2005–2010 to $7.55 Billion. Consequently, product placement growth is expected to significantly outpace that of traditional advertising and marketing. By 2010, the overall value of paid and unpaid product placement is expected to increase 18.4% compounded annually to $13.96 Billion. Television product placements are the dominant choice of brand marketers, accounting for 71.4% of global spending in 2006. Advertisement spending on product placement in games in the U.S. is likely to reach $1 Billion by 2010.

The U.S. is the largest and fastest growing paid product placement market, $1.5 Billion in 2005, $2.9 Billion in 2007, and $3.7 Billion in 2008. Marketers increased the dollars spent on branded content in 2009, double the 2008 figures. Branded content comprised 32% of overall marketing, advertising, and communications budgets. These numbers are expected to jump significantly in 2010. Some 75% of U.S. prime-time network shows use product placements. This number is expected to increase due to the fact that 41% of U.S. homes are expected to have and use digital video recorders that can skip through commercials. Hence, communicating core marketing messages is vital and difficult. Consider the following data:

- "90% of people with digital video recorders skip TV ads."
- "To be seen, brands now have to get inside the content."
- "Consumer consumption of entertainment increases when economic times get tough."
- "ITV reported an increase of 1.1% in TV viewing in the first quarter of 2009."
- "Cinema admissions for 2009 to April 30 stand at 55.2 million, a 14.2% increase on the same periods in 2008."
- "Research shows product placement in content boosts brand awareness, raises brand affinity and encourages prospective purchasers."
- "60% of viewers felt more positive about brands they recognized in a placement."
- "45% said they would be more likely to make a purchase."

Product placements can be a cost-effective method for reaching target customers. Because of this, product placements are likely to eclipse traditional advertising messages.

In terms of specific numbers, U.S. product placement occurrences for January 1–November 30, 2008 broadcast network programming for the Top 10 programs featured 29,823 product placements. *Biggest Loser* was the leader in terms of the number of product placements (6,248 occurrences), followed by *American Idol, Extreme Makeover Home Edition, America's Toughest Jobs, One Tree Hill, Deal or No Deal, America's Next Top Model, Last Comic Standing, Kitchen Nightmares*, and *Hells Kitchen*. The Top 10 brands that featured product placements for January 1–November 30, 2008 were CVS Pharmacy, TRESemme, El, Pollo Loco, Bluefly.com, Sears, Glad, Whole Foods Market, Food & Wine Magazine, GQ Magazine, and Hugo Boss.

The use of product placements in recorded music also is growing. As noted by Plambeck

"According to a report released last week by PQ Media, a research firm, the money spent on product placement in recorded music grew 8 percent in 2009 compared with the year before, while overall paid product placement declined 2.8 percent, to $3.6 Billion."

"The money is often used to offset the video's cost, which is usually shared by the artist and label."

"Patrick Quinn, chief executive of PQ Media, said that revenue from product placement in music videos totaled $15 million to $20 million last year, more than double the amount in 2000, and he expected that to grow again this year."

"The Lady Gaga video, which has been viewed 62 million (updated: 91.8 million as of November 14, 2010) times on YouTube, included product placements from Miracle Whip and Virgin Mobile."

Another area of growing product placements is placed-based video ads in stores, shopping malls, restaurants, medical offices, bars, airports, or health clubs. Approximately 29.6% of U.S. adults or 67.4 million adults have viewed these types of video ads in the last 30 days. Both young men and young women, in general, are more likely than the population as a whole to report they viewed place-based video ads. Young men aged 18–34 are 28% more likely (young women are 13% more likely) than the population as a whole to have viewed a placebased video ad in the last 30 days. This is important because these young consumers are difficult to reach via traditional media. "Video advertising in stores and shopping malls garnered the largest audience, at nearly 19% and 15% of the U.S. adult population, respectively. This was followed by nearly 11% of U.S. adults who saw a video ad in the last 30 days in a restaurant or medical office, nearly 9% who saw a video ad in a bar/pub or at an airport, and 7% who saw a video ad while at the gym or health club."

Generally, U.S. product placement markets are much more advanced than other countries such that other countries often aspire to the U.S. model. The next largest global markets are Brazil, Australia, France, and Japan. China is forecast to be the fastest growing market for product placements this year, up 34.5%. Product placement methods differ widely by country given varying cultures and regulations. Most product placements are in five product areas: transportation and parts, apparel and accessories, food and beverage, travel and leisure, and media and entertainment.

Purposes of Product Placement

Product placement can be very useful. Ultimately, product placements among entertainment firms, corporate brands, and agencies are all monetarily driven, either directly or indirectly. At the very least, entertainment firms and independent production companies are hoping to reduce their budgets so that more dollars can be invested elsewhere. Its purposes include achieving prominent audience exposure, visibility, attention, and interest; increasing brand awareness; increasing consumer memory and recall; creating instant recognition in the media vehicle and at the point of purchase; changing consumers' attitudes or overall evaluations of the brand; changing the audiences' purchase behaviors and intent; creating favorable practitioners' views on brand placement; and promoting consumers' attitudes towards the practice of brand placement and the various product placement vehicles. As noted by van Reijmersdal, Neijens, and Smit, a substantial part of the effects and interactions of product placement is still unknown.

(1) To achieve prominent audience exposure, visibility, attention, and interest

Product placements can have a significant effect on message receptivity. The sponsor of product placements is likely to gain goodwill by associating itself with a popular program targeted to a specific audience. The more successful the program, the longer shelf life of the product placement. Interest in advertising appearing in product placement in movies is reported to be of "considerable" or "some" interest to 31.2% of consumers. More frequent viewers and viewers who enjoy the program pay more attention to product placements. Brands need to be visible just long enough to attract attention, but not too long to annoy the audience.

(2) To increase brand awareness

Nielsen Media Research has shown that product placement in television shows can raise brand awareness by 20%. Tsal, Liang, and Liu found that higher brand awareness results in a greater recall rate, more positive attitudes, and a stronger intention of buying. When brand awareness is high, a positive attitude toward the script leads to a higher recall rate. Also, when a brand gains a certain level of awareness, the more positive the attitude toward product placement, the stronger its effect on recall rate, attitude, and intention of buying. However, when product/brand awareness is not high enough, consumers typically fail even to remember the names of the advertised products.

(3) To increase consumer memory and recall of the brand or product

Product placements can have a significant effect on recall. For example, memory improves when visual/auditory modality and plot connection are congruent. Pokrywczynski has found that viewers can correctly recognize and recall placed brands in movies, using aided recall measures and free recall measures. Also, brands placed prominently in a movie scene enjoy higher brand recall than those that are not. Verbal and visual brand placements are better recalled than placements having one or the other. In addition, showing the brand early and often with at least one verbal mention enhances brand recall. Also, sitcoms rather than reality shows tend to spark better recall for product placements. Hong, Wang, and de los Santos, found that product placement upholds brand salience or the order in which brands come to mind. They note that to build brand salience, product placement strategies should focus on how a product can explicitly convey the product's superiority, durability, performance, and specification. That is, marketers should focus on how a product can be noticed, even if it is perceived as artificially inserted for commercial purpose. As such, marketers need to give as much attention to product placements as they do to the insertion of commercials into a television program. To achieve higher brand salience, they also found that products should be placed more in negative-context programming than in positive ones and should not excessively interfere with the plot. In addition, Gupta and Gould found that greater recall can be obtained by smart placement of product placements in game shows, in particular, placements that appear at the beginning of a game show command higher recall. Brand recall is typically no higher than 30%. Or, as summarized by van Reijmersdal, "Prominent brand placement affects memory positively, but affects attitudes negatively when audiences are involved with the medium vehicle, when they like the medium vehicle, or when they become aware of the deliberate brand placement (selling attempt).

(4) To create instant recognition of the product/brand in the media vehicle and at the point of purchase

Product placement can have a significant effect on recognition. Familiar brands achieve higher levels of recognition than unfamiliar brands. In addition product or brand placement recognition levels received from audio-visual prominent placements exceed the recognition rates achieved by visual-only prominent placements. Some 57.5% of viewers recognized a brand in a placement when the brand also was advertised during the show. That number is higher than the 46.5% of viewers who recognized the brand from watching only a television spot for the brand. While prominence of the placement leads to increased recognition, if the placement is too long or too prominently placed,

viewers might become suspicious, elaborate on the commercial purpose of the placement, counter-argue, and form negative attitudes or behaviors. In addition, star liking, cognitive effect, and pleasure affect recognition for product placements. Specifically, brand recognition due to product placements increased 29% during highly enjoyable programs.

(5) To bring desired change in consumers' attitudes or overall evaluations of the brand

The influence of product placement on attitudes, preferences, and emotions toward a product or brand has not been researched very much. With this in mind, however, no differences have been found in viewers attitudes toward a product or brand. On the other hand, initial evidence suggests that consumers align their attitudes toward products with the characters' attitudes to the products. In addition, this process is driven by the consumers' attachment to the characters. Argan, Velioglu, and Argan suggest that the audience pays attention to and accepts brand placement in movies and takes celebrities as references when shopping. However, the movie should not be over commercialized. At the same time, initial studies find that attitudes toward product placements do not differ based on gender, age, income, or education. However, as discussed later, more recent studies have found differences. Authors van Reijmersdal, Neijens, and Smit have found that as consumers watch more episodes, the brand image becomes more in agreement with the program image. This confirms that learning and human association memory are important to brand placement. It also has been noted that product placements on emotionally engaging programs were recognized by 43% more viewers.

(6) To bring a change in the audiences' purchase behaviors and intent

Product placements are associated with increased purchase intent and sales, particularly when products appear in sitcoms, for example *Ally McBeal* in Nick and Nora pajamas, *Frasier and Friends* in Starbucks and New World Coffee, and Cosmopolitan martinis in *Sex and the City*. In one example, Dairy Queen was featured on *The Apprentice*. The contestants needed to create a promotional campaign for the Blizzard. During the week of the broadcast, Blizzard sales were up more than 30%. Website hits also were up significantly on the corporate and Blizzard Fan Club sites as well as the Blizzard promotional site. While DQ had six minutes of screen time, the overall tone was a little harsh with two contestants arguing. So, it was not the most positive environment for good, old-fashioned DQ. However, it cost DQ in the "low seven figures" to appear on the show and run its supporting promotion. Not bad for a 30% increase in sales. Controversy does seem to generate attention.

(7) To create favorable practitioners' views on brand placement

Practitioners' views on product placement generally are favorable or else the product placement market would not continue to increase. Practitioners remain positive about product placements as long as no harm is done, sales and brand image go up, and consumers are positive about the product and brand. Also, product placements help the practitioner make up for an increasingly fragmented broadcast market due to technology such as TiVo and DVD recorders.

(8) To promote consumers' attitudes towards the practice of brand placement and the various product placement vehicles

In general, attitudes toward product placement are favorable across media types. Additionally, viewers tend to like product placements as long as they add realism to the scene. Snoody has found that viewer enjoyment of product placements actually increased for media vehicle versions of product placements where products were an integral part of the script. He conjectures that peoples' lives are so saturated with brands that the inclusion of identifiable products adds to the sense of reality, that is, validates the individual's reality. Also, product placements are preferred to fictitious brands and are understood to be necessary for cost containment in the making of programs and movies. About half of respondents said that they would be more likely to buy featured products. People with more fashionable and extroverted lifestyles typically have more positive attitudes toward product placement. Sung and de Gregorio found that college students' attitudes toward brand placement are positive overall across media, but that brand placements in songs and video games are less acceptable than within films and television programs. So, marketers need to take into account the appropriateness of the specific genre of the particular media program into which they intend to place brands. Non-students are more neutral toward the practice than students. In general, consumers are positively disposed toward product placement, value the realism of the ad, and do not consider the ad to be unethical or misleading as long as the product is not ethically charged, for example, alcohol. Also, while there is a generally positive perception of the practice overall, there are reservations regarding the insertion of certain ethically charged products such as firearms, tobacco, and alcohol. Also, if brand image is positive, then consumers' brand evaluations toward the product placement seem to be more positive. Older consumers are more likely to dislike product placements and more likely to consider the practice as manipulation.

Overall, the managerial implications have been stated eloquently and succinctly by van Reijmersdal, Neijens, and Smit:

'To create brand placements that are positively evaluated, they should be placed within programs, movies, games, or magazines that are involving for the audience. Placements are also positively evaluated when the placement format is more editorial rather than commercial.

"To increase brand memory, brands should be prominently placed and be accompanied by an actor in films or television programs. Brand evaluations can become more positive when the placement is more editorial instead of commercial and when non-users of the brand are reached. Behavior and behavioral intentions are influenced best when the audience has positive evaluations of brand placement, when placements are presented in editorial formats, and when placements are repeated."

Use of Product Placement in Specific Media

Researchers have studied product placement in various media advergames, computer/video games, digital games, movies, television, television magazines, novels, online games, simulation games, sporting events, game shows, radio, physical environments such as hotel rooms, rental cars, or ships (Weaver, 2007), virtual/online environments, and songs. Most product placement studies have focused on film (33.87%), television (32.25%), and video games (20.21%). In actuality, most product placement is done through television, film, and video games. However, regardless of the media used, the brand's image and the content vehicle need to fit in such a way that the product/brand image will not be harmed and that attention will be brought to the product or brand. Also, because advertisers continue to look for ways to stay in touch with consumers, they easily could follow their audiences into less-regulated media such as the Internet and 3-G mobile phones. As web-connected television becomes a practical reality, a user-driven environment and peer-to-peer file swapping is being reinforced. While new platforms such as 4G and MPEG-4 create greater opportunities for interactivity, successful product placement still must be relevant to its host content.

Television

Television viewing is complicated with the use of zipping, zapping, TiVo, and DVRs. That is, the audience can shift the channel, change the program, and slow down or fast-forward the program to avoid advertising. In addition, media clutter, similarity of programming across channels, and channel switching behavior all compound the advertising effectiveness of television. As a result, top-rated television shows are not necessarily the best places for product placements. Product placements depend on a number of factors, including length of the time on air, when and how products are woven into the story line, and targeted audience.

Plot connection (Russell, 1998) is the degree to which the brand is woven into the plot of the story. Lower plot placements do not contribute much to the story. Higher plot placements comprise a major thematic element. Essentially, verbally mentioned brand names that contribute to the narrative structure of the plot need to be highly connected to the plot. Lower plot visual placements need to serve an accessory role to the story that is lower in plot connection. Visual placements need to be lower in plot connections, and audio and visual placements need to be even higher in plot connection. Also, prominent brand placements in television have a more significant advantage than subtle brand placements.

Film

What is the effect of Tom Cruise chewing Hollywood gum or Agent 007 using a BMW? These are typical examples of product placement in movies. Higher involvement is required to view a movie than for viewing television. Television viewers can multi-task in the home setting thereby reducing their attention span and brand retention. Moviegoers actively choose the experience, movie, time, and cost. As such, they are much more receptive to the brand communication during the movie. A majority of movie watchers have a positive attitude toward this form of marketing communication, feeling it is preferable to commercials shown on the screen before the movie. More frequent viewers and viewers who enjoy the movie more, pay attention to product placements in the movie.

Shapiro has classified four types of product placements in movies: (1) provides only clear visibility of the product or brand being shown without verbal reference, for example, a bottle of Coca-Cola sitting on the counter; (2) used in a scene without verbal reference, for example, actor drinks a Coca-Cola but does not mention anything about it; (3) has a spoken reference, for example, "Boy, I'm thirsty for a Coke"; and (4) provides brand in use and is mentioned by a main star, for example, actor says "This Coke tastes so refreshing" while drinking the Coke. The star using and speaking about the brand in the film is assumed to have higher impact than the mere visual display of the brand. That is, meaningful stimuli become more integrated into a person's cognitive structure and are processed deeply and generate greater recall. Yang and Raskos-Ewoldsen found that higher levels of placements influence recognition of the brand and attitudes toward the brand. However, single placement of the brand within the movie influenced implicit memory and the implicit choice task. To gain greater audience recognition, the brand needs to be used by the main character or needs to play a role in the unfolding story. That is, prominence and plot connection are important. Product placements may have a long-term effect on implicit memory and perceptions of familiarity.

Computer/Video Games

Products and brands are expanding into video games and even creating their own games. Active product placement in computer games can have positive effects. For example, exposure to a particular brand in a computer game can increase the brand attitude among consumers whose original attitude toward the brand is fairly low. Product placement within computer games has been found to be an effective means of building high spontaneous brand recall and even of influencing consumers less positively predisposed towards a brand, that is, non-users. Product placements in computer/video games are becoming powerful marketing tools that form an active part of the gamers' play experience. In particular, they can be used to target the elusive younger male consumer segment with brands woven into near real-life situations that provide a means of interacting with the brand. Lee and Faber note that the location or proximity of the brand messages in the game, game involvement, and prior-game experience interact to influence brand memory. A highly incongruent brand Is better recalled than either a moderately incongruent brand or a highly congruent brand. As experienced players' involvement increases, brand recognition decreases, that is, they are paying attention to the game. Also, product placement seems to grow on the second exposure, that is, when a consumer sees the movie, then the DVD comes out, and in actually playing the game. The multiple viewings may reduce the intrigue in the storyline and give more time to notice the props.

Essentially, there are three general approaches to game advertising: (1) traditional product placements, signs, and billboard ads that are just in the games from the beginning and cannot be changed later, (2) dynamic advertising wherein new ads can be inserted at anytime via the Internet, and (3) advergames or rebranded versions of current games that blatantly promote a single product throughout, Until now, advergames and product placements have been the leading forms of in-game advertising. For example, Burger King created three games suitable for the whole family: racing, action, and adventure, featuring The King, Subservient Chicken, and Brooke Burke. Their target market of young males meshes well with the Xbox audience, given that 18–34 year old men have been a hard group for marketers to get their product or name in front of.

However, dynamic advertising is taking off and is probably the wave of the future. In dynamic advertising, a marketer can specify where ads are put, can set times when ads will run, can choose which audience type your ad goes to, and can get the tracking available for Internet ads. Approximately 62% of gamers are playing online at least some of the time. Researchers can track how long each ad is on the screen, how much of the screen the ad occupies and from what angle the gamer is viewing the ad. Companies pay for ad impressions—one ad impression constitutes 10 seconds of screen time. For example, about half of video games are suitable for ads and could be contextually relevant to the game. More than 50 games already are receiving dynamic ad content, with another 70 set to go by year-end.

Another wave of the future is 3D ads that are twice as powerful as billboards. Also, the latest version of digital video standard MPEG-4 offers the possibility to personalize storylines or even hyperlink from tagged content, so viewers can click on objects they want to buy. Whatever the future brings, advertising and product placements need to fit with the game. That is, video game developers need to incorporate advertising in an ambient way that will not distract players. In addition, the center of the screen gets the most attention based on eye-tracking research.

Summary

Product placement has become an increasingly popular way of reaching potential customers who are able to zap past commercials. To reach these retreating audiences, advertisers use product placements increasingly in clever, effective ways that do not cost too much. The result is that the average consumer is exposed to 3,000 brands a day including billboards, T shirts, tattoos, schools, doctor's office, ski hills, and sandy beaches. While some preliminary conclusions with regard to product placements have been reached, the industry is far from a comprehensive analysis and testing of all the antecedents and consequences of product placement. In the interim, however, a wise caveat to consider for product and brand placement is "Our philosophy is if the brand doesn't make the show better, the brand doesn't make the show. People must not notice the integration, but they must remember it. That's the test." The ideal product placement situation is win-win-win-win: customer gets to know about new and established products and their benefits, client gets relatively inexpensive branding of their product, media vehicle gets a brand for free or can reduce its production budget, and the product placement agency gets paid for bringing the parties together.

KAYLENE WILLIAMS, ALFRED PETROSKY, and EDWARD HERNANDEZ are all professors at California State University, Stanislaus, and ROBERT PAGE, JR., is a professor at Southern Connecticut State University, New Haven, CT.

Ekaterina V. Karniouchina, Can Uslay, and
Grigori Erenburg

 **NO**

Do Marketing Media Have Life Cycles? The Case of Product Placement in Movies

For better or worse (e.g., more than four dozen brands in *The Departed* [2006]), product placement in the movies has become a part of the contemporary marketing arsenal, lending its power to offerings ranging from pregnancy tests to luxury cars. Gupta and Gould (1997, p. 37) define product placement as a marketing strategy that "involves incorporating brands in movies in return for money or for some promotional or other consideration." Industry sources boast that it can do wonders and significantly boost sales of featured brands. For example, Ray-Ban considered the lifespan of its Wayfarer model sunglasses to be almost over when it placed them in *Risky Business* (1983). Before the release of the movie, the declining sales were at approximately 18,000 units a year; following the movie release, the annual sales of the revived product jumped to 360,000 units. By 1989, following a number of successive placements (e.g., *Top Gun* [1986]), sales reached 4 million units. Despite the abundance of such success stories, the evidence for the tangible benefits of product placement is mostly anecdotal, and studies that empirically demonstrate its economic worth are scant at best. Nevertheless, firms can take extreme measures to establish strategic dominance in branded entertainment. At the peak of the "cola wars" in the early 1980s, Coca-Cola went as far as purchasing Columbia Pictures to control the entertainment arena.

Product placement originally fell under the umbrella of covert marketing because viewers were often unaware of the commercial persuasion effort. Many early marketing research efforts concentrated on the subliminal and covert nature of this marketing medium. However, as consumers have become more marketing savvy and the technique more prominent, it has shifted closer to the realm of conventional marketing. At present, the question remains whether this tactic is still as effective as it was in the past; it is commonly believed that when advertisers cross the line and overwhelm the audience with blatant product placements, their efforts will backfire.

In this article, we adopt a longitudinal perspective and examine the evolution of the effectiveness of product placement in the movies over a 40-year time frame.... We conclude with managerial implications, future research directions, and limitations.

An Historical Perspective on Product Placement

Although many researchers believe that product placement was born when a little boy made an extraterrestrial friend by laying a trail of Reese's Pieces in *E.T.* (1982), other sources are starkly divided on its true origins. For example, Karrh, McKee, and Pardun (2003) argue that product placement originated in the 1940s, while others suggest that this marketing medium can be traced back to the end of nineteenth century, when Lever Brothers' Sunlight soap was placed in several films. However, most sources agree that the practice emerged as a legitimate marketing instrument in the mid-1970s and has been rapidly expanding since that time. The biggest surge has arguably been during first decade of the twenty-first century. Product placement spending in the United States grew at an annual rate of almost 34% to $2.9 billion in 2007 and was projected to reach $5.6 billion in 2010.

In the early stages of its development, product placement was governed by ad hoc decisions and intuition. Branded placement was a casual process, in which branded items were donated, loaned, or purchased at a discount for particular scenes. However, in the new millennium, the process of placing branded consumer products in feature films has gained mass appeal, becoming orderly and institutional, with clearly defined roles involving multiple parties and intermediaries. For example, Next Medium has propelled itself as a leader in the product placement arena by automating the process of product placement in the movies, television shows, and video games and even allowing product placement needs to be filled using an auction-based platform. With more than 80% of national marketers using branded placement, the practice is certainly a part of today's mainstream marketing arsenal.

Because of the proliferation of this marketing medium, consumers are becoming aware of product placement tactics and have started to show evidence of resistance to persuasion. In addition, in an ironic twist, product placements have now created a cluttered environment, which marketers initially designed the tactic to avoid. Furthermore, consumers and industry participants are beginning to question whether the overabundance of placements detracts from the viewing experience and interferes with filmmakers' creative vision (e.g., Writers Guild of America West 2005). Numerous Internet blogs are devoted to dissecting and mocking placement-heavy films (e.g., http://www.brandspotters.com). Multiple consumer advocacy groups are calling on the Federal Trade Commission and other government agencies to curb and/or regulate product placement practices (e.g., Commercial Alert 2003). . . .

Product Placement Efficacy

Researchers have traditionally attributed the efficacy of product placement as a marketing medium to its ability to cut through advertising clutter by relying on transference mechanisms. Instead of competing against a plethora of competitive advertisements in more traditional advertising channels, product placement acts in a more unobtrusive way by evoking the positive associations, aspirations, and symbolic meanings connected with the underlying movie content. Excitation transfer theory also suggests that the excitement associated with film sequences can be transferred to other subsequently presented objects, including embedded products. Labeled by the industry as "the anti-TiVo," product placements are also believed to be more effective in reaching the target audience than traditional advertising spots because they are immune to ad skipping. Finally, product placements might circumvent consumer resentment by blurring the lines between commercial content and entertainment, thereby providing "advertainment." . . .

At present, the consensus is that, despite the large spectrum of research on product placement, the economic value of a placement remains a pressing research question. We are aware of only one study that has attempted to evaluate the effect of product placement in movies on firm value: In a cross-sectional study, Wiles and Danielova (2009) investigate price reactions for stocks of publicly traded companies that placed their brands in the 24 most popular movies of 2002. Their daily event study indicates that product placement in these movies resulted in .89% positive abnormal return over the (–2, 0) movie release event window. Surprisingly, the cumulative abnormal return (CAR) over the (–2, 1) time window was not significant, indicating a possible price reversal that takes place immediately after the movies' release. Therefore, additional research on the efficacy of such a heavily used marketing medium is warranted. In this study, we examine both blockbuster and non-blockbuster movies and extend this emerging research stream with a longitudinal examination of the value of product placements and related tie-in campaigns (i.e., concurrent advertisement campaigns marketers use to accentuate the effect of placements).

Conceptual Framework

A possible explanation why so little research has been done to estimate the financial worth of product placements is the complex lagged effects of product placement on firms' cash flows. Moreover, other concurrent activities affect cash flows and revenues, making it difficult to tease out the value product placement adds specifically. We attempt to overcome this problem by analyzing stock market reaction to product placement.

The efficient market theory (EMT) stipulates that stock prices reflect available information regarding a firm's future cash flows. According to this theory, once information about the product placement is available to investors, the resulting change in stock price should reflect investors' expectations of the total change in future cash flows due to the product placement. Our conceptual framework builds on the EMT, which posits that investors' responses to product placements are contingent on their expectations regarding customer behavior. By measuring stock price reaction to the release of the movie in which the company's brand is featured, we estimate the incremental value that the investors place on that product placement. We introduce several factors related to the placements' ability to resonate with moviegoers, and produce the desired effect. In addition, we introduce information-processing effects and market-related controls because they can influence investors' willingness and ability to invest in brands that are placed in feature films and our ability to detect abnormal returns. Next, we discuss the conceptual framework and its key factors in more detail. . . .

Srinivasan and Hanssens (2009) note that product innovation has a greater impact on firm value when coupled with greater advertising support. It is possible that product placements that are tied to concurrent traditional advertising/sales promotion campaigns also generate higher returns because they can create more traction with consumers. To control for this, we incorporate promotional tie-in campaigns into the framework. The framework also recognizes that the effectiveness of the tie-in campaigns can follow a certain trajectory over time and be affected by additional drivers such as A-list celebrity participation.

To account for the awareness of the movie before its release, we incorporate adjusted production budget, which research has found to be highly correlated with advertising spending because advertising data are not available for the majority of time frame covered by our study. Moreover, the framework includes brand familiarity because it can influence the awareness and acceptance of the placement effort.

Acceptance

In addition to exposure, consumers should also be receptive to buying the products placed in the movies. More prominent placements could be more memorable; at the same time, consumers can show resistance to over-the-top marketing efforts and exhibit general anticonsumption tendencies in various settings. Some placements can be so overt (e.g., repeated placements of the same brand within the film) that the centrality of the brand/product to the plot can alert the viewers to the placement effort and even cause resentment. Therefore, we incorporate overtness of the placement in our framework.

Meanwhile, growing resentment of product placements could give rise to negative time effects, and familiarity with the medium and increased product placement expertise of marketers could give rise to positive time effects. We also include the actors' star power in the framework because it can influence the acceptance level of the placed brands if the stars are perceived as endorsers. The degree of annoyance might be greater when placements are embedded in poor-quality films. In addition, we anticipate that certain movies and movie genres are less suitable for product placement. . . .

Data and Methods

In this study, we employ the Brand Hype Movie Mapper data set. Brand Hype (University of Concordia) is an educational resource that includes a searchable movie/brand placement data set starting with 1968. Our investigation is based on the 1968–2007 time frame and uses 928 product placement observations (linked to 159 films) that

have sufficient financial data for our analysis. The average opening box office revenue in our sample is $18.3 million, which is significantly lower than the $44.8 million average Wiles and Danielova (2009) report. Therefore, the sample used in this study represents a broader cross-section of small and blockbuster films. . . .

Discussion of Findings

Event Study Results

[Event study results] reveal a gradual stock price buildup that begins approximately ten days before the movie release and continues for approximately three business weeks (i.e., 16 days) after the release date, followed by price stabilization. Over the price buildup period (i.e., the [–10, 16] event window), the stocks gain .75% on average. The returns to product placements in the movies are positive and significant. . . .

In line with recent marketing research, the documented price pattern suggests that investors' new information processing takes time; delayed stock market response to marketing-related information may be a more common phenomenon than previously believed. For example, Pauwels et al. (2004) find that it takes six weeks in the automobile sector to absorb new product introductions. This finding is also consistent with traditional finance literature that notes that it takes time for the information to be fully reflected in stock prices.

Although stock prices can be driven by informed trading, they can also be affected by uninformed noise trading. If the latter is the case, stock price reaction would only be temporary, and the change in stock prices would not be a good measure of the value of product placement. . . . We also note the potential presence of noise trading, which results in a minor price adjustment in the post event window. . . .

Other Significant Findings

The variable (NUMBER OF APPEARANCES WITH MAIN CHARACTER) has a significant negative coefficient. (An alternative measure of overtness using time on screen with the main character generated qualitatively the same results.) There is anecdotal evidence suggesting that blatant product placements can be detrimental. For example, FedEx drew criticism for the relentless abundance of FedEx references in the movie *Cast Away* (2000). Our result is consistent with the literature that suggests that "in your face," overt placements may not be as effective as their more subtle counterparts. . . .

Differences Across Movies and Industries

The results indicate that our sample has significant movie and industry specific heterogeneity ($p < .01$). The implication is that picking appropriate films for placement is a relevant managerial concern. Further examination of the industry-related random effects revealed additional dynamics associated with industry differences. . . .

Two industries are characterized by large positive residuals and low posterior variance: electronics and automotive placements enjoy .8% and .2% higher returns, respectively, when compared with other placements. At the same time, other popular placements, such as those for soft and alcoholic drinks, media and entertainment, and food processing, do not enjoy similar advantages. Alcoholic beverages lag almost half a percentage point behind average placements. Although it is possible that some of the alcohol-related placements do not present the product in a positive light, the examination of our sample offers another explanation. The vast majority of placements are for inexpensive domestic beer, a relatively mundane product category. We also note that, across the board, the "unexciting" product categories (e.g., food processing; telecom; retail, which captures retail "super-chains" and large box stores) have lower returns. . . .

[D]ynamics of the prices around the movie release date separately for the three groups of movies. The significant price increases for the high-grossing films start 30 trading days before the release of the film, with most of the CARs taking place before Day 4; then, a period of insignificant price movements are followed by the downward adjustment. The price reaction for the movies with lower box office revenues starts later (right after the release date) but takes less time to complete. Prices stabilize on the new level within two weeks. The price pattern for the blockbuster films suggest that, while the investors' reaction to the placements in such movies reaches a higher magnitude than the reaction to the lower-grossing films, some of the initial reaction may be driven by uninformed trading and, to that degree, is not indicative of the potential increase in companies' future revenues. The earlier prerelease price run-up for high-grossing movies is consistent with this explanation because hype among the noise traders could be driven by the intense prerelease advertising campaigns associated with these high-grossing/high-budget films. Nevertheless, the permanent price impact of the placement in high-grossing movies does not seem to be different from that in low-grossing movies.

The combined results from this study and that of Wiles and Danielova (2009) indicate that blockbuster films may be associated with higher initial CARs to product placements in films but also with a strong downward adjustment that takes place when the movie opens. Blockbuster films may generate more hype, encouraging noise trading. However, this increased hype does not lead to an additional sustainable increase in the firm's economic value.

Finally, we considered the possibility that longitudinal changes in advertising spending at both film and brand level could influence the relationship between time and placement effectiveness. We performed this robustness check with the 1994–2007 subsample by including advertising expenditure across all media for brands and total advertising budget for films. (Our source, ACNielsen, began collecting both types of data in 1994.) The quadratic curve produced similar estimates to the linear trend (also similar to results for the full sample). . . .

Including both advertising related variables (i.e., movie and brand related advertising spending) did not affect the inverted U-shaped trend or the timing of the peak in the effectiveness of the tie-in campaigns. First-order conditions indicated that the peak in effectiveness of the tie-in campaigns took place in 2000 (as we found in the full data set results). Although inclusion of advertising-related variables did not affect the underlying time related trends, it enriches our understanding of tie-in effectiveness. For example, negative and significant interaction between the tie-ins and brand-level advertising spending suggest that tie-ins are more effective for brands with lower advertising intensity. . . .

Implications for Managers

Our findings suggest that, just as products go through a life cycle, so too do the instruments used to market them. When a new technique shows promise, innovators and early adopters expand its use and start perfecting its application, which lead to growth and increased effectiveness. In the case of product placement in the movies, it seems this happened before the 1990s. However, as a new marketing technique gains wider acceptance, lack of novelty may diminish its effectiveness and consumers may start showing resistance to persuasion. They turn to consumer advocacy groups (e.g., Media Awareness Network, Commercial Alert) and technologies that enable them to avoid exposure to advertising (e.g., DVR) and even lobby for blanket legislation (e.g., do-not-call lists). Even in the absence of regulatory action, consumers seem to learn to tune out the messages, or they become savvy and impervious to the new type of marketing media. It is also possible that the costs of effective forms of marketing media increase, rendering them less profitable. Regardless of the exact mechanism, our findings indicate the presence of inverted U-shaped relationship over time in the returns for a new marketing practice and reinforce the need for the marketing industry to reinvent itself as new tactics lose their luster. The inverted U-shaped relationship holds true not only for product placements themselves but also for promotional tie-in campaigns used to support them.

DeLorme, Reid, and Zimmer (1994) report negative attitudes toward placements involving overexposed brands. Our results suggest that overexposing the brand within the same film (as measured by the number of appearances with the main character) can be detrimental. Furthermore, we find that tie-in campaigns are less effective for brands with larger advertising budgets. Counterintuitively, lower-intensity, fleeting placements can be more profitable than repetitive and potentially more expensive marquee placements with main characters. This finding is consistent with previous literature that suggests that "visual-only placements, typically the lower-priced placements, are processed by viewers at a low level of cognition and therefore may lead to stronger emotional and purchase intent effects than more elaborate placements that mention the product by name or show the product in use." Moreover, romance movies in particular seem to be less suitable for placements. This finding suggests that movies that require deep emotional involvement do not necessarily make the best platforms for placements, because they could be perceived as disruptive.

Previous literature has suggested that too many brand placements can result in less attention devoted to each individual placement due to clutter and information overload. Surprisingly, it seems that this insight from traditional advertising research does not transfer to the product placement arena. . . . Perhaps movies that are more suitable for placements attract more placements, potentially masking the underlying relationship. We considered other functional forms representing various types of curvilinear relationships but failed to detect any significant empirical regularity. Therefore, more product placement in a movie does not necessarily affect the value of a given placement in a negative way. Marketers may actually benefit from aligning themselves with a movie with other placements: Given the confirmed importance of selecting the movie for placement, existing placement agreements can signal suitability and serve as qualifiers.

Future Research Directions and Limitations

It is an ongoing challenge for marketers to constantly develop, identify, experiment with, and adopt novel media and techniques to reach and persuade their audiences. Meanwhile, marketers must gauge, decrease, and abandon

less effective media activity just to remain competitive. Is it inevitable that all marketing media ultimately succumb to a life cycle (introduction, growth, maturity, and decline), just as products do? To our knowledge, this study represents a first attempt to investigate the longitudinal effectiveness of a successful marketing medium through its life cycle and could be viewed as a building block toward a theory of marketing medium life cycle. We advocate the longitudinal examination of the economic worth of both traditional and emerging media.

Extant literature has primarily concentrated on product placements in the movies consistent with Gupta and Gould's (1997) definition. However, product placements have found several additional outlets, such as traditional television shows, reality shows, newscasts, video games, music videos, lyrics, catalogs, comic strips, novels, live broadcasts, Internet casting, and even magazine editorials. There is a need to develop an integrated definition that incorporates the variety of current and emerging product placement domains and forms. It would be of interest to examine the extent to which such alternative placement media registers abnormal returns and whether they are also subject to a curvilinear relationship (i.e., life cycle). If so, what would be the expected trajectory of their effectiveness over time? Future studies would also benefit from incorporating various placement-related factors that have been shown to have an impact on advertising effectiveness, such as brand/plot/genre congruity, execution-related factors, and attitude toward sponsor, which we did not explore in this study. These factors may explain how some companies manage to achieve success through placements despite life-cycle considerations.

Although the data set we used in this study represents a great resource for product placement researchers, it is not without limitations. For example, because the data collection was led by film scholars, critically acclaimed and mature content movies were overrepresented in the data set. Although most differences are relatively mild, the high critical acclaim of the movies included in the Brand Hype data set may have led to more conservative estimates of the economic worth of product placements because Wiles and Danielova's (2009) and our findings suggest that the placements in such films are associated with lower CARs.

Despite the tremendous growth and volume of product placements in recent years, Balasubramanian, Karrh, and Patwardhan (2006) note that only 29% of these placements are paid. It seems to be important to examine the antecedents and consequences of barter, gratis, and hybrid forms of product placements to improve the return on investment of this marketing medium and to determine best practices. An interesting caveat is that the Federal Communication Commission currently requires the disclosure of paid product placements but does not penalize the omission of such disclosures unless there is a deliberate nonobjective claim or deception related to the product. This means creative room for the interpretation of regulation regarding barter and gratis placements. It is likely that nonpaid product placements (which do not have to be disclosed) not only offer greater return on investment but also can be more effective. Still, nonpaid placements can come at a cost: It is not uncommon for a marketer to pay six-figure fees to product placement agencies for annual service contracts. It would be worthwhile to distinguish between paid and nonpaid forms of product placements in further research.

Our focus in this study was on assessing the effect of product placement in the movies on the value of the companies that owned the advertised brands. An interesting research question is the flip side of this issue: What is the impact of product placements on the movie's success? In the context of print advertising, it has been shown that too much advertising relative to editorial content can be detrimental to consumers' perceptions of editorial quality and can have a negative impact on circulation. Mandese (2006, p. 3) cites industry sources who argue that in the television context, "when consumers grow wary of product placement . . . they may not simply react negatively about the brands involved but may actually turn the shows off." Consistent with the literature on distrust, Wei, Fischer, and Main (2008) find that audience members who recognized a paid placement not only lowered their evaluations of the placed brand but also lowered their evaluations of the hosts, show, and radio station. We did not find any evidence of such a relationship in our sample. Organically integrated brands in a movie may actually enhance a film's artistic qualities by creating a more realistic setting and providing a connection between the story and the "real world." A more detailed investigation that considers endogeneity between movie quality, placement volume, and placement quality is warranted.

This article draws generalizations regarding the effectiveness of product placements over time. However, other areas of longitudinal exploration remain to be addressed. For example, is there a value in lasting relationships between movie stars and brands? For example, Will Smith seems to have a long-standing relationship with Ray-Ban (e.g., *Men in Black* [1997]; *Men in Black II* [2002]; *Bad Boys II* [2003]; *Hancock* [2008]). Do these continuous relationships benefit advertisers by allowing the brand to adhere to the star's persona and capitalize on celebrity appeal, thereby enhancing the realism of the placement? Similar questions could be asked about the enduring relationships between the brands and movie franchises. For example, the James Bond franchise has had a long engagement with the Rolex brand since the 1960s; however, starting with *Golden Eye* (1995), the franchise switched to Omega. Whether the effective formation and management of such relationships can result in tangible benefits to firms' bottom lines remains to be explored. . . .

References

Balasubramanian, Siva K., James A. Karrh, and Hemant Patwardhan (2006), "Audience Response to Product Placements: An Integrative Framework and Future Research Agenda," *Journal of Advertising*, 35 (3), 115–27.

DeLorme, Denise E., Leonard Reid, and Mary R. Zimmer (1994), "Brands in Films: Young Moviegoers' Experiences and Interpretations," in *Proceedings of the 1994 Conference of the American Academy of Advertising*, Karen W. King, ed. Athens, GA: American Academy of Advertising, 60.

Gupta, Paula B. and Stephen J. Gould (1997), "Consumers Perceptions of the Ethics and Acceptability of Product Placements in Movies: Product Category and Individual Differences," *Journal of Current Issues and Research in Advertising*, 19 (1), 37–50.

Mandese, Joe (2006), "When Product Placement Goes Too Far," *Broadcasting and Cable*, (January 1), (accessed January 10, 2011), [available at http://www.broadcastingcable.com/article/102250-When_Product_Placement_Goes_Too_Far.php].

Pauwels, Koen, Jorge M. Silva-Russo, Shuba Srinivasan, and Dominique M. Hanssens (2004), "New Products, Sales Promotions, and Firm Value: The Case of the Automobile Industry," *Journal of Marketing*, 68 (October), 142–56.

Wei, Mei-Ling, Eileen Fischer, and Kelley J. Main (2008), "An Examination of the Effects of Activating Persuasion Knowledge on Consumer Response to Brands Engaging in Covert Marketing," *Journal of Public Policy & Marketing*, 27 (Spring), 34–44.

Wiles, Michael A. and Anna Danielova (2009), "The Worth of Product Placement in Successful Films: An Event Study Analysis," *Journal of Marketing*, 73 (July), 44–63.

Writers Guild of America West (2005), "Entertainment Guilds Call for Industry Code of Conduct of FCC Regulation for Product Integration in Programming and Film: Guilds Issue White Paper Report on the Runaway Use of Stealth Advertising in Television and Film," (accessed May 1, 2010), [available at http://www.wga.org/subpage_newsevents.aspx?id=1422].

EKATERINA V. KARNIOUCHINA and CAN USLAY are both assistant professors of marketing at the Argyros School of Business and Economics, Chapman University.

GRIGORI ERENBURG is an assistant professor of finance at King's University College, University of Western Ontario, Canada.

EXPLORING THE ISSUE

Is Product Placement an Effective Form of Advertising?

Critical Thinking and Reflection

1. Though product placement has become more common, do you think advertisers are operating ethically when they pay to have certain products featured in media content?
2. How and in what way(s) can product placement influence the flow of a media program or media content?
3. Is product placement as popular in new media as it has been in traditional television and film content?
4. Would you be willing to pay more for media content that did not include subsidized images through product placement? Would the production company/companies have to change their business models?
5. Over time, do audiences become anaesthetized to this type of advertising?

Is There Common Ground?

For the authors of the two selections in this issue, product placement is an accepted advertising technique, but the authors differ in how deeply one can examine the functionality or dysfunctionality of the way product placement achieves its desired result—which is to blur the difference between advertising and program content. These authors do not involve themselves with questions of morality, ethics, or whether product placement actually could harm the public, but rather, keep their eyes on the success of the advertising campaign through this technique.

The common ground these authors tread upon is the normalization of advertising and advertising techniques that are so prominent in our society today. As such, they avoid problems that the advertising industry has had to deal with for decades—and those questions deal with whether advertising operates in the public good or not.

What are your perspectives on the role of advertising techniques to attract audiences, and the role of advertising in our society?

Additional Resources

Scott Donaton, *Madison and Vine: Why the Entertainment and Advertising Industries Must Converge to Survive* (Crain Communications, 2004).

Mary-Lou Galician, ed., *Handbook of Product Placement in the Mass Media: New Strategies in Marketing Theory, Practice, Trends, and Ethics* (Best Business Books, 2004).

Jean-Marc Lehu, *Branded Entertainment: Product Placement & Brand Strategy in the Entertainment Business* (Kogan-Page, 2009).

Internet References . . .

American Marketing Association, Statement of Ethics

http://www.marketingpower.com/AboutAMA/Pages
/Statement%20of%Ethics.aspx

American Psychological Association, "Advertising to Children: Is It Ethical?"

http://www.apa.org/monitor/sep00/advertising.aspx

An Ethical Evaluation of Product Placement—A Deceptive Practice?

http://www.academia.edu/600330/An_ethical
_evaluation_of_product_placement
_a_deceptive_practice

Selected, Edited, and with Issue Framing Material by:
Alison Alexander, *University of Georgia*
and
Jarice Hanson, *University of Massachusetts—Amherst*

ISSUE

Is There Any Harm In Taking Selfies?

YES: Elizabeth Day, from "How Selfies Became a Global Phenomenon," *The Guardian* (2013)

NO: Jenna Wortham, from "My Selfie, Myself," *New York Times Sunday Review* (2013)

Learning Outcomes

After reading this issue, you will be able to:

- Consider the many aspects of taking selfies as a cultural phenomenon.
- Think about how one presents one's self to others.
- Consider whether some selfies divulge too much personal information to others.
- Explore how one creates a digital persona and digital identity in online form.
- Reflect on the meaning of self-portraiture over time.

ISSUE SUMMARY

YES: British journalist Elizabeth Day thinks of selfies as modern-day self-portraits. Despite their popularity, she sides with critics who consider selfies to be narcissistic and expressions of our self-absorbed lifestyles.

NO: *The New York Times* reporter Jenna Wortham claims that our predilection for responding to faces is just a part of a more technologized world, and that while we shouldn't discount the selfie phenomenon, we should also keep in mind that selfies are a type of visual diary.

On the surface, selfies—those self-portraits often taken with a cell phone camera and posted online—seem innocuous, but in recent years the number of selfies taken and the possible meaning that those images have for the person in the picture and the social statement he or she makes have begun to stir the interests of social scientists and cultural critics. Certainly, the taking of self-portraits is nothing new, but the frequency with which they are taken and posted for others to see has resulted in a popular activity. When Ellen DeGeneres took a selfie at the 2014 Oscar Awards with Jared Leto, Jennifer Lawrence, Meryl Streep, Bradley Cooper, Peter Nyong'o Jr., Channing Tatum, Julia Roberts, Kevin Spacey, Brad Pitt, Lupita Nyong'o, and Angelina Jolie (how did they all fit on that small screen?), Twitter crashed as the image was simultaneously sent to 37 million people worldwide. Of course, this action made Samsung, a sponsor of the Oscar Awards, very happy! The word "selfie" became one of the "words of the

year" in *Time* magazine's 2012 annual collection of new, trending topics. In 2013, the Oxford English Dictionary also added the word to its compendium of words in the English language.

The photo capabilities of cell phones have fueled interest in selfies, and a number of social media outlets—Instagram in particular—have helped selfies become a part of our culture. Some selfies are carefully crafted, and some follow the style of Kim Kardashian, who introduced the pouty mouthed, head turned classic selfie image. Though celebrity selfies are popular and help the celebrity stay in the media spotlight (think of how often Justin Bieber tweets selfies of himself), selfies themselves have become cultural icons of self-representation.

Some scholars have focused on the types of problems selfies address, such as the narcissistic desire to be seen, and the denigration of one's body image when one compares their selfies to those that have been carefully crafted by celebrities and their publicists, but once you get beyond the fun of a quick snap of the camera, selfies may well make a number of statements about the subject, and the way the subject thinks of himself/herself in relationship to friends, and others in society. The Pew Internet and American Life Project conducted a study in 2014 and found that people of all ages say they have posted a selfie of themselves at some time, but that millennials (people who reached young adulthood around the year 2000) post significantly more than any other age group. And, as social media usage increases among all ages every year, we can expect the selfie to become even more apparent in the next few years as cell phone manufacturers make better cameras, and social networks make it easier to upload and distribute selfies on a variety of platforms.

In this issue, the two authors cite different evidence to argue the question of whether selfies can be harmful. Elizabeth Day discusses how and why selfies caught on, and suggests that we project a good deal of biographical information about ourselves when we take and post selfies. In arguing that selfies are a prime example of a narcissistic age, she outlines the statement selfies make about our sexuality and our sense of worth in society. She quotes many selfie takers who justify their actions based upon wanting to look good when they go out, or who actually contribute to a "pornification" of our culture in terms of constructing images that suggest that people create images that self-objectify themselves. These questions she raises ask us to think twice about why we take selfies, and the way other people may "read" those images.

On the other hand, Jenna Wortham discusses how selfies mediate a person's sense of self and the outer environment. She is less willing to examine the rise of sexual selfies and those that create objectified images, and instead discusses some of the ways that selfies connect people to others. As components of "visual diaries," selfies reflect how visual our culture has become, and how we've begun to rely on our impressions of faces as modes of communication.

Selfies themselves have been grouped into a number of subgroups. After-sex selfies, selfies with celebrities and politicians, selfies in different geographical regions, and selfies that mimic the positions of statues and public exhibitions have been collected on some social media sites and tend to elicit a number of responses from viewers. For many of these types of selfies, comments can range from admiration to disgust. Though neither of our authors discusses the number of "likes" people may get from posting their pictures, this quasi-measure of popularity has a lot to do with the way selfie-posters think about their behaviors when they do post pictures on social media platforms.

The ease of snapping a selfie with a cell phone that requires no special lighting and gives instant results is also a factor in thinking about how technology today is often used for purposes for which it was not originally intended. For many people, the selfie is a type of mirror that lets them see how they might be perceived by others. As a result, many selfie-snappers openly talk about how much time they devote to getting just the right look, and expressing the mood they want to the world. A number of websites exist that discuss the aesthetics of taking a good selfie so that the self-portrait has the right look and the right tone to express one's personality and elicit the desired effect.

Among some of the most recent academic studies of selfies, we learn that men may actually exhibit more antisocial traits than women when taking selfies. With the headline, "Hey, Guys: Posting a Lot of Selfies Doesn't Send a Good Message," researchers at Ohio University conducted a large study that shows that men who posted a number of online photos of themselves often scored more highly on measures of narcissism and psychopathy. In other research, men's selfies were grouped according to the selfie "type," suggesting that expressions of masculinity and competition were often the subtexts for the types of selfies men take, and post. Yet another study discussed how selfies actually annoy friends, who feel that they have to look at pictures that make them see their friends as more self-absorbed than they want to believe. Undoubtedly, the longer we live with the selfie phenomenon, the more studies will emerge that delve into the behavior of those who take and post selfies.

YES ↵

Elizabeth Day

How Selfies Became a Global Phenomenon

. . .

It starts with a certain angle: a smartphone tilted at 45 degrees just above your eyeline is generally deemed the most forgiving. Then a light source: the flattering beam of a backlit window or a bursting supernova of flash reflected in a bathroom mirror, as preparations are under way for a night out.

The pose is important. Knowing self-awareness is conveyed by the slight raise of an eyebrow, the sideways smile that says you're not taking it too seriously. A doe-eyed stare and mussed-up hair denotes natural beauty, as if you've just woken up and can't help looking like this. Sexiness is suggested by sucked-in cheeks, pouting lips, a nonchalant cock of the head and a hint of bare flesh just below the clavicle. Snap!

Afterwards, a flattering filter is applied. Outlines are blurred, colours are softened, a sepia tint soaks through to imply a simpler era of vinyl records and VW camper vans.

All of this is the work of an instant. Then, with a single tap, you are ready to upload: to Twitter, to Facebook, to Instagram, each likeness accompanied by a self-referential hashtag. Your image is retweeted and tagged and shared. Your screen fills with thumbs-up signs and heart-shaped emoticons. You are "liked" several times over. You feel a shiver of—what, exactly? Approbation? Reassurance? Existential calm? Whatever it is, it's addictive. Soon, you repeat the whole process, trying out a different pose. Again and again, you offer yourself up for public consumption.

This, then, is the selfie: the self-portrait of the digital age. We are all at it. Just type "selfie" into the Twitter search bar. Or take a look at Instagram, where over 90m photos are currently posted with the hashtag #me.

Adolescent pop poppet Justin Bieber constantly Tweets photos of himself with his shirt off to the shrieking delight of his huge online following. Rihanna has treated her fans to Instagrammed selfies of her enjoying the view at a strip club, of her buttocks barely concealed by a tiny denim thong and of her posing with two oversize cannabis joints while in Amsterdam. Reality TV star Kim Kardashian overshares to the extent that, in March, she posted a picture of her own face covered in blood after undergoing a so-called "vampire facial." In the same month, the selfie-obsessed model and actress Kelly Brook banned herself from posting any more of them (her willpower lasted two hours).

The political classes have started doing it too. President Obama's daughters, Sasha and Malia, took selfies at his second inauguration. In June, Hillary Clinton got in on the act after her daughter, Chelsea, tweeted a joint picture of them taken on her phone at arm's length. Earlier this month, three sisters from Nebraska stormed the field of a college baseball match and filmed themselves while doing so, eventually being removed by security guards. Stills from the six-second Vine video clip became known as "the most expensive selfie of all time" after it emerged that the sisters were facing a $1,500 fine.

. . .

"The selfie is revolutionising how we gather autobiographical information about ourselves and our friends," says Dr Mariann Hardey, a lecturer in marketing at Durham University who specialises in digital social networks. "It's about continuously rewriting yourself. It's an extension of our natural construction of self. It's about presenting yourself in the best way . . . [similar to] when women put on makeup or men who bodybuild to look a certain way: it's an aspect of performance that's about knowing yourself and being vulnerable."

. . .

Although photographic self-portraits have been around since 1839, when daguerreotype pioneer Robert Cornelius took a picture of himself outside his family's store in Philadelphia (whether he had the help of an assistant is not known), it was not until the invention of the compact digital camera that the selfie boomed in popularity. There was some experimentation with the selfie in the 1970s—most notably by Andy Warhol—when the Polaroid camera came of age and freed amateur photographers from the tyranny of the darkroom. But film was expensive and it wasn't until the advent of digital that photographs became truly instantaneous.

The fact that we no longer had to traipse to our local chemist to develop a roll of holiday snaps encouraged us to experiment—after all, on a digital camera, the image could be easily deleted if we didn't like the results. A selfie could be done with the timer button or simply by holding the camera at arm's length, if you didn't mind the looming tunnel of flesh dog-earing one corner of the image.

As a result, images tagged as #selfie began appearing on the photo-sharing website Flickr as early as 2004. But it was the introduction of smartphones—most crucially the iPhone 4, which came along in 2010 with a front-facing camera—that made the selfie go viral. According to the latest annual Ofcom communications report, 60% of UK mobile phone users now own a smartphone and a recent survey of more than 800 teenagers by the Pew Research Centre in America found that 91% posted photos of themselves online—up from 79% in 2006.

Recently, the Chinese manufacturer Huawei unveiled plans for a new smartphone with "instant facial beauty support" software which reduces wrinkles and blends skin tone.

"A lot of the cameras on smartphones are incredibly good," says Michael Pritchard, the director general of the Royal Photographic Society. "The rise of digital cameras and the iPhone coincided with the fact that there are a lot more single people around [than before]. The number of single-occupancy households is rising, more people are divorcing and living single lives and people go on holiday by themselves more and don't have anyone else to take the picture. That's one reason I take selfies: because I do actually want to record where I am."

But if selfies are simply an exercise in recording private memories and charting the course of our lives, then why do we feel such a pressing need to share them with hundreds and thousands of friends and strangers online? To some, the selfie has become the ultimate symbol of the narcissistic age. Its instantaneous nature encourages superficiality—or so the argument goes. One of the possible side-effects has been that we care more than ever before about how we appear and, as a consequence, social acceptance comes only when the outside world accepts the way we look, rather than endorsing the work we do or the way we behave off-camera.

The American writer John Paul Titlow has described selfie-sharing as: "a high school popularity contest on digital steroids." In an article published on the website ReadWrite earlier this year, Titlow argued that selfie users "are seeking some kind of approval from their peers and the larger community, which thanks to the internet is now effectively infinite."

Indeed, although many people who post pictures of themselves on the internet do so in the belief that it will only ever be seen by their group of friends on any given social network, the truth is that the images can be viewed and used by other agencies. There are now entire porn sites devoted to the "amateur" naked selfie and concerns have recently been raised that jilted lovers can seek their revenge by making explicit images of their ex publicly available online.

The preponderance of young women posing for selfies in a state of undress is a potentially worrying issue. When the model Cara Delevingne Instagrammed a picture of her nipples poking through a black lace top, it rapidly got over 60,000 "Likes."

According to Gail Dines, the author of *Pornland: How Porn Has Hijacked Our Sexuality*: "Because of porn culture, women have internalised that image of themselves. They self-objectify, which means they're actually doing to themselves what the male gaze does to them."

Dines argues that although men can "gain visibility" in a variety of ways, for women the predominant way to get attention is "fuckability." And it is true that a lot of female selfie aficionados take their visual vernacular directly from pornography (unwittingly or otherwise): the pouting mouth, the pressed-together cleavage, the rumpled bedclothes in the background hinting at opportunity.

But Rebecca Brown, a 23-year-old graduate trainee from Birmingham, believes her penchant for selfies is neither degrading nor narcissistic. Instead, she explains, it is a simple means of self-exploration.

"It's almost like a visual diary," she says. "I can look back and see what I looked like at a particular time, what I was wearing. It's exploring your identity in digital form. To me it's not about nudity or having a raunchy or raw kind of look . . . People think if you take pictures of yourself, you're self-obsessed but that's like saying if you write a diary or an autobiography, you're self-obsessed. Not necessarily. A selfie is a format and a platform to share who you are."

Does she feed off the social approval that a selfie can generate?

"I suppose you take photos to see what you look like," Brown concedes. "Before I go out, I'll take a couple of pictures almost to see how I look in other people's eyes.

In the same way that if you wrote a really good piece of work and had people commenting about how good it was, or if you put something on Twitter that people retweeted, if people start liking your selfie, then obviously you're going to get a natural buzz. It gives you a nice boost and you can walk with that little bit more confidence."

. . .

The popularity of the selfie is, says Mariann Hardey, "an extension of how we live and learn about each other" and a way of imparting necessary information about who we are. By way of an example, Hardey says that when her father died suddenly last year, she took refuge in her Instagram feed.

"I couldn't bear the conversations but one way to prove to friends that I was OK was to take a picture of myself," she says. "That revealed something very important to my friends—one, that I was still functioning and, two, I was out doing stuff. An image can convey more than words."

The idea that young women are self-objectifying by posing semi-pornographically for selfies is, she believes, a dangerous one.

"When we're talking about what is acceptable for women in terms of constructing an image, we need to be very careful of not heading down into the territory of 'she was wearing a short skirt, so she was asking to be raped'. We should avoid that argument because it's probably an extension of more patriarchal demands."

"Women should be allowed to portray themselves in a way they feel enhanced by. Who didn't experiment with cutting their hair off and dying it pink when they were younger? This is just a natural progression of experimenting with the changing interfaces of being young and one of these interfaces, yes, is sexual identity."

A selfie can, in some respects, be a more authentic representation of beauty than other media images. In an article for *Psychology Today* published earlier this year, Sarah J Gervais, an assistant professor of psychology, wrote that: "Instagram (and other social media) has allowed the public to reclaim photography as a source of empowerment . . . [it] offers a quiet resistance to the barrage of perfect images that we face each day. Rather than being bombarded with those creations . . . we can look through our Instagram feed and see images of real people—with beautiful diversity."

"Instagram also allows us the opportunity to see below the surface. We capture a glimpse into the makings of people's daily lives. We get a sense of those things that make the everyday extraordinary."

The appeal for celebrities like Bieber, Kardashian et al is connected to this. The expansion of social networking has enabled them to communicate directly with their fanbase and to build up large, loyal followings among people who believe they are getting a real glimpse into the lives of the rich and famous.

. . .

The key is the idea of "manageable reality": celebrities can now exercise more control than ever over the dissemination of their image. The paradox at the heart of the selfie is that it masquerades as a "candid" shot, taken without access to airbrushing or post-production, but in fact, a carefully posed selfie, edited with all the right filters, is a far more appealing prospect than a snatched paparazzo shot taken from a deliberately unflattering angle.

"It's about self-exposure and control," says artist Simon Foxall, whose work questions the parameters of individuality and self-expression. "A selfie blurs the line between 'reality' and the performance of a fantasy self, so one collapses into the other."

Beyond that, a judicious use of selfies can make good business sense too: Alexa Chung and Florence Welch have both used selfies to post daily updates on what they are wearing, thereby cementing their position as modern style icons and guaranteeing, no doubt, the continuation of a series of lucrative fashion deals. (Chung, for one, has designed a womenswear line for the fashion brand Madewell for the last three years.)

The website What I Wore Today began as a site that featured young entrepreneur Poppy Dinsey posing for a daily selfie, in a different outfit for every day of the year. It became an internet hit and has now expanded to allow users to upload their own images, as well as generating advertising revenue by featuring online links to clothing retailers.

"People like the control selfies give them," says Dinsey. "Sometimes it's just a practical matter of not having anyone around to shoot you and that's why I always took my own pictures in mirrors for WIWT. But you're deciding how to frame yourself—you're not trusting someone else to make you look good. With front-facing cameras on iPhones, and so on, you can see the picture you're taking and frame it perfectly to show yourself off as best as possible—your mate isn't going to make the same effort when taking your picture. Plus, you can retake and retake without anyone having to know how much vanity has gone into that 'casual' pose."

In some ways, of course, the notion of control is disingenuous: once a selfie is posted online, it is out there for public delectation. Future employers can see it. Marketers can use it. A resentful former lover could exploit it.

You can use digital technology to manipulate your own image as much as you like. But the truth about selfies is that once they are online, you can never control how other people see you.

ELIZABETH DAY is a British journalist, broadcaster, and novelist. Since 2007, she has been a feature writer for *The Observer*. She has also written three novels: *Scissors, Paper, Stone*; *Home Fires*; and *Paradise City*.

Jenna Wortham

➡ **NO**

My Selfie, Myself

RECENTLY, I came across a great find in a Vermont antiques store: an old black-and-white photograph of a female pilot on a mountaintop, her aviator glasses pushed up on her forehead, revealing a satisfied, wind-burned face, the wings of her plane just visible behind her. But the best part of the discovery was the slow realization that she was holding the camera herself. It was, for lack of a better word, a "selfie."

It reminded me of another self-portrait of sorts, one I've been watching evolve online of the mysterious Benny Winfield Jr.

I don't know Mr. Winfield personally, but I've seen his face most days for the past few months, in dozens of photographs he shares on the social networking application Instagram. He calls himself the "leader of the selfie movement" and each image is hypnotically the same—his grinning face fills the frame, and is usually accompanied by a bit of inspirational text.

The self-portraits are worlds—and decades—apart. But they are threaded together by a timeless delight in our ability to document our lives and leave behind a trace for others to discover.

"There is a primal human urge to stand outside of ourselves and look at ourselves," said Clive Thompson, a technology writer and the author of the new book "Smarter Than You Think: How Technology Is Changing Our Minds for the Better."

Selfies have become the catchall term for digital self-portraits abetted by the explosion of cellphone cameras and photo-editing and sharing services. Every major social media site is overflowing with millions of them. Everyone from the pope to the Obama girls has been spotted in one. In late August, Oxford Dictionaries Online added the term to its lexicon. One of the advertisements for the new Grand Theft Auto V video game features a woman in a bikini taking a photograph of herself with an iPhone. In a recent episode of Showtime's "Homeland," one of the main characters snaps and sends a topless selfie to her boyfriend. Snapchat, a photo-based messaging service, is processing 350 million photos each day, while a recent project on Kickstarter raised $90,000 to develop and sell a small Bluetooth shutter release for smartphones and tablets to help people take photographs of themselves more easily.

It is the perfect preoccupation for our Internet-saturated time, a ready-made platform to record and post our lives where others can see and experience them in tandem with us. And in a way, it signals a new frontier in the evolution in social media.

"People are wrestling with how they appear to the rest of the world," Mr. Thompson said. "Taking a photograph is a way of trying to understand how people see you, who you are and what you look like, and there's nothing wrong with that."

At times, it feels largely performative, another way to polish public-facing images of who we are, or who we'd like to appear to be. Selfies often veer into scandalous or shameless territory—think of Miley Cyrus or Geraldo Rivera—and at their most egregious raise all sorts of questions about vanity, narcissism and our obsession with beauty and body image.

But it's far too simplistic to write off the selfie phenomenon. We are swiftly becoming accustomed to—and perhaps even starting to prefer—online conversations and interactions that revolve around images and photos. They are often more effective at conveying a feeling or reaction than text. Plus, we've become more comfortable seeing our faces on-screen, thanks to services like Snapchat, Skype, Google Hangout and FaceTime, and the exhilarating feeling of connectedness that comes from even the briefest video conversation. Receiving a photo of the face of the person you're talking to brings back the human element of the interaction, which is easily misplaced if the interaction is primarily text-based.

"The idea of the selfie is much more like your face is the caption and you're trying to explain a moment or tell a story," said Frédéric della Faille, the founder and designer of Frontback, a popular new photo-sharing application that lets users take photographs using both front- and rear-facing cameras. "It's much more of a moment and a story than a photo." And more often than not, he added, "It's not about being beautiful."

In other words, it is about showing your friends and family your elation when you're having a good day or opening a dialogue or line of communication using an image the same way you might simply text "hi" or "what's up?"

And selfies strongly suggest that the world we observe through social media is more interesting when people insert themselves into it—a fact that many social media sites like Vine, a video-sharing tool owned by Twitter, have noticed. Dom Hofmann, one of the founders of Vine, said the first iteration of the application didn't let people shoot videos using the front-facing camera, partly because of technical constraints. His co-founder, Rus Yusupov, was in favor of adding the feature to the service, but Mr. Hofmann had concerns that it might denigrate the quality of the content people were sharing through the service.

"Rus felt that it would open up a lot of creative possibilities," said Mr. Hofmann. "But I thought it would be a lot of vanity. I didn't see much value in it."

But after some discussion, and repeated requests from users, the company decided to release the front-camera capability as an update. It turned out that his partner was right. Users loved it, Mr. Hofmann said.

"It wasn't really about vanity at all," he said. "It's not really about how you look. It's about you doing something else, or you in other places. It's a more personal way to share an experience."

The feedback loop that selfies can inspire doesn't hurt, either. As an early Instagram user, I rarely turned the camera on myself. I preferred sharing pictures of sunsets, crazy dance parties and bodega cats to showing off a new haircut or outfit. But over the last year or so, I've watched as all my peers slowly began turning their cameras inward on themselves. It's made my feed more interesting and entertaining. And I'd much rather see my friends' faces as they prepare food than a close-up photo of the finished meals instead. The rare occasion when I feel bold enough to post a full-face frontal, I see spikes in comments and feedback, the kind that pictures of a park or a concert photo rarely get.

In fact, I've even noticed that the occasional selfie appears to nudge some friends who I haven't seen in a while to get in touch via e-mail or text to suggest that we meet for a drink to catch up, as if seeing my face on a screen reminds them it's been awhile since they've seen it in real life.

Dr. Pamela Rutledge, director of the nonprofit Media Psychology Research Center, says that's how the human brain works.

"We are hard-wired to respond to faces," she said. "It's unconscious. Our brains process visuals faster, and we are more engaged when we see faces. If you're looking at a whole page of photos, the ones you will notice are the close-ups and selfies."

As for the well-worn assertion that selfies foster vanity and somehow court stalkers, "There are some people who put themselves at a certain amount of risk by exposing too much," Dr. Rutledge said. "But that's not about the selfie. That's about someone who is not making good choices."

Rather than dismissing the trend as a side effect of digital culture or a sad form of exhibitionism, maybe we're better off seeing selfies for what they are at their best—a kind of visual diary, a way to mark our short existence and hold it up to others as proof that we were here. The rest, of course, is open to interpretation.

JENNA WORTHAM is a technology writer for the *New York Times*. She specializes in stories that focus on the way people use technology, on start-ups, and digital culture. Prior to writing for the *Times*, she was a writer with *Wired* magazine.

EXPLORING THE ISSUE

Is There Any Harm In Taking Selfies?

Critical Thinking and Reflection

1. Consider whether selfies are more culturally important than just snapping a picture for fun.
2. Think about the way celebrities have used selfies for self-promotion, and measure our own behavior against theirs.
3. Reflect on the digital trail we leave by posting selfies and personal information online.
4. Think of whether selfies are a reflection of self-indulgence that may actually reflect a person's attitudes toward others.

Is There Common Ground?

Both authors represented in this issue discuss the rise of the visual image and the role selfies play in the long history of self-portraiture. They differ, though, on the range of cultural readings that selfies sometimes prompt. Undoubtedly, selfies are a part of a culture that is obsessed with taking and sharing pictures, and the excellent cameras that come with today's cell phones and file sharing apps and social networks help spread those images.

We might question whether selfies are just popular forms of expression that will die out over time, or whether they really do constitute a new art form. Perhaps someday there will be great collections of selfies exhibited in museums, or collected in books and journals. If that happens, we can be sure that cultural critics will continue to examine selfies and what they say about the people who take them and share them.

Additional Resources

Jack Linshi, "Men Who Share Selfies Online Show More Signs of Psychopathy, Study Says," *Time*

Magazine, January 11, 2015. This report addresses the Ohio University study that reports on men's use of selfies.

Kate Losse, "The Return of the Selfie," *The New Yorker*, May 31, 2013. Taking the position that the selfie is becoming a cultural reference point, Losse discusses what selfies say about a person's self-image.

Gwendolyn Seidman, Ph.D. "Are Selfies a Sign of Narcissism and Psycopathy?" *Psychology Today* (January 15, 2015). In this short article, Seidman examines some of the more common assumptions supporting academic research in the effects of selfies.

P. Sorakowski, A Sorokawska, A. Oleszkiewics, T. Frackowiak, A. Huk, and K. Pisanski, "Selfie Posting Behaviors are Associated with Narcissism Among Men," *Personal Individual Differences*, 85 (2015), pp. 123–127. This article focuses on men and narcissism in particular, and discusses how male behavior may be influenced by issues of masculinity.

Internet References . . .

BBC News, Self-portraits and Social Media: The Rise of the 'Selfie'

www.bbc.com/news/magazine-22511650

Heriot Watt University, "Sharing Photographs on Facebook Could Damage Relationships, New Study Shows" (October 26, 2015)

www.hw.ac.uk/news/sharing-photographs-facebook -could-damage-13069.htm

Jerry Saltz (2014) "At Arm's Length: The History of the Selfie," *Vulture.com*

www.vulture.com/2014/01/history-of-the-selfie.html#

Selfiecity (a comparison of selfies taken in five major cities)

http://selfiecity.net/

The Selfies Research Network is an international group of academics studying the social and cultural implications of the selfie.

www.selfiesresearchers.com

Unit 3

UNIT

News and Politics

*A*t one time, one of the most hotly debated questions about media was whether media content demonstrated a liberal or conservative bias. In recent years, this question has shifted to questions of whether some media institutions provide "fake news" or not. How do we make distinctions about what is truth, and what is misleading, or slanted news? Is fake news as big of a problem as President Trump seems to think it is? In recent years we've also been faced with questions about whether media institutions actually contribute to violence rather than simply reporting what occurs. And, as newer technologies and distribution forms target different audiences, is there any way to successfully monitor what is happening in our environment? Do some media applications, like Twitter, actually present us with serious news? Although all of these issues have been debated in some form for years – and, in some cases, decades – we approach this set of questions with a contemporary lens that focuses on the meaning of these issues as the nature of what is political expands.

Selected, Edited, and with Issue Framing Material by:
Alison Alexander, *University of Georgia*
and
Jarice Hanson, *University of Massachusetts—Amherst*

ISSUE

Is Networking Through Social Media Contributing to the Growth of Fake News?

YES: Farhad Manjoo, from "Can Facebook Fix Its Own Worst Bug?" *The New York Times Magazine* (2017)

NO: David Uberti, from "The Real History of Fake News," *Columbia Journalism Review* (2016)

Learning Outcomes

After reading this issue, you will be able to:

- Think critically about the history, impact, and importance of what constitutes "fake" news.
- Be more thoughtful about the range of topics that are often subsumed under the name "fake" news.
- Have a better concept of how social media spreads information.
- Consider the role of ethics in the creation and dissemination of important (and unimportant) topics in media.
- Understand the concepts of filter bubbles, echo chambers, and clickbait.

ISSUE SUMMARY

YES: Technology writer Farhad Manjoo has interviewed Mark Zuckerberg, founder of Facebook, on many occasions. In this article, he discusses how Zuckerberg and the Facebook staff reacted to what was being written and said about Facebook's role in disseminating "fake news" prior to, and during the 2016 Presidential election. The article discusses whether Facebook's attempts to create connections among users have actually contributed to the spread of lies, misinformation, and fake news, and whether social media has a responsibility to monitor information that can mislead the public, particularly through its News Feed feature.

NO: Providing an overview of news gathering and dissemination processes for the last hundred years, David Uberti highlights some of the historical precedents that stirred up controversy about whether the news media spreads misinformation or not. He shares the perspective that over time, different forms of media have participated in misleading the public. Even though he cites PolitiFact as the source of calling fake news in 2016 the "Lie of the Year," he is critical of how mainstream media have contributed to the public's distrust of all forms of news media.

Since the lead up to the Presidential election of 2016 and since that time, Donald Trump and many others have used the term "fake news" to mean several different things. Trump's predilection toward calling any news organization that was critical of him or unflattering to him "fake news" was only one of the uses of the term, but now we know that "fake news" actually encompasses a broad range of information that includes misinformation (intentionally slanted to influence consumers); disinformation (intentionally misleading information); and bogus information (untrue information, like lies).

Mainstream media outlets have fought battles for years about whether their news and information is thoroughly researched, verified, or whether, in the rush to get something printed, or on the air, factually checked.

Additionally, there has been for a very long time, the claim that different news media sources demonstrate a bias. There is a long history of bias in the news, originally emanating from the influence of the publisher in newspapers and magazines, like the examples in the Uberti article, to the beliefs and principles of a specific news organization. Talk radio, which became even more focused on political information after the FCC abolished the Fairness Doctrine in 1987, became a ready source for local and national news and information that featured personality-driven content that sometimes blurred the distinction between news, information, and the opinions of the radio personality.

When Fox Broadcasting began their television network in 1986, there were only three other television networks producing national news: ABC, CBS, and NBC. When the "big three" dominated televised news, there were subtle differences, but those networks took great pride in trying to verify information and remain as objective as possible. Fox, however, never even tried to be objective, though they used the slogan "fair and balanced" as a way to suggest their content was accurate—the television news division followed the format of opinion radio and strongly emphasized the personal political viewpoints of their on-air hosts, which were undoubtedly and unabashedly conservative. The CEO of Fox television was Roger Ailes, who had been a political consultant for Republican candidates for governorships and presidencies, and at the time of his death in 2017, had just finished helping then candidate Donald Trump prepare for the 2016 Presidential Debates.

What really contributed to the growth and dissemination of really "fake news" however, was the number of online sites that were constructed to mislead or lie to the public with the hope of swaying the 2016 Presidential election. At the time of this writing, there is an investigation into the role of Russian hackers who may have influenced the outcome of the Presidential election by creating truly fake news sites online that could be picked up by social media, or sent from one person to their entire group of friends with one click. Many social media sites (including Facebook) have acknowledged that they accepted advertising during the run up to the election and since then from sites that have turned out to be the work of political interest groups, including Russian hackers. If the theories about Russian hackers are found to be true, the validity of the Presidential election could be in jeopardy. But whether hackers manipulated electronic voting machines, or focused attempts to discredit candidates (particularly Hilary Clinton), the reality of fake news has become a subject that warrants investigation and understanding.

One problem for online media is that it is now easy enough for anyone (or anyone with a political agenda) to create a site that looks as professional as real professional sites are. Software can be used to create pop-ups, or a user's attention can be attracted to clickbait (which routes them to other sites that are often bogus or intended to engage them in different content for a longer period of time). Through social media, particularly Facebook, users can easily send this type of content to friends, therefore perpetuating the misinformation or "fake" information but giving it the imprimatur of coming from someone who might be thought to be an opinion leader. The more a person sees a message, the more likely they may be to think it's accurate, even if it bears no resemblance to truth.

Facebook has had to deal with the way its News Feed sends messages through a person's social network, and the organization has made some weak attempts to label unsubstantiated stories, but as Manjoo writes in his article, Facebook was originally intended to connect people. Now that it produces a News Feed, the responsibility for accuracy must be addressed somehow, or, Facebook must take responsibility for the inaccuracies that it perpetuates online.

There are many problems associated with sending any type of information over social media, and that stems from the fact that social networks were originally created for a different purpose than to act as sources of verified, factual news. And, as we know, most people tend to seek out opinions and information that have the same values they already believe, therefore, creating an environment of news and information that may resemble gossip and innuendo. There are sites to which a person can turn for verification about information that they believe, might be fake. Snopes (http://www.snopes.com/), Politico (http://www.politico.com/), Factcheck (http://www.factcheck.org/), and PolitiFact (http://www.politifact.com/) are all sites that have excellent reputations for fact checking and explaining the truth behind many of the stories in media.

As the two selections in this issue attest, "fake news" can mean a number of things, but the idea of misleading, or biased news that is intended to influence someone's beliefs has a long history in the use of media for news and information. The bigger question is, "what can we do to stop the spread of fake news, and educate consumers about how to identify the truth?" The push for more media literacy is one small approach toward trying to help people understand the way media operate, but now, a new technological literacy may need to be developed too, so that people maintain a healthy skepticism about what they see and hear, and how their thought processes are influenced by that type of information transmitted over social networks. Many of the same principles are the same, but the details in exchanging online information (especially over social media forms, or through personal networks) makes verifying information much more difficult.

One of the other areas of great contention these days is exactly who believes fake news and why do they do so? There have been so many studies of the spread of news since the Presidential election, we seem to be learning more about the topic every day. In the additional resources and the Internet references, we have identified a number of studies that provide some of the answers for these questions. Undoubtedly, the spread of news and information (verified or untrue) is something that will continue to be with us for many years. Books will be written about the 2016 election and the public's attention will remain focused on how media communicate to us, and with what impact. For scholars of media, news consumption, and news production, these issues will remain absolutely critical in the future.

YES ⤶

Farhad Manjoo

Can Facebook Fix Its Own Worst Bug?

In early January [2017], I went to see Mark Zuckerberg at MPK20, a concrete-and-steel building on the campus of Facebook's headquarters, which sits across a desolate highway from the marshy salt flats of Menlo Park, Calif. The Frank Gehry-designed building has a pristine nine-acre rooftop garden, yet much of the interior—a meandering open-plan hallway—appears unfinished. There are exposed air ducts and I-beams scribbled with contractors' marks. Many of the internal walls are unpainted plywood. The space looks less like the headquarters of one of the world's wealthiest companies and more like a Chipotle with standing desks. It's an aesthetic meant to reflect—and perhaps also inspire employee allegiance to—one of Facebook's founding ideologies: that things are never quite finished, that nothing is permanent, that you should always look for a chance to take an ax to your surroundings.

The mood in overwhelmingly liberal Silicon Valley at the time, days before Donald Trump's inauguration, was grim. But Zuckerberg, who had recently returned from his 700-acre estate on the Hawaiian island of Kauai, is preternaturally unable to look anything other than excited about the future. "Hey, guys!" he beamed, greeting me and Mike Isaac, a Times colleague who covers Facebook. Zuckerberg wore a short-sleeve gray T-shirt, jeans and sneakers, which is his Steve Jobsian daily uniform: Indoor Zuck.

Zuckerberg used to be a nervous speaker, but he has become much less so. He speaks quickly but often unloads full paragraphs of thought, and sometimes his arguments are so polished that they sound rehearsed, which happened often that morning. "2016 was an interesting year for us," he said as the three of us, plus a P.R. executive, sat around a couple of couches in the glass-walled conference room where he conducts many of his meetings. (There are many perks to working at Facebook, but no one, not even Zuckerberg, has a private office.) It was an understatement and a nod to the obvious: Facebook, once a mere app on your phone, had become a global political and cultural force, and the full implications of that transformation had begun to come into view last year. "If you

look at the history of Facebook, when we started off, there really wasn't news as part of it," Zuckerberg went on. But as Facebook grew and became a bigger part of how people learn about the world, the company had been slow to adjust to its new place in people's lives. The events of 2016, he said, "set off a number of conversations that we're still in the middle of."

Nearly two billion people use Facebook every month, about 1.2 billion of them daily. The company, which Zuckerberg co-founded in his Harvard dorm room 13 years ago, has become the largest and most influential entity in the news business, commanding an audience greater than that of any American or European television news network, any newspaper or magazine in the Western world and any online news outlet. It is also the most powerful mobilizing force in politics, and it is fast replacing television as the most consequential entertainment medium. Just five years after its initial public offering, Facebook is one of the 10 highest market-capitalized public companies in the world.

As recently as a year ago, Zuckerberg might have proudly rattled off these facts as a testament to Facebook's power. But over the course of 2016, Facebook's gargantuan influence became its biggest liability. During the U.S. election, propagandists—some working for money, others for potentially state-sponsored lulz—used the service to turn fake stories into viral sensations, like the one about Pope Francis' endorsing Trump (he hadn't). And fake news was only part of a larger conundrum. With its huge reach, Facebook has begun to act as the great disseminator of the larger cloud of misinformation and half-truths swirling about the rest of media. It sucks up lies from cable news and Twitter, then precisely targets each lie to the partisan bubble most receptive to it.

After studying how people shared 1.25 million stories during the campaign, a team of researchers at M.I.T. and Harvard implicated Facebook and Twitter in the larger failure of media in 2016. The researchers found that social media created a right-wing echo chamber: a "media network anchored around Breitbart developed as a distinct and insulated media system, using social media as a backbone to transmit a hyperpartisan perspective to the world." The findings partially echoed a long-held worry about social news: that people would use sites like Facebook to cocoon themselves into self-reinforcing bubbles of confirmatory ideas, to the detriment of civility and a shared factual basis from which to make collective, democratic decisions. A week and a half after the election, President Obama bemoaned "an age where there's so much active misinformation and it's packaged very well and it looks the same when you see it on a Facebook page or you turn on your television."

After the election, Zuckerberg offered a few pat defenses of Facebook's role. "I'm actually quite proud of the impact that we were able to have on civic discourse over all," he said when we spoke in January. Misinformation on Facebook was not as big a problem as some believed it was, but Facebook nevertheless would do more to battle it, he pledged. Echo chambers were a concern, but if the source was people's own confirmation bias, was it really Facebook's problem to solve?

It was hard to tell how seriously Zuckerberg took the criticisms of his service and its increasingly paradoxical role in the world. He had spent much of his life building a magnificent machine to bring people together. By the most literal measures, he'd succeeded spectacularly, but what had that connection wrought? Across the globe, Facebook now seems to benefit actors who want to undermine the global vision at its foundation. Supporters of Trump and the European right-wing nationalists who aim to turn their nations inward and dissolve alliances, trolls sowing cross-border paranoia, even ISIS with its skillful social-media recruiting and propagandizing—all of them have sought in their own ways to split the Zuckerbergian world apart. And they are using his own machine to do it.

In Silicon Valley, current events tend to fade into the background. The Sept. 11 attacks, the Iraq war, the financial crisis and every recent presidential election occurred, for the tech industry, on some parallel but distant timeline divorced from the everyday business of digitizing the world. Then Donald Trump won. In the 17 years I've spent covering Silicon Valley, I've never seen anything shake the place like his victory. In the span of a few months, the Valley has been transformed from a politically disengaged company town into a center of anti-Trump resistance and fear. A week after the election, one start-up founder sent me a private message on Twitter: "I think it's worse than I thought," he wrote. "Originally I thought 18 months. I've cut that in half." Until what? "Apocalypse. End of the world."

Trump's campaign rhetoric felt particularly personal for an industry with a proud reliance upon immigrants.

Stephen K. Bannon, Trump's campaign chief executive and now chief White House strategist, once suggested that there were too many South Asian chief executives in tech. More than 15 percent of Facebook's employees are in the United States on H-1B visas, a program that Trump has pledged to revamp. But the outcome also revealed the depth of the Valley's disconnection with much of the rest of the country. "I saw an election that was just different from the way I think," says Joshua Reeves, a Bay Area native who is a co-founder of Gusto, a human-resources software start-up. "I have this engineering brain that wants to go to this analytical, rational, nonemotional way of looking at things, and it was clear in this election that we're trending in a different direction, toward spirited populism."

Underneath it all was a nagging feeling of complicity. Trump had benefited from a media environment that is now shaped by Facebook—and, more to the point, shaped by a single Facebook feature, the same one to which the company owes its remarkable ascent to social-media hegemony: the computationally determined list of updates you see every time you open the app. The list has a formal name, News Feed. But most users are apt to think of it as Facebook itself.

If it's an exaggeration to say that News Feed has become the most influential source of information in the history of civilization, it is only slightly so. Facebook created News Feed in 2006 to solve a problem: In the social media age, people suddenly had too many friends to keep up with. At the time, Facebook was just a collection of profiles, lacking any kind of central organization. To figure out what any of your connections were up to, you had to visit each of their profiles to see if anything had changed. News Feed fixed that. Every time you open Facebook, it hunts through the network, collecting every post from every connection—information that, for most Facebook users, would be too overwhelming to process themselves. Then it weighs the merits of each post before presenting you with a feed sorted in order of importance: a hyperpersonalized front page designed just for you.

Scholars and critics have been warning of the solipsistic irresistibility of algorithmic news at least since 2001, when the constitutional-law professor Cass R. Sunstein warned, in his book "Republic.com," of the urgent risks posed to democracy "by any situation in which thousands or perhaps millions or even tens of millions of people are mainly listening to louder echoes of their own voices." (In 2008, I piled on with my own book, "True Enough: Learning to Live in a Post-Fact Society.") In 2011, the digital activist and entrepreneur Eli Pariser, looking at similar issues, gave this phenomenon a memorable name in the title of his own book: "The Filter Bubble."

Facebook says its own researchers have been studying the filter bubble since 2010. In 2015, they published an in-house study, which was criticized by independent researchers, concluding that Facebook's effect on the diversity of people's information diet was minimal. News Feed's personalization algorithm did filter out some opposing views in your feed, the study claimed, but the bigger effect was users' own choices. When News Feed did show people views contrary to their own, they tended not to click on the stories. For Zuckerberg, the finding let Facebook off the hook. "It's a good-sounding theory, and I can get why people repeat it, but it's not true," he said on a call with analysts last summer.

Employees got the same message. "When Facebook cares about something, they spin up teams to address it, and Zuck will come out and talk about it all the time," one former executive told me. "I have never heard of anything close to that on the filter bubble. I never sensed that this was a problem he wanted us to tackle. It was always positioned as an interesting intellectual question but not something that we're going to go focus on."

Then, last year, Facebook's domination of the news became a story itself. In May, Gizmodo reported that some editors who had worked on Facebook's Trending Topics section had been suppressing conservative points of view. To smooth things over, Zuckerberg convened a meeting of conservative media figures and eventually significantly reduced the role of human editors. Then in September, Facebook deleted a post by a Norwegian writer that included the photojournalist Nick Ut's iconic photo of a naked 9-year-old girl, Phan Thi Kim Phuc, running in terror after a napalm attack during the Vietnam War, on the grounds that it ran afoul of Facebook's prohibition of child nudity.

Facebook, under criticism, reinstated the picture, but the photo incident stuck with Zuckerberg. He would bring it up unbidden to staff members and to reporters. It highlighted, for him, the difficulty of building a policy framework for what Facebook was trying to do. Zuckerberg wanted to become a global news distributor that is run by machines, rather than by humans who would try to look at every last bit of content and exercise considered judgment. "It's something I think we're still figuring out," he told me in January. "There's a lot more to do here than what we've done. And I think we're starting to realize this now as well."

It struck me as an unsatisfying answer, and it later became apparent that Zuckerberg seemed to feel the same way. On a Sunday morning about a month after the first meeting, I got a call from a Facebook spokesman. Zuckerberg wanted to chat again. Could Mike and I come back on Monday afternoon?

We met again in the same conference room. Same Zuck outfit, same P.R. executive. But the Zuckerberg who greeted us seemed markedly different. He was less certain in his pronouncements than he had been the month before, more expansive and questioning. Earlier that day, Zuckerberg's staff had sent me a draft of a 5,700-word manifesto that, I was told, he spent weeks writing. The document, "Building Global Community," argued that until now, Facebook's corporate goal had merely been to connect people. But that was just Step 1. According to the manifesto, Facebook's "next focus will be developing the social infrastructure for community—for supporting us, for keeping us safe, for informing us, for civic engagement, and for inclusion of all." If it was a nebulous crusade, it was also vast in its ambition.

The last manifesto that Zuckerberg wrote was in 2012, as part of Facebook's application to sell its stock to the public. It explained Facebook's philosophy—what he called "the hacker way"—and sketched an unorthodox path for the soon-to-be-public company. "Facebook was not originally created to be a company," he wrote. "It was built to accomplish a social mission: to make the world more open and connected."

What's striking about that 2012 letter, read through the prism of 2017, is its certainty that a more "open and connected" world is by definition a better one. "When I started Facebook, the idea of connecting the world was not controversial," Zuckerberg said now. "The default assumption was that the world was incrementally just moving in that direction. So I thought we can connect some people and do our part in helping move in that direction." But now, he said, whether it was wise to connect the world was "actually a real question."

Zuckerberg's new manifesto never quite accepts blame for any of the global ills that have been laid at Facebook's feet. Yet by the standards of a company release, it is remarkable for the way it concedes that the company's chief goal—wiring the globe—is controversial. "There are questions about whether we can make a global community that works for everyone," Zuckerberg writes, "and whether the path ahead is to connect more or reverse course." He also confesses misgivings about Facebook's role in the news. "Giving everyone a voice has historically been a very positive force for public discourse because it increases the diversity of ideas shared," he writes. "But the past year has also shown it may fragment our shared sense of reality."

At the time of our second interview, the manifesto was still only a draft, and I was surprised by how unsure Zuckerberg seemed about it in person. He had almost as many questions for us—about whether we understood what he was trying to say, how we thought it would land in the media—as we had for him. When I suggested that it might be perceived as an attack on Trump, he looked dismayed. He noted several times that he had been noodling over these ideas since long before November. A few weeks earlier, there was media speculation, fueled by a postelection tour of America by Zuckerberg and his wife, that he was laying the groundwork to run against Trump in 2020, and in this meeting he took pains to shoot down the rumors. When I asked if he had chatted with Obama about the former president's critique of Facebook, Zuckerberg paused for several seconds, nearly to the point of awkwardness, before answering that he had.

Facebook's spokespeople later called to stress that Obama was only one of many people to whom he had spoken. In other words: Don't read this as a partisan anti-Trump manifesto. But if the company pursues the admittedly airy aims outlined in "Building Global Community," the changes will echo across media and politics, and some are bound to be considered partisan. The risks are especially clear for changes aimed at adding layers of journalistic ethics across News Feed, which could transform the public's perception of Facebook, not to mention shake the foundations of its business.

The Facebook app, and consequently News Feed, is run by one of Zuckerberg's most influential lieutenants, a 34-year-old named Chris Cox, the company's chief product officer. Ten years ago, Cox dropped out of a graduate program in computer science at Stanford to join Facebook. One of his first assignments was on the team that created News Feed. Since then, he has become an envoy to the media industry. Don Graham, the longtime publisher of *The Washington Post* who was for years a member of Facebook's board, told me that he felt Cox, among Facebook staff, "was at the 99.9th percentile of interest in news. He thought it was important to society, and he wanted Facebook to get it right."

For the typical user, Cox explained when I met him on a morning in October at MPK20, News Feed is computing the relative merits of about 2,000 potential posts in your network every time you open the app. In sorting these posts, Facebook does not optimize for any single metric: not clicks or reading time or likes. Instead, he said, "what you really want to get to is whether somebody, at the end of the day, would say, 'Hey, my experience today was meaningful.'" Personalizing News Feed, in other words, is a very big "math problem," incorporating countless metrics in extraordinarily complicated ways. Zuckerberg calls it "a modern A.I. problem."

Last summer, I sat in on two meetings in another glass-walled MPK20 conference room, in which News Feed's engineers, designers, user-research experts and managers debated several small alterations to how News Feed displays certain kinds of posts. The conversations were far from exciting—people in jeans on couches looking at PowerPoints, talking quietly about numbers—and yet I found them mesmerizing, a demonstration of the profound cultural differences between how news companies like The Times work and how Facebook does. The first surprise was how slowly things move, contrary to the freewheeling culture of "the hacker way." In one meeting, the team spent several minutes discussing the merits of bold text in a certain News Feed design. One blessing of making social software is that you can gauge any potential change to your product by seeing how your users react to it. That is also the curse: At Facebook, virtually every change to the app, no matter how small or obviously beneficial, is thoroughly tested on different segments of the audience before it's rolled out to everyone.

The people who work on News Feed aren't making decisions that turn on fuzzy human ideas like ethics, judgment, intuition or seniority. They are concerned only with quantifiable outcomes about people's actions on the site. That data, at Facebook, is the only real truth. And it is a particular kind of truth: The News Feed team's ultimate mission is to figure out what users want—what they find "meaningful," to use Cox and Zuckerberg's preferred term—and to give them more of that.

This ideal runs so deep that the people who make News Feed often have to put aside their own notions of what's best. "One of the things we've all learned over the years is that our intuition can be wrong a fair amount of the time," John Hegeman, the vice president of product management and a News Feed team member, told me. "There are things you don't expect will happen. And we learn a lot from that process: Why didn't that happen, and what might that mean?" But it is precisely this ideal that conflicts with attempts to wrangle the feed in the way press critics have called for. The whole purpose of editorial guidelines and ethics is often to suppress individual instincts in favor of some larger social goal. Facebook finds it very hard to suppress anything that its users' actions say they want. In some cases, it has been easier for the company to seek out evidence that, in fact, users don't want these things at all.

Facebook's two-year-long battle against "clickbait" is a telling example. Early this decade, the internet's headline writers discovered the power of stories that trick you into clicking on them, like those that teasingly withhold information from their headlines: "Dustin Hoffman Breaks Down Crying Explaining Something That Every Woman Sadly Already Experienced." By the fall of 2013, clickbait had overrun News Feed. Upworthy, a progressive activism site co-founded by Pariser, the author of "The Filter Bubble," that relied heavily on teasing headlines, was attracting 90 million readers a month to its feel-good viral posts.

If a human editor ran News Feed, she would look at the clickbait scourge and make simple, intuitive fixes: Turn down the Upworthy knob. But Facebook approaches the feed as an engineering project rather than an editorial one. When it makes alterations in the code that powers News Feed, it's often only because it has found some clear signal in its data that users are demanding the change. In this sense, clickbait was a riddle. In surveys, people kept telling Facebook that they hated teasing headlines. But if that was true, why were they clicking on them? Was there something Facebook's algorithm was missing, some signal that would show that despite the clicks, clickbait was really sickening users?

To answer these questions, Cox and his team hired survey panels of more than a thousand paid "professional raters" around the world who answer questions about how well News Feed is working. Starting in 2013, Facebook began adding first dozens and then hundreds and then thousands of data points that were meant to teach the artificial-intelligence system that runs News Feed how people were reacting to their feeds. Facebook noticed that people would sometimes click open a clickbaity story but spend very little time on it. In other cases, lots of people would click on a story but few would share or Like it. Headlines on stories that people seemed to reject often contained a set of signature phrases ("you'll never believe," "this one trick," etc.) or they came from a set of repeat-offender publishers.

The more such signals Facebook incorporated into the feed, the more clickbait began to drop out of the feed. Since its 2013 peak, Upworthy's traffic has declined; it now averages 17.5 million visitors a month. The site has since disavowed clickbait. "We sort of unleashed a monster," Peter Koechley, Upworthy's co-founder, told a conference in 2015. "Sorry for that."

Cox suggested that it was not exactly correct to say that Facebook, as a company, decided to fight clickbait. What actually happened was that Facebook found better ways to listen to users, who were themselves rejecting clickbait. "That comes out of good-quality panels and measurement systems, rather than an individual decision saying, 'Hey, I really want us to care about clickbait,'" he says.

This approach—looking for signs of user dissatisfaction—could curb stories that constitute the most egregious examples of misinformation. Adam Mosseri, Facebook's vice president in charge of News Feed, says that Facebook has begun testing an algorithm change that would look at whether people share an article after reading it. If few of the people who click on a story decide to share it, that might suggest people feel misled by it and it would get lower billing in the feed.

But the solution to the broader misinformation dilemma—the pervasive climate of rumor, propaganda and conspiracy theories that Facebook has inadvertently incubated—may require something that Facebook has never done: ignoring the likes and dislikes of its users. Facebook believes the pope-endorses-Trump type of made-up news stories are only a tiny minority of pieces that appear in News Feed; they account for a fraction of 1 percent of the posts, according to Mosseri. The question the company faces now is whether the misinformation problem resembles clickbait at all, and whether its solutions will align as neatly with Facebook's worldview. Facebook's entire project, when it comes to news, rests on the assumption that people's individual preferences ultimately coincide with the public good, and that if it doesn't appear that way at first, you're not delving deeply enough into the data. By contrast, decades of social-science research shows that most of us simply prefer stuff that feels true to our worldview even if it isn't true at all and that the mining of all those preference signals is likely to lead us deeper into bubbles rather than out of them.

After the election, Margaret Sullivan, *The Washington Post* columnist and a former public editor of The Times, called on Facebook to hire an executive editor who would monitor News Feed with an eye to fact-checking, balance and editorial integrity. Jonah Peretti, the founder of Buzz-Feed, told me that he wanted Facebook to use its data to create a kind of reputational score for online news, as well as explore ways of strengthening reporting through monetary partnerships.

"At some point, if they really want to address this, they have to say, 'This is good information' and 'This is bad information,'" says Emily Bell, the director for the Tow Center for Digital Journalism at Columbia Journalism School. "They have to say, 'These are the kinds of information sources that we want to privilege, and these others are not going to be banned from the platform, but they are not going to thrive.' In other words, they have to create a hierarchy, and they're going to have to decide how they're going to transfer wealth into the publishing market."

There aren't many technical reasons Facebook could not implement such plans. The hurdles are institutional and philosophical, and ultimately financial too. Late last year, Facebook outlined a modest effort to curb misinformation. News Feed would now carry warning labels: If a friend shares a viral story that has been flagged and shot down by one of Facebook's fact-checking partners (including Snopes and PolitiFact), you'll be cautioned that the piece has been "disputed." But even that slight change has been met with fury on the right, with Breitbart and The Daily Caller fuming that Facebook had teamed up with liberal hacks motivated by partisanship. If Facebook were to take more significant action, like hiring human editors, creating a reputational system or paying journalists, the company would instantly become something it has long resisted: a media company rather than a neutral tech platform.

In many ways, the worry over how Facebook changes the news is really a manifestation of a grander problem with News Feed, which is simply dominance itself. News Feed's aggressive personalization wouldn't be much of an issue if it weren't crowding out every other source. "To some degree I feel like the Pottery Barn Rule applies," says Pariser, the Upworthy chief executive. "They play a critical role in our information circulatory system, and so—lucky them—all of the problems therein are significantly on their shoulders."

During our first meeting in January, I posed this question to Zuckerberg: "When you see various problems in the media, do you say to yourself, 'I run Facebook, I can solve that?'"

"Um," he started, and then paused, weighing his words as carefully as American presidents once did. "Not usually." He argued that some of Facebook's critics' proposed fixes for news on the service, such as hiring editors, were impractical due to Facebook's scale and global diversity. Personalization, he said, remained a central tenet. "It really gets back to, like, what do people want at a deep level," he said. "There's this oversimplified narrative that a company can get very successful by just scratching a very superficial itch, and I don't really think that's right over the long term."

Yet by our second meeting, Zuckerberg's position seemed to have evolved. Facebook had by then announced plans for the Facebook Journalism Project, in which the company would collaborate with news companies on new products. Facebook also created a project to promote "news literacy" among its users, and it hired the former CNN news anchor Campbell Brown to manage the partnership between it and news companies. Zuckerberg's tone toward critics of Facebook's approach to news had also grown far more conciliatory. "I think it's really important to get to the core of the actual problem," he said. "I also really think that the core social thing that needs to happen is that a common understanding needs to exist. And misinformation I view as one of the things that can possibly erode common understanding. But sensationalism

and polarization and other things, I actually think, are probably even stronger and more prolific effects. And we have to work on all these things. I think we need to listen to all the feedback on this."

Still, in both our conversation and his new manifesto, Zuckerberg remained preoccupied with the kind of problems that could be solved by the kind of hyperconnectivity he believed in, not the ones caused by it. "There's a social infrastructure that needs to get built for modern problems in order for humanity to get to the next level," he said. "Having more people oriented not just toward short-term things but toward building the long-term social infrastructure that needs to get built across all these things in order to enable people to come together is going to be a really important thing over the next decades." By way of example, he pointed to Safety Check, Facebook's system for letting people tell their friends that they've survived some kind of dangerous event, like a natural disaster or terrorist attack.

"We're getting to a point where the biggest opportunities I think in the world . . . problems like preventing pandemics from spreading or ending terrorism, all these things, they require a level of coordination and connection that I don't think can only be solved by the current systems that we have," Zuckerberg told me. What's needed, he argues, is some global superstructure to advance humanity.

This is not an especially controversial idea; Zuckerberg is arguing for a kind of digital-era version of the global institution-building that the Western world engaged in after World War II. But because he is a chief executive and not an elected president, there is something frightening about his project. He is positioning Facebook — and, considering that he commands absolute voting control of the company, he is positioning himself — as a critical enabler of the next generation of human society. A minor problem with his mission is that it drips with megalomania, albeit of a particularly sincere sort. With his wife, Priscilla Chan, Zuckerberg has pledged to give away nearly all of his wealth to a variety of charitable causes, including a long-term medical-research project to cure all disease. His desire to take on global social problems through digital connectivity, and specifically through Facebook, feels like part of the same impulse.

Yet Zuckerberg is often blasé about the messiness of the transition between the world we're in and the one he wants to create through software. Building new "social infrastructure" usually involves tearing older infrastructure down. If you manage the demolition poorly, you might undermine what comes next. In the case of the shattering media landscape, Zuckerberg seems finally to have at least noticed this problem and may yet come up with fixes for it. But in the meantime, Facebook rushes headlong into murky new areas, uncovering new dystopian possibilities at every turn.

A few months after I spoke with Zuckerberg, Facebook held its annual developer conference in San Jose, Calif. At last year's show, Zuckerberg introduced an expanded version of Facebook's live streaming service which had been promised to revolutionize how we communicate. In the year since, Live had generated iconic scenes of protest, but it was also used to broadcast a terrorist attack in Munich and at least one suicide. Hours before Zuckerberg's appearance at the conference, police announced that a Cleveland man who had killed a stranger and posted a video on Facebook had shot himself after a manhunt.

But as he took the stage in San Jose, Zuckerberg was ebullient. He started with a few dad jokes and threatened to read his long manifesto on stage. For a brief moment, there was a shift in tone: Statesman Zuck. "In all seriousness, this is an important time to work on building community," he said. He offered Facebook's condolences to the victim in Cleveland; the incident, he said, reminded Facebook that "we have a lot more to do."

Just as quickly, though, Zuckerberg then pivoted to Facebook's next marvel, a system for digitally augmenting your pictures and videos. The technical term for this is "augmented reality." The name bursts with dystopian possibilities — fake news on video rather than just text — but Zuckerberg never mentioned them. The statesman had left the stage; before us stood an engineer.

Farhad Manjoo is a journalist specializing in media, politics, and technology topics. He has written for the *New York Times*, *Wall Street Journal*, and *Slate*, and he is a contributing writer to National Public Radio. His most recent book is *True Enough: Learning to Live in a Post-Fact Society* (2008).

David Uberti

➡ **NO**

The Real History of Fake News

In an 1807 letter to John Norvell, a young go-getter who had asked how to best run a newspaper, Thomas Jefferson penned what today would make for a fiery Medium post condemning fake news.

"It is a melancholy truth, that a suppression of the press could not more completely [sic] deprive the nation of its benefits, than is done by its abandoned prostitution to falsehood," the sitting president wrote. "Nothing can now be believed which is seen in a newspaper. Truth itself becomes suspicious by being put into that polluted vehicle."

That vehicle grew into a commercial powerhouse in the 19th century and a self-reverential political institution, "the media," by the mid-20th. But the pollution has been described in increasingly dire terms in recent months. PolitiFact named fake news its 2016 "Lie of the Year," while chagrined Democrats have warned about its threat to an honest public debate. The pope compared consumption of fake news to eating feces. And many of the wise men and women of journalism have chimed in almost uniformly: Come to us for the real stuff.

"Whatever its other cultural and social merits, our digital ecosystem seems to have evolved into a near-perfect environment for fake news to thrive," New York Times CEO Mark Thompson said in a speech to the Detroit Economic Club on Monday.

A little bit of brake-tapping may be in order: It's worth remembering, in the middle of the great fake news panic of 2016, America's very long tradition of news-related hoaxes. A thumbnail history shows marked similarities to today's fakery in editorial motive or public gullibility, not to mention the blurred lines between deliberate and accidental flimflam. It also suggests that the recent fixation on fake news has more to do with macro-level trends than any new brand of faux content.

Macedonian teenagers who earn extra scratch by concocting conspiracies are indeed new entrants to the American information diet. Social networks allow smut to hurtle through the public imagination—and into pizza parlors—at breakneck speed. People at or near the top of the incoming administration have shared fake news casually. And it's appearing in news organizations' own programmatic ads.

But put aside the immediate election-related PTSD and the rampant self-loathing by journalists, which has led to cravings for a third-party, perhaps Russian-speaking, fall guy. The broader issue driving the paranoia is the tardy realization among mainstream media that they no longer hold the sole power to shape and drive the news agenda. Broadsides against fake news amount to a rearguard action from an industry fending off competitors who don't play by the same rules, or maybe don't even know they exist.

"The existence of an independent, powerful, widely respected news media establishment is an historical anomaly," Georgetown Professor Jonathan Ladd wrote in his 2011 book, Why Americans Hate the Media and How it Matters. "Prior to the twentieth century, such an institution had never existed in American history." Fake news is but one symptom of that shift back to historical norms, and recent hyperventilating mimics reactions from eras past.

Take Jefferson's generation. Our country's earliest political combat played out in the pages of competing partisan publications often subsidized by government printing contracts and typically unbothered by reporting as we know it. Innuendo and character assassination were standard, and it was difficult to discern content solely meant to deceive from political bomb-throwing that served deception as a side dish. Then, like now, the grey-beards grumbled about how the media actually inhibited the fact-based debate it was supposed to lead.

"I will add," Jefferson continued in 1807, "that the man who never looks into a newspaper is better informed than he who reads them; inasmuch as he who knows nothing is nearer to truth than he whose mind is filled with falsehoods & errors."

Decades later, when Alexis de Tocqueville penned his seminal political analysis, Democracy in America, he also assailed the day's content producers as men "with a scanty education and a vulgar turn of mind" who played on readers' passions. "What [citizens] seek in a newspaper is a knowledge of facts," de Tocqueville wrote, "and it is only by altering or distorting those facts that a journalist can contribute to the support of his own views." His concerns weren't for passive failures of journalism, but active manipulation of the truth for political ends.

While circulation in those days was relatively low—high publishing costs, low literacy rates—proliferation of multiple titles in each major city provided a menu of worldviews that's similar to today. The infant republic nevertheless managed to survive the fake news scourge of early 19th-century newspapermen. "The large number of news outlets, the heterogeneity of the coverage, the low public esteem toward the press, and the obvious partisan leanings of publishers limited the power of the press to be influential," political scientist Darrell M. West wrote in his 2001 book, The Rise and Fall of the Media Establishment.

With the growth of the penny press in the 1830s, some newspapers adopted advertising-centric business models that required much larger audiences than highbrow partisan opinions would attract. So the motivation to mislead shifted slightly more toward commercially minded sensationalism, spurring some of the most memorable media fakes in American history.

In 1835, The New York Sun ran a six-part series, "Great Astronomical Discoveries Lately Made," which detailed the supposed discovery of life on the Moon. The hoax landed in part because the Sun's circulation was huge by standards of the day, and the too-good-to-be-true story supposedly enticed many new readers to fork over their pennies as well.

Edgar Allan Poe, who weeks before had published his own moon hoax in the Southern Literary Messenger, quickly criticized the Sun story's unbelievability—and the public's gullibility. "Not one person in 10 discredited it," Poe recounted years later. He went on to chastise the Sun's fake news story for what he saw as low production value:

> Immediately upon completion of the 'Moon story' . . . I wrote an examination of its claims to credit, showing distinctly its fictitious character, but was astonished at finding that I could obtain few listeners, so really eager were all to be deceived, so magical were the charms of a style that served as a vehicle of an exceedingly clumsy invention. . . . Indeed, however rich the imagination displayed in this fiction, it wanted much of the force that might have been given to it by a more scrupulous attention to analogy and fact.

Many other newspapers were skeptical of the Sun's moon story. But public backlash was muted in part because of the lack of widely accepted standards for the content appearing in readers' news feeds, not unlike today. Objective journalism had yet to settle in, and there were no clear dividing lines between reporting, opinions, and nonsense. The public's credulity—potentially embellished by Poe and other contemporaneous accounts—became part of the legend, particularly given elites' apprehension of Jacksonian populism.

These historic purveyors of fake news were by no means obscure publications from the 19th-century equivalent of the digital gutter. In 1874, the widely read New York Herald published a more than 10,000-word account of how animals had broken out of the Central Park Zoo, rampaged through Manhattan, and killed dozens. The Herald reported that many of the escaped animals were still at large as of press time, and the city's mayor had installed a strict curfew until they could be corralled. A disclaimer, tucked away at the bottom of the story, admitted that "the entire story given above is a pure fabrication. Not one word of it is true."

Many readers must have missed it. The hoax quickly spread through real-life social networks, as historian Hampton Sides described in his 2014 book, In the Kingdom of Ice: The Grand and Terrible Polar Voyage of the USS Jeannette:

> Alarmed citizens made for the city's piers in hopes of escaping by small boat or ferry. Many thousands of people, heeding the mayor's 'proclamation,' stayed inside all day, awaiting word that the crisis had passed. Still others loaded their rifles and marched into the park to hunt for rogue animals.

Even as the late-19th and early-20th centuries saw the early stages of the shift toward a more professionalized media, corruption of the information that reached readers remained common. In his 1897 book critiquing American news coverage of the Cuban War of Independence, Facts and Fakes about Cuba, George Bronson Rea outlined the stages of embellishment between minor news events outside of Havana to seemingly fictionalized front-page stories in New York. Cuban sources wanted to turn public opinion against Spain, while American correspondents were eager to sell newspapers.

"But the truth is a hard thing to suppress," Rea wrote, "and will sooner or later come to light to act as a boomerang on the perpetrators of such outrageous 'fakes,' whose only aim is to draw this country into a war with Spain to attain their own selfish ends."

There are fewer glaring examples of fake news stretching toward the mid-20th century, as journalistic norms—as we conceive of them today—began to emerge. Commercial monopolies, coupled with lack of political partisanship, gave news organizations daylight to professionalize and police themselves. But that's not to say this golden era was free from myths.

Indeed, many uncorrected stories concern the news media itself, which could provide clues as to why today's notion of fake news seems to have so much cultural currency. As American University Professor W. Joseph Campbell debunks in his book, Getting It Wrong: Ten of the Greatest Misreported Stories in American Journalism, a remark by Walter Cronkite wasn't actually the first domino to fall en route to ending the Vietnam War. *The Washington Post* didn't really bring down Nixon. (Media coverage and public opinion toward the war had already gone south; Nixon was felled by subpoena-wielding authorities and a wide array of other constitutional processes.)

"They're neat and tidy, easy to remember, fun to tell, and media centric," Campbell says in an interview. "They serve to elevate media actors. There is an aspirational component to these myths that help keep them alive."

The opposite force could be at play in today's fake news debate. Public trust of the media has been in decline for decades, though the situation now feels particularly cataclysmic with the atomization of media consumption, partisan criticism from all corners, and the ascension of Donald Trump to the White House. Just as Watergate gave the media a bright story to tell about itself, fake news provides a catchall symbol–and a scapegoat–for journalists grappling with their diminished institutional power.

It's telling that the most compelling reporting on fake news has focused on distribution networks—what's new—even if those stories have yet to prove they've exacerbated the problem en masse. In the meantime, let's retire the dreaded moniker in favor of more precise choices: misinformation, deception, lies. Just as the media has employed "fake news" to discredit competitors for public attention, political celebrities and partisan publications have used it to discredit the press wholesale. As hard as it is to admit, that's an increasingly unfair fight.

David Uberti is a former senior staff writer for the *Columbia Journalism Review*. He now writes for the Gizmodo Media Group.

EXPLORING THE ISSUE

Is Networking Through Social Media Contributing to the Growth of Fake News?

Critical Thinking and Reflection

1. How have different styles of journalism changed over the years, and what impact have those changes made on the way the public regard the honesty of news media?
2. Who do you consider the most trustworthy sources of news and information? On what do you base your criteria?
3. As news consumers change their news consumption habits, what role do traditional mainstream media outlets play in adequately vetting their information?
4. Do you think it would be possible to create a form of "news literacy" that required people consult several different sources of news before they form an opinion?
5. How much pressure are news organizations under to produce "news" quickly, before confirming their sources?

Is There Common Ground?

The authors of these two selections acknowledge that the whole controversy of "fake" news is tied to the way individuals consume news, and through specific channels (or forms of media). Both argue that the public has a responsibility for thinking critically about what type of news is accessed or disseminated. Each also discusses how time in history contributes to the way news articles are produced and distributed, and imply that the public needs to take more responsibility for consuming and sharing news. Despite the fact that one article (by Uberti) focuses more on mainstream news, both authors are not only aware that the public's consumption habits have changed, but they take as a given that the public's credulity always contributes to the spread of anything that might conceivably be called "fake" news.

In looking back at the 2016 election and the way the President has continued to label many news organizations (like CNN, for example) "fake" news, one wonders how much President Trump's continued emphasis on "fake" news keeps the controversy in the spotlight. The more research that is conducted on the topic, the better we understand how large a problem misleading news may be, how vulnerable media are (especially online media) to the "planting" of misinformation or disinformation by others who have a specific agenda to convey, and who, in society, may be the most vulnerable to believing the range of what constitutes "fake" news.

These authors and their perspectives on truth (or the "untrue") in news harken to early days of mass media in which some people thought that the public would absorb information like a "magic bullet"—meaning that the message sent would be received exactly as it had been intended to be received by the public. Over one hundred years have passed, but some of the same questions remain: what is the function of the press; what must an informed citizen do to be wary of misinformation; and what ethical responsibilities do news organizations have to ensure that they are not spreading incorrect information?

Additional Resources

Hunt Allcott and Matthew Gentzkow, "Social Media and Fake News in the 2016 Election," *Journal of Economic Perspectives*, 31, Spring 2017, pp. 211–236.

The authors of this article define "fake news" as information that is intentionally and verifiably false, and possibly misleading to readers. Based upon survey data, they make several conclusions concerning the impact this type of news could have on the political process, and by extension, on democracy.

W. Joseph Campbell, *Getting It Wrong: Ten of the Greatest Misreported Stories in American Journalism* (2010).

The author won the Society of Professional Journalists' Sigma Delta Chi award for research about journalism. A former practicing journalist, Campbell is now a Professor in the School of Communication at American University in Washington, DC. In this book, Campbell examines key media myths in American history and explains the context in which they took place, and the impact they had.

Walter Lippmann, *Public Opinion*, (1922).

In this early argument for objectivity in journalism, Lippmann identifies the need for journalists to be objective news gatherers and interpreters. He discusses the need for journalism that provides objective truth, even though he knows that truth and accuracy are important, but sometimes unobtainable. It is interesting to read his arguments in light of today's multi-media news environment and within the context of the responsibility of the press.

Eli Pariser, *The Filter Bubble: What the Internet Is Hiding From You* (2011).

In this book, Pariser, who is also the CEO of the online site *Upworthy*, intended to spread "worthwhile" viral content, discusses how people choose to make sense of media from the sources they access, and how those sources are skewed to make money and prey on the way people browse online content.

Internet References . . .

Adam Entous, "Obama Tried To Give Zuckerberg a Wake-up Call Over Fake News on Facebook, Chicago Tribune, September 24, 2017.

http://www.chicagotribune.com/bluesky/technology/
ct-obama-zuckerberg-facebook-20170924-story.html

Berkman Klein Center for Internet and Society at Harvard University.

https://cyber.harvard.edu/research/mediacloud

Eli Pariser, "Beware Online Filter Bubble," Ted Talk (2011)

https://www.ted.com/talks/eli_pariser_beware_
online_filter_bubbles

Jason Shwartz, "Tagging Fake News on Facebook Doesn't Work, Study Says," Politico, September 11, 2017.

http://www.politico.com/story/2017/09/11/facebook-
fake-news-fact-checks-242567

Yochi Benkler, "The Right-Wing Media Eco-system," Harvard Kennedy Center, Shorenstein Center on Media, Politics, and Public Policy, April 7, 2017.

https://shorensteincenter.org/benkler/

Selected, Edited, and with Issue Framing Material by:
Alison Alexander, *University of Georgia*
and
Jarice Hanson, *University of Massachusetts—Amherst*

ISSUE

Does Media Coverage Encourage Mass Shootings and Terrorist Attacks?

YES: Mark Follman, from "How the Media Inspires Mass Shooters," *Mother Jones* (2015)

NO: Charlie Beckett, from "Fanning the Flames: Reporting on Terror in a Networked World," *Tow Center for Digital Journalism at Columbia's Center for Digital Journalism* (2016)

Learning Outcomes

After reading this issue, you will be able to:

- Define the issues surrounding the coverage of terroristic or mass shooting events.
- Advocate for the standards of coverage that should be adopted by news organizations.
- When considering the causes of terrorism and mass shootings, describe how important journalism is among these causes.
- Discuss how framing influences coverage.

ISSUE SUMMARY

YES: Journalist and editor Mark Follman reports that mass shooters claim to be inspired by previous massacres. A desire for fame is enhanced by the coverage achieved in previous shootings. Copycats plan their actions to be seen by the media and the public. Changing how media covers these stories may reduce the likelihood of subsequent copycats. Follman urges media organizations to create industry standards for coverage of mass shootings.

NO: Professor Charlie Beckett acknowledges that terrorism relies on publicity to disrupt society, provoke fear, and demonstrate power. Journalism has a responsibility to help society cope with this complicated problem, but faces challenges of verification, dealing with propaganda, and the speed of the news cycle. Better reporting is needed, but journalists cannot shirk the responsibility to be independent, critical, and trustworthy.

Domestic and international terrorist attacks and mass shootings elicit comprehensive, extensive coverage by traditional news media. Although significantly different in motivation, both terrorists and mass shooters seek news media coverage of their actions. Whether these events are deemed a mass shooting or a terrorist attack, the same journalistic norms need to inform coverage.

Defining mass shootings or terrorism is not clear-cut. An incident involving four or more people, not counting the perpetrators, is defined as a mass shooting, though this definition does not include gang slayings or family killings.

Definitions, however, vary. An event is defined as terroristic if it appears to be intended to intimidate or to coerce people. There is a large body of literature that examines the motivations for these attacks. Terrorists aim to create terror in order to fulfill their agenda, whether the motive is political, religious or ideological. Mass shooting agendas are varied including the killing of coworkers, students, and strangers. Individuals' motives for shooting vary.

Follman argues that the media inspire mass shooters. He describes sensational coverage of a number of shootings. The FBI uses a strategy of threat assessment, and according to an agent has found evidence of a copycat effect wherein perpetrators use past attacks for inspiration and operational details. Social media may be particularly at fault with both the speed and pervasiveness of their reports. Follman recommends some changes in news media reporting including minimizing the use of attacker's name and image, resisting frames that make the violence seem glamorous, and limiting coverage.

Another research takes a social science perspective to study imitation. A "contagion" effect suggests that a mass shooting increases the chance of another shooting occurring in the near future. Meindl and Ivy (see Additional Resources) offer a generalized imitation model that explores how one incident can influence another person to behave in a similar behavior. There is a long history of exploring imitation of behavior seen in media. These authors suggest that the way media cover mass shooting events can increase the probability of imitation.

Where Follman focused on mass shootings, Beckett focuses on terrorism. While it may seem strange to put these together, both present journalists with similar pragmatic and ethical challenges. Beckett describes a number of international terrorist events and notes that in the age of instant news and social media, terrorism is a "different beast." Not unlike in a mass shooting, the flow of information includes not only the information from journalists, but through social media from observers, citizens, authorities and even the terrorists themselves.

Beckett acknowledges the need for journalistic standards, but concedes that little can be done to create standards that apply to social media sites. Rather than limiting coverage of names, faces, and limiting extensiveness of coverage, the keys to transforming coverage of terrorism are in not eliminating coverage but in expanding it with more transparency, verification, attention to how the story is framed, and a commitment to handle these stories honestly and with appropriate depth. He gives examples of how scrambling to provide wall-to-wall coverage of events leads to amplifying terrorist messages, mislabeling groups, and even provoking more terroristic responses.

To oversimplify, while both argue for changed coverage, Follman urges a subtractive model that limits the exposure of the attacker to the public. This, he and others argue, limits the likelihood of contagion, by refusing to make the shooter a media "star." Beckett urges expanding coverage and applying strong standards of verification, minimizing uninformed speculation, and honesty to the reporting process.

As we examine the coverage of these mass murders, you will find many examples of media organizations creating ethical guidelines and standards for coverage of these events. The Internet References section shows you several examples from journalism organizations' Web sites. However, James Warren notes that television news has mass death down to a melancholy routine. His listing of the routine seems all too familiar: The "chyrons, logos, the speculating terrorism specialists, the instant search for motive, the repetition of others' reporting and rumors, the show hosts airlifted into the scene . . . and the inevitable broaching of whether this event will shock the nation into prodding legislators to enact new gun control laws" (https://www.vanityfair.com/news/2017/10/the-media-turns-to-a-familiar-mass-shooting-script). If television coverage is routine, social media is anything but predictable as it churns out pictures, accounts, speculation, rumors, and hoaxes. People pushing an agenda create some of these hoaxes, and many are spread by individuals retweeting or forwarding them widely. The problem is distinguishing the hoaxes from everything else. Some advice for spotting misreporting in found at http://www.wnyc.org/story/breaking-news-consumers-handbook-pdf/ that offers some cautions, such as "In the immediate aftermath, news outlets will get it wrong," "Don't trust anonymous sources," " Compare multiple sources," and be aware that "Big news brings out the fakers. And Photoshoppers." Their site gives readers explanations of each point and offers a printable PDF to remind users of their tips.

As we return to the initial question of whether coverage inspires terrorists and mass shooters, we find the answer to be complex. The answer advocated by both authors is to improve coverage, although they vary significantly in what they advocate. Rarely, however, do those who study violence list media coverage as an important impetus for those who commit these crimes. Although the forms of reporting may be all too familiar, these are standards of coverage that may be very hard to change. Common to all the exhortation is the theme of critical, careful coverage that does not turn these actions into media spectacles. That seems sensible, but something that does not happen when a terrorist attack or mass shooting occurs. The media are voracious. They are looking for news to fill their pages, their broadcast airtime, and their Internet sites. No matter how much traditional media adopt guidelines for coverage, it is doubtful that social media will do the same. As readers and viewers and, for some of you, as future journalists these questions address multiple important issues: Does media coverage inspire mass murder events? If so, how do traditional media address this concern? And finally, how can traditional media deal with the onslaught of social media with their sometimes valuable and sometimes erroneous messages?

YES ←

Mark Follman

How the Media Inspires Mass Shooters

And 6 ways news outlets can help prevent copycat attacks

In late August, not 10 hours after a disgruntled former TV reporter posted video on Twitter and Facebook of himself gunning down two ex-colleagues in Virginia, the New York Daily News tweeted a preview of its front page for the next day. It featured a triptych of stills from the killer's horrifying footage. Readers saw the attack from the shooter's perspective—looking down the barrel of his Glock 19 at the flash of the muzzle and a victim's terrified face, just moments before her death.

It was a gut punch to the victims' loved ones. Journalists and the public responded with a torrent of tweets decrying the cover as "repulsive" and "despicable" and saying that "the victims deserve better." The Daily News said that it published the images "to convey the true scale" of the attack "at a time when it is so easy for the public to become inured to such senseless violence."

Journalism can be a powerful force for change, and news organizations should not flinch at reporting on mass shootings. But what the Daily News editors didn't realize was that this sensational approach can possibly do more than perturb or offend. Such images provide the notoriety mass killers crave and can even be a jolt of inspiration for the next shooter.

The next one struck just five weeks later, in Oregon. The 26-year-old man who murdered nine and wounded nine others at Umpqua Community College last Thursday had posted comments expressing admiration for the Virginia killer, apparently impressed with his social-media achievement: "His face splashed across every screen, his name across the lips of every person on the planet, all in the course of one day. Seems like the more people you kill, the more you're in the limelight."

Since the 1980s, forensic investigators have found examples of mass killers emulating their most famous predecessors. Now, there is growing evidence that the copycat problem is far more serious than is generally understood.

Ever since the 1999 massacre at Colorado's Columbine High School, the Federal Bureau of Investigation has been studying what motivates people to carry out these crimes. Earlier this year, I met with supervisory special agent Andre Simons, who until recently led a team of agents and psychology experts who assist local authorities in heading off violent attacks around the country, using a strategy known as threat assessment. Since 2012, according to Simons, the FBI's unit has taken on more than 400 cases—and has found evidence of the copycat effect rippling through many of them.

Evidence amassed by the FBI and other threat assessment experts shows that perpetrators and plotters look to past attacks both for inspiration and operational details, in hopes of causing even greater carnage. Would-be attackers frequently emulate the Columbine massacre; one high-level law enforcement agent told me that he's encountered dozens of students around the country who say they admire the Columbine killers. "Some of these kids now weren't even born when that happened," he said. The 2007 massacre at Virginia Tech and other attacks that generated major publicity have also spawned many copycats, according to several law enforcement officials I spoke with.

As part of our investigation into threat assessment, Mother Jones documented the chilling scope of the "Columbine effect": We found at least 74 plots and attacks across 30 states in which suspects and perpetrators claimed to have been inspired by the nation's worst high school massacre. Their goals ranged from attacking on the anniversary of Columbine to outdoing the original body count. Law enforcement stopped 53 of these plots before anyone was harmed. Twenty-one of them evolved into attacks, with a total of 89 victims killed, 126 injured, and nine perpetrators committing suicide. (See more about this data here.)

As they plan to strike, many mass shooters now express their desire for fame in comments and manifestos posted online. "They do this to claim credit and to articulate the grievance behind the attack," Simons told me. "And we believe they do it to heighten the media attention that will be given to them, the infamy and notoriety they believe they'll derive from the event."

Despite whatever delusions or obsessive grievances they may be experiencing, many perpetrators are keenly aware of how their actions will be seen by the media and the public. "A lot of times they thrive on posing," says Reid Meloy, a forensic psychologist at the University of California-San Diego and a leading researcher on targeted violence who has interviewed and evaluated mass killers. He cites the police booking photo of Jared Loughner, who shot Rep. Gabrielle Giffords and 18 others in Tucson, Arizona, in 2011. "He's got that contemptuous smile, like it's a great pose. The savvy of these individuals to capitalize on visual exposure should not be underestimated."

A month before the Tucson rampage, Loughner posted what he called "a foreshadow" of his attack in comments on his MySpace page: "I'll see you on National TV!" He got what he wanted—and then some. His booking photo "flashed around the world, at once haunting and fascinating," Washington Post media reporter Paul Farhi wrote three days after the massacre. "Dozens of newspapers placed the photo atop their front pages, burning Loughner's visage into the American consciousness." (The Daily News ran a "nearly life-sized" version on its front page, Farhi noted, with the headline "Face of Evil," while the New York Post ran a similar front page that blared "Mad Eyes of a Killer.") Several of the nation's largest news outlets have continued using the image in stories and broadcasts ever since.

The media faces a growing challenge in how its content is spread and recycled. When I asked various law enforcement and forensic psychology experts what might explain America's rising tide of gun rampages, I heard the same two words over and over: social media. Although there is no definitive research yet, widespread anecdotal evidence suggests that the speed at which social media bombards us with memes and images exacerbates the copycat effect.

Meloy and other threat assessment experts recommend some specific changes by the news media to address the copycat problem. Attackers' names should be used minimally—and their images even less so. "Their use can have a dangerous effect on other young men vulnerable to dark and violent identifications with the perpetrators," Meloy says. "When real life for these individuals is so blighted in terms of love and work, they turn to the anti-heroes." The narcissism running through many copycat cases is even more troubling in this regard: "They don't

just want to be like them—they are envious and want to one-up them," Meloy explains. Copycats will aim to accomplish that either by going for a higher body count, he says, or, as in the Virginia case, killing in a more sensational way.

Meloy argues the media should also rethink some of its language. "Stop using the term 'lone wolf' and stop using 'school shooter'," he says. "In the minds of young men this makes these acts of violence cool. They think, 'This has got some juice behind it, and I can get out there and do something really cool—I can be a lone wolf. I can be a shooter'." Instead, Meloy suggests using terms such as "an act of lone terrorism" and "an act of mass murder."

Changing how the media covers these stories may be especially important when it comes to preventing gun rampages in schools, according to John Van Dreal, a psychologist who helped build a pioneering threat assessment program in Oregon's Salem-Keizer school district, which has more than 40,000 students. "I hear how all the kids talk about it," Van Dreal says. "When it gets played up so much in the media, it becomes heroic to the kids who are thinking about doing it." No one can control what explodes across social media platforms. But news organizations remain powerful magnifiers of content and could work toward "an ethical best practice to leave out the imagery and the name as much as possible," Van Dreal says.

In January, Caren and Tom Teves—whose son Alex was one of the 12 people murdered in the July 2012 massacre in Aurora, Colorado—launched a "No Notoriety" campaign admonishing the media never to use mass shooters' names. There is a similar movement stirring among police officers: The Oregon sheriff handling the response to last week's attack (whose views on gun regulations and the Sandy Hook massacre raised some eyebrows) vowed in a press conference that he would not say the shooter's name—and the town of Roseburg rallied around the idea. His move echoed the recommendations of a FBI-endorsed law enforcement training program on active shooters at Texas State University, which recently began a "Don't Name Them" campaign.

Though laudable, such absolutism is unrealistic in terms of the media's duty to report. As the Poynter Institute's chief media correspondent Jim Warren explained.

Sunday on CNN's Reliable Sources, reporting on the killers is crucial to public understanding of the problem—and for knocking down the rampant misinformation that ricochets around the internet in the aftermath of an attack. (Rumors swirled late last week that the Umpqua killer was a Muslim, for example, which was false.)

But some journalists and news organizations are beginning to recast their coverage of mass shooters with the recognition that they should avoid glamorizing them, and that proportionality matters. The day of the Virginia murders, CNN said it would show a segment of the killer's footage only once per hour; if that sounded odd in its own right, it was an improvement over the sensationalism of the constant looping so common on cable news networks. Since Aurora, CNN's Anderson Cooper has at times declined to name on the air the perpetrators of high-profile massacres.

There is precedent for establishing the type of industry standard that threat assessment experts suggest. Rape victims and juveniles charged with crimes are rarely named in news reports. Ditto people who commit suicide—another problem with a potent contagion effect. When American journalists are taken hostage overseas, news organizations usually agree not to report on their plight due to fears that it would undermine their safety and jeopardize negotiations for their release. Perhaps a rising awareness of the copycat problem will lead to a similar change in how the media covers gun rampages.

We made similar choices with our newly published cover package on threat assessment and the Columbine effect. With most of our major investigations into gun violence, we have published our underlying datasets so that anyone can use them for further study and analysis. But we are only providing summary data and analysis from our research on Columbine copycats. Though much of the case-level data we've collected is publicly available, we decided not to make it easily accessible in one place, where it could potentially be used by aspiring attackers searching for inspiration or tactical information.

Below, we've compiled half a dozen recommendations based on interviews with and research from threat assessment experts concerned about this issue. Not all of these ideas will go over well in newsrooms, and as journalists, we can see arguments for and against these practices.

But given the scope of the copycat problem, they are worthy of serious consideration and debate.

Report on the perpetrator forensically and with dispassionate language. Avoid terms like "lone wolf" and "school shooter," which may carry cachet with young men aspiring to attack. Instead use "perpetrator," "act of lone terrorism," and "act of mass murder."

Minimize use of the perpetrator's name. When it isn't necessary to repeat it, don't. And don't include middle names gratuitously, a common practice for distinguishing criminal suspects from others of the same name, but which can otherwise lend a false sense of their importance.

Keep the perpetrator's name out of headlines. Rarely, if ever, will a generic reference to him in a headline be any less practical.

Minimize use of images of the perpetrator. This is especially important both in terms of aspiring copycats' desire for fame, and the psychology of vulnerable individuals who identify with mass shooters.

Avoid using "pseudocommando" or other posed photos of the perpetrator. This should apply especially after these images are outdated, such as showing the Aurora killer again with his red "Joker" hair during his trial three years later, when he was heavier and wore glasses and a beard.

Avoid publishing the perpetrators' videos or manifestos except when clearly necessary or valuable to the reporting. Instead, paraphrase, cite sparingly, and provide analysis. The guiding question here may be: Is this evidence already easily accessible online? If so, is there a genuine reason to reproduce and spread it, other than to generate page views?

Mark Follman is the National Affairs Editor of *Mother Jones* magazine. He is widely published in national magazines and covers issues of media, politics, and culture.

Charlie Beckett

Fanning the Flames: Reporting on Terror in a Networked World

The Problem With Covering Terrorism

By its very nature, terrorism challenges normal narrative frames and processes. The basic facts themselves are often difficult to establish after a terrorist incident, much less analyze: What happened? Who did it? Why? What is the reaction of the authorities and the public? What policy or political change might it provoke? How can we report it without making it more likely to happen again?

Historical Coverage of Terrorism

Terrorism is always a relative term, and its application has changed over time. Former UK Prime Minister Margaret Thatcher once labeled Nelson Mandela's anti-apartheid African National Congress party as a "terrorist" organization before later going on to urge his release. The American extreme left-wing group the Weathermen, founded in 1969, began as an anti-imperialist group that bombed government buildings and ended up as a counter-cultural cult. The nationalist Irish Republican Army (IRA) was highly organized along military lines which Thatcher also described as terrorist, but with whom she initiated negotiations. Hamas has won elections and has a strong social service network but has also carried out attacks, including suicide bombings on civilians. The American government describes Hamas as terrorist, while others such as Turkey are prepared to treat it as a political actor in the Middle East and give it support.

Because of the term's subjective nature, some people argue terrorism should not be used at all by journalists. But semantics are only part of the problem. For journalists, part of the challenge has always been how to reflect the perspectives of the authorities and public in their own countries. This is only made more complex with international terrorism and transnational media. For example, this year Turkey was subject to a series of attacks by different groups killing civilians. The way those narratives are framed by Western news media has not been consistent, according to Azzam Tamimi, editor in chief of the London-based Arabic channel Al Hiwar:

> Whereas the Islamic State [Daesh] is considered a menace, the PKK and its affiliates are seen as legitimate actors or even freedom fighters. Few Western journalists can resist the temptation to take sides on ideological or cultural basis. The inherited fear or hate of Islam and Muslims usually manifests itself.

Terrorism has always had a symbiotic relationship with news media, one that predates the internet. Journalist and terrorism expert Jason Burke points out that those involved in violent struggle soon realized the opportunity provided by the arrival of mass media:

> In 1956, the Algerian political activist and revolutionary Ramdane Abane wondered aloud if it was better to kill 10 enemies in a remote gully "when no one will talk of it" or "a single man in Algiers, which will be noted the next day" by audiences in distant countries who could influence policymakers.

As Burke writes, the same technological advances such as communications satellites which created a globalized media also gave opportunities for expanded publicity for terrorism:

> In 1972, members of the Palestinian Black September group attacked Israeli athletes at the Munich Olympics, the first games to be broadcast live and the first to be the target of a terrorist attack. The cameras inevitably switched their focus from the sports to the ongoing hostage crisis.

The September 11 attacks were, of course, a watershed moment. Observing the attacks unfold in real time was a communal event, shared by tens of millions of people around the world. A report by Annenberg on journalism and terror published two years later recognized the internet had become a significant factor. It points out that the internet allowed the public to "aggregate bits of information" independently and extended "reach" for smaller media organizations. It also notes that "problematic information is now available on non-journalistic sites."

Al-Qaeda also exemplified the way that terror organizations have become media producers as well as media subjects. Most famously, Osama bin Laden made a series of videos that allowed him to speak through the world's media. But as Burke has chronicled, from 2005 onwards with the expansion of the internet, the Al-Qaeda network with its widespread, diffuse organization of cells and affiliates prioritized the recording of its activities and the dissemination of its propaganda online. Some of this ended up in mainstream news media, such as the video of the beheading in 2004 of the American contractor Nick Berg in Iraq..

A few years later, the transformative effect of Web 2.0 and the meteoric rise of Facebook, Twitter, and other social networks would utterly reshape that digital context. Although the core editorial concerns of the report would remain, the media landscape in which terror attacks now unfold is on a very different scale.

Terrorism in the age of instant news and social media is a "different beast," said former BBC Global News Director Richard Sambrook in an interview. He has worked through the last three decades and insists the subject is now more complex:

> Twenty years ago . . . reporting terror was simpler. You knew who had done it. A car bomb goes off outside Harrods, and the IRA communicate directly with code words. The police would know. The issues were more straightforward, and you knew who you were dealing with. Now it's much more complicated. Terrorism is a different beast, and the fact that it is networked or that it is more likely to be indigenous raises a raft of issues.

The Challenging New Context for the Journalist and Audience

Social platforms are increasingly the place where terrorism is reported first. From ISIS beheadings to video from inside the Bataclan Paris nightclub, these sites are a key news player, sometimes shaping coverage.

There has been a fundamental shift, from news media having control over the flow of information to a more distributed set of sources and plat forms. The journalist is no longer the primary gatekeeper. Today's audiences

have vastly more immediate and direct access to a greater volume of material and variety of sources online. The public can get information directly from other citizens, the authorities, or even terrorists themselves. The relative ease with which the news media are able to report events quickly and graphically—thanks to digital technology—means that audiences often report they feel overwhelmed and even repulsed by the onslaught of "bad news" events.

Around terror events, live broadcasting, and particularly television, remains the dominant news information source for a majority of the media-consuming public. However, over the last decade, those reports are becoming more reliant on social media. Coverage of the London bombings in 2005 featured grainy mobile phone video of survivors walking away from the wrecked train carriages down underground tunnels. In the wake of that, the BBC set up a user-generated content (UGC) hub specifically to gather and verify content created by citizens for use in its news. By the attacks in Mumbai in 2008, journalists were able to find imagery and information from citizen photography sites such as Flickr and the 900 tweets published every minute. Traditional news distribution agencies such as Reuters became clearing houses for UGC. AP appointed its first social media editor in 2012.

In 2016, the first phase of broadcast coverage of the attacks in urban centers such as Paris, Brussels, Munich, and Ankara was dominated by both video and stills harvested from social media. ABC News's International Managing Editor Jon Williams, who has been making broadcast news for more than 30 years, points out that this is an historical change in the visibility of news events:

> Clearly in the 1970s and 80s very often incidents would happen without pictures. In 1996 the only imagery of the IRA Manchester bombing came from CCTV some time after the event. Today there would be any number of people recording that on cellphones and inundating social media with it in real time.

Framing the Narrative: Definitions of "Terrorism"

There is enormous pressure with a major breaking story to come up with a fresh line amidst the surge of information. Audience expectations of instant reportage combined with the increasing market competition add to that need for journalists to work quickly and at the limits of their abilities and resources. This rush to certainty can lead to false leads from mainstream as well as social media. Journalists and audiences inevitably seek to fit terrorist incidents into a pattern. This is exacerbated by group think among journalists, especially on social media. In the race to publish and in the midst of a dangerous situation it is difficult to maintain a critical attitude to those dispensing authoritative information.

One manifestation of this is the expert commentator, who is often chosen as much for their closeness to a TV studio as for their relevant insights. Live broadcasters are developing a language that relativizes its statements: "this is what is being reported," "this is what we are being told," and "reports on social media suggest." The danger is the audience does not understand the precise nature of the qualifications involved.

Adding qualifiers such as "appears to be" or "potential" to "terrorism" is highly risky in a breaking news story. "Terrorism" has traditionally been seen as an external threat, such as 9/11, but as the London Bombings of 2005 and many of the incidents of 2016 show, there are "homegrown" terrorists who draw upon international networks as well as "domestic" terrorists with a local or national agenda. Individuals who carry out terror attacks are not necessarily a "lone wolf." Someone with mental health issues might also be a terrorist. The descriptions are rarely clear. Section two makes the case for greater reflection on terminology and sets out some principles.

One option is to never use the word. Al Jazeera English made it clear that its journalists should not use the term, along with others such as "jihadist." BBC guidelines do not ban the use of the term, but admit it is problematic:

> The word "terrorist" itself can be a barrier rather than an aid to understanding. We should convey to our audience the full consequences of the act by describing what happened. We should use words which specifically describe the perpetrator such as "bomber," "attacker," "gunman," "kidnapper," "insurgent," and "militant." We should not adopt other people's language as our own; our responsibility is to remain objective and report in ways that enable our audiences to make their own assessments about who is doing what to whom.

Avoiding Harm: The News Media's Relationship to Terrorism

Terrorists are now media producers themselves. Anders Breivik was acutely conscious of the role the media would have in promoting his beliefs. He sent a 1,500-word manifesto to more than a thousand people just before his first

bomb went off. ISIS has an extensive media production capacity, creating videos and articles that are distributed through highly-developed social media activities. They use the kidnapped British journalist John Cantlie as a subject of their videos and then as a presenter. Much of the material is English-language targeted at potential sympathizers or recruits online internationally. To tell the story of what the terrorist is thinking, saying, and doing it is often useful to use this material. But the danger is that even in a critical context this effectively relays and amplifies the terrorist's message.

There is always a danger of media giving terrorists details about security operations that help them improve their work. This is particularly relevant in the midst of a terrorist operation. Live video or pictures of a scene may endanger security forces or hamper their work. It is essential that, when the public is at risk, the news media works closely with security officials.

There is also a wider problem that those authorities, especially politicians, frame their commentary on terror events to suit their own interests. Journalists have an obligation to report what powerful people say but they do not have an obligation to replicate their perspective. As British journalist and former *London Times* editor Simon Jenkins argues, politicians have their own agendas:

> To the media, terrorism is meat and drink. To politicians, it is an opportunity to flex muscles, brandish guns, boast revenge. Talk of war adds ten points to an approval rating. It saved George Bush as it is now saving France's Francois Hollande. Counter-terror theory may advise caution and an emphasis on normality. Political necessity counsels the opposite; the trumpets and drums of battle. It requires the terrorist's deeds to be amplified, headlined, exaggerated to justify a warlike response.

At what point does a "hate crime" such as the Charleston church shooting become categorized as "terrorism"? Breivik had active links with extreme right-wing groups and used his actions to promote his anti-Islamic, anti-liberal ideology. His convictions included "terrorism." However, in the media, he was most often referred to as a mass murderer or mass killer, not a terrorist. Likewise, Ali Sonboly , the 2016 Munich shooter was described by police as "inspired" by Breivik, but they said the incident was not "terror-related." Sonboly had been receiving psychiatric treatment, raising the definitional problem around terror and mental health. In considering the mix of mot ives, it does seem that mainstream media has a propensity to describe events as " terror" if they have some element of jihadist or lslamist ideological ingredient.

Even if a recognized terrorist organization does claim responsibility, journalists may need to fine-tune the language. There was evidence that the 2016 Wurzburg train attacker was " inspired" by ISIS propaganda rather than controlled by them, yet ISIS still claimed it as part of their campaign in Europe. The Ansbach bomber Mohammed Daleel had stronger links to ISIS including a propaganda video he made pledging allegiance to the ISIS leader Abu Bakr al-Baghdadi. His preparation for the bombing was more sophisticated and planned. Does that make him more of a terrorist? What significance should journalists have given to the fact that several of this summer's German attackers were asylum seekers or refugees? As soon as perpetrators are identified with a minority group, the danger is that community will be impugned in a way that does not happen when perpetrators are seen to be from the majority population. In a political environment where in many regions there are tensions over ethnic identity, immigration, and cultural values, it is even more important that the news media does not make unqualified connect ions between race, religion, and terror acts.

Boston Marathon bombing in 2013, leading to a manhunt before police were able to rule him out. But in that four-hour period many journalists disseminated the rumor on their own social media accounts. They appeared to accept a lower standard of verification then they would have done for publication on their regular news channels or sites.

The primary function of journalism is still to get facts right. The volume of social media content and the fact that some of it is inaccurate or misleading should not make professional journalists complacent. News media content is now blended into the audience's news feeds and audiences often do not discriminate between "amateur" and "official" or journalistic content online. Research shows that on social media people trust their peers as much as the news media (although that includes their peers sharing news media content).

Reshaping the Newsroom

New skills are needed to understand user-generated imagery from social networks, terrorist propaganda on specialist websites (often not English language), government or security communications, expert and academic analysis/research blogs and websites, local, specialist, international, and foreign language news media organizations, aggregators, bots and campaign groups.

Yet a guiding philosophy through this complex network of information should be simple: Only report as facts what you know to be true. We can put aside philosophical debates over truth and focus on the journalistic process of identifying some kind of evidence-related process that gives us the best, most reliable account of who, what, where, when, and why.

Getting to the Truth

CNN took a serious reputational hit for its mistake in coverage of the Boston Marathon. Like almost all major news organizations, it has adopted a more effective way of reconciling the competing demands from audiences for instant news and verified information. It now has a more coordinated editorial management structure with digital platforms integrated with broadcast.

The business as well as the ethical case for journalism in a media environment so full of false, partial, or provisional information must be based on trust. Citizens now have social media feeds full of messages, often from peers not professionals, that alert them to breaking terror news. When they click onto the mainstream news media material, they expect something more reliable. Journalists cannot police the internet for truth, but as well as getting their own facts right, journalists can also have a role helping to identify fake or mistaken information on social media. This kind of "myth-busting" helps arrests the spread of false information and can educate the audience in online verification.

Journalists covering breaking terror news are adapting their language and being humbler in publicly sharing their ignorance as well as their knowledge-something once unimaginable to newsroom culture. To say that something has not been confirmed is not adequate as a final narrative, but in the early stages of an incident it is as important to identify uncertain information. Authority is enhanced, not diminished, by making sources as clear and precise as possible. A general statement such as "reports on social media" is at the worse vague end of the spectrum, but if the platform and social media account is identified then that helps build a more nuanced picture. This is part of building much needed media literacy in the audience. Detailed, continual transparency helps promote public understanding of the process of news as well as building trust in its outputs.

Avoiding Harm and Relations with Authorities

Reporting on terror events must also be sensitive to security considerations. Journalists have a duty to report as fully as possible but in a terror-related scenario the news media has a responsibility to avoid causing harm. Journalists can legitimately not report facts if doing so would increase risks or hamper a security operation. This means responding to requests from the authorities to not report particular facts or not to show certain images. There should always be a due process within the news organization of making that decision. Ideally, the fact of any decision to restrict reporting should be reported.

During the 2004 school siege in Beslan, Chechnya, the BBC decided to go on a time delay for its live feed because of the danger of showing graphic imagery of hostages including children. During the security operation following the 2015 attacks on the Charlie Hebdo offices in Paris and the siege of a supermarket where hostages had been taken, the French broadcast regulator issued a notice to domestic newsrooms asking them to show "discretion." Paris police on the scene told TV crews not to broadcast their officers in act ion. At the same time broadcasters were regulating themselves. Paris-based BFM TV chose not to broadcast the police rescue operation live. It also did not air an audio interview it recorded with the hostage-takers themselves until after the incident was over. BFM TV journalist Ruth Elkrief said it was a series of decisions they had to make for themselves in the newsroom:

> It's very difficult. We have to move fast. But are we undermining the investigation? Are we being manipulated? We're asking ourselves these questions constantly. We had several emergency meetings during the day to debate what to do. We're always checking ourselves.

Transparency about making those judgments helps build the understanding and confidence of the audience. Clearly, journalists cannot give a running commentary on all their editorial decisions, but a similar approach could be adopted to that when embedded with the military during conflicts, as suggested in BBC guidelines:

> We should normally say if our reports are censored or monitored or if we withhold information, and explain, wherever possible, the rules under which we are operating.

Journalists have a civic duty to cooperate in the interests of public safety, but this does not mean automatically complying with police or security requests. The seizing of the laptop of BBC journalist Secunder Kermani—who had made contacts with extremists—appeared to challenge in principle the idea that journalists can ever talk to terrorists or their Associates.

Not Helping the Terrorist

There is also a long-term issue about how detailed media coverage might help terrorists improve their operational effectiveness. As Javier Delgado Rivera has written, thanks to news media reports, terrorists now know how the FBI tracked the network of the San Bernardino shooters with information from their damaged cell phones. They know that French police linked one of the Paris attackers to the Brussels attacks through parking tickets. Perhaps future terrorists will be more careful:

> Detailed media reporting on police investigations can inadvertently help attackers avoid past miscalculations and refine their modus operandi. Journalists would argue that their job is to protect society's right to know. Yet in such exceptional circumstances, editors should ensure that the latest information they feed to their audience is useless to fundamentalists seeking to do harm.

This is especially important as terrorists become increasingly self radicalized and train themselves partly through the study of previous incidents. Overall, it would be impossible for the news media not to report any circumstantial detail that could help a future terrorist, but as with the reporting of suicide, where journalists refrain from describing methods of self-killing, discretion around the depth of information on methods and countermeasures is possible.

In a breaking crisis situation, we usually set up a thread for "myth-busting" that will point out fake images or correct false leads and give basic background information. People expect us to do that and they trust us to do it.

Journalism must be independent, critical, and realistic, but there is opportunity for narratives of resistance, solidarity, and com passion. This would also help a fearful or jaded public engage with the issues and generate a more positive discussion about resilience in the face of the threat and a better quality of debate around "solutions," according to media researcher Arda Bilgen:

> Implementing certain [editorial] policies that are different than the previous failed policies can facilitate the breaking of that cycle by forcing at

least one side of the equation-the media-to act in a more responsible, more conscious , and more cooperative manner. Only then starving the terrorists of the oxygen of publicity on which they depend can become possible and more robust steps can be taken to win the ideological and actual battle against terrorism.

Humanizing Terror's Victims and their Communities may be the Best Counter-Extremist Measure Media can Provide

Journalism around terror events also has a role in mediating the emotional impact for the audience. There is an element of useful ritual about the creation of instant shrines at the scene of incidents, the memorial services, and the expressions of condolence. Social media and platforms now play a part in that, with special hashtags or profile flags to show solidarity. By showing this process of grieving, the news media helps communities recover from the trauma. By focusing on the victims rather than the perpetrators, journalists can bring humanity and dignity back into a narrative of destruction and fear. Samantha Barry of CNN explains:

> Our audience tells us in a number of ways that they want us to focus on the victims. One of the most powerful pieces we did which achieved unprecedented levels of engagement across all platforms was when Anderson Cooper choked up reading the names of the Orlando victims. We try to be impersonal in how we report, but we are not robots. And the audience needs good news, too. Survivor stories are important as are those stories of personal courage such as the people who went back into the Bataclan nightclub to save their friends.

Emotion used to be seen as an indulgence in hard news journalism, but when it comes to terrorism it is important to treat it as more than a commodity, especially with the advent of social media. Part of this is acknowledging the emotional impact of terrorist events on the journalist themselves. Anderson Cooper's tears over the Orlando massacre run the risk of appearing too personally involved with the story. But it is possible to include feelings as part of storytelling without diluting factual and critical perspective. BuzzFeed's Gibson says news organizations should be able to operate in different modes without compromising overall integrity:

> With these events we are operating in three dimensions at the same time. We are simultaneously doing the breaking news, the analysis, and we are also sending reporters without a specific deadline to go find out what is going on-not to talk to the police but to talk to people to get the emotion behind the story. To go to vigils to talk to people to get their testimony but also to get the reasons why people were out and about in the wake of the event-seeing it from bottom up.

Perhaps most important is to ensure that this is inclusive of the wider communities involved, be they the LBGT population of Florida or the Muslims of Europe. Humanizing terror's victims and their communities may be the best counter-extremist measure media can provide.

CHARLIE BECKETT is a professor in the Department of Media and Communications at the London School of Economics. Before joining the LSE, he was a journalist at the BBC and ITN.

EXPLORING THE ISSUE

Does Media Coverage Encourage Mass Shootings and Terrorist Attacks?

Critical Thinking and Reflection

1. Is ignorance better than information in some cases?
2. What are the obstacles to change in news coverage?
3. How can we balance the public's right to know with limited coverage of such events?
4. Social media is the wild card in these discussions. How should the legacy media handle social media accounts and can or should social media be controlled in any way?
5. Should there be different standards for covering terrorism vs. mass shootings?

Is There Common Ground?

Some might argue that there is no common ground between covering mass shootings versus covering terrorist attacks. Yet while the authors discuss the differences in these events, they also discuss common issues about how to cover such violence. Nonetheless, they come from very different motivations and history. It will always be important to acknowledge these differences.

Not all journalists agree with putting any form of limitation on, for example, sharing the name of the perpetrator. They argue for the public's right to know and for preventing endless speculation about identity. Even police differ on this issue. Although there may never be agreement on issues such as releasing names and pictures, news professional associations will probably have some success in influencing coverage if they discuss and create industry guidelines.

Framing remains both crucial and difficult. We particularly see this in defining some form of attack as a mass shooting versus a terrorist event. As we in despair watch coverage of some man-made disaster, one of the first questions is "Is this a terrorist, a lone wolf, a madman or an accident?" From the beginning we look for frames to put around each event, helping us to place this in an unfortunately familiar frame. Both authors agree that we must be much more careful in attribution. Careless labels can short circuit the in-depth and critical reporting that is crucial.

Additional Resources

Nicole Dahmen, Jesse Abdenour, Karen McIntyre & Krystal Noga-Styron, "Covering Mass Shootings: Journalists' Perceptions of Coverage and Factors Influencing Attitudes," *Journalism Practice*, (published online May 31, 2017), retrieved from http://www.tandfonline.com/doi/abs/10.1080/17512786.2017.1326832

Using data from a national survey authors examine journalists' attitudes toward news coverage of mass shootings. Participants generally agreed that coverage had become routine. Journalists were largely supportive of coverage of perpetrators and were concerned about any possible "copycat," effect.

Ruth DeFoster, Terrorizing the Masses: Identity, Mass Shootings, and the Media Construction of "Terror." Peter Lang Inc. (2017)

In this book the author examines the history of media coverage of terrorizing the mass public, and discusses the role media play in shaping attitudes and beliefs about harm in society.

Des Freedman and Daya Thussu (eds.), Media and Terrorism: Global Perspectives. Sage (2012)

In the 18 chapters in this book, the editors have collected essays that fit into four groups: Contexts,

Global Representations of Terrorism, Terrorist from the Home Front, and Journalists and the "War on Terror."

James Meindi and Jonathan Ivy, "Mass Shootings: The Role of the Media in Promoting Generalized Imitation," *American Journal of Public Health*, (March 2017)

Authors examine the situation in the United States and the potential problem of contagion that often seems to come with any form of media coverage of horrific events.

Joanne Zalatoris, Why the Media Must Report on Shooters and Terrorists, (August 25, 2016), retrieved from https://www.newamerica.org/weekly/edition-132/why-media-must-report-shooters-and-terrorists/

In this article the author discusses the ethical dilemma in reporting certain aspects of shooters and terrorists, including the names of the alleged perpetrators and their methods of creating havoc.

Internet References . . .

Ethical Journalism Network

http://ethicaljournalismnetwork.org/tag/terrorism

Journalist's Toolbox: School Violence and Covering Mass Killings

http://www.journaliststoolbox.org/2017/09/12/school_violence/

Radio Television Digital News Association

https://www.rtdna.org/content/shooting_hostage_situation

United Nations Educational, Scientific and Cultural Organization Terrorism and the Media: A Handbook for Journalists

http://unesdoc.unesco.org/images/0024/002470/247074E.pdf

Selected, Edited, and with Issue Framing Material by:
Alison Alexander, *University of Georgia*
and
Jarice Hanson, *University of Massachusetts—Amherst*

ISSUE

Are Polls an Accurate Assessment
of Public Opinion?

YES: Sheldon R. Gawiser and G. Evans Witt, from "20 Questions a Journalist Should Ask about Poll Results," *National Council of Public Polls* (2012)

NO: Herbert J. Gans, from "Public Opinion Polls Do Not Always Report Public Opinion," *Nieman Reports* (2013)

Learning Outcomes

After reading this issue, you will be able to:

- Consider the type of poll, become aware of the size of the population sampled, and think about the credibility of the pollster.
- Become more aware of how media use polls for their intended effects.
- Think about alternative or minority viewpoints that are not reflected in polls.
- Reflect on whether poll reports further the agenda of the news organization.

ISSUE SUMMARY

YES: Sheldon R. Gawiser and G. Evans Witt have a vast experience in developing polls and analyzing the results of polls. Their belief in the accuracy of polls to reflect public opinion is grounded in decades of experience, and in the scientific accuracy of the poll. They provide advice to journalists on how to measure the worth of a poll in terms of its scientific rigor as opposed to its casual approach toward accuracy.

NO: Herbert J. Gans discusses how news media personnel often portray public opinion through polls inaccurately. He makes an important distinction between the way people answer polls and the definition of public opinion.

The rise of public opinion polling owes a debt to the technologies that facilitated many of the techniques that are still used in polling today. The telephone certainly made it possible to call someone and ask his or her opinion, and in the days of phone books that listed names, addresses, and phone numbers of people who had phones, this treasure of a resource was invaluable for conducting polls that were randomized (every fifth name might be called, for example), or for those who lived in geographic proximity, as could be detected by the telephone exchange numbers. Radio was a medium that often distributed national newscasts, prior to television and the Internet, and some of the earliest polling companies polled public opinion based on what people either read in the newspapers, or perhaps heard on radio. Therefore, the entire history of polling is conditioned by the technologies that made survey sampling possible.

Politicians have always wanted to understand what the public thinks, and how policies can be crafted to gain favor by an electorate. Public opinion polling in the United States owes much to the pioneering work of George Gallup, who founded the American Institute of Public Opinion in 1936. Princeton University started the academic journal *Public Opinion Quarterly* in 1937 to focus on emerging techniques and applications of polling criteria. Soon, the Roper, Crossley, and Harris Polls were also established to help monitor public opinion about a wide range of things, from politics to product marketing. The National Opinion

Research Center was founded in 1941 and was the first noncommercial polling company. Today, however, many colleges and universities provide homes to polling companies, and it is not unusual for major companies to use any number of commercial marketing firms to test their products and ideas.

The authors of these selections have insider knowledge about what it takes to conduct a good, scientifically rigorous poll, and all of them criticize the types of polls that are conducted using nonscientific models. In general, the authors agree that polls that reflect rigorous methodological standards can be scientifically and statistically important, but that when methods are distorted by the sponsor's desire to find what it is looking for, or when good social science is not being applied, the results can be very misleading.

Understanding public opinion has long been a critical component of considering the relationship between the press and the public. In 1922, Walter Lippmann, himself a journalist and keen observer of the way media shaped the images in the minds of the audience, wrote a very influential book called *Public Opinion*. In this book he called for the principle of objectivity to be a value that every journalist should strive for, but at the same time, he knew that the words of journalists often influenced what he called the "manufacture of consent," which created images for the audience that influenced audience members' psychological interpretation of meaning. Lippmann's pioneering work helped create the academic study of the media, and provided both a philosophical and moral imperative for the training of journalists.

Today, however, the number of communication technologies we use and have access to has changed the nature of some types of polling. Have you ever been asked for your opinion online, and once you start a questionnaire, you wonder who this poll is for, and what the polling organization might do with your information? Online polls are often "click bait" for companies that may be trying to find out more information about you, rather than what answers you provide to a simple, easy-to-use interactive online service. And yet, there seems to be something compelling about offering our perspective. Sometimes we want to air our viewpoints. Other times we find ourselves caught up in answering questions because they are constructed to really seem as though our opinions matter. The problem with the number of nonscientific polls, though, is that they sometimes diminish what a poll really means and affect the interpretation of the meaning of the responses elicited by the poll.

In a recent *New Yorker* article, journalist Jill Lepore wrote that "From the late 1990s to 2012, twelve hundred polling organizations conducted nearly 37,000 polls by making more than three billion phone calls" (Lepore, November 16, 2015). These numbers are staggering, and we can probably assume that not all of these polls were conducted scientifically, or with rigorous methods. Interestingly, she provides the history of polls that once equated the "poll" to mean the top of a person's head; therefore, when people went to be polled, the result was a head-count. Eventually, "the polls" were the places where voting would take place. As Lepore develops the thesis of her article, she explains how, over time, "polling" began to mean both surveys of opinions as well as forecasts of election results.

Certainly what constitutes a poll has changed over the years, but today, there are also many kinds of polls. "Push polls" use terms that might sway a person's response toward a calculated result so that the "pollster" manipulates the result. "Straw polls" are unofficial expressions of tendencies to lean certain ways in discussions, or toward political "votes" or expressions of opinion. "Benchmark polls" are often done to provide insights on how a candidate's popularity is tracked over time, and "entrance" or "exit" polls ask voters what they think they will vote on, or for whom, and later, on what they said they did (which may not always be what they really did).

One problem with the reporting of public opinion is that sometimes respondents say what they think the pollster wants to hear, whether they really believe the statement or not. For example, a person might be asked how she intends to vote, and she may want to provide an answer even though she is not registered to vote. The assertion actually hides the fact that the person is not political, but she doesn't want to be perceived as not being politically active. Many psychological studies have focused on why people sometimes respond by telling someone what they think that person wants to hear. The actual measurement of public opinion often is blurred by a number of psychological and sociological factors.

But despite the wide range of interpretations and applications of polls today, the authors of the selections in this issue remind us that there are a host of issues that should be addressed when we rely on polls for information. It is ultimately the responsibility of the reader or viewer of poll data to ask important questions about the validity of the poll, and what it means in the larger context of things.

YES ↵

Sheldon R. Gawiser and G. Evans Witt

20 Questions a Journalist Should Ask about Poll Results

Polls provide the best direct source of information about public opinion. They are valuable tools for journalists and can serve as the basis for accurate, informative news stories. For the journalist looking at a set of poll numbers, here are the 20 questions to ask the pollster before reporting any results. This publication is designed to help working journalists do a thorough, professional job covering polls. It is not a primer on how to conduct a public opinion survey.

The only polls that should be reported are "scientific" polls. A number of the questions here will help you decide whether or not a poll is a "scientific" one worthy of coverage—or an unscientific survey without value.

Unscientific pseudo-polls are widespread and sometimes entertaining, but they never provide the kind of information that belongs in a serious report. Examples include 900-number call-in polls, man-on-the-street surveys, many Internet polls, shopping mall polls, and even the classic toilet tissue poll featuring pictures of the candidates on each roll.

One major distinguishing difference between scientific and unscientific polls is who picks the respondents for the survey. In a scientific poll, the pollster identifies and seeks out the people to be interviewed. In an unscientific poll, the respondents usually "volunteer" their opinions, selecting themselves for the poll.

The results of the well-conducted scientific poll provide a reliable guide to the opinions of many people in addition to those interviewed—even the opinions of all Americans. The results of an unscientific poll tell you nothing beyond simply what those respondents say.

By asking these 20 questions, the journalist can seek the facts to decide how to report any poll that comes across the news desk.

. . .

1. Who Did the Poll?

What polling firm, research house, political campaign, or other group conducted the poll? This is always the first question to ask.

If you don't know who did the poll, you can't get the answers to all the other questions listed here. If the person providing poll results can't or won't tell you who did it, the results should not be reported, for their validity cannot be checked.

Reputable polling firms will provide you with the information you need to evaluate the survey. Because reputation is important to a quality firm, a professionally conducted poll will avoid many errors.

2. Who Paid for the Poll and Why Was It Done?

You must know who paid for the survey, because that tells you—and your audience—who thought these topics are important enough to spend money finding out what people think.

Polls are not conducted for the good of the world. They are conducted for a reason—either to gain helpful information or to advance a particular cause.

It may be the news organization wants to develop a good story. It may be the politician wants to be re-elected. It may be that the corporation is trying to push sales of its new product. Or a special-interest group may be trying to prove that its views are the views of the entire country.

All are legitimate reasons for doing a poll.

The important issue for you as a journalist is whether the motive for doing the poll creates such serious doubts about the validity of the results that the numbers should not be publicized.

Private polls conducted for a political campaign are often unsuited for publication. These polls are conducted solely to help the candidate win—and for no other reason. The poll may have very slanted questions or a strange sampling methodology, all with a tactical campaign purpose. A campaign may be testing out new slogans, a new statement on a key issue or a new attack on an opponent. But since the goal of the candidate's poll may not be a straightforward, unbiased reading of the public's sentiments, the results should be reported with great care.

Likewise, reporting on a survey by a special-interest group is tricky. For example, an environmental group trumpets a poll saying the American people support strong measures to protect the environment. That may be true, but the poll was conducted for a group with definite views. That may have swayed the question wording, the timing of the poll, the group interviewed and the order of the questions. You should carefully examine the poll to be certain that it accurately reflects public opinion and does not simply push a single viewpoint.

3. How Many People Were Interviewed for the Survey?

Because polls give approximate answers, the more people interviewed in a scientific poll, the smaller the error due to the size of the sample, all other things being equal. A common trap to avoid is that "more is automatically better." While it is absolutely true that the more people interviewed in a scientific survey, the smaller the sampling error, other factors may be more important in judging the quality of a survey.

4. How Were Those People Chosen?

The key reason that some polls reflect public opinion accurately and other polls are unscientific junk is how people were chosen to be interviewed. In scientific polls, the pollster uses a specific statistical method for picking respondents. In unscientific polls, the person picks himself to participate.

The method pollsters use to pick interviewees relies on the bedrock of mathematical reality: when the chance of selecting each person in the target population is known, then and only then do the results of the sample survey reflect the entire population. This is called a random sample or a probability sample. This is the reason that interviews with 1,000 American adults can accurately reflect the opinions of more than 210 million American adults.

Most scientific samples use special techniques to be economically feasible. For example, some sampling

methods for telephone interviewing do not just pick randomly generated telephone numbers. Only telephone exchanges that are known to contain working residential numbers are selected, reducing the number of wasted calls. This still produces a random sample. But samples of only listed telephone numbers do not produce a random sample of all working telephone numbers.

But even a random sample cannot be purely random in practice as some people don't have phones, refuse to answer, or aren't home.

Surveys conducted in countries other than the United States may use different but still valid scientific sampling techniques, for example, because relatively few residents have telephones. In surveys in other countries, the same questions about sampling should be asked before reporting a survey.

5. What Area (Nation, State, or Region) or What Group (Teachers, Lawyers, Democratic Voters, etc.) Were These People Chosen From?

It is absolutely critical to know from which group the interviewees were chosen. You must know if a sample was drawn from among all adults in the United States, or just from those in one state or in one city, or from another group. For example, a survey of business people can reflect the opinions of business people—but not of all adults. Only if the interviewees were chosen from among all American adults, can the poll reflect the opinions of all American adults.

In the case of telephone samples, the population represented is that of people living in households with telephones. For most purposes, telephone households are similar to the general population. But if you were reporting a poll on what it was like to be homeless, a telephone sample would not be appropriate. The increasingly widespread use of cell phones, particularly as the only phone in some households, may have an impact in the future on the ability of a telephone poll to accurately reflect a specific population. Remember, the use of a scientific sampling technique does not mean that the correct population was interviewed.

Political polls are especially sensitive to this issue.

In pre-primary and pre-election polls, which people are chosen as the base for poll results is critical. A poll of all adults, for example, is not very useful for a primary race where only 25 percent of the registered voters actually turn out. So look for polls based on registered voters, "likely voters," previous primary voters and such. These distinctions are important and should be included in the story, for one of the most difficult challenges in polling is trying to figure out who actually is going to vote.

The ease of conducting surveys in the United States is not duplicated around the world. It may not be possible or practical in some countries to conduct surveys of a random sample throughout the country. Surveys based on a smaller group than the entire population—such as a few larger cities—can still be reliable if reported correctly—as the views of those in the larger cities, for example, but not those of the country—and may be the only available data.

6. Are the Results Based on the Answers of All the People Interviewed?

One of the easiest ways to misrepresent the results of a poll is to report the answers of only a subgroup. For example, there is usually a substantial difference between the opinions of Democrats and Republicans on campaign-related matters. Reporting the opinions of only Democrats in a poll purported to be of all adults would substantially misrepresent the results.

Poll results based on Democrats must be identified as such and should be reported as representing only Democratic opinions.

Of course, reporting on just one subgroup can be exactly the right course. In polling on a primary contest, it is the opinions of those who can vote in the primary that count—not those who cannot vote in that contest. Primary polls should include only eligible primary voters.

7. Who Should Have Been Interviewed and Was Not? Or Do Response Rates Matter?

No survey ever reaches everyone who should have been interviewed. You ought to know what steps were undertaken to minimize non-response, such as the number of attempts to reach the appropriate respondent and over how many days.

There are many reasons why people who should have been interviewed were not. They may have refused attempts to interview them. Or interviews may not have been attempted if people were not home when the interviewer called. Or there may have been a language problem or a hearing problem.

In recent years, the percentage of people who respond to polls has diminished. There has been an increase in those who refuse to participate. Some of this is due to the increase in telemarketing and part is due to Caller ID and other technology that allows screening of incoming calls. While this is a subject that concerns pollsters, so far careful study has found that these reduced response rates have not had a major impact on the accuracy of most public polls.

Where possible, you should obtain the overall response rate from the pollster, calculated on a recognized basis such as the standards of the American Association for Public Opinion Research. One poll is not "better" than another simply because of the one statistic called response rate.

8. When Was the Poll Done?

Events have a dramatic impact on poll results. Your interpretation of a poll should depend on when it was conducted relative to key events. Even the freshest poll results can be overtaken by events. The President may have given a stirring speech to the nation, pictures of abuse of prisoners by the military may have been broadcast[ed], the stock market may have crashed or an oil tanker may have sunk, spilling millions of gallons of crude on beautiful beaches.

Poll results that are several weeks or months old may be perfectly valid, but events may have erased any newsworthy relationship to current public opinion.

9. How Were the Interviews Conducted?

There are four main possibilities: in person, by telephone, online or by mail. Most surveys are conducted by telephone, with the calls made by interviewers from a central location. However, some surveys are still conducted by sending interviewers into people's homes to conduct the interviews.

Some surveys are conducted by mail. In scientific polls, the pollster picks the people to receive the mail questionnaires. The respondent fills out the questionnaire and returns it.

Mail surveys can be excellent sources of information, but it takes weeks to do a mail survey, meaning that the results cannot be as timely as a telephone survey. And mail surveys can be subject to other kinds of errors, particularly extremely low response rates. In many mail surveys, many more people fail to participate than do. This makes the results suspect.

Surveys done in shopping malls, in stores or on the sidewalk may have their uses for their sponsors, but publishing the results in the media is not among them. These approaches may yield interesting human-interest stories, but they should never be treated as if they represent public opinion.

Advances in computer technology have allowed the development of computerized interviewing systems that dial the phone, play taped questions to a respondent and then record answers the person gives by punching numbers on the telephone keypad. Such surveys may be more vulnerable to significant problems including uncontrolled selection of respondents within the household, the ability of young children to complete the survey, and poor response rates.

Such problems should disqualify any survey from being used unless the journalist knows that the survey has proper respondent selection, verifiable age screening, and reasonable response rates.

10. What About Polls on the Internet or World Wide Web?

The explosive growth of the Internet and the World Wide Web has given rise to an equally explosive growth in various types of online polls and surveys.

Online surveys can be scientific if the samples are drawn in the right way. Some online surveys start with a scientific national random sample and recruit participants while others just take anyone who volunteers. Online surveys need to be carefully evaluated before use.

Several methods have been developed to sample the opinions of those who have online access. The fundamental rules of sampling still apply online: the pollster must select those who are asked to participate in the survey in a random fashion. In those cases where the population of interest has nearly universal Internet access or where the pollster has carefully recruited from the entire population, online polls are candidates for reporting.

However, even a survey that accurately sampled all those who have access to the Internet would still fall short of a poll of all Americans, as about one in three adults do not have Internet access.

But many Internet polls are simply the latest variation on the pseudo-polls that have existed for many years. Whether the effort is a click-on Web survey, a dial-in poll or a mail-in survey, the results should be ignored and not reported. All these pseudo-polls suffer from the same problem: the respondents are self-selected. The individuals choose themselves to take part in the poll—there is no pollster choosing the respondents to be interviewed.

Remember, the purpose of a poll is to draw conclusions about the population, not about the sample. In these pseudo-polls, there is no way to project the results to any larger group. Any similarity between the results of a pseudo-poll and a scientific survey is pure chance.

Clicking on your candidate's button in the "voting booth" on a Web site may drive up the numbers for your candidate in a presidential horse-race poll online. For most such efforts, no effort is made to pick the respondents, to limit users from voting multiple times or to reach out for people who might not normally visit the Web site.

The dial-in or click-in polls may be fine for deciding who should win on *American Idol* or which music video is the *MTV Video of the Week*. The opinions expressed may be real, but in sum the numbers are just entertainment. There is no way to tell who actually called in, how old they are, or how many times each person called.

Never be fooled by the number of responses. In some cases a few people call in thousands of times. Even if 500,000 calls are tallied, no one has any real knowledge of what the results mean. If big numbers impress you, remember that the *Literary Digest's* non-scientific sample of 2,000,000 people said Landon would beat Roosevelt in the 1936 Presidential election.

Mail-in coupon polls are just as bad. In this case, the magazine or newspaper includes a coupon to be returned with the answers to the questions. Again, there is no way to know who responded and how many times each person did.

Another variation on the pseudo-poll comes as part of a fund-raising effort. An organization sends out a letter with a survey form attached to a large list of people, asking for opinions and for the respondent to send money to support the organization or pay for tabulating the survey. The questions are often loaded and the results of such an effort are always meaningless.

This technique is used by a wide variety of organizations from political parties and special-interest groups to charitable organizations. Again, if the poll in question is part of a fund-raising pitch, pitch it—in the wastebasket.

11. What Is the Sampling Error for the Poll Results?

Interviews with a scientific sample of 1,000 adults can accurately reflect the opinions of nearly 210 million American adults. That means interviews attempted with all 210 million adults—if such were possible—would give approximately the same results as a well-conducted survey based on 1,000 interviews.

What happens if another carefully done poll of 1,000 adults gives slightly different results from the first survey? Neither of the polls is "wrong." This range of possible results is called the error due to sampling, often called the margin of error.

This is not an "error" in the sense of making a mistake. Rather, it is a measure of the possible range of approximation in the results because a sample was used.

Pollsters express the degree of the certainty of results based on a sample as a "confidence level." This means a sample is likely to be within so many points of the results one would have gotten if an interview were attempted with the entire target population. Most polls are usually reported using the 95% confidence level.

Thus, for example, a "3 percentage point margin of error" in a national poll means that if the attempt were made to interview every adult in the nation with the same questions in the same way at the same time as the poll was taken, the poll's answers would fall within plus or minus 3 percentage points of the complete count's results 95% of the time.

This does not address the issue of whether people cooperate with the survey, or if the questions are understood, or if any other methodological issue exists. The sampling error is only the portion of the potential error in a survey introduced by using a sample rather than interviewing the entire population. Sampling error tells us nothing about the refusals or those consistently unavailable for interview; it also tells us nothing about the biasing effects of a particular question wording or the bias a particular interviewer may inject into the interview situation. It also applies only to scientific surveys.

Remember that the sampling error margin applies to each figure in the results—it is at least 3 percentage points plus or minus for each one in our example. Thus, in a poll question matching two candidates for President, both figures are subject to sampling error.

12. Who's on First?

Sampling error raises one of the thorniest problems in the presentation of poll results: For a horse-race poll, when is one candidate really ahead of the other?

Certainly, if the gap between the two candidates is less than the sampling error margin, you should not say that one candidate is ahead of the other. You can say the race is "close," the race is "roughly even," or there is "little difference between the candidates." But it should not be called a "dead heat" unless the candidates are tied with the same percentages. And it certainly is not a "statistical tie" unless both candidates have the same exact percentages.

And just as certainly, when the gap between the two candidates is equal to or more than twice the error margin—6 percentage points in our example—and if there are only two candidates and no undecided voters, you can say with confidence that the poll says Candidate A is clearly leading Candidate B.

When the gap between the two candidates is more than the error margin but less than twice the error margin, you should say that Candidate A "is ahead," "has an advantage" or "holds an edge." The story should mention that there is a small possibility that Candidate B is ahead of Candidate A.

When there are more than two choices or undecided voters—virtually in every poll in the real world—the question gets much more complicated.

While the solution is statistically complex, you can fairly easily evaluate this situation by estimating the error margin. You can do that by taking the sum of the percentages for each of the two candidates in question and multiplying it by the total respondents for the survey (only the likely voters if that is appropriate). This number is now the effective sample size for your judgment. Look up the sampling error in a table of statistics for that reduced sample size, and apply it to the candidate percentages. If they overlap, then you do not know if one is ahead. If they do not, then you can make the judgment that one candidate has a lead.

And bear in mind that when subgroup results are reported—women or blacks or young people—the sampling error margin for those figures is greater than for results based on the sample as a whole. Be very careful about reporting results from extremely small subgroups. Any results based on fewer than 100 respondents are subject to such large sampling errors that it is almost impossible to report the numbers in a meaningful manner.

13. What Other Kinds of Factors Can Skew Poll Results?

The margin of sampling error is just one possible source of inaccuracy in a poll. It is not necessarily the source of the greatest possible error; we use it because it's the only one that can be quantified. And, other things being equal, it is useful for evaluating whether differences between poll results are meaningful in a statistical sense.

Question phrasing and question order are also likely sources of flaws. Inadequate interviewer training and supervision, data processing errors and other operational problems can also introduce errors. Professional polling operations are less subject to these problems than volunteer-conducted polls, which are usually less trustworthy. Be particularly careful of polls conducted by untrained and unsupervised college students. There have been several cases where the results were at least in part reported by the students without conducting any survey at all.

You should always ask if the poll results have been "weighted." This process is usually used to account for unequal probabilities of selection and to adjust slightly the demographics in the sample. You should be aware that a poll could be manipulated unduly by weighting the numbers to produce a desired result. While some weighting may be appropriate, other weighting is not. Weighting a scientific poll is only appropriate to reflect unequal probabilities or to adjust to independent values that are mostly constant.

14. What Questions Were Asked?

You must find out the exact wording of the poll questions. Why? Because the very wording of questions can make major differences in the results.

Perhaps the best test of any poll question is your reaction to it. On the face of it, does the question seem fair and unbiased? Does it present a balanced set of choices? Would most people be able to answer the question?

On sensitive questions—such as abortion—the complete wording of the question should probably be included in your story. It may well be worthwhile to compare the results of several different polls from different organizations on sensitive questions. You should examine carefully both the results and the exact wording of the questions.

15. In What Order Were the Questions Asked?

Sometimes the very order of the questions can have an impact on the results. Often that impact is intentional; sometimes it is not. The impact of order can often be subtle.

During troubled economic times, for example, if people are asked what they think of the economy before they are asked their opinion of the president, the presidential popularity rating will probably be lower than if you had reversed the order of the questions. And in good economic times, the opposite is true.

What is important here is whether the questions that were asked prior to the critical question in the poll could sway the results. If the poll asks questions about abortion just before a question about an abortion ballot measure, the prior questions could sway the results.

16. What About "Push Polls"?

In recent years, some political campaigns and special-interest groups have used a technique called "push polls" to spread rumors and even outright lies about opponents. These efforts are not polls, but political manipulation trying to hide behind the smokescreen of a public opinion survey.

In a "push poll," a large number of people are called by telephone and asked to participate in a purported survey. The survey "questions" are really thinly-veiled accusations against an opponent or repetitions of rumors about a candidate's personal or professional behavior. The focus here is on making certain the respondent hears and understands the accusation in the question, not in gathering the respondent's opinions.

"Push polls" are unethical and have been condemned by professional polling organizations.

"Push polls" must be distinguished from some types of legitimate surveys done by political campaigns. At times, a campaign poll may ask a series of questions about contrasting issue positions of the candidates—or various things that could be said about a candidate, some of which are negative. These legitimate questions seek to gauge the public's reaction to a candidate's position or to a possible legitimate attack on a candidate's record.

A legitimate poll can be distinguished from a "push poll" usually by:

The number of calls made—a push poll makes thousands and thousands of calls, instead of hundreds for most surveys; The identity of who is making the telephone calls—a polling firm for a scientific survey as opposed to a telemarketing house or the campaign itself for a "push poll"; The lack of any true gathering of results in a "push poll," which has as its only objective the dissemination of false or misleading information.

17. What Other Polls Have Been Done on This Topic? Do They Say the Same Thing? If They Are Different, Why Are They Different?

Results of other polls—by a newspaper or television station, a public survey firm or even a candidate's opponent—should be used to check and contrast poll results you have in hand.

If the polls differ, first check the timing of the interviewing. If the polls were done at different times, the differing results may demonstrate a swing in public opinion.

If the polls were done about the same time, ask each poll sponsor for an explanation of the differences. Conflicting polls often make good stories.

18. What About Exit Polls?

Exit polls, properly conducted, are an excellent source of information about voters in a given election. They are the only opportunity to survey actual voters and only voters.

There are several issues that should be considered in reporting exit polls. First, exit polls report how voters believe they cast their ballots. The election of 2000 showed that voters may think they have voted for a candidate, but their votes may not have been recorded. Or in some cases, voters actually voted for a different candidate than they thought they did.

Second, absentee voters are not included in many exit polls. In states where a large number of voters vote either early or absentee, an absentee telephone poll may be combined with an exit poll to measure voter opinion. If in a specific case there are large numbers of absentee voters and no absentee poll, you should be careful to report that the exit poll is only of Election Day voters.

Third, make sure that the company conducting the exit poll has a track record. Too many exit polls are conducted in a minimal number of voting locations by people who do not have experience in this specialized method of polling. Those results can be misleading.

19. What Else Needs to Be Included in the Report of a Poll?

The key element in reporting polls is context. Not only does this mean that you should compare the poll to others taken at the same time or earlier, but it also means that you need to report on what events may have impacted on the poll results.

A good poll story not only reports the results of the poll, but also assists the reader in the interpretation of those results. If the poll shows a continued decline in consumer confidence even though leading economic indicators have improved, your report might include some analysis of whether or not people see improvement in their daily economic lives even though the indicators are on the rise.

If a candidate has shown marked improvement in a horse race, you might want to report about the millions of dollars spent on advertising immediately prior to the poll.

Putting the poll in context should be a major part of your reporting.

20. So I've Asked All the Questions. The Answers Sound Good. Should We Report the Results?

Yes, because reputable polling organizations consistently do good work.

However, remember that the laws of chance alone say that the results of one poll out of 20 may be skewed away from the public's real views just because of sampling error.

Also remember that no matter how good the poll, no matter how wide the margin, no matter how big the sample, a pre-election poll does not show that one candidate has the race "locked up." Things change—often and dramatically in politics. That's why candidates campaign.

If the poll was conducted correctly, and you have been able to obtain the information outlined here, your news judgment and that of your editors should be applied to polls, as it is to every other element of a story.

In spite of the difficulties, the public opinion survey, correctly conducted, is still the best objective measure of the state of the views of the public.

SHELDON R. GAWISER, PH.D., is the Director of Elections at NBC News. G. Evans Witt is the CEO of Princeton Survey Research Associates International. Both Gawiser and Witt are the cofounders of the Associated Press/NBC News Poll.

Herbert J. Gans  **NO**

Public Opinion Polls Do Not Always Report Public Opinion

Polls have long been newsworthy, but never more so than when their conclusions can be compared to contrary politician behavior, the recent gun control debate being a particularly dramatic example. The pollsters' finding that 90 percent of their respondents said they favored universal background checks for guns was juxtaposed (except by Fox News) with the Senate's filibustered rejection of such legislation.

More interesting and important, the news media turned poll respondents' answers to pollsters' questions into the expression of public opinion. In effect, the news media, and later many politicians, including President Obama, seemed to imply that the Republicans refused to listen to *vox populi*. Some may even have been thinking that the polls were sometimes a better instrument of American democracy than its elected officials.

In one respect, the polls *are* more democratic; they report the opinions of a random sample of the entire population, while elected officials have been chosen by an electorate which at best includes 60 percent of the eligible voters and at worst many fewer. Thus, when 90 percent of poll respondents agree on the answers to polling questions, the polls are sending a message about majoritarian democracy.

In other respects, however, polls are not the best representative of the popular will, for people's answers to pollster questions are not quite the same as their opinions—or, for that matter, public opinion.

The pollsters typically ask people whether they favor or oppose, agree or disagree, approve or disapprove of an issue, and their wording generally follows the centrist bias of the mainstream news media. They offer respondents only two sides (along with the opportunity to say "don't know" or "unsure"), thus leaving out alternatives proposed by people with minority political views. Occasionally, one side is presented in stronger or more approving language—but by and large, poll questions maintain the balanced neutrality of the mainstream news media.

The pollsters' reports and press releases usually begin with the asked question and then present tables with the statistical proportions of poll respondents giving each of the possible answers. However, the news media stories about the polls usually report only the results, and by leaving out the questions and the don't knows, transform answers into opinions. When these opinions are shared by a majority, the news stories turn poll respondents into the public, thus giving birth to public opinion.

Normally, the news story tells what proportion of that public favors the legislation being questioned or rejected by the Beltway politicians. Indeed, such polls are newsworthy in large part because the reportage is framed as a conflict between majoritarian opinions and politicians' rejection of the popular will.

To be sure, poll respondents favor what they tell the pollsters they favor. But still, poll answers are not quite the same as their opinions. While their answers may reflect their already determined opinions, they may also express what they feel, or believe they ought to feel, at the moment. Pollsters should therefore distinguish between respondents with previously determined opinion and those with spur-of-the-moment answers to pollster questions.

However, only rarely do pollsters ask whether the respondents have thought about the question before the pollsters called, or whether they will ever do so again. In addition, polls usually do not tell us whether respondents have talked about the issue with family or friends, or whether they have expressed their answer *cum* opinion in other, more directly political ways.

In fact, respondents incur no responsibilities with their answers, no subsequent obligation to vote or do anything else. Conversely, politicians can lose the next election with a vote that angers their base.

If poll results can be interpreted as opinion, they are pollster-evoked or *passive* opinions. They are not the *active* opinions of citizens who feel strongly about, or participate in some way in the debates about forthcoming legislation or a presidential decision.

Elected officials may take passive opinions into account but they pay far more attention to active opinions. Above all, however, politicians listen most closely to the usual suspects with power: influential citizens, Congressional leaders and whips, lobbies, and campaign funders.

Jennifer Steinhauer of *The New York Times* was right on target when she described the poll results as an expression of "national sentiment," which she then contrasted with the Senate's "political dynamic."

Some Corrective Fixes

Since polls will continue to be used as indicators of public opinion, the news media should be adding some context to their reporting of the results. From time to time, they should remind the news audience that polls are answers to questions rather than opinions, just as they now remind audiences of the polls' error margins.

In addition, the pollsters should be urged to pose and report intensity questions, telling the politicians and the public how strongly respondents feel about what they tell pollsters, and whether they have been politically active in behalf of these feelings.

At the same time, the news media should keep track of other kinds of intensity measures. For about 30 years, the Pew Research Center has been reporting what news stories a national sample says it follows very closely. Some respondents may exaggerate that closeness, but not many stories are followed closely by more than 50 percent of the sample. Over the years, stories that touch people emotionally and personally relevant ones have always scored highest.

In 2012, the Sandy Hook tragedy was followed very closely by 57 percent, and rising gas prices by 52 percent. In late January 2013, the gun control debate reached a high of 42 percent and stood at 37 percent in early April. The debates over the debt limit and immigration were followed very closely by just under 25 percent of the Pew sample, but 63 percent followed the Boston Marathon bombing very closely.

Better ways the news media can put the passivity of poll opinions into context include the following:

- Report news about active citizen expressions of opinion, at local town halls, organized debates, demonstrations, teach ins, and the like. Gatherings involving predominantly adult and older mainstream Americans are particularly important; and some politically conscientious websites could be counting and reporting the number of such active expressions, large and small, all across the country.
- Keep track of the number, content, and tone of phone calls, letters, and other communications to elected officials, particularly those directly involved in an issue. Spontaneous communications have priority over organized ones, notably the now ubiquitous petitions requiring only single clicks on a website.

  In fact, the mainstream news media, journalistic websites, and other enterprising fact-finders should regularly be asking elected and appointed officials about communications and visits from citizens on currently debated political and social issues.
- Plan follow-up stories after legislation dealing with major problems and issues has been approved or disapproved. Such stories are already being reported, but for the purpose of putting poll results in context, they should emphasize what citizen communications politicians received and try to find out which ones they took into account.

  Regular reporting of such stories would add to public understanding of which kinds of citizen participation and active opinion the politicians consider. That would also help people understand the place of polls in democratic politics, and perhaps lead to debates about whether they can or should play a larger role in politics. Such debates might even stimulate journalistic and other discussions of the pros and cons of majoritarian democracy.

HERBERT J. GANS is a distinguished sociologist from Columbia University who conducts work in urban affairs, policy research, and the use of news media, particularly as the decisions about what constitute news become manifest in news content.

EXPLORING THE ISSUE

Are Polls an Accurate Assessment of Public Opinion?

Critical Thinking and Reflection

1. Think about how often you hear polls reported and consider the sponsor of the poll as well as the results.
2. Consider whether polls become the focus of news stories or are used to set our agenda (agenda setting theory) about what is important.
3. Reflect on the rigor of conducting a strong, statistically relevant poll.
4. Understand the difference between public opinion and public statements reflecting a topic.
5. Develop a more critical eye to understanding how public opinion influences public policy.

Is There Common Ground?

The authors of these two selections agree that some polls, when carefully constructed to measure public opinion, can be accurate, but they differ on how news media report the results of polls and on whether polls are scientifically or casually constructed. The potential for measuring public opinion is important, but the application and use of polls sometimes skew the real meaning of the data that appear to represent public opinion.

The authors of both selections believe that with care, polls can be more accurate, and with a critical eye, journalists and the public can understand the authority of the pollsters and their products. They also agree that when polls are conducted correctly, they play an important role in the democratic process.

Additional Resources

James N. Druckman and Lawrence R. Jacobs, *Who Governs?: Presidents, Public Opinion and Manipulation* (University of Chicago Press, 2015). The authors of this book examine the way Presidents largely ignore public opinion of the masses and cater instead, to the whims of a few affluent citizens and political insiders.

Patrick Fisher, *Demographic Gaps in American Political Behavior* (New York: Westview Press, 2014). In this book, the author discusses how different political groups influence public opinion and the creation of policy.

Arthur S. Hayes, *Press Critics Are the Fifth Estate: Media Watchdogs in America* (Westport, CT and London: Praeger, 2008). Hayes discusses the rise of new media that make bloggers and other press critics a part of the political system by influencing public opinion through their roles as critics of mainstream media.

Jill Lepore, "Politics and the New Machine: What the Turn from Polls to Data Science Means for Democracy," *The New Yorker* (November 16, 2015). The author provides a rich history of polling and talks about how the methods of polling have not kept up with new technology.

Stacey Margolis, *Fictions of Mass Democracy in Nineteenth-Century America* (New York: Cambridge University Press, 2015). Before there were polls, public opinion was measured in very different ways. Margolis explores the impact of this type of governance, so predominant in the nineteenth century, and how that has affected today's belief in understanding public opinion.

Internet References . . .

Gallup Polls

www.gallup.com/home.aspx

Pew Internet Research

www.pewinternet.org/

Polling Report

http://www.pollingreport.com/

Rassmusen Reports

www.rasmussenreports.com/

Selected, Edited, and with Issue Framing Material by:
Alison Alexander, *University of Georgia*
and
Jarice Hanson, *University of Massachusetts—Amherst*

ISSUE

Are Twitter and Other Social Media a Good Source of Political Information?

YES: John H. Parmelee and Shannon L. Bichard, from *Politics and the Twitter Revolution: How Tweets Influence the Relationship between Political Leaders and the Public,* Lexington Books (2012)

NO: Clay Shirky, from "The Political Power of Social Media: Technology, the Public Sphere and Political Change," *Foreign Affairs* (2011)

Learning Outcomes

After reading this issue, you will be able to:

- Consider how social media, especially Twitter, is being used for political purposes.
- Reflect on how individuals use forms of media for political information.
- Think about the range of activities that constitute democratic participation.
- Consider how Twitter may persuade users to examine their own civic participation.

ISSUE SUMMARY

YES: In these sections of their longer study on the role of Twitter and politics, Professors John H. Parmelee and Shannon L. Bichard examine how political leaders use Twitter to influence the public. While politicians establish personal relationships with followers, some tweets are intended to influence policy. The authors examine the potential for the one-way form of communication provided by Twitter to engage with the public.

NO: Clay Shirky turns this issue around by asking about the use of social media to effect change within authoritarian regimes. He describes situations in which protests have been arranged by text. It is in the use of social media to coordinate actions and develop shared awareness that their power resides. But, he warns that these tools can be ineffective and cause as much harm as good.

T witter may be a unique form of media in that it is intended to be short-form communication (limited to 140 characters) and immediate (anyone with a Twitter account can send or receive messages). These messages are not filtered through the traditional "gatekeeper" of editor or production process and therefore can appear to be very personal. As we've learned over time, Twitter messages credited to an individual might actually be written and disseminated by someone else—either a public relations person, or someone else employed by (or posing as) the sender of the tweet. At the same time, much of Twitter is retweeted by the receivers of messages and passed on from one person to another. So, how is information via Twitter used and understood, and does this form of communication really matter?

There are many different approaches to understanding the power and impact of a new medium like Twitter. A number of people look at social networking in general as a boon to the democratic process of information sharing and exchange, while many others remain skeptical of short-form communications, like Twitter. The authors of both of these selections agree that studies investigating the real impact of Twitter and other social media's communicative potential in political life are only starting to emerge. Parmelee and Bichard focus on one aspect of Twitter use, to help us understand not only the potential for Twitter and politics, but also illuminate a number of realities and misconceptions about how prominent Twitter is, or how prominent it may become, in political life. Shirky looks at the life and death situations in which social media play a role.

One of the underlying premises of the use of any social network is the question of whether social media operate in the public sphere or not. Do social media, and Twitter in particular, contribute to a more democratic society by bypassing big media and allowing users a more direct form of communication from sender to receiver? Are tweets and retweets a form of political information dissemination, or are they public relations opportunities? Who tweets, and why? And most importantly, as our media landscape grows to encompass social media as well as legacy media, can short-form communications like tweets really influence the way the public thinks and behaves?

The selection from Parmelee and Bichard is taken from the Introduction and the Conclusion of their book, *Politics and the Twitter Revolution: How Tweets Influence the Relationship between Political Leaders and the Public*. It could be said that their position is an optimistic one. In this selection we learn who uses political tweets, and who, within the U.S. public, pays attention to them. The authors take the perspective that in the realm of political communication in the United States, Twitter followers tend to be from an older and more professional demographic than groups who use other forms of social media. They discuss the issues of followers' political ideologies, demographics, and the relative influence of Twitter vis-à-vis traditional media and interpersonal sources of information. They also warn that there is little research to date on whether Twitter actually influences political beliefs. They conclude that even though Twitter essentially operates as one-way communication from political leaders to the public, the relationship between political leaders and their followers is quite powerful.

Shirky takes an entirely different approach to examining the impact of social media use across a variety of protest situations. Rather than looking at how politicians use social media for political support, Shirky's article examines how those challenging authoritarian governments use social media and the consequences. He does not see social media as a good tool for immediate change, and particularly is concerned that social media campaigns can expose protesters. He argues that access to information is not a primary way that social media constrains government action. Social media are useful for coordinating action and creating social awareness, but they also can do as much harm as good. Shirky argues that the Internet and social media are much better at promoting long-term change, and argues instead for the support of local public speech and assembly to effect shorter-term change.

Together these selections help us understand the range of issues behind Twitter as a medium of information, and its role in the very important process of using media forms for democratic purposes such as understanding political information, changing political structure, and influencing users' beliefs, attitudes, and behaviors. Will Twitter and other social media evolve over time, and will more people gravitate to messages from political leaders as Twitter use spreads? Will new ways of using Twitter evolve to capture the attention of users, and ultimately make Twitter an even more important medium of information dissemination? What are the limits of Twitter as a medium? Will social media be able to foster social change, rather than just promote immediate protest?

Like many "new" forms of communication, we have a lot to learn as the technology and social use of the medium grow over time. For those Twitter users as well as those who contemplate using Twitter, it will be important to think of Twitter (and other social media) as elements within our larger media landscape.

For students and scholars who wish to pursue the persuasive capacity of the medium, there is a strong desire to compare Twitter to other forms of media; because Twitter continues to evolve, the potential for examining Twitter's impact on our society and in the world is a fascinating social phenomenon. Shirky's warning that we should remember that not every culture adopts technology and uses it in the way we do in the United States is an important point.

YES ↵

John H. Parmelee and Shannon L. Bichard

Politics and the Twitter Revolution: How Tweets Influence the Relationship between Political Leaders and the Public

. . . **P**olitical tweeting raises many questions for those who study political communication. For example, to what degree do political tweets influence follower's political views and behavior? . . . Do followers have certain characteristics that make some followers more easily influenced than others? Who can be most easily influenced may rest on characteristics such as demographics, ideology, interest in politics, trust in government, and followers' motives for using Twitter. To measure the impact of tweets, it is possible to find these connections by constructing a detailed profile of the people who choose to follow political leaders on Twitter. Measuring the impact of tweets also means comparing the effects of political tweets with more traditional forms of political influence: friends, family, acquaintances, and co-workers. Are tweeted messages from political leaders (whom most followers have usually never met) more or less politically influential than messages that are communicated by family or acquaintances?

. . .

Now is a good time to examine how Twitter is used in politics. . . . Twitter has enjoyed an exponential increase in popularity that compares only to social networking sites such as Facebook and YouTube. Twitter is used by more than 175 million people worldwide, and more than 30 billion tweets have been sent. Politicians are increasingly using it, too. Today, the president and most governors, members of Congress, and mayors of large metropolitan areas have Twitter accounts. President Barack Obama has the most Twitter followers of any political leader, with more than 7 million. Other political leaders tend to have between 10,000 and 100,000 followers, though some governors, mayors, and other officials have more

than 1 million followers. The number of followers that a political leader has varies considerably and often does not depend on the size of the leaders' constituency. For example, the mayor of New York (which has a population of 8 million), has about 83,000 followers. In comparison, the mayor of Newark, New Jersey (which has a population of less than 300,000), has more than 1 million followers.

When political leaders and their followers engage on Twitter, they are part of the power and promise of Web 2.0, which refers to websites and social networking platforms that enable users to create their own content and share it with other users. Just one example of Web 2.0 is the video-sharing site YouTube, a service where anyone can post video messages to be seen, commented on, and forwarded by millions of viewers literally overnight. In terms of politics, the participatory and interactive nature of Web 2.0, including Twitter, has the potential to promote a more open exchange of ideas across a wide audience concerning key issues.

. . .

Twitter's Features

While Twitter messages can be only 140 characters, a lot can be communicated in that small space. Tweets can include links to websites that provide additional information. Political leaders often use this linking function to direct followers to sites such as the following:

- online news sites or blogs that validate their policies
- websites for their campaign or an ally's campaign
- petitions
- photos of themselves on the job
- government-based sites that provide services to constituents

The following is an example of a tweet from Massachusetts Governor Duval Patrick that includes such a link:

- MassGovernor: Before grabbing your helmet, learn how the rules of the road have changed. http://cot.ag/dCnemg

Clicking the link sends the user to an official Commonwealth of Massachusetts site that explains a new law regarding vehicle safety. As can be seen in this example, a link's Web address often is shortened on Twitter to save valuable space.

Hashtags are another important aspect of political tweets. A *hashtag* is a word or abbreviation (designated in a tweet by the "#" sign) that can be searched on Twitter's website. The tweets of anyone who includes that hashtag are grouped together on Twitter. Hashtags have political value because political leaders, or anyone else, can spark dialog on an issue by giving the issue a hashtag in their tweets. Twitter users can search the hashtag, see what has been said about the issue, and they can also contribute to the conversation. The following tweet from the White House Twitter account shows how hashtags are used:

- whitehouse: President Obama: "the long battle to stop the leak and contain the oil is finally close to coming to an end" "#oilspill

Clicking (or searching for) the hashtag "#oilspill" directs users to hundreds of tweets from a wide cross-section of people who are talking about the 2010 British Petroleum (BP) oil spill in the Gulf of Mexico. Often, those tweets include additional links to websites and hashtags, which allow users to learn and discuss even more about BP, oil drilling, and the environmental impact of the spill.

Leaders also can spread their influence beyond their band of followers if they are included on "lists" that are made by Twitter users. Any user can create a list, which is simply a grouping of other Twitter users that is based on some commonality: a hobby, a musical taste, or an interest in politics. Users who click a list that is labeled, say, "influential political leaders," see a stream of tweets from the leaders on that list, regardless of whether the users are followers. Also, users can add leaders to a list even if the users are not the leaders' followers.

. . .

Since its founding in 2006, Twitter's popularity and use has skyrocketed. The service went from about 5 million users at the end of 2008 to 75 million users one year later. In addition, users are becoming increasingly active. Users went from sending 1 billion tweets a month in the fall of 2008,

to 2 billion tweets per month during the summer of 2010. According to media commentator Jolie O'Dell "Twitter's growth curve is clearly accelerating." Twitter is considered important enough that the Library of Congress is archiving every public tweet since the company's inception.

. . .

Some applications are designed especially to help political leaders and followers to be more influential (and influenced). The website TweetCongress displays the tweets of all congressional members, shows trending keywords and hashtags, and provides a directory to find which members tweet and how frequently. TweetCongress calls its site "a grass-roots effort to get our men and women in Congress to open up and have a real conversation with us." GovTwit, which focuses on the tweets of government agencies, has many of the same features as TweetCongress.

Twitter's early success also has come with some problems. The service has occasionally crashed due to the high volume of tweets. Also, hackers have had some success in hijacking user accounts. The most high-profile example came in January 2009, when hackers were able to send a phony tweet from the account of then-President-elect Obama. Other people simply set up a Twitter account and pretend to be somebody famous. As a result, Twitter now does "verified accounts" for celebrities and other high-profile users, including political leaders. This process requires a background check to establish the authenticity of the user. Despite some setbacks, Twitter has grown considerably since its founding and it attracts an audience that political leaders find valuable.

. . .

The Content of Political Tweets

What goes into leaders' tweets? There is research on that question. So far, the findings suggest that political leaders use tweets primarily to broadcast information about their policies and their personality. Interacting with followers is a secondary priority. One analysis of more than 6,000 tweets of members of Congress showed these results:

> Congresspeople are primarily using Twitter to disperse information, particularly links to news articles about themselves and to their blog posts, and to report on their daily activities. These tend not to provide new insights into government or the legislative process or to improve transparency: rather, they are vehicles for self-promotion.

Political leaders at the state level also focus heavily on disseminating information to followers about themselves and about their issues. A case study of one particularly prolific tweeter, Minnesota State Representative Laura Brod, found mentions of policy issues to be the most frequently occurring category of tweet. In second place were tweets she made that dealt with what the study called "personal life and musings."

Those politicians who are particularly successful at using Twitter make an effort to have more than one-way communication with followers. By replying to and retweeting followers' tweets, leaders are able to create a conversation on Twitter that keeps existing followers satisfied and attracts more followers. That strategy is one reason why Newark's Mayor Booker has more than twice as many followers as there are residents in the city he runs. Booker's tweets often include two-way communication with followers, and he does not focus solely on policy. A study by Donia found that his tweets are designed to meet the needs of a busy social media audience:

> Mayor Booker realizes that there are literally hundreds of thousands of people reading what he says on a daily basis and they likely give his page or profile a quick scroll before moving on to something else, so his information has to captivate them, if even for a few seconds. He is able to captivate them by mixing up his types of posts—not just events or quotations—but also links, videos, pictures, and stories.

Some other political leaders conduct two-way communication on Twitter. Congressman Michael Burgess of Texas invited the public to ask questions via Twitter during a health policy forum that was being broadcast online. In another example, to field questions about budgetary issues, Democrats conducted a "Twitter town hall" in which members of Congress responded to comments sent to the hashtag #AskDems.

The "personality" of the writing in political tweets can range considerably. Some messages are formal and read like short press releases, such as the following from New York Mayor Michael Bloomberg:

- MikeBloomberg: Dangerous heat forecast for NYC this weekend. For info on cooling centers call 311, visit http://nyc.gov/oem or follow @notifyNYC

Others tweets have a homespun, personal style. Missouri Senator Claire McCaskill is an exemplar of this approach, as can be seen in her response to a followers' tweet:

- Clairecmc: Yes @tigeranniemac that was me at Target in the soap aisle. You shoulda said hi. Was with my daughter Lily. We're very friendly.

Still others' tweets include humor or sarcasm to get the point across. Senator John McCain, who has long been known for fighting what he sees as wasteful federal spending, uses sarcasm frequently when tweeting about such spending:

- SenJohnMcCain: $1,427,250 for genetic improvements of switchgrass—I thought switchgrass genes were pretty good already, guess I was wrong.

Sometimes the content in political tweets has gotten political leaders in trouble, and the following are some famous illustrations of that fact. For example, New York Congressman Anthony Weiner was forced to resign after he tweeted a lewd photo. Michigan Congressman Peter Hoekstra caused a security risk when he tweeted that his congressional delegation had just landed in Iraq. Missouri Senator Claire McCaskill had to apologize after being criticized, even by her own mother, for tweeting on the House floor during Obama's first State of the Union address. Problems sometimes arise because of the speed and ease at which leaders can send a tweet, combined with the desire to make their followers feel connected.

. . .

Reasons to Tweet

Tweeting serves several purposes for political leaders. The main purpose is that Twitter allows leaders to communicate directly to a mass audience. Politicians are always looking for ways to get their message across without having it filtered and potentially altered by others, such as news media. Twitter, along with other social networks, can fill that need. That reason is why many inside and outside politics, such as former House Speaker Newt Gingrich, encourage its use: "Using Twitter to bypass traditional media and directly reach voters is definitely a good thing." Some political leaders are unable to get as much press coverage as they desire, or go through periods of limited power. Spreading the word on Twitter is essential for these politicians. One media consultant noted that Republicans (GOP) used Twitter far more than Democrats in the months after Obama's inauguration solidified Democratic control of the legislative and executive branches of government.

Because the GOP's power was at low ebb, they found that their ideas and issues were not being covered; thus Twitter became an alternate venue to disseminate their message. In addition, strategic use of Twitter can increase the amount of press coverage that a politician gets. Journalists often follow the politicians they cover, so tweets that include newsworthy information can lead to a story in traditional media outlets.

Tweeting can serve to mobilize action. Many political tweets include requests for followers to take some action, such as contributing to a campaign or signing a petition. A leader's tweet followers are an ideal group to contact to take part in such action because they may be more likely to be motivated to do what they are asked than the average person. The very act of choosing to be a follower suggests a significant interest and commitment to that leader.

The rise of the Tea Party is one case study of how Twitter can be used to mobilize political activists. Members of the Tea Party (whose main cause is to reduce federal spending) are part of a movement that has little centralized authority and is spread across the country. Yet without the organizational structure and resources of a major political party, they have staged numerous large protests and elected candidates to office. Sarno found that Tea Party members' use of Twitter was instrumental in their ability to share ideas on how to build up the movement and attract people to their protests:

> Much of the sharing is now facilitated by the fast-growing messaging site Twitter, where today the keyword "teaparty" was one of the most frequently used terms. Users sent out a flurry of updates about attendance, links to photos on Flickr and Photobucket, and videos on YouTube and other sites.

Mobilizing activists to sign petitions is regularly done on Twitter. Act.ly is one such site that has found success among progressives who want to sway political leaders. After creating a petition on act.ly and tweeting it, anyone who receives the petition can "sign" it by retweeting. The petition tweets are then sent via Twitter to the political leaders being targeted. Leaders can respond to the petitions if they choose. Speed and the ability to reach out to many people are two great advantages of using Twitter for political petitions (further, it is free). "You can go from outrage to petition idea to people signing in about 2 minutes," according to Gilliam, the site's creator. "There is huge potential to tweet change." One environmental interest group used the Twitter petition concept

to pressure Massachusetts Senator Scott Brown to vote its way on pending energy legislation.

Speed of idea dissemination is why many politicians use Twitter. When the then House Speaker Nancy Pelosi wanted to call back Congress early from a recess to vote on Medicaid and education funding, she broke the news on Twitter. In the modern 24-hour news cycle, there is no faster way to transmit information. According to journalist Michael O'Brien,

> Her office said they opted to use Twitter to break the news, instead of a conventional press release, because of the intense interest in the vote. "We wanted to get the word out quickly on the decision that the House will be voting to keep teachers on the job. The Senate cloture vote was a major topic that was being followed closely on Twitter, the blogs, online news site, newspapers, TV, and wires," said Nadeam Elshami, a spokesman for the speaker. "So that is why we used Twitter, and we e-mailed the news release within minutes."

Twitter is used differently by the major political parties. Republicans took an early lead over Democrats in terms of joining Twitter, tweeting frequently, and attracting followers. In Congress, for example, the list of members who send the most tweets per day includes few Democrats. The Democrats also lag behind Republicans when it comes to the number of followers and amount of influence. Republicans hold 70 of the 100 most influential congressional Twitter accounts. However, the Democrats are beginning to use Twitter more. In fall of 2009, fewer than 60 Democratic members used Twitter; but 156 used it as of the summer of 2011. In comparison, 229 Republican members tweet.

. . .

The Impact of Twitter: Research Results

Now that billions of tweets are being sent by more than 100 million people worldwide, some researchers and companies are devoted to measuring the ways in which Twitter use influences politics and other facets of society. One of the most difficult aspects of this research work is determining what constitutes "influence" on Twitter. There are many possible definitions of the concept of influence. In terms of politics, for example, one measure of influence is to simply count the number of followers that leaders have and then conclude that those politicians with the most followers have the most influence. By that measure, Obama's 7 million followers make him the most influential leader. However, this measure ignores many important features of Twitter that, if used effectively, can increase a leader's influence. Features such as retweeting, replying, and linking to URLs are especially useful to examine. For example, a leader with 10,000 followers may be able to spread his or her ideas further than a leader with 20,000 followers, depending on how actively the two leaders' messages are retweeted by followers. In addition, leaders who often reply to followers' tweeted questions and comments can create an appreciative and loyal group of followers who may be more willing to fulfill leaders' requests for action. One of those actions is clicking links; these links direct followers to websites that a leader deems politically useful. Such links often are embedded in a leader's tweets.

Because of the different ways in which influence can be measured, some social media analytics companies (such as Sysomos, Twitalyzer, and Klout) have examined the concept of influence by using a variety of definitions. For instance, Sysomos looked at the Twitter influence of political leaders such as Obama, celebrities such as Britney Spears, and news organizations such as *The New York Times*. Sysomos found that a follower count is not as meaningful a measure of influence as one would think. Sysomos's calculation of influence, which is called an *authority ranking*, was based on several factors, including these characteristics: number of followers, frequency of updates, and retweets. By this measure by Sysomos, Obama has less influence than *The New York Times*, even though the news organization has far fewer followers than the president. In another example, in measuring the amount of replying that leaders do to followers' tweets, Twitalyzer found that many politicians, including senators McCain and McCaskill, took more time to address questions and comments than Obama. Klout has still other ways to measure the impact of leaders on the microblog. One of Klout's calculations of influence is called *true reach*, a measure that reveals how many of a leader's followers are paying attention to the tweets they receive. Another Klout calculation of influence is called a *network influence score*, which takes into account that some followers are more important to a leader than other followers. Some followers are highly influential in terms of who follows them and how engaged they are. A leader whose network of followers is highly influential is likely to find Twitter a more valuable political tool than a leader with followers who have a low network influence score.

. . .

Who Follows Political Leaders on Twitter—And Why?

Research shows that followers who use Twitter for general purposes are from an older and more professional demographic than those who use other forms of social media. But no studies [to date] have examined the demographic makeup of those who follow political leaders on Twitter. This lack of studies is important because certain demographic and psychographic groups, such as those who are highly educated and interested in politics, are potentially more politically influential and valuable to leaders than other groups. Even more fundamental is to discover what types of people and organizations are considered to be political leaders who are worth following. Certain individuals, such as elected public officials, are an obvious choice of who might be worth following. But to what degree do followers choose to follow people who fall outside that narrow definition? Today some of the most politically influential people hold no office. Al Gore (a former U.S. vice president) and Sarah Palin (a former candidate for U.S. vice president) are two good examples. Gore is arguably more powerful today in terms of environmental politics than when he was vice president. As a private citizen, Palin has reached a larger audience and influenced the national agenda more than when she was governor of Alaska.

In addition to finding out who is being followed, it also would be helpful to know what motivates users in choosing which political leaders to follow. Do they follow leaders primarily as a means to receive political information? If so, that would be an information-seeking motive. Or do they follow leaders because they want to interact with leaders or fellow political junkies? If so, that would be a social and self-expressive motive. Further, does a follower's motivation affect how much influence a leader's tweets have?

How Influential Are Political Tweets?

Political leaders tweet for many reasons, including going over the heads of the mass media (such as television) to reach the public. By tweeting, they wish to generate media coverage. At other times, these leaders want to mobilize their political "troops" of followers to take action on their behalf. Leaders could suggest to followers a wide variety of actions: take part in a petition or protest, read a recommended blog post or news story, spread the word to others to vote for a candidate, or support legislation. Spreading the word is especially easy on Twitter because of its features such as retweeting, mentioning, hashtags, and website linking. While previous research has found that Twitter users are eager to share opinions and often do so regarding brands they like or dislike it is not clear whether followers of political tweets are as willing to spreading the word about politicians and policies. Because there is no research on how influential political tweets are on followers, it is impossible to know how often followers take actions that are requested by leaders. In addition, it is not clear how much influence political tweets have on shaping followers' political views. Is that influence greater than more traditional sources of political influence, such as friends, family, and co-workers? It may even be that the influence of political tweets varies depending on a follower's ideology or demographic makeup.

. . .

How Twitter Influences the Relationship between Political Leaders and the Public

. . . Because of the number of people using the microblogging service for politics, how they use it, and how they are affected by it, Twitter influences how political leaders and the public relate in a number of crucial ways:

- The relationship that followers have with their leaders is quite powerful. Political leaders' tweets regularly cause followers to look up information and take other actions that the leaders request. In addition, the relationship that followers have with the leaders often influences followers' political views as much as or more than their family and friends.
- From the followers' perspective, the relationship goes beyond receiving information from leaders; it is about sharing leaders' information with others. Leaders tweet political information to followers, and followers pass that information along. Leaders' tweets give followers something to talk and tweet about with others, which is a popular activity among followers. This relationship is beneficial for followers and leaders. Followers now have access to more political information to share, and leaders have their views spread by followers to an increasingly wide audience.
- From the leaders' perspective, the relationship is based on using Twitter mainly as a one-way communication vehicle to transmit their policies and ideas. However, their followers want to use Twitter as a forum for two-way communication with

leaders and other politically interested individuals. As a result, many followers crave engagement with leaders but often are left disappointed.
- One of Twitter's great strengths is that it forces political leaders (and anyone else) to quickly get to the point. Politicians, for example, are notoriously longwinded in their speeches, press releases, and other forms of communication. Those followers who receive politicians' brief tweets, however, are able to see elected officials in a new light. The 140-character limit of tweets means that politicians and other leaders must be succinct in their writing, and that brevity is a refreshing change. As writing teacher William Zinsser noted: "Clutter is the disease of American writing. We are a society strangling in unnecessary words, circular construction, pompous frills and meaningless jargon. . . . The secret of good writing is to strip every sentence to its cleanest components." Twitter imposes that kind of brevity.
- While the average political Twitter user often seeks a politically diverse range of leaders to follow, those who are extremely ideological tend to avoid diverse viewpoints on Twitter. This practice may not be healthy.

. . .

So what makes political leaders' tweets so influential? Participants in the in-depth interviews said there are nine elements that cause leaders' tweets to be acted upon: clarity, a call to action, personal relevance, professional usefulness, helpful links and hashtags, including a political counterpoint, humor, interactivity, and outrageousness. Some of these elements are important for fairly obvious reasons; for example, tweets that are written clearly and include politically useful information have a better chance to persuade than tweets that are confusing or irrelevant. Other elements, however, deserve further discussion. The fact that participants said they were looking for political counterpoints indicates they are open to having their political views influenced by an ideologically wide range of leaders. The desire for humorous political tweets dovetails with the finding that many followers have an entertainment motivation in following political leaders. Also, other research has found humor to be quite persuasive. One study on why some e-mail messages are forwarded frequently found that humor was a key determinant because humor can "spark strong emotion." Interactivity, as has been noted previously, is an important element because followers like to see their leaders engaging with their audiences (not merely transmitting to them). One form of interactivity happens when leaders solicit advice from their followers. The last element mentioned, outrageousness, underscores the point that leaders' tweets can have unintended consequences. A tweet that seems exaggerated or false often causes followers to react, sometimes by criticizing the leader who sent it.

Taken together, the findings add to what is known about the persuasiveness of word-of-mouth communication. While past research shows that companies can harness the power of WOM to create buzz marketing campaigns around their products, far less is known about whether political leaders can use Twitter to create political buzz. Surveys and in-depth interviews with followers indicate that political leaders can be proactive in using their tweets to generate a lot of interest in an issue. What leaders want to avoid, however, is using Twitter to do political "astroturf" campaigns, which are "campaigns disguised as spontaneous, popular 'grassroots' behavior that are in reality carried out by a single person or organization." Astroturfers achieve this effect on Twitter by creating many fake user accounts to initially spread a leader's message. However, such a practice is not necessary on Twitter because followers seem quite willing to spread leaders' ideas without any deception needed.

Followers' motives play a major role in how influential political leaders' tweets can be. Those followers with social and self-expressive motives were the most likely to respond to leaders' tweets by retweeting, looking for recommended information, or taking suggested actions. With that knowledge in mind, it becomes even clearer why political leaders can benefit by interacting more with their followers. Those followers with social and self-expressive motives are the individuals who interact the most on Twitter and expect engagement with the leaders they follow. As a result, leaders who engage in two-way communication on Twitter stand the best chance of attracting and keeping those followers with social and self-expressive motives—the very individuals most influenced by leaders.

JOHN H. PARMELEE is an associate professor in the Department of Communication at the University of North Florida. Most of his research involves political communication and journalism in emerging democracies.

SHANNON L. BICHARD is an associate professor in the College of Mass Communications at Texas Tech University. She teaches advertising, and her research interests focus on public opinion and consumer behavior.

Clay Shirky  **NO**

The Political Power of Social Media: Technology, the Public Sphere and Political Change

On January 17, 2001, during the impeachment trial of Philippine President Joseph Estrada, loyalists in the Philippine Congress voted to set aside key evidence against him. Less than two hours after the decision was announced, thousands of Filipinos, angry that their corrupt president might be let off the hook, converged on Epifanio de los Santos Avenue, a major crossroads in Manila. The protest was arranged, in part, by forwarded text messages reading, "Go 2 EDSA. Wear blk." The crowd quickly swelled, and in the next few days, over a million people arrived, choking traffic in downtown Manila.

The public's ability to coordinate such a massive and rapid response—close to seven million text messages were sent that week—so alarmed the country's legislators that they reversed course and allowed the evidence to be presented. Estrada's fate was sealed; by January 20, he was gone. The event marked the first time that social media had helped force out a national leader. Estrada himself blamed "the text-messaging generation" for his downfall.

Since the rise of the Internet in the early 1990s, the world's networked population has grown from the low millions to the low billions. Over the same period, social media have become a fact of life for civil society worldwide, involving many actors—regular citizens, activists, nongovernmental organizations, telecommunications firms, software providers, governments. This raises an obvious question for the U.S. government: How does the ubiquity of social media affect U.S. interests, and how should U.S. policy respond to it?

As the communications landscape gets denser, more complex, and more participatory, the networked population is gaining greater access to information, more opportunities to engage in public speech, and an enhanced ability to undertake collective action. In the political arena, as the protests in Manila demonstrated, these increased freedoms can help loosely coordinated publics demand change.

The Philippine strategy has been adopted many times since. In some cases, the protesters ultimately succeeded, as in Spain in 2004, when demonstrations organized by text messaging led to the quick ouster of Spanish Prime Minister José María Aznar, who had inaccurately blamed the Madrid transit bombings on Basque separatists. The Communist Party lost power in Moldova in 2009 when massive protests coordinated in part by text message, Facebook, and Twitter broke out after an obviously fraudulent election. Around the world, the Catholic Church has faced lawsuits over its harboring of child rapists, a process that started when The Boston Globes 2002 expose of sexual abuse in the church went viral online in a matter of hours.

There are, however, many examples of the activists failing, as in Belarus in March 2006, when street protests (arranged in part by e-mail) against President Aleksandr Lukashenko's alleged vote rigging swelled, then faltered, leaving Lukashenko more determined than ever to control social media. During the June 2009 uprising of the Green Movement in Iran, activists used every possible technological coordinating tool to protest the miscount of votes for Mir Hossein Mousavi but were ultimately brought to heel by a violent crackdown. . . .

The use of social media tools—text messaging, e-mail, photo sharing, social networking, and the like—does not have a single preordained outcome. Therefore, attempts to outline their effects on political action are too often reduced to dueling anecdotes. If you regard the failure of the Belarusian protests to oust Lukashenko as paradigmatic, you will regard the Moldovan experience as an outlier, and vice versa. Empirical work on the subject is also hard to come by, in part because these tools are so new and in part because relevant examples are so rare. The safest characterization of recent quantitative attempts to answer the question, Do digital tools enhance democracy? (such as those by Jacob Groshek and Philip Howard) is that these tools probably do not hurt in the short run and might help in the long run—and that they have the most dramatic effects in states where a public sphere already constrains the actions of the government.

Despite this mixed record, social media have become coordinating tools for nearly all of the world's political movements, just as most of the world's authoritarian governments (and, alarmingly, an increasing number of democratic ones) are trying to limit access to it. In response, the U.S. State Department has committed itself to "Internet freedom" as a specific policy aim. Arguing for the right of people to use the Internet freely is an appropriate policy for the United States, both because it aligns with the strategic goal of strengthening civil society worldwide and because it resonates with American beliefs about freedom of expression. But attempts to yoke the idea of Internet freedom to short-term goals—particularly ones that are country-specific or are intended to help particular dissident groups or encourage regime change—are likely to be ineffective on average. And when they fail, the consequences can be serious.

Although the story of Estrada's ouster and other similar events have led observers to focus on the power of mass protests to topple governments, the potential of social media lies mainly in their support of civil society and the public sphere—change measured in years and decades rather than weeks or months. The U.S. government should maintain Internet freedom as a goal to be pursued in a principled and regime-neutral fashion, not as a tool for effecting immediate policy aims country by country. It should likewise assume that progress will be incremental and, unsurprisingly, slowest in the most authoritarian regimes.

The Perils of Internet Freedom

In January 2010, U.S. Secretary of State Hillary Clinton outlined how the United States would promote Internet freedom abroad. She emphasized several kinds of freedom, including the freedom to access information (such as the ability to use Wikipedia and Google inside Iran), the freedom of ordinary citizens to produce their own public media (such as the rights of Burmese activists to blog), and the freedom of citizens to converse with one another (such as the Chinese public's capacity to use instant messaging without interference).

Most notably, Clinton announced funding for the development of tools designed to reopen access to the Internet in countries that restrict it. This "instrumental" approach to Internet freedom concentrates on preventing states from censoring outside Web sites, such as Google, YouTube, or that of The New York Times. It focuses only secondarily on public speech by citizens and least of all on private or social uses of digital media. According to this vision, Washington can and should deliver rapid, directed responses to censorship by authoritarian regimes.

The instrumental view is politically appealing, action-oriented, and almost certainly wrong. It overestimates the value of broadcast media while underestimating the value of media that allow citizens to communicate privately among themselves. It overestimates the value of access to information, particularly information hosted in the West, while underestimating the value of tools for local coordination. And it overestimates the importance of computers while underestimating the importance of simpler tools, such as cell phones.

The instrumental approach can also be dangerous. Consider the debacle around the proposed censorship-circumvention software known as Haystack, which, according to its developer, was meant to be a "one-to-one match for how the [Iranian] regime implements censorship." The tool was widely praised in Washington; the U.S. government even granted it an export license. But the program was never carefully vetted, and when security experts examined it, it turned out that it not only failed at its goal of hiding messages from governments but also made it, in the words of one analyst, "possible for an adversary to specifically pinpoint individual users." . . . The challenges of . . . Haystack demonstrate how difficult it is to weaponize social media to pursue country-specific and near-term policy goals.

New media conducive to fostering participation can indeed increase the freedoms Clinton outlined, just as the printing press, the postal service, the telegraph, and the telephone did before. One complaint about the idea of new media as a political force is that most people simply use these tools for commerce, social life, or self-distraction, but this is common to all forms of media. Far more people in the 1500s were reading erotic novels than Martin Luther's "Ninety-five Theses," and far more people before the American Revolution were reading Poor Richard's Almanack than the work of the Committees of Correspondence. But those political works still had an enormous political effect.

Just as Luther adopted the newly practical printing press to protest against the Catholic Church, and the American revolutionaries synchronized their beliefs using the postal service that Benjamin Franklin had designed, today's dissident movements will use any means possible to frame their views and coordinate their actions; it would be impossible to describe the Moldovan Communist Party's loss of Parliament after the 2009 elections without discussing the use of cell phones and online tools by its opponents to mobilize. Authoritarian governments stifle communication among their citizens because they fear, correctly, that a better-coordinated populace would constrain their ability to act without oversight.

Despite this basic truth—that communicative freedom is good for political freedom—the instrumental mode of Internet statecraft is still problematic. It is difficult for outsiders to understand the local conditions of dissent. External support runs the risk of tainting even peaceful opposition as being directed by foreign elements. Dissidents can be exposed by the unintended effects of novel tools. A government's demands for Internet freedom abroad can vary from country to country, depending on the importance of the relationship, leading to cynicism about its motives.

The more promising way to think about social media is as long-term tools that can strengthen civil society and the public sphere. In contrast to the instrumental view of Internet freedom, this can be called the "environmental" view. According to this conception, positive changes in the life of a country, including pro-democratic regime change, follow, rather than precede, the development of a strong public sphere. This is not to say that popular movements will not successfully use these tools to discipline or even oust their governments, but rather that U.S. attempts to direct such uses are likely to do more harm than good. Considered in this light, Internet freedom is a long game, to be conceived of and supported not as a separate agenda but merely as an important input to the more fundamental political freedoms.

The Theater of Collapse

Any discussion of political action in repressive regimes must take into account the astonishing fall of communism in 1989 in eastern Europe and the subsequent collapse of the Soviet Union in 1991. Throughout the Cold War, the United States invested in a variety of communications tools, including broadcasting the Voice of America radio station, hosting an American pavilion in Moscow (home of the famous Nixon-Khrushchev "kitchen debate"), and smuggling Xerox machines behind the Iron Curtain to aid the underground press, or samizdat. Yet despite this emphasis on communications, the end of the Cold War was triggered not by a defiant uprising of Voice of America listeners but by economic change. As the price of oil fell while that of wheat spiked, the Soviet model of selling expensive oil to buy cheap wheat stopped working. As a result, the Kremlin was forced to secure loans from the West, loans that would have been put at risk had the

government intervened militarily in the affairs of non-Russian states. In 1989, one could argue, the ability of citizens to communicate, considered against the background of macroeconomic forces, was largely irrelevant.

. . .

The ability of these groups to create and disseminate literature and political documents, even with simple photocopiers, provided a visible alternative to the communist regimes. For large groups of citizens in these countries, the political and, even more important, economic bankruptcy of the government was no longer an open secret but a public fact. This made it difficult and then impossible for the regimes to order their troops to take on such large groups.

Thus, it was a shift in the balance of power between the state and civil society that led to the largely peaceful collapse of communist control. The state's ability to use violence had been weakened, and the civil society that would have borne the brunt of its violence had grown stronger. When civil society triumphed, many of the people who had articulated opposition to the communist regimes—such as Tadeusz Mazowiecki in Poland and Vaclav Havel in Czechoslovakia—became the new political leaders of those countries. Communications tools during the Cold War did not cause governments to collapse, but they helped the people take power from the state when it was weak.

The idea that media, from the Voice of America to samizdat, play a supporting role in social change by strengthening the public sphere echoes the historical role of the printing press. As the German philosopher Jürgen Habermas argued in his 1962 book, The Structural Transformation of the Public Sphere, the printing press helped democratize Europe by providing space for discussion and agreement among politically engaged citizens, often before the state had fully democratized, an argument extended by later scholars, such as Asa Briggs, Elizabeth Eisenstein, and Paul Starr.

Political freedom has to be accompanied by a civil society literate enough and densely connected enough to discuss the issues presented to the public. In a famous study of political opinion after the 1948 U.S. presidential election, the sociologists Elihu Katz and Paul Lazarsfeld discovered that mass media alone do not change people's minds; instead, there is a two-step process. Opinions are first transmitted by the media, and then they get echoed by friends, family members, and colleagues. It is in this second, social step that political opinions are formed. This is the step in which the Internet in general, and social media in particular, can make a difference. As with the printing press, the Internet spreads not just media consumption but media production as well—it allows people to privately and publicly articulate and debate a welter of conflicting views.

A slowly developing public sphere, where public opinion relies on both media and conversation, is the core of the environmental view of Internet freedom. As opposed to the self-aggrandizing view that the West holds the source code for democracy—and if it were only made accessible, the remaining autocratic states would crumble—the environmental view assumes that little political change happens without the dissemination and adoption of ideas and opinions in the public sphere. Access to information is far less important, politically, than access to conversation. Moreover, a public sphere is more likely to emerge in a society as a result of people's dissatisfaction with matters of economics or day-to-day governance than from their embrace of abstract political ideals.

To take a contemporary example, the Chinese government today is in more danger of being forced to adopt democratic norms by middle-class members of the ethnic Han majority demanding less corrupt local governments than it is by Uighurs or Tibetans demanding autonomy. Similarly, the One Million Signatures Campaign, an Iranian women's rights movement that focuses on the repeal of laws inimical to women, has been more successful in liberalizing the behavior of the Iranian government than the more confrontational Green Movement.

For optimistic observers of public demonstrations, this is weak tea, but both the empirical and the theoretical work suggest that protests, when effective, are the end of a long process, rather than a replacement for it. Any real commitment by the United States to improving political freedom worldwide should concentrate on that process—which can only occur when there is a strong public sphere.

The Conservative Dilemma

Disciplined and coordinated groups, whether businesses or governments, have always had an advantage over undisciplined ones: they have an easier time engaging in collective action because they have an orderly way of directing the action of their members. Social media can compensate for the disadvantages of undisciplined groups by reducing the costs of coordination. The anti-Estrada movement in the Philippines used the ease of sending and forwarding text messages to organize a massive group with no need (and no time) for standard managerial control. As a result, larger, looser groups can now take on some kinds of coordinated action, such as protest movements and public media campaigns, that were previously reserved for formal organizations. For political movements, one of the main forms of coordination is what the military calls "shared

awareness," the ability of each member of a group to not only understand the situation at hand but also understand that everyone else does, too. Social media increase shared awareness by propagating messages through social networks. . . .

The Chinese anticorruption protests that broke out in the aftermath of the devastating May 2008 earthquake in Sichuan are another example[s] of such ad hoc synchronization. The protesters were parents, particularly mothers, who had lost their only children in the collapse of shoddily built schools, the result of collusion between construction firms and the local government. . . . The consequences of government corruption were made broadly visible, and it went from being an open secret to a public truth.

The Chinese government originally allowed reporting on the post-earthquake protests, but abruptly reversed itself in June. Security forces began arresting protesters and threatening journalists when it became clear that the protesters were demanding real local reform and not merely state reparations. From the government's perspective, the threat was not that citizens were aware of the corruption, which the state could do nothing about in the short run. Beijing was afraid of the possible effects if this awareness became shared: it would have to either enact reforms or respond in a way that would alarm more citizens. After all, the prevalence of camera phones has made it harder to carry out a widespread but undocumented crackdown.

This condition of shared awareness—which is increasingly evident in all modern states—creates what is commonly called "the dictator's dilemma" but that might more accurately be described by the phrase coined by the media theorist Briggs: "the conservative dilemma," so named because it applies not only to autocrats but also to democratic governments and to religious and business leaders. The dilemma is created by new media that increase public access to speech or assembly, with the spread of such media, whether photocopiers or Web browsers, a state accustomed to having a monopoly on public speech finds itself called to account for anomalies between its view of events and the public's. The two responses to the conservative dilemma are censorship and propaganda. But neither of these is as effective a source of control as the enforced silence of the citizens. The state will censor critics or produce propaganda as it needs to, but both of those actions have higher costs than simply not having any critics to silence or reply to in the first place. But if a government were to shut down Internet access or ban cell phones, it would risk radicalizing otherwise pro-regime citizens or harming the economy.

The conservative dilemma exists in part because political speech and apolitical speech are not mutually exclusive. Many of the South Korean teenage girls who turned out in Seoul's Cheonggyecheon Park in 2008 to protest U.S. beef imports were radicalized in the discussion section of a Web site dedicated to Dong Bang Shin Ki, a South Korean boy band. DBSK is not a political group, and the protesters were not typical political actors. But that online community, with around 800,000 active members, amplified the second step of Katz and Lazarsfeld's two-step process by allowing members to form political opinions through conversation.

Popular culture also heightens the conservative dilemma by providing cover for more political uses of social media. Tools specifically designed for dissident use are politically easy for the state to shut down, whereas tools in broad use become much harder to censor without risking politicizing the larger group of otherwise apolitical actors. Ethan Zuckerman of Harvard's Berkman Center for Internet and Society calls this "the cute cat theory of digital activism." Specific tools designed to defeat state censorship (such as proxy servers) can be shut down with little political penalty, but broader tools that the larger population uses to, say, share pictures of cute cats are harder to shut down.

For these reasons, it makes more sense to invest in social media as general, rather than specifically political, tools to promote self-governance. The norm of free speech is inherently political and far from universally shared. To the degree that the United States makes free speech a first-order goal, it should expect that goal to work relatively well in democratic countries that are allies, less well in undemocratic countries that are allies, and least of all in undemocratic countries that are not allies. But nearly every country in the world desires economic growth. Since governments jeopardize that growth when they ban technologies that can be used for both political and economic coordination, the United States should rely on countries' economic incentives to allow widespread media use. In other words, the U.S. government should work for conditions that increase the conservative dilemma, appealing to states' self-interest rather than the contentious virtue of freedom, as a way to create or strengthen countries' public spheres.

Social Media Skepticism

There are, broadly speaking, two arguments against the idea that social media will make a difference in national politics. The first is that the tools are themselves ineffective, and the second is that they produce as much harm as good, because repressive governments are becoming better at using these tools to suppress dissent.

The critique of ineffectiveness, most recently offered by Malcolm Gladwell in The New Yorker, concentrates on examples of what has been termed "slacktivism," whereby casual participants seek social change through low-cost activities, such as joining Facebook's "Save Darfur" group, that are long on bumper-sticker sentiment and short on any useful action. The critique is correct but not central to the question of social media's power; the fact that barely committed actors cannot click their way to a better world does not mean that committed actors cannot use social media effectively. Recent protest movements . . . have used social media not as a replacement for real-world action but as a way to coordinate it. As a result, all of those protests exposed participants to the threat of violence, and in some cases its actual use. In fact, the adoption of these tools (especially cell phones) as a way to coordinate and document real-world action is so ubiquitous that it will probably be a part of all future political movements.

This obviously does not mean that every political movement that uses these tools will succeed, because the state has not lost the power to react. This points to the second, and much more serious, critique of social media as tools for political improvement—namely, that the state is gaining increasingly sophisticated means of monitoring, interdicting, or co-opting these tools. The use of social media, the scholars Rebecca MacKinnon of the New America Foundation and Evgeny Morozov of the Open Society Institute have argued, is just as likely to strengthen authoritarian regimes as it is to weaken them. The Chinese government has spent considerable effort perfecting several systems for controlling political threats from social media. The least important of these is its censorship and surveillance program. Increasingly, the government recognizes that threats to its legitimacy are coming from inside the state and that blocking the Web site of The New York Times does little to prevent grieving mothers from airing their complaints about corruption.

The Chinese system has evolved from a relatively simple filter of incoming Internet traffic in the mid-1990s to a sophisticated operation that not only limits outside information but also uses arguments about nationalism and public morals to encourage operators of Chinese Web services to censor their users and users to censor themselves. Because its goal is to prevent information from having politically synchronizing effects, the state does not need to censor the Internet comprehensively; rather, it just needs to minimize access to information.

Authoritarian states are increasingly shutting down their communications grids to deny dissidents the ability to coordinate in real time and broadcast documentation of an event. This strategy also activates the conservative dilemma, creating a short-term risk of alerting the population at large to political conflict. When the government of Bahrain banned Google Earth after an annotated map of the royal family's annexation of public land began circulating, the effect was to alert far more Bahrainis to the offending map than knew about it originally. So widely did the news spread that the government relented and reopened access after four days.

. . .

In the most extreme cases, the use of social media tools is a matter of life and death, as with the proposed death sentence for the blogger Hossein Derakhshan in Iran (since commuted to 19 and a half years in prison). . . . Indeed, the best practical reason to think that social media can help bring political change is that both dissidents and governments think they can. All over the world, activists believe in the utility of these tools and take steps to use them accordingly. And the governments they contend with think social media tools are powerful, too, and are willing to harass, arrest, exile, or kill users in response. One way the United States can heighten the conservative dilemma without running afoul of as many political complications is to demand the release of citizens imprisoned for using media in these ways. Anything that constrains the worst threats of violence by the state against citizens using these tools also increases the conservative dilemma.

Looking at the Long Run

To the degree that the United States pursues Internet freedom as a tool of statecraft, it should de-emphasize anti-censorship tools, particularly those aimed at specific regimes, and increase its support for local public speech and assembly more generally. Access to information is not unimportant, of course, but it is not the primary way social media constrain autocratic rulers or benefit citizens of a democracy. Direct, U.S. government—sponsored support for specific tools or campaigns targeted at specific regimes risk creating backlash that a more patient and global application of principles will not.

This entails reordering the State Departments Internet freedom goals. Securing the freedom of personal and social communication among a state's population should be the highest priority, closely followed by securing individual citizens' ability to speak in public. This reordering would reflect the reality that it is a strong civil society—one

in which citizens have freedom of assembly—rather than access to Google or YouTube, that does the most to force governments to serve their citizens.

As a practical example of this, the United States should be at least as worried about Egypt's recent controls on the mandatory licensing of group-oriented text-messaging services as it is about Egypt's attempts to add new restrictions on press freedom. The freedom of assembly that such text-messaging services support is as central to American democratic ideals as is freedom of the press. Similarly, South Korea's requirement that citizens register with their real names for certain Internet services is an attempt to reduce their ability to surprise the state with the kind of coordinated action that took place during the 2008 protest in Seoul. If the United States does not complain as directly about this policy as it does about Chinese censorship, it risks compromising its ability to argue for Internet freedom as a global ideal.

More difficult, but also essential, will be for the U.S. government to articulate a policy of engagement with the private companies and organizations that host the networked public sphere. Services based in the United States, such as Facebook, Twitter, Wikipedia, and YouTube, and those based overseas, such as QQ. (a Chinese instant-messaging service), WikiLeaks (a repository of leaked documents whose servers are in Sweden), Tuenti (a Spanish social network), and Naver (a Korean one), are among the sites used most for political speech, conversation, and coordination. And the world's wireless carriers transmit text messages, photos, and videos from cell phones through those sites. How much can these entities be expected to support freedom of speech and assembly for their users?

The issue here is analogous to the questions about freedom of speech in the United States in private but commercial environments, such as those regarding what kind of protests can be conducted in shopping malls. For good or ill, the platforms supporting the networked public sphere are privately held and run; Clinton committed the United States to working with those companies, but it is unlikely that without some legal framework, as exists for real-world speech and action, moral suasion will be enough to convince commercial actors to support freedom of speech and assembly.

It would be nice to have a flexible set of short-term digital tactics that could be used against different regimes at different times. But the requirements of real-world statecraft mean that what is desirable may not be likely. Activists in both repressive and democratic regimes will use the Internet and related tools to try to effect change in their countries, but Washington's ability to shape or target these changes is limited. Instead, Washington should adopt a more general approach, promoting freedom of speech, freedom of the press, and freedom of assembly everywhere. And it should understand that progress will be slow. Only by switching from an instrumental to an environmental view of the effects of social media on the public sphere will the United States be able to take advantage of the long-term benefits these tools promise—even though that may mean accepting short-term disappointment.

Reference

Shirky [CC]. The Political Power of Social Media: Technology, the Public Sphere and Political Change. *Foreign Affairs-New York-*, 2011[;] *90*(1)[:] 28–41.

CLAY SHIRKY is Professor of New Media at New York University and the author of *Cognitive Surplus: Creativity and Generosity in a Connected Age*.

EXPLORING THE ISSUE

Are Twitter and Other Social Media a Good Source of Political Information?

Critical Thinking and Reflection

1. How pervasive is Twitter (and the Internet) in different regions of the world? Does the public's trust in the forms of media available to them provide any insight into whether Twitter is considered important within that culture, or not?
2. How is Twitter similar to or different from other forms of social media? Do these similarities or differences suggest different ways of thinking about Twitter's role within specific cultural contexts?
3. How might Twitter become an even more powerful medium of dissemination of information? Who would benefit from this/these change(s)?
4. When other forms of media were new, were they also subject to the same questions that Twitter poses? What is the next step in social media as a political tool?

Is There Common Ground?

The authors of these two selections examine the use of Twitter for political purposes, but they ask significantly different questions to contextualize Twitter within the public sphere. It should be stressed that the first selection comes from a longer, more theoretically and methodologically rigorous study, so to be fair to the authors we should remember that their book provides many more details than can be encapsulated in a short, edited segment. However, both selections examine emerging media for the purpose of helping us understand the power of Twitter and other social media as unique forms of political communication. They help us understand that as an emerging phenomenon, Twitter and other social media are likely to be used differently in different cultural settings, and that they should be viewed with respect to the communication and information infrastructure available in any specific country.

As more studies emerge we can expect to see that there is not one uniform use or understanding of how social media communicate political information or are used for political purposes that are easily applied to different cultures or regions. History, economy, and technological availability influence how Twitter, and any form of medium, is perceived by the people within a country or region and quite often, as the research in *Taking Sides* clearly illuminates, there are often multiple ways of understanding media use, and many different individual perspectives on using media and technology for purposes of communication. Both the technology and social use of Twitter will evolve, and though we can't project how the medium may change over the years, we can be sure there will be multiple perspectives on how it is used, by whom, and for what purpose.

Additional Resources

Jason Gainous and Keven M. Wagner, *Tweeting to Power: The Social Media Revolution in American Politics* (Oxford University Press, 2013).

Jurgen Habermas, *The Structural Transformation of the Public Sphere: An Inquiry Into a Category of Bourgeois Society* (MIT Press, 1989).

Eric Schmidt and Jared Cohen, "The Digital Disruption: Connectivity and the Diffusion of Power," *Foreign Affairs* (November 2010)

Shanto Iyengar, M*edia Politics: A Citizen's Guide,* 3rd ed. (W. W. Norton and Company, 2015)

Internet References . . .

E-Democracy.org

forums.e-democracy.org/about

Lindsay Hoffman, "Reflecting on Twitter and its Implications for Democracy"

www.huffingtonpost.com/lindsay-hoffman/twitter
-elections_b_2568989.html

Pew Research Center

Amy Mitchell and Pul Hitlin, "Twitter Reaction to Events Often at Odds with Overall Public Opinion"

www.pewresearch.org/2013/03/04/twitter-reaction-to
-events-often-at-odds-with-overall-public-opinion/

Marc A. Smith, Lee Rainie, Ben Shneiderman, and Itai Himelboim, "Mapping Twitter Topic Networks: From Polarized Crowds to Community Clusters"

www.pewinternet.org/2014/02/20/mapping-twitter
-topic-networks-from-polarized-crowds-to
-community-clusters/

Kentaro Toyama, "Twitter Isn't Spreading Democracy—Democracy Is Spreading Twitter"

www.theatlantic.com/technology/archive/2013/11
/twitter-isnt-spreading-democracy-democracy-is
-spreading-twitter/281368/

Unit 4

UNIT

Law and Policy

*N*ew technology influences the interpretation of laws and policies that were crafted in earlier times. In many cases, we use private technology in public places. When we do that, do we willingly give up personal privacy? When we transport our communication technologies to different places, are we violating our own right to privacy, or influencing the privacy of others? The issues in this section deal with important topics, such as privacy and security, corporate accountability, drones and personal privacy, and the actions of trolls that may contribute to creating a hostile environment online.

Selected, Edited, and with Issue Framing Material by:
Alison Alexander, *University of Georgia*
and
Jarice Hanson, *University of Massachusetts—Amherst*

ISSUE

Does Technology Invade Our Privacy?

YES: Daniel J. Solove, from "The All-or-Nothing Fallacy," in *Nothing to Hide: The False Tradeoff between Privacy and Security,* Yale University Press (2011)

NO: Stewart Baker, from "The Privacy Problem: What's Wrong with Privacy," Tech Freedom (2010)

Learning Outcomes

After reading this issue, you will be able to:

- Explain the limitations of the "nothing to hide"and the "all-or-nothing" fallacies.
- Identify the trade-offs of security versus privacy from the point of view of each author.
- Describe the definitions of privacy used by these authors.
- Evaluate the solutions suggested by both authors.
- Agree or disagree: You have zero privacy anyway. Get over it.

ISSUE SUMMARY

YES: Daniel J. Solove, professor of law at George Washington University and authority on privacy issues, argues that privacy is too often sacrificed for security concerns. He argues that there are often solutions that do not involve such sacrifices, but that they are dismissed by an all-or-nothing attitude.

NO: Stewart Baker, former Assistant Secretary for Policy at Homeland Security, argues vigorously for better collection and use of technological information. Its importance in preventing acts of terrorism, in tracking potential criminals, and in protecting the interests of the country far outweighs privacy concerns of individuals.

New technologies allow unprecedented invasions of privacy. We are familiar with some of the concerns: Can employers really make us open our Facebook page before they hire us? What if I end up on-screen in one of the views captured by Google Street View technology? What if an unflattering picture taken by a friend or in a public space goes viral before I even know about it? What if a stalker uses the Internet to track down information about me? What if my search for medical information is used by Google to target ads to me—and anyone who might see those ads?

What unites these concerns? All these "what if" questions are about the control of personal information.

Although there is a great agreement on the importance of privacy, there is little agreement on how it can be accomplished. The most effective way of controlling privacy comes from efforts to exercise control over personal information. The Electronic Frontier Forum (EFF.org) has several web pages dedicated to explaining that anonymity is a right, conferred by the U.S. Constitution, and it criticizes many organizations for challenging or violating rights. In 2011, EFF criticized Facebook's new policy on selling personal information of Facebook users to advertisers, and claimed that it violated the trust of users. Others are less concerned. Scott McNealy, cofounder of Sun Microsystems, is famously reported saying, "You have zero privacy anyway. Get over it."

An important feature of this issue is that often people leave "trails" of information that can actually identify them, even when users assumed they were anonymous. We rarely consider the technological structures of news media (such as the Internet and cell phones), nor do we realize that the idea of using technology in public places actually records our use, including the time, and often, our identifying information. Think for a moment of a situation in which someone who was using a public computer terminal in a library types in his or her password, perhaps a credit card number, and the many websites he or she visited. If the person forgets to logoff or to clear the cache of the computer, this information is easily accessible to the next user who can easily view the recent history of the computer's use. In *I Know Who You Are and I Saw What You Did*, Lori Andrews tells a chilling story of a school district that activated webcams on school-issued laptops using software designed to help recovery if the laptops were stolen. Instead district personnel collected screenshots of the room where the laptop was located, often a bedroom, where these high school students were studying, dressing, or sleeping.

As you can see, the issues go far beyond overhearing someone on a cell phone in a public place or accidentally hitting "reply all" on an indiscrete email. There is always the possibility of someone forwarding electronic messages to others, as we have seen recently in the scandals surrounding political figures using cell phones for sexting, or in the British *News of the World* cell phone-hacking scandals—both situations in which their perpetrators thought they could hide behind their online anonymity, only to be disgraced and humiliated once the information so easily came to light.

The problems of privacy become even more important when we move from the realm of the personal control of information to public or governmental uses of that information. Digital technologies have created surprisingly robust pictures of our lives. At this time, the National Security Agency (NSA) is embroiled in a global scandal surrounding data collection of information about U.S. and international figures. Much of this emerges from the loosening of restrictions and the subsequent cover activities that emerged after 9/11 and the Patriot Act. Although this scandal is much too complex to unravel in this issue, the result has put the issue of governmental surveillance in the spotlight.

In this digital world, how do we weight the benefits and the consequences of government surveillance of its citizens, as well as its allies? Daniel Solove argues that privacy is too often sacrificed in the name of security. His book is titled *Nothing to Hide*, a phrase that is used to minimize the violation of privacy. "I've got nothing to hide. Only if you're doing something wrong should you worry." Solove attacks these and other arguments about the value of security and the negligible loss of privacy in times of crisis or when national security is threatened. He deplores the "all-or-nothing" governmental approach that implies that every security measure must be taken, no matter what the personal cost or the possibility of other less invasive solutions.

Stewart Baker asks "What's Wrong with Privacy" and proceeds to tell us just exactly what concerns about privacy do to disable national security. He argues that privacy groups discourage actions that could prevent terrorist activity such as occurred on 9/11/2001. Baker talks about the early establishment of right to privacy doctrine and the spirit of the privacy movement today, which he describes as reactionary, Luddite, and anti-technology. He is particularly concerned about efforts to narrow the ability of databases to "talk" to one another, thus preventing the creation of big data sources that can amass incredible amounts of information about the objects of surveillance. Baker also discusses his solutions to these privacy concerns. He dismisses several ideas that don't work, and argues finally for accountability: investigations and punishment of those who misuse data.

We are used to thinking about privacy as a concern for personal information. And, we are used to thinking about big data as something that scientists collect or perhaps the 24/7 information that Nielsen can collect about viewing habits with recent technological advances. The stakes are much higher when we talk about combating terrorism or protecting the security of our country. Certainly, the current NSA scandals make it clear that careful judgment is required; loosening the constraints on surveillance can result in highly unfavorable outcomes. These authors will challenge you, with highly contrasting points of view, to envision the solutions to these concerns.

YES ↵

Daniel J. Solove

The All-or-Nothing Fallacy

"**I**'d gladly give up my privacy if it will keep me secure from a terrorist attack." I hear this refrain again and again. The debate is often cast as an all-or-nothing choice, whether we should have privacy or a specific security measure. Consider the way the government defended the NSA surveillance program, which involved secret wiretapping of phone calls without any oversight. In a congressional hearing, Attorney General Alberto Gonzales stated: "Our enemy is listening, and I cannot help but wonder if they are not shaking their heads in amazement at the thought that anyone would imperil such a sensitive program by leaking its existence in the first place, and smiling at the prospect that we might now disclose even more or perhaps even unilaterally disarm ourselves of a key tool in the war on terror."

Notice his language. He's implying that if we protect privacy, it will mean that we must "disarm" ourselves of some really valuable security measures. He's suggesting that even terrorists would consider us crazy for making such a tradeoff.

I constantly hear arguments like this when officials justify security measures or argue that they shouldn't be regulated. They point to the value of the surveillance and the peril we'd be in without it. "We're hearing quite a lot of chatter about terrorist attacks," they say. "Do you want us to stop listening? Then the terrorists could talk about how they plan to blow up a plane, and we won't know about it. Is a little privacy really worth that cost?"

Those defending the national-security side of the balance often view security and liberty as a zero-sum tradeoff. The legal scholars Eric Posner and Adrian Vermeule contend that "any increase in security requires a decrease in liberty." The argument is that security and civil liberties such as privacy can never be reconciled. Every gain in privacy must be a loss in security. Every gain in security must be a loss in privacy.

But this argument is flawed. The argument that privacy and security are mutually exclusive stems from what I call the "all-or-nothing fallacy." Sacrificing privacy doesn't automatically make us more secure. Not all security measures are invasive of privacy. Moreover, no correlation has been established between the effectiveness of a security measure and a corresponding decrease in liberty. In other words, the most effective security measures need not be the most detrimental to liberty. . . .

Security and privacy need not be mutually exclusive. For example, one security response to the September 11 attacks was to lock the cockpit doors on airplanes. This prevents a terrorist from gaining control of the plane. Does it invade privacy? Hardly at all. . . .

The all-or-nothing fallacy causes tremendous distortion in the balance between privacy and security. In fact, I believe that many courts and commentators who balance security measures against privacy rights conduct the balance wrongly because of this fallacy. . . . On one side of the scale they weigh the benefits of the security measure. On the other side they weigh privacy rights.

At first blush, this seems like a reasonable approach—balance the security measure against privacy. Yet it is quite wrong. Placing the security measure on the scale assumes that the *entire security measure, all-or-nothing, is in the balance*. It's not. Protecting privacy seldom negates the security measure altogether. Rarely does judicial oversight or the application of the Fourth Amendment prohibit a government surveillance activity. Instead, the activity is allowed subject to oversight and sometimes a degree of limitation.

Most constitutional and statutory protections work this way. The Fourth Amendment, for example, allows all sorts of very invasive searches. Under the Fourth Amendment, the government can search your home. It can search your computer. It can do a full body-cavity search. It can search nearly anything and engage in nearly any kind of surveillance. How can this be so? Because the Fourth Amendment doesn't protect privacy by stopping the government from searching; it works by requiring judicial oversight and mandating that the government justify its measures. So under the Fourth Amendment, the government can engage in highly invasive searches if it justifies the need to do so beforehand to a judge.

Like the Fourth Amendment, electronic-surveillance law allows for wiretapping, but limits the practice by mandating judicial supervision, minimizing the breadth of the wiretapping, and requiring law-enforcement officials to report back to the court to prevent abuses. Thus the protection of privacy might demand the imposition of oversight and regulation but need not entail scrapping an entire security measure. . . .

Far too often, however, discussions of security and liberty fail to assess the balance this way. Polls frequently pose the question as an all-or-nothing tradeoff. A 2002 Pew Research poll asked American citizens:

> Should the government be allowed to read e-mails and listen to phone calls to fight terrorism?

A 2005 poll from Rasmussen Reports posed the question:

> Should the National Security Agency be allowed to intercept telephone conversations between terrorism suspects in other countries and people living in the United States?

Both these questions, however, neglect to account for warrants and court orders. Few would contend that the government shouldn't be allowed to conduct a wide range of searches when it has a search warrant or court order. So the questions that *should* be posed are:

> Should the government be allowed to read emails and listen to phone calls *without a search warrant or the appropriate court order required by law* to fight terrorism?

> Should the National Security Agency be allowed to intercept telephone conversations between terrorism suspects in other countries and people living in the United States *without a court order or judicial oversight?*

The choice is not between a security measure and nothing, but between a security measure with oversight and regulation and a security measure at the sole discretion of executive officials. In many cases, oversight and regulation do not diminish a security measure substantially, so the cost of protecting privacy can be quite low. Unfortunately, the balance is rarely assessed properly. When the balance is measured under the allor-nothing fallacy, the scale dips dramatically toward the security side. The costs

of protecting privacy are falsely inflated, and the security measure is accorded too much weight.

The National-Security Argument

Many people argue that the government should be regulated much less when it pursues matters of national security than when it investigates ordinary crime. They contend that national-security threats are quite different from the dangers of crime. For example, as Andrew McCarthy, senior fellow of the Foundation for the Defense of Democracies and former federal prosecutor, testified to Congress:

> We want constitutional rights to protect Americans from oppressive executive action. We do not, however, want constitutional rights to be converted by enemies of the United States into weapons in their war against us. We want courts to be a vigorous check against overbearing governmental tactics in the investigation and prosecution of Americans for ordinary violations of law; but we do not—or, at least, we should not—want courts to degrade the effectiveness of executive action targeted at enemies of the United States who seek to kill Americans and undermine their liberties.

Those who maintain the exceptionalism of national-security threats propose weaker Fourth Amendment requirements or none at all. They contend that matters involving national security must be kept secret and should be insulated from close scrutiny. Should matters of national security be given special treatment? I argue that the distinction between matters of national security and regular crime is too fuzzy and incoherent to be workable.

The Law of National Security

In 1969 the three founding members of a group called "the White Panthers" bombed a CIA office in Michigan. The group wasn't a white supremacist group; in fact, they supported the goals of the Black Panther Party. They also advocated radical anarchist goals, arguing that everything should be free and that money should be abolished. The group's manifesto stated: "We demand total freedom for everybody! And we will not be stopped until we get it. . . . ROCK AND ROLL music is the spearhead of our attack because it is so effective and so much fun."

During its investigation of the crime, the government wiretapped calls made by one of the bombers. The wiretapping was conducted without warrants supported by probable cause required by the Fourth Amendment.

The case made its way up to the U.S. Supreme Court in 1972. The Nixon administration argued that because the bombing involved a threat to national security, the government wasn't bound by the Fourth Amendment. The administration argued the U.S. Constitution grants the president special national-security powers to "preserve, protect and defend the Constitution of the United States," and these powers trump the regular protections of the Fourth Amendment.

The Supreme Court rebuffed President Nixon's claim that he could ignore Fourth Amendment rights in the name of national security:

> [W]e do not think a case has been made for the requested departure from Fourth Amendment standards. The circumstances described do not justify complete exemption of domestic security surveillance from prior judicial scrutiny. Official surveillance, whether its purpose be criminal investigation or ongoing intelligence gathering, risks infringement of constitutionally protected privacy of speech. Security surveillances are especially sensitive because of the inherent vagueness of the domestic security concept, the necessarily broad and continuing nature of intelligence gathering, and the temptation to utilize such surveillances to oversee political dissent. We recognize, as we have before, the constitutional basis of the President's domestic security role, but we think it must be exercised in a manner compatible with the Fourth Amendment. In this case we hold that this requires an appropriate prior warrant procedure.

The Court noted that the Fourth Amendment might require slightly different procedures for matters of national security depending upon practical considerations. Thus Fourth Amendment regulation is flexible to the particular needs of the situation.

Despite the Supreme Court's rejection of the argument that national security should entail a dramatic departure from constitutional protections, the national-security argument is still invoked. The legal scholar Stephen Vladeck notes that the concept of national security has a distorting effect on the law: "[O]ne can find national security considerations influencing ordinary judicial decision making across the entire gamut of contemporary civil and criminal litigation." Although claims of national security don't directly eliminate rights or civil liberties, they severely weaken them. National-security claims are often accompanied by calls for deference, as well as demands for secrecy. . . .

Improper Invocations of "National Security"

"National security" has often been abused as a justification not only for surveillance but also for maintaining the secrecy of government records as well as for violating the civil liberties of citizens. The Japanese internment during World War II, as well as many other abuses, was authorized in the name of national security. As the court noted in *United States v. Ehrlichman,* the Watergate burglary was an example of the misuse of national-security powers: "The danger of leaving delicate decisions of propriety and probable cause to those actually assigned to ferret out 'national security' information is potent, and is indeed illustrated by the intrusion undertaken in this case."

The government has often raised national-security concerns to conceal embarrassing and scandalous documents from the public—documents which often turned out to be harmless, such as the Pentagon Papers, a study of the U.S. military and political involvement in Vietnam. Daniel Ellsberg, an analyst who worked on the study, gave the Pentagon Papers to the *New York Times.* The government sought to prevent publication by claiming that disclosing the Pentagon Papers would create a "grave and immediate danger to the security of the United States." But this claim was false. The U.S. Supreme Court rejected the government's attempt to stop the Pentagon Papers from being disclosed, and national security wasn't harmed after they were published. Solicitor General Edwin Griswold, who wrote the government's brief, later recanted, stating that he hadn't seen "any trace of a threat to national security" in the Pentagon Papers. The dire claims the government made about national security were bogus, just a way to cover up what the Pentagon Papers revealed—that the government had made deceptive claims about the Vietnam War.

After the September 11 attacks, the government began using a tactic called the "state secrets privilege" to exclude evidence in a case if it will reveal a classified secret. Even if the government isn't a party to the case, it can swoop in and invoke the privilege. Many times, the case gets dismissed because a person can't prove her case without the evidence. Tom Blanton, director of George Washington University's National Security Archive, says that the state secrets privilege acts like a "neutron bomb" on a case, effectively wiping it out. . . .

Ironically, the case that gave rise to the state secrets privilege involved an improper use of secrecy. In *United States v. Reynolds,* a U.S. Air Force plane exploded in flight, killing nine people. Only four people were able to parachute to safety. The widows of three civilians who died in the accident sued the government for negligence. In a civil lawsuit, plaintiffs are ordinarily entitled to see documents pertaining to an accident, and the plaintiffs in this case wanted to see the Air Force's accident report and other evidence surrounding the incident But the government withheld these documents due to national-security concerns. The government wouldn't even allow the trial judge to examine the documents to evaluate the government's claim that their disclosure would undermine national security.

The U.S. Supreme Court upheld the government's actions under the state secrets privilege, declaring that "when the formal claim of privilege was filed by the Secretary of the Air Force, under circumstances indicating a reasonable possibility that military secrets were involved, there was certainly a sufficient showing of privilege to cut off further demand for the document." The Court deferred to the government's assertions; indeed, it even refused to examine the accident report. When the report was eventually declassified forty-seven years later, it revealed no state secrets. Instead, it showed that the government had been negligent. In his book about the case, Louis Fisher, a senior scholar at the Library of Congress, concludes that the government "falsely described" the documents and "misled" the courts.

Certainly, there are times where the government has a compelling reason to keep information secret, But it is currently far too easy for the government to cry "national security" to conceal unseemly information. Claims of secrecy in the name of national security must be subjected to rigorous scrutiny. . . .

Should the Government Engage in Data Mining?

I like to shop on Amazon.com. Every time I visit Amazon.com, they say to me: "Welcome, Daniel." They know me by name! And then they say: "We've got recommendations for you." I love their recommendations. They suggest various books and products I might like, and they're pretty good at it.

Amazon.corn's recommendations are the product of a form of "data mining." Data mining involves creating profiles by amassing personal data and then analyzing it for nuggets of wisdom about individuals. Amazon looks at my buying pattern and compares it to similar patterns of other people. If I bought a *Lord of the Rings* movie, it might recommend a *Harry Potter* movie. Why? Because a high percentage of people buying a *Lord of the Rings* movie

also bought a *Harry Potter* movie. Despite our desire to be authentic and unique, we're often similar to other people, and we're frequently quite predictable.

Some government officials think that if data mining works so well for Amazon and other companies, then it might work well for law enforcement. If data mining can predict whether I'm likely to buy a *Harry Potter* movie, maybe it can also predict whether I'm likely to commit a crime or engage in terrorism.

Generally, law enforcement is investigative, focusing on apprehending perpetrators of past crimes. When it comes to terrorism, law enforcement shifts to being more preventative, seeking to identify terrorists before they act. This is why the government has become interested in data mining—to predict who might conduct a future terrorist attack.

Proponents of data mining argue that examining information for patterns will greatly assist in locating terrorists because certain characteristics and behaviors are likely to be associated with terrorist activity. As Judge Richard Posner argues, in "an era of global terrorism and proliferation of weapons of mass destruction, the government has a compelling need to gather, pool, sift, and search vast quantities of information, much of it personal."

Data mining supporters contend that because it involves computers analyzing data, the information is rarely seen by humans, so there's no privacy harm. They also argue that there's no privacy harm because much of the data already exists in databases, so nothing new is being disclosed. And as the law professor Eric Goldman argues, in many cases people don't even know their data is being analyzed. He declares: "This situation brings to mind the ancient Zen parable: if a tree falls in a forest and no one is around to hear it, does it make a sound?". . .

The Problems of Data Mining

Defenders of data mining insist that it causes only minimal privacy harms. As Richard Posner argues:

> The collection, mainly through electronic means, of vast amounts of personal data is said to invade privacy. But machine collection and processing of data cannot, as such, invade privacy. Because of their volume, the data are first sifted by computers, which search for names, addresses, phone numbers, etc., that may have intelligence value. This initial sifting, far from invading privacy (a computer is not a sentient being), keeps most private data from being read by any intelligence officer.

The potential harm from data mining, according to Posner, is use of the information to blackmail an "administration's critics and political opponents" or to "ridicule or embarrass." This argument defines the privacy problems with data mining in narrow ways that neglect to account for the full panoply of problems created by the practice. Posner focuses on the problems of disclosure and the threat of disclosure (blackmail). But data mining involves many other kinds of problems, which I'll now discuss.

Inaccuracy

Data mining isn't very accurate in the behavioral predictions it makes. The difficulty is that while patterns repeat themselves, they don't do so with perfect regularity. We can be fairly confident in predicting that gravity will still work tomorrow. But predicting the weather isn't as easy—and certainly, human behavior is far more unpredictable than the weather.

Consider the following profiles:

1. "John" was a young man who was born and raised in Egypt. His parents were Muslim, though not strongly religious. His father was a successful attorney and his mother came from a wealthy family. He had two sisters, one of whom became a doctor, the other a professor. John studied architecture at Cairo University. He later lived in Germany and worked at an urban-planning firm. He had a number of close friends, and he lived with roommates. He increasingly became more religious, eventually founding a prayer group. After five years in Germany, he came to the United States. He decided to enroll in flying school to learn how to fly airplanes.

2. "Matt" was a young man who was born and raised near Buffalo, New York. His parents were Catholic, but Matt later became an agnostic. He had two sisters. His parents were middle class, and his father worked at a General Motors factory. He was a good student in high school, but he dropped out of college. He liked to collect guns, and he strongly believed in gun rights. Matt enjoyed computer programming. He enlisted in the U.S. Army. After leaving the army, he worked as a security guard. He maintained close ties with several friends he met in the army.

3. "Bill" was a middle-aged man born in Chicago to middle-class parents. He was admitted at an early age to Harvard. He received a Ph.D. in math from Michigan, and then became a professor at Berkeley. He later quit the professorship and moved to a cabin in the woods. He enjoyed reading history books, riding his bike, and gardening.

"John" is Mohammed Atta, the ringleader of the September 11 attacks. "Matt" is Timothy McVeigh, who bombed the Alfred P. Murrah Federal Building in Oklahoma City in 1995, killing 168 people. "Bill" is Theodore Kaczynski, the Unabomber, who mailed bombs to people for a period of nearly twenty years. These three individuals had very different backgrounds and beliefs. Atta had radicalized Islamic beliefs, McVeigh was an agnostic who believed the power of the U.S. government was running amok, and Kaczynski was an atheist who hated modern technology and industry.

Terrorists come not in just one flavor but in many, making it more difficult to construct an accurate profile. Atta, McVeigh, and Kaczynski had vastly different political beliefs, childhoods, families, socioeconomic backgrounds, levels of intelligence, and religions. Interestingly, all came from apparently normal families. Many other individuals have similar backgrounds, similar religious and political beliefs, and similar behavior patterns, but no desire to commit terrorist acts.

The things terrorists of the future do may be similar to the things done by terrorists of the past, but they, also may be different. By focusing on patterns based on past experience, we may ignore new characteristics and behaviors of the terrorists of the future.

Data mining proponents might reply that although not all terrorists repeat the past, they nonetheless might have some things in common, so looking at behavior patterns might still help us identify them. The problem is that even if data mining identifies some terrorists correctly, it is effective only if it doesn't have too many "false positives"—people who fit the profile but who aren't terrorists.

More than two million people fly each day worldwide. A data mining program to identify terrorists with a false positive rate of 1 percent (which would be exceptionally low for such a program) would flag more than twenty thousand false positives every day. This is quite a large number of innocent people who will be wrongly snagged by the system.

Why is the government so interested in data mining when the accuracy and workability of the practice remain uncertain? Part of the government's interest in data mining stems from the aggressive marketing efforts of database companies. After September 11, database companies met with government officials and made a persuasive pitch about the virtues of data mining. The technology, which often works quite well in the commercial setting, can sound dazzling when presented by skillful marketers.

The problem, however, is that just because data mining might be effective for businesses trying to predict customer behavior, it isn't necessarily effective for government officials trying to predict who will engage in terrorism. A high level of accuracy is not essential when data mining is used by businesses to target marketing for consumers, because the cost of error to individuals is minimal. If Amazon.com makes a poor book recommendation to me, there's little harm. I just move on to the next recommendation. But the consequences of government data mining are vastly greater: being singled out for extra investigation, repeatedly being subjected to extra screening at the airport, being stranded while on a no-fly list, or even being arrested.

First Amendment Concerns

Another potential threat posed by data mining is that it can target people based on their First Amendment–protected activities. . . . Suspicious profiles might involve information about people's free speech, free association, or religious activity. Singling people out for extra investigation, for denial of the right to travel by plane, or for inclusion in a suspicious-persons blacklist is more troubling if the action is based even in part on protected First Amendment activities. How do we know that the profiles aren't based on a person's free expression? What if a person is singled out for extra investigation based on his unpopular political views? How do we know that the profiles aren't based upon a person's religious activity? If people are members of unpopular political groups, do they get singled out for extra screening at the airport?

Information gathering about First Amendment-protected activities involving people's reading habits and speech might chill the exercise of these rights. There doesn't need to be a leak to deter people from reading unpopular books or saying unpopular things. People might be deterred by the fact that the government can readily learn about what a person reads and says—and that the government might mine this data to make predictions about a person's behavior.

Suppose I perform the following searches on Google about ricin, a poison made from castor beans that can be lethal if ingested or inhaled:

> obtain ricin
> where to buy castor beans lethal dosage of ricin
> how to administer ricin
> how to make ricin from castor beans

Suppose I also buy a book on Amazon called *The Idiot's Guide to Using Poison*. Looks quite suspicious, doesn't it? But I have an innocent explanation: I'm 'writing a novel about a character who murders someone with ricin. Although I have no intent to do evil, I certainly wouldn't want some nervous government law-enforcement officials to see my activities. Nor would I want some computer to start beeping because of my odd buying and Web-surfing behavior. Even though there's an innocent explanation, I shouldn't have to worry about explaining myself or being subjected to an investigation or extra scrutiny at the airport.

Perhaps I might be undeterred and still do the searches and buy the book. But not everyone would feel as comfortable. Some people might refrain from researching ricin or other things because of a fear of potential consequences, and that's a problem in a society that values robust freedom to speak, write, and read.

Equality

Data mining also implicates the principle that people should be treated equally under the law regardless of their race, ethnicity, or religion. How do we know the extent to which race or ethnicity is used in the profiles?

Some argue that data mining helps to eliminate stereotyping and discrimination. Computers can minimize the human element, thus preventing bias and racism from entering into the process. Whereas some data mining techniques involve a human-created profile of a terrorist and seek to identify people who match the profile, other data mining techniques ostensibly let the computer compose the profile by analyzing patterns of behavior from known terrorists. Even this technique, however, involves human judgment. Somebody has to make the initial judgment about who qualifies as a known terrorist and who does not. Profiles can contain pernicious assumptions hidden in the architecture of computer code and embedded in algorithms so that they appear to be the decision of neutral computers.

On the other hand, one might argue, profiling via data mining might be better than the alternatives. The legal scholar Frederick Schauer aptly notes that there is no escape from profiling, for without data mining, officials will be making their own subjective judgments about who is suspicious. These judgments are based on an implicit profile, though one that isn't overt and articulated. "[T]he issue is not about whether to use profiles or not but instead about whether to use (or to prefer) formal written profiles or informal unwritten ones." Although it is true that formal profiles constructed in advance have their virtues over discretionary profiling by officials, formal profiles contain some disadvantages. They are more systematic than the discretionary approach, thus compounding the effects of information tied to race, ethnicity, religion, speech, or other factors that might be problematic. Those profiling informally are subject to scrutiny, as they have to answer in court about why they believed a person was suspicious. Data mining, however, lacks such transparency. . . . Formal written profiles cease to have an advantage over informal unwritten ones if they remain hidden and unsupervised. . . .

Transparency

The key problem with data mining is that it is hard to carry out with transparency. Transparency, or openness, is essential to promote accountability and to provide the public with a way to ensure that government officials are not engaging in abuse. "Sunlight is said to be the best of disinfectants," Justice Brandeis declared, "electric light the most efficient policeman." As James Madison stated: "A popular government without popular information or the means of acquiring it is but a prologue to a farce or a tragedy or perhaps both. Knowledge will forever govern ignorance. And a people who mean to be their own governors must arm themselves with the power which knowledge gives."

One problem with many data mining programs is that they lack adequate transparency. The programs are secret because revealing the patterns that trigger identification as a possible future terrorist will tip off terrorists about what behaviors to avoid. This is indeed a legitimate concern. . . . Without public accountability, unelected bureaucrats can administer data mining programs in ways often insulated from any scrutiny at all. For example, the information gathered about people for use in data mining might be collected from sources that don't take sufficient steps to maintain accuracy. Without oversight, it is unclear what level of accuracy the government requires for the information it gathers and uses. . . . If a person is routinely singled out based on a profile and wants to challenge the profile, there appears to be no way to do so unless the profile is revealed.

The lack of transparency in data mining programs makes it nearly impossible to balance the privacy and security interests. Given the significant potential privacy issues and other constitutional concerns, combined with speculative and unproven security benefits as well as the availability of many other alternative means of promoting security, should data mining still be on the table as a viable policy option? One could argue that data mining at least should be investigated and studied. There is nothing wrong with doing so, but the cost must be considered in light of alternative security measures that might already be effective and present fewer potential problems. . . .

Daniel J. Solove is a Research Professor of Law at George Washington University. He is an expert in Privacy Law, and the author of several books on privacy and over 40 law review articles.

Stewart Baker   **→ NO**

The Privacy Problem: What's Wrong with Privacy

Why are privacy groups so viscerally opposed to government action that could reduce the risks posed by exponential technologies? The cost of their stance was made clear on September 11, 2001. That tragedy might not have occurred if not for the aggressive privacy and civil liberties protection imposed by the Foreign Intelligence Surveillance Court and the Department of Justice's Office of Intelligence; and it might have been avoided if border authorities had been able to use airline reservation data to screen the hijackers as they entered the United States.

But even after 9/11, privacy campaigners tried to rebuild the wall and to keep the Department of Homeland Security (DHS) from using airline reservation data effectively. They failed; too much blood had been spilled.

But in the fields where disaster has not yet struck—computer security and biotechnology—privacy groups have blocked the government from taking even modest steps to head off danger.

I like to think that I care about privacy, too. But I had no sympathy for privacy crusaders' ferocious objection to any new government use of technology and data. Where, I wondered, did their objection come from?

So I looked into the history of privacy crusading. And that's where I found the answer.

The Birth of the Right of Privacy

In the 1880s, Samuel Dennis Warren was near the top of the Boston aristocracy. He had finished second in his class at Harvard Law School. He founded a law firm with the man who finished just ahead of him, Louis Brandeis, and they prospered mightily. Brandeis was a brilliant, creative lawyer and social reformer who would eventually become a great Supreme Court justice.

But Samuel Dennis Warren was haunted. There was a canker in the rose of his life. His wife was a great hostess, and her parties were carefully planned. When Warren's cousin married, Mabel Warren held a wedding breakfast and filled her house with flowers for the event. The papers described her home as a "veritable floral bower."

No one should have to put up with this. Surely you see the problem. No? Well, Brandeis did.

He and Warren both thought that, by covering a private social event, the newspapers had reached new heights of impertinence and intrusiveness. The parties and guest lists of a Boston Brahmin and his wife were no one's business but their own, he thought. And so was born the right to privacy.

Angered by the press coverage of these private events, Brandeis and Warren wrote one of the most frequently cited law review articles ever published. In fact, "The Right to Privacy," which appeared in the 1890 Harvard Law Review, is more often cited than read—for good reason, as we'll see. But a close reading of the article actually tells us a lot about the modern concept of privacy.

Brandeis, also the father of the policy-oriented legal brief, begins the article with a candid exposition of the policy reasons why courts should recognize a new right to privacy. His argument is uncompromising:

> The press is overstepping in every direction the obvious bounds of propriety and of decency. Gossip is no longer the resource of the idle and of the vicious, but has become a trade, which is pursued with industry as well as effrontery . . . To occupy the indolent, column upon column is filled with idle gossip, which can only be procured by intrusion upon the domestic circle. The intensity and complexity of life, attendant upon advancing civilization, have rendered necessary some retreat from the world, and man, under the refining influence of culture, has become more sensitive to publicity, so that solitude and privacy have become more essential to the individual; but modern enterprise and invention have, through invasions upon his privacy, subjected him to mental pain and distress, far greater than could be inflicted by mere bodily

injury . . . Even gossip apparently harmless, when widely and persistently circulated, is potent for evil . . . When personal gossip attains the dignity of print, and crowds the space available for matters of real interest to the community, what wonder that the ignorant and thoughtless mistake its relative importance . . . Triviality destroys at once robustness of thought and delicacy of feeling.

What does Brandeis mean by this? To be brief, he thinks it should be illegal for the newspapers to publish harmless information about himself and his family. That, he says, is idle gossip, and it distracts "ignorant and thoughtless" newspaper readers from more high-minded subjects. It also afflicts the refined and cultured members of society—like, say, Samuel Dennis Warren and his wife—who need solitude but who are instead harassed by the fruits of "modern enterprise and invention."

What's remarkable about "The Right to Privacy" is that the article's title still invokes reverence, even though its substance is, well, laughable.

Is there anyone alive who thinks it should be illegal for the media to reveal the guest-list at a prominent socialite's dinner party or to describe how elaborate the floral arrangements were? . . .

Equally peculiar is the suggestion that we should keep such information from the inferior classes lest they abandon self-improvement and wallow instead in gossip about their betters. That makes Brandeis sound like a wuss and a snob.

He does sound quite up-to-date when he complains that "modern enterprise and invention" are invading our solitude. That is a familiar complaint. It's what privacy advocates are saying today about Google, not to mention the National Security Agency (NSA). Until you realize that he's complaining about the scourge of "instantaneous photographs and newspaper enterprise." Huh? Brandeis evidently thinks that publishing a private citizen's photo in the newspaper causes "mental pain and distress, far greater than could be inflicted by mere bodily injury."

If we agreed today, of course, we probably wouldn't have posted 5 billion photographs of ourselves and our friends on Flickr.

Spirit of the Privacy Movement Today

Anachronistic as it seems, the spirit of Brandeis's article is still the spirit of the privacy movement. The right to privacy was born as a reactionary defense of the status quo, and so it remains. Then, as now, new technology suddenly made it possible to spread information more cheaply and more easily. This was new, and uncomfortable. But apart from a howl of pain—pain "far greater than . . . mere bodily injury"—-Brandeis doesn't tell us why it's so bad. I guess you had to be there—literally. . . .

We should not mock Brandeis too harshly. His article clearly conveys a heartfelt sense of invasion. But it is a sense of invasion we can never share. The sensitivity about being photographed or mentioned in the newspapers, a raw spot that rubbed Brandeis so painfully, has calloused over. So thick is the callous that most of us would be tickled, not appalled, to have our dinner parties make the local paper, and especially so if it included our photos.

And that's the second thing that Brandeis's article can tell us about more contemporary privacy flaps. His brand of resistance to change is still alive and well in privacy circles, even if the targets have been updated. Each new privacy kerfuffle inspires strong feelings precisely because we are reacting against the effects of a new technology. Yet as time goes on, the new technology becomes commonplace. Our reaction dwindles away. The raw spot grows a callous. And once the initial reaction has passed, so does the sense that our privacy has been invaded. In short, we get used to it.

At the beginning, of course, we don't want to get used to it. We want to keep on living the way we did before, except with a few more amenities. And so, like Brandeis, we are tempted to ask the law to stop the changes we see coming. There's nothing more natural, or more reactionary, than that.

Most privacy advocates don't see themselves as reactionaries or advocates for the status quo, of course. Right and left, they cast themselves as underdogs battling for change against the entrenched forces of big government. But virtually all of their activism is actually devoted to stopping change—keeping the government (and sometimes industry) from taking advantage of new technology to process and use information.

But simply opposing change, especially technological change, is a losing battle. At heart, the privacy groups know it, which may explain some of their shrillness and lack of perspective. Information really does "want to be free"—or at least cheap. And the spread of cheap information about all of us will change our relationship to the world. We will have fewer secrets. Crippling government by preventing it from using information that everyone else can get will not give us back our secrets.

In the 1970s, well before the personal computer and the Internet, privacy campaigners persuaded the country that the FBI's newspaper clipping files about U.S. citizens were a threat to privacy. Sure, the information was public, they acknowledged, but gathering it all in one file was viewed as vaguely sinister. The attorney general banned the practice in the absence of some legal reason for doing so, usually called an investigative "predicate."

So, in 2001, when Google had made it possible for anyone to assemble a clips file about anyone in seconds, the one institution in the country that could not print out the results of its Google searches about Americans was the FBI. This was bad for our security, and it didn't protect anyone's privacy either.

The privacy campaigners are fighting the inevitable. The "permanent record" our high school principals threatened us with is already here—in Facebook. Anonymity, its thrills and its freedom, has been characteristic of big cities for centuries. But anonymity will also grow scarce as data becomes easier and easier to gather and correlate. We will lose something as a result, no question about it. The privacy groups' response is profoundly conservative in the William F. Buckley sense—standing athwart history yelling, "Stop!" . . .

That might work if governments didn't need the data for important goals such as preventing terrorists from entering the country. After September 11, though, we can no longer afford the forced inefficiency of denying modern information technology to government. In the long run, any effective method of ensuring privacy is going to have to focus on using technology in a smart way, not just trying to make government slow and stupid.

The Evolution of Technology & the "Zone of Privacy"

That doesn't mean we have to give up all privacy protection. It just means that we have to look for protections that work with technology instead of against it. We can't stop technology from making information cheap and reducing anonymity, but we can deploy that same technology to make sure that government officials can't misuse data and hide their tracks. This new privacy model is partially procedural—greater oversight and transparency—and partly substantive—protecting individuals from actual adverse consequences rather than hypothetical informational injuries.

Under this approach, the first people who should lose their privacy are the government workers with access to personal data. They should be subject to audit, to challenge, and to punishment if they use the data for improper purposes. That's an approach that works with emerging technology to build the world we want to live in. In contrast, it is simple Luddism to keep government from doing with information technology what every other part of society can do.

The problem is that Luddism always has appeal. "Change is bad" is a slogan that has never lacked for adherents, and privacy advocates sounded alarm after alarm with that slogan as the backdrop when we tried to put in place a data-based border screening system.

But would we really thank our ancestors if they'd taken the substance of Brandeis's article as seriously as its title? If, without a legislature ever considering the question, judges had declared that no one could publish true facts about a man's nonpolitical life, or even his photograph, without his permission?

I don't think so. Things change. Americans grow less private about their sex lives but more private about financial matters. Today, few of us are willing to have strangers living in our homes, listening to our family conversations, and then gossiping about us over the back fence with the strangers who live in our friends' homes. Yet I'll bet that both Brandeis and Warren tolerated without a second thought the limits that having servants put on their privacy.

Why does our concept of privacy vary from time to time? Here's one theory: Privacy is allied with shame. We are all ashamed of something about ourselves, something we would prefer that no one, or just a few people, know about. We want to keep it private. Sometimes, of course, we should be ashamed. Criminals always want privacy for their acts. But we're also ashamed—or at least feel embarrassment, the first cousin of shame—about a lot of things that aren't crimes.

We may be ashamed of our bodies, at least until we're sure we won't be mocked for our physical shortcomings. Privacy is similar; we are often quite willing to share information about ourselves, including what we look like without our clothes, when we trust our audience, or when the context makes us believe that our shortcomings will go unnoticed. . . .

The things that Brandeis considered privacy invasions are similar. Very few of us are happy the first time we see our photograph or an interview in the newspaper. But pretty soon we realize it's just not that big a deal. Our nose and our style of speech are things that the people we know have already accepted, and no one else cares enough to embarrass us about them. The same is true when we Google ourselves and see that a bad review of our dinner-theater performance is number three on the list. Our first reaction is embarrassment and unhappiness, but the reaction is oddly evanescent.

If this is so, then the "zone of privacy" is going to vary from time to time and place to place—just as our concept of physical modesty does. The zone of privacy has boundaries on two sides. We don't care about some information that might be revealed about us, probably because the revelation causes us no harm—or we've gotten used to it. If the information is still embarrassing, we want to keep it private, and society may agree. But we can't expect privacy for information that society views as truly shameful or criminal.

Over time, information will move into and out of the zone of privacy on both sides. Some information will simply become so unthreatening that we'll laugh at the idea that it is part of the privacy zone. . . .

The biggest privacy battles will often be in circumstances where the rules are changing. The subtext of many Internet privacy fights, for example, is whether some new measure will expose the identities of people who download pornography or copyrighted music and movies. Society is divided about how shameful it is to download these items, and it displaces that moral and legal debate into a fight about privacy.

Divorce litigation, for instance, is brutal in part because information shared in a context of love and confidence ends up being disclosed to the world in a deliberately harmful way. Often the activity in question (like making a telephone call or a credit card purchase) is something that the individual does freely, with clear knowledge that some other people (his bank or his phone company) know what he is doing. . . .

In those cases, the privacy concern is not that the bank or the phone company (or our spouse) actually has the information, but rather what they will do with the information they have—whether they will use the data in ways we didn't expect or give the data to someone who can harm us. We want to make sure the data will not be used to harm us in unexpected ways.

And that helps explain why privacy advocates are so often Luddite in inclination. Modern technology keeps changing the ways in which information is used. Once, we could count on practical obscurity—the difficulty of finding bits of data from our past—to protect us from unexpected disclosures. Now, storage costs are virtually nil, and processing power is increasing exponentially. It is no longer possible to assume that your data, even though technically public, will never actually be used. It is dirt cheap for data processors to compile dossiers on individuals, and to use the data in ways we didn't expect.

Some would argue that this isn't really "privacy" so much as a concern about abuse of information. However it's defined, though, the real question is what kind of protection is it reasonable for us to expect. Can we really write a detailed legislative or contractual pre-nup for each

disclosure, setting forth exactly how our data will be used before we hand it over? I doubt it. Maybe we can forbid obvious misuses, but the more detailed we try to get, the more we run into the problem that our notions of what is private, and indeed of what is embarrassing, are certain to change over time. If so, does it make sense to freeze today's privacy preferences into law?

In fact, that's the mistake that Brandeis made—and the last lesson we can learn from the odd mix of veneration and guffawing that his article provokes. Brandeis wanted to extend common law copyright until it covered everything that can be recorded about an individual. The purpose was to protect the individual from all the new technologies and businesses that had suddenly made it easy to gather and disseminate personal information: "the too enterprising press, the photographer, or the possessor of any other modern device for rewording or reproducing scenes or sounds." . . .

Every year, information gets cheaper to store and to duplicate. Computers, iPods, and the Internet are all "modern devices" for "reproducing scenes or sounds," which means that any effort to control reproduction of pictures, sounds, and scenes becomes extraordinarily difficult if not impossible. In fact, it can't be done.

There is a deep irony here. Brandeis thought that the way to ensure the strength of his new right to privacy was to enforce it just like state copyright law. If you don't like the way "your" private information is distributed, you can sue everyone who publishes it. One hundred years later, the owners of federal statutory copyrights in popular music and movies followed this prescription to a T. They began to use litigation to protect their data rights against "the possessor[s] of any other modern device for . . . reproducing scenes or sounds," a class that now included many of their customers. The Recording Industry Association of America (RIAA) sued consumers by the tens of thousands for using their devices to copy and distribute songs.

Unwittingly, the RIAA gave a thorough test to Brandeis's notion that the law could simply stand in front of new technology and bring it to a halt through litigation. There aren't a lot of people who think that that has worked out well for the RIAA's members, or for their rights. . . .

It's one thing to redirect the path of technological change by a few degrees. It's another to insist that it take a right angle. Brandeis wanted it to take a right angle; he wanted to defy the changes that technology was pressing upon him. So did the RIAA.

Both were embracing a kind of Luddism—a reactionary spasm in the face of technological change. They were doomed to fail. The new technologies, after all, empowered ordinary citizens and consumers in ways that could not be resisted. If the law tries to keep people from enjoying the new technologies, in the end it is the law that will suffer.

But just because technologies are irresistible does not mean that they cannot be guided, or cannot have their worst effects offset by other technologies. The solutions I'm advocating will only work if they allow the world to keep practically all the benefits of the exponential empowerment that new technology makes possible.

Privacy for the Real World: Proposed Solutions

So what's my solution to the tension between information technology and our current sense of privacy? . . .

But before talking about what *might* work, let's take a closer look at some of the ideas that don't.

Ownership of Personal Data

The first privacy solution is one we've already seen. It's the Brandeisian notion that we should all "own" our personal data. That has some appeal, of course. If I have a secret, it feels a lot like property. I can choose to keep it to myself, or I can share it with a few people whom I trust. And I would like to believe that sharing a secret with a few trusted friends doesn't turn it into public property. It's like my home. Just because I've invited one guest home doesn't mean the public is welcome.

But in the end, information is not really like property. Property can only be held by one person at a time, or at most by a few people. But information can be shared and kept at the same time. And those with whom it is shared can pass it on to others at little or no cost. If you ever told a friend about your secret crush in junior high, you've already learned that information cannot be controlled like property. As Ben Franklin is credited with saying, "Three may keep a secret if two of them are dead." . . . The recording and movie industries discovered the same thing. If these industries with their enormous lobbying and litigation budgets cannot control information that they own as a matter of law, the rest of us are unlikely to be able to control information about ourselves. Gossip is not going to become illegal simply because technology amplifies it. . . .

In fact, so transformed is Brandeis's privacy doctrine that it is now described, accurately, as a "right of publicity," which surely would have him turning in his grave. Currently, most states honor Brandeis by allowing lawsuits for unauthorized commercial use of a person's likeness, either by statute or judge-made law. . . .

Judges began shrinking the [property] right until it only had bite in the one set of circumstances where the right to control one's image actually feels like a property right—when the image is worth real bucks. Thus, the courts require disgorgement of profits made when a celebrity's name, face, voice, or even personal style is used without permission to sell or endorse products. As a result, the right to exploit a celebrity's image really is property today; it can be sold, transferred, and even inherited.

There's only one problem with this effort to turn privacy into property: it hasn't done much for privacy. It simply protects the right of celebrities to make money off their fame. In fact, by monetizing things like celebrity images, it rewards those who have most relentlessly sacrificed their privacy to gain fame.

The right of publicity is well named. It is the right to put your privacy up for sale. Not surprisingly, a lot of people have been inspired to do just that. Ironically, Brandeis's doctrine has helped to destroy the essence of what he hoped to preserve.

Oh, and in the process, Brandeis's approach has stifled creativity and restricted free speech—muzzling artists, social commentators, and businesspeople who want to make creative use of images that are an essential part of our cultural environment. It's a disaster. Slowly, courts are waking up to the irony and limiting the right of publicity.

The same "private information as property" approach has also made a modest appearance in some consumer privacy laws, and it's worked out just as badly. At bottom, consumer privacy protection laws like the Right to Financial Privacy Act treat a consumer's data like a consumer's money: You can give your data (or your money) to a company in exchange for some benefit, but only if you've been told the terms of the transaction and have consented. Similarly, the Cable Communications Policy Act of 1984 prevents cable providers from using or releasing personal information in most cases unless the providers get the customer's consent. The fruit of this approach is clear to anyone with a bank account or an Internet connection. Everywhere you turn, you're confronted with "informed consent" and "terms of service" disclosures; these are uniformly impenetrable and non-negotiable. No one reads them before clicking the box, so the "consent" is more fiction than reality; certainly it does little to protect privacy. Indeed, it's turning out a lot like the right of publicity. By treating privacy as property, consumer privacy protection law invites all of us to sell our privacy.

And we do. Only for most of us, the going price turns out to be disconcertingly cheap.

Mandatory Predicates for Information Access

The second way of protecting privacy is to require what's called a "predicate" for access to information. That's a name only a lawyer could love. In fact, the whole concept is one that only lawyers love.

Simply put, the notion is that government shouldn't get certain private information unless it satisfies a threshold requirement—a "predicate" for access to the data. Lawyers have played a huge role in shaping American thinking about privacy, and the predicate approach has been widely adopted as a privacy protection. But its value for that purpose is quite doubtful.

The predicate approach to privacy can be traced to the Fourth Amendment, which guarantees that "no Warrants shall issue, but upon probable cause." Translated from legalese, this means that the government may not search your home unless it has a good reason to do so. When the government asks for a search warrant, it must show the judge "probable cause"—evidence that the search will likely turn up criminal evidence or contraband. Probable cause is the predicate for the search.

When a flap arose in the 1970s over the FBI practice of assembling domestic security dossiers on Americans who had not broken the law, the attorney general stepped in to protect their privacy. He issued new guidelines for the FBI. He was a lawyer, so he declared that the FBI could not do domestic security investigations of Americans without a predicate.

The predicate wasn't probable cause; that was too high a standard. Instead, the attorney general allowed the launching of a domestic security investigation only if the bureau presented "specific and articulable facts giving reason to believe" that the subject of the investigation may be involved in violence.

Actually, the story of the FBI guidelines shows why the predicate approach often fails. The dossiers being assembled by the FBI were often just clippings and other public information. They usually weren't the product of a search in the classic sense; no federal agents had entered private property to obtain the information. Nonetheless, the FBI guidelines treated the gathering of the information itself as though it were a kind of search.

In so doing, the guidelines were following in Brandeis's footsteps—treating information as though it were physical property. The collection of the information was equated to a physical intrusion into the home or office of the individual. Implicitly, it assumes that data can be locked up like property.

But that analogy has already failed. It failed for Brandeis and it failed for the RIAA. It failed for the FBI guidelines, too. As clippings became easier to retrieve, clippings files became easier to assemble. Then Google made it possible for anyone to assemble an electronic clips file on anyone. There was nothing secret about the clippings then. They were about as private as a bus terminal.

But the law was stuck in another era. Under the guidelines, only the FBI and CIA needed a predicate to do Google searches. You have to be a pretty resilient society to decide that you want to deny to your law enforcement agencies a tool that is freely available to nine-year-old girls and terrorist gangs. Resilient, but stupid. (Not surprisingly, the guidelines were revised after 9/11.)

That's one reason we shouldn't treat the assembling of data as though it were a search of physical property. As technology makes it easier and easier to collect data, the analogy between doing that and conducting a search of a truly private space will become less and less persuasive. No one thinks government agencies should have a predicate to use the White Pages. Soon, predicates that keep law enforcement from collecting information in other ways will become equally anachronistic, leaving law enforcement stuck in the 1950s while everyone else gets to live in the twenty-first century.

Limits on Information Use

That leaves the third approach to privacy, one we've already seen in action. If requiring a predicate is the lawyer's solution; this third approach is the bureaucrat's solution. It is at heart the approach adopted by the European Union: Instead of putting limits on when information may be collected, it sets limits on how the information is used. The European Union's data protection principles cover a lot of ground, but their unifying theme is imposing limits on how private data is used. Under those principles, personal data may only be used in ways that are consistent with the purposes for which the data were gathered.

Any data that is retained must be relevant to the original purposes and must be stored securely to prevent misuse.

The EU's negotiating position in the passenger name records conflict was largely derived from this set of principles. The principles also explain Europe's enthusiasm for a wall between law enforcement and intelligence. If DHS gathered reservation data for the purpose of screening travelers when they cross the border, why should any other agency be given access to the data? This also explains the EU's insistence on short deadlines for the destruction of PNR data. Once it had been used to screen passengers, it had served the purpose for which it was gathered and should be promptly discarded.

There is a core of sense in this solution. It focuses mainly on the consequences of collecting information, and not on the act of collection. It doesn't try to insist that information is property. It recognizes that when we give information to others, we usually have an expectation about how it will be used, and as long as the use fits our expectations, we aren't too fussy about who exactly gets to see it. By concentrating on how personal information is used, this solution may get closer to the core of privacy than one that focuses on how personal information is collected.

It has another advantage, too. In the case of government databases, focusing on use also allows us to acknowledge the overriding importance of some government data systems while still protecting against petty uses of highly personal information.

Call it the deadbeat-dad problem, or call it mission creep, but there's an uncomfortable pattern to the use of data by governments. Often, personal data must be gathered for a pressing reason—the prevention of crime or terrorism, perhaps, or the administration of a social security system. Then, as time goes on, it becomes attractive to use the data for other, less pressing purposes—collecting child support, perhaps, or enforcing parking tickets. No one would support the gathering of a large personal database simply to collect unpaid parking fines; but "mission creep" can easily carry the database well beyond its original purpose. A limitation on use prevents mission creep, or at least forces a debate about each step in the expansion.

That's all fine. But in the end, this solution is also flawed.

It, too, is fighting technology, though less obviously than the predicate and property approaches. Data that has already been gathered is easier to use for other purposes. It's foolish to pretend otherwise. Indeed, developments in information technology in recent years have produced real strides in searching unstructured data or in finding relationships in data without knowing for sure that the data will actually produce anything useful. In short, there are now good reasons to collate data gathered for widely differing purposes, just to see the patterns that emerge.

This new technical capability is hard to square with use limitations or with early destruction of data. For if collating data in the government's hands could have prevented a successful terrorist attack, no one will congratulate the agency that refused to allow the collation because

the data was collected for tax or regulatory purposes, say, and not to catch terrorists.

What's more, use limitations have caused great harm when applied too aggressively. The notorious "wall" between law enforcement and intelligence was at heart a use limitation. It assumed that law enforcement agencies would gather information using their authority, and then would use the information only for law enforcement purposes. Intelligence agencies would do the same. Or so the theory went. But strict enforcement of this use limitation was unimaginably costly. In August 2001, two terrorists were known to have entered the United States. As the search for them began, the government's top priority was enforcing the wall—keeping intelligence about the terrorists from being used by the "wrong" part of the FBI. Government lawyers insisted that law enforcement resources could not be used to pursue intelligence that two known al Qaeda agents were in the United States in August 2001. This was a fatal blunder. The criminal investigators were well-resourced and eager. They might have found the men. The intelligence investigators, in contrast, had few resources and did not locate the terrorists, at least not until September 11, when the terrorists' names were discovered on the manifests of the hijacked planes. It was a high price to pay for the modest comfort of "use" limitations.

Like all use limitations, the "wall" between law enforcement sounded reasonable enough in the abstract. While no one could point to a real privacy abuse arising from cooperation between the intelligence and law enforcement agencies in the United States, it was easy to point to the Gestapo and other totalitarian organizations where there had been too much cooperation among agencies.

So, what might have been a sensible, modest use restriction preventing the dissemination of information without a good reason became an impermeable barrier.

That's why the bureaucratic system for protecting privacy so often fails. The use restrictions and related limits are abstract. They make a kind of modest sense, but if they are enforced too strictly, they prevent new uses of information that may be critically important.

And often they are enforced too strictly. You don't have to tell a bureaucrat twice to withhold information from a rival agency. Lawsuits, bad press, and Congressional investigations all seem to push against a flexible reading of the rules. If a use for information is not identified at the outset, it can be nearly impossible to add the use later, no matter how sensible the change may seem. This leads agencies to try to draft broad uses for the data they collect, which defeats the original point of setting use restrictions.

It's like wearing someone else's dress. Over time, use restrictions end up tight where they should be roomy—and loose where they should be tight. No one is left satisfied.

The Audit Approach: Enforced Accountability

So what will work? Simple: accountability, especially electronically-enforced accountability.

The best way to understand this solution is to begin with Barack Obama's passport records—and with "Joe the Plumber." These were two minor flaps that punctuated the 2008 presidential campaign. But both tell us something about how privacy is really protected these days.

In March of 2008, Barack Obama and Hillary Clinton were dueling across the country in weekly primary showdowns. Suddenly, the campaign took an odd turn. The Bush administration's State Department announced that it had fired or disciplined several contractors for examining Obama's passport records.

Democrats erupted. It wasn't hard to jump to the conclusion that the candidate's files had been searched for partisan purposes. After an investigation, the flap slowly deflated. It soon emerged that all three of the main presidential candidates' passport files had been improperly accessed. Investigators reported that the State Department was able to quickly identify who had examined the files by using its computer audit system. This system flagged any unusual requests for access to the files of prominent Americans. The fired contractors did not deny the computer record. Several of them were charged with crimes and pleaded guilty. All, it turned out, had acted purely out of "curiosity."

Six months later, it was the Republicans' turn to howl about privacy violations in the campaign. Samuel "Joe" Wurzelbacher, a plumber, became an overnight hero to Republicans in October 2008 after he was practically the only person who laid a glove on Barack Obama during the campaign. The candidate made an impromptu stop in Wurzelbacher's Ohio neighborhood and was surprised when the plumber forced him into a detailed on-camera defense of his tax plan. Three days later, "Joe the Plumber" and his taxes were invoked dozens of times in the presidential debates.

The price of fame was high. A media frenzy quickly stripped Wurzelbacher of anonymity. Scouring the public record, reporters found that the plumber had been hit with a tax lien; they also found government data that raised doubts about the status of his plumbing license.

Reporters weren't the only ones digging. Ohio state employees also queried confidential state records about Wurzelbacher. In all, they conducted eighteen state records checks on Wurzelbacher. They asked whether the plumber owed child support, whether he'd ever received welfare or unemployment benefits, and whether he was in any Ohio law enforcement databases. Some of these searches were proper responses to media requests under Ohio open records laws; others looked more like an effort to dig dirt on the man.

Ohio's inspector general launched an investigation and in less than a month was able to classify all but one of the eighteen records searches as either legitimate or improper. Thirteen searches were traced and deemed proper, but three particularly intrusive searches were found improper; they had been carried out at the request of a high-ranking state employee who was also a strong Obama supporter. She was suspended from her job and soon stepped down. A fourth search was traced to a former information technology contractor who had not been authorized to search the system he accessed; he was placed under criminal investigation.

What do these two flaps have in common? They were investigated within weeks of the improper access, and practically everyone involved was immediately caught. That's vitally important. Information technology isn't just taking away your privacy or mine. It's taking away the privacy of government workers even faster. Data is cheap to gather and cheap to store. It's even getting cheap to analyze.

So it isn't hard to identify every official who accessed a particular file on a particular day. That's what happened here. And the consequences for privacy are profound.

If the lawyer's solution is to put a predicate between government and the data and the bureaucrat's solution is to put use restrictions on the data, then this is the auditor's solution. Government access to personal data need not be restricted by speed bumps or walls. Instead, it can be protected by rules, so long as the rules are enforced.

What's new is that network security and audit tools now make it easy to enforce the rules. That's important because it takes the profit motive out of misuse of government data. No profit-motivated official is going to take the risk of stealing personal data if it's obvious that he'll be caught as soon as people start to complain about identity theft. Systematic misuse of government databases is a lot harder and more dangerous if good auditing is in place.

If the plight of government investigators trying to prevent terrorist attacks doesn't move you, think about the plight of medical technicians trying to keep you alive after a bad traffic accident.

The Obama administration has launched a longoverdue effort to bring electronic medical records into common use. But the privacy problem in this area is severe. Few of us want our medical records to be available to casual browsers. At the same time, we can't personally verify the bona fides of the people accessing our records, especially if we're lying by the side of the road suffering from what looks like brain or spine damage.

But the electronic record system won't work if it can't tell the first responders that you have unusual allergies or a pacemaker. It has to do that quickly and without a lot of formalities. Auditing access after the fact is likely to be our best answer to this problem, as it is to the very similar problem of how to let law enforcement and intelligence agencies share information smoothly and quickly in response to changing and urgent circumstances.

These technologies can be very flexible. This makes them especially suitable for cases where outright denial of data access could have fatal results. The tools can be set to give some people immediate access, or to open the databases in certain situations, with an audit to follow. They can monitor each person with access to the data and learn that person's access patterns—what kinds of data, at what time, for how long, with or without copying, and the like. Deviations from the established pattern can have many consequences. Perhaps access will be granted but the person will be alerted that an explanation must be offered within twenty-four hours. Or access could be granted while a silent alarm sounds, allowing systems administrators to begin a real-time investigation.

There's a kind of paradox at the heart of this solution. We can protect people from misuse of their data, but only by stripping network users of any privacy or anonymity when they look at the data. The privacy campaigners aren't likely to complain, though. In our experience, their interest in preserving the privacy of intelligence and law enforcement officers is pretty limited.

In the end, that's the difference between a privacy policy that makes sense and one that doesn't. We can't lock up data that is getting cheaper every day. Pretending that it's property won't work. Putting "predicates" between government and the data it needs won't work, and neither will insisting that they may only be used for purposes foreseen when it was collected.

What we *can* do is use new information technology tools to deter government officials from misusing their access to that data.

As you know by now, I think that some technology poses extraordinary risks. But we can avoid the worst risks if we take action early. We shouldn't try to stop the trajectory of new technology. But we can bend it just a little. Call it a course correction on an exponential curve.

That's also true for privacy. The future is coming—like it or not. Our data will be everywhere. But we can bend the curve of technology to make those who hold the data more accountable. Bending the exponential curve a bit—that's a privacy policy that could work. And a technology policy that makes sense.

STEWART BAKER was the first Assistant Secretary for Policy at the Department of Homeland Security. He has served as counsel for the National Security Agency and is currently a partner in the law office of Steptoe & Johnson.

EXPLORING THE ISSUE

Does Technology Invade Our Privacy?

Critical Thinking and Reflection

1. Analyze a situation in which technology leads us to think one thing (providing an illusion of anonymity or privacy) while creating a situation in which anonymity/privacy can be easily violated. Should new laws be created to solve these problems?
2. Consider the varying definitions of privacy presented by these authors. Can you create one of your own?
3. Is privacy becoming less "important" in a society in which we use so many technologies in public places?
4. Should the NSA have warrantless access to digital records?

Is There Common Ground?

The selections on this issue are just the tip of the iceberg when it comes to considering the implications of surveillance access to the many ways in which we communicate digitally every day. Wiki Leaks, the NSA scandals, even the attention you are likely to attract if you begin searching the net for information on building bombs reveals that we have no real understanding of the information that can and has been created about any of us. This is an issue that goes far beyond protecting our personal information.

The rights of the individual will often suffer in times of crisis. It is only through constant vigilance that such rights can be protected. Traditionally, we have invoked the Fourth Amendment to the Constitution as providing us our right to personal privacy in our own home, but how does that hold up when we use technologies to communicate in public settings? Warrants are required to search our homes and must show probable cause for the search. What is the appropriate level of legal requirements to gain access to our personal communications? It seems unlikely that these opposing viewpoints will easily find common ground.

Additional Resources

Lori Andrews, *I Know Who You Are and I Saw What You Did: Social Networks and the Death of Privacy* (Free Press, 2011)

James Bamford, *The Shadow Factory: The NSA from 9/11 to the Eavesdropping on America* (Anchor, 2009)

Yves-Alexandre de Montjoye, César A. Hidalgo, Michel Verleysen, and Vincent D. Blondel. "Unique in the Crowd: The Privacy Bounds of Human Mobility," *Nature* (March 2013)

Erik Sofge and Davin Coburn, *Popular Mechanics: Who's Spying on You? The Looming Threat to Your Privacy, Identity, and Family in the Digital Age* (Hearst, 2012)

Siva Vaidhyanathan, *The Googlization of Everything (And Why We Should Worry)* (University of California Press, 2011)

Internet References . . .

American Civil Liberties Union (ACLU)

http://aclu-wa.org/student-rights-and-
responsibilitiesdigital-age-guide-public-school-
studentswashington-state

**Pew Internet & American Life Project:
Anonymity, Privacy and Security Online**

www.pewinternet.org/Reports/2013/Anonymityonline
.aspx

**Privacy.Org: The Site for News,
Information and Action**

http://privacy.org/

Privacy Rights Clearinghouse

www.privacyrights.org/fs/fs18-cyb.htm

Shorenstein Center's Journalist's Resource

http://journalistsresource.org/studies/society/
internet/thestate-of-internet-privacy-in-2013-
research-roundupIssue

Selected, Edited, and with Issue Framing Material by:
Alison Alexander, *University of Georgia*
and
Jarice Hanson, *University of Massachusetts—Amherst*

ISSUE

Should Corporations Be Allowed to Finance Political Campaigns?

YES: Thomas R. Eddlem, from "Citizens United Is Breaking Up Corporate Dominance of Elections," *The New American* (2012)

NO: David Earley and Ian Vandewalker, from "Transparency for Corporate Political Spending: A Federal Solution," Brennan Center for Justice at New York University School of Law (2012)

Learning Outcomes
After reading this issue, you will be able to:
• Consider the impact of money and freedom of speech in political campaigns.
• Evaluate the impact of political campaign donations.
• Compare the way media industries and special interest groups influence what we know and their influence in the democratic process.

ISSUE SUMMARY

YES: Conservative author Thomas R. Eddlem makes the case that corporate media institutions influence the messages that the public sees and hears. As a result, the Supreme Court's 2010 *Citizens United* decision, which gives corporations the right to make political contributions and creates the possibility of the establishment of SuperPACs, also results in the exercise of freedom of speech.

NO: David Earley and Ian Vandewalker, two counsels at the Brennan Center for Justice at the New York University School of Law, argue that the rise of political spending that resulted from the Supreme Court's *Citizens United* decision has created a situation in which political elections can be "bought" by corporate donors. Because of the new law, they argue that the only way to ensure transparency is to create a situation in which all political donations are disclosed to the public.

The 2012 presidential election, which pitted incumbent Barack Obama against Mitt Romney, was the most costly in history. According to most reports, the two candidates spent over 2 billion dollars on their campaigns. When added to the cost of all other campaigns in the 2012 congressional elections, the sum total reached 8 billion dollars. These historic figures were largely the result of changes to traditional campaign finance practices, and attributed to the 2010 Supreme Court's *Citizens United* decision, which lifted restrictions on the amount of money corporate donors and special interest groups could donate to political candidates, issues, and campaigns, and allowed the formation of SuperPACs (political action committees).

The relationship of campaign donors and the cost of running a political campaign have always been controversial. In the United States, at the federal level, Congress has the responsibility of enacting campaign finance laws, and they are enforced by an independent federal agency called the Federal Election Commission (FEC). Traditionally, individual donors could contribute to a political candidate's campaign, but were restricted by certain dollar amounts. Typically, an individual could give up to $2,500 to a candidate. But in 2008, an independent organization called Citizens United wanted to air a film that was critical of Hillary Clinton, who was then a candidate for president. The film was called *Hillary: The Movie*, and Citizens United wanted to advertise the film during television broadcasts close to a Democratic primary, which was prohibited by the 2002 Bipartisan Campaign Reform Act (known as the McCain-Feingold Act).

Though the U.S. District Court for the District of Columbia originally prohibited Citizens United from advertising their film within 30 days of the convention, the case was appealed to the Supreme Court, and in 2010 the court overturned the District Court's decision (on a vote of 5-4) and found that the First Amendment prohibited the government from restricting political expenditures by corporations and unions. Many people criticized the Court for giving corporations the same freedom of speech that individual citizens are guaranteed, but the end result of the *Citizens United* decision was that the amount of money raised for candidates or to oppose candidates or certain positions could now be raised through organizations of donors, called political action committees (PACs), or very large organizations called SuperPACs that can accept unlimited amounts of money from corporations, unions, and associations. In the 2012 campaigns, it was found that much of the SuperPAC money was spent on negative advertising, and major criticism was leveled at millionaire and billionaire donors who appeared to be trying to "buy" political influence by backing certain candidates, and certain issues.

The controversy even found its way to Comedy Central, where Stephen Colbert used his show *The Colbert Report* to announce that by following the new FEC rules, he could start his own SuperPAC, Americans for a Better Tomorrow, Tomorrow, which raised 1.2 million dollars from viewers in 15 months. By publicizing the weaknesses in the new system, Colbert's SuperPAC demonstrated how weak the new decision was, and how it could be subject to manipulation. In 2012, Colbert was awarded a Peabody Award for how well he had used his SuperPAC parody as an "innovative means of teaching American viewers about the landmark court decision."

No doubt, some people like the idea of contributing to organizations that support their views, but in the case of the *Citizens United* decision and the increased power of SuperPACs, many say that the Supreme Court made a terrible decision because it equates corporate power with freedom of speech, in effect, giving the loudest megaphone to those who have the most money. John McCain, former candidate for president called it the "worst decision ever," and President Obama criticized the decision in his 2010 State of the Union address. In the YES and NO selections, conservative author Thomas R. Eddlem equates the *Citizens United* decision with the same power that media industries have been exerting over what the public knows, and claims that if we really want to see who influences politics, we should look to the news media and the members of the Council on Foreign Relations, a group of high-powered members of the media who influence politics in their own ways. Two attorneys, David Earley and Ian Vandewalker, who work for the Brennan Center for Justice at the New York University School of Law, remind us that even though the Citizens United organization supported the idea of disclosure laws to make campaign donations more transparent for the public, the Supreme Court and Congress did not act to make those disclosure rules a part of the practice of the decision, and as a result, opened the door to misuse and manipulation.

YES ↵

Thomas R. Eddlem

Citizens United Is Breaking Up Corporate Dominance of Elections

With the 2012 political season heating up, many people are calling for a ban on the SuperPacs created in the wake of the 2010 Supreme Court *Citizens United* decision. A few on the left have even called for a constitutional amendment to ban corporations from making political advertisements, for fear that corporations have come to dominate elections in the United States.

In one sense, they are right. But it's not the Super-Pacs. The corporations that have been dominating the public debate for decades are the media empires. Right now, six corporations control most of the television, radio, and print publishing networks that Americans see on a daily basis. They drive the debate, and the social issues behind the debate.

- **ABC/Disney** runs ABC News, as well as a large number of local and cable television stations, theme parks, and movie studios.
- **Time-Warner** owns CNN, TNT, and a whole slew of cable television stations, Warner Brothers movie studios, plus a large number of magazines, including *Time, People,* and *Sports Illustrated.*
- **NewsCorp** runs Fox News, a radio news network, 20th Century Fox movie studios, and dozens of newspapers and book publishers.
- **NBCUniversal** is jointly owned by Comcast and General Electric, one of the largest corporations in America. It runs the NBC network, MSNBC, a large selection of cable channels, Universal theme parks, and digital media.
- **Viacom** owns a variety of cable television channels and Paramount Pictures movie studios.
- **CBS Corporation** owns CBS television network, Showtime, a number of cable television stations, and a radio news network.

Even the Left admits that a few corporations control the message most Americans see.

What they don't talk about is that these few corporations are associated with each other in the New York-based Council on Foreign Relations, and that they have a tight relationship with government and establishment corporate leadership across the country. The Council on Foreign Relations has only 4,500 members, out of a national population of some 300 million. But they boast some of the most powerful media personalities and media corporate leaders in the country.

Corporate Members of the CFR include NewsCorp, Google, Time-Warner, Verizon, Microsoft, McGraw-Hill (publishing), General Electric (49 percent of NBC), and Thomson-Reuters (publishing/news network). And many of the personalities that Americans see every day on television are CFR members. For *example*:

NBC/MSNBC: Brian Williams (NBC anchor), Mika Brzezinski (MSNBC anchor), Maria Bartiromo (CNBC anchor), Tom Brokaw (former anchor), and Jonathan Alter (NBC News/*Newsweek* magazine)

CBS: Bob Schieffer (anchor) and Dan Rather (former anchor)

CNN: Fareed Zakaria (CNN anchor), Erin Burnett (CNN anchor), and commentators David Gergen, Jonathan Karl, and Jeffrey Toobin

ABC/Disney: George Stephanopoulos (anchor), Diane Sawyer (anchor), Katie Couric (former anchor), and commentators Peggy Noonan and George Will

Fox/NewsCorp: Rupert Murdoch (CEO of News-Corp) and commentators Morton Kondracke and Charles Krauthammer

Even movie stars are CFR members, such as Angelina Jolie, Warren Beatty, and George Clooney.

But it's not just full-time journalists and Hollywood bigshots from the CFR that get network airtime. The CFR member/anchors call CFR member/"experts" to affirm their positions. CFR President Richard Haass *boasted* in the CFR's 2011 Annual Report that the "CFR has been active on the full range of U.S. foreign policy concerns. Experts published five hundred and seventy op-eds and articles in the *New York Times, Washington Post, Wall Street Journal, Financial Times, Newsweek, Time,* and the *Atlantic,* among others, and made nearly five hundred media appearances on major U.S. and international news networks. CFR experts also testified before Congress fourteen times and briefed U.S. and foreign government officials over four hundred times."

So go ahead: Change the channel and pretend you can get a different perspective. In reality, it doesn't matter what channel you flip to; the CFR limits on acceptable debate are evident on every national channel, something that many freedom-lovers witnessed with the media ignoring or—later—demeaning Ron Paul in the presidential race. There's no national debate on eliminating all foreign aid, even though some *three-fourths of Americans want to do it.* Why not? Because it's not on the CFR talking points. There's no debate about bringing Americans home from hundreds of military bases abroad, even though a clear majority of Americans want it. Why not? Because it's not on the CFR talking points.

Imagine if such a concentration of top media personalities were found to be members of the National Rifle Association or the Teamsters Union, both of which have a membership nearly 1,000 times that of the Council on Foreign Relations. Wouldn't there be an outcry about bias or corruption?

We also saw the mainstream media coalesce around the idea that we had to bail out the banks in 2008 and 2009. Why was that? The CFR and its members led the people to bail out companies that were headed by their fellow CFR members. CFR corporate membership includes major banks such as Goldman Sachs, Morgan Stanley, Citibank, Bank of America—and did include AIG—until it went bankrupt despite the bailouts.

And it's not surprising that they got the bailouts either, since the CFR was *holding policy discussions* with Treasury Department officials throughout the conference. They *still are.*

Of course, it's easy to get a *phone-in from the Treasury Secretary* before he heads out to the G-20 conference if he's already a member. Indeed, it's not just Timothy Geithner who's a member, but just about all the past Treasury secretaries have been members of the Council on Foreign Relations for 50 years—from Bush's Hank Paulson to Clinton's Lawrence Summers and Robert Rubin (the latter a former CEO of Goldman Sachs).

This is true across the spectrum of government. Obama's Secretary of State Hillary Clinton is a member, just as Condi Rice and Colin Powell were under the Bush administration, and Madeleine Albright and Warren Christopher were under the Clinton administration.

The point of all this discussion is not to beat up on the Council on Foreign Relations, though its members probably deserve it. It's to point out that our media and our elections are already tightly controlled by a handful of well-connected multi-billion-dollar media corporations. And they were controlled that way long before the *Citizens United* decision. That's how they've been able to get the bailout deals done at the expense of the middle-class taxpayers—despite protests by the Tea Party and the Occupy movement. In this battle, it's a fight not just between the 99 percent and the one percent, but between the 99.999 percent and the 0.001 percent, who are practiced and very good at robbing the 99.999 percent through the agency of government authority.

But the stranglehold of these five corporations is breaking. The Internet started the breakup, but *Citizens United* tore that media oligopoly wide open. Under *Citizens United,* people have only to find one millionaire to fund their views and they can get around the mainstream media with grass-roots campaigning, Internet ads, or even conventional television advertisements. This happened with Liberty For All SuperPac, which helped guide Ron Paul fan Thomas Massie to a Republican primary win in an open Kentucky congressional district. And Freedom-Works SuperPac has shaken up Utah politics with its "Retire Hatch" campaign to stop TARP bailout Republican Orrin Hatch. A six-term senator, Hatch would never have had to have been in a run-off election against Dan Liljenquist without FreedomWorks SuperPac's help.

The Left implores the nation to repeal *Citizens United* in order to "take money out of politics." But the only way to do this is to ban freedom of the press. The *New York Times condemned* the *Citizens United* decision when it came out in 2009, complaining that corporations should not be involved in politics. This was just days after the *Times'* corporate subsidiary, the *Boston Globe,* had *endorsed* the Democrat in the Massachusetts U.S. Senate race to replace the late Ted Kennedy.

No corporations involved in politics?

. . . except themselves.

As James Madison noted in *Federalist #10,* political disagreements can be decided by either government censorship or allowing everyone to broadcast their views and trusting the people to make the right decisions at the ballot box. He chose the latter, stating:

> There are two methods of curing the mischiefs of faction: the one, by removing its causes; the other, by controlling its effects.
>
> There are again two methods of removing the causes of faction: the one, by destroying

the liberty which is essential to its existence; the other, by giving to every citizen the same opinions, the same passions, and the same interests.

It could never be more truly said than of the first remedy, that it was worse than the disease. Liberty is to faction what air is to fire, an aliment [element] without which it instantly expires. But it could not be less folly to abolish liberty, which is essential to political life, because it nourishes faction, than it would be to wish the annihilation of air, which is essential to animal life, because it imparts to fire its destructive agency.

Destroying essential liberty is precisely what the critics of *Citizens United* want to do. The attitude of the repeal-*Citizens-United* crowd can be summed up accurately as "totalitarian paternalism." They don't trust the people to come to the right conclusions. The people must be safely shepherded by the guardians of acceptable opinion, as represented by the five or six giant corporations that run the establishment media. Or perhaps they remain blissfully unaware that repealing *Citizens United* would put the same old establishment back in charge.

In the end it is an attitude of censorship worthy of Joseph Stalin. More importantly, it is flatly contradictory to the *First and Tenth Amendments* to the U.S. Constitution.

The cry on the Left is that corporations are not people. That's true; corporations and SuperPacs are associations of people. And this too was part of the First Amendment, which protected the right of the people to assemble and associate.

During congressional debate on the Bill of Rights in 1789, Connecticut Congressman Theodore Sedgwick *opposed* the First Amendment because he thought adding freedom of assembly to freedom of speech and press was redundant. According to the Annals of Congress, Sedgwick "feared it would tend to make them appear trifling in the eyes of their constituents; what, said he, shall we secure the freedom of speech, and think it necessary, at the same time, to allow the right of assembling? If people freely converse together, they must assemble for that purpose; it is a self-evident, unalienable right which the people possess; it is certainly a thing that never would be called in question; it is derogatory to the dignity of the House to descend to such minutiae. . . ."

The right to band together for a political cause and spend money was well-entrenched in the American constitutional system by the 1830s, when Alexis de Tocqueville *noted* in his *Democracy in America* that:

> In no country in the world has the principle of association been more successfully used or applied to a greater multitude of objects than in America. Besides the permanent associations which are established by law under the names of townships, cities, and counties, a vast number of others are formed and maintained by the agency of private individuals. . . . An association consists simply in the public assent which a number of individuals give to certain doctrines and in the engagement which they contract to promote in a certain manner the spread of those doctrines. The right of associating in this fashion almost merges with freedom of the press, but societies thus formed possess more authority than the press.

While the Left demonizes the label "corporations," it's nothing more than a label, a bogeyman. Call them associations of Americans exercising their rights to freedom of the press and freedom of speech, and the bogeyman is banished. The *Citizens United* decision allows more speech, not less. And for that reason, the Founding Fathers were probably smiling down from heaven when the decision was released.

THOMAS R. EDDLEM is a freelance writer and former newspaper editor who often writes for *The New American*, a conservative magazine. A native of Boston, he also contributes to other magazines and blogs, and has a radio show in the southeastern region of Massachusetts.

David Earley and Ian Vandewalker  **NO**

Transparency for Corporate Political Spending: A Federal Solution

American elections are awash in cash as never before. Spending in the 2012 presidential election will shatter all historic records, as will spending in Congressional races. But the most significant money won't be in the candidates' campaign coffers. The money transforming contemporary elections is that flowing into—and being spent by—outside groups that are legally independent of the candidates. Many of these outside groups are able to raise funds in unlimited amounts from wealthy individuals, unions, and corporations.

As the law stands today, corporations and unions can spend unlimited amounts of money in order to influence the outcome of elections. If individuals, unions, or corporations choose to spend political money directly—by producing television advertising and buying air time, for example—they must publicly disclose the expenditures and their contributors. But it is easy to evade such disclosure by simply routing political contributions through intermediary groups that purchase the ad time. The end result is that wealthy individuals, corporations, and unions can spend millions on political advertising to influence voters' choices at the ballot box, without disclosing this spending to the public.

After the Supreme Court decided *Citizens United v. FEC*, Americans were outraged at the invitation extended to corporations to spend unlimited sums to influence elections. But in addition to expanding corporations' ability to make political expenditures, *Citizens United* strongly approved of disclosure requirements. The court emphasized the importance of such disclosure, explaining that through it "[s]hareholders can determine whether their corporation's political speech advances the corporation's interest in making profits, and citizens can see whether elected officials are 'in the pocket' of so-called moneyed interests."

Unfortunately, a disclosure regime that would accomplish these goals did not exist at the time *Citizens United* was decided. Nor does it exist now: more than two years after *Citizens United*, Congress has done nothing to improve our nation's disclosure laws. The DISCLOSE Act of 2012, which would have required groups spending more than $10,000 during an election cycle to identify donors of more than $10,000, was filibustered in the Senate.

But the failure of Congress to act does not necessarily mean that Americans' calls for accountability in political spending must go unanswered. Instead, the Securities and Exchange Commission ("SEC") can take action, having both the authority and the responsibility to protect shareholders and the public by mandating the disclosure of political expenditures by publicly-traded corporations. Indeed, one of the SEC commissioners, Luis Aguilar, recently came forward in support of disclosure rules and urged the full Commission to act. The rest of the Commission should follow his lead. . . .

The Pressure on Corporate Decision Makers to Engage in Political Spending Has Risen with the Increasing Cost of American Elections

The Supreme Court's 2010 decision in *Citizens United v. FEC* ushered in a new era of spending in our nation's elections. The Court opened the door for unions and corporations to spend unlimited amounts to influence the outcomes of elections. While *Citizens United* enabled companies to spend treasury funds on political advertisements, lower court decisions expanded the ruling to strike down contribution limits on outside groups that exist solely to air political advertisements. Most significant was a decision by the United States Court of Appeals for the D.C. Circuit, *SpeechNow.org v. FEC*, which permitted individuals, corporations, and unions to give unlimited amounts to groups called independent-expenditure-only committees, more commonly known as "super PACs." Super PACs can accept unlimited contributions and spend unlimited sums on political advertisements.

The capacity to raise and spend unlimited sums on elections has ratcheted up the demand for political dollars—and political fundraisers have increasingly targeted corporate managers. In a 2010 Zogby International poll of business leaders, almost half of respondents said that pressure has increased to give to politicians since 2008. Seventy-two percent of respondents explained that their businesses gave money to either "gain access to influence the legislative process (55 percent) or to avoid adverse legislative consequences (17 percent)." Indeed, "members of the business community . . . face 'shake downs' for political contributions" from aggressive politicians.

> For example, in a 2010 meeting with 80 corporate PAC leaders, one Republican Party official candidly put these leaders on notice by stating, "we're evaluating giving patterns." He admitted that he tells corporate donors, "I understand you have to give money to Democrats. But I want to be back in the majority. You don't have to give [this Democrat] $5,000. Give them $2,000. You can give $3,000 elsewhere. Now let me show you some open seats where you can make an investment" in a suitable candidate.

Businesses face real pressure from politicians to make political expenditures, a problem made worse by *Citizens United.*

Given these increased pressures on corporate leaders, it is unsurprising that corporate political spending is growing along with the costs of elections. In recent years, spending in federal elections has exploded. Contributions to federal candidates have more than doubled from $781 million in 1998 to an astounding $1.9 billion in 2010. As a result of *Citizens United* in particular, outside spending in the 2010 federal elections quadrupled relative to the last midterm elections held in 2006. . . .

Even though the cash flowing into elections after *Citizens United* has the potential to determine winners and losers at the polls, Americans are often in the dark about who controls the spigot. Current law offers various avenues by which corporations can engage in political spending without public disclosure. Closing these loopholes, and bringing transparency to corporate political activities, would yield benefits to shareholders, investors, and voters.

There are several ways under current law for corporations to engage in political electioneering without revealing their donors. *First,* although super PACs must report

their donors, donations can be veiled by shunting them through shell corporations. For example, journalists investigating two corporations that each gave $1 million to the super PAC supporting Mitt Romney discovered that the corporations had the same address, but neither seemed to actually have an office there, and neither appeared to engage in any business. Both companies were tied to a Utah multimillionaire, Steven Lund, who later acknowledged using them to donate in support of Romney.

Second, corporations can pass their political spending through nonprofit "social welfare" groups organized under section 501(c)(4) of the tax code. Many of these organizations are spending large sums on elections, and there is no requirement that they publicly disclose their donors. At least some of these groups appear to have little social purpose aside from spending to influence elections. One 501(c)(4), Crossroads GPS, has spent tens of millions of dollars on television ads in swing states attacking President Obama: it announced a $25 million ad campaign in May and another $25 million blitz in July. Among its donations, Crossroads GPS has reported two valued at $10 million each, but the group did not publicly disclose the source of either donation.

Third, corporations underwrite substantial amounts of political advertising by routing donations through nonprofit trade organizations organized under section 501(c)(6) of the tax code. One of the largest 501(c)(6) spenders on elections is the U.S. Chamber of Commerce. Corporations donate millions to the Chamber, which is not required to report the identities of its donors. The Chamber is then able to leverage huge sums of corporate money to influence electoral outcomes, and intends to spend more $100 million in the 2012 elections. After a court decision required the disclosure of donors who support the type of political ad on which the Chamber has historically relied, the organization announced that it would no longer sponsor that type of advertising and would switch to another that allows it to keep its donors secret.

Disclosure of corporate political spending protects both shareholders and the proper functioning of American democracy. Corporate managers are currently largely free to make political expenditures according to their own interests because shareholders have little or no control over such spending; without disclosure, shareholders don't know about political spending, and so are unable to use corporate democracy to rein it in.

Half of American households own shares in major corporations—many through mutual funds, pensions, 401 (k) accounts, and the like. An increase in oversight of corporate political spending by shareholders, as well as the sunshine of public disclosure, would act as a democratizing influence on that spending. It would give a larger and more diverse portion of Americans influence over the financing of elections. That oversight cannot be exercised without information about spending. . . .

Corporate disclosure of political expenditures presents a number of benefits, both to investors and to the market broadly. As an example of the latter, it can shed light on companies' practice of securing market advantages by cashing in on elected officials' gratitude for donations. This practice distorts the operation of the marketplace and can create a suboptimal distribution of capital because advantage is gained through political influence rather than genuine market value. Disclosure can also help to ensure that corporations do not violate campaign finance laws; violations would be far easier to detect if details about companies' spending were publicly available.

In addition to these broader benefits, disclosure of political expenditures by corporations would directly protect investors in two ways: (1) empowering investors' oversight concerning political spending and its effect on profits, and (2) allowing shareholders to ensure their money is not used to support candidates or causes that conflict with their personal beliefs. Both issues are clearly relevant to those who own stock in a given company, who have various ways to react to actions by corporate management, including voting against retention of the board and divesting their shares. But these issues also matter to *potential* investors who are deciding whether to buy stock in a particular company and seek to make an informed decision. Responsible investors learn about the companies whose stock they are considering buying as they attempt to ensure a return on their investment.

As an initial matter, transparency in political spending by corporations allows current and potential shareholders to monitor whether spending choices by corporate managers benefit a firm's bottom line. An example involving News Corporation illustrates how this dynamic plays out. In June 2010, News Corporation—which owns Fox News among many other media entities—donated $1 million to the Republican Governors Association. Rupert Murdoch, the founder, chairman, and CEO of the company, at first explained: "It had nothing to do with Fox News. The RGA [gift] was actually [a result of] my friendship with John Kasich." Kasich had previously hosted his own program on Fox News and, at the time, was a Republican candidate for governor of Ohio; Kasich went on to narrowly defeat Democratic incumbent Ted Strickland by a two point margin. Murdoch later explained that the donation was "in the interest of the country and of all

the shareholders" and that his previous explanation was a "foolish throwaway line." When asked whether shareholders might be permitted to be involved in the process of choosing political expenditures, Murdoch dismissed the possibility, saying: "No. Sorry, you have the right to vote us off the board if you don't like that."

News Corporation's conduct is a glaring example of a manager acting in his own interest rather than the company's. Managers have considerable decision-making power regarding how to spend money, and shareholders have an interest in decisions about spending being made in the pursuit of corporate returns. Some political scientists have concluded that companies that spend money on elections have lower returns, and that their returns decrease as political spending rises. Corporations making political donations may come close to—or venture over—the lines demarcating violations of campaign finance laws or prohibited pay-to-play activities. Criminal liability would obviously affect profits. In order to make well-informed decisions, investors must have information about actions by corporate management so they can assess whether a corporation's political spending helps or hurts the company's bottom line.

Distinct from their financial interest in the company's profit, shareholders also have a political or expressive interest in refraining from financially supporting political activities with which they disagree. Robust disclosure of corporate political spending gives shareholders the tools to ensure they invest only in companies with whose political spending they agree. In 2010, Target Corporation contributed $150,000 to MN Forward, a PAC "that backs pro-business candidates in [Minnesota] statewide races, including a candidate for governor who opposes samesex marriage." As a result of the contribution, Target was the subject of boycotts and extensive negative publicity. Beyond having concern with how political expenditures could harm Target's corporate image and profitability, shareholders asked the company to consider when contributing to political candidates "whether a candidate espouses policies that conflict with the company's values." At least one Target shareholder, a foundation that funds groups fighting against prejudice against gay, lesbian, bisexual, and transgender people, liquidated its stock in protest. As Target Chairman, President, and CEO Gregg Steinhafel later explained in an apology letter to "Target Leaders," he was "genuinely sorry" because the "decision affected many . . . in a way [he] did not anticipate." At the 2011 annual shareholder meeting, Steinhafel was so exasperated from receiving questions about Target's political contributions that he said, "Does anybody have a question relating to our business that is unrelated to political giving? I would love to hear any question related to something else."

Target was not the only company to receive negative feedback as a result of its political activities. Replacements, Ltd., a North Carolina company that sells china, silver, and glassware, lobbied legislators, made monetary contributions, and even sold T-shirts in its showroom in an effort to oppose the state's Amendment One, which would ban same-sex marriage. Numerous customers expressed disagreement with the company's actions and vowed to conduct no further business with the company. As this example shows, harm to a company's bottom line can occur for engaging in any political activity, regardless of the viewpoint expressed. . . .

The informational interest. As the Supreme Court noted, voters have an interest in knowing "where political campaign money comes from and how it is spent by the candidate in order to aid the voters in evaluating those who seek . . . office." Knowing who is speaking allows voters to better understand the messages they receive and "to place each candidate in the political spectrum more precisely than is often possible solely on the basis of party labels and campaign speeches."

Outside political spenders have a storied history of hiding behind deceptive organization names to obfuscate the true source of funds. A few years ago in Colorado, an organization named "'Littleton Neighbors Voting No' spent $170,000 to defeat a restriction that would have prevented Wal-Mart from coming to town." While the name of this organization might evoke images of a grassroots group of people coming together in the small Colorado town of about 41,000 people, it was later revealed that the organization was funded exclusively by Wal-Mart. Indeed, this is just one of the latest examples in a long line of misleading monikers that has been extensively documented, including by the Supreme Court. In rejecting an earlier challenge to a disclosure law, the Court explained:

> Curiously, Plaintiffs want to preserve the ability to run these advertisements while hiding behind dubious and misleading names like: 'The Coalition—Americans Working for Real Change' (funded by business organizations opposed to organized labor) [and] 'Citizens for Better Medicare' (funded by the pharmaceutical industry). . . . Given these tactics, Plaintiffs never satisfactorily answer the question of how 'uninhibited, robust, and wideopen' speech can occur when organizations hide themselves from the scrutiny of the voting public.

Disclosure prevents companies from masking their spending, allowing the public to know the sources of electoral advertising. . . .

How to Achieve Disclosure of Corporate Political Spending

Requiring disclosure of corporate political spending would produce numerous benefits for the investor community and the body politic. *How* to achieve full transparency around corporate political spending, however, presents a separate question. Various solutions are available at least in theory: disclosure policies could be adopted by companies voluntarily, through regulation by the states, or through federal regulation. Federal regulation is the superior option because of the nationwide application that federal rules would have and the uniformity they would bring to a system of disclosure. . . .

Federally Mandated Disclosure: The Best Solution

Federal regulation would not suffer from the same limitations as state-by-state regulation. The federal government already engages in significant oversight of publicly held corporations through federal securities laws. Given the keen interest of investors and the public in the issue, the SEC clearly has the statutory authority to add political spending to the disclosures required of publicly held corporations. The Securities Exchange Act of 1934 created the SEC and gives it "complete discretion . . . to require in corporate reports . . . such information as it deems necessary or appropriate in the public interest or to protect investors." A "philosophy of full disclosure" is the "fundamental purpose" of the Securities Exchange Act; disclosure is necessary "to achieve a high standard of business ethics in the securities industry." . . .

The SEC should promulgate regulations requiring public corporations to disclose all of their political expenditures on a periodic basis. As SEC Commissioner Aguilar has said, "[a]rming investors with the information they need to facilitate informed decision-making is a core responsibility of the SEC. In fact, it is one of the factors that led to the creation of the SEC." In particular, such disclosures should include political contributions, independent expenditures, electioneering communications, and contributions to organizations that undertake these activities. Political expenditures at all levels of government—federal, state, and local—should all be reported. Each entry should include specific information, including the identity of any candidates involved, whether the payment supports or opposes the candidate, the amount of the expenditure, and the date of the expenditure. Similar information should be collected with regard to ballot initiatives, referenda, and other issues put to a public vote.

Political expenditures should be reported quarterly on a company's Form 10-Q filing with the SEC. A central database that included all disclosures nationwide would be far easier for shareholders and voters alike to navigate than fifty separate databases maintained by the states. Reviewing disclosure forms can be an involved, labor-intensive process. While private efforts have been made to consolidate state disclosures into one central database, regulation that created a nationwide database would be uniform and dependable. The SEC can easily incorporate the collection of this information into its preexisting EDGAR filing system, which already receives thousands of electronic filings daily. This information would then be freely available to shareholders and voters through the Internet, with many filings being posted on the same day they are submitted.

Recent legal changes have created an electoral environment fraught with new risks for shareholders and voters alike. Corporate spending on elections may impact the fiscal health of corporations and has the potential to distort the operation of the market. Shareholders may unknowingly fund activity that conflicts with their political beliefs. Voters can be kept in the dark about the sources of advertisements designed to influence their votes. Disclosure, however, would minimize these risks: shareholders would know how their companies are spending money and voters would know who is funding political speech.

While *Citizens United* prompted increased corporate spending on politics, the decision also contained the seeds of the solution. The Supreme Court strongly approved of laws requiring disclosure of political expenditures and noted the importance of well-functioning corporate democracy. As the Court succinctly put it, "prompt disclosure of expenditures can provide shareholders and citizens with the information needed to hold corporations and elected officials accountable for their positions and supporters." Such prompt disclosure is not required by current law, but an SEC rule would change that. In the words of SEC Commissioner Aguilar, "Investors are not receiving adequate disclosure, and as the investors' advocate, the Commission should act swiftly to rectify the situation by requiring transparency."

David Earley is an attorney at the Brennan Center for Justice at the New York University School of Law where he focuses on campaign finance reform. He is a former article editor for the *New York University Annual Survey of American Law*.

Ian Vandewalker works on issues of voting rights and campaign finance reform at the Brennan Center for Justice at the New York University School of Law. An attorney, he graduated from the NYU School of Law where he was senior article editor for the *New York University Review of Law and Social Change*.

EXPLORING THE ISSUE

Should Corporations Be Allowed to Finance Political Campaigns?

Critical Thinking and Reflection

1. Does our political process give too much power to those who can make large campaign donations?
2. What arguments are there for giving corporations the same rights as individuals, and should corporations or special interest groups be subject to caps on how much money they can contribute?
3. Do negative political ads really work?
4. How complex are the relationships of campaigns, democracy, and using media to inform the public?

Is There Common Ground?

Several groups, like the ACLU, have put pressure on the Supreme Court to reverse the *Citizens United* decision, and several citizens groups have started grassroots campaigns to have the decision changed, but even if the Court revisits the decision, most pundits are expecting that elections in the near future will continue to raise exorbitant amounts of money, and that campaigning is likely to become even more negative in the future. At the same time, members of Congress have offered additional modifications to campaign finance reform, and we can expect to see this debate heating up in the future.

Other countries have different ways of dealing with the relationship of money and influence; some limit the amount of time before an election for media coverage, while some have specific limits of what parties can spend on elections. If the United States were to radically overhaul the way campaigns are run, and how they are run, the negotiations would very likely take years. Perhaps the best we can expect is that voters become educated to understand the process and impact of the money spent on political campaigns.

Additional Resources

The American Civil Liberties Union (ACLU) has long been concerned with the relationship of money and politics. Their website focuses on their interpretation of the history of campaign finance reform, and provides periodic updates to keep the public informed of their efforts to monitor political money flow:

www.aclu.org/free-speech/campaign-finance-reform

Stephen Colbert of *The Colbert Report* has an online archive of his efforts to start and maintain his own SuperPAC, Americans for a Better Tomorrow, Tomorrow, which includes updates of his financial filings:

www.colbertsuperpac.com/home.php

The Washington Post kept a running total of the money spent in the 2012 presidential campaign by month:

www.washingtonpost.com/wp-srv/special/politics/ campaign-finance/

Greg Palast with illustrations by Ted Rall, *Billionaires & Ballot Bandits: How to Steal an Election in 9 Easy Steps* (Seven Stories Press, 2012). In this collection of previously published essays from a variety of publications, the author takes a light-hearted, but nonetheless, serious approach to understanding how the 2012 election unfolded.

Internet References . . .

The Conference Board

www.conference-board.org/politicalspending/

Selected, Edited, and with Issue Framing Material by:
Alison Alexander, *University of Georgia*
and
Jarice Hanson, *University of Massachusetts—Amherst*

ISSUE

Does Drone Journalism Challenge Journalistic Norms of Privacy?

YES: Margot E. Kaminski, from "Enough with the 'Sunbathing Teenager' Gambit," *Slate* (2016)

NO: United States of America National Transportation Safety Board, from "Brief of Amicus Curiae to Safeguard the Public's First Amendment Interest in the Free Flow of Information," *www.hklaw.com* (2014)

Learning Outcomes

After reading this issue, you will be able to:

- Articulate the privacy norms of traditional journalism.
- Explain the issues surrounding intrusion with drones.
- Define "plain view."
- Clarify the relevance of the FAA to drone journalism.

ISSUE SUMMARY

YES: The access afforded by drones is rewriting privacy laws according to Law Professor Kaminski. She explores the complexity of privacy issues, including the range of national, state, and local regulations and practices that often conflict. Drone regulation, she notes, is about much more than sunbathing teenagers.

NO: The Amici Curiae brief filed with the Federal Aviation administration represents media industries arguments to protect First Amendment rights of newsgathering organizations in the evolving regulatory environment. They warn against the "chilling effect" on news of several actions including banning the use of drones for newsgathering.

What are the norms of privacy in journalism? They have been long established and are relatively complex. Reporting news stories will often publicize facts or show images that will anger individuals. Often such disagreements end up in court, with the consequence that interpretations of invasion of privacy can change over time and jurisdiction. The concept of a "reasonable expectation of privacy" is a legal, but often amorphous, standard.

According to the Reporters Committee For Freedom of the Press in their Photographers Guide to Privacy, courts have recognized four major types of privacy law: (1) unreasonable instruction upon seclusion; (2) unreasonable revelation of private facts; (3) unreasonably placing another person in a false light before the public; and (4) misappropriation of a persons' name or likeness. Thus photographers cannot trespass nor can they take pictures from outside your home with a zoom lens where you have every reasonable expectation of privacy. Intrusion is the most common claim, particularly when dealing with still or video materials. Private facts may come into play if, for example, photographs are taken from private property without permission. False light can occur when a photograph is not captioned property or when images are used to support a story unrelated to the initial reason for the photograph. Finally misappropriation involves using a photograph for commercial use without permission.

To be more specific, what can be seen in a "plain view" from public place can be photographed. "In plain view" is not as simple as it may sound. If a photograph or video is taken in a public place where the average person could see what is happening, consent is not required. However, if photographs are taken in places where an individual would have a reasonable expectation of privacy—such as their home, consent is required. But let's complicate this a bit. What if you, a photojournalist, are standing on top of a mountain with a powerful zoom lens? Can you use pictures taken of people below? Most photographers would say no, because you are using the lens to enhance viewing and therefore this would not be what an average person could see. Taking these practices into account, consider what changes may be wrought by using drone technology for newsgathering.

As a culture we are already under scrutiny from above. Google Earth uses pictures of private property from satellite images. Helicopters frequently try to obtain shots of celebrities on a beach or at their wedding. Some events may have large tents, so that pictures from above cannot be taken. Now, drones can get much closer to events and obtain pictures previously unavailable and at a much more reasonable cost. The issues are not only about privacy but about legal regulations. Legally, airspace is public space. You do not own the air above your property. The Federal Aviation Administration (FAA) regulates air traffic, and has been holding hearings and working on crafting a series of guidelines and regulations about drone pilots and flights. Much of the discussion about drones has to do with establishing requirement to license drone pilots, as well as to set regulations about altitudes allowed and issues concerning flights over people and their property. Drone pilots must be certified, and must know the limitations on flights restricted airspace, temporary flight restrictions, and regulations on notification of air towers about flight plans. Certain limitations on drone flight are required: the individual operating the drone must keep it within his/her line of sight at all times, altitude requirements seem to be set at a maximum of 400 feet from the ground or from the structure over which they fly (so far there seem to be no minimum drone flight requirements, such as for example that drones must fly at least a minimum height above the ground), and that flights cannot be over people unless they are involved in the flight itself (e.g., someone on the ground relaying information to the drone pilot). This final restriction is for safety to legally protect people from having a drone drop on them from the sky.

Very importantly, the FAA defines drones as an aircraft. While one would never shoot down an airplane or helicopter, there have been instances of individuals capturing or shooting down a drone that was flying too low and/or too intrusively near their home, as exemplified in the Yes selection of this issue. According to the FAA this is a felony; as an aircraft, you are not allowed to shoot it down.

Beyond the legal issues are the ethical ones revolving around drone journalism. The difference between what can be done and what should be done has become more complex with drone technology. There are a number of organizations working to create guidelines for ethical drone journalism; many are represented or discussed in the Internet References section.

Kaminski offers an insightful analysis that explores the complexity of privacy issues, which range from protecting consumers to cyber security problems if drone are hacked. If the issues are complex, the range of national, state, and local regulations and practices that often conflict make these problems even more difficult. Although Kaminski's concerns range far beyond the realm of newsgathering, they reflect the regulatory issues that will impact the practice of journalism in the future. And of course, these issues remind us that this about much more than sunbathing teenagers.

The Amici Curiae brief filed with the Federal Aviation administration represents media industries arguments to protect First Amendment rights of newsgathering organizations in the evolving regulatory environment. They warn against the "chilling effect" on news of several actions including banning the use of Unmanned Aerial Systems (UAS) for newsgathering. They note the benefit for the public of information that can be achieved by drones. Given the limited authority of the FAA in regulating privacy, they encourage the FAA to avoid creating policy in that area. They finally urge that the cease and desist process used by the FAA be replaced by rulemaking procedures.

Drones create both legal and ethical challenges. They create the capacity for intrusions on privacy as well as the capacity for more and better reporting in arenas ranging from natural disasters to local festivals. We are already under much more scrutiny than most of us are aware of. What journalists can do and should do are quickly evolving legal and ethical dilemmas.

YES ←

Margot E. Kaminski

Enough with the "Sunbathing Teenager" Gambit

Drone privacy is about much more than protecting girls in bikinis

Last July, a Kentucky father spotted a drone hovering over his backyard, where his two daughters were purportedly sunbathing. He took out his shotgun and shot the drone down. Later he ruminated that "[w]e don't know if they're pedophiles looking for kids, we don't know if they're thieves. We don't know if it's ISIS."

Drones embody surveillance. They provide a visual and sometimes physical target for privacy fears. Drones have catalyzed state privacy lawmaking and prompted numerous conversations about coming privacy concerns. Intriguingly, however, the driving drone privacy narrative hasn't been about location tracking, or pervasive government surveillance. It's been about sunbathing young women.

Advertisement

The Kentucky father protecting his daughters is in good company. A New Jersey man also shot down a drone to protect his family's privacy. A woman in Virginia Beach, Virginia, told a drone operator that hovering over sunbathers on a private beach was "creepy." A Connecticut woman assaulted a drone hobbyist for taking pictures of people on the public beach with his "helicopter plane." A California man threw his T-shirt over a drone on a public beach, explaining that "[w]e had like a peeping Tom." A Florida resident alleged that drones had been spying on her sunbathing teenage neighbor: "They're recording children in bathing suits or they're recording the teenager across the street, who lays out in her front yard in her bikini." (By the way, that narrative about the Kentucky father protecting his daughters has been challenged since

his arrest. He won in state court but a federal suit filed by the drone owner is pending.)

The sunbather narrative has made its way to the United Kingdom, where a Bristol woman quickly covered up after seeing a drone overhead. And it has made its way into academic and policy work. Drone expert Gregory McNeal talks about the sunbathing woman in his Brookings Institution report "Drones and Aerial Surveillance," writing, "While the police are overhead photographing 123 Main Street, they look down and see a woman sunbathing in the adjacent property at 125 Main Street. . . ." Arizona State University law professor Troy Rule, in proposing a localized zoning system for drone use of airspace, discusses how "[i]ndividuals flying camera-fitted drones above residential neighborhoods have disturbed sunbathers in their private yards."

With all we know about the complexities of information privacy, why is the female sunbather the story that keeps capturing attention?

Maybe it's because the sunbather narrative is easy; it's concrete. A woman or girl who otherwise wouldn't expose herself in a bikini suddenly has a much wider audience than intended. Maybe it's because the sunbather narrative is actually happening at a greater frequency than other privacy issues; people are perverts, and prurience is a great motivator. Or maybe the sunbather narrative is just the latest spin on the old, old tale of Lady Godiva: Peeping Tom takes a look at the nude woman and is consequently struck blind or dead.

The sunbather story fails us because it ignores issues of information privacy.

The story of Lady Godiva is a myth filled with fascinating gender dynamics. Most scholars believe that the ride didn't actually happen. According to legend, Lady Godiva pleaded with her husband, Count Leofric, to lower taxes. He told her he would do so the day she rode nude through town at noon. When in protest she did just that, the people of the town of Coventry stayed indoors out of respect, to preserve her modesty. But Peeping Tom ignored the social contract, gazed at her out of lust, and was punished. According to professor Daniel Donoghue, who has tracked the development of the Godiva myth, the story evolved over time to include Peeping Tom. Donoghue explains, "Tom would become the scapegoat and bear the symbolic guilt for people's desire to look at this naked woman." Peeping Tom became a point of resolution for conflicting impulses over freedom, control, and lust.

The sunbather disrupted by drones is a Lady Godiva story, of sorts, without the tax policy. A young woman expresses liberation by wearing a bikini in her backyard or on the beach. Everyone generally follows social norms and refrains from staring for too long, or taking photos or video. But the hovering drone breaks that agreement and must be punished, just like Tom. Often it's dad who does the punishing, but sometimes it's just a Good Samaritan. Law isn't very helpful. Existing state Peeping Tom laws mostly do not cover these incidents, because many require trespassing or peeping in through the windows of an actual house.

The problem with letting the sunbather narrative dominate drone privacy coverage is that it provides a woefully incomplete account of the kinds of privacy concerns that drones raise. If we legislate to protect the modesty of sunbathers, we risk letting significant issues fall by the wayside. That's leaving aside questions of whether privacy and modesty are equivalent (they're not), and whether the father–daughter dynamic that results in a shot-down drone is a healthy one (take a guess).

The sunbather story fails us because it ignores issues of information privacy. Drones will collect enormous amounts of information and absent federal omnibus data privacy law, which we don't have in the United States, there is next to nothing to govern that data's processing or use. This includes combining data from one drone with data from other devices, to create a near-complete portrait of somebody's physical interactions. Retailers and insurance companies, just as examples, could certainly be motivated to create these kinds of data portraits of people. (As of publication, insurance companies had received 276 special permissions from the Federal Aviation Administration to use drones.) We are already profiled online by data brokers; companies have every incentive to try to extend that profiling to physical space. And they don't want to have to ask for permission to get it.

Our current federal privacy regime, depending on enforcement actions by the Federal Trade Commission, is premised on protecting consumers from broken promises and unfair actions by the companies with which they transact. The problem with drones and other new technologies is that a person who gets tracked by a drone usually won't be the drone's owner. He or she thus won't have the consumer relationship with the drone company that triggers FTC protection. The FTC is ill-equipped to govern this, in the same way it is ill-equipped to govern the "Internet of Other Peoples' Things."

The sunbather narrative fails us in other respects as well. For instance, it doesn't address facial recognition technology. Our inescapable biometric identifiers mean we can lose the practical obscurity in which we usually operate in physical spaces. People out there in public might not recognize or identify us—but drones will. This allows those in possession of drone video to much more readily profile particular individuals. The sunbather story also doesn't address that many times, drones will be gathering information using superhuman senses, like thermal imaging, that we aren't accustomed to acknowledging and can't practically shield ourselves from. And the sunbather narrative fails to capture cybersecurity problems. If you think drones are disruptive now, just wait until they're hacked.

However, the sunbather narrative isn't completely wrong. It resonates precisely because drones, like an array of other new technologies, sit at the intersection of spatial and information privacy. The sunbather story illustrates a spatial privacy problem: Once, fathers thought their daughters were protected by the six-foot privacy fence. (The daughters themselves may or may not have cared.) Now, drones make that fence irrelevant. Physical architecture once constrained people from seeing into others' backyards or upstairs windows; now drones, like thermal-imaging technology, can discern information that was otherwise obtained only at great cost. The question is whether or when the law should intervene to impose legal costs where the physical and financial constraints have fallen. Law can enable us to continue to manage our privacy using features of the real world that we've grown up with—and grown dependent on.

As social actors, we regularly use cues from our physical and social environments to decide how much we want to disclose in a particular setting. Technologies like drones disrupt environments. They take down walls. They distance the human operator from the enforcement of social norms in a particular setting (like the beach). They disrupt our ability to calculate how much we've disclosed by potentially tracking behavior over time, at far lower cost than a helicopter.

The Supreme Court is starting to understand these things, although it took some time. In 2001, the court found police use of a thermal-imaging device violated the Fourth Amendment because it "might disclose, for example, at what hour each night the lady of the house takes her daily sauna and bath." (There's Godiva again.) The court hinged its decision about new information technology and spatial privacy on whether the new technology had been widely and publicly adopted. This reasoning raised a host of concerns about a downward ratchet in privacy law; would we lose Fourth Amendment protection just by widely adopting new technology?

By 2012, however, five justices understood that using GPS technology to persistently track somebody's location over nearly a month, even in public places, and even though GPS technology is certainly in widespread public use, could violate a reasonable expectation of privacy and thus the Fourth Amendment. These justices recognized that we calibrate behavior based on the assumption that it's just too hard or too expensive for someone to follow us that consistently, over that amount of time. And persistent tracking over time and space can disclose sensitive information, such as religious beliefs, or sexual or political preferences.

The Fourth Amendment applies to law enforcement, not to private actors. But current developments provide better ways of thinking about data-gathering technologies such as drones. Like GPS, drones make it cheaper and easier for creepy neighbors to follow someone over an extended period of time. Like thermal imaging (and sometimes using thermal imaging), they make the physical barriers that we rely on less effective. Drones pose a hybrid of information and spatial privacy problems. That hybrid of issues is increasingly the problem of this age.

Currently, there's no regulatory regime in place to handle drone privacy. (There are a number of state privacy laws, but most states have no privacy laws that would cover the sunbather, or persistent tracking by drone, or drone data use.) The Federal Aviation Administration has said it wants to stay out of privacy issues; a court just this month refused to weigh in to compel the FAA to address privacy before its final rules have come down. Last year, the president instructed the National Telecommunications and Information Administration to host the development of industry best practices for drone use. That process is ongoing, but many public interest groups have chosen not to participate in it after the failure of the NTIA's best practices for facial recognition.

In April, the Senate approved a bill reauthorizing the Federal Aviation Administration. The bill would, among many other things, suggest (but not require) that drone operators "for compensation or for hire, or in the furtherance of a business enterprise" create a privacy policy enforceable by the FTC. The bill provides no substantive requirements for those policies, allowing companies to set their own low standards—or not set them at all. Absent consumer relationships with those tracked by drones, it's unclear what would motivate companies to put good privacy policies in place. The bill also instructs the NTIA to submit a report to Congress on industry best practices that may serve as the basis of federal legislation. Again, given the weaknesses of the NTIA process (in which I've been involved), this is not a good source of substantive privacy recommendations. The Senate bill pre-empts drone-specific state laws, which would foreclose local experimentation with drone policy, including privacy. This is ill-advised. It remains to be seen what will happen in the House, but its controversial Aviation, Innovation, Reform, and Reauthorization Act similarly leans heavily on the NTIA.

Drones have many, many positive uses, from safety inspections to environmental research to monitoring police behavior. But when we're discussing the privacy problems they raise, it's about time we got away from the bikinis.

MARGOT E. KAMINSKI is an Assistant Professor of law at The Ohio State University Moritz College of Law and affiliated fellow of the Yale Information Society Project.

**United States of America National
Transportation Safety Board**

Brief of Amicus Curiae to Safeguard the Public's First Amendment Interest in the Free Flow of Information

Introduction

Since 2007, the Federal Aviation Administration ("FAA"), through ad hoc administrative actions rather than through properly enacted and promulgated federal regulation, has applied an overly broad policy prohibiting the unlicensed use of unmanned aerial systems ("UAS") for "business purposes" in the United States national airspace. In applying agency posture in the guise of regulatory rule, the FAA has never distinguished between "business operations" and the use of UAS technology for the First Amendment-protected purpose of gathering and disseminating news and information. Indeed, just last month, the FAA indicated that a newspaper's mere posting on the Internet of photographs provided to it by a non-commercial UAS hobbyist might subject the media company to federal regulatory fines for using a UAS for "business purposes."

The News Media Amici remain concerned that—in addition to the deficiencies in enactment and the inconsistencies in application that Administrative Law Judge Patrick G. Geraghty correctly noted in granting Respondent's Motion to Dismiss—the FAA still has not given appropriate consideration to the First Amendment interests at stake. Indeed, despite a 2012 mandate from Congress to issue a comprehensive plan for integrating UAS into the air traffic system by February 2013, the FAA has failed to issue a notice of proposed rulemaking to address the use of even small UAS, or any other segment of the UAS population other than for experimental and public aircraft purposes. The FAA also has taken very little action to grant licenses to private parties to use the technology. As a result, the almost complete prohibition on the civilian use of UAS for any purpose, including First Amendment purposes, remains the current de facto policy.

This overly broad policy, implemented through a patchwork of regulatory and policy statements and an ad hoc cease-and-desist enforcement process, has an impermissible chilling effect on the First Amendment newsgathering rights of journalists, including News Media Amici.

The federal government has deprived its citizens and a free and independent news media of the opportunity to participate in the rulemaking process required under U.S. law when the government seeks to regulate, restrict, or curtail otherwise proper lawful activity. The federal government, through the FAA and with the NTSB's encouragement, should move forward with the development of polices that protect, rather than hinder, freedom of speech and of the press.

The FAA should develop a rule to regulate small UAS, using appropriate notice-and-comment procedures to provide the news media with input into the development of UAS regulations that will provide carefully tailored safety restraints and maximum First Amendment freedom to lawfully gather news.

Argument

I. A Complete Ban on the Use of Unmanned Aerial Systems Violates the First Amendment Right to Gather News.

The FAA, in a series of threats of administrative sanction, and in derogation of the First Amendment rights of the public to receive news and information, has flatly banned the use of UAS for newsgathering purposes. The FAA will not approve licenses for UAS use for news operations. It has threatened fines against university-conducted student experimentation with drone journalism. And it has even suggested that a newspaper "err on the side of caution"—a chilling warning of impending punishment—and refrain from lawfully publishing photographs taken independently by a UAS hobbyist and provided after the fact to the newspaper. In each case, the FAA has averred to its restrictions on the use of UAS for "business purposes." The FAA's position is untenable as it rests on a fundamental misunderstanding about journalism. News gathering is not a "business purpose": It is a First Amendment right. Indeed, contrary to the FAA's complete shutdown of an entirely new means to gather the news, the remainder of the federal government, in legislation, regulation and adjudication, has recognized that, in the eyes of the law, journalism is not like other businesses. The government in a myriad of measures has long accommodated the bedrock First Amendment principle that "without some protection for seeking out the news, freedom of the press could be eviscerated."

Unlike the FAA, for example, the Supreme Court recognizes that the publication of news is not a "commercial" activity comparable to the sale of goods and services. The First Amendment fully protects both for-profit and non-profit gathering and dissemination of news and information. "Of course, the degree of First Amendment protection is not diminished merely because the newspaper or speech is sold rather than given away."; Pacific Gas & Elec. Co. v. Public Utils. Comm'n, "extends well beyond speech that proposes a business transaction" and thus is fully protected by the First Amendment the fact that "books newspapers, and magazines are published and sold for profit does not prevent them from being a form of expression whose liberty is safeguarded by the First Amendment." The right to use the press for expressing one's views is not to be measured by the protection afforded commercial handbills. It should be remembered that the pamphlets of Thomas Paine were not distributed free of charge. The Supreme Court has noted that the First Amendment is implicated whenever a "commercial" regulation encroaches on news gathering and dissemination.

. . . When UAS operated by hobbyists in Ohio captured video footage of a recent fire, the FAA cautioned a news publication from airing the footage, stating through a spokesperson that it "would require more legal review to determine if it was a fineable offense to publish the video on [a news] site." The spokesperson also warned the journalists to "err on the side of caution." The FAA thus has interrupted the free flow of information guaranteed to all U.S. citizens that is so vital to our "profound national commitment to the principle that debate on public issues should be uninhibited, robust, and wide-open[.]"

II. The Potential Public Benefit of News Media Reporting by Unmanned Aerial Systems Counsels in Favor of Restrained Regulatory Rulings

A. Unmanned Aerial Systems Have The Potential To Improve News Coverage

The public stands to benefit enormously from the news media's use of UAS, as many news stories are told best from an aerial perspective. For example, reports on traffic, hurricanes, wildfires, and crop yields could all be told more safely and cost-effectively with the use of UAS. Lower-cost aerial photography would help more newsrooms across the country bring more accurate and useful information to the public.

A recent study by Amicus Curiae the National Press Photographers Association illustrates the beneficial uses for which news organizations and individual journalists would deploy UAS in their reporting. As set forth in this study, survey respondents indicated that UAS will be used to help journalists obtain footage despite obstructions, safety concerns, police restrictions, or hazardous environments, improving their ability to report on fires, accidents, weather conditions, natural disasters, and construction sites.

For example:

- One respondent indicated that UAS could have helped his station's reporting on a news story about ice jams in a river and the threat of flooding. News crews were not able to safely get close-ups of the problem, but a UAS could have achieved a clearer picture of the issue from a closer and safer vantage point.
- Other respondents noted that UAS could help cover wildfires, which spread rapidly and also pose safety concerns to news crews.
- Another respondent noted that UAS could be used to obtain better footage of sprawling facilities. In reporting on the anniversary of a GM plant closure, without the ability to use a UAS, the respondent said that the news crew drove by the fence of the closed plant and shot video.
- Another respondent noted that the use of UAS would help address what might be considered a more routine issue, where limited access and roadblocks prevent photographers from capturing images of major news events. This respondent noted that companies with helicopters may be able to capture these types of images, but with shrinking news budgets, this is becoming less likely.

Hobbyists have already begun using UAS in some of these circumstances, receiving the approval and accolades of some first responders. Recently, during a fire in Dayton, Ohio, a UAS hobbyist rather than a news organization, obtained an aerial view of the burning building.

According to news reports, the fire chief overseeing the incident noted that " . . . in a case like this, if you can get an aerial view of the burning building, it is very helpful. That's why we have 110-foot ladder trucks. But it's a lot easier if you could fly a drone over." Similarly, other hobbyists flew UAS to obtain coverage of fires in Harlem and Brooklyn.

International coverage of protests, like those in Kiev, has likewise benefitted from the use of UAS. As these examples demonstrate, UAS have the currently unrealized potential to facilitate better access to news events at a more reasonable cost, allowing news organizations to continue to report on important stories that they might not be able to cover without these tools.

B. Privacy Concerns Involving Journalists' Use of UAS Are Adequately Addressed in State Law and Do Not Warrant Federal Regulatory Oversight

In light of the public benefit UAS may provide in newsgathering, regulatory efforts, including the FAA's small UAS rulemaking and enforcement proceedings like this one, should cautiously approach privacy issues. The Administrative Law Judge wisely avoided privacy issues in adjudicating this dispute. For many reasons, the Board should do the same.

First, the FAA lacks the expertise to develop or enforce policies pertaining to privacy or civil liberties. Instead, the FAA's authority is limited to ensuring safety and efficiency in the aviation system. Recognizing its specific mission, the FAA pointedly disclaimed authority to regulate based on alleged privacy interests when it released a "roadmap" for integrating unmanned aerial systems into the national airspace. As the FAA itself has recognized, privacy concerns have no bearing on safety enforcement matters like this one.

Second, much of the public debate concerning the domestic use of UAS has centered on law enforcement agencies. Certainly, use of UAS to conduct surveillance for law enforcement purposes raises constitutional privacy issues that may be appropriate for legislation, court review, or even civil litigation. However, constitutional concerns about the appropriate role of law enforcement agencies and their use of developing technologies should play no role in determining how the news media (and other private citizens) may deploy UAS. The privacy issues inherent in the constitutional limitations on law enforcement present entirely separate issues and should not be considered in this civil penalty dispute.

Third, any privacy concerns that may arise from the news media's use of UAS already are taken into account in the common law and statutory regimes of the states. Since the Kodak Camera was first introduced in the late 1800s, and future Supreme Court Justice Louis D. Brandeis and co-author Samuel D. Warren raised the fear that "the press is overstepping in every direction the obvious bounds of propriety and of decency," state law has "[grown] to meet the demands of society." State legislatures and courts, as Brandeis and Warren recommended, have developed invasion of privacy laws flexible enough to respond to issues raised by developing technologies. Privacy concerns are best addressed by these existing state tort laws and statutes, which provide sufficient remedies to address allegedly invasive uses of UAS. The types of laws that may address the improper use of UAS include invasion of privacy laws, as well as trespass laws, nuisance laws, state electronic eavesdropping or wiretapping laws, and anti-stalking laws. Through litigation, journalists continue to attempt to help courts strike the appropriate balance between privacy and the First Amendment. The results have not always been favorable for the news media, and obviously each case will turn on its specific facts. The state courts, and legislatures, remain the appropriate place for the resolution of this balance as new technologies emerge. Therefore, relying on state laws is favorable to beginning anew with a federal regulatory regime, promulgated by an agency that admits it lacks the necessary experience.

As the FAA recognized in its roadmap, it is critical that policy determinations addressing privacy be based on a discussion among policy makers, privacy advocates and industry. Any dialogue about UAS must include the news media, so that important and practical First Amendment considerations can be taken into account. Moreover, any resulting rules must be based on factual considerations of the public policy issues, rather than generalized theories, fears or concerns about the use of a new technology. Our laws have always been flexible enough to incorporate new technologies—from the printing press, to cameras, to radio, to television, to the Internet—without banning them and while still protecting basic rights and freedoms. Likewise, UAS technologies should be integrated into our society through reasonable regulations without infringing on the rights and freedoms of citizens, including the rights to gather, disseminate and receive news.

III. The Ad Hoc Cease-And-Desist Process Used by the Faa is an Inappropriate Substitute for Notice-and-Comment Rulemaking Procedures

The FAA's use of an ad hoc cease-and-desist process and inconsistent enforcement regime to regulate UAS is particularly concerning in light of the First Amendment implications of the agency's decisions restricting the use of UAS.

As the ALJ correctly determined, the FAA's "Notice of Policy" prohibiting the use of UAS for "business purposes" without a license is not a proper regulation that can bind the public. The policy indicates on its face that it is a statement of policy, which cannot establish a rule or enforceable regulation. An agency cannot escape its responsibility to present evidence and reasoning supporting its substantive rules by announcing binding precedent in the form of a general statement of policy.). If, despite its plain language, the FAA intended this statement of policy as a binding regulation, it failed to meet the requirements of the Administrative Procedure Act, which requires advance notice and the opportunity to comment.

The FAA's alternative theory of regulatory authority is similarly problematic. The basis for this theory is that the FAA may exercise regulatory authority over small UAS and model aircraft operations under general Federal Aviation Regulations.

This is based on the definition of the term "aircraft" as a "device that is used or intended to be used for flight in the air." This policy is inconsistent with the FAA's historical position, which has been that small UAS, like model aircraft, are excluded from the regulatory and statutory definitions. Where an agency's position deviates from its long-standing practice and is announced in an enforcement proceeding, it is entitled only to deference "proportional to the 'thoroughness evident in its consideration, the validity of its reasoning, its consistency with earlier and later pronouncements, and all of those factors which give it power to persuade'."

Here, the FAA's position that its general Federal Aviation Regulations apply to UAS, including model airplanes, is inconsistent with its historical position that model aircraft operations are subject only to voluntary compliance with guidance. Likewise, its position could easily lead to absurd results. As ALJ Geraghty stated, the FAA's position in this matter "would lead to a conclusion that those definitions include as an aircraft all types of devices/contrivances intended for, or used for, flight in the air. The extension of that conclusion would then result in the risible argument that a flight in the air of, e.g. a paper aircraft, or a toy balsa wood glider, could subject the 'operator' to the regulatory provisions of FAA Part 91, Section 91.13(a)." Accordingly, ALJ Geraghty correctly concluded that the FAA's position that it could use its pre-existing Federal Aviation Regulations to govern the use of UAS should not be credited.

Yet, despite ALJ Geraghty's ruling that the FAA's policy prohibiting the use of UAS is unenforceable, news organizations and the general public remain at risk that the FAA will pursue an enforcement action for the allegedly purely commercial use of UAS. Indeed, the day after ALJ Geraghty's decision was announced, the FAA indicated that it was appealing the decision, which has the affect of staying the decision until the Board rules on the appeal. At the same time, the FAA directed individuals to a web site stating the use of UAS for business purposes is almost entirely prohibited.

Likewise, following the fire in Dayton, Ohio, the FAA indicated to the Dayton Business Journal through a spokesperson that it "would require more legal review to determine if it was a fineable offense to publish the video on [a news] site." The spokesperson also told the newspaper that she "would err on the side of caution." The FAA took this position even though the UAS were operated by hobbyists, who provided the video to the fire department and news media at no charge and as a public service. Moreover, regardless of the enforceability of the FAA policy generally, the Constitution entitled the media to publish UAS footage that it lawfully obtained from the hobbyists. The FAA spokesperson's advice to "err on the side of caution" was intended to chill free speech and, therefore, was flatly unconstitutional.

These anecdotes demonstrate the confusion caused by the FAA's ad hoc approach and illustrate why the FAA's actions are inappropriate substitutes for notice-and-comment rulemaking. The FAA's approach is particularly concerning given the First Amendment newsgathering interests involved. "A fundamental principle in our legal system is that laws which regulate persons or entities must give fair notice of conduct that is forbidden or required . . . . A statute which either forbids or requires the doing of an act in terms so vague that men of common intelligence must necessarily guess at its meaning and differ as to its application violates the first essential of due process of law." These due process requirements are applicable in all cases, but, as the Supreme Court has recognized, "when speech is involved, rigorous adherence to those requirements is necessary to ensure that ambiguity does not chill speech."

Indeed, as the Supreme Court has noted, specificity in regulation is particularly important so that citizens exercising their First Amendment rights are not forced to "err on the side of caution." "Where a vague statute abut(s) upon sensitive areas of basic First Amendment freedoms, it operates to inhibit the exercise of (those) freedoms. Uncertain meanings inevitably lead citizens to steer far wider of the unlawful zone . . . than if the boundaries of the forbidden areas where clearly marked."

As these cases demonstrate, where First Amendment rights are implicated, it is critical that Congress and regulatory agencies provide clear, constitutional standards that avoid improperly limiting the rights to free speech and a free press. The FAA's ad hoc restrictions on the use of UAS do not currently provide clear standards. As a result, media organizations are at risk of facing enforcement actions like that brought against Mr. Pirker. This risk flatly contravenes the First Amendment. The FAA must undertake a proper notice-and-comment rulemaking to establish a workable regulatory framework for the safe and legal use of UAS and to provide clear, constitutional guidance to the public and the media about when UAS may be used.

A legal brief from media companies who wish to ensure that U.S. law provides maximum opportunities and narrow restraints on the use of unmanned aerial system (UAS) for newsgathering purposes. Companies signatory to this brief include Associated Press, Cox, Gannett, Hearst, McClatchy, National Press Photographers Association, National Press Club, New York Times, and others.

EXPLORING THE ISSUE

Does Drone Journalism Challenge Journalistic Norms of Privacy?

Critical Thinking and Reflection

1. What are the limits of privacy in the modern age?
2. How would you regulate drones? What privacy restrictions should be enforced and by whom?
3. How will the definition of drones as aircraft influence journalism?
4. What are the legal and ethical issues facing journalism regarding drone usage?
5. What are the different points of view of journalists and the general public about the difference between what journalists can do and what they should do?

Is There Common Ground?

Significant legal concerns about the regulation of flight can impede journalists in the use of drones for newsgathering. Media companies fear restrictive regulation and point, already, to times where local police have restricted the use of drones even when there were no regulations to prevent their use. Some regulations are already in place and more are expected; if issues of privacy are left to existing laws, this conflict will subside significantly. If not, the debate will continue for a very long time.

Ethical issues in the use of drones for newsgathering are already generating multiple statement of drone journalism ethical guidelines. It is crucial to media organizations to solve these problems and establish norms of journalist behavior and access. Digital innovations of the future will almost certainly offer similar challenges. It is in the interest of media organizations to begin to outline clear standards for the future.

In an era of the Internet of Things everything that can be connected will be connected. When practically every device we own from refrigerators to our e-readers are enabled to collect and exchange data, the issues of privacy will reach far beyond what journalists can "see." This will have ongoing consequences not just for journalists, but also for society as a whole.

Additional Resources

Phillip Chamberlain, Drones and Journalism: *How the Media is Making Use of Unmanned Aerial Vehicles*. Routledge (2016).

This book addresses the use of drones in investigative reporting as well as covering the topic of drones and personal privacy rights. The author has conducted a number of interviews with experts to provide a well-rounded academic study of drones, journalism, and privacy rights.

Kathleen Culver, "From Battlefield to Newsroom: Ethical Implications of Drone Technology in Journalism," *Journal of Mass Media Ethics* (2014), 52–64.

This article examines ethical considerations as technologists and practitioners envisioned drones to be used for information gathering purposes. It explores utilitarian ethical theory to suggest multiple layers of reasoning that accompany the issue of drones and reporting.

Leah Davis, "Without a Pilot: Navigating the Space between the First Amendments and State and Federal Directives Affecting Drone Journalism," 49 *Ga. L. Rev. 1159*, 1192 (2015).

Both states and the federal government have guidelines pertaining to the use of drones for information gathering. The author investigates a number of issues related to the topic and considers the First Amendment principles that influence legal interpretation.

Konstantin Kakaes, "Drones Can Photograph Almost Anything. But Should They?" *Columbia Journalism Review*. (April 21, 2016) retrieved at https://www.cjr.org/the_feature/drones_can_photograph_almost_anything_but_should_they.php

Starting with the situation of drones investigating disasters, such as fires or hurricanes, the author expands the range of issues that drones could help or hinder. Drones challenge traditional legal principles because they fly in space that has previously been unregulated. The article asks provocative questions about what issues must be addressed to safeguard personal privacy.

David Wolfgang, "Droning On," *Quill*, (March/Spr 2013).

Wolfgang reminds us that few journalists will have the opportunity (in the near future) to avail themselves of drones for information gathering, but he discusses the greater problem of normalizing drones for work that can be done in other ways.

Internet References . . .

Drone Advisory Committee (DAC)

https://www.rtca.org/content/drone-advisory-committee

Poynter Institute

https://www.poynter.org/news/poynter-workshops-produce-new-drone-journalism-ethics-policy

Professional Society of Drone Journalists

http://www.dronejournalism.org/code-of-ethics

Reporters Committee for Freedom of the Press

https://www.rcfp.org/photographers-guide-privacy/primer-invasion-privacy

Society of Professional Journalists

https://www.spj.org/quill_issue.asp?ref=1998

Selected, Edited, and with Issue Framing Material by:
Alison Alexander, *University of Georgia*
and
Jarice Hanson, *University of Massachusetts—Amherst*

ISSUE

Can Anything Be Done about Trolls and Online Harassment?

YES: Andy Greenberg, from "Inside Google's Internet Justice League and It's AI-Powered War on Trolls," *Wired* (2016)

NO: Elisabeth Witchel, from "Why a Troll Trolls," *The Committee to Protect Journalists* (2016)

Learning Outcomes

After reading this issue, you will be able to:

- Think more critically about how anti-social behavior is more common in online formats.
- Consider whether technological solutions to problems are ever adequate solutions for bad behavior.
- Become more aware of anti-social uses of online communication, like racism, homophobia, sexism.
- Critically think about whether censorship should be a part of social media.
- Examine the social impact of online abuse and online abusers.

ISSUE SUMMARY

YES: Technology writer Andy Greenberg discusses the problem of online harassment and argues that many people are being driven off of the Internet because they cannot speak or write what they feel, even in jest, because social media organizations are not set up to police personal expressions. But now, Google has a subsidiary called Jigsaw that can moderate political or personally motivated cyberattacks through artificial intelligence. Drawing heavily on the experiences of a number of women, some of whom were victims of online harassment through Gamergate, Greenberg believes that technological solutions may be found to curb online trolling and personal harassment.

NO: Elisabeth Witchel consults with the Committee to Protect Journalists, an independent nonprofit dedicated to journalistic integrity and protecting the rights of journalists around the world. In this article, she discusses the problem of trolling from some people who have acted as trolls, but also, from people whose lives have been affected by trolls. She addresses the psychology of people who troll, and addresses the question of whether trolling is a manifestation of cultural sickness. She also identifies people who have been the victims of trolls and their responses.

One of the first questions posed in the history of media research was whether seeing violent images in film would cause someone to become violent. Today, especially with social media, that early problem has become much greater in scope and in effect. Now, that early problem has grown to encompass a number of different questions that still focus on the relationships of what type of behavior might be enacted in response to images or words that have the potential to incite violence.

We know that online forms of communication have the potential to create hostile environments through bullying, stalking, harassing, or attacking other users. Some of the most extreme cases took place in what came to be known as the "Gamergate" problems that began in 2014 that resulted in (mostly) men who were symbolically, verbally, and physically attacking women who were taking a stand for more positive images of women in videogames. Some of the women who were becoming active gamers, designers, and critics were speaking out about sexism in videogames, and many, like Anita Sarkeesian, Kaitlin Tremblay, Zoë Quinn, and Brianna Wu, were violently threatened for the way they spoke out for stronger images of women. Some of them received death threats and had to go to extremes to protect themselves against the violent threats they received.

Persons who intentionally create threats, start quarrels, or post inflammatory messages in an online community such as in user comments, chat rooms, or forums, are called trolls. Trolls intentionally try to stir up controversy and sometimes seem to have no boundaries with regard to the physical and/or psychological harm they inflict upon the people involved. The troll tries to exert power over others by creating a hostile environment or by threatening others with physical harm. Witchel cites the study conducted by the Pew Research Center in 2014 that found that over 40 percent of the people in any cyber community has probably experienced some form of online harassment, with men experiencing online insults more than women, but with women experiencing more severe threats of violence. Some trolls stalk Facebook pages, Twitter feeds, and other forms of social media—and each organization has rules and procedures for how to block trolls, but these procedures are often useless. As the authors of these selections state, any form of online harassment can be harmful to victims, and First Amendment principles of "freedom of speech" do not necessarily furnish answers for what legal steps we might take to punish trolls.

A common sense approach to avoiding trolls is known as the "do not feed the troll" approach, but many authors agree that this approach doesn't work. In "Why a Troll Trolls," Elisabeth Witchel profiles "Jim," a troll who admits that he would escalate his abuse of anyone who might "snipe back" to the comments he leaves in the messages he trolls. In some high profile cases, the International News Safety Institute and the International Women's Media Foundation found that women journalists are often attacked online for the work they do—even when that work is not related to anything that might seemingly provoke sexist responses. For example, writer Caroline Criado-Perez wrote about why she thought Jane Austen should be on the 10-pound note in Britain, and was then attacked with online rape and death threats by several people. Authorities located two trolls who had threatened her with explicit harm, and those individuals are now in jail. But journalists cannot always do the work of policing who threatens them, and Witchell quotes Michele Ferrier, the founder of TrollBusters who wrote, "If your job is being public as a journalist, you cannot avoid social media as part of your job."

Online harassment takes many other forms as well. Children in particular are often bullied, and the problem of cyberbullying has been well studied. Though some solutions have been offered, such as telling a parent, or a teacher—children are often afraid to tell tales of other children, lest they be seen as "cry-babies" or "snitches." Parents often do what seems natural—they tell the children not to use their cell phones or social media, but for a child who is so dependent upon peer connections, not using social media may be worse than the bullying. But through the years, we have at least learned how to identify harassment online a little more clearly. Because of the attempt of the mother of young Meagan Meier, who committed suicide after being bullied online, Congress passed the Megan Meier Cyberbullying Prevention Act that amends the federal criminal code to impose criminal penalties on anyone who transmits communication intended to "coerce, intimidate, harass, or cause substantial emotional distress to another person, using electronic means to support severe, repeated, and hostile behavior." Through efforts like this, we have started to draw clearer guidelines about what online harassment can be, and what it can do.

Online harassment takes many forms and targets many people, but it often attacks someone's sense of identity. Who we are is critical to the way we think of ourselves and how we interact with others. Bullies, for example, often exhibit bullying behavior in face to face situations as well as in mediated communication forms. Humiliating, harassing, or threatening someone is not the act of someone who is really powerful, but rather, someone who wants power and has internal fears about not having power, or losing what little power they feel they have. Bullies can often hide behind technology, thus demonstrating what is considered to be a dysfunctional use of communication media.

Andy Greenberg is more optimistic that machine learning might help prevent trolls from operating through social media. With the help of some of the new programs and artificial intelligence (AI), he thinks that there might be a future in online comment moderation. His article addresses many of the attempts that have been made by companies and individuals to deal with abrasive and abusive comments. While his biggest concern is whether these systems influence freedom of speech, he does feel that attempts to find technological solutions to behavioral problems is a worthy avenue of inquiry.

Early developers of the Internet intentionally kept the distribution system open so that interaction would be stimulated and encouraged, but they failed to see how often some of the architecture of an online environment could be abused by those who are intent on exhibiting their own power, and sometimes hiding behind the anonymity the Internet affords. It has taken a long time to find the precedents that contribute to adequate laws, practices, and policies about two-way communication in social networks, and there is a long road ahead of us full of speed bumps as we debate what can, should, or cannot be done.

This topic is likely to stir up a lot of controversy, and some people may be reticent to participate. Perhaps they have been victims of online harassment, or maybe the subject stirs up a lot of unwanted feelings for people. But whether we find the topic comfortable or uncomfortable, it remains to be an issue that we can expect to see, or perhaps experience, sometime, ourselves.

YES ⬅

Andy Greenberg

Inside Google's Internet Justice League and its AI-Powered War on Trolls

Around midnight one Saturday in January, Sarah Jeong was on her couch, browsing Twitter, when she spontaneously wrote what she now bitterly refers to as "the tweet that launched a thousand ships." The 28-year-old journalist and author of The Internet of Garbage, a book on spam and online harassment, had been watching Bernie Sanders boosters attacking feminists and supporters of the Black Lives Matter movement. In what was meant to be a hyperbolic joke, she tweeted out a list of political caricatures, one of which called the typical Sanders fan a "vitriolic cryptoracist who spends 20 hours a day on the Internet yelling at women."

The ill-advised late-night tweet was, Jeong admits, provocative and absurd—she even supported Sanders. But what happened next was the kind of backlash that's all too familiar to women, minorities, and anyone who has a strong opinion online. By the time Jeong went to sleep, a swarm of Sanders supporters were calling her a neoliberal shill. By sunrise, a broader, darker wave of abuse had begun. She received nude photos and links to disturbing videos. One troll promised to "rip each one of [her] hairs out" and "twist her tits clear off."

The attacks continued for weeks. "I was in crisis mode," she recalls. So she did what many victims of mass harassment do: She gave up and let her abusers have the last word. Jeong made her tweets private, removing herself from the public conversation for a month. And she took a two-week unpaid leave from her job as a contributor to the tech news site Motherboard.

For years now, on Twitter and practically any other freewheeling public forum, the trolls have been out in force. Just in recent months: Trump's anti-Semitic supporters mobbed Jewish public figures with menacing Holocaust "jokes." Anonymous racists bullied African American comedian Leslie Jones off Twitter temporarily with pictures of apes and Photoshopped images of semen on her face. Guardian columnist Jessica Valenti quit the service after a horde of misogynist attackers resorted to rape threats against her 5-year-old daughter. "It's too much," she signed off. "I can't live like this." Feminist writer Sady Doyle says her experience of mass harassment has induced a kind of permanent self-censorship. "There are things I won't allow myself to talk about," she says. "Names I won't allow myself to say."

Mass harassment online has proved so effective that it's emerging as a weapon of repressive governments. In late 2014, Finnish journalist Jessikka Aro reported on Russia's troll farms, where day laborers regurgitate messages that promote the government's interests and inundate opponents with vitriol on every possible outlet, including Twitter and Facebook. In turn, she's been barraged daily by bullies on social media, in the comments of news stories, and via email. They call her a liar, a "NATO skank," even a drug dealer, after digging up a fine she received 12 years ago for possessing amphetamines. "They want to normalize hate speech, to create chaos and mistrust," Aro says. "It's just a way of making people disillusioned."

All this abuse, in other words, has evolved into a form of censorship, driving people offline, silencing their voices. For years, victims have been calling on—clamoring for—the companies that created these platforms to help slay the monster they brought to life. But their solutions generally have amounted to a Sisyphean game of whack-a-troll.

Now a small subsidiary of Google named Jigsaw is about to release an entirely new type of response: a set of tools called Conversation AI. The software is designed to use machine learning to automatically spot the language of abuse and harassment—with, Jigsaw engineers say, an accuracy far better than any keyword filter and far faster than any team of human moderators. "I want to use the best technology we have at our disposal to begin to take on trolling and other nefarious tactics that give hostile voices disproportionate weight," says Jigsaw founder and president Jared Cohen. "To do everything we can to level the playing field."

Jigsaw is applying artificial intelligence to solve the very human problem of making people be nicer on the Internet. Conversation AI represents just one of Jigsaw's wildly ambitious projects. The New York–based think tank and tech incubator aims to build products that use Google's massive infrastructure and engineering muscle not to advance the best possibilities of the Internet but to fix the worst of it: surveillance, extremist indoctrination, censorship. The group sees its work, in part, as taking on the most intractable jobs in Google's larger mission to make the world's information "universally accessible and useful."

Cohen founded Jigsaw, which now has about 50 staffers (almost half are engineers), after a brief high-profile and controversial career in the US State Department, where he worked to focus American diplomacy on the Internet like never before. One of the moon-shot goals he's set for Jigsaw is to end censorship within a decade, whether it comes in the form of politically motivated cyberattacks on opposition websites or government strangleholds on Internet service providers. And if that task isn't daunting enough, Jigsaw is about to unleash Conversation AI on the murky challenge of harassment, where the only way to protect some of the web's most repressed voices may be to selectively shut up others. If it can find a path through that free-speech paradox, Jigsaw will have pulled off an unlikely coup: applying artificial intelligence to solve the very human problem of making people be nicer on the Internet.

Jigsaw is the outgrowth of an earlier effort called Google Ideas, which Google's then-CEO Eric Schmidt and Cohen launched in 2010 as a "think/do tank." But aside from organizing conferences and creating fancy data visualizations, Ideas didn't actually do much at first. "People would come around and talk a bunch of bullshit for a couple days," one Google Ideas conference attendee remembers. "Nothing came out of it."

But slowly, the group's lofty challenges began to attract engineers, some joining from other parts of Google after volunteering for Cohen's team. One of their first creations was a tool called uProxy that allows anyone whose Internet access is censored to bounce their traffic through a friend's connection outside the firewall; it's now used in more than 100 countries. Another tool, a Chrome add-on called Password Alert, aims to block phishing by warning people when they're retyping their Gmail password into a malicious look-alike site; the company developed it for Syrian activists targeted by government-friendly hackers, but when it proved effective, it was rolled out to all of Google's users.

In February, the group was renamed Jigsaw to reflect its focus on building practical products. A program called Montage lets war correspondents and nonprofits crowdsource the analysis of YouTube videos to track conflicts and gather evidence of human rights violations. Another free service called Project Shield uses Google's servers to absorb government-sponsored cyberattacks intended to take down the websites of media, election-monitoring, and human rights organizations. And an initiative, aimed at deradicalizing ISIS recruits, identifies would-be jihadis based on their search terms, then shows them ads redirecting them to videos by former extremists who explain the downsides of joining an ultraviolent, apocalyptic cult. In a pilot project, the anti-ISIS ads were so effective that they were in some cases two to three times more likely to be clicked than typical search advertising campaigns.

The common thread that binds these projects, Cohen says, is a focus on what he calls "vulnerable populations." To that end, he gives new hires an assignment: Draw a scrap of paper from a baseball cap filled with the names of the world's most troubled or repressive countries; track down someone under threat there and talk to them about their life online. Then present their stories to other Jigsaw employees.

At one recent meeting, Cohen leans over a conference table as 15 or so Jigsaw recruits—engineers, designers, and foreign policy wonks—prepare to report back from the dark corners of the Internet. "We are not going to be one of those groups that sits in our offices and imagines what vulnerable populations around the world are experiencing," Cohen says. "We're going to get to know our users." He speaks in a fast-forward, geeky patter that contrasts with his blue-eyed, broad-shouldered good looks, like a politician disguised as a Silicon Valley executive or vice versa. "Every single day, I want us to feel the burden of the responsibility we're shouldering."

We hear about an Albanian LGBT activist who tries to hide his identity on Facebook despite its real-names-only policy, an administrator for a Libyan youth group wary of government infiltrators, a defector's memories from the digital black hole of North Korea. Many of the T-shirt-and-sandal-wearing Googlers in the room will later be sent to some of those far-flung places to meet their contacts face-to-face.

"They'll hear stories about people being tortured for their passwords or of state-sponsored cyberbullying," Cohen tells me later. The purpose of these field trips isn't simply to get feedback for future products, he says. They're about creating personal investment in otherwise distant, invisible problems—a sense of investment Cohen says he himself gained in his twenties during his four-year stint in the State Department, and before that during extensive travel in the Middle East and Africa as a student.

Cohen reports directly to Alphabet's top execs, but in practice, Jigsaw functions as Google's blue-sky, human-rights-focused skunkworks. At the group's launch, Schmidt declared its audacious mission to be "tackling the world's toughest geopolitical problems" and listed some of the challenges within its remit: "money laundering, organized crime, police brutality, human trafficking, and terrorism." In an interview in Google's New York office, Schmidt (now chair of Alphabet) summarized them to me as the "problems that bedevil humanity involving information."

Jigsaw, in other words, has become Google's Internet justice league, and it represents the notion that the company is no longer content with merely not being evil. It wants—as difficult and even ethically fraught as the impulse may be—to do good.

In September of 2015, Yasmin Green, then head of operations and strategy for Google Ideas, the working group that would become Jigsaw, invited 10 women who had been harassment victims to come to the office and discuss their experiences. Some of them had been targeted by members of the antifeminist Gamergate movement. Game developer Zoë Quinn had been threatened repeatedly with rape, and her attackers had dug up and distributed old nude photos of her. Another visitor, Anita Sarkeesian, had moved out of her home temporarily because of numerous death threats.

At the end of the session, Green and a few other Google employees took a photo with the women and posted it to the company's Twitter account. Almost immediately, the Gamergate trolls turned their ire against Google itself. Over the next 48 hours, tens of thousands of comments on Reddit and Twitter demanded the Googlers be fired for enabling "feminazis."

"It's like you walk into Madison Square Garden and you have 50,000 people saying you suck, you're horrible, die," Green says. "If you really believe that's what the universe thinks about you, you certainly shut up. And you might just take your own life."

To combat trolling, services like Reddit, YouTube, and Facebook have for years depended on users to flag abuse for review by overworked staffers or an offshore workforce of content moderators in countries like the Philippines. The task is expensive and can be scarring for the employees who spend days on end reviewing loathsome content—yet often it's still not enough to keep up with the real-time flood of filth. Twitter recently introduced new filters designed to keep users from seeing unwanted tweets, but it's not yet clear whether the move will tame determined trolls.

The meeting with the Gamergate victims was the genesis for another approach. Lucas Dixon, a wide-eyed Scot with a doctorate in machine learning, and product manager CJ Adams wondered: Could an abuse-detecting AI clean up online conversations by detecting toxic language—with all its idioms and ambiguities—as reliably as humans?

To create a viable tool, Jigsaw first needed to teach its algorithm to tell the difference between harmless banter and harassment. For that, it would need a massive number of examples. So the group partnered with The New York Times, which gave Jigsaw's engineers 17 million comments from Times stories, along with data about which of those comments were flagged as inappropriate by moderators. Jigsaw also worked with the Wikimedia Foundation to parse 130,000 snippets of discussion around Wikipedia pages. It showed those text strings to panels of 10 people recruited randomly from the CrowdFlower crowdsourcing service and asked whether they found each snippet to represent a "personal attack" or "harassment." Jigsaw then fed the massive corpus of online conversation and human evaluations into Google's open source machine learning software, TensorFlow.

Machine learning, a branch of computer science that Google uses to continually improve everything from Google Translate to its core search engine, works something like human learning. Instead of programming an algorithm, you teach it with examples. Show a toddler enough shapes identified as a cat and eventually she can recognize a cat. Show millions of vile Internet comments to Google's self-improving artificial intelligence engine and it can recognize a troll.

In fact, by some measures Jigsaw has now trained Conversation AI to spot toxic language with impressive accuracy. Feed a string of text into its Wikipedia harassment-detection engine and it can, with what Google describes as more than 92 percent certainty and a 10 percent false-positive rate, come up with a judgment that matches a human test panel as to whether that line represents an attack. For now the tool looks only at the content of that single string of text. But Green says Jigsaw has also looked into detecting methods of mass harassment based on the volume of messages and other long-term patterns.

Wikipedia and the Times will be the first to try out Google's automated harassment detector on comment threads and article discussion pages. Wikimedia is still considering exactly how it will use the tool, while the Times plans to make Conversation AI the first pass of its website's comments, blocking any abuse it detects until it can be moderated by a human. Jigsaw will also make its work open source, letting any web forum or social media platform adopt it to automatically flag insults, scold harassers, or even auto-delete toxic language, preventing an intended harassment victim from ever seeing the offending comment. The hope is that "anyone can take these models and run with them," says Adams, who helped lead the machine learning project.

What's more, some limited evidence suggests that this kind of quick detection can actually help to tame trolling. Conversation AI was inspired in part by an experiment undertaken by Riot Games, the videogame company that runs the world's biggest multiplayer world, known as League of Legends, with 67 million players. Starting in late 2012, Riot began using machine learning to try to analyze the results of in-game conversations that led to players being banned. It used the resulting algorithm to show players in real time when they had made sexist or abusive remarks. When players saw immediate automated warnings, 92 percent of them changed their behavior for the better, according to a report in the science journal Nature.

My own hands-on test of Conversation AI comes one summer afternoon in Jigsaw's office, when the group's engineers show me a prototype and invite me to come up with a sample of verbal filth for it to analyze. Wincing, I suggest the first ambiguously abusive and misogynist phrase that comes to mind: "What's up, bitch?" Adams types in the sentence and clicks Score. Conversation AI instantly rates it a 63 out of 100 on the attack scale. Then, for contrast, Adams shows me the results of a more clearly vicious phrase: "You are such a bitch." It rates a 96.

In fact, Conversation AI's algorithm goes on to make impressively subtle distinctions. Pluralizing my trashy greeting to "What's up bitches?" drops the attack score to 45. Add a smiling emoji and it falls to 39. So far, so good.

For a tech executive taking on would-be terrorists, state-sponsored trolls, and tyrannical surveillance regimes, Jigsaw's creator has a surprisingly sunny outlook on the battle between the people who use the Internet and the authorities that seek to control them. "I have a fundamental belief that technology empowers people," Jared Cohen says. Between us sits a coffee table covered in souvenirs from his travels: a clay prayer coin from Iraq, a plastic-wrapped nut bar from Syria, a packet of North Korean cigarettes. "It's hard for me to imagine a world where there's not a continued cat-and-mouse game. But over time, the mouse might just become bigger than the cat."

The story Cohen's critics focus on, however, is his involvement in a notorious piece of software called Haystack, intended to provide online anonymity and circumvent censorship. They say Cohen helped to hype the tool in early 2010 as a potential boon to Iranian dissidents. After the US government fast-tracked it for approval, however, a security researcher revealed it had egregious vulnerabilities that put any dissident who used it in grave danger

of detection. Today, Cohen disclaims any responsibility for Haystack, but two former colleagues say he championed the project. His former boss Slaughter describes his time in government more diplomatically: "At State there was a mismatch between the scale of Jared's ideas and the tools the department had to deliver on them," she says. "Jigsaw is a much better match."

But inserting Google into thorny geopolitical problems has led to new questions about the role of a multinational corporation. Some have accused the group of trying to monetize the sensitive issues they're taking on; the Electronic Frontier Foundation's director of international free expression, Jillian York, calls its work "a little bit imperialistic." For all its altruistic talk, she points out, Jigsaw is part of a for-profit entity. And on that point, Schmidt is clear: Alphabet hopes to someday make money from Jigsaw's work. "The easiest way to understand it is, better connectivity, better information access, we make more money," he explains to me. He draws an analogy to the company's efforts to lay fiber in some developing countries. "Why would we try to wire up Africa?" he asks. "Because eventually there will be advertising markets there."

"We're not a government," Eric Schmidt says slowly and carefully. "We're not engaged in regime change. We don't do that stuff."

Wikileaks founder Julian Assange has accused Cohen of continuing to work as a de facto State Department employee, quietly advancing the government's foreign policy goals from within Google, and labeled him the company's "director of regime change." When I raise that quote with Schmidt, he visibly tenses, then vehemently rejects the notion. "We're not a government," he says slowly and carefully. "We're not engaged in regime change. We don't do that stuff. But if it turns out that empowering citizens with smartphones and information causes changes in their country . . . you know, that's probably a good thing, don't you think?"

Beyond the issue of Jigsaw's profit motives or imagined government ties, however, another point nags at Cohen's optimistic digital interventionism: Technology has unintended consequences. A tool like Haystack that was intended to help Iranians could have put them in danger. Twitter, with all its revolutionary potential, enabled new forms of abuse. And Conversation AI, meant to curb that abuse, could take down its own share of legitimate speech in the process.

DURING HER WORST DAYS of being targeted by a gang of misogynists last year, feminist writer Sady Doyle would look down at her phone after an hour and find a hundred new Twitter notifications, many of them crude sexual comments and attacks on her history of mental health issues. But when I present her with the notion of Conversation AI as a solution, she hesitates. "People need to be able to talk in whatever register they talk," she says. "Imagine what the Internet would be like if you couldn't say 'Donald Trump is a moron.'" In fact, when I run the phrase though the Conversation AI prototype, I find that calling someone a moron scores a full 99 out of 100 on its personal attack scale.

The example highlights Conversation AI's potential for false positives or suppressing the gray areas of speech. After all, even without automated flagging, Twitter and Facebook have been criticized for blocking legitimate, even politically powerful, content: Last year Twitter banned Politwoops, a feed that collected the deleted tweets of political figures to catch damning off-the-cuff statements. Facebook blocked photos of drowned migrant children intended to make Americans more aware of the tragedy of Syria's refugee crisis.

Sarah Jeong, the Motherboard writer who was silenced by Bernie bros, says she supports the notion of Conversation AI, in theory. "The Internet needs moderation," she says. But she warns that no one should be foolish enough to let Conversation AI run wild with automated comment deletion: "These are human interactions." Any fix for the worst of those interactions, she says, will need to be human too. "An automated detection system can open the door to the delete-it-all option," adds Emma Llansó, director of the Free Expression Project at the nonprofit Center for Democracy and Technology, "rather than spending the time and resources to identify false positives."

My tests of Conversation AI do in fact produce outright false positives. "I shit you not" somehow got an attack score of 98 out of 100, the same as the far more offensive "you are shit." The rather harmless phrase "you suck all the fun out of life" scored a 98, just a point shy of "you suck." And most problematic of all, perhaps: "You are a troll"—the go-to response for any troll victim—was flagged with an attack score of 93.

"When you're looking at curbing online harassment and at free expression, there's a tension between the two. We don't claim to have all the answers."

Throwing out well-intentioned speech that resembles harassment could be a blow to exactly the open civil society Jigsaw has vowed to protect. When I ask Conversation AI's inventors about its potential for collateral damage, the engineers argue that its false positive rate will improve over time as the software continues to train itself. But on the question of how its judgments will be enforced, they say that's up to whoever uses the tool. "We want to let communities have the discussions they want to have," says Conversation AI cocreator Lucas Dixon. And if that favors a sanitized Internet over a freewheeling one? Better to err on the side of civility. "There are already plenty of nasty places on the Internet. What we can do is create places where people can have better conversations."

ANDY GREENBERG is a senior writer at *Wired* magazine. He specializes in technology journalism, and has formerly worked as a writer for *Forbes* magazine.

Elisabeth Witchel

NO

Why a Troll Trolls

"Yeah... I went too far," he said, which by most accounts would be an understatement.

Among the Twitter comments this Internet troll posted to or about a female writer and activist were:

"Rape her nice ass."

"I will find you."

"The police will do nothing."

The man, who agreed to be interviewed only under a pseudonym–we'll call him Jim–said he did not start off with the intention of menacing anyone. Yet it is hard to imagine a public milieu where an individual might consider casually uttering such words–to a stranger no less.

Jim's comments are, however, disturbingly representative of Internet trolling, a practice that has become a major concern for activists and journalists, particularly females.

A troll, or more specifically a cyber troll, is commonly described as a person who intentionally posts provocative messages to cause arguments or disruptions. The term has come to be applied broadly to a range of online behaviors, from those that are provocatively contrarian to others that are criminally menacing. Trolls may target specific individuals and they may stand out in a virtual crowd or operate like a mob, tearing apart anyone whose views, appearance, or attitude they don't like.

Online hectoring directly affects nearly half the cyber community, according a 2014 study by the US-based Pew Research Center, which found that 40 percent of Internet users have personally experienced mild to severe online harassment. Men are more often subject to insults online, according to the study, but forms of online abuse toward women tend to be far more severe, including sexual harassment and threats of violence. "The kinds of threats women get online are in sync with the real-world threats they face," said feminist activist and writer Soraya Chemaly.

This special brand of online abuse is becoming a de facto occupational hazard for many female journalists. Sri Lankan journalist Sonali Samarasinghe describes the negative comments she has received online as typically criticizing not her words, but her womanhood. "One person wrote that I had no uterus," she recalled.

Samarasinghe is not alone. A March 2014 survey on violence and harassment against women in media conducted by the International News Safety Institute and the International Women's Media Foundation found that a quarter of the work related-threats and intimidation directed at female journalists took place online.

Though the impact and prevalence of Internet abuse and trolling is increasingly well documented and aired in public forums, less is known about those who engage in it and why. The anonymity and fluidity of social media, and the fact that trolls come in many shapes and sizes, make it hard to pin down an archetype. "It's really important to remember that underneath all their abuse, trolls are complex human beings just like the rest of us," noted Claire Hardaker, a linguist at Lancaster University who has written extensively on trolls. "They can be women in their twenties, men in their twenties, or thirties, or sixties–mothers, fathers, privately educated, or from any walk of life at all."

Despite their penchant for inserting themselves into online threads, contacting trolls directly for this report proved challenging. Many accounts had been shut down or banned and several trolls did not respond to or refused interview requests.

In a phone interview, Jim said that he began tweeting comments when he was a newcomer to social media exploring topics that were trending on Twitter. "I decided for some stupid reason to join in," he said. Once the retweets and responses began flowing, he felt a strong personal validation and so embarked upon what soon became an ugly trajectory. His explanation of how that happened doesn't fully account for the brutishness that resulted, but it does provide insight into the pull of trolling.

Another troll–though he does not approve of that appellation–who identifies himself on Twitter as @SageCommander, also known as John Blackout, calls himself an "irritant," not a troll. "I like to 'troll' certain accounts, especially when they tweet something stupid," he said in an interview via Twitter. "But I don't consider myself a troll. My tweets are maybe 20 percent trolling."

Blackout sees his online comments not as harassment, but as a needed counterweight to opinions and news items he believes are flawed. "I can make people uncomfortable when confronting them with their own positions," he wrote. For him, it is dialectic without boundaries. "I might ask someone who considers themselves 'pro-choice' if they are ok with aborting babies at nine months so long as at least part of them is still in the mother. That isn't trolling, it's asking them to examine the courage and extremes of their position."

For some, such comments border on, or cross over into, hate speech. While women are often victims of online aggression, some of the worst trolling targets race.

Andrew Auernheimer, as he identifies himself, also known as @rabide, and sometimes as weev, revels in the opportunity provided by social media and the blogosphere to tout his Aryan causes, among them #WhiteGenocide. "I've never harassed anyone in legal definitions, but some people see Aryan opinions as harassment," he said in a phone interview. Though Auernheimer now focuses on nationalist and racist complaints, he said his interest in trolling escalated with the emergence in 2014 of #gamergate, an online campaign against several women in the gaming industry that spun into a rash of serious cyber harassment, including threats of violence and doxxing, the practice of revealing personal information, such as home addresses, online.

Auernheimer was imprisoned for more than three years for hacking and identity fraud. On his account he has posted, "The thing I missed most in prison was Twitter. Seriously." He said Twitter gives him an entrée he never had into the pop culture fray. Prior to Twitter, "there was not a single outlet to represent us; we were shunned by the mainstream." He has more than 29,000 followers.

Auernheimer explained trolling as a weapon in his war against "SJWs," or Social Justice Warriors. One of its most powerful functions, he said, is to push the "Overton window"–a political theory developed by American public policy analyst Joseph Overton to describe the range of ideas the public will accept. Auernheimer claims the numbers of likeminded "netizens" is growing. "It's a great time to be a white nationalist!" he said.

Some efforts have been made in recent years to identify the social and psychological causes behind trolling. According to one study, "Trolls Just Want to Have Fun," which looks into the personality traits of trolls, they are simply bad people. The study, published

in 2014 by Canadian psychology academics Erin E. Buckels, Paul D. Trapnell, and Delroy L. Paulhus, found "trolling correlated positively with sadism, psychopathy, and Machiavellianism," with sadism showing the most "robust" associations with trolling. "Cyber-trolling appears to be an Internet manifestation of everyday sadism," the authors concluded.

But there is a danger, others contend, in marginalizing trolls as malevolent outliers or social aberrations. "It lends itself to a mythology, but in fact they are 'normal,' reflecting a dimension of human nature that is ugly," said Chemaly, who writes on gender for The Huffington Post, the Guardian and other publications. Trolls frequently target women and, "The word itself evokes some little monster, but we are talking about the misogynists next door," she said.

Trolling has become so pervasive that one UK insurance company offers policies that include coverage of the costs of legal action, relocation, and other actions necessitated by cyber bullying.

Whitney Phillips, author of the book This Is Why We Can't Have Nice Things: Mapping the Relationship between Online Trolling and Mainstream Culture, argues that trolling is a manifestation of deeper societal problems, such as pervasive sexism. "This isn't a 'trolling' issue, in other words, it's evidence of a cultural sickness," Phillips said in an email. "I would argue that more commonplace, everyday expressions of sexism are just as dangerous as more extreme, obvious examples of violent misogyny."

Hardaker, the Lancaster University linguistics lecturer, agrees, though for different reasons, that viewing trolls through a more universal lens is the best approach to understanding their behavior. "Very few of us look at ourselves in the mirror that morning and say, 'Today I'm going to attack a child online till they cry, self-harm, or even commit suicide,'" she said. "Instead, they're likely to be thinking of their behavior in other, more socially acceptable ways–they're correcting people who are wrong, they're sticking it to the man, they're righting a perceived wrong, they're just being funny for their friends, and so forth."

How, then, to deal with the problem of trolls, which sometimes threatens to escalate into actual violence? And at what point do gender-based trolling attacks actually encourage the kind of pervasive sexism Phillips evoked?

A handful of women have confronted their cyber persecutors successfully, either directly or through legal action. In 2014, Seattle-based writer and editor Lindy West wrote an open letter online to one of her trolls. Her antagonist had made derogatory comments while impersonating West's recently deceased father. Surprisingly, the troll apologized via email. West chronicled the exchange for National Public Radio's "This American Life" program, during which the two also spoke by phone. He explained that his actions stemmed from his offense at seeing a highly confident woman at a time when he was professionally frustrated and had recently broken up with a girlfriend.

"I think my anger towards you stems from your happiness with your own being," he wrote in an email to West. "It offended me because it served to highlight my unhappiness with my own self. It is the lowest thing I have ever done."

Women's activist and writer Caroline Criado-Perez, whose campaign to put Jane Austen on Great Britain's 10-pound note brought her a maelstrom of online rape and death threats, brought charges against two of her worst trollers, including a woman, Isabella Sorley. Both were jailed in January 2014 for making "extreme threats." In a public apology on BBC, Sorley read some of her tweets aloud. They included "Rape is the last of your worries" and "Go kill yourself before I do." She described her behavior as "utterly appalling." "It's disgusting, it's venomous," she said, and though she attributed it to alcohol, she admitted there must be more to it. "Am I mental? I've got to question," she said in the interview.

The conventional wisdom, however, is that "feeding the troll" by responding or confronting him typically leads to more aggressive activities, rather than trolls' remorse. Jim said he escalated the vehemence of his comments the moment his target began to snipe back, though he did not say why.

"They want attention. If you respond, they win," is how University of Pennsylvania professor Anthea Butler sees it. Butler said she has had to block thousands of accounts due to hostile comments.

Those who troll often say that anyone unhappy with what is being said can simply leave the conservation. John Blackout said that in his opinion it is up to the individual user to draw the line of what he or she will tolerate. "Other people can decide whether to follow/fave/retweet/mute/block and control their own timeline," he said.

For journalists, that is easier said than done, according to US journalist and founder of TrollBusters Michele Ferrier, who chronicles her own experience with hateful readers elsewhere in this book. "If your job is being public as a journalist, you cannot avoid social media as part of your job," she said. "It's expected to be online in many capacities. Or if you are an independent online news provider, who are you going to call to step in for you?" Ignoring physical threats can be risky, she said. "There is no safe space online and limited recourse to just block or get off the computer."

So the trolling continues. Jim said he plans to stop trolling, but whether he will manage to overcome the urge remains to be seen.

ELISABETH WITCHEL is a consultant with the Committee to Protect Journalists, an international nonprofit organization founded to investigate violations in repressive countries, conflict zones, and established democracies. She previously worked with the CPJ as a journalistic assistant coordinator.

EXPLORING THE ISSUE

Can Anything Be Done about Trolls and Online Harassment?

Critical Thinking and Reflection

1. What is it about the act of using technologies for communication in private places that allows or even encourages some people to "act out" and exert power over others by creating a hostile environment online?
2. Is online harassment any different than face-to-face harassment?
3. Why do some people become bullies, or cyberharassers?
4. Are there any social or political institutions that should become responsible for policing online communication to prevent, or punish people who create a hostile online environment? Which one(s) could be considered to be most effective?
5. Does communicating online require any adherence to ethical principles of equality or fairness for those who express opinions online?

Is There Common Ground?

Both of the authors of these selections examine real-world situations and the experiences of women and people of color who have been made to be targets of online harassment. They agree that the consequences of threats, verbal attacks, cyberstalking, and other forms of creating hostile environments online are dangerous and highly threatening (sometimes life threatening) to those people who receive the messages of individuals who attempt to exert power over others through their online postings.

Each author also examines the potential for online technological methods of catching trolls and possibly punishing them, but both differ in what they think the consequences of using online techniques could be. Though they agree that online harassment is a serious problem with major sociological and legal consequences, they do not agree that we can be optimistic about finding a technological solution.

Both authors also cite a number of high-profile stories that have provided the public with examples of trolling behavior and the harm inherent in online harassment. These stories lead us toward thinking about who the trolls are, and how their behavior influences the quality of life for the person or persons whom they attack.

Additional Resources

Anita Bernstein, "Abuse and Harassment Diminish Free Speech." *Pace Law Review* 1 (2014). By examining the notion of Freedom of Speech, Bernstein

approaches anti-social speech as a problem that could, over time, erode First Amendment principles of noncensorship.

Danielle Keats Citron, *Hate Crimes in Cyberspace* (2014). Citron is the Morton & Sophia Macht Professor of Law at the University of Maryland in the Francis King Carey School of Law. A legal scholar and privacy rights expert, she writes about the impact and the laws that influence contemporary thought on cyberstalking and cyberharassment.

Sarah Kessler, "Why Online Harassment Is Still Ruining Lives—And How We Can Stop It. Fast Company (June 3, 2015). Though the Supreme Court has made it more difficult to prosecute online threats, and police are having a harder time tracking down trolls, sharing stories and strategies for how individuals deal with harassment can be powerful. Focused on Anita Sarkeesian, who was given death threats in the "gamergate" controversy, this article examines the possibility for greater controlling of cyberstalkers and cyberharassers in the future.

Marlisse Silver Sweeney, "What the Law Can (and Can't) Do About Online Harassment," *The Atlantic*, November 12, 2014. This article discusses the federal guidelines that are in place concerning cyberbullying, cyberstalking, and online harassment.

Internet References . . .

Bullying and Cyberbullying

https://www.youthbeyondblue.com/understand-what's-going-on/bullying-and-cyberbullying

Cyberstalking Tool Kit

https://www.fightcyberstalking.org/

Ashley Judd, "How Online Abuse of Women Has Spiraled Out of Control, Ted Talks, October, 2016.

https://www.ted.com/talks/ashley_judd_how_online_abuse_of_women_has_spiraled_out_of_control

Elise Moreau, "10 Types of Internet Trolls You'll Meet Online: Haters gonna hate, trolls gonna troll," *Lifewire*, May 19, 2017.

https://www.lifewire.com/types-of-internet-trolls-3485894

Rebecca Venema and Katarina Lobinger, "Online Harassment & Cyberstalking," *Privacy Rights Clearinghouse*, 2016.

https://www.privacyrights.org/printpdf/67531

Unit 5

UNIT

Media Business

*I*t is important to remember that media industries are businesses and that they must be profitable in order to thrive. Changes in ownership rules have resulted in a new group of media companies and corporations. Newspapers may be the first major industry to fail. Most have retooled and have focused on smaller, targeted audiences. In this section, we discuss what has changed in traditional media outlets, and whether some of those changes are really good for the artists who participate in them. Are some forms of media, like streaming music, print journalism, or news sharing sites able to survive in such a highly competitive marketplace? These questions lead us to ask what media will be available to us in the future. Are there evolving models of business for the digital age? What aspects of law, regulation, and business practices have come together to change the nature of the media "playing field"? How likely are new services to survive? Is the era of mass media now over?

Selected, Edited, and with Issue Framing Material by:
Alison Alexander, *University of Georgia*
and
Jarice Hanson, *University of Massachusetts—Amherst*

ISSUE

Is Streaming the Future of the Music Industry?

YES: Joan E. Solsman, from "Attention, Artists: Streaming Music Is the Inescapable Future. Embrace It," CNET News (2014)

NO: Charles Arthur, from "Streaming: The Future of the Music Industry, or Its Nightmare?," *The Guardian* (2015)

Learning Outcomes

After reading this issue, you will be able to:

- Better understand how streaming has changed the distribution system for music.
- Understand the impact on industries as more technologies use wireless, digital forms.
- Consider how important revenue is to the ongoing maintenance of an industry.
- Better judge the impact of music piracy.
- Consider how business models influence what type of content becomes available to us.

ISSUE SUMMARY

YES: Journalist Joan E. Solsman discusses the rise of streaming services like Pandora and Spotify, and identifies three business models that are emerging from the number of streaming services. Her article shows how divergent the forms of distribution for music have become, and the impact on artist revenue for some of those new services.

NO: Journalist Charles Arthur discusses some of the same streaming services, but identifies how little profit many of them are making because consumer tendency to download free music cuts into the revenue of many of the emerging services.

When an industry is forced to change because of new technology or new business practices, the term used to describe the event is *disruption*. The disruption to the traditional recorded music industry has been monumental in scope and suggests that other media technologies may well be disrupted themselves, as digital technology makes it easier to share, distribute, and even illegally access content that had previously tightly controlled the distribution to maximize revenue. In these two selections that explore the disruptive aspects of streaming music services, we get a sense that the recorded music industry is in for even more disruption as different streaming services compete against

each other for customers, and as revenue models change the way we access music.

The recorded music industry has changed more than any other media-related industry because the shift to digital distribution of music has resulted in a variety of new formats for delivery. Streaming content over the Internet is inexpensive and highly accessible. In part, the biggest challenge for the recorded music industry today is the illegal piracy of signals that are possible through some forms of downloading content. Although there have been many attempts to curb this type of piracy of content, streaming technologies all tend to challenge our traditional concepts of copyright, ownership, and fair compensation for the artists whose content is digitally distributed.

The music industry faced its first challenge to the traditional business model (in which record labels controlled the content of those artists who had signed with their companies) in 1998, when 19-year-old Shawn Fanning developed a free Internet-based, peer-to-peer (P2P) service called Napster that allowed people to share music files through MP3 technology. By 2001, Fanning had been taken to court by the Recording Industry Association of America (RIAA) for copyright infringement, and Napster was shut down. Fanning then sold the logo and name to Roxio, a company that legally sold music through the Internet, and since that time, the recording industry has been in flux and new business models have emerged to promote musicians and music. The former record companies have not given up hope that they could survive the technical shift to digital music and have come up with a number of new services and methods of distributing content, but this plethora of competition has also presented a number of challenges to artists and the industry.

Of course, we can't even talk about streaming without commenting on how the same technologies can be used to pirate content. When this happens, no one in the recording industry makes a profit (except perhaps the pirates themselves, through the sale of their music libraries). So although the two selections in this issue focus on commercial streaming services, we should remember that the same technology can undermine the profit motive within an industry as well.

One of the biggest challenges for commercial services is that streaming services often pay artists different types of royalties for music that someone streams over their service. Some artists receive fractions of a penny for each download of their music, while more established artists may make a bit more—but rarely more than a penny per download. And if an artist's music is being streamed by different companies, those companies are likely to have different scales of royalties. The result is an extremely complicated system of reporting the number of songs streamed, by which companies, and at which rates.

At the same time, some services have actually helped new artists become known. Companies like SoundCloud, BandCamp, and even the re-imagined MySpace (for example) have developed services that allow artists to freely share with each other, and introduce new artists to music aficionados. Despite these possible uses of streaming technology to open the market to new artists, some established artists feel that they no longer can allow their music to be streamed at all, because of the potential loss of revenue that can affect best-selling artists. Singers like Taylor Swift, David Byrne, and Radiohead (for example) have all chosen not to license

their music to streaming services, and Jay-Z launched a service called Tidal, which pays the highest royalties possible to artists. No matter how you look at it, the number of services and the complicated structure of payment to artists have changed the nature of the music industry forever.

Streaming is an important distribution form, since it is highly likely to affect film and television content as well. Many of the companies that are already streaming music now have some video and gaming services, like The Pirate Bay, and many more have plans to roll out video and interactive gaming services in the near future. So the upset in the recorded music industry is very likely to affect film, television, and gaming industries as well.

The media industries are, after all, businesses that cannot thrive for long if they don't make a profit, and performing artists need to be able to control the distribution of their own material. In many ways, the shift from physical records or CDs to streaming music has created an even larger market for artists to go on the road, perform live, and make the bulk of their income from ticket sales and the sale of merchandise when they do perform live. Those high prices to attend a live concert are, in part, due to the relative lack of income generated by streaming technology and the sharing of free content among users.

If you think about other media industries also affected by the changes to the music industry, you start to see how one major change impacts another. Radio and airplay of music are still possible, but royalty payments for radio may be very different from streaming services targeting individual consumers. Many artists license their work for other forms of media, such as when their songs are used in films, or even for the theme songs of television programs. One of the first groups to make a significant income from licensing their previously recorded material was They Might Be Giants, who licensed their song "You're Not the Boss of Me" for the popular TV show *Malcolm in the Middle*, which ran from 2001 to 2006. And the Canadian group Bare Naked Ladies began the trend of establishing their own record label so that they could better control the distribution of their music and how it might be used by other media forms.

As you read these selections, it may be helpful to think about issues of copyright and who (or which jobs) are actually affected by streaming, as well as the technologies that disrupt established industries. The corner "mom-and-pop" record store is no longer the mainstay of any community, and all of the people who were involved in the promotion, distribution, and marketing of traditional recorded music have seen their jobs disappear or radically change. As time passes, we may see that streaming is only a small part of music distribution, or, perhaps we may see streaming become the major distribution form for all sorts of media content.

YES ↵

Joan E. Solsman

Attention, Artists: Streaming Music Is the Inescapable Future. Embrace It

Music's Bedrock Business will be Selling Access to Streams, Not Ownership of Tunes. So What Does That Mean for the Artists You Love? It Should be Music to Their Ears.

Eric Hutchinson long cherished his alphabetized treasury of CDs, but when he began gravitating to streaming-music sites like Pandora, he packed his music collection into four suitcases. That all fits in a pocket now, he remembers thinking, as he shoved the suitcases into a taxi to take to a secondhand CD store.

If you subscribe to the anti-Spotify gospel of Taylor Swift, Hutchinson's actions should strike fear in the hearts of artists: a music lover moving from money-making purchases to the feels-like-free universe of streaming tunes. The only wrinkle: Hutchinson is a musician himself.

A recording artist for more than a decade, Hutchinson is headlining a 30-date cross-country tour, playing theaters that can accommodate 1,000 or more people. The singer-songwriter also listens to 7 to 10 hours of streaming music a week. "The model is not perfect yet for sure, but the more people stream, it's an exciting time to be making music as a result," he said.

The rise of streaming services like Spotify and Pandora is spurring a fundamental change in how the industry makes money, from selling ownership of music to selling access to it. This shift fogs the career path for artists: Beside complicating royalties, it hasn't been around long enough to prove it can sustain careers. Plus, stars looking down from on high—like Swift, Radiohead's Thom Yorke and The Talking Heads' David Byrne—proclaim the model cheapens music and rips musicians off. But artists who look past the high-profile preaching will find that streaming actually levels the playing field, giving more musicians than ever a fighting chance.

Maybe that's what Swift is afraid of. The pop star made herself the poster girl for the anti-streaming set this month, yanking her entire catalog off Spotify just as her album "1989" pulled off the best debut-week sales of any

record in 12 years. Her life's work shouldn't be the guinea pig in an experiment that doesn't fairly compensate creators, she said.

But the streaming takeover is inevitable. In the US, streamed music accounted for 27 percent of music sales in the first half of the year, up from just 3 percent in 2007 and 15 percent in 2012, according to the Recording Industry Association of America. Streaming sales have nearly surpassed sales from physical music—mostly CDs—which stand at 28 percent. Digital downloads made up the biggest chunk at 41 percent of total revenue, but both downloads and physical sales are dwindling.

"Will subscription and access models be the de facto way that the majority of people will end up consuming music at some point in the future? Yes, 100 percent, I'm absolutely convinced that that will be the case," said Rob Wells, the head of global digital business at the world's biggest record-label company, Universal Music Group, who added that downloads and physical purchases aren't going away.

And being paid for sound recordings has never been how artists really make bank. Albums and singles are essential, but the boon for the musician was the merchandise, touring and sponsorships, or that 30-second snippet of song in a national commercial. Streaming actually bolsters those, but it's not easy getting people to take a leap of faith that something so different will work.

"When you've got this new system, you're asking people to learn," said Lars Murray, Pandora's head of label relations. "It's human nature to not want to reset the table."

The Curse of Complications

The biggest stumbling block for artists is that the streaming-music future complicates a business that's already baffling in its complexity.

For one, the blanket term "streaming music" applies to a diverse lineup of services, all of which pay musicians and songwriters differently.

There are three main models. The ad-supported product like Pandora, the Internet's biggest online radio service, pays royalties mostly determined by the US government or government-related bodies. Another category is on-demand, paid-subscription services, such as Apple's Beats Music. You pay a monthly fee for all-you-can-eat listening from a catalog of millions of songs. These services pay royalties based on confidential licensing deals with rights holders, such as labels. The third is a hybrid of the two, like Spotify, which offers a free, ad-supported option and a paid tier with privileged features like offline listening on your phone.

Other platforms defy those categorizations. SoundCloud, an audio YouTube, lets anyone upload and listen to sound files. SoundCloud hit 250 million registered users late last year, on par with Pandora.

Confused yet? Try to untangle the knot of royalties in the music world. Royalties before streaming were already dizzying, with payments for physical products differing from those for performances. Now every kind of streaming service pays different rates to different people under different circumstances in different countries—and many of these rates aren't public.

An artist looking at the sum of her royalty checks from streaming for the year will mostly see a reflection of her contract—not a full picture of what streaming services pay to rights holders. In addition, the royalty rates for a stream of a single song are much smaller than for the purchase of a single song. That's where people like Swift cry foul.

A Leap of Faith

Artists' top criticism of the streaming-music future is that it just won't pay as well. Swift's label, Big Machine, put a number to that argument Wednesday: $496,044. That's how much the label received for US streams of Swift's music in the last 12 months. That's much smaller than the $6 million a year Spotify founder and Chief Executive Daniel Ek said an artist of Swift's stature was on track to earn.

The consensus response to this complaint: just wait until streaming goes mainstream.

"When the CD was three years old, people were complaining that you couldn't build a career on CD sales," said Charles Caldas, chief executive of Merlin, a group that represents more than 20,000 independent labels worldwide. "It took years for that format to get to scale."

While a per-song payment for a download is much higher than the per-song payment of a stream, downloads are a onetime deal. That makes streaming the gift that keeps on giving. "Revenues look small because there are relatively few subscribers," said Alex Pollock, who has handled tour accounting for bands like Coldplay, Maroon 5 and the Beastie Boys. "But if you buy into the concept that subscriber base will continue to grow, the money will grow exponentially."

Evidence is building that streaming services, particularly subscription, will pay material sums to the industry as they get bigger. Spotify, for example, will pay out more [than] $1 billion to rights holders this year, double its payments of 2013.

"Spotify is the single biggest driver of growth in the music industry, the No. 1 source of increasing revenue, and the first or second biggest source of overall music revenue in many places," Ek wrote Tuesday.

The Opportunity for the Open-Minded

While streaming does complicate the business side for artists, it also gives musicians unprecedented power. Streaming puts global distribution to a massive audience at the fingertips of social-savvy artists, at the same time technology made it easier to record a song on a shoestring budget.

Alina Baraz last year recorded a song on her laptop and uploaded it to SoundCloud. "I remember sitting on my couch and realizing that today is going to be the day I release my first song," she said. Over the year, she's accumulated 29,000 followers and had her most popular song played 2.8 million times. She connected with a producer in Denmark through the platform, with whom she collaborates through Skype, email and shared audio files.

"I don't know how I knew that SoundCloud would be the best opportunity for me, but I don't think anything else would have suited," she said.

Soundcloud co-founder Eric Wahlforss said streaming creates a path for more people like Baraz. "Being a musician was never easy, especially if you're doing music that doesn't appeal to a huge audience," he said. "This is a way to make it sustainable for a larger part of musicians than it has before."

True, but the 2.8 million streams of Baraz's songs are 2.8 million times she gave away her music. As painful as it may be for artists to accept that their invaluable music may not be what listeners want to pay for, the big money doesn't stem from the recordings themselves anyway—it comes from things like concerts.

"It started off you would tour to support an album," Pollock said of legacy bands like his client Depeche Mode.

"That's now shifted to putting out an album to create a reason to justify a tour."

Live performance revenue is the biggest money-maker in the business, and it's getting bigger. Live music sales are expected to grow to 64 percent of the US music industry by 2018, from 59 percent share last year, according to PwC's entertainment and media outlook.

Another perk of streaming: it can tell artists where they'll probably pack venues. After Pandora showed Hutchinson the top 10 cities that listen to him most, he was surprised to see the list include[s] places like Seattle, where he gets less radio play. He made sure to put it on his tour. High-priced VIP tickets sold out weeks in advance.

Streaming music platforms are also allowing artists to widen their "merch table" to include intangible experiences such as selling a one-on-one Skype chat with a fan. Smule, the music-app maker behind Sing Karaoke, has begun a program of promotional partnerships with artists. Emerging artist Todd Carey, for example, offered a contest to Smule-app users: upload a cover of his single for the chance to win an iPad. Because people ended up buying his music to practice, the business effect was immediate and obvious, said manager Jason Spiewak. Carey went from selling 100 or so singles a week to a thousand-plus, and his views on YouTube and social following jumped.

None of these forms of making money—contests, concerts, VIP experiences—are new for musicians, but streaming music puts them within reach of more independent and emerging artists. "Engagement is the most important thing," Spiewak said. When thousands of people interact with his client's music, "if we can convert 1 percent of those people to be ticket holders, for an independent artist like Todd, that's a win," he said.

Carey isn't a solitary case. Indie-label group Merlin surveyed a subset of its members this summer and found that nearly half saw streaming revenue increase more than 50 percent in 2013 from a year ago, while the number of those reporting sales increases in downloads fell. Though Swift argues streaming perpetuates a perception that music has no value, 73 percent of indie labels surveyed were optimistic about the future of their business as they watched their streaming sales increase.

Previously, "those with institutional money could buy the storefronts, and it was easier to herd consumers," Merlin's CEO Caldas said. The stream and the download changed that. "That's why independents perform better in a digital world."

The Freedom of the Streaming-Music Future

Singer-songwriter Hutchinson, who personified today's morphing listening habits, also embodies the journey of an artist as the world shifts to streaming and subscriptions. Signed to Madonna's Maverick Records in 2005 only for the label to collapse and freeze his album in the middle of its creation, he put out his next record on his own. Its top-selling single went gold.

This year, he released his latest album, "Pure Fiction," through a label-services business that doesn't touch the master rights to his recordings—that lets artists keep more control of their work and retain more of their royalties, including the revenue they bank from streaming services.

Now when people approach him and say they were just listening to his music on Spotify or Pandora, Hutchinson takes no notice that they didn't say they heard him on the radio, on iTunes or on CD.

"I only hear the first half of the sentence: 'I was just listening to you.'"

JOAN E. SOLSMAN is a senior writer for CNET who specializes in digital media coverage. She formerly wrote for *The Wall Street Journal* and *Dow Jones Newswires*. She is based in New York.

Charles Arthur

Streaming: The Future of the Music Industry, or Its Nightmare?

If you wonder what the person next to you on the bus or train wearing headphones and looking at their mobile screen is listening to, it is probably the new radio—a streaming service.

According to the music business body, the British Phonographic Industry (BPI), Britons streamed 14.8 bn tracks last year, almost double the 7.5 bn of 2013, as internet connectivity improves and becomes pervasive.

Compared to buying music downloads, streaming services have a number of advantages. Listeners can range over millions of tracks—the "universal jukebox," create and share playlists socially, discover new artists effortlessly through "artist radio," and listen anywhere (even downloading temporarily for times when their smartphone gets no signal).

This year Apple is expected to muscle in on the scene using the Beats brand it bought for $3 bn (£2 bn) in May 2014, as is Google's YouTube, which last November launched a paid-for, ad-free music and video streaming service, YouTube Music Key.

Snapchat, best known for its self-destructing photos and videos that are a hit with teenagers, is also planning a music feature, according to emails leaked as part of the hack of Sony Pictures. A partnership with the music video service Vevo could be incorporated into future versions—which surely helped the Silicon Valley darling raise another $485m, valuing it at more than $10 bn, in the past few weeks.

Sometimes it seems as if everyone is planning a music streaming service, just as a decade ago everyone down to HMV and Walmart offered music downloads.

But unlike downloads, musicians do not universally love streaming.

At the start of November, Taylor Swift removed her new album and back catalogue from Spotify and the other streaming services, having complained in a Wall Street Journal column in July: "Valuable things should be paid for. It's my opinion that music should not be free."

Ed Sheeran, Beyoncé and Coldplay have used similar tactics, offering CDs and digital downloads for sale before putting them on streaming services—the opposite of the way radio has been used for promotion for decades.

Yet streaming revenues are rising fast, according to the BPI's figures: they have zoomed from zero in 2007 to £76.7m in 2013. Data released by the Entertainment Retailers Association and BPI this week suggested wholesale streaming revenues were £125m for 2014. (The ERA reported streaming revenues of £175m, but typically its values show a 40% retail markup over the BPI's wholesale figures.) The problem with streaming services, though, is that they seem remarkably ineffective at persuading people to hand over their money. If they are the new radio, well, who pays to listen to the radio? And unlike radio, advertising cannot cover the cost of the service.

Spotify, for example, is available to nearly 1.1 billion internet users around the world, yet it can claim only 12.5 million paying users and 50m ad-supported accounts. So only 1% of potential subscribers actually pay. Another service, Deezer, claims to be in 182 countries, giving it about as many potential users (and payers) as Spotify; in mid-2013 it reported 16 million monthly active users, and 5 million subscribers.

The US-only Pandora claims 250 million users, but only 3.3 million paying its $5 a month subscription.

Mark Mulligan of Midia Consulting[,] who has a long track record watching the music business, reckons there are only about 35 million paying subscribers worldwide for all streaming services, out of more than a billion potential users.

Mulligan thinks the problem is the price. Even before the digital revolution, the average person spent less than £5 a month on music, with most spending accounted for by a small number of big buyers. Cutting subscription prices would entice many more to pay, he thinks, easily making up for lost revenues. "I've been banging the pricing drum for so long the stick has broken," he said recently. "Unfortunately there was pitifully little progress in 2014, with label fears of cannibalising 9.99"—the price of a standard album, in dollars or euros, on iTunes—"dominating thoughts." Something needs to change. The figures suggest streaming is eating into digital downloads rather than CD sales: its revenue growth is almost exactly matched by a fall in digital download revenues, now at their lowest level since 2011. In the US, Nielsen SoundScan has confirmed the same pattern, with paid song downloads down 12% in 2014, from 1.26 bn to 1.1bn, while song streaming rocketed from 106 bn to 164 bn.

There's another difficulty: streaming services tend to lose money.

Pandora, the market-listed US streaming service, hasn't made an annual profit since it floated in 2011. Spotify still records losses—even though it is expected to seek a flotation this year.

The main problem is that for each song streamed, the service has to pay a set amount to the record labels; the more songs streamed, the greater the payment, creating a cost barrier that never shrinks. Spotify says it pays out 70% of its revenues to artists.

That could be about to change with the arrival of Apple. Its acquisition of Dr Dre's Beats was seen as a defensive move after a dramatic fall in iTunes music downloads and revenues. "Apple had to address streaming," Syd Schwartz, a former EMI Music executive, told Rolling Stone in May.

When Apple introduces Beats Music outside the US, it could galvanise the market. Music industry figures are eager to see what effect it could have because data suggest iPhone owners are typically higher spenders (and so easier to convert to paying subscribers) than the average smartphone buyer. "We've reached a very interesting point where there are important changes to come," a BPI spokesman said. "It seems that we're moving towards a time of people understanding that streaming is the future."

Apple is understood to be seeking lower per-song payments from the music labels, so it can offer lower subscription rates. Google's paid-for YouTube Music Key service launched in November with a six-month free trial and a discounted £7.99-a-month cost (down from £9.99). Mulligan expects that discount to continue, and pricing tiers to fall in line.

Yet YouTube itself might be a key obstacle to boosting subscriptions, because it is unofficially the world's largest ad-supported music streaming service. Teenagers use it to find songs and related artists exactly as they do the normal streaming services. (Snapchat's user demographic is a perfect match for that sort of service—which Vevo may seek to capitalise on.) When Swift removed her content from streaming services, it created a media uproar—but all her songs, including new album 1989, could still be found on YouTube.

Mulligan thinks artists and labels will have to swallow their pride and accept the world of change—and lower payments.

"The whole 'changing download dollars into streaming cents' issue continues to haunt streaming though," he said. "With streaming services struggling to see a route to operational profitability the perennial issue of sustainability remains a festering wound. The emerging generation of artists such as Avicii and Ed Sheeran who have never known a life of platinum album sales will learn how to prosper in the streaming era. The rest will have to learn to reinvent themselves, fast—really fast."

CHARLES ARTHUR was *The Guardian's* technology editor for nine years and is now a contributing writer for that online service based in the United Kingdom. He writes on technology, business, science, and health.

EXPLORING THE ISSUE

Is Streaming the Future of the Music Industry?

Critical Thinking and Reflection

1. When an industry is *disrupted*, are there new opportunities for people to work in the industries, or are those opportunities fewer in number? What types of jobs are most likely to change?
2. When technology can be used for legal purposes, but also illegal purposes, should there be guidelines, regulations, or laws to punish those who circumvent the legal uses?
3. How reliant are we on other technology industries when we stream music? For example, how important is the Internet? How important is your smartphone carrier? Or even, how important is electrical energy to your ability to stream music?
4. Have you ever considered whether streaming music actually costs you more than the purchase of a CD? Think about the amount of money that a subscription service costs, and whether you use it enough to pay for the cost of the service?
5. Many streaming services include a number of advertisements. Does this change your listening enjoyment or the price you are willing to pay for services that don't include ads?

Is There Common Ground?

Both of the authors' perspectives in this issue acknowledge that streaming is an important part of today's music industry, but each has a different perspective on whether streaming will ultimately make enough money to sustain the business models that are currently emerging. But even though media industries continue to evolve as new distribution services emerge, the smaller companies are often acquired by the bigger firms. If streaming continues at the rate projected by each of these journalists, what might be the future of recorded music?

"Hit" records are almost a rare commodity now, as the music industry focuses on "micro-hits" and local distribution rather than the mass distribution, which created a "hit-machine" in earlier days. Although new business models are emerging, we can expect others also to rise over time. Is this type of disruption likely to become the norm in other media industries too?

Additional Resources

Greg Bensinger, "Amazon Launches Music-Streaming Service," *Wall Street Journal* (June 12, 2014). This article discusses the business behind Amazon's development of a streaming service that will also affect sales for other branches of the Amazon business.

Greg Kot, *Ripped: How the Wired Generation Revolutionized Music* (Scribner, 2009). This book takes an early look at streaming services starting with Napster, and discusses how the traditional music industry has had to adapt to digital distribution.

Donald S. Passman, *All You Need to Know About the Music Business,* 8th ed. (Simon and Schuster, 2012). Taking a long-view perspective, Passman provides advice to musicians who want to break into the music industry.

Bob Stanley, *Yeah, Yeah, Yeah, Yeah: The Story of Pop Music from Bill Haley to Beyonce* (W.W. Norton, 2014). In this historical document of the explosive growth of pop music since the 1960s, Stanley addresses distribution forms and the flow of music from one country to another.

Internet References . . .

BMI, "Types of Copyright"

www.bmi.com/licensing/entry/types_of_copyrights

Pharrell's advice for today's artist . . . beware

https://www.youtube.com/watch?v=MrFPWE2TnrM

Recording Industry Association of America (RIAA)

www.riaa.com

U.S. Copyright Office, "Copyright and the Music Marketplace" (February 2015)

copyright.gov/policy/musiclicensingstudy/copyright -and-the-music-marketplace.pdf

Selected, Edited, and with Issue Framing Material by:
Alison Alexander, *University of Georgia*
and
Jarice Hanson, *University of Massachusetts—Amherst*

ISSUE

Is There a Future for Digital Newspapers?

YES: **Gabriel Snyder**, from "Keeping Up with the *Times*," *Wired* (2017)

NO: **Michael Rosenwald**, from "Print Is Dead. Long Live Print," *Columbia Journalism Review* (2016)

Learning Outcomes

After reading this issue, you will be able to:

- Identify the changes that threaten traditional newspapers.
- Identify the benefits and costs of moving to a digital model.
- Discuss the organizational climate for change in a traditional newsroom.
- Support your prediction for digital versus print.

ISSUE SUMMARY

YES: An in-depth analysis of *The New York Times* digital strategies by Gabriel Snyder illustrates how traditional companies can move into the world of digital newspapers. The *Times* strategy is to invest heavily in their core journalism offerings while continually adding new online features. By 2016, the *Times* was making nearly $500 million in digital revenues. They now believe they can make the economics work.

NO: Michael Rosenwald quotes early digital journalist, "I have come to realize that replicating print in a digital device is much more difficult than what anybody, including me, imagined." Digital editions have not proved to be the replacement revenue stream that was envisioned and the assumption that readers prefer the immediacy of digital now seems questionable. To this author, the future of print journalism will be the traditional newspaper.

W e've heard the bad news. Newspaper revenue from advertising continues to slide as classified ads move online, along with lucrative employment, auto and retail advertising. Subscriptions are declining, particularly among the younger generations. Reductions in the work force have followed with newsrooms significantly reduced in size. The Pew Report on the State of the Media 2016 (https://assets.pewresearch.org/wp-content/uploads/sites/13/2016/06/30143308/state-of-the-news-media-report-2016-final.pdf) reports that the current workforce is 20,000 jobs smaller than 20 years ago. Expensive printing presses have a limited lifespan, and some believe that when they die they will not be replaced. Consider for a moment your own news consumption, do you read a print

newspaper every day? Every week? Is there a newspaper delivered to your home or the home of your parents? Where else do you get news? Where do you get most of your news? Your answers should give you some insight into the issues the newspaper industry is facing.

As we examine this issue, we should not lose track of the importance of the press. The Pew Report mentioned above supports pessimism about the influence of newspapers, reporting that a January 2016 survey found that just 5 percent of US adults who had learned about the presidential election in the past week named print newspapers as their "most helpful" source, trailing cable, TV, radio, social media, and news websites. The report ends with an telling statement: ". . . it is important to keep in mind that the result [of changing delivery systems for news] is about far more than who captures the upper hand or the revenue base. It is determining how and with what kinds of story-telling Americans learn about the issues and events facing society and the world. "

James Fallows (The Atlantic, April 2011) worries about the consequences of newspapers becoming ever more market minded. He fears unintended consequences if newspapers become focused on giving people what they want, but not giving people what they need to know. He fears something that many of us are worried about in this moment: a babble of "truthiness" where there are no arbiters of reality or fact, therefore allowing people to withdraw into their own information spheres. Alex Jones in Losing the News, 2009, describes the iron core of journalism. It is a fact-based accountability journalism, an expensive, intensive search for information that holds those with power accountable. This is the "heavy lifting" of journalism and is borne in large part by newspapers. Without newspapers he argues we will have to answer questions such as who will do the reporting? What principles, if any, will guide them? And, what organizations will be strong enough to serve as a counterweight to big government and large corporations? Who, in short, will speak truth to power?

Whatever the ultimate outcome for journalism, most newspapers are still profitable, although not at the same level as in the past. Surprisingly, newspapers coming on the market are finding buyers. Some investors argue that the traditional newspaper will not die. Warren Buffet, billionaire investor, is buying newspapers with the argument that many readers are 50 and over, and that provides a market for at least the next forty years. He's 87.

For many publishers, the hope for the future lies in digital publication. Print newspaper requires printing physical copy using expensive ink, paper and printing machines and transporting them daily to people's homes at a substantial deliver cost. Digital production puts that information online for virtually no reproduction or distribution costs. It is no surprise that all but the smallest newspaper have a digital presence, and many now offer digital only subscriptions.

There are challenges to the digital newspaper model. Digital advertising revenue has not kept pace with analog revenue. Even now, most newspapers find digital revenue a fraction of the amount received from print ads. Readers have numerous choices of information sources from the Internet, and many are reluctant to pay for digital information. This has been one of the biggest challenges for publishers trying to move to digital formats.

Snyder details the story of The New York Times as it pursues its goal of transforming their digital subscriptions into the main engine of their business. They want to augment their traditional news content with ever-changing online features and services. They want the Times to become indispensable to their reader's lives. He details the rocky road to a "digital first" organization. Their chosen method of revenue collection was the paywall, requiring payment for full access to the digital editions. The paywall has not been well received in many other locations, but for the Times it has worked with more than 1.5 million subscribers paying more than $299 million by 2015. The digital first shift required significant attention, with programmers developing a suite of editorial products and with executives talking with many Internet organizations to develop partnerships. In short, this was an expensive and intensive project, but the Times is finally are able to conclude as Sulzberger notes "it is profitable on subscription alone, and we can make the economics work, I suspect, for a long time. "

Rosenwald argues that in the decades since newspapers launched websites none have matched the success of print in revenue or readership. He now finds the notion that readers will prefer digital copy to be questionable. Publishers are concerned that young readers are not subscribers and thus digital must be the future of news. Chyi, see Additional Resources, argues, "They have killed print, their core product, with all of their focus online." The assumption that the future is online seems, in his judgment, not to be inevitable.

Did newspapers jump on the bandwagon too quickly? Have they given up their core business? And, what would help a digital newspaper compete with the many other digital forms of journalism and information? From your perspective, what would it take to keep you reading print newspapers? What is the solution to the dire straits that plague print journalism today?

YES

Gabriel Snyder

Keeping Up with the *Times*

The New York Times Claws Its Way into the Future

Arthur Gregg Sulzberger doesn't remember the first time he visited the family business. He was young, he says, no older than 6, when he shuffled through the brass-plated revolving doors of the old concrete hulk on 43rd Street and boarded the elevator up to his father's and grandfather's offices. He often visited for a few minutes before taking a trip to the newsroom on the third floor, all typewriters and moldering stacks of paper, and then he'd sometimes go down to the subbasement to take in the oily scents and clanking sounds of the printing press. This was the early 1980s, when *The New York Times* was nothing but ink on paper and was printed in the same building where the journalism was created. His memories are hazy, perhaps because he's 36 now and it was a long time ago, and perhaps because that building, like the *Times*, was always just there, a fact of life.

The *Times* building is still there, except it's not the *Times* building anymore. It's been sold off and sliced up, and the top two floors are presently occupied by Snapchat, while the bottom two were bought by Kushner Companies, the family business of Jared Kushner, son-in-law extraordinaire of Donald J. Trump. A few blocks—but more like a century—away from that old building, Sulzberger sits in his office in the newish glass-and-steel-lattice-encased headquarters of the *Times*. He looks the picture of a young tech executive—close-cropped hair, tortoiseshell glasses, considered stubble—and I ask him point-blank if he worries about whether *The New York Times* will ever cease to be a fact of life. "No," he says, equally point-blank, which is exactly the party line one expects to hear from the deputy publisher of the *Times*—a recent appointment that put him next in line to lead the paper when the current publisher and chair, his father, retires. But there could be another reason for his confidence. Sulzberger, like more than three dozen other executives and journalists I interviewed and shadowed at the *Times*, is working on the biggest strategic shift in the paper's 165-year history, and he believes it will

strengthen its bottom line, enhance the quality of its journalism, and secure a long and lasting future.

The main goal isn't simply to maximize revenue from advertising—the strategy that keeps the lights on and the content free at upstarts like the Huffington Post, BuzzFeed, and Vox. It's to transform the *Times'* digital subscriptions into the main engine of a billion-dollar business, one that could pay to put reporters on the ground in 174 countries even if (OK, when) the printing presses stop forever. To hit that mark, the *Times* is embarking on an ambitious plan inspired by the strategies of Netflix, Spotify, and HBO: invest heavily in a core offering (which, for the *Times*, is journalism) while continuously adding new online services and features (from personalized fitness advice and interactive newsbots to virtual reality films) so that a subscription becomes indispensable to the lives of its existing subscribers and more attractive to future ones. "We think that there are many, many, many, many people—millions of people all around the world—who want what *The New York Times* offers," says Dean Baquet, the *Times'* executive editor. "And we believe that if we get those people, they will pay, and they will pay greatly."

How they reach those people, and how they make them pay, is now the work of hundreds of journalists, designers, engineers, data scientists, and product managers. At stake isn't just the future of a very old newspaper that has seen its advertising revenue cut in half in less than a decade—it's the still unresolved question of whether high-impact, high-cost journalism can thrive in a radically changing landscape. Newspaper companies today employ 271,000 fewer people than they did in 1990—around the population of Orlando—and with fewer journalists working with fewer resources, and more Americans getting their news on platforms where the news could very well be fake, the financial success of the *Times* isn't an incidental concern for people who care about journalism. It's existential, especially in the context of the new American president.

Just days after the election, Trump suggested that the *Times*—or, per his preferred Twitter epithet, "the failing @nytimes"—would be a frequent target of his administration, calling an article "dishonest" for citing something he had said on CNN (which was odd, since he did actually say it, in public, on video) and adding (also falsely) that the *Times* "is losing thousands of subscribers because of their very poor and highly inaccurate coverage." In fact, it's been the exact opposite: Four weeks after the election, *Times* chief executive Mark Thompson told an industry conference that subscriptions had surged at 10 times their usual rate. To Thompson, the likeliest explanation wasn't that the *Times* did a bang-up job covering the final days of the election—like everyone else, they failed to anticipate Trump's victory—or that readers were looking to hedge against fake news. He suggests a simpler reason: "I think the public anxiety to actually have professional, consistent, properly funded newsrooms holding politicians to account is probably bigger than all of the other factors put together." In other words, the president's hostility to the press and the very notion of facts themselves seems to have reminded people that nothing about *The New York Times*— or the kind of journalism it publishes—is inevitable.

On May 25, 1994, Arthur Ochs Sulzberger Sr., who had stepped down as publisher of the *Times* two years prior but was still the company's chair, was delivering a speech in Kansas City, Missouri, and turned to the burgeoning "information highway." He didn't like it much. "Far from resembling a modern interstate," he predicted, it "will more likely approach a roadway in India: chaotic, crowded, and swarming with cows."

That same day, back in New York City, Arthur Ochs Sulzberger Jr., who succeeded his father as publisher (which he remains to this day), was also giving a speech about technological change. "If they want it on CD-ROM, I'll try to meet that need. The internet? That's fine with me," he said. "Hell, if someone would be kind enough to invent the technology, I'll be pleased to beam it directly into your cortex." It was a line the young publisher liked to repeat. "He said that in my job interview," says Martin Nisenholtz, who was hired in 1995 as the original architect of the *Times*' digital strategy.

Arthur Gregg Sulzberger, who goes by Arthur but is known as A.G. around the *Times*, was 16 at the time, and the bulk of what happened next in journalism—the rise of blogs, social media, podcasts, and mobile; the fall of print circulation, advertising, and prestige—happened while he was learning how to be a journalist. He graduated from Brown with a degree in political science in 2003 and started writing for The Providence Journal and The Oregonian before joining the *Times* as a metro reporter in

2009. The financial crisis that coincided with his homecoming so damaged the *Times*' advertising revenue that many started to speculate about when the *Times* would go bankrupt. Though digital advertising increased from an asterisk in financial reports to well over $100 million between 2005 and 2010, it wasn't nearly enough to offset the $600 million loss in print advertising over the same period. The *Times* managed to survive through savvy financial maneuvering—taking out a $250 million loan from Mexican billionaire Carlos Slim in exchange for what is now a 17 percent stake in the company; selling its gleaming Renzo Piano–designed Manhattan headquarters and leasing it back from the buyer; shedding assets like About.com and a stake in the Boston Red Sox—but its continued existence was no longer a foregone conclusion. "The former *Times* executive editor Abe Rosenthal often said he couldn't imagine a world without the *Times*," one critic wrote in The Atlantic. "Perhaps we should start."

Over the next few years, finding new digital revenue became the *Times*' top business priority, and in 2014, Sulzberger, by then an editor on the metro desk, was tasked with overseeing an internal assessment of the paper's digital efforts to date. The result was a 97-page document known as the Innovation Report, which found that editors too often said no to programmers and product designers from the technology group. "The newsroom has historically reacted defensively by watering down or blocking changes," read the report, "prompting a phrase that echoes almost daily around the business side: 'The newsroom would never allow that.' " Initially intended for only a handful of senior managers, most *Times* employees first learned of the report from a grainy photocopy that was leaked to BuzzFeed; one employee said they cried when they first read it because, as Harvard's Nieman Lab reported, "it surfaced so many issues about *Times* culture that digital types have been struggling to overcome for years."

The BuzzFeed leak was devastating for Sulzberger— "a moment of panic," he says. "We had written a pretty frank and candid document expressly for a small group of leaders of this organization, and suddenly it felt like our dirty laundry was being aired." Even worse: It was a Sulzberger, of the Sulzbergers, doing the airing. Still, he realized within a few days that the public scrutiny had turned an administrative white paper into a media rallying cry. "You couldn't read that report and think that the status quo was an option. Once it's clear that that is not an option, then the conversation all of a sudden becomes much more productive. It's not should we change, it's how do we change."

The privileging of print journalism over the web, the sclerotic approach to change, the lack of coordination between the growing number of digital disciplines and specialists—Sulzberger and his team laid it all bare, lighting a digital-first fuse that still burns today. "It's not like I'm the first person who came into this newsroom and said, 'Social media is something that needs to be accounted for in our future,'" Sulzberger says. "But it wasn't until the Innovation Report that those points really landed."

The Innovation Report was also the first time that most people outside of the *Times* had ever heard of Sulzberger, though *Times* watchers had for several years pitted him against two of his cousins—David Perpich and Sam Dolnick, an executive and an editor at the *Times*, respectively—as a leading candidate for the publisher's job when Sulzberger's father eventually retired.

The *Times* is a big organization, with about 1,300 journalists, and management has created a number of task forces to workshop new approaches to reporting and storytelling. One committee, the 2020 Group, studied the newsroom for a year, and its report, published in January, detailed how *Times* journalism should evolve over the next three years. (Among the recommendations: Greater emphasis on visuals, greater variety of formats and voices. They also announced that the *Times* would be introducing an alternative metric to pageviews that would "measure an article's value to attracting and retaining subscribers.") Another division, Story[X], was created last spring to experiment with emerging technology like machine learning and translation. And then there is the Beta Group, which has become a hub for most of the *Times*' digital initiatives. Beta was launched by Sulzberger's 39-year-old cousin, Perpich, who, after working at two tech startups out of college, helped launch a DJ training school called Scratch Academy. He went on to Harvard Business School for an MBA and landed at Booz & Company as a management consultant. When he joined the family business in 2010 as an executive director for paid products, he and his team oversaw the rollout of the paywall that for the first time required people to shell out cash for full and regular access to NYTimes.com. The project has become the *Times*' biggest business success of late. Five years on, more than 1.5 million people pay more than $200 million every year for a subscription.

Even with the success of the paywall, though, "it's a very, very steep uphill battle to simply sell people on the idea of buying one more news story," Kinsey Wilson, the *Times*' executive vice president for product and technology, admitted at a conference last year. He later told me: "I believe that the only way you create value is if you're able to bundle various services together." Which is where the members of the Beta Group come in. They're tasked with developing a new suite of editorial products (apps, blogs, verticals) that, in the way of expensive original programming on HBO and Netflix, keep existing subscribers coming back and new subscribers coming in. Central to Perpich's original vision was having Beta's product people work alongside designers, developers, and—most radically for the *Times*—editors. No one on Beta has an office; instead, each product is assigned its own conference room lined with whiteboards covered in colorful diagrams, design mock-ups, and Post-it notes where members of the team immerse themselves in what they are trying to build.

In addition to Cooking and Crosswords—two of the original Beta apps—the group is now working on Real Estate, an app for home listings; Well, a health and fitness blog the group wants to turn into a suite of personalized training and advice services; and Watching, a vertical dedicated to TV and movie recommendations. The newest addition to Beta was an acquisition: In October, *The New York Times* paid $30 million for the Wirecutter, a gadget review site. (In a show of confidence in the deal, Perpich stepped back from the Beta Group earlier this year to become general manager of the Wirecutter.)

"Working hour by hour, day by day, with software developers and designers and product managers—to me that was a real revolution, a kind of epiphany," says Clifford Levy, who won two Pulitzers at the *Times* before being promoted to the assistant managing editor overseeing digital platforms. "This is standard operating procedure in Silicon Valley, but it was radical here."

And the radical shift was felt, and heard, throughout the newsroom. "It is not incorrect for me to say that I had no idea what people were talking about in my first couple months," says Sam Sifton, the *Times*' food editor, who started working with the Beta Group to launch the Cooking app back in 2013. "'We can iterate on that.' What? We spoke different languages, different cultures." Still, Sifton has embraced his new digital mission, agreeing this past November to host a text message experiment called "Turkey Talk" to help cooks with their Thanksgiving dinners.

This shift toward personality-driven personal service echoes an earlier chapter in *Times* history, when, in the 1970s, the paper rolled out an array of advertiser-friendly sections like Weekend, Home, and Living. The goal, according to then-executive–editor Abe Rosenthal, was to figure out "ways that would get more revenue, more readers." Just as those new sections were greeted with howls of derision both inside and outside the paper—James Reston, a *Times* elder statesman, said, "It goes against my original concept of what the *Times* ought to be"—today's emphasis on news you can use ("What We Know and Don't Know About the Trump–Russia Dossier," "15 Ways to Be a Better Person") has provoked accusations of clickbait.

To Jill Abramson, who ran the newsroom between 2011 and 2014 (and whose firing was, as firings go, public and acrimonious), the choice between publishing quality journalism and clickbait is a false one. "In my years, I used to laugh that everything you agreed to in terms of lighter or more advertising–friendly content would be because we needed that advertising revenue to support the Baghdad Bureau," she says. "So if a certain audience wants lighter content, they can click on it. If others don't want it, there's still plenty of great international or investigative reporting at the *Times*."

"There's this fashion for media companies to call themselves technology companies," says Jake Silverstein, editor of *The New York Times* Magazine. "Our job isn't to make technology. Our job is to figure out how to use technologies." Or, as Sam Dolnick puts it: "We're not going to create augmented reality. We're going to figure out how to use that in a journalistic way."

Which is to say, a "Timesian" way, a shorthand you frequently hear for what the *Times* can and cannot do in the interest of protecting its exalted status (and nowhere is it more exalted than within the *Times* itself). What Timesian means or doesn't mean often depends on who's defining it, but it's typically in the same general neighborhood as authoritative, or maybe stuffy. Editors are infamous for their lengthy divinations on whether new headline styles are sufficiently Timesian, and, per the Innovation Report, nothing slowed down a new initiative more than when management deliberated on just how Timesian it was or wasn't.

It's been Dolnick's mission to drum up enthusiasm in the newsroom for testing out new applications, from VR to livestreaming, without worrying too much about the Timesian thing. After stints at the Staten Island Advance and the Associated Press, Dolnick started at the *Times* in 2009 as a metro reporter—the same year as his cousin A.G.—and wrote a prizewinning series on halfway houses before becoming a senior editor for mobile and then an associate editor. Inside the *Times* these days, he is known for the regular companywide email newsletter "Digital Highlights."

One such highlight: At the Olympics last summer, deputy sports editor Sam Manchester sent short, frequently humorous text messages to the 20,000 readers who had signed up for the service. One, which sparked a viral meme, was a photo of a lifeguard watching swimmers practice, with a caption: "You know who has the most useless job in Rio? She does. That's right, they have lifeguards in case Olympic swimmers need saving."

"A generation ago, or even five years ago," says Dolnick, "there'd be a lot of this Timesian stuff, 'Oh, The

New York Times doesn't do that. We don't make jokes in text messages.' " The audience responded, though, and Manchester buckled under the thousands of questions that readers texted him. That explains why, for its next engagement experiment with readers, the *Times* turned to artificial intelligence. Running up to the election, they created a Facebook Messenger chatbot that offered daily updates on the race in the voice of political reporter Nick Confessore. Running the backend was a tool created by Chatfuel that combined natural language parsing (so it could understand the questions posed to Confessore) with a conversation tree (so that the bot could respond to readers' queries using prewritten answers).

One of the biggest initiatives Dolnick has been involved in is virtual reality. He says it started with an email he sent to Silverstein last year: "Hey man, want to see something cool?" Dolnick had just visited a VR production company called Vrse. Works (since renamed Here Be Dragons1) and brought one of their films, Clouds Over Sidra, into his office. The *Times* has since jumped into VR, partnering with Google to send its Cardboard VR viewers to all of its 1.1 million Sunday print-edition subscribers, creating an NYT VR app that's been downloaded more than 1 million times, and producing 16 (and counting) original films about topics as varied as displaced refugees (The Displaced), floating movie stars (Take Flight), and battling ISIS in Iraq (The Fight for Falluja). It remains a working experiment. The floating movie stars, for example: "People liked it, it got pretty good views," Silverstein says. "But it didn't feel like we were advancing the ball. It had a little whiff of 'Look at us. We have VR'."

Even as Sulzberger boasts, "We employ more journalists who can write code than any other news organization," there are some at the *Times*—usually those who can't write code—who chafe at these endless waves of experimentation. "When we're told this is the new best practice, everyone marches in lockstep," says one editor who asked to remain anonymous. "Facebook Live? Yep! Video? On it! *The New York Times* isn't a place where people say no, and we're flat-out exhausted."

In March of 2016, Alex MacCallum, the *Times'* senior vice president for video (and at the beginning of her career, one of the first three hires at the Huffington Post), went to Baquet with a proposition from Facebook: If the *Times* would commit to producing dozens of livestreams a month for Facebook Live, its new video platform, the social media giant would pay the *Times* $3 million a year. Like most major media companies, the *Times* has a complicated relationship with Facebook—a 2015 deal to publish *Times* journalism directly on Facebook Instant led some in the newsroom to worry about cannibalizing subscriptions and losing control of their content—but following the Innovation Report, the pull of a new social platform was hard to resist. Baquet gave the green light. "We spun up a team and started producing within two weeks, which is like a land speed record in this organization," MacCallum says.

Over the next few months, the Live team recruited more than 300 *Times* journalists to livestream anything and everything: press conferences, protests, political conventions. It was too much for some, and the public editor of the *Times*, Liz Spayd, said as much in a column headlined "Facebook Live: Too Much, Too Soon." Spayd complained that some of the videos were "plagued by technical malfunctions, feel contrived, drone on too long . . . or are simply boring." She urged editors to slow down, regroup, and wait until the *Times* could stay true to its past model of "innovating at a thoughtful, measured pace, but with quality worthy of its name." (Timesian!)

MacCallum concedes that some of the early efforts may have fallen short, but today she puts them in the perspective more common in tech circles than media organizations. "I disagree that it's possible to have every single thing be up to the standard. Otherwise you can't take any risks." What's more, Baquet says, the project helped train hundreds in his newsroom in how to frame a shot, speak on camera, and all the other skills necessary to produce journalism in the years to come. "If you buy that our future is the phone, and you buy that that means our future is going to be more visual than it's been in the past, then *New York Times* journalists have to be comfortable with video."

The alternative is stark. For most of the last year, the *Times* offered buyouts to employees, in part to make room for new, digitally focused journalists. As one editor (fearful of being quoted by name) put it: "One of the anxieties I heard throughout the *Times* is that they can get the journalism absolutely right, execute the technology perfectly, and still not find the hundreds of millions it costs every year to line the walls with Pulitzers. While other media companies collapse or implode—witness the once-proud Tribune Company's devolution into national punch line "Tronc"—there is unease over the possibility that when (or if) the *Times* emerges from its digital rebirth, it might be scarcely recognizable. Even Sulzberger admits to long-term doubts for the industry, though, he says, "We feel like we're closer to cracking the code than anyone else."

In 2010, the *Times* was making about $200 million in digital revenue, almost entirely from advertising; by 2016 that number had more than doubled, to nearly $500 million, with almost all of the gains coming from digital subscriptions. The internal *Times* goal for total digital revenue is $800 million by 2020—which, according to senior management, would be enough to fund the *Times'* global news-gathering operation with or without a print edition.

To find that additional $300-plus million, they need to sign up new subscribers across all its different platforms. The site's metered paywall remains its most powerful incentive to subscribe, which is why most new subscribers sign up once they've maxed out their monthly allowance on *NYTimes.com*. (Subscriptions through mobile and social media continue to lag behind desktop.) They also need five straight years of 13 percent growth in digital revenue, which would seem more doable if, in the first three quarters of 2016 (before the postelection bump), growth hadn't been tracking at only 8 percent. "Look, nobody said this was going to be a straight line," CEO Mark Thompson says.

Still: credit where credit is due. The *Times* has had more success at building its digital subscriber base than any other publication. Its nearly $500 million in digital revenue not only dwarfs what any print publication has managed online, it also far exceeds leading digital-only publishers. At *The Washington Post*, which has invested heavily in digital growth since it was acquired by Amazon founder Jeff Bezos, digital revenue was reported in 2016 to be in the neighborhood of $60 million. In 2015, BuzzFeed brought in a reported $170 million, while the Huffington Post's 2014 revenue, the most recent reported figure, was $146 million. "Today we have the largest and most successful pay model for journalism in the world," says Meredith Kopit Levien, the *Times'* chief revenue officer. "Our digital subscriber number is a tiny fraction of Netflix's or Spotify's numbers, so it still has to be proven that it can be done around news. I think it can." None of that even accounts for the revenue that comes in from the print edition, which Sulzberger says isn't going anywhere any time soon. "It is profitable on subscription revenue alone, and we can make the economics work, I suspect, for a long time."

As long as he's there, anyway. Family control is one of the competitive advantages of The *New York Times*—there is no plan B for Sulzberger or his family. Bezos' support brought fresh hope to The Washington Post after he bought it from the Graham family for $250 million in 2013; two years later, it surpassed the *Times* in unique visitors for the first time. But there is no reason why Bezos can't wake up tomorrow and decide to dedicate all of his personal fortune to colonizing Mars instead of saving journalism. Chris Hughes, one of the founders of Facebook, bought The New Republic in 2012 with the goal of revolutionizing the century-old periodical for the digital age, spending millions of his own money in the process. Four years later, when I was editor in chief, he sold it and walked away.

Sulzberger can't just walk away. Much of the family's fortune is tied up in *Times* stock, for starters, but there is also a pronounced, and profound, sense of obligation among him and his cousins to *The New York Times* as both a business and a public good. They have to figure this out. Whether or not they succeed, and whether Bezos is in the journalism game for the long haul, is the stuff of tomorrow's headlines. Today's news is all we know for sure, and today the Post has a billionaire behind it, and the *Times* has hundreds of thousands of subscribers it didn't have six months ago, and the president of the United States has a Twitter account. The journalists have plenty of work ahead.

GABRIEL SNYDER is a former top editor at *The New Republic, The Atlantic Wire, Newsweek* and *Gawker.*

Michael Rosenwald   **NO**

Print Is Dead. Long Live Print

ROGER FIDLER IS THE FOREFATHER of digital journalism. In the early 1980s, he wrote and illustrated an essay on the future of news. When Fidler presented his ideas around Knight Ridder, his co-workers sometimes laughed. "It was not quite like Roger had descended from another planet," a colleague of his once told me, "but he was saying some things that were simply very hard to believe at the time."

The idea he spoke of most was one Steve Jobs would have many years later—a tablet on which to read electronic newspapers. Fidler's design and execution of a prototype were so similar to the eventual iPad that when Apple sued Samsung over design infringements, Samsung used Fidler's early device to argue the idea was in the public domain.

In Fidler's vision of the future, news and information were headed to the nascent internet, where stories would be instantly published from one computer to millions more, eliminating the need to operate an expensive press run by expensive workers. A tablet, he thought, was the perfect device to replace paper. Readers could click on boxes that revealed data or more information about a particular subject. Advertisers could produce immersive, interactive ads. And the tablet could be slipped into a briefcase or bag. Fidler was right, of course. Apple has sold several hundred million iPads, and more than a billion phones that serve much the same purpose.

Now, Fidler wonders if he was wrong. "I have come to realize that replicating print in a digital device is much more difficult than what anybody, including me, imagined," he told me this summer, and he wasn't just referring to tablets. Fidler is equally concerned about the reading experience and economics of all forms of digital news. Now retired from teaching journalism at the University of Missouri, he has watched newspapers struggle to move their content and business online. The idea of interactive advertising has clearly not panned out, he says. Readers are annoyed and distracted by it, so many block it with browser extensions. He and others have observed that print offers a limited amount of ad space, which is infinite online, driving down ad prices and sending publishers racing around a hamster wheel. To make money, they need more content to advertise against. Some of this content is—how to put this?—lousy, giving readers another reason not to pay for news.

Even though his iPad is never far away, Fidler still subscribes to the print editions of *The New York Times*, the Columbia Daily Tribune and the Columbia Missourian. "I have been wondering," Fidler says, "whether we have completely underestimated the viability and usefulness of the print product."

Me too.

I am not a dinosaur; I'm a tech dork who waits in line outside the Apple Store for new iPhones. If my wife ever divorces me, she will testify that I spent too much time on Facebook and Twitter. I've been an enthusiastic and vocal supporter of digital news at my workplace, The Washington Post, so much so that my colleagues and bosses might be surprised I'm even posing the following question: What if everything we've been led to believe about the future of journalism is wrong?

Two decades have passed since newspapers launched websites, and yet here we are. Big city papers have gone under, thousands of journalists have lost their jobs, and the idea that digital news will eventually become a decent business feels like a rumor. The reality is this: No app, no streamlined website, no "vertical integration," no social network, no algorithm, no Apple, no Apple Newsstand, no paywall, no soft paywall, no targeted ad, no mobile-first strategy has come close to matching the success of print in revenue or readership. And the most crucial assumption publishers have made about readers, particularly millennials—that they prefer the immediacy of digital—now seems questionable, too.

I wish I were being hyperbolic, but Iris Chyi, a University of Texas associate professor and new media researcher, has been collecting facts to support these assertions. Like me, Chyi is not anti-technology. She enjoys her travels around the Web. While pursuing her PhD in the late 1990s, Chyi conducted audience research for the Austin American-Statesman. But looking at reader metrics nearly a decade later, it became clear to Chyi that online penetration and engagement weren't growing. This got her wondering, like Fidler, whether newspapers were pursuing a future that would never come.

Chyi began conducting surveys and collecting readership data, analyzing it all in academic papers and a recent book titled, Trial and Error: U.S. Newspapers' Digital Struggles Toward Inferiority. She has come to believe that the digital shift has been a disaster for media organizations, and that there is no evidence online news will ever be economically or culturally viable. "They have killed print, their core product, with all of their focus online," Chyi told me in an interview.

To help explain her position, Chyi devised a metaphorical symbol for news online: Ramen noodles. Compared to dinner in a nice restaurant, ramen noodles are an inferior good. They are cheap. You can cook and consume them just about anywhere, including a dorm room sink, in five minutes. To make them profitable, you have to sell them by the metric ton. As for their taste, typing the phrase "Ramen noodles taste like..." into the Google search box produces this result: "Ramen noodles taste like soap."

In her book, Chyi writes that "the (supposedly dying) print edition still outperforms the (supposedly hopeful) digital product by almost every standard, be it readership, engagement, advertising revenue," and especially willingness to actually pay for the product. In a paper published earlier this year, Chyi examined data collected by Scarborough, a market research firm owned by Nielsen, for the 51 largest US newspapers, finding that the print edition reaches 28 percent of circulation areas, while the digital version reaches just 10 percent. Digital readers don't linger. Pew Research Center data shows that readers coming directly to news sites stay less than five minutes. Readers coming from Facebook are gone in less than two minutes.

Publishers argue that print readers are just getting older while younger readers move further away from even considering print, but Pew surveys and Chyi's analysis of the Scarborough data show that considerable interest in print still persists, even among young readers. Pew reports that print-only is still the most common way of reading news, with more than half of readers last year opting for ink on their hands every day. The percentage who only read news via a computer? Five percent in 2014 . . . and in 2015? Also 5 percent.

Chyi's findings show that among 18- to 24-year-old news readers, 19.9 percent had read the print edition of a newspaper during the past week. Less than 8 percent read it digitally.

Chyi has been making this argument for several years, but when I spoke to her this past summer she told me that few people in the industry were paying attention, including media reporters. Now they are. Jack Shafer, a sharp media critic at Politico, highlighted her research in an October column on the enduring value of print, but missed the larger context—that her numbers don't exist in a vacuum. Print is rebounding or stabilizing in other areas of daily life. Sales of print books have risen every year since 2013, while e-books have leveled off and in some genres declined. University students prefer printed textbooks over electronic ones, according to surveys. And independent and used bookstores have made a comeback. Yet as book publishers double down on print—even raising the price of e-books to make paper more attractive—the cost of printed newspapers is going up, not down. Publishers are watering down the lemonade and asking for more quarters. You don't have to be an economist to see this won't end well.

It's undoubtedly true that Americans read less print news year after year. In fairness to the digital gurus, I won't hide this fact: The number of print newspaper readers has been halved in the last 20 years. But what if the big decline in print readership has more to do with a lack of quality than a lack of interest? By cutting staff, eliminating sections, and moving up deadlines hours (further aging the news before it's delivered), publishers have communicated that print really is only useful for lining the bottoms of bird cages.

Corporate titans often say that you must be willing to sacrifice your best products to develop new and potentially bigger ones. Apple killed the iPod with the iPhone. We all know how that worked out. But what if newspapers are killing their iPod without an iPhone in sight?

Newspapers still get the vast majority of their revenue from print. Meanwhile, a growing number of online readers use ad blockers, less than 10 percent of readers are willing to pay for more content online, and the digital advertising business stinks—and not just because of the oversupply of ad space. In October, executives at The Guardian bought ads on their own website to see how much money they were left with after Google and the various ad auction companies took their cuts. The result? Thirty cents on the dollar. Given all this, you might think there would be some serious soul searching in the industry. You would be wrong.

Instead, there is evidence that publishers are ignoring the writing on their monitors. Chyi writes in her book that "a well-known newspaper association, which is supposed to inform its members with research relevant to the state of the industry, once declined to publish a research synopsis they invited me to write." In a letter explaining why, the group told her that because her findings showed that moving to digital might not be the best strategy for newspapers, the organization didn't want to share them with its members.

Fidler, Chyi, and others concerned about digital news aren't just worried about the future of journalism; they're worried about society. In recent years, a flurry of studies has shown that the reading experience online is less immersive and enjoyable than print, which has implications for how we consume and retain information. Studies show that readers tend to skim and jump around online more than they do in print—not just within individual stories, but from page to page and site to site. Print provides a more linear, less distracting way of reading, which in turn increases comprehension

"The cornerstone of democracy," Thomas Jefferson once wrote, "rests on the foundation of an educated electorate." But how educated can a society of skimmers really be? A 2013 study in the Newspaper Research Journal found that *Times* readers recalled more stories and specific details in print than they did online. The study's authors blamed the poor online results on distractions (ads, links, etc.) and fewer design cues about which articles were newsy and significant. The results are important, the study said, in elucidating "the modern role newspapers play in maintaining an informed citizenry." The electorate has never been fully informed, but that's typically by voter choice. Online news, the research says, could make it impossible to be informed—even for those who want to be.

In her book, Chyi quotes a study in which an unnamed newspaper publisher says, "Our website wouldn't exist if we didn't have the print edition, because it wouldn't make money." The publisher was then asked, "Would the print product exist without the online edition?" The publisher was a bit perplexed. "Now that's a good question," he said, "and one that I'm sure has occurred to everybody in our industry: 'What if we just didn't do it?' We are batting our heads against the wall. All the effort that is going into the website is hurting the print edition. Could we just not do it? I don't know."

At least one publisher is trying. Michael Gerber is not a scion of the Sulzberger family. He has never worked at a newspaper. He's a humor writer. Last year, he launched The American Bystander, a humor magazine publishing some of the biggest names in comedy writing, including George Meyer, the genius behind The Simpsons, and cartoonists such as Roz Chast. Gerber has a website, but there is no writing from the magazine on it. The site exists solely to let readers pay for printed copies, which are then mailed to them.

"If you put quality content online, you are tethering it to a business model that is cratering and dying," Gerber told me, adding that it's undeniable that "very, very few formerly print publications are better off now than they were prior to the Web."

The American Bystander is printed on thick paper and looks and feels substantial. The first two issues had more than 100 pages each. Gerber just raised nearly $40,000 for the magazine on Kickstarter. He gets the irony, but "[w]e are going for it," Gerber says. "We're going where everyone else isn't."

By that, he means paper. He's placing a bet on the future by choosing the past. "There's this assumption that online is inevitable, that it is like the steam engine or something," Gerber says. "Maybe it is. But maybe it's not. Maybe it can't be."

I logged into Kickstarter the other night and made a pledge.

MICHAEL ROSENWALD is a reporter at the *Washington Post*. He has also written for *The New Yorker, Esquire,* and *The Economist.*

EXPLORING THE ISSUE

Is There a Future for Digital Newspapers?

Critical Thinking and Reflection

1. Are the threats to print newspaper insurmountable?
2. Are the obstacles to adopting digital news insurmountable?
3. Can younger readers be lured into traditional news reading, whether print or digital?
4. What do you think will be the outcome of this issue in 20 years?

Is There Common Ground?

The stark contrast between digital or print editions ignores the possibility of publishers choosing to support both print and digital. Certainly, *The New York Times* is still printing their paper daily. They are, however, ready to move to a digital format if necessary. Most newspapers are operating in that dual state. One concern is that unlike the *Times* most publications are not deriving enough revenue from digital to even support that product, much less to move the entire enterprise to digital. Nonetheless, it is almost inevitable that producing both digital and print is the transitional state for most of the industry.

Rarely do small and middle-sized towns have the deep pockets of the *Times*. While the *Times* experiments may inform the future of many newspapers, there are few that have the capacity to create such an innovative product.

Finally, the answer to this issue may be "none of the above." There are many alternatives to newspapers in whatever form: from Breitbart to Facebook, Twitter, and Google and including others like the *Huffington Post*, *Buzz Feed*, and *Politico*. Also network and cable news poses alternative sources of information. What you will notice is that all of these are focused on national and international news. Rarely are local communities covered and that is almost always in a feature or during a disaster. One of the real challenges of moving away from local newspapers, whether digital or print, is that localism can be lost.

Additional Resources

Hsiang Iris Chyi and Ori Tenenboim, "Reality Check: Multiplatform newspaper readership in the United States, 2007–2015." *Journalism Practice* (September 2017).

The authors conduct a longitudinal analysis of 51 US newspapers' readership data from 2007 through 2015 to investigate the growth and potential of online readership in relation to reader habits and preferences.

Jim Rutenberg, "Yes the News Can Survive the Newspaper," *New York Times*, (Sept. 4, 2016) Retrieved at https://www.nytimes.com/2016/09/05/business/yes-the-news-can-survive-the-newspaper.html.

Based on the premise that the word "newspaper" no longer has meaning, the Newspaper Association of America is changing its name to the News Media Alliance. Additionally, "readers" are now being thought to be "viewers." These changes are addressed to help illuminate what this means for society.

David M. Ryfe, *Can Journalism Survive: An Inside Look at American Newsrooms*. Polity (2012)

Based on a number of visits to newsrooms and interviews with journalists, Ryfe discusses what digital platforms have done to the business of newsgathering and dissemination, and he examines the fiscal problems caused by migration to new platforms.

Internet References . . .

American Press Institute

https://www.americanpressinstitute.org/
publications/reports/digital-subscriptions-
future/

American Society of News Editors

asne.org

News Media Alliance

https://www.newsmediaalliance.org/about-us/

Pew Research Center: State of the News Media

http://www.pewresearch.org/topics/state-of-the-
news-media/

Selected, Edited, and with Issue Framing Material by:
Alison Alexander, *University of Georgia*
and
Jarice Hanson, *University of Massachusetts—Amherst*

ISSUE

Are Digital News Services Good for the News Business?

Yes: David Weinberger, from "The Rise, Fall, and Possible Rise of Open News Platforms: The Twisty Path towards a Net Ecosystem That Makes News More Discoverable, Reusable, and Relevant," Shorenstein Center on Media, Politics, and Public Policy (2015)

No: Jonathan Stray, from "The Age of the Cyborg," *Columbia Journalism Review* (2016)

Learning Outcomes

After reading this issue, you will be able to:

- Think about how news gathering is changing with the ability to share data and stories electronically.
- Consider whether news sharing sites that are based on algorithms "report" stories differently than individuals do.
- Imagine what the future of journalism might be as more open source news sharing sites are used to gather and report news.
- Think of how journalism has evolved and the drive for cheaper ways to gather and disseminate news quickly.
- Consider how the web increasingly drives what we know, and how we know it.

ISSUE SUMMARY

YES: When he was a Shorenstein Fellow at Harvard University, David Weinberger investigated the brief history and impact of open source news gathering and dissemination. His study of how open source architecture influenced the quality of news at National Public Radio, the *New York Times*, and *The Guardian*. Calling the system API (application programming interface), Weinberger examines the impact of sharing information with other media companies and individuals over the Internet. Though the systems started slowly, he is optimistic that in time most news gathering will be conducted with APIs.

NO: Jonathan Stray, a technology writer and teacher at Columbia Journalism School addresses the technologies and sharing sites as a more automated method of gathering and disseminating news and information. With artificial intelligence (AI) and algorithms that scour social media (like Twitter and Google), these "cyborg" technologies notice what is trending and what people are sharing. This type of topical news generation can result in stories and videos that are put together more quickly than a person could assemble the pieces for a finished story. However, Stray thinks that it will be a long time before AI can be effectively used to replace human journalists.

In recent years digital technologies have infiltrated the newsrooms of traditional, mainstream media organizations as well as social media platforms. One thing digital technologies can do is target specific individuals with news and information that is interesting to them alone. These types of news feeds (like Facebook's News Feed system) are culled from the frequency with which news stories are downloaded and shared, but the algorithm can also create an individualized News Feed just for you, based upon your browsing history and the number of stories and topics you "like" when you register your interest. As we wrote in the beginning of this book, we've gone a long way from "mass media" that distributed news and information to the "masses" to targeting individuals, groups of people who have common interests, and much more toward those who are likely to share information over social media. When we see news and information targeted to us, the news organization has streamlined the process so that we get the news and information we are most likely to read.

There is a term used to describe the micro-targeting of information to individuals and like-minded groups. They are called "engagement" stories (or "engagement ads") because they have the buzz words, or "hook" to attract your attention and involve you in the story. Sometimes that involvement is by asking you to repost to your group of friends, or to comment on the article, but the point is, we are more likely to respond to content that engages our attention and interest more than skimming a massive amount of information for the few stories or ads that appeal to us.

There are many commercial products that cull information for us and we sometimes refer to these groups as "news brokers." Each uses an algorithm to search multiple platforms for information you might like, and then package it for your attention. As Jonathan Stray writes, this is similar to having a robot or "bot" comb the news for you and prepare your news feed. Stray uses the generic name "cyborg" to impress upon us the meaning of artificially created stories, and he discusses the impact of artificial intelligence to search, package, deliver, and monetize the process of targeting individuals. While he is skeptical about the effective use of AI technology and claims it doesn't work well yet, he sees the future as a place where we will undoubtedly see more means of artificial intelligence doing what human journalists have always done in the past.

David Weinberger has charted the growth of APIs (application programming interfaces) that provide the basic programming for websites and applications to communicate with each other, no matter what platform is used. While there are both open source and proprietary APIs, Weinberger discusses the effectiveness and potential for open source sites to improve the quality of news in a timely manner. And because digital news depends on rapid response, he is optimistic that APIs will continue to be used for some of the best sites, especially if they continually tweak the algorithms as they master the ability

to share news across platforms in a very brief manner of time.

Undoubtedly, journalism and news organizations have to respond to new technologies all of the time, but we do know that the disruption of a process can create instability in the business. For example, due to new digital news services and applications, the news organizations lose any credibility they may have had in the past, in lieu of trying to respond to events quickly. Perhaps even more importantly for mainstream media, there is a loss of audience data that undermines advertising and revenue sharing. Some fear that in the interest of timely news, the rapid gathering of trending topics can hurt the veracity of news. For example, In March, 2017, a number of stories about Fox newscaster Megyn Kelly claimed she was fired from NBC before she even began her new job. The information turned out to be a hoax, but not until many news organizations published the information as though it were true. Likewise, within hours of a Las Vegas shooter's violent attack of concert-goers in October, 2017, conspiracy theories and hoaxes began to flood social media organizations, spreading misinformation about the shooter's motives, the number of people killed or wounded, and the possible number of additional shooters who were contributing to the melee.

As news businesses respond to newer techniques of gathering and sharing news, the importance of accurate news grows. We have seen how easy it is for fake news to be generated and perpetuated, but to be an informed citizenry, we need to have faith in the sources that we consult for important information that is critical to the public. In the future we may see labeling of unsubstantiated news, or mentions that the story has been "tagged" as problematic, but social media organizations are trying to find ways to let consumers know what is true, and what may be disputed. This is particularly difficult for them because many social media organizations were not founded to be news and information disseminators, but rather, social tools for connecting individuals for social reasons.

Mainstream media organizations have to take note of what is happening on multiple platforms, and they have to be as vigilant as possible to maintain their integrity. There are plenty of biased organizations that exist to try to influence news consumers and enhance their preconceived beliefs, but we know that despite people choosing sources that already confirm their belief system, news and information are vital to maintaining democracy. Undoubtedly, the plethora of digital technologies used for news consumption and those marketed for meeting the needs of news organizations to be fast, timely, and relevant may clash, but news organizations and consumers both have to take responsibility for what they contribute to the public.

Digital news services like those discussed by Weinberger and Stray are just some of the most recent interventions in the news business. Over time we can expect to see many more—particularly if they can be monetized and made more effective. What other changes might you expect in the future? For those of you hoping to have a career in journalism and media, the answers could very well influence your future career prospects.

YES ⤶

David Weinberger

The Rise, Fall, and Possible Rise of Open News Platforms: The Twisty Path towards a Net Ecosystem That Makes News More Discoverable, Reusable, and Relevant

A Failed Vision in Common

"It was a success in every dimension except the one we thought it would be." That's Daniel Jacobson's tweet-length summary of his experience opening up National Public Radio's vast resources to any software developer anywhere in the world who had a good—or bad—idea for an app that could use it. It's a tweet that could have been sent by other pioneers of open news platforms, including The New York Times and The Guardian, with the only difference that the Times' expectations were lower.

The vision was idealistic. Imagine any Internet site, service, or application that had even a passing interest in saying something reliable about what's happening easily getting the news it needed. Imagine a world in which news has an ever wider impact as clever software developers put it to work in ways the news organization itself would not have come up with, and could not have afforded to implement. The vision was humble as well, for it assumed that some of the best ideas for putting a news organization's stories to use would not come from that news organization itself.

So, in July 2008, NPR opened up its resources to external developers, followed by The New York Times in October of that year, and The Guardian in March 2009. And then the air went out of the vision. The Renaissance of News Apps became just another failed dream of cyber utopians.

They launched software platforms that used the most up-to-date industry standards. The platforms were constructed to be robust and reliable. Documentation and tools introduced external developers to the bounty. When the platforms were ready, press releases were emitted. The occasional "hackathon" was held at which developers were

given the space, time, and pizza required to slap together apps over the course of a weekend or even a single day. There was a flurry of enthusiastic articles in the technical press and conference presentations. These platforms embodied the Internet's best values.

Yet, the platform architects at NPR, The Guardian and The New York Times still use words like "transformative" and "revolutionary." But it's not the world that's been transformed. It's the news organizations themselves.

If these major news media outlets went down the platform path in large part to enable an Internet vision of an open information ecosystem, only to discover that these platforms are justified by straightforward business benefits, are there less utopian ways of achieving the utopian dream? Might there be ways of creating a far more open news environment on the Net by following business imperatives?

The Triumph of Abstraction

There is no single reason why 2008 was the year that three of the most important news organizations developed open platforms.

Facebook had done something similar in August 2006[2] when it permitted external developers to build applications that integrated with Facebook's data and services, creating everything from games that run within Facebook to apps that track users' vitamin intake.

Or perhaps having to bring news to the Internet in all the ways the Net demands simply broke the back of the news organizations' existing systems. Facebook's success was influential.

It was a long time coming. As early as 2001, NPR's Dan Jacobson had headed down the platform path, prompted by thinking, "How many more times are we going to redesign the site?"

By then, NPR.org was no longer just an adjunct to NPR's on-air programming. It was crucial that the site keep up with the cascade of new content types and services users demanded. For example, RSS4 was becoming the accepted standard for open content syndication, but RSS was undergoing rapid evolution, and soon spawned Atom, a competing standard. Then podcast versions of on-air stories become de rigueur, requiring new extensions to NPR program pages. In just a few years, the rise of smartphones would necessitate producing and syncing parallel sites where users expected to swipe, tap, pinch, and type with their on tiny fake keyboards displayed on small screens that can rotate from landscape to portrait.

The content management systems (CMS) used by all three news organizations were beginning to fray under the pressure. They were designed to manage the workflow of the production of content, and then to output it in a few relatively stable formats: a print version, an audio file, a website. But the Web ecosystem never slept and was placing a new premium on flexible and rapidly changing outputs. That required an approach that Jacobson and his colleague Rob Holt early on expressed as the COPE approach: Create Once, Publish Everywhere. Graham Tackley, a leader of the technical team at The Guardian, understates it when he says that by 2007, "We were beginning to face a number of scalability issues." The demands were increasing, and the riskiness of experimenting with solutions was rising: the team at The Guardian was worried that if something they tried went terribly wrong, it might break the CMS and slow down or even disable the organization's existing sites. Reaction to that would be swift and chilling. Concerns like these came to a head at NPR in 2007 when the network wanted to launch a cross-program site dedicated to music to be called, reasonably, NPR Music.

An abstraction layer hides the details of how a task is accomplished. Evan Sandhaus—director for search, archives, and semantics for the Times—explains it using a restaurant metaphor. A customer who wants a dish doesn't have to go into the kitchen and tell the chef to grate an ounce of cheddar cheese, beat two eggs with a tablespoon of milk, heat up a 9 inch pan, etc. Instead, the customer can simply ask for the cheese omelet that's on the menu. The menu provides a layer of abstraction.

"It was a very different user interface, different presentation, different assets associated with each piece," says Jacobson. It would have been relatively easy to extend the CMS to accommodate the new needs, but how about for the next new site? And the next? And the next? "It would

be better if we could create an abstraction layer that the site could draw from."

This makes life easier for the customer, but the systems benefit is at least as important. The restaurant can hire a new cook, replace the stove, switch food suppliers, or tinker with the recipe, and the customer can continue ordering the omelet without knowing or caring about what exactly is going on in the kitchen. The whole place runs more smoothly.

Rajiv Pant, the New York Times chief technology officer, gives a concrete example. Subscribers have to register to make it through the Times' pay wall, so the Times built a behind-the-scenes registration system that serves all the for-pay services the Times offers, on all the devices those services run on. Creating a new user registration system for each new service would be a waste of resources, and having to use a new system for each new service would frustrate subscribers. So in 2007 both NPR and the Times built APIs—application programming interfaces— to serve as their abstraction layers. Matt McAlister, who was in charge of The Guardian's API development, points to exactly the same benefits of putting an API on top of their CMS. Around 2007 their CMS was "very, very big" and complicated. His team wanted to ensure that the burgeoning applications and services would be stable, robust and very fast. They needed an API.

The API stands between an application and the information that application needs. A command like "Check the password the user just entered" is like "omelet" on a menu. The developer doesn't care how the user registration system actually does that check. The people maintaining the registration system could change which database they're using—which in fact was one of the considerations that drove NPR to put an abstraction layer in place—and the app developer wouldn't have to change a single line of code. The "Check this password" command to the API will continue to work without a hiccup.

APIs have been around for decades, but modern APIs tend to have two distinctive features. First, they don't talk directly to the CMS (or other database application) but to a full text index of the content of the CMS. A full text index serves the same purpose as the index at the back of a book: rather than requiring the reader to skim through all the text every time she wants to find where the book talks about some topic, the book's index provides a "precomputed" tool for rapidly looking but modern APIs.

An online full text index lets the API operate at Google-like speeds and adds some flexibility in the sorts of requests it can field.

But it is from the second distinctive characteristic of modern APIs that the vision of an open news ecosystem arose: The APIs adopted by NPR, the Times and The Guardian, as well as many other content-producing organizations, use the Web as the medium for sending requests for data and for receiving data back. This means that you can think of a typical modern API as a website designed to be accessed not by humans looking for pages, but by computer applications looking for data. So, without much work, the set of clever developers doing good things with news media content could be expanded to any developer with an Internet connection.

Why not?

The Open Impulse

NPR's Jacobson says "We built an API for the music site, and then thought about having all our news sites draw from the same API." That thought led immediately to another: "If we have this API, it's a relatively small step to get it to be public." It would hardly be rocket science. They'd have to provide an automated way of issuing ID codes, called "keys," that developers can insert in their API requests so that there is a modicum of protection against miscreants. They might also want to set reasonable limits on how many requests per second and per day would be permitted. And they'd have to decide which information they would give access to. Licensing issues and concerns about constraining misuse can make content problematic, but information about the content—metadata—generally is not. Jacobson says that the biggest technical challenge was "making sure we had content tagged with correct rights information and then have the API be smart enough to prune or modify the content that hit certain rights issues."

But why go to even that much trouble?

The three organizations had overlapping reasons for putting up public APIs. "NPR has a public service mission," explains Jacobson. Graham Tackley, The Guardian's director of architecture, also points to the corporate mission, saying that the creation of APIs in the first place was prompted by the organization's commitment to the sort of collaborative sharing the Web enables. "Our editor-in-chief Alan Rusbridger absolutely believes that...engaging with other people on the Web is an important part of being a news organization."

Rajiv Pant at the Times makes the same point: creating public APIs "lets others build and benefit from what we do," which is "consistent with the New York Times mission—it's good not only for our company but for society overall." But Pant's hopes were never high: "We did external APIs in part because it's the right thing to do," without expecting it would spur all that much development.

By 2008 the Times had been using APIs internally for over a year. But Tackley says "The [Guardian's] initial creation of the content API was about enabling other people to access our content and do interesting things with it." Likewise at NPR, Daniel Jacobson recalls, "If you look at the article and interviews from the time, the quotes were about us being really excited about the magic that would be developed by people in their garages."

Behind this a set of cultural values was at work. In July 2008, Wired.com ran an interview with Derek Gottfrid of the Times and NPR's Jacobson in which Gottfrid makes this explicit:

> We're geared to whoever is going to find the content interesting. Anyone that's interested in it, we're interested in making it accessible and having them use it. This isn't something that's driven off of market research or anything like that. This is fulfilling a basic gut-level instinct that this is how the internet works.

McAlister had come to The Guardian from Yahoo! and the Silicon Valley where building "open APIs seemed like the right thing to do." But he found that it wasn't as obvious to a news organization. The Guardian under Rusbridger's leadership was willing to listen, "but there needed to be at least an understandable benefit to it. That took a lot of work," he says, "and a lot of slides showing the value of openness.

One slide McAlister used in many meetings laid out the most basic dynamic: "While we were in an unsustainable decline in print, there was strong growth in digital, but not enough to put The Guardian or any media organization back into a position as strong as before the decline of print."

Therefore, McAlister urged, "media organizations needed to extend beyond their domain to grow, and to be present in all the places that readers are." Some of those extensions would be built by The Guardian, using their API as their way to connect their own apps to their own data. But some would be built by developers outside of The Guardian. "The open innovation pitch was an important part of this," he says, "but a little harder to justify."

As a result, all three organizations opened up public APIs within months of each other. Javaun Moradi, a product manager at NPR at the time, recalls: "The 2008 conventional wisdom on APIs was that it would let a thousand flowers bloom. People in our community would rise up and build mashups that we couldn't even imagine."

Sure enough, the community of developers responded. Wanly.

Moradi remembers a visual app that displayed a "globe that spun that popped up stories from around the world." People wrote some syndication apps that made it easier to distribute NPR stories. McAlister recalls that there were about fifty apps from independent developers in The Guardian's gallery. For example, GoalRun.com integrated Guardian content into its niche football websites. There were some interesting political sites, too, he says, including one that used Guardian political data "to create an index to understand how powerful your vote is, given the strength of the political parties in your area." Joe Fiore, Manager of Technology at the Times, recalls an app a high school history teacher wrote that's like a fantasy football league except you draft countries, not players. "Any time one of your players is mentioned in the New York Times, you get a point."

It was thrilling when developers built permission-free apps. Moradi says, "We got a call saying there's an NPR app in the iTunes store that isn't ours. We used that gentleman's name for years as a shorthand for when someone disrupts you with the technology you invented." He adds, "It was meant as the highest possible praise."

So, a lot of excitement and some excellent examples. But, after an initial spurt, growth flattened. Development of the public APIs and of the supporting documentation and tools slowed at all three organizations.

But that is far from the end of the story. Jacobson points to the iTunes app that Moradi referred to: "We learned about it because all of a sudden we saw a lot of traffic coming from a single app. You could navigate through our topics and programs to listen to our stories. I think the app was downloaded somewhere around 500,000 times. It told us that the iPhone was a really important space. It gave us a kick in the pants"—a prod for NPR itself to develop for the iPhone. "The public developers have been fine historically," Jacobson concludes, but "it wasn't transformative in the way we expected. It was hugely successful in letting us see the internal uses."

The Indoor API

If the external story is one of disappointment, the internal story is about exceeding expectations.

NPR and The Guardian tell matching accounts about the moment they understood the value that APIs could bring to their organizations. On January 27, 2010, Steve Jobs introduced the first iPad at one of his trademark on-stage demos. According to Jacobson, three weeks earlier NPR had received a call from Apple inviting them to

participate in the launch by showing off an NPR app for this first-of-its-kind piece of hardware. Three weeks later, NPR had a native iPad app ready for the launch. In fact, in those three weeks it also produced an app for the Safari Web browser—"Different technologies leveraging the same API infrastructure," Jacobson says.

McAlister says The Guardian got a similar call and was just as eager to share in the excitement. Five or six weeks later The Guardian had an app for the iPad.21 Typically when developing software of this sort, there will be a team working on the data the app will use (the back end) and another team working on how the Without an API, development time would have taken months. Moradi explains, "Having the API meant we already had all the technical problems about getting content solved. We spent the few weeks we had designing the user experience and coding the app."

An API enables the front end developers to work independently of the back end team. They can try out an interface, tweak it, implement a new idea for a feature, drop it or change it, all without ever asking for anything from the back end folks.

"No way we could have gotten that done without an API," says Jacobson. McAlister agrees. "We worked hard to be in their inner circle as a launch partner," he says. "Because we had the API we knew we'd be able to build something amazing quickly." The app they built, EyeWitness, In September 2014 The Guardian announced it was no longer supporting the EyeWitness app because that functionality had been rolled into a new suite of apps. provided access to the hundred most recent photos in their EyeWitness series, along with "pro tips" from The Guardian's team. In the end, "Jobs hauled it on stage" at the launch. The claims of the early adopters that their APIs were "transformative" and "revolutionary" are supported by the range of overlapping benefits they have brought to their organizations:

That's a good run for an app, especially one created so quickly. And it's an unqualified success story for the Guardian API, since the new suite that obviated the EyeWitness app uses that API as well..

In September 2011, The Guardian decided to bring the news to social media, announcing on its blog that the Guardian Facebook app would enable "Facebook users to read and experience Guardian content without leaving Facebook." If you clicked on a link within the app, the Guardian's content would be shown on a Facebook page so you can see "what your friends are also reading from the Guardian…"

In December of the following year, the success of the new direction motivated The Guardian to tack. As the announcement on the company's blog said:

> In the months following the launch, we saw tremendous volumes of traffic being generated by the app. Over 12 million Facebook users have authenticated the Guardian Facebook app since launch, and at its peak (April 2012) we were seeing 6 million active monthly users.

With that many users, The Guardian decided they'd rather have clicks take users to the articles on The Guardian site, rather than defaulting to embedding the article into Facebook pages. "The Facebook app has given us access to a hard to reach audience and has helped us learn much more about our new and existing readership which, as a digital first organisation, is crucial," says the blog post. No mention is made of the increase in ad revenue the switch would bring.

Jacobson cities NPR's own evidence of the effect an API can have on traffic:

> Around 2009–2010 there was a one year stretch in which traffic to all of NPR's traffic increased 100%. Eighty-five percent was due to the platform development by the API. That tells a powerful story about the power of APIs.

The use of persistent, unique identifiers for the things that news articles talk about enables information from all around the Web to cluster. We can discover more and more about the things the news cares about. The contribution of news media to our knowledge of those things then becomes part of our web of knowledge, discussion, and understanding. And, not so incidentally, the news articles about those things are more discoverable, including by people who didn't know they were interested in them.

A computer that sees metadata on two separate Web pages that both link to the same Wikipedia page can be quite confident that they're talking about the same thing. Additional sources are emerging for linking to disambiguated people, places, and things.

Conclusion: Utopia Redux?

With interoperability, we may get to something like the failed utopia but for pragmatic, non-altruistic reasons.

News media's internal APIs have succeeded beyond expectation because they make the content development and distribution processes far more resilient, lower the cost of building and maintaining sites, provide more granular access to content, enable experimentation, and are the backbone of powerful strategic partnerships.

Interoperable content from multiple news media can be treated computationally as a single distributed database representing many views on the events of our times. It can be traversed by algorithms looking for latent connections. It can be made more traversable by incorporating the latent meanings discovered by human beings.

This brings us significantly closer to what in clickbait fashion we might call "The News Singularity" in which news is undammed and forms an ocean of information, ideas, and human expression ever richer with meaning. Such an ocean opens far more opportunities for synthesizing value than any one news source ever could, even three as august as NPR, The New York Times, and The Guardian.

The rise of internal APIs brings us one step closer. The experiences of the three major news organizations we've looked at proves the business benefits of APIs. Once in place, reconfiguring them for external access is not a significant problem. Making the business decision to do so is a far greater obstacle, since it involves a leap of faith (Will anyone develop anything worthwhile?), a risk (Will our content be ripped off or abused?), and a commitment to some level of support for developers (How much technical help and community development are we signing up for?).

It is probable, indeed likely, that news media will continue to see public APIs as an investment that brings them too little direct benefit. The industry's experience may convince the news media that there is no real demand for public APIs: they built them in 2008 and few came.

But the technical barriers are lower than ever and conceivably go as low as altering a few lines in a configuration file. The benefits might increase if enough news media open up public APIs creating a critical mass of content and metadata. Perhaps most important, as the news media become ever more concerned that their "product" is under-valued on the Net—the kids don't read newspapers, Facebook is filtering out news stories—they could view the development of an open ecosystem of news as an environmental concern. By opening up portions of their internal APIs for public access and making their stories interoperable, news media could create a deep, rich, and lively resource that would enable the engine of the Internet to engage with that content, making the news an irreplaceable component of the infrastructure of the Net.

David Weinberger was a Joan Shorenstein Fellow and senior researcher at Harvard's Berkman Center, in Spring, 2015.

Jonathan Stray   **NO**

The Age of the Cyborg

Fall/Winter 2016

You've probably heard that news organizations such as AP, Reuters, and many others are now turning out thousands of automated stories a month. It's a dramatic development, but today's story-writing bots are little more than Mad Libs, filling out stock phrases with numbers from earnings reports or box scores. And there's good reason to believe that fully automated journalism is going to be very limited for a long time.

At the same time, quietly and without the fanfare of their robot cousins, the cyborgs are coming to journalism. And they're going to win, because they can do things that neither people nor programs can do alone.

Apple's Siri can schedule my appointments, Amazon's Alexa can recommend music, and IBM's Watson can answer Jeopardy questions. I want interactive AI for journalism too: an intelligent personal assistant to extend my reach. I want to analyze superhuman amounts of information, respond to breaking news with lightning reflexes, and have the machine write not the last draft, but the first. In short, I want technology to make me a faster, better, smarter reporter.

Let's call this technology Izzy, after the legendary American muckraker I. F. Stone, who found many of his stories buried in government records. We could build Izzy today, using voice recognition to drive a variety of emerging journalism technologies. Already, computers are watching social media with a breadth and speed no human could match, looking for breaking news. They are scanning data and documents to make connections on complex investigative projects. They are tracking the spread of falsehoods and evaluating the truth of statistical claims. And they are turning video scripts into instant rough cuts for human review.

"This is a speed game, clearly, because that's what the financial markets are looking for," says Reg Chua, executive editor for data and innovation at Reuters. Reuters produced its first automated stories in 2001, publishing computer-generated headlines based on the American Petroleum Institute's weekly report. That report contains key oil production figures closely watched by energy traders who need new information as fast as possible, certainly faster than their competitors. Automation is a no-brainer when seconds count. Today, the news organization produces automated stories from all kinds of corporate and government data, something like 8,000 automated items a day, in multiple languages.

Automated systems can report a figure, but they can't yet say what it means; on their own, computer-generated stories contain no context, no analysis of trends, anomalies, and deeper forces at work. Reuters's newest technology goes deeper, but with human help: It still writes words, but isn't meant to publish stories on its own. Reuters's "automation for insights" system, currently under development, summarizes interesting events in financial data and alerts journalists. Instead of supplying what Chua calls "the headline numbers—the index was at this number, up/down from yesterday's close," the machine surfaces "more sophisticated analyses, the biggest rise since whenever, that sort of thing."

The system could look for changes in analysts' ratings, unusually good or bad performance compared to other companies in the same industry, or company insiders who have recently sold stock. Rather than being a sentence generator, it's meant to "flag journalists to things that might be of interest to them," says Chua, "helpfully done in the form of a sentence."

But not all breaking news comes through financial data feeds, so Reuters's most sophisticated piece of automation finds news by analyzing social media. Internal research showed that something like 10 or 20 percent of news breaks first on Twitter, so the company decided to monitor Twitter. All of it.

At the end of 2014, Reuters started a project called News Tracer. The system analyzes every tweet in real time—all 500 million or so each day. First it filters out spam and advertising. Then it finds similar tweets on the same topic, groups them into "clusters," and assigns each a topic such as business, politics, or sports. Finally it uses natural language processing techniques to generate a readable summary of each cluster.

There have been social media monitoring systems before, mostly built for marketing and finance professionals. DataMinr is a powerful commercial platform that also ingests every tweet, and there's quite a bit of overlap with Reuters's internal tool, which is good news for journalists who don't work at Reuters. But News Tracer was built from the ground up for reporters, and perhaps what most distinguishes it are the "veracity" and "newsworthiness" ratings it assigns to each cluster.

Newsroom standards are rarely formal enough to turn into code. How many independent sources do you need before you're willing to run a story? And which sources are trustworthy? For what type of story? "The interesting exercise when you start moving to machines is you have to start codifying this," says Chua. Much like trying to program ethics for self-driving cars, it's an exercise in turning implicit judgments into clear instructions.

News Tracer assigns a credibility score based on the sorts of factors a human would look at, including the location and identity of the original poster, whether he or she is a verified user, how the tweet is propagating through the social network, and whether other people are confirming or denying the information. Crucially, Tracer checks tweets against an internal "knowledge base" of reliable sources. Here, human judgment combines with algorithmic intelligence: Reporters handpick trusted seed accounts, and the computer analyzes who they follow and retweet to find related accounts that might also be reliable.

"A bomb goes off in a certain place, and then ultimately the verified account of that police station says, or the mayor's office says, or the verified account of the White House says," explains Chua. If Reuters has that, it might be ready to run the story, and a reporter should know it.

News Tracer also must decide whether a tweet cluster is "news," or merely a popular hashtag. To build the system, Reuters engineers took a set of output tweet clusters and checked whether the newsroom did in fact write a story about each event—or whether the reporters would have written a story, if they had known about it. In this way, they assembled a training set of newsworthy events. Engineers also monitored the Twitter accounts of respected journalists, and others like @BreakingNews, which tweets early alerts about verified stories. All this became training data for a machine-learning approach to newsworthiness. Reuters "taught" News Tracer what journalists want to see.

The results so far are impressive. Tracer detected the bombing of hospitals in Aleppo and the terror attacks in Nice and Brussels well before they were reported by other media. Chua estimates the tool enabled Reuters to begin its reporting eight to 60 minutes ahead of the competition, a serious head start.

For Chua, the significance of Tracer is not just what the machine can do, but what it frees reporters to spend more time doing: "Talk to people, pose questions that haven't been posed before, make leaps of insight that machines don't do as well."

It's tempting to ask our hypothetical reporter AI to work on its own. "Izzy, investigate this data," we'd want to say, but it will be a long time before a computer can write anything but the most formulaic stories by itself.

In 2012, Michael Sedlmair, an assistant professor in the Visualization and Data Analysis Group at the University of Vienna, co-published a paper that helps explain why so many things are so hard for computers to do.

"The problem is the problem," says Sedlmair. "The underlying assumption behind automatic approaches is that the problem is well defined. In other words, we know exactly what the task is and have all the data available to solve the problem."

Sedlmair sorts problems on a diagram with two axes. The first axis is task clarity, meaning how well defined the problem is. Buying a train ticket, deciding whether an email is spam, or checking whether someone's name appears in a database are clear problems with clear solutions.

But lots of really interesting problems—including most of those posed by journalism—are not at all clear. There's no one-size-fits-all recipe for doing research, following a hunch, or seeing a story in the data. As Sedlmair puts it, "there is no single optimal solution to these problems."

What if a computer could monitor every word uttered by politicians and media alike, to trace the genesis and spread of falsehoods?

The other axis represents the location of the information needed to solve the problem. Computer scientists frequently assume that all necessary information is already stored in the computer as data, but this is rarely true in journalism. "To fulfill certain tasks, data often needs to be combined with information that is not computerized but still 'locked' in people's heads," says Sedlmair.

Consider the *Wall Street Journal* story that revealed EMC Corporation's CEO routinely used company jets to fly to his vacation homes. This came from analysis of FAA flight records, but the data is not a story until you combine it with some additional information, namely, the locations of the CEO's vacation homes, and the fact that he's not supposed to be using these jets for personal travel. That information was in the reporter's head, perhaps gleaned from interviews or late nights spent reading disclosure documents. There will never be an algorithm that can find this story—and many others that might be lurking there—from FAA data alone, for the simple reason that identifying the suspicious flight pattern requires information that is not in the data.

"Fully automatic solutions are good when the task is clear and we have all, or at least most of the necessary information to solve this task available on our computer," says Sedlmair. For everything else—for most of journalism—we need human-machine cooperation.

Instead of asking computers to do human work, we must learn to meet them in the middle, breaking our reporting work into relatively concrete, self-contained tasks. Fortunately, that's still extraordinarily useful.

'Izzy, make a rough cut.'

Just as computers have found a niche producing automated stories from data, journalists are already using software to cut stock footage together. In goes the script, out comes an edit.

Israeli startup Wibbitz began with the idea of creating a "personal video newscaster." In 2013 it launched an app that pulled articles from a variety of news sources, cut the text down to video script length, and read the stories in a synthesized voice accompanied by computer-selected images. The company has since added human curators and voice actors, and focused more on helping publishers produce their own videos quickly.

"What we've created in Wibbitz is a technology that can automate the majority of the production process," says co-founder and CEO Zohar Dayan. The majority, not the entirety.

Wibbitz turns text articles into video rough cuts. First it creates a script by using natural language processing techniques to select key sentences. That is, the computer doesn't actually write anything, it just edits the human to length. Then it scans the text for "entities," which include people and companies, but also things like sports leagues and notable events. It assembles a video by searching for footage of those entities in licensed sources such as Getty Images and Reuters, or the publisher's own archives. These repositories, with their carefully tagged images and videos, are the critical data source that underlies the intelligence.

The point is scalable video production, which sits squarely in the digital media zeitgeist. Wibbitz is one of a few computer-assisted video companies currently selling to media organizations, the other major one being Wochit.

"I could make a 35- to 40-second video, cradle to grave, in probably seven to 10 minutes," says Neal Coolong, a senior editor for USA Today's network of NFL sports sites. He supervises four people whose primary task is making videos with Wibbitz, each producing six or seven per day. All told, they add a video to about one in 10

articles published on the network. The videos are designed for sound-off viewing on phones and social media, with subtitles instead of narration.

Yet Wibbitz's value may be more about workflow and less about sophisticated AI. Coolong prefers writing the video scripts himself to using the auto-summarization feature, and finds that the computer doesn't always choose the best images. "For me there's a certain way that I want to have it," says Coolong, noting that Wibbitz does better with straight news writing, while his team more often does opinion pieces.

To get a feel for Wibbitz's level of intelligence, I asked Dayan to demonstrate the system starting with a recent article on EpiPen price hikes. He copied five paragraphs of text from the story, from which the system generated a 94-second video in moments. It consisted entirely of similar shots of EpiPen manufacturer Mylan's CEO, mostly taken from the same interview, plus one image of the Capitol building to go with a mention of attention from Congress. We were able to include shots of the product itself by searching for "EpiPen" within the editing interface.

Dayan says Wibbitz works best when the story is about popular people and things, suggesting that EpiPen price hikes are a bit niche. But he notes that the system learns from its users. During the Olympics, the system learned about previously obscure athletes because they were mentioned in articles processed by the platform. Knowing that Conor Dwyer is an American swimmer in the men's 200-meter freestyle lets the computer pull up related swimming photos even if the script never says "swimming." "The more content flows through the system, the smarter it gets, the better it knows how to make connection between certain types of things," says Dayan. There's the importance of data to train the computer, again.

Coolong believes that automatically generated videos will augment, not replace, traditional video production at USA Today. "We don't have a TV crew on standby waiting for breaking news," he notes. When the Colin Kaepernick story broke, for instance, Wibbitz allowed Coolong's team to produce a video much more quickly than the couple hours it would have taken a human being to write up a script and shoot it. The big drawback of automated systems, of course, is that they can only use footage that has already been shot.

The titans of AI have so far ignored reporters. Google is working on self-driving cars, image understanding, and health applications. IBM's Watson division has invested $1 billion in "cognitive computing" in the hope of selling software to practitioners of law, medicine, marketing, and intelligence. Journalism doesn't make the list; it simply isn't a big enough market.

But a few people are building AI for journalism anyway, or at least the component parts. I've described a few major examples, but dozens of simpler systems operate throughout journalism: alert systems that watch for court filings; automated campaign finance monitoring; and all manner of single-purpose bots that write stories about earthquakes or stock prices or crime waves.

We could build Izzy today. The pieces exist. With commercial voice recognition technology, we could tie them together to create a powerful reporter's assistant, the other half of a human-plus-machine journalism team. What we're lacking is a place to integrate all the features that journalist-programmers are already creating for their own work, and all the data they're able to share. Without such a platform, newsroom developers' work will remain fragmented.

Inspiration for Izzy might come from bots like Amazon's Alexa, which can be upgraded by installing "skills." Reporters should be able to add "organized crime" or "campaign finance" or "seismic monitoring" skills. And perhaps before long, we will. The individual skills are being worked out by innovative news organizations, one story at a time.

AI is definitely coming to journalism, but perhaps not the way you might have imagined. It will be a long time before a machine beats humans at reporting, but reporters augmented with intelligent software—cyborg reporters—have already pushed past the ancient limitations of a single human brain.

(FORMERLY IPYTHON NOTEBOOK) is the data scientist's fairytale come true: an interactive journal where you can mix notes and code, with the computer drawing the charts and filling in the tables automatically. Journalists use a lot of different software for data analysis, everything from traditional spreadsheets to specialized tools like the R programming language. Doing a story has always involved an awkward dance, going back and forth between different programs, struggling to keep track of multiple versions. No more. Doing an entire project in a single notebook fills me with delight. I end up with a step-by-step journal of my analysis and visualization work, complete with all my sketches and experiments. It's intuitive to use, easy to dig up later when new data comes in, and you can publish the whole thing online, a godsend for journalistic transparency.

JONATHAN STRAY is a research scholar at Columbia Journalism School. He has written about technology and journalism for the *New York Times*, *Associated Press*, *Foreign Policy*, *ProPublica*, and *Wired* Magazine.

EXPLORING THE ISSUE

Are Digital News Services Good for the News Business?

Critical Thinking and Reflection

1. Given the problems with the cost of newsgathering and the current controversy over "fake news," do you expect news organizations to continue to seek automated methods of news gathering and news sharing?
2. How would the economics of news organizations change with increased reliance on open source, data-driven news?
3. Can you think of other new technologies that have dramatically changed the way news organizations do business?
4. Can machines, AI, and open architecture emulate objectivity in news gathering?
5. If all stories (or most stories) could be gathered using machine intelligence, what is the future of journalism and the journalistic profession?

Is There Common Ground?

Journalism has always adapted to new technologies, though sometimes the transition to multiplatform news and changing audience news consumption has shaken the foundation of many media and news organizations. Business models have had to change and those changes have not always been easy. These two authors provide us with very recent methods of news gathering that will undoubtedly change the way journalist gather news, and the way stories are generated.

Both of the authors discuss how news organizations will change internally, and dynamically, but they differ on which organizations might make the most successful transition to using algorithms and artificial intelligence to gather topics and produce quality news that has the traditional values we have come to expect. Based on the experiences of different news organizations that have experimented with the methods Weinberger and Stray discuss, we might expect other organizations to have a wide range of experiences once they delve more deeply into using the technologies and methods discussed by these authors.

Both authors take the position that change in news organizations is inevitable, but they differ on when we might expect to see agencies roll out new processes and products that influence what we know, and how we know it.

Additional Resources

Klint Finley, "In the Future, Robots Will Write News That's All About You," *Wired* Magazine, March 6, 2015.

Finley provides information on a data-driven program (API) that combs data that is specifically targeted for a particular audience. If this process is widely adopted, we can expect to see individually-targeted news feeds.

Mario Haim and Andreas Graefe, "Automated News: Better Than Expected?" *Digital Journalism*, 5, 2017, pp. 1044-1059.

In this study, the authors had people read news stories that were written by human journalists, and automated stories. People found the stories written by humans to be more readable and interesting, but stories created through automation, more credible.

Joe Keohane, "What News-Writing Bots Mean for the Future of Journalism," *Wired* Magazine, February 16, 2017.

In this article, Keohane discusses how APIs generate news stories without much human intervention. He sees this move as a way to provide information on a wider range of topics, but that would appeal to a broader group of news consumers who prefer short news stories that appeal to their own interests.

Adrienne LaFrance, "A Computer Tried (and Failed) to Write This Article," *The Atlantic*, June 8, 2016.

In this humorous account of the author trying to have a computer glean information from her past articles to write this article, LaFrance demonstrates that at times a computer can generate gibberish, and that only a human can make logical connections to develop a story.

Internet References . . .

American Press Institute, *How Millennials Get News: Inside the Habits of America's First Digital Generation*, March 16, 2015.

https://www.americanpressinstitute.org/publications/reports/survey-research/millennials-news/

Emily Bell and Taylor Owen, "The Platform Press: How Silicon Valley Reengineered Journalism," Tow Center for Digital Journalism, March 29, 2017.

https://towcenter.org/research/the-platform-press-how-silicon-valley-reengineered-journalism/

April Glaser, "Google Is Funding A New Software Project that Will Automate Writing Local News," Recode, July 7, 2017.

https://www.recode.net/2017/7/7/15937436/google-news-media-robots-automate-writing-local-news-stories

Tom Rosenstiel, "The Future of Journalism," TEDx Talks Atlanta, May 28, 2013

https://www.youtube.com/watch?v=RuBE_dP900Y

Wendell Santos, 81 News APIs: Digg, FanFeedr and ClearForest, ProgrammableWeb, February 1, 2012,

https://www.programmableweb.com/news/81-news-apis-digg-fanfeedr-and-clearforest/2012/02/01

Unit 6

UNIT

Life in the Digital Age

*P*redictions of a world that is increasingly reliant upon media and communication technologies have generally provided either utopian or dystopian visions about what our lives will be like in the future. New media distribution technologies present new options for traditional ways of doing things. Not too many years ago, people were talking about the possibility of an information superhighway. Today, people talk about Facebook, Twitter, and Instagram. Although we are still learning how electronic communication may change our lives and the ways in which we work and communicate, many questions have not changed. Will new ways of communication change the way individuals interact? In an era in which the Internet and web seemingly offer boundless information, will we lose those repositories of information that preceded them? Perhaps most importantly, will the First Amendment survive current attacks on freedom of the press in the United States and elsewhere?

Selected, Edited, and with Issue Framing Material by:
Alison Alexander, *University of Georgia*
and
Jarice Hanson, *University of Massachusetts—Amherst*

ISSUE

Can Digital Libraries Replace Traditional Libraries?

YES: Robert Darnton, from "A World Digital Library Is Coming True!" *The New York Review of Books* (2014)

NO: Jill Lepore, from "The Cobweb: Can the Internet Be Archived?," *The New Yorker* (2015)

Learning Outcomes

After reading this issue, you will be able to:

- Think about the future of information access and the number of forms it could take.
- Evaluate whether the traditional model of publication and the dissemination of research is viable.
- Consider the options for digital storage of material; the lifespan of e-content; and how we may need to develop new search strategies.
- Think about the role of the library as a place for learning and as a community resource.
- Reflect on what it means when valuable information is not appropriately stored for future generations.

ISSUE SUMMARY

YES: Harvard University Library Director Robert Darnton suggests that a new model of publishing scholarly work may need to be created to preserve ideas in electronic form. The traditional library, he says, relies on a financial model that is no longer sustainable. The result, he suggests, is to continue to convert scholarly research to digital data and for libraries to specialize and cooperate in their lending processes.

NO: Historian and Harvard University Professor Jill Lepore examines the efforts to collect digital information—particularly websites—through the Internet Archive, but provides frightening data on how incomplete the archive of digital data is, why that happens, and what consequences occur because of incomplete records of digital data.

Electronic repositories of information are libraries of a sort, but the traditional library, complete with books, stacks, periodicals for browsing, and reference books for consultation, may be changing. The ability to convert print into electronic form is revolutionizing the publishing industries, and nowhere is this more important than in academic and scholarly libraries, where new ideas are collected and preserved for anyone to consult. The basis of the traditional "borrowing" library is that of making work available to all. And yet, as business models of academic (and popular) publishing begin to favor the lower cost of electronic publishing, we fear that something may be lost. Whether it is the joy of coming across something you didn't expect as you peruse the stacks in a library, or the ease of access in what appears to be a World Wide Web of "everything"—we know there are situations in which information we suspect is out there, but just may not be found. Whether we don't use the right keywords to access what we want, we experience "click fatigue" and give up, or whether the information is buried or has been dumped, information access and information availability is changing.

According to the Director of the Harvard Library, Robert Darnton, we only need to look at the high cost of producing academic journals to understand that the budgets of traditional libraries can't keep pace. It is more cost-effective to change the model of publishing so that specialized libraries are in charge of types of information, and that trained librarians become sleuths to help us find what we're looking for. In this article, Darnton discusses the role of academic publishing and suggests that a new model would be for the author to pay for publishing, and then later, after the initial period of time has passed, the work become that of public domain in a more open system. While students may not realize this, many colleges and universities have a "publish or perish" culture in which faculty members must, by contract, continue to do research that adds to general knowledge. In these "publish or perish" institutions, the quality of the journals in which you publish (i.e., the quality of the peer-reviewed journals) is often the arbiter of solid, quality work. But the cost for libraries to subscribe to the many academic journals is a problem for budgets, and therefore, Darnton envisions a different model for the dissemination of scholarly work and a different structure for institutions (like libraries) to access that information.

On the other hand, Jill Lepore investigates the *Internet Archive*, an electronic library of Web-based information that references a significant amount of the Web, but not all of it. In examining the evolution of the *Archive*, she shows how much digital information has already been lost and what the implications are for original material that was published in electronic form. Her evaluation of the content of the *Archive* is frighteningly inaccurate and incomplete, despite the best efforts of the staff of the Internet Archive to be as thorough as they can be with information that proliferates at such incredible speed.

The publishing industry is experiencing a shift in the way it does business in the same way the recording industry has already experienced a revolution in the way it records and distributes music. Scholarly libraries are specifically concerned with material that chronicles our history and culture, but even the popular press is not immune to shifting to an electronic form. Project Gutenberg is the oldest digital library of public domain books (those for which a copyright is not active) and already has made more than 50,000 items available to the public at no charge.

Once the digitization of books and periodicals became technologically possible, the number of ways people read information also began to shift. Certainly electronic text that is available online can be read on any computer or smartphone, but electronic copies of both popular and scholarly books can be downloaded to any number of tablets or electronic reading devices. Amazon is a commercial company that has benefitted greatly from electronic books, in part because it started as an online bookstore that easily had a distribution system in place for the browsing, ordering, and financial aspects of delivering traditional books to readers, but also because it marketed the Kindle reader, which encouraged users to request the electronic form of the book. The portability of the e-reader is a valuable feature for the casual reader, but it doesn't necessarily serve the purpose of someone who is conducting research and engaging with electronic text for that reason.

The term *information literacy* is increasingly being used with regard to the way users of electronic text evaluate the credibility of the author and the statements being made. With today's technology, the writer of a blog can produce and "publish" content on the Web that looks so professionally produced that the reader may have a hard time separating fact from opinion. The proliferation of opinions online makes it more difficult for people to weigh the merits of an argument. Often, when people search for information online they look for something that confirms their own belief system, and think, therefore, that what they are reading is proof of their own preconceived notions. What this means, though, is that the more we recognize the potential for electronic text to mislead, or provide opinion rather than fact, the more we need some arbiters of judgment.

We should also remember that libraries in communities also serve a special function. Often they are the community centers for people. Not only are books and popular periodicals available, many libraries serve important social functions too. Literacy programs, locations for voting, discussion groups for people who like to talk about current events, literature, or any subject really, often take place in the cultural center that is the traditional library.

As you think about the issues raised by these authors, you might want to think about the range of libraries and the way they function in a number of contexts. From the academic library to the local public library, we've formed certain expectations of what the institution does, and what it means in our lives. Will the shift to more digital distribution of information radically change our concept of the library? Will traditional libraries be able to continue to exist and offer services to the public? Like other industries and institutions in the midst of technological change, the library is likely to undergo change. How important might those changes be?

YES ←

Robert Darnton

A World Digital Library Is Coming True!

In the scramble to gain market share in cyberspace, something is getting lost: the public interest. Libraries and laboratories—crucial nodes of the World Wide Web—are buckling under economic pressure, and the information they diffuse is being diverted away from the public sphere, where it can do most good.

Not that information comes free or "wants to be free," as Internet enthusiasts proclaimed twenty years ago. It comes filtered through expensive technologies and financed by powerful corporations. No one can ignore the economic realities that underlie the new information age, but who would argue that we have reached the right balance between commercialization and democratization?

Consider the cost of scientific periodicals, most of which are published exclusively online. It has increased at four times the rate of inflation since 1986. The average price of a year's subscription to a chemistry journal is now $4,044. In 1970 it was $33. A subscription to the *Journal of Comparative Neurology* cost $30,860 in 2012—the equivalent of six hundred monographs. Three giant publishers—Reed Elsevier, Wiley-Blackwell, and Springer—publish 42 percent of all academic articles, and they make giant profits from them. In 2013 Elsevier turned a 39 percent profit on an income of £2.1 billion from its science, technical, and medical journals.

All over the country research libraries are canceling subscriptions to academic journals, because they are caught between decreasing budgets and increasing costs. The logic of the bottom line is inescapable, but there is a higher logic that deserves consideration—namely, that the public should have access to knowledge produced with public funds.

Congress acted on that principle in 2008, when it required that articles based on grants from the National Institutes of Health be made available, free of charge, from an open-access repository, PubMed Central. But lobbyists blunted that requirement by getting the NIH to accept a twelve-month embargo, which would prevent public accessibility long enough for the publishers to profit from the immediate demand.

Not content with that victory, the lobbyists tried to abolish the NIH mandate in the so-called Research Works Act, a bill introduced in Congress in November 2011 and championed by Elsevier. The bill was withdrawn two months later following a wave of public protest, but the lobbyists are still at work, trying to block the Fair Access to Science and Technology Research Act (FASTR), which would give the public free access to all research, the data as well as the results, funded by federal agencies with research budgets of $100 million or more.

FASTR is a successor to the Federal Research Public Access Act (FRPAA), which remained bottled up in Congress after being introduced in three earlier sessions. But the basic provisions of both bills were adopted by a White House directive issued by the Office of Science and Technology Policy on February 22, 2013, and due to take effect at the end of this year. In principle, therefore, the results of research funded by taxpayers will be available to taxpayers, at least in the short term. What is the prospect over the long term? No one knows, but there are signs of hope.

The struggle over academic journals should not be dismissed as an "academic question," because a great deal is at stake. Access to research drives large sectors of the economy—the freer and quicker the access, the more powerful its effect. The Human Genome Project cost $3.8 billion in federal funds to develop, and thanks to the free accessibility of the results, it has already produced $796 billion in commercial applications. Linux, the free, open-source software system, has brought in billions in revenue for many companies, including Google. Less spectacular but more widespread is the multiplier effect of free information on small and medium businesses that cannot afford to pay for information hoarded behind subscription walls. A delay of a year in access to research and data can be prohibitively expensive for them. According to a study completed in 2006 by John Houghton, a specialist in the economics of information, a 5 percent increase in the accessibility of research would have produced an increase in productivity worth $16 billion.

Yet accessibility may decrease, because the price of journals has escalated so disastrously that libraries—and also hospitals, small-scale laboratories, and data-driven enterprises—are canceling subscriptions. Publishers respond by charging still more to institutions with budgets strong enough to carry the additional weight. But the system is breaking down. In 2010, when the Nature Publishing Group told the University of California that it would increase the price of its sixty-seven journals by 400 percent, the libraries stood their ground, and the faculty, which had contributed 5,300 articles to those journals during the previous six years, began to organize a boycott. . . .

In the long run, journals can be sustained only through a transformation of the economic basis of academic publishing. The current system developed as a component of the professionalization of academic disciplines in the nineteenth century. It served the public interest well through most of the twentieth century, but it has become dysfunctional in the age of the Internet. In fields like physics, most research circulates online in prepublication exchanges, and articles are composed with sophisticated programs that produce copy-ready texts. Costs are low enough for access to be free, as illustrated by the success of arXiv, a repository of articles in physics, mathematics, computer science, quantitative biology, quantitative finance, and statistics. (The articles do not undergo full-scale peer review unless, as often happens, they are later published by conventional journals.)

The entire system of communicating research could be made less expensive and more beneficial for the public by a process known as "flipping." Instead of subsisting on subscriptions, a flipped journal covers its costs by charging processing fees before publication and making its articles freely available, as "open access," afterward. That will sound strange to many academic authors. Why, they may ask, should we pay to get published? But they may not understand the dysfunctions of the present system, in which they furnish the research, writing, and refereeing free of charge to the subscription journals and then buy back the product of their work—not personally, of course, but through their libraries—at an exorbitant price. The public pays twice—first as taxpayers who subsidize the research, then as taxpayers or tuition payers who support public or private university libraries.

By creating open-access journals, a flipped system directly benefits the public. Anyone can consult the research free of charge online, and libraries are liberated from the spiraling costs of subscriptions. Of course, the publication expenses do not evaporate miraculously, but they are greatly reduced, especially for nonprofit journals, which do not need to satisfy shareholders. The processing fees, which can run to a thousand dollars or more, depending on the complexities of the text and the process of peer review, can be covered in various ways. They are often included in research grants to scientists, and they are increasingly financed by the author's university or a group of universities.

At Harvard, a program called HOPE (Harvard Open-Access Publishing Equity) subsidizes processing fees. A consortium called COPE (Compact for Open-Access Publishing Equity) promotes similar policies among twenty-one institutions, including MIT, the University of Michigan, and the University of California at Berkeley; and its activities complement those of thirty-three similar funds in institutions such as Johns Hopkins University and the University of California at San Francisco.

The main impediment to public-spirited publishing of this kind is not financial. It involves prestige. Scientists prefer to publish in expensive journals like *Nature*, *Science*, and *Cell*, because the aura attached to them glows on CVs and promotes careers. But some prominent scientists have undercut the prestige effect by founding open-access journals and recruiting the best talent to write and referee for them. Harold Varmus, a Nobel laureate in physiology and medicine, has made a huge success of *Public Library of Science*, and Paul Crutzen, a Nobel laureate in chemistry, has done the same with *Atmospheric Chemistry and Physics*. They have proven the feasibility of high-quality, open-access journals. Not only do they cover costs through processing fees, but they produce a profit—or rather, a "surplus," which they invest in further open-access projects.

The pressure for open access is also building up from digital repositories, which are being established in universities throughout the country. In February 2008, the Faculty of Arts and Sciences at Harvard voted unanimously to require its members (with a proviso for opting out or for accepting embargoes imposed by commercial journals) to deposit peer-reviewed articles in a repository, DASH (Digital Access to Scholarship at Harvard), where they can be read by anyone free of charge.

DASH now includes 17,000 articles, and it has registered three million downloads from countries in every continent. Repositories in other universities also report very high scores in their counts of downloads. They make knowledge available to a broad public, including researchers who have no connection to an academic institution; and at the same time, they make it possible for writers to reach far more readers than would be possible by means of subscription journals.

The desire to reach readers may be one of the most underestimated forces in the world of knowledge. Aside from journal articles, academics produce a large numbers of books, yet they rarely make much money from them. Authors in general derive little income from a book a year or two after its publication. Once its commercial life has ended, it dies a slow death, lying unread, except for rare occasions, on the shelves of libraries, inaccessible to the vast majority of readers. At that stage, authors generally have one dominant desire—for their work to circulate freely through the public; and their interest coincides with the goals of the open-access movement. A new organization, Authors Alliance, is about to launch a campaign to persuade authors to make their books available online at some point after publication through nonprofit distributors like the Digital Public Library of America, of which more later.

All sorts of complexities remain to be worked out before such a plan can succeed: How to accommodate the interests of publishers, who want to keep books on their backlists? Where to leave room for rights holders to opt out and for the revival of books that take on new economic life? Whether to devise some form of royalties, as in the extended collective licensing programs that have proven to be successful in the Scandinavian countries? It should be possible to enlist vested interests in a solution that will serve the public interest, not by appealing to altruism but rather by rethinking business plans in ways that will make the most of modern technology.

Several experimental enterprises illustrate possibilities of this kind. Knowledge Unlatched gathers commitments and collects funds from libraries that agree to purchase scholarly books at rates that will guarantee payment of a fixed amount to the publishers who are taking part in the program. The more libraries participating in the pool, the lower the price each will have to pay. While electronic editions of the books will be available everywhere free of charge through Knowledge Unlatched, the subscribing libraries will have the exclusive right to download and print out copies. By the end of February, more than 250 libraries had signed up to purchase a pilot collection of twenty-eight new books produced by thirteen publishers, and Knowledge Unlatched headquarters, located in London, announced that it would soon scale up its operations with the goal of combining open access with sustainability.

OpenEdition Books, located in Marseille, operates on a somewhat similar principle. It provides a platform for publishers who want to develop open-access online collections, and it sells the e-content to subscribers in formats that can be downloaded and printed. Operating from Cambridge, England, Open Book Publishers also charges for PDFs, which can be used with print-on-demand technology to produce physical books, and it applies the

income to subsidies for free copies online. It recruits academic authors who are willing to provide manuscripts without payment in order to reach the largest possible audience and to further the cause of open access.

The famous quip of Samuel Johnson, "No man but a blockhead ever wrote, except for money," no longer has the force of a self-evident truth in the age of the Internet. By tapping the goodwill of unpaid authors, Open Book Publishers has produced forty-one books in the humanities and social sciences, all rigorously peer-reviewed, since its foundation in 2008. "We envisage a world in which all research is freely available to all readers," it proclaims on its website.

The same goal animates the Digital Public Library of America, which aims to make available all the intellectual riches accumulated in American libraries, archives, and museums. As reported in these pages, the DPLA was launched on April 18, 2013. Now that it has celebrated its first anniversary, its collections include seven million books and other objects, three times the amount that it offered when it went online a year ago. They come from more than 1,300 institutions located in all fifty states, and they are being widely used: nearly a million distinct visitors have consulted the DPLA's website (dp.la), and they come from nearly every country in the world (North Korea, Chad, and Western Sahara are the only exceptions).

At the time of its conception in October 2010, the DPLA was seen as an alternative to one of the most ambitious projects ever imagined for commercializing access to information: Google Book Search. Google set out to digitize millions of books in research libraries and then proposed to sell subscriptions to the resulting database. Having provided the books to Google free of charge, the libraries would then have to buy back access to them, in digital form, at a price to be determined by Google and that could escalate as disastrously as the prices of scholarly journals.

Google Book Search actually began as a search service, which made available only snippets or short passages of books. But because many of the books were covered by copyright, Google was sued by the rights holders; and after lengthy negotiations the plaintiffs and Google agreed on a settlement, which transformed the search service into a gigantic commercial library financed by subscriptions. But the settlement had to be approved by a court, and on March 22, 2011, the Southern Federal District Court of New York rejected it on the grounds that, among other things, it threatened to constitute a monopoly in restraint of trade. That decision put an end to Google's project and cleared the way for the DPLA to offer digitized holdings—but nothing covered by copyright—to readers everywhere, free of charge.

Aside from its not-for-profit character, the DPLA differs from Google Book Search in a crucial respect: it is not a vertical organization erected on a database of its own. It is a distributed, horizontal system, which links digital collections already in the possession of the participating institutions, and it does so by means of a technological infrastructure that makes them instantly available to the user with one click on an electronic device. It is fundamentally horizontal, both in organization and in spirit.

Instead of working from the top down, the DPLA relies on "service hubs," or small administrative centers, to promote local collections and aggregate them at the state level. "Content hubs" located in institutions with collections of at least 250,000 items—for example, the New York Public Library, the Smithsonian Institution, and the collective digital repository known as HathiTrust—provide the bulk of the DPLA's holdings. There are now two dozen service and content hubs, and soon, if financing can be found, they will exist in every state of the union.

Such horizontality reinforces the democratizing impulse behind the DPLA. Although it is a small, nonprofit corporation with headquarters and a minimal staff in Boston, the DPLA functions as a network that covers the entire country. It relies heavily on volunteers. More than a thousand computer scientists collaborated free of charge in the design of its infrastructure, which aggregates metadata (catalog-type descriptions of documents) in a way that allows easy searching.

Therefore, for example, a ninth-grader in Dallas who is preparing a report on an episode of the American Revolution can download a manuscript from New York, a pamphlet from Chicago, and a map from San Francisco in order to study them side by side. Unfortunately, he or she will not be able to consult any recent books, because copyright laws keep virtually everything published after 1923 out of the public domain. But the courts, which are considering a flurry of cases about the "fair use" of copyright, may sustain a broad-enough interpretation for the DPLA to make a great deal of post-1923 material available for educational purposes.

A small army of volunteer "Community Reps," mainly librarians with technical skills, is fanning out across the country to promote various outreach programs sponsored by the DPLA. They reinforce the work of the service hubs, which concentrate on public libraries as centers of collection-building. A grant from the Bill and Melinda Gates Foundation is financing a Public Library Partnerships Project to train local librarians in the latest digital technologies. Equipped with new skills, the librarians will invite people to bring in material of their own—family letters, high school yearbooks, postcard collections stored in trunks and attics—to be digitized, curated, preserved, and made accessible online by the DPLA. While developing local community consciousness about culture and history, this project will also help integrate local collections in the national network.

Spin-off projects and local initiatives are also favored by what the DPLA calls its "plumbing"—that is, the technological infrastructure, which has been designed in a way to promote user-generated apps or digital tools connected to the system by means of an API (application programming interface), which has already registered seven million hits. Among the results is a tool for digital browsing: the user types in the title of a book, and images of spines of books, all related to the same subject, all in the public domain, appear on the screen as if they were aligned together on a shelf. The user can click on a spine to search one work after another, following leads that extend far beyond the shelf space of a physical library. Another tool makes it possible for a reader to go from a Wikipedia article to all the works in the DPLA that bear on the same subject. These and many other apps have been developed by individuals on their own, without following directives from DPLA headquarters.

The spin-offs offer endless educational opportunities. For example, the Emily Dickinson Archive recently developed at Harvard will make available digitized copies of the manuscripts of all Dickinson's poems. The manuscripts are essential for interpreting the work, because they contain many peculiarities—punctuation, spacing, capitalization—that inflect the meaning of the poems, of which only a few, badly mangled, were published during Dickinson's lifetime. Nearly every high school student comes across a poem by Dickinson at one time or other. Now teachers can assign a particular poem in its manuscript and printed versions (they often differ considerably) and stimulate their students to develop closer, deeper readings. The DPLA also plans to adapt its holdings to the special needs of community colleges, many of which do not have adequate libraries.

In these and other ways, the DPLA will go beyond its basic mission of making the cultural heritage of America available to all Americans. It will provide opportunities for them to interact with the material and to develop materials of their own. It will empower librarians and reinforce public libraries everywhere, not only in the United States. Its technological infrastructure has been designed to be interoperable with that of Europeana, a similar enterprise that is aggregating the holdings of libraries in the twenty-eight member states of the European Union. The DPLA's collections include works in more than four hundred languages, and nearly 30 percent of its users come from outside the US. Ten years from now, the DPLA's first year of activity may look like the beginning of an international library system.

It would be naive, however, to imagine a future free from the vested interests that have blocked the flow of information in the past. The lobbies at work in Washington also operate in Brussels, and a newly elected European Parliament will soon have to deal with the same issues that remain to be resolved in the US Congress. Commercialization and democratization operate on a global scale, and a great deal of access must be opened before the World Wide Web can accommodate a worldwide library.

ROBERT DARNTON is the Carl H. Pforzheimer University Professor and Director of the University Library at Harvard University. His primary area of research is eighteenth-century France, but he also writes extensively about print culture.

Jill Lepore    **NO**

The Cobweb: Can the Internet Be Archived?

Malaysia Airlines Flight 17 took off from Amsterdam at 10:31 A.M. G.M.T. on July 17, 2014, for a twelve-hour flight to Kuala Lumpur. Not much more than three hours later, the plane, a Boeing 777, crashed in a field outside Donetsk, Ukraine. All two hundred and ninety-eight people on board were killed. The plane's last radio contact was at 1:20 P.M. G.M.T. At 2:50 P.M. G.M.T., Igor Girkin, a Ukrainian separatist leader also known as Strelkov, or someone acting on his behalf, posted a message on VKontakte, a Russian social-media site: "We just downed a plane, an AN-26." (An Antonov 26 is a Soviet-built military cargo plane.) The post includes links to video of the wreckage of a plane; it appears to be a Boeing 777.

Two weeks before the crash, Anatol Shmelev, the curator of the Russia and Eurasia collection at the Hoover Institution, at Stanford, had submitted to the Internet Archive, a nonprofit library in California, a list of Ukrainian and Russian Web sites and blogs that ought to be recorded as part of the archive's Ukraine Conflict collection. Shmelev is one of about a thousand librarians and archivists around the world who identify possible acquisitions for the Internet Archive's subject collections, which are stored in its Wayback Machine, in San Francisco. Strelkov's VKontakte page was on Shmelev's list. "Strelkov is the field commander in Slaviansk and one of the most important figures in the conflict," Shmelev had written in an e-mail to the Internet Archive on July 1st, and his page "deserves to be recorded twice a day."

On July 17th, at 3:22 P.M. G.M.T., the Wayback Machine saved a screenshot of Strelkov's VKontakte post about downing a plane. Two hours and twenty-two minutes later, Arthur Bright, the Europe editor of the *Christian Science Monitor*, tweeted a picture of the screenshot, along with the message "Grab of Donetsk militant Strelkov's claim of downing what appears to have been MH17." By then, Strelkov's VKontakte page had already been edited: the claim about shooting down a plane was deleted. The only real evidence of the original claim lies in the Wayback Machine.

The average life of a Web page is about a hundred days. Strelkov's "We just downed a plane" post lasted barely two hours. It might seem, and it often feels, as though stuff on the Web lasts forever, for better and frequently for worse: the embarrassing photograph, the regretted blog (more usually regrettable not in the way the slaughter of civilians is regrettable but in the way that bad hair is regrettable). No one believes any longer, if anyone ever did, that "if it's on the Web it must be true," but a lot of people do believe that if it's on the Web it will stay on the Web. Chances are, though, that it actually won't. In 2006, David Cameron gave a speech in which he said that Google was democratizing the world, because "making more information available to more people" was providing "the power for anyone to hold to account those who in the past might have had a monopoly of power." Seven years later, Britain's Conservative Party scrubbed from its Web site ten years' worth of Tory speeches, including that one. Last year, BuzzFeed deleted more than four thousand of its staff writers' early posts, apparently because, as time passed, they looked stupider and stupider. Social media, public records, junk: in the end, everything goes.

Web pages don't have to be deliberately deleted to disappear. Sites hosted by corporations tend to die with their hosts. When MySpace, GeoCities, and Friendster were reconfigured or sold, millions of accounts vanished. (Some of those companies may have notified users, but Jason Scott, who started an outfit called Archive Team—its motto is "We are going to rescue your shit"—says that such notification is usually purely notional: "They were sending e-mail to dead e-mail addresses, saying, 'Hello, Arthur Dent, your house is going to be crushed.'") Facebook has been around for only a decade; it won't be around forever. Twitter is a rare case: it has arranged to archive all of its tweets at the Library of Congress. In 2010, after the announcement, Andy Borowitz tweeted, "Library of Congress to acquire entire Twitter archive— will rename itself Museum of Crap." Not long after that, Borowitz abandoned that Twitter account. You might, one day, be able to find his old tweets at the Library of

Congress, but not anytime soon: the Twitter Archive is not yet open for research. Meanwhile, on the Web, if you click on a link to Borowitz's tweet about the Museum of Crap, you get this message: "Sorry, that page doesn't exist!"

The Web dwells in a never-ending present. It is—elementally—ethereal, ephemeral, unstable, and unreliable. Sometimes when you try to visit a Web page what you see is an error message: "Page Not Found." This is known as "link rot," and it's a drag, but it's better than the alternative. More often, you see an updated Web page; most likely the original has been overwritten. (To overwrite, in computing, means to destroy old data by storing new data in their place; overwriting is an artifact of an era when computer storage was very expensive.) Or maybe the page has been moved and something else is where it used to be. This is known as "content drift," and it's more pernicious than an error message, because it's impossible to tell that what you're seeing isn't what you went to look for: the overwriting, erasure, or moving of the original is invisible. For the law and for the courts, link rot and content drift, which are collectively known as "reference rot," have been disastrous. In providing evidence, legal scholars, lawyers, and judges often cite Web pages in their footnotes; they expect that evidence to remain where they found it as their proof, the way that evidence on paper—in court records and books and law journals—remains where they found it, in libraries and courthouses. But a 2013 survey of law- and policy-related publications found that, at the end of six years, nearly fifty percent of the URLs cited in those publications no longer worked. According to a 2014 study conducted at Harvard Law School, "more than 70% of the URLs within the Harvard Law Review and other journals, and 50% of the URLs within United States Supreme Court opinions, do not link to the originally cited information." The overwriting, drifting, and rotting of the Web is no less catastrophic for engineers, scientists, and doctors. Last month, a team of digital library researchers based at Los Alamos National Laboratory reported the results of an exacting study of three and a half million scholarly articles published in science, technology, and medical journals between 1997 and 2012: one in five links provided in the notes suffers from reference rot. It's like trying to stand on quicksand.

The footnote, a landmark in the history of civilization, took centuries to invent and to spread. It has taken mere years nearly to destroy. A footnote used to say, "Here is how I know this and where I found it." A footnote that's a link says, "Here is what I used to know and where I once found it, but chances are it's not there anymore." It doesn't matter whether footnotes are your stock-in-trade. Everybody's in a pinch. Citing a Web page as the source for something you know—using a URL as evidence—is ubiquitous. Many people find themselves doing it three or four times before breakfast and five times more before lunch. What happens when your evidence vanishes by dinnertime?

The day after Strelkov's "We just downed a plane" post was deposited into the Wayback Machine, Samantha Power, the U.S. Ambassador to the United Nations, told the U.N. Security Council, in New York, that Ukrainian separatist leaders had "boasted on social media about shooting down a plane, but later deleted these messages." In San Francisco, the people who run the Wayback Machine posted on the Internet Archive's Facebook page, "Here's why we exist."

The address of the Internet Archive is archive .org, but another way to visit is to take a plane to San Francisco and ride in a cab to the Presidio, past cypresses that look as though someone had drawn them there with a smudgy crayon. At 300 Funston Avenue, climb a set of stone steps and knock on the brass door of a Greek Revival temple. You can't miss it: it's painted wedding-cake white and it's got, out front, eight Corinthian columns and six marble urns.

"We bought it because it matched our logo," Brewster Kahle told me when I met him there, and he wasn't kidding. Kahle is the founder of the Internet Archive and the inventor of the Wayback Machine. The logo of the Internet Archive is a white, pedimented Greek temple. When Kahle started the Internet Archive, in 1996, in his attic, he gave everyone working with him a book called "The Vanished Library," about the burning of the Library of Alexandria. "The idea is to build the Library of Alexandria Two," he told me. (The Hellenism goes further: there's a partial backup of the Internet Archive in Alexandria, Egypt.) Kahle's plan is to one-up the Greeks. The motto of the Internet Archive is "Universal Access to All Knowledge." The Library of Alexandria was open only to the learned; the Internet Archive is open to everyone. In 2009, when the Fourth Church of Christ, Scientist, decided to sell its building, Kahle went to Funston Avenue to see it, and said, "That's our logo!" He loves that the church's cornerstone was laid in 1923: everything published in the United States before that date lies in the public domain. A temple built in copyright's year zero seemed fated. Kahle hops, just slightly, in his shoes when he gets excited. He says, showing me the church, "It's *Greek!*"

. . .

When Kahle was growing up, some of the very same people who were building what would one day become the Internet were thinking about libraries. In 1961, in

Cambridge, J. C. R. Licklider, a scientist at the technology firm Bolt, Beranek and Newman, began a two-year study on the future of the library, funded by the Ford Foundation and aided by a team of researchers that included Marvin Minsky, at M.I.T. As Licklider saw it, books were good at displaying information but bad at storing, organizing, and retrieving it. "We should be prepared to reject the schema of the physical book itself," he argued, and to reject "the printed page as a long-term storage device." The goal of the project was to imagine what libraries would be like in the year 2000. Licklider envisioned a library in which computers would replace books and form a "network in which every element of the fund of knowledge is connected to every other element."

In 1963, Licklider became a director at the Department of Defense's Advanced Research Projects Agency (now called DARPA). During his first year, he wrote a seven-page memo in which he addressed his colleagues as "Members and Affiliates of the Intergalactic Computer Network," and proposed the networking of ARPA machines. This sparked the imagination of an electrical engineer named Lawrence Roberts, who later went to ARPA from M.I.T.'s Lincoln Laboratory. (Licklider had helped found both B.B.N. and Lincoln.) Licklider's two-hundred-page Ford Foundation report, "Libraries of the Future," was published in 1965. By then, the network he imagined was already being built, and the word "hyper-text" was being used. By 1969, relying on a data-transmission technology called "packet-switching" which had been developed by a Welsh scientist named Donald Davies, ARPA had built a computer network called ARPANET. By the mid-nineteen-seventies, researchers across the country had developed a network of networks: an internetwork, or, later, an "internet."

Kahle enrolled at M.I.T. in 1978. He studied computer science and engineering with Minsky. After graduating, in 1982, he worked for and started companies that were later sold for a great deal of money. In the late eighties, while working at Thinking Machines, he developed Wide Area Information Servers, or WAIS, a protocol for searching, navigating, and publishing on the Internet. One feature of WAIS was a time axis; it provided for archiving through version control. (Wikipedia has version control; from any page, you can click on a tab that says "View History" to see all earlier versions of that page.) WAIS came before the Web, and was then overtaken by it. In 1989, at CERN, the European Particle Physics Laboratory, in Geneva, Tim Berners-Lee, an English computer scientist, proposed a hypertext transfer protocol (HTTP) to link pages on what he called the World Wide Web. Berners-Lee toyed with the idea of a time axis for his protocol, too. One reason it was

never developed was the preference for the most up-to-date information: a bias against obsolescence. But the chief reason was the premium placed on ease of use. "We were so young then, and the Web was so young," Berners-Lee told me. "I was trying to get it to go. Preservation was not a priority. But we're getting older now." Other scientists involved in building the infrastructure of the Internet are getting older and more concerned, too. Vint Cerf, who worked on ARPANET in the seventies, and now holds the title of Chief Internet Evangelist at Google, has started talking about what he sees as a need for "digital vellum": long-term storage. "I worry that the twenty-first century will become an informational black hole," Cerf e-mailed me. But Kahle has been worried about this problem all along.

"I'm completely in praise of what Tim Berners-Lee did," Kahle told me, "but he kept it very, very simple." The first Web page in the United States was created at SLAC, Stanford's linear-accelerator center, at the end of 1991. Berners-Lee's protocol—which is not only usable but also elegant—spread fast, initially across universities and then into the public. "Emphasized text like this is a hypertext link," a 1994 version of SLAC's Web page explained. In 1991, a ban on commercial traffic on the Internet was lifted. Then came Web browsers and e-commerce: both Netscape and Amazon were founded in 1994. The Internet as most people now know it—Web-based and commercial—began in the mid-nineties. Just as soon as it began, it started disappearing.

And the Internet Archive began collecting it. The Wayback Machine is a Web archive, a collection of old Web pages; it is, in fact, the Web archive. There are others, but the Wayback Machine is so much bigger than all of them that it's very nearly true that if it's not in the Wayback Machine it doesn't exist. The Wayback Machine is a robot. It crawls across the Internet, in the manner of Eric Carle's very hungry caterpillar, attempting to make a copy of every Web page it can find every two months, though that rate varies. (It first crawled over this magazine's home page, newyorker.com, in November, 1998, and since then has crawled the site nearly seven thousand times, lately at a rate of about six times a day.) The Internet Archive is also stocked with Web pages that are chosen by librarians, specialists like Anatol Shmelev, collecting in subject areas, through a service called Archive It, at archive-it.org, which also allows individuals and institutions to build their own archives. (A copy of everything they save goes into the Wayback Machine, too.) And anyone who wants to can preserve a Web page, at any time, by going to archive.org/web, typing in a URL, and clicking "Save Page Now." (That's how most of the twelve screenshots of Strelkov's

VKontakte page entered the Wayback Machine on the day the Malaysia Airlines flight was downed: seven captures that day were made by a robot; the rest were made by humans.)

I was on a panel with Kahle a few years ago, discussing the relationship between material and digital archives. When I met him, I was struck by a story he told about how he once put the entire World Wide Web into a shipping container. He just wanted to see if it would fit. How big is the Web? It turns out, he said, that it's twenty feet by eight feet by eight feet, or, at least, it was on the day he measured it. How much did it weigh? Twenty-six thousand pounds. He thought that *meant* something. He thought people needed to *know* that.

Kahle put the Web into a storage container, but most people measure digital data in bytes. This essay is about two hundred thousand bytes. A book is about a megabyte. A megabyte is a million bytes. A gigabyte is a billion bytes. A terabyte is a million million bytes. A petabyte is a million gigabytes. In the lobby of the Internet Archive, you can get a free bumper sticker that says "10,000,000,000,000,000 Bytes Archived." Ten petabytes. It's obsolete. That figure is from 2012. Since then, it's doubled.

The Wayback Machine has archived more than four hundred and thirty billion Web pages. The Web is global, but, aside from the Internet Archive, a handful of fledgling commercial enterprises, and a growing number of university Web archives, most Web archives are run by national libraries. They collect chiefly what's in their own domains (the Web Archive of the National Library of Sweden, for instance, includes every Web page that ends in ".se"). The Library of Congress has archived nine billion pages, the British Library six billion. Those collections, like the collections of most national libraries, are in one way or another dependent on the Wayback Machine; the majority also use Heritrix, the Internet Archive's open-source code. The British Library and the Bibliothèque Nationale de France backfilled the early years of their collections by using the Internet Archive's crawls of the .uk and .fr domains. The Library of Congress doesn't actually do its own Web crawling; it contracts with the Internet Archive to do it instead.

The church at 300 Funston Avenue is twenty thousand square feet. The Internet Archive, the building, is open to the public most afternoons. It is, after all, a library. In addition to housing the Wayback Machine, the Internet Archive is a digital library, a vast collection of digitized books, films, television and radio programs, music, and other stuff. Because of copyright, not everything the Internet Archive has digitized is online. In the lobby of the church, there's a scanning station and a listening room: two armchairs, a coffee table, a pair of bookshelves, two iPads, and two sets of headphones. "You can listen to anything here," Kahle says. "We can't put all our music on the Internet, but we can put everything here."

Copyright is the elephant in the archive. One reason the Library of Congress has a very small Web-page collection, compared with the Internet Archive, is that the Library of Congress generally does not collect a Web page without asking, or, at least, giving notice. "The Internet Archive hoovers," Abbie Grotke, who runs the Library of Congress's Web-archive team, says. "We can't hoover, because we have to notify site owners and get permissions." (There are some exceptions.) The Library of Congress has something like an opt-in policy; the Internet Archive has an opt-out policy. The Wayback Machine collects every Web page it can find, unless that page is blocked; blocking a Web crawler requires adding only a simple text file, "robots.txt," to the root of a Web site. The Wayback Machine will honor that file and not crawl that site, and it will also, when it comes across a robots.txt, remove all past versions of that site. When the Conservative Party in Britain deleted ten years' worth of speeches from its Web site, it also added a robots.txt, which meant that, the next time the Wayback Machine tried to crawl the site, all its captures of those speeches went away, too. (Some have since been restored.) In a story that ran in the *Guardian*, a Labour Party M.P. said, "It will take more than David Cameron pressing delete to make people forget about his broken promises." And it would take more than a robots.txt to entirely destroy those speeches: they have also been collected in the U.K. Web Archive, at the British Library. The U.K. has what's known as a legal-deposit law; it requires copies of everything published in Britain to be deposited in the British Library. In 2013, that law was revised to include everything published on the U.K. Web. "People put their private lives up there, and we actually don't want that stuff," Andy Jackson, the technical head of the U.K. Web Archive, told me. "We don't want anything that you wouldn't consider a publication." It is hard to say quite where the line lies. But Britain's legal-deposit laws mean that the British Library doesn't have to honor a request to stop collecting.

. . .

In 2002, Kahle proposed an initiative in which the Internet Archive, in collaboration with national libraries, would become the head of a worldwide consortium of Web archives. (The Internet Archive collects from around the world, and is available in most of the world. Currently, the biggest exception is China—"I guess because we have materials on the archive that the Chinese government would rather not have its citizens see," Kahle says.)

This plan didn't work out, but from that failure came the International Internet Preservation Consortium, founded in 2003 and chartered at the BnF. It started with a dozen member institutions; there are now forty-nine.

. . .

The plan to found a global Internet archive proved unworkable, partly because national laws relating to legal deposit, copyright, and privacy are impossible to reconcile, but also because Europeans tend to be suspicious of American organizations based in Silicon Valley ingesting their cultural inheritance. Illien told me that, when faced with Kahle's proposal, "national libraries decided they could not rely on a third party," even a nonprofit, "for such a fundamental heritage and preservation mission." In this same spirit, and in response to Google Books, European libraries and museums collaborated to launch Europeana, a digital library, in 2008. The Googleplex, Google's headquarters, is thirty-eight miles away from the Internet Archive, but the two could hardly be more different. In 2009, after the Authors Guild and the Association of American Publishers sued Google Books for copyright infringement, Kahle opposed the proposed settlement, charging Google with effectively attempting to privatize the public-library system. In 2010, he was on the founding steering committee of the Digital Public Library of America, which is something of an American version of Europeana; its mission is to make what's in libraries, archives, and museums "freely available to the world . . . in the face of increasingly restrictive digital options."

Kahle is a digital utopian attempting to stave off a digital dystopia. He views the Web as a giant library, and doesn't think it ought to belong to a corporation, or that anyone should have to go through a portal owned by a corporation in order to read it. "We are building a library that is us," he says, "and it is ours."

When the Internet Archive bought the church, Kahle recalls, "we had the idea that we'd convert it into a library, but what does a library look like anymore? So we've been settling in, and figuring that out."

From the lobby, we headed up a flight of yellow-carpeted stairs to the chapel, an enormous dome-ceilinged room filled with rows of oak pews. There are arched stained-glass windows, and the dome is a stained-glass window, too, open to the sky, like an eye of God. The chapel seats seven hundred people. The floor is sloped. "At first, we thought we'd flatten the floor and pull up the pews," Kahle said, as he gestured around the room. "But we couldn't. They're just too beautiful."

On the wall on either side of the altar, wooden slates display what, when this was a church, had been the listing of the day's hymn numbers. The archivists of the Internet have changed those numbers. One hymn number was 314. "Do you know what that is?" Kahle asked. It was a test, and something of a trick question, like when someone asks you what's your favorite B track on the White Album. "Pi," I said, dutifully, or its first three digits, anyway. Another number was 42. Kahle gave me an inquiring look. I rolled my eyes. Seriously? But it is serious, in a way. It's hard not to worry that the Wayback Machine will end up like the computer in Douglas Adams's "Hitchhiker's Guide to the Galaxy," which is asked what is the meaning of "life, the universe, and everything," and, after thinking for millions of years, says, "Forty-two." If the Internet can be archived, will it ever have anything to tell us? Honestly, isn't most of the Web trash? And, if everything's saved, won't there be too much of it for anyone to make sense of any of it? Won't it be useless?

The Wayback Machine is humongous, and getting humongouser. You can't search it the way you can search the Web, because it's too big and what's in there isn't sorted, or indexed, or catalogued in any of the many ways in which a paper archive is organized; it's not ordered in any way at all, except by URL and by date. To use it, all you can do is type in a URL, and choose the date for it that you'd like to look at. It's more like a phone book than like an archive. Also, it's riddled with errors. One kind is created when the dead Web grabs content from the live Web, sometimes because Web archives often crawl different parts of the same page at different times: text in one year, photographs in another. In October, 2012, if you asked the Wayback Machine to show you what cnn.com looked like on September 3, 2008, it would have shown you a page featuring stories about the 2008 McCain-Obama Presidential race, but the advertisement alongside it would have been for the 2012 Romney-Obama debate. Another problem is that there is no equivalent to what, in a physical archive, is a perfect provenance. Last July, when the computer scientist Michael Nelson tweeted the archived screenshots of Strelkov's page, a man in St. Petersburg tweeted back, "Yep. Perfect tool to produce 'evidence' of any kind." Kahle is careful on this point. When asked to authenticate a screenshot, he says, "We can say, 'This is what we know. This is what our records say. This is how we received this information, from which apparent Web site, at this IP address.' But to actually say that this happened in the past is something that we can't say, in an ontological way." Nevertheless, screenshots from Web archives have held up in court, repeatedly. And, as Kahle points out, "They turn out to be much more trustworthy than most of what people try to base court decisions on."

You can do something more like keyword searching in smaller subject collections, but nothing like Google searching (there is no relevance ranking, for instance), because the tools for doing anything meaningful with Web archives are years behind the tools for creating those archives. Doing research in a paper archive is to doing research in a Web archive as going to a fish market is to being thrown in the middle of an ocean; the only thing they have in common is that both involve fish.

· · ·

The footnote problem, though, stands a good chance of being fixed. Last year, a tool called Perma.cc was launched. It was developed by the Harvard Library Innovation Lab, and its founding supporters included more than sixty law-school libraries, along with the Harvard Berkman Center for Internet and Society, the Internet Archive, the Legal Information Preservation Alliance, and the Digital Public Library of America. Perma.cc promises "to create citation links that will never break." It works something like the Wayback Machine's "Save Page Now." If you're writing a scholarly paper and want to use a link in your footnotes, you can create an archived version of the page you're linking to, a "permalink," and anyone later reading your footnotes will, when clicking on that link, be brought to the permanently archived version. Perma.cc has already been adopted by law reviews and state courts; it's only a matter of time before it's universally adopted as the standard in legal, scientific, and scholarly citation.

Perma.cc is a patch, an excellent patch. Herbert Van de Sompel, a Belgian computer scientist who works at the Los Alamos National Laboratory, is trying to reweave the fabric of the Web. It's not possible to go back in time and rewrite the HTTP protocol, but Van de Sompel's work involves adding to it. He and Michael Nelson are part of the team behind Memento, a protocol that you can use on Google Chrome as a Web extension, so that you can navigate from site to site, and from time to time. He told me, "Memento allows you to say, 'I don't want to see this link where it points me to today; I want to see it around the time that this page was written, for example.'" It searches not only the Wayback Machine but also every major public Web archive in the world, to find the page closest in time to the time you'd like to travel to. ("A world with one archive is a really bad idea," Van de Sompel points out. "You need redundancy.") This month, the Memento group is launching a Web portal called Time Travel. Eventually, if Memento and projects like it work, the Web will have a time dimension, a way to get from now to then, effortlessly, a fourth dimension. And then the past will be inescapable, which is as terrifying as it is interesting.

JILL LEPORE writes regularly for the *New Yorker*, but also is the Chair of the History and Literature Department at Harvard University. Her specialty is American History, and she has written a number of books. Her first book, *The Name of War*, won the Bancroft Prize and her 2005 book, *New York Burning*, was a finalist for the Pulitzer Prize.

EXPLORING THE ISSUE

Can Digital Libraries Replace Traditional Libraries?

Critical Thinking and Reflection

1. Though it may be odd to think that academic researchers may have to pay to be published, what benefit would there be to humanity if this model of publication of scholarly work were adopted?
2. What is necessary to keep us from experiencing information overload, and information relativity?
3. If we lose the original sources of some of our laws and policies, how can we continue to build a system of rational decision making?
4. Libraries and collections of information often exist for the public good. What would happen if libraries of some types of information were privatized?
5. Community and academic libraries often are much more than repositories of printed materials. What other functions do libraries serve?

Is There Common Ground?

Both of the authors for this issue recognize the role of digital media in shaping and reshaping concepts about publishing, books, and libraries. As critics of American culture, they understand the relationship among publishing houses, the role of the academic press, and the costs of maintaining current collections of printed material. The most common fear they both project is a future in which valuable original material is lost or relegated to a space where no one will ever see it again.

They differ, however, in what the future of the library will be in American culture. Electronic print is very different than the traditional print market, and while students may not always understand the nature of the commitment to published research that many academics share, the idea that some work will not be published because of the cost is frightening. Even more frightening though is that it may be published, only to be lost or misplaced because keywords no longer can index the information in an organized, rationale way.

Certainly, the cost of books and periodicals will affect academic and public libraries, but it is important for any civilization to build upon the repository of laws, regulations, and research that advances our shared knowledge of our surroundings and the really important chronology of what matters to humanity. The selections in this issue remind us that as technology and distribution forms change, we need to pay attention to the important information that can be lost or misplaced along the way.

Additional Resources

Ashley Dawson, "DIY Academy: Cognitive Capitalism, Humanist Scholarship, and the Digital Transformation," in *The Social Media Reader*, edited by Michael Mandiberg (New York: New York University Press, 2012, pp. 257–274). In this book chapter, the author discusses the open source model for academic publishing.

Laura Mandell, *Breaking the Book: Print Humanities in the Digital Age* (Hoboken, New Jersey, 2015). In this book, the author examines the relationship readers have with traditional print versus the electronic version of the word.

Alexander Starre, *Metamedia: American Book Fictions and Literary Print Culture After Digitization* (Iowa City, IA, 2015). The author compares the aesthetics and format of traditional books and digital books, and the experience of reading different formats.

Richard Thompson, *Merchants of Culture: The Publishing Business in the Twenty-first Century,* 2nd ed. (London: Plume, 2012). In this book, Thompson discusses the changing business models of the publishing industry.

Internet References . . .

American Library Association (ALA)

www.ala.org/

Net Literacy

www.netliteracy.org/?gclid=Cj0KEQiAjpGyBRDgrt-LqzbHayb8BEiQANZauhy7OzKjxDhylyMnLBATttrUW-dURv7y9NPC7U4bX1AggaAvn48P8HAQ

Project Gutenberg

www.gutenberg.org/

Public Broadcasting Service (PBS), "Literacy Link" for Adults

http://litlink.ket.org/

Selected, Edited, and with Issue Framing Material by:
Alison Alexander, *University of Georgia*
and
Jarice Hanson, *University of Massachusetts—Amherst*

ISSUE

Can Journalism Stand Up to Attacks on Freedom of the Press?

YES: Marvin Kalb, from "Current Challenges to the Freedom of the Press," *Shorenstein Center on Media, Politics and Public Policy* (2017)

NO: Philip Bennett and Moises Naim, from "21st-Century Censorship," *Columbia Journalism Review* (2015)

Learning Outcomes

After reading this issue, you will be able to:

- Describe what freedom of the press has traditionally meant in the United States.
- Discuss what constitutes attacks on freedom of the press.
- Evaluate the consequences of social media for an informed society.
- Explain the strategies employed to curtail media influence in other countries.

ISSUE SUMMARY

YES: Marvin Kalb finds Trump's dismissive treatment of news media a significant attack on freedom of the press. His judgment in calling media "enemies of the American people" was reminiscent of the language of Mao Zedong and Stalin. Undercutting the media is a strategy of authoritarianism; preserving democracy requires a free press.

NO: Philip Bennett and Moises Naim look at press freedom in a global and digital context and find censorship on the rise. They argue that governments are having success in disrupting and undercutting independent media to determine the information that reaches the society.

The First Amendment to the US Constitution says that, "Congress shall make no law ... abridging the freedom of speech, or of the press...." Freedom of the press protects the right to publish information or opinions without government censorship. Typically, among other things, this means that the government cannot prevent publication of information, force newspapers to publish information against their will, criminalize the publication of truthful information, require licensing by the government of journalists or newspapers, or compel journalists to reveal sources. Freedom of the press is an evolving concept that now must encompass broadcast and digital reporting. Libel allows individuals to sue a journalistic organization which they deem has published false statement(s).

The libertarian theory of the press informed the creation of the First Amendment. This concept sees human kind as rational beings, deserving of individual liberties. Central to freedom of the press is the belief that in the marketplace of ideas these rational beings will make intelligent decisions within a climate of free expression. Interference from government should be restrained, allowing the press to function as a watchdog to the executive, legislative, and judicial branches of government and therefore act as a fourth branch of government (sometimes called the Fourth Estate). During this time, the press was highly partisan with newspapers deeply involved in political battles. It was only in the 20th century that newspapers began taking a stance that privileged accuracy and evenness. In the last few decades, we have again seen the rise of partisan press.

Thomas Jefferson is famously quoted as saying, "… were if left to me to decide whether we should have a government without newspapers or newspaper without a government, I should not hesitate a moment to prefer the latter." Calvin Coolidge in 2015 stated that, "Wherever the cause of liberty is making its way, one of its highest accomplishment is the guarantee of the freedom of the press." Kalb quotes President Bush as saying that media is "indispensable to democracy." Why are these presidents so supportive of the press? The core is their belief that freedom of expression is crucial for successful democracy because the free flow of information allows the public to participate in informed decisions. Senator John McCain has said "without a free press, we would lose so much of our individual liberties over time."

Marvin Kalb's speech detailed his concerns about freedom of the press under the Trump administration. His attacks on the press have been far ranging and often nebulous: a disgrace, terrible, lies, fake. Kalb describes his strategy for the 16 other GOP candidates in the Presidential race—to diminish and destroy. This may be his strategy with the press. Many agree that a free press is essential to democracy. But when he belittles and humiliates the press, Kalb asserts, he does more than bolster his self-esteem and appeal to his supporters, he begins to undermine an institution central to democracy. The American press, Kalb asserts, must have the spunk and the support to stand up to Trump.

Bennett and Naim talk about these issues in a global context and paint a gloomy worldwide picture of government using the Internet to undercut traditional media and determine the information that reaches society. Censorship is on the rise in the information age. Much of contemporary censorship is hidden. It includes gaining power over media by using anonymous buyers or shell corporations In Venezuela. In Hungary, the Media Authority levies fines, taxes, and licensing to pressure media. Turkey has used huge fine for critical coverage; Russia launched its own media outlets, while limiting outlets with foreign investment; In Egypt and in China, journalists have been jailed.

The examples are many, and their application to the United States seems limited. Yet the techniques of weakening and suppressing print and broadcast in order to control the news seems increasingly possible. "To weaken the institutions that exist to prevent the concentration of power" is the tactic of those determined to do whatever it takes to keep power. Bennett and Naim are pessimistic that independent media can thrive in this environment.

By now some of you must be saying, yes but what we do when we don't know whom to believe. Fake news presents a troubling threat to the press in this era of social media. Fake news is not legitimately labeled when it is simply something that you do not like. Fake news is a real problem that happens in at least two ways: legacy media pick up stories from social media that are later proved false or individuals or organizations post fake stories that are picked up virally and soon become "truth" around the globe. One tragic example occurred during the 2016 presidential race when an individual came armed to a DC pizza parlor to rescue children held in a sex ring operated by Hillary Clinton. His source: a right wing radio personality. The abashed perpetrator later offered, "The intel on this wasn't 100 percent." An extreme example, but one that is worrisome in an environment where truth and fiction can be hard to separate. Not only must we be concerned about coverage that is biased from the left or the right wing. Now we must also be worried about stories, sometimes planted by foreign governments, that are designed to undermine our society and that sometimes cannot be distinguished from legitimate news.

This issue becomes more complex the more it is discussed. I assume, and I hope not incorrectly, that all of you say you believe in the First Amendment and in the freedom of the press. Yet, the press can certainly be criticized. When does criticism become undermining the institution? Perhaps it is when presidents criticize without context and without ever correcting that which is proved incorrect. Perhaps it is when truth is abandoned. It seems we are living in an age of opinion. What will it mean for society when "truth" and "fact" are meaningless terms? Will this mean the demise of news?

YES ⤶

Marvin Kalb

Current Challenges to the Freedom of the Press

On March 30, 2017, Marvin Kalb, former Shorenstein Center director, delivered commentary on the threats to US democracy posed by the Trump administration. The talk was sponsored by the Press Freedom Committee of the National Press Club Journalism Institute.

Thank you, Mike, and thank you, Barbara Cochran and Julie Schoo, of the Journalism Institute of the National Press Club for giving me this opportunity to express my thoughts—mine, no one else's—about President Donald Trump's troubling, and at times frightening, relations with the American press.

I have been in this business of journalism now for more than 60 years, most of the time doing straight news, not commentary. But what you will hear tonight is commentary, certain no doubt to offend some of you, while prompting others to nod in agreement.

I believe that after a few rapid-fire months in office it's fair to say that President Trump has launched a style of governance, utterly unfamiliar to the American experience. Experts in politics, diplomacy, and journalism have been left shaking their heads in dismay and bewilderment, unable in their wanderings through American history to come up with a parallel. What we have now could be called creeping authoritarianism. It may yet fail, and there have been some indications (most recently on health care) that it will fail; but we cannot dismiss the possibility that it may, at some point, actually succeed. And, if it does succeed, this glorious experiment in American democracy will have failed.

Nowhere, it seems, is this new style of un-American governance more pronounced than in President Trump's dealings with the press. His angry attacks, his "running war" with the media, as it's called, have raised more than a few eyebrows. The press, overall, he says, is a "disgrace." Reporters are "very dishonest people." Their coverage he describes as an "outrage." The New York Times is a "failing newspaper." CNN—"terrible." Buzzfeed, one of the relatively new websites, he dismisses as "garbage." When a story is critical of him or his policies, he calls it "fake news,"

often written in his tweets with capital letters. When public opinion polls produce numbers that violate his rosy image of himself, they are described as "fake polls."

Stephen Bannon, his Darth Vader shadow, gleefully reminds reporters that their coverage of the 2016 presidential race was so awful they ought to feel "embarrassed and humiliated and keep [their] mouths shut and just listen for a while." He, whose experience in journalism extends no further than a few years at Breitbart News. For him, the press is nothing more, nothing less, than the "opposition party."

But perhaps most important to any understanding of the president's judgment of the press was his recent comment that they are all "enemies of the American people," a comment that shocked not only the reporters but also anyone with an even passing familiarity with recent world history.

Josef Stalin often used that loaded expression when he arrested and killed enemies of his people in the old Soviet Union, then governed by communists.

Mao Zedong liked to divide the Chinese people into two groups: one group, that favors his communist rule; and the other group that opposes his rule, he denounced as "enemies of the people."

Adolf Hitler loved Henrik Ibsen's play, "Enemy of the People," and his Nazi cohorts denounced Jewish critics of his regime as "enemies of the people," and 6-million of them were murdered during World War Two.

When the president used this phrase, did he know the history of its use by these 20th century killers? Or did the phrase just pop into his mind as an appropriate description of the American press? We are not apt to get an answer to these questions from his spokesman Sean Spicer.

But others did have an answer. Former President George W. Bush, still a Republican last I heard, when asked whether he considers the media to be "enemies of the American people," he replied that the media is "indispensable to democracy." With Trump obviously very much on his mind, Bush continued, "power can be very addictive and it can be corrosive, and it's important for the media to call to account people who abuse their power."

Senator John McCain, the Republican who ran and lost his race for the presidency in 2008, was even more blunt. "When you look at history," he said, "the first thing that dictators do is shut down the press." He then rushed to add, "I'm not saying that President Trump is trying to be a dictator. I'm just saying we need to learn the lessons of history." The Senator from Arizona, once a prisoner of war in Vietnam, obviously feels that he has learned the lessons of history. "We need a free press. It's vital," he said, choosing his words carefully. "If you want to preserve democracy, as we know it, you have to have a free and many times adversarial press. Without it, I'm afraid, we would lose so much of our individual liberties over time. That's how dictators get started."

It is important to note that at the recent Gridiron dinner Vice President Mike Pence told reporters that he, and the president, he added, both support the first amendment. How nice! There was a sprinkling of applause in the ballroom, but a few of the reporters noted privately that there was no retraction of the president's comment about the press being "enemies of the people;" nor was there an explanation of how reporters can enjoy both the benefits of the first amendment and at the same time be "enemies of the American people." Maybe, in retrospect, what the Vice-President said was better than nothing.

What we know, so far, is that Donald Trump is a self-absorbed, impulsive, ego-driven, former tv-reality president, narcissistic in a big way, obsessed with cable news (for him, the fount of all knowledge, past and present), an outsider, a real estate magnate, who never, before now, held political office, never served in the military, and yet managed, in a totally unpredictable presidential campaign, the closest to political madness in recent history, to diminish and then demolish 16 other GOP candidates, and finally, against all odds, slip past his democratic opponent, Hillary Clinton, and end up sitting in the Oval Office, where, as president, he is the only one in the United States whose finger is on the nuclear button.

Trump is, some say, a damaged president, but still, arguably, the most powerful politician in the country, perhaps the world, and that is why his approach to governance, to democracy and to a free press, is so crucially important.

In my view, a free press, which is what we still have, is the best guarantor of a free and open society. That should be obvious to any politician, as the sun at high noon…which, by the way, might explain why, after his health care defeat, the first thing he did was telephone not Fox News or Breitbart but a Washington Post reporter to put his spin on his defeat. Not his fault, he said; it was the fault of the Democrats. And a few days later, it was the fault of the right wing of the Republican Party. It's always somebody else's fault, never his.

But when President Trump makes it a habit of belittling and humiliating the mainstream press, he is doing more than playing to his gallery of supporters, for whom journalism in any case is a kind of social disease, tolerated but not appreciated; he is also trying, in my judgment, to emasculate, to destroy, the 4th branch of government, as it was once called, and to rob it of the legitimacy it used to enjoy among many Americans.

And why would the president do this? Is his purpose simply to score a point in his never-ending battle for public approval? Yes and no, I think. For a president with the lowest public approval rating of any at this stage of his tenure, every point matters, of course. But there is a larger purpose, and it is consistent with his tilt towards authoritarianism. If he can persuade enough people that what they read in their newspapers, watch on television or listen to on radio, is all "fake," all "lies," not worthy of a second thought, "horrible," garbage," as he put it, then he feels he can govern as he wishes, without any institutional red lights flashing in his eyes—for example, without the judiciary imposing any legal constraints on his Oval Office proclamations about immigration, and without the media raising any embarrassing questions about his latest tweets, or his family business operations (which, by the way, scream out for a diligent investigation), or his strange willingness to look the other way when a Russian autocrat like Putin engages in aggressive action. It's interesting, really–President Trump has been openly critical of the Germans, the French, the Iranians, the Chinese, his predecessor, Barack Obama, but never the Russian autocrat, Putin. Why? Trump provides no real answers to the Russia questions, and Congress, though it's trying, has failed so far to come up with a meaningful explanation.

When reporters ask other questions—such as, why he has not released his income tax returns, as he promised he would do during the campaign and as all other recent presidents have done, he resorts, for an excuse, to a mysterious and apparently never ending audit.

Thanks to Rachel Maddow of MSNBC, a few details from his 2005 return have now been revealed to the public, but we still know comparatively little.

In the Mafia handbook, there is an old saying about "follow the money." Clearly the president feels that if we were to follow it too far–to Trump Tower, or to some mysterious address in Moscow, or a bank in Cyprus, for example–we may all learn too much. And that he clearly does not want.

Trump makes fun of reporters for asking questions about his tax returns. The public, he says, doesn't really care about them. And, in this respect, maybe he is right. And if he is right, who can blame him for feeling that, as president, he can consider himself to be above the law, and act accordingly.

In 1974, another president, Richard Nixon by name, might have thought he stood above the law too, only to be forced to resign days ahead of almost certain impeachment by an angry, disappointed Congress. As former President Bush warned, power can become "addictive" and "corrosive." It can be "abused."

Let us hope that this president comes to understand, as quickly as possible, that there is a vast difference between campaigning, when winning an election defines success, and governing, when balancing competing interests at home and abroad defines success. At this point in his presidency, though, the evidence strongly suggests that Trump, by his actions and statements, has begun to undercut and thus to jeopardize the very foundations of American democracy.

If there is an explanation for this sudden and disturbing flipflop in American politics, it may lie (and this is the charitable explanation) in the way Trump and his colleagues view media coverage of the presidential campaign that brought them to power. Kellyanne Conway, the president's ubiquitous spokesperson, who has a ready explanation for anything, literally anything, Trump has ever said or done, claims that her boss, during the campaign, was the most "vilified and attacked politician" ever, subject to blistering, "negative coverage." The press, she says, "suspended the objective standards of journalism," putting "their fingers on the scales" to favor Hillary Clinton. They were "unfair," she concludes, using one of the president's favorite words. What was he to do except fight back, in his way?

A humble word of dissent is now in order. When Trump described the Mexicans as "rapists," the press reported his comment, accurately. When Trump was caught on tape using what he later called "locker room talk" about a woman's private parts, the press reported it, accurately. When Trump, as president, boasted that more people showed up at his inauguration than did at Barack Obama's, the press reported it, accurately, before adding that the president was dead wrong on his facts. He also said the sun was shining when, in fact, it had begun to rain. This president does have a habit of vastly exaggerating everything, even to the extent of absolute fantasy, stuff no one can believe. "Innocent hyperbole," he calls it.

If your media world consists, for the most part, of Fox News, Rush Limbaugh, Laura Ingraham, Mark Levin and Breitbart, which Stephen Bannon once ran, and if you rarely read a book, you may very well indulge in a form of make-believe, which may be comforting for a child but can be a very dangerous toy for a sitting president.

For example, you may conclude that Sweden was attacked by terrorists, when it wasn't, or that former President Obama wiretapped your phones (Trump charged in a tweet: "This is Nixon/Watergate. Bad, or sick guy"); after Sweden and Obama, you may then rush to your twitter account, and inform the world—you may do this, even though there is not a shred of evidence connecting these dreary fantasies to the real world. We seem to be living in Trump's postfact world.

And yet, despite all this, press coverage of President Trump, while far from ideal, has been, for the most part, balanced and accurate. If, as Kellyanne Conway said, the coverage has been unfair, then the fault, dear Brutus, lies with the president, with his words, his actions, his policies, and not with the press, for reporting them.

When confronted with a mistake or a lie, of which there have been many in this administration, rather than admit the lie, Trump usually doubles-down. Facts and polls that are unflattering are obviously "fake." In other words, in Trump's judgment, news can only be regarded as truthful and reliable if it describes him in glowing terms. Over the years, many autocrats have felt essentially the same way.

A Trump surrogate, Scottie Nell Hughes, explained that the "American people" have now developed their own way of knowing whether a fact is true or not. "Unfortunately," she said, "there's no such thing anymore as facts," thus contradicting the wisdom of the late Senator Daniel Patrick Moynihan that we can all have our own opinions, but we cannot have our own facts. This White House assumes, in other words, that the American people no longer care if the president lies. They will pick and choose whatever "alternative facts" conform to their already locked-in political views. "Alternative facts," by the way, is a Conway concoction.

The big question of our time, in my opinion, is whether the media, in its daily tussle with an impatient, powerful president has the spunk, the stuff, and the public support to stand up and say, Mr. President, this far and no further. If the media, for whatever reason, fails to meet this challenge, then democracy, as we have known it, will slowly die. Weaken the press, and you weaken freedom; weaken freedom, and you weaken democracy, and open the door to an American authoritarianism—and maybe more. In this downward spiral from democracy to authoritarianism, Congress can be crucially important; so too the judiciary; but it starts with the press—with the daily headline, or broadcast bulletin. That is where the political wars are now fought—and won or lost.

In recent decades, the press has become increasingly influential in presidential campaigns, in legislative battles, in covering wars—so much so that a politician must deal with the press if he has any hope of advancing his agenda. Trump is no exception. He would have been wise to make nice to the press, but I fear he may not be capable of that.

Recently, a Post columnist speculated that Trump would not survive four years in the White House. She thinks he will leave after two. Howard Stern, the shock jock, has interviewed Trump many times, knows him quite well. Stern says he advised his friend not to run for the presidency. "This is something that is going to be very detrimental to his mental health," Stern said. "He (Trump) wants to be liked, he wants to be loved, he wants people to cheer for him." Stern added, after noting that criticism of the president has been mounting steadily, "I don't think this is going to be a healthy experience for him."

Since Trump's inauguration, many speculative stories have appeared, suggesting that his reported narcissism, defined as an excessive love of oneself, may complicate his decision-making process and ultimately force a confrontation between the White House and Congress.

What is fascinating about Trump is that he always places himself in the center of every story. He especially loves television, which is natural since he was once a tv-reality star. During the campaign, he dominated television. According to the respected Tyndall Report, the three tv news networks—ABC, CBS and NBC—helped elect Trump, giving him 1,144 minutes of free tv coverage, compared to 506 free minutes for Clinton, more than double the time. On cable news, even more so, with Trump the candidate seen and heard anywhere and at any time. The upshot—cable news made more money in 2016 than ever before. Trump was treated as the star of American television. He was often his own tv producer, deciding when and how he would appear, and the networks almost always obliged.

A remarkable irony is that the more Trump disparages the press, the more money the press makes. In recent months, subscriptions for the so-called "failing New York Times" have skyrocketed; same for the *Washington Post*, *Politico*, the *New Yorker* and the *Atlantic* magazines. Trump remains a big story, even as he roars against the press. With his roars, he would like to topple the press; but so far he has only made them richer.

The president seems to want and need enemies, someone or some group to blame if and when his presidency runs into serious trouble, as it almost certainly will.

Trump seems to represent a populist rebellion against the entire establishment, including the press, here and around the world. Bannon, up to now anyway, has been able to whisper sweet nothings into the president's ear. He defines the aim of the Trump presidency as "the deconstruction of the administrative state," meaning, I think, deconstructing or transforming the government, as we have known it, into a white, nationalist nation, driven by an America First ideology, locked in an existential struggle with a radical Islamic fanaticism. In this struggle, oddly, Russia is seen by Trump and Bannon as an ally. If their concept of a free press is demolished in this apocalyptic confrontation, they would shed no tears.

For reporters, Trump is a great news story, but very difficult to cover. They have discovered that they have to get up early and stay up late. They have to watch what Trump watches on cable news, from dawn to midnight and beyond—that is his world, his reality. He operates mostly by instinct, not the soundest way of deciding war and peace issues. Careful notes must be taken of his fusillade of tweets–they provide insights into his thinking.

Trump is erratic. He hates the press, and yet cannot live without it. It is his oxygen; it is what keeps him alive, emotionally and politically.

It may be too dramatic to say that American democracy rests in the hands of a free, though at the moment, uncertain press. But I believe it does. I also believe that the press will ultimately prevail in this dangerous, running war the president launched.

I come to a close on this note of moderate optimism. Reporters, by their work, bring the neighborhood and the world to us. They deserve our praise and admiration. We depend on them. Young women cover wars in the Middle East, and often they are stringers working without life insurance, open to being kidnapped or killed. That is courage.

Resourceful organizations, such as the Pulitzer Center, where I currently hang my hat, help fill the hole left by budgetary shortfalls. The Center gives money to reporters to cover stories all over the world. The Shorenstein Center at Harvard gives hefty annual prizes to investigative reporters, who spend months covering official corruption and governmental malfeasance. Journalism is an honorable and rewarding craft, and must be so recognized. Every day, it seems, foundations are giving more money to news organizations to cover the news, fact-based news—it's that vital.

One day, Donald Trump will be gone, but the United States will still be here, a free nation. The free press will still be here too, the essential pillar of our democracy, carved into the First Amendment to the US Constitution, as valid today as it was yesterday or the day before. A free press, if supported by the public, can still perform miracles, and it does so every day, Trump or no Trump.

Marvin Kalb is a distinguished American journalism. He was the founding director of the Shorenstein Center on Media Politics and Public Policy at Harvard. He was an award-winning reporter for CBS and NBC News, as well as long time moderator of Meet the Press.

Philip Bennett and Moises Naim  **NO**

21st-Century Censorship

Governments Around the World Are Using Stealthy Strategies to Manipulate the Media

Two beliefs safely inhabit the canon of contemporary thinking about journalism. The first is that the Internet is the most powerful force disrupting the news media. The second is that the Internet and the communication and information tools it spawned, like YouTube, Twitter, and Facebook, are shifting power from governments to civil society and to individual bloggers, netizens, or "citizen journalists."

It is hard to disagree with these two beliefs. Yet they obscure evidence that governments are having as much success as the Internet in disrupting independent media and determining the information that reaches society. Moreover, in many poor countries or in those with autocratic regimes, government actions are more important than the Internet in defining how information is produced and consumed, and by whom.

Illustrating this point is a curious fact: Censorship is flourishing in the information age. In theory, new technologies make it more difficult, and ultimately impossible, for governments to control the flow of information. Some have argued that the birth of the Internet foreshadowed the death of censorship. In 1993, John Gilmore, an Internet pioneer, told Time, "The Net interprets censorship as damage and routes around it."

Today, many governments are routing around the liberating effects of the Internet. Like entrepreneurs, they are relying on innovation and imitation. In countries such as Hungary, Ecuador, Turkey, and Kenya, officials are mimicking autocracies like Russia, Iran, or China by redacting critical news and building state media brands. They are also creating more subtle tools to complement the blunt instruments of attacking journalists.

As a result, the Internet's promise of open access to independent and diverse sources of information is a reality mostly for the minority of humanity living in mature democracies.

How is this happening? As journalists, we've seen firsthand the transformative effects of the Internet. It seems capable of redrafting any equation of power in which information is a variable, starting in newsrooms. But this, it turns out, is not a universal law. When we started to map examples of censorship, we were alarmed to find so many brazen cases in plain sight. But even more surprising is how much censorship is hidden. Its scope seems hard to appreciate for several reasons. First, some tools for controlling the media are masquerading as market disruptions. Second, in many places Internet usage and censorship are rapidly expanding at the same time. Third, while the Internet is viewed as a global phenomenon, censorship can seem a parochial or national issue—in other words, isolated. Evidence suggests otherwise.

In Venezuela, a case that we examine below in depth, all three of these factors are in play. Internet usage there is among the fastest-growing in the world, even as the government pursues an ambitious program of censorship. Many methods used by the state are beneath the waterline, and have surfaced in other countries. They include, as we and others have discovered, gaining influence over independent media by using shell companies and phantom buyers. According to Tamoa Calzadilla, until last year the investigations editor at Ultimas Noticias, Venezuela's largest-circulation newspaper, the array of pressures on journalists in her country is not well understood in Europe or the United States. She resigned in protest after anonymous buyers took control of the paper, and a new editor demanded what she considered to be politically motivated changes in an investigative story about anti-government protests. "This is not your classic censorship, where they put a soldier in the door of the newspaper and assault the journalists," Calzadilla told us. "Instead, they buy the newspaper, they sue the reporters and drag them into court, they eavesdrop on your communications and then broadcast them on state television. This is censorship for the 21st century."

The new censorship has many practitioners, and increasingly refined practices:

- In Hungary, the government's Media Authority has the power to collect detailed information about journalists as well as advertising and editorial content. Prime Minister Viktor Orban's regime uses fines, taxes, and licensing to pressure critical media, and steers state advertising to friendly outlets. A comprehensive report by several global press freedom organizations concluded: "Hungary's independent media today faces creeping strangulation."

- In Pakistan, the state regulatory authority suspended the license of Geo TV, the most popular channel in the country, after a defamation claim against it was made by the intelligence services following a shooting of one of the station's best-known journalists. The channel was off the air for 15 days starting in June 2014. Pakistani journalists say that self-censorship and bribery are rife.

- In Turkey, a recent amendment to the Internet law gave the Telecommunications Directorate the authority to close any website or content "to protect national security and public order, as well as to prevent a crime." President Recep Tayyip Erdogan has been criticized for jailing dozens of journalists, and for using tax investigations and huge fines in retaliation for critical coverage (in 2009, for instance, tax authorities fined a leading media group $2.5 billion). More recently, the government blocked Twitter and other social media allegedly in response to a corruption scandal that implicated Erdogan and other senior officials.

- In Russia, President Vladimir Putin is remaking the media landscape in the government's image. In 2014, multiple media outlets were blocked, shuttered, or saw their editorial line change overnight in response to government pressure. While launching its own media operations, the government approved legislation limiting foreign investment in Russian media. The measure took aim at publications like Vedomosti, a daily newspaper respected for its standards and independence and owned by three foreign media groups: Dow Jones, the Financial Times Group and Finland's Sanoma.

Graphic Deleted

Traditional censorship was basically an exercise of cut and paste. Government agents inspected the content of newspapers, magazines, books, movies, or news broadcasts, often prior to release, and suppressed or altered them so that only information judged acceptable would reach the public. For dictatorships, censorship meant that an uncooperative media outlet could be shut down or that unruly editors and journalists exiled, jailed, or murdered.

Starting in the early 1990s, when journalism went online, censorship followed. Filtering, blocking and hacking replaced scissors and black ink. Some governments barred access to Web pages they didn't like, redirected users to sites that looked independent but which in fact they controlled, and influenced the conversation in chat rooms and discussion groups via the participation of trained functionaries. They directed anonymous hackers to vandalize the sites and blogs, and disrupt the Internet presence of critics, defacing, or freezing their Facebook pages or Twitter accounts.

Tech-savvy activists quickly found ways to protect themselves and evade digital censorship. For a while it looked like agile, hyperconnected, and decentralized networks of activists, journalists, and critics had the upper hand in a battle against centralized, hierarchal, and unwieldy government bureaucracies. But governments caught up. Many went from spectators in the digital revolution to sophisticated early adopters of advanced technologies that allowed them to monitor content, activists, and journalists, and direct the flow of information.

No place shows the contradictions of this contest on as grand a scale as China. The country with the most Internet users and the fastest-growing connected population is also the world's most ambitious censor. Of the three billion Internet users in the world, 22 percent live in China (nearly 10 percent live in the United States). The government maintains the "Great Firewall" to block unacceptable content, including foreign news sites. An estimated two million censors police the Internet and the activities of users. Yet the BBC reports that a 2014 poll found that 76 percent of Chinese questioned said they felt free from government surveillance. This was the highest rate of the 17 countries polled.

The Internet has allowed Chinese authorities to deploy censorship strategies that are subtle and harder for the public to see. In Hong Kong, where China is obligated by treaty to respect a free press, Beijing has used an array of measures to limit independent journalism, including selective violence against editors and the arrest of reporters. But it has also arranged the firing of critical reporters and columnists and the withdrawal of advertising by state and private sources, including multinationals, and launched cyberattacks on websites. The Hong Kong Journalists Association described 2014 as "the darkest for press freedom in several decades."

National security policies place the United States and other mature democracies in the same discussion as countries, like Russia, that see the Internet as both a threat and a means of control.

China's actions demonstrate the emerging censorship menu: It can be direct and visible, or indirect and stealthy. These stealth strategies have become important as more governments try to hide their efforts to control the media. Stealth censorship can involve creating entities that look like private companies, or government-organized, non-governmental organizations, known as GONGOS. These organizations purport to represent civil society, but in practice are government agencies. The approach allows the anonymous hackers in Russia or China who attack the networks of critics at home, or governments abroad, to be portrayed as mysterious members of the sprawling global civil society, rather than allies of the regime.

Stealth censorship appeals to authoritarian governments that want to appear like democracies—or at least not like old-style dictatorships. And they have more options available to them than ever.

In illiberal democracies, how a government censors often reflects the tension between projecting an image of democracy and ruthlessly suppressing dissent. Some governments are trying to reconcile this contradiction by outsourcing censorship to groups they secretly control. Or they use currency controls to starve publishers of newsprint. Or they promote the migration of irritating journalists from major papers to online startups, where they have to build new audiences. This allows the government to keep a grip on the news media while concealing its fingerprints.

That is the story today in Venezuela. The country of 30 million has become a laboratory for testing ways to control the flow of news and information. As a case study in how governments disrupt independent media, the Venezuelan model offers several compelling ingredients: a feisty and courageous independent media, a press establishment serving elite audiences, a socialist revolution that claims to be building a popular democracy, and a deeply polarized citizenry that is witness to a near constant information war.

Recently, as a political and economic crisis has deepened, the state and its allies appear to have unveiled a new weapon: quieting critical reporting through the shadowy purchase of some of the private media companies most vexing to the government.

At first, the deals looked similar to the changing of the guard that is happening at old-line media institutions around the world. They have involved Venezuela's best-selling but financially troubled newspaper, Ultimas Noticias, and its oldest daily, El Universal. But with time the sales seem less the result of market disruption, and more like political meddling using government-friendly buyers, dark money, and a web of foreign companies, some of them created overnight in order to conceal the identities of the new owners.

It is naive to assume there is a technological fix for governments that are determined to concentrate power and do whatever it takes to keep it.

The legal strategies used in the acquisitions make them hard to trace and evaluate. No evidence of a direct connection to government funds has surfaced. But the highly irregular structure of the deals, followed by changes in the editorial lines of the publications, have convinced journalists that their papers have lost their independence.

In the case of Ultimas Noticias and its parent chain, for instance, the buyer was Latam Media Holding, a shell company created in Curaçao less than a month before the sale, according to documents that we've examined. The price, which was not made public at the time, was at least $97 million, a huge sum for newspapers in Venezuela's anemic economy. According to the documents, two days before the sale, one original shareholder sold her stock for $11 million to a Latin American currency fund of opaque ownership, a transaction not disclosed publicly. The biggest paper in the country had changed hands, and questions about the origin of the funds and the identities of the owners were met with silence.

The intrigue thickened when it was revealed that Latam Media Holding is controlled by Robert Hanson, a British businessman with no evident experience investing in media or in Latin America. Hanson is the multimillionaire son of the late British industrialist Lord Hanson, and a familiar figure in London society columns (the "raffish blade about town" in one memorable description in The Times of London). He has declined to talk about the purchase.

The new editors of Ultimas Noticias reassured the staff that the paper's standards would not change. But within weeks, reporters say, they were told to soften pieces critical of the government or pressured not to write them at all, a charge the current editor has denied. Since the purchase, more than 50 journalists have resigned.

Journalists and media executives in Venezuela are used to rough treatment from authorities. The late President Hugo Chávez and his handpicked successor, the current President Nicolás Maduro, have attacked private news media for supporting the opposition and accused them of destabilizing the country. The government has passed legislation limiting press freedom, restricted access to public information, levied fines and taxes on media companies, withheld broadcast licenses, forced programs off the air, and used foreign currency controls to create a scarcity of newsprint, which is imported. At least a dozen newspapers have closed for lack of printing supplies.

The state has a long record of harassing, detaining, and beating reporters, and suing them for defamation. Officials routinely take to state media to excoriate individual reporters or news outlets. Reporters know they run high personal risks for writing about corruption or covering shortages of basic necessities, from toilet paper to medicine or food staples, in ways that reflect badly on the government. In a survey of journalists by the Venezuelan branch of the Institute for Press and Society, which supports press freedom, 42 percent reported being pressured by officials to change a story.

Cracking down directly on the media has proven costly to the government, sparking domestic protests and bringing international condemnation. And it has never worked for long. Until recently, Venezuelans could find vigorous coverage of such sensitive topics as Chávez's health (he died of cancer in 2013), shocking crime statistics (the second-highest murder rate in the world), and state management of the energy sector (including the world's largest oil reserves).

Then came the violent clashes between protesters and police during the first half of 2014. Students started the protests in response to a crime on a provincial campus, but they quickly grew into a full-blown crisis for Maduro. As the protests spread, and with them pictures of the dead and wounded, the government banned NTN24, an international cable channel covering the violence. It blocked all images on Twitter. Reporters, photographers, and camera operators were detained and beaten. State media scarcely covered the violence or the motives behind the protests. Particularly startling to some viewers was the lack of tough coverage on Globovision, a 24-hour news channel. It had been the last television station that was critical of the government. But several months earlier, it had been bought by an insurance firm reportedly close to the Maduro regime.

At Ultimas Noticias, the investigative team run by Tamoa Calzadilla obtained an electrifying scoop: a video showing police and men in civilian clothes firing on fleeing protesters, killing one. Despite the recent sale of the paper, Calzadilla and her team put the video online. Their report led to the first arrests of members of the security forces. But a short time later, the president of the chain that owns the newspaper resigned and was replaced by an ally of the ruling party.

The following month, Calzadilla presented the new editor with an inside look at the protesters and the police squaring off in Caracas. She says that he refused to run the piece unless it was changed to say that protesters were financed by the United States (there is no evidence of this). Instead, Calzadilla resigned, going into a bathroom in the newsroom and tweeting, "journalism first," before exiting the building.

A month after the protests subsided last June, the owners of El Universal (whom Maduro had described on television as "rancid oligarchy") announced that they had sold the 106-year-old daily.

If the purchase of Ultimas Noticias was mysterious, the sale of El Universal in July 2014 contained elements of farce. It was bought by a Spanish investment firm that had been founded a year earlier with an initial capital of about $4,000. According to documents published by the blogger Alek Boyd, the sole shareholder in the Spanish firm was a Panama-registered corporation called Tecnobreaks, Inc. But when Boyd contacted the founders of Tecnobreaks, a Venezuelan father and son apparently in the auto repair business, they said they had no idea of the sale and were not people of means. It was as if The New York Times had been bought by a Midas franchisee.

Months later, it is still a mystery who is behind the purchase of El Universal or how much they paid (estimates range from $20 million to $100 million). The Spanish firm remains the purchaser of record. But the impact on the journalism has been clear. In the month after the sale, at least 26 journalists said they were dismissed over critical coverage. Rayma Suprani, a popular editorial cartoonist, was fired for a cartoon that mocked Chávez's famous signature, trailing off in a flat line, to depict the demise of healthcare in Venezuela. "We don't know who bought El Universal or who pays the salaries," she told CNN en Español after her dismissal. "But now we know they are bothered by the critical editorial line. So we can presume that it wasn't some invisible man but the government got its hands on it."

Suprani now posts her cartoons on Twitter, where she has more than half a million followers. Many of Venezuela's most enterprising journalists have migrated online. Tamoa Calzadilla is now investigations editor of runrun.es, an independent news site with reporters in Caracas, where, she told us, "we are doing the journalism that needs to be done." But while Internet usage is growing sharply in Venezuela, less than half the population has access to the Web. In a country divided down the middle by politics, most Venezuelans are now getting half the story.

Despite the economic crisis, the government is investing aggressively to build its own media empire. State-owned Telesur has become the largest 24-hour television news channel in Latin America. Started by Chávez "to lead and promote the unification of the peoples of the SOUTH," it now employs 800 reporters. The company reached a milestone last year with the launch of an English-language website and newscast, which it promoted in a full-page ad in The New Yorker.

For a moment in 2011, during the Arab spring, social media seemed to give democracy activists an advantage against entrenched regimes. As protesters triumphed in Egypt, Google executive and activist Wael Ghonim famously told Wolf Blitzer, "If you want to liberate a government, give them the Internet." Although the complex dynamics of the uprising went far beyond a "Facebook Revolution," the term captured a sense that something important had changed.

Four years later, media freedom in Egypt is under withering assault. Dozens of journalists have been jailed, according to the Committee to Protect Journalists. And last summer, Amnesty International reported having obtained internal documents that describe a government contract to build a system to spy on Facebook, Twitter, WhatsApp, and other social media.

This might be a slogan for the Facebook counter-revolution: To empower a government, give it the Internet.

The Edward Snowden leaks made clear that the Internet is a tool for peering into the lives of citizens, including journalists, for every government with the means to do so. Whether domestic spying in the United States or Great Britain qualifies as censorship is a matter of debate. But the Obama administration's authorization of secret wiretaps of journalists and aggressive leak prosecutions has had a well-documented chilling effect on national-security reporting. At the very least, electronic snooping by the government means that no journalist reporting on secrets can promise in good conscience to guarantee a source anonymity.

National security policies place the United States and other mature democracies in the same discussion with countries, like Russia, that see the Internet as both a threat and a means of control. Most of these countries have not tried to hide from charges that they perform surveillance over the Internet. Instead, Russia, India, Australia, and others have approved security legislation that writes the practice into law.

Journalists legitimately fear being swept up in this electronic dragnet. But frequently they are its specific targets. China has hacked foreign journalists' email accounts, presumably to vacuum up their sources, and broke into the servers of leading US newspapers. The NSA hacked into Al Jazeera. The Colombian government spied on communications of foreign journalists covering peace talks with rebels. Ethiopia's Information Network Security Agency has tracked journalists in the United States. Belarus, Russia, Saudi Arabia, and Sudan all routinely monitor reporters' communications, according to Reporters Without Borders.

Joel Simon, executive director of the Committee to Protect Journalists, describes the sinister consequences of surveillance in his recent book, The New Censorship. Simon recounts in chilling detail how Iran turned journalists' reliance on the Internet into a weapon against protesters in 2009. Security agents tortured journalists like Maziar Bahari (the subject of the Jon Stewart film Rosewater) until they divulged their social media and email passwords, and then combed through their networks, identifying and arresting sources. Iranian officials also created fake Facebook accounts to lure activists. "The use of Facebook and other social media platforms by governments to dismantle political networks has become a standard practice," Simon writes.

It's not only states that are using these techniques. In Mexico, drug cartels run grotesque online media operations to intimidate rivals, the government, and the public. They have viciously silenced efforts to report anonymously on their activities on social media. In October 2014, cartel members kidnapped a citizen journalist in Reynosa, Maria del Rosario Fuentes Rubio, and then posted pictures of her dead body on her Twitter account.

It is little wonder why governments would pursue a strategy of weakening print and broadcast companies if it meant journalists moved to a platform the state can control and monitor. In Russia and elsewhere, there is a pattern of independent media being pressured not just by markets but by the state to move online, where they must rebuild their audience and the state is a powerful tenant, if not the landlord. If independent media grow too big online, like the popular Russian news site Lenta.ru, they can see their editors suddenly dismissed, the editorial line changed, and the site crumble.

One disturbing trend is the banding together of governments to create an Internet that is easier to police. China has advised Iran on how to build a self-contained "Halal" Internet. Beijing has also been sharing know-how with Zambia to block critical Web content, according to Reporters Without Borders. Private surveillance firms advertise their wares to countries that want to upgrade their encryption penetrating software.

If that is not enough, some governments can still count on self-censorship to do the work for them. Last October, after a deadly attack on the army by Islamic militants, top editors at more than a dozen Egyptian newspapers pledged to withhold criticism of the government and block "attempts to doubt state institutions or insult the army or police or judiciary." The ownership of Al Nahar television added: "Freedom of expression cannot ever justify belittling the Egyptian Army's morale."

For every government that succeeds in controlling the free flow of information or repressing journalists, there is a counterexample. Courageous citizens have found ways to circumvent or undermine official controls. Or they are willing simply to risk opposing a government's claims that it has the sole authority to write history. This power struggle is far from over, and its outcome will vary among countries and over time. Technological innovation will create new options that enable individuals and organizations to counteract government censorship, even as governments adopt technologies that enhance their ability to censor.

Pressures on governments for transparency, accountability, access to public information, and more citizen participation in public decisions will not go away. Autocratic states face populations that are more politically awake, restless, and harder to silence. Ukrainians showed recently that citizens fed up with the way they are governed could topple a president, even if he has the support of neighboring Russia. Or in Hong Kong, as the world witnessed last fall, a leaderless group of activists can defy China's immense power.

But states retain extraordinary capacities to alter the flow of information to suit their interests. And a growing number of governments are undermining the checks and balances that constrain chief executives. From Russia to Turkey, Hungary to Bolivia, leaders are packing Supreme Courts and the judiciary with loyalists and staging elections that reward their allies. They are weakening the institutions that exist to prevent the concentration of power. In such a political environment, independent media cannot survive for long.

The Internet can redistribute power. But it is naïve to assume that there is a simple technological fix for governments and their leaders who are determined to concentrate power and do whatever it takes to keep it. Censorship will rise and fall as technological innovation and the hunger for freedom clash with governments bent on controlling their citizens, starting with what they read, watch, and hear.

PHILIP BENETT is director of the DeWitt Wallace Center for Media Democracy at Duke. He is a former managing editor of the *Washington Post* and *Frontline*.

MOISES NAIM is a distinguished fellow at the Carnegie Endowment for International Peace and a contributing editor at *The Atlantic*. He was editor in chief of *Foreign Policy*.

EXPLORING THE ISSUE

Can Journalism Stand Up to Attacks on Freedom of the Press?

Critical Thinking and Reflection

1. What does freedom of the press mean in the information/digital age?
2. To what standards should we hold the press?
3. How can we manage the intractable social media?
4. How serious are the current threats to freedom of the press?
5. Does the libertarian ideal of a free marketplace of ideas have validity in this age?

Is There Common Ground?

Ironically in an issue where truth versus opinion is so important, the crux of the matter is one of optimism versus pessimism. Do we believe that the press can stand up to attacks on freedom of the press or do we not? What will be the consequence of the constant hammering of the press? Will its credibility be destroyed? Will only the immediate targets be affected or will all media be harmed? If so, what will become the alternative? Certainly Bennett and Naim point to many countries where restriction of information has become the norm. Can it happen here?

Yet, there is common ground. Many US presidents and citizens believe in the importance of the press in a society. Abroad, courageous journalists continue to fight authoritarian government. They all share a belief in the power of the press. We must remember that "the press" is an ambiguous term. The press is not monolithic; there are many voices and many more platforms than ever before. When some denigrates the press, it is always a good idea to ask what they mean.

Is there a serious threat to freedom of the press in the United States at this time? I think many will say no, and that these warnings are overwrought. Clearly many in the press think the way journalists are treated and journalism is demeaned is something they must stand against. Only time will tell.

Additional Resources

Alex Jones, *Losing the News*, Oxford University Press (2009).

Written by controversial author Alex Jones, this book investigates whether news can and will survive in a future of multiple platforms and highly targeted news stories.

Marvin Kalb, Trump's Troubling Relationship with the Press, *Brookings Institute* (2/21/2017) Retrieved at https://www.brookings.edu/blog/upfront/2017/02/21/trumps-troubling-relationship-with-the-press/

Respected former news man Marvin Kalb discusses the way President Trump talks about the news and the impact of degrading newscasters and media have on democratic values and the need to support a free press.

Andrew Marantz, "Trolling the Press Corps." *The New Yorker* (3/20/2017).

In this thoughtful article, Marantz examines the White House Press Corps and discusses how difficult it is for them to do their job when President Trump continually undermines their work.

Internet References . . .

Brookings Institute

https://www.brookings.edu/blog/fixgov/2017/09/18/
views-among-college-students-regarding-the-first-
amendment-results-from-a-new-survey/

**CQ Researcher: Trust in Media and
Journalism Under Fire**

http://library.cqpress.com/cqresearcher/document.
php?id=cqresrre2017060900

**Knight First Amendment Institute at
Columbia University**

https://knightcolumbia.org

Newseum Institute

http://www.newseuminstitute.org/first-amendment-
center/first-amendment-faq/#press

Reporters without Borders

https://rsf.org/en